Machine Translation Summit 2023

Volume 1: Research Track

Macau, China
4-8 September 2023

ISBN: 978-1-7138-9040-9

Printed from e-media with permission by:

Curran Associates, Inc.
57 Morehouse Lane
Red Hook, NY 12571

Some format issues inherent in the e-media version may also appear in this print version.

Printed with permission by Curran Associates, Inc. (2024)

For permission requests, please contact the Association for Computational Linguistics at the address below.

Association for Computational Linguistics
209 N. Eighth Street
Stroudsburg, Pennsylvania 18360

Phone: 1-570-476-8006
Fax: 1-570-476-0860

acl@aclweb.org

Additional copies of this publication are available from:

Curran Associates, Inc.
57 Morehouse Lane
Red Hook, NY 12571 USA
Phone: 845-758-0400
Fax: 845-758-2633
Email: curran@proceedings.com
Web: www.proceedings.com

MT Summit 2023

MTS Machine Translation Summit 2023

September 4-8, 2023 Macau SAR, China

Proceedings of Machine Translation Summit XIX
Vol. 1: Research Track

September 4 - 8, 2023

Introduction

The research track at MT Summit 2023 has a wide range of topics with 33 papers selected from entire 50 submissions. The part of subjects covered by the research track, as indicated by the keywords in the titles below:

- Low-Resource, Zero-resource MT
- Document-Level, Coherent, Context-aware NMT
- Quality Estimation
- Multi-domain, Domain Robustness, Domain Adaptation
- Unsupervised NMT
- Robust NMT, Markup Translation
- MT Evaluation
- Annotation
- Poetry, Compounds, Dialectal
- Post-editing
- Sign Language, Multimodal

Among the 33 papers, 19 papers are accepted as oral presentations and 14 as poster presentations. The most popular subject is "Low-Resource" MT. The subjects of "Context-aware" NMT and "Quality Estimation" are also popular. We also have unique topics like Myanmar Sign Language, Translation with Markup, Robust NMT, Dialectal Arabic-Turkish MT, and Poetry Translation. These indicate we have both popular topics and unique topics, which could be overlooked in the larger general NLP conferences.

We thank the authors, reviewers, and MT Summit organizing committee for making a good conference happen. We also thank our invited speakers for the research track for sharing their interesting experiences: Min Zhang, Ondřej Bojar, Mitesh Khapra, Tong Xiao, and Isao Goto.

Sincerely,
Masao Utiyama and Rui Wang (Research Track Co-Chairs)

Organizing Committee

General Chair

Eiichiro Sumita, National Institute of Information and Communications Technology

Steering Committee

Eiichiro Sumita, National Institute of Information and Communications Technology
Kozo Moriguchi, Kawamura International Co. Ltd.
Derek Wong, University of Macau
Sadao Kurohashi, National Institute of Informatics & Kyoto University
Hideki Tanaka, National Institute of Information and Communications Technology

Research Track Chair

Masao Utiyama, National Institute of Information and Communications Technology
Rui Wang, Shanghai Jiao Tong University

Users Track Chair

Masaru Yamada, Rikkyo University
Félix do Carmo, University of Surrey

Workshop Chair

Jiajun Zhang, Chinese Academy of Sciences
Thepchai Supnithi, The National Electronics and Computer Technology Center

Local Arrangement Chair

Derek Wong, University of Macau
Hou Pong Chan, University of Macau

Publication Chair

Katsuhito Sudoh, Nara Institute of Science and Technology
Xuebo Liu, Harbin Institute of Technology, Shenzhen

Sponsorship Chair

Kozo Moriguchi, Kawamura International Co. Ltd.
Jaap van der Meer, TAUS
Tong Xiao, Northeastern University

Conference Manager

Andrew Jiang, Macau Expo Group

Program Committee

Sweta Agrawal
Loic Barrault
Pushpak Bhattacharyya
Houda Bouamor
Michael Carl
Abhisek Chakrabarty
Xingyu Chen
Colin Cherry
Chenhui Chu
Chenchen Ding
Kevin Duh
Marcello Federico
Christian Federmann
Minwei Feng
Markus Freitag
Ruize Gao
Isao Goto
Barry Haddow
Zhiwei He
MukendiI Kalamba
Rebecca Knowles
Philipp Koehn
Mamoru Komachi
Shankar Kumar
Lemao Liu
Qun Liu
Wolfgang Macherey
Arne Mauser
Arul Menezes
Hideya Mino
Makoto Morishita
Masaaki Nagata
Hiromi Nakaiwa
Toshiaki Nakazawa
Takashi Ninomiya
Shantipriya Parida
Tharindu Ranasinghe
Raphael Rubino
Fatiha Sadat
Michel Simard
Haiyue Song
Katsuhito Sudoh
Akihiro Tamura
Hajime Tsukada
Yiming Wang
Xiaolin Wang
Taro Watanabe
Muyun Yang
François Yvon
Rabih Zbib
Jiajun Zhang
Pei Zhang
Bing Zhao

Table of Contents

Conference Program

Wednesday, 6th September

11:15–12:15 Session RP1: Research Track Posters (1)

Multiloop Incremental Bootstrapping for Low-Resource Machine Translation
Wuying Liu, Wei Li and Lin Wang

Joint Dropout: Improving Generalizability in Low-Resource Neural Machine Translation through Phrase Pair Variables
Ali Araabi, Vlad Niculae and Christof Monz

A Study of Multilingual versus Meta-Learning for Language Model Pre-Training for Adaptation to Unseen Low Resource Languages
Jyotsana Khatri, Rudra Murthy, Amar Prakash Azad and Pushpak Bhattacharyya

Data Augmentation with Diversified Rephrasing for Low-Resource Neural Machine Translation
Yuan Gao, Feng Hou, Huia Jahnke and Ruili Wang

A Dual Reinforcement Method for Data Augmentation using Middle Sentences for Machine Translation
Wenyi TANG and Yves Lepage

16:00–17:30 Session RS1: Quality Estimation

Perturbation-based QE: An Explainable, Unsupervised Word-level Quality Estimation Method for Blackbox Machine Translation
Tu Anh Dinh and Jan Niehues

Semi-supervised Learning for Quality Estimation of Machine Translation
Tarun Bhatia, Martin Kraemer, Eduardo Vellasques and Eleftherios Avramidis

Learning from Past Mistakes: Quality Estimation from Monolingual Corpora and Machine Translation Learning Stages
Thierry Etchegoyhen and David Ponce

Thursday, 7th September

10:30–12:00 Session RS2: Transfer Learning Approach

Exploring Domain-shared and Domain-specific Knowledge in Multi-Domain Neural Machine Translation
Zhibo Man, YUJIE ZHANG, Yuanmeng Chen, Yufeng Chen and Jinan Xu

Enhancing Translation of Myanmar Sign Language by Transfer Learning and Self-Training
Hlaing Myat Nwe, Kiyoaki Shirai, Natthawut Kertkeidkachorn, Thanaruk Theeramunkong, Ye Kyaw Thu, Thepchai Supnithi and Natsuda Kaothanthong

Improving Embedding Transfer for Low-Resource Machine Translation
Van Hien Tran, Chenchen Ding, Hideki Tanaka and Masao Utiyama

10:30–12:00 Session RS3: Training with Auxiliary Information

Boosting Unsupervised Machine Translation with Pseudo-Parallel Data
Ivana Kvapilíková and Ondřej Bojar

A Study on the Effectiveness of Large Language Models for Translation with Markup
Raj Dabre, Bianka Buschbeck, Miriam Exel and Hideki Tanaka

A Case Study on Context Encoding in Multi-Encoder based Document-Level Neural Machine Translation
Ramakrishna Appicharla, Baban Gain, Santanu Pal and Asif Ekbal

Thursday, 7th September (continued)

15:00–16:00 Session RP2: Research Track Posters (2)

In-context Learning as Maintaining Coherency: A Study of On-the-fly Machine Translation Using Large Language Models
Suzanna Sia and Kevin Duh

Beyond Correlation: Making Sense of the Score Differences of New MT Evaluation Metrics
Chi-kiu Lo, Rebecca Knowles and Cyril Goutte

Bad MT Systems are Good for Quality Estimation
Iryna Tryhubyshyn, Aleš Tamchyna and Ondřej Bojar

Improving Domain Robustness in Neural Machine Translation with Fused Topic Knowledge Embeddings
Danai Xezonaki, Talaat Khalil, David Stap and Brandon Denis

Instance-Based Domain Adaptation for Improving Terminology Translation
Prashanth Nayak, John Kelleher, rejwanul haque and Andy Way

16:00–17:30 Session RS4: Feedback and Evaluation

Learning from Mistakes: Towards Robust Neural Machine Translation for Disfluent L2 Sentences
Shuyue Stella Li and Philipp Koehn

The Role of Compounds in Human vs. Machine Translation Quality
Kristyna Neumannova and Ondřej Bojar

Benchmarking Dialectal Arabic-Turkish Machine Translation
Hasan Alkheder, Houda Bouamor, Nizar Habash and Ahmet Zengin

Friday, 8th September

Friday, 8th September (continued)

16:00–17:00 Session RP3: Research Track Posters (3)

Multiloop Incremental Bootstrapping for Low-Resource Machine Translation

Wuying Liu [1,2] wyliu@ldu.edu.cn
[1] Shandong Key Laboratory of Language Resources Development and Application, Ludong University, Yantai, 264025, China
[2] Center for Linguistics and Applied Linguistics, Guangdong University of Foreign Studies, Guangzhou, 510420, China
Wei Li 676471162@qq.com
School of Computer and Big Data Science, Jiujiang University, Jiujiang, 332005, China
Lin Wang * lwang@xdsisu.edu.cn
Xianda College of Economics and Humanities, Shanghai International Studies University, Shanghai, 200083, China
* Corresponding Author

Abstract

Due to the scarcity of high-quality bilingual sentence pairs, some deep-learning-based machine translation algorithms cannot achieve better performance in low-resource machine translation. On this basis, we are committed to integrating the ideas of machine learning algorithm improvement and data augmentation, propose a novel multiloop incremental bootstrapping framework, and design the corresponding semi-supervised learning algorithm. This framework is a meta-frame independent of specific machine translation algorithms. This algorithm makes full use of bilingual seed data of appropriate scale and super-large-scale monolingual data to expand bilingual sentence pair data incrementally, and trains machine translation models step by step to improve the translation quality. The experimental results of neural machine translation on multiple language pairs prove that our proposed framework can make use of continuous monolingual data to raise itself. Its effectiveness is not only reflected in the easy implementation of state-of-the-art low-resource machine translation, but also in the practical option to quickly establish precise domain machine translation systems.

1. Introduction

Machine Translation (MT) is an algorithmic computing process that uses a target natural language form to paraphrase the semantics of a source natural language. After the Bronze Age marked by Rule-based MT (RBMT) and the Silver Age marked by Statistical MT (SMT), the Golden Age marked by deep-learning-based Neural MT (NMT) has begun. After more than 70 years of unremitting exploration around the three generations of MT, many excellent algorithms and practical products have been produced (Garg and Agarwal, 2018).

If the formal language theory and context-free grammar derived from the development of compilers have achieved MT based on transformation generation rules, then language data has become the backbone of MT in the post-rule era. The Bayes conditional probability formula explicitly quantifies the language model and translation model contained in large-scale language data, which makes the noise channel model to decrypt an encrypted message become a

Proceedings of Machine Translation Summit XIX, Vol. 1: Research Track, pages 1–11
September 4–8, 2023, Macau SAR, China.

statistical MT paradigm. The deep neural network performs fine-grained characterization of super-large-scale language data, and uses many parameters to simulate the end-to-end NMT model that can generate fluent target language (Tan, Wang, Yang, Chen, Huang, Sun and Liu, 2020).

RBMT is time-consuming and labor-intensive, and it is not easy to guarantee the self-consistency among many rules, so it is difficult to popularize into practical applications. SMT often needs more than 5 million sentence pairs to train a good model, while NMT requires at least 20 million sentence pairs to train an excellent model. The effect of NMT rolling that of RBMT and SMT is the result of the interaction of computing power, algorithm and data. It is precisely because the vector computing component has greatly accelerated the parallel computing ability, which makes the early proposed artificial neural network algorithm can burst out amazing deep intelligence on the data of super-large-scale bilingual sentence pairs (Stahlberg, 2020).

Among the more than 7,000 existing languages in the world, the vast majority of less commonly taught languages, such as indigenous languages, endangered languages, and dialects that are not widely spoken, have difficulties in data scarcity of super-large-scale bilingual sentences to varying degrees. Therefore, there is still huge room for improvement in low-resource MT with limited training data (Ranathunga, Lee, Skenduli, Shekhar, Alam and Kaur, 2021). At present, low-resource MT has gradually evolved into two mainstream research ideas, data augmentation centric idea and machine learning algorithm improvement centric idea. There is an overlap between the two ideas since the latter one may also use various language data.

2. Related Works

Reviewing the research history of low-resource MT, the data augmentation centric idea mainly focuses on how to expand the training corpus. While the machine learning algorithm improvement centric idea often explores how to use transfer learning, unsupervised learning, adversarial learning, and so on to improve the effect of low-resource MT.

Typical data augmentations include: **(1)** By pairing monolingual training data with an automatic back-translation, the approach can treat it as additional parallel training data, and obtain substantial improvements on the low-resource MT task (Sennrich, Haddow and Birch, 2016). **(2)** The method starts with a small amount of parallel data and iteratively improves the model by training it on the current data and using it to generate translations for additional monolingual data. (Hoang, Koehn, Haffari and Cohn, 2018). **(3)** Some studies use a bilingual lexicon to build a phrase-table, combine it with a language model, and use the resulting MT system to generate a synthetic parallel corpus, which does not require any additional resource besides the monolingual corpus used to train the embeddings (Artetxe, Labaka and Agirre, 2019).

Classical machine learning algorithm improvements include: **(1) Transfer learning**. The earlier technique is transfer learning between vocabulary, grammar and cognate languages mainly based on the characteristics of the language itself. Some studies first train a high-resource language pair (the parent model), then transfer some of the learned parameters to the low-resource pair (the child model) to initialize and constrain training (Zoph, Yuret, May and Knight, 2016). Then there are studies that relieve the vocabulary mismatch by using cross-lingual word embedding, train a more language-agnostic encoder by injecting artificial noises, and generate synthetic data easily from the existing data, so as to implement transfer learning between languages with different vocabulary and grammar (Kim, Gao and Ney, 2019). Some studies prove that the cognate parallel corpus can improve the low-resource language NMT effectively, which mainly depends on the morphological similarity and semantic equivalence between the cognate languages (Liu, Xiao, Jiang and Wang, 2018). Recent technique tends to adopt pre-trained models in related languages to bootstrap the training of a low-resource MT model. According to the language affinity, the research also found that the use of multi-round fine-tuning of highly related multiple high-resource language pairs can further improve the effect of low-resource MT (Maimaiti, Liu, Luan and Sun, 2019). Some studies have systematically compared multistage fine-tuning, and relevant experiments have confirmed that multi-parallel corpora are extremely useful, and their multistage fine-tuning can give 3~9 BLEU score gains over a simple one-to-one model (Dabre, Fujita and Chu, 2019). A study has proposed a XLNet based pre-training method, that corrects the defects of the pre-training model, and enhance NMT model for context feature extraction. Experimental results on minority languages to Chinese tasks show that the generalization ability and BLEU scores of this method are improved, which fully verifies the effectiveness of the method (Wu, Hou, Guo and Zheng, 2021). There are also studies aimed at two related very low resource Sorbian languages. On the one hand, the authors pretrain the German-Upper-Sorbian model using masked sequence to sequence objective and then finetune using iterative back-translation. On the other hand, they use final German-Upper-Sorbian model as initialization of the German-Lower-Sorbian model, and then the same vocabulary in the two languages is used in the further training of iterative back-translation (Khatri, Murthy and Bhattacharyya, 2021). **(2) Unsupervised learning**. This technique involves training a MT model without using any labeled data. Different from the unsupervised method in the above data augmentation, some studies have proposed a novel method to train a NMT system in a completely unsupervised manner, relying on nothing but monolingual corpus, which completely removes the need of parallel data (Artetxe, Labaka, Agirre and Cho, 2018). Some studies propose two knowledge distillation methods and empirically introduce a simple method to translate between thirteen languages using a single encoder and a single decoder, making use of multilingual data to improve unsupervised neural MT for all language pairs (Sun, Wang, Chen, Utiyama, Sumita and Zhao, 2020). Some studies add an adapter layer with a denoising objective on top of pre-trained model, and implement multilingual unsupervised MT that only has monolingual data by using auxiliary parallel language pairs (Üstün, Berard, Besacier and Gallé, 2021). **(3) Adversarial learning**. This technique adopts an interesting idea of alternate promotion of both two sides of contradiction. Some studies have put forward a unique idea of training the NMT model to generate human-like translations directly by using the generative adversarial net (Yang, Chen, Wang and Xu, 2018). The method builds a conditional sequence generative adversarial net which comprises of two adversarial sub models, a generative model which translates the source sentence into the target sentence as the traditional NMT models do and a discriminative model which discriminates the machine-translated target sentence from the human-translated one. The two sub models play a minimax game and achieve a win-win situation when reaching a Nash Equilibrium.

Overall, low-resource MT algorithms are still an active area of research, and there are many promising techniques being developed to improve the quality of translations for low-resource languages. We propose a novel multiloop incremental bootstrapping (MIB) meta framework independent of specific MT algorithms, and hope to integrate the advantages of data augmentation and machine learning algorithm improvements from a higher level of abstraction to achieve concise and efficient industrial practical methods.

3. Multiloop Incremental Bootstrapping

The MIB we proposed is a semi-supervised incremental learning data augmentation idea that can promote the advantages of supervised learning and unsupervised learning. The idea adopts a rolling snowball strategy: Firstly, good bidirectional MT models are trained by using bilingual corpus of appropriate scale. Then, through fully tapping the potential of the Internet monolingual big data, the trained MT models translate monolingual sentences twice to incrementally construct a bilingual pseudo-corpus. Then, the bilingual pseudo-corpus is used to enhance the initial bilingual corpus. Finally, the above process is loop-repeated based on the enhanced bilingual corpus, until the trained MT model meets the optimal performance requirements.

3.1. Framework

According to the MIB idea, we give full play to the advantages of super-large-scale unlabeled corpora, and propose a MIB framework for low-resource MT as shown in Figure 1. The framework mainly includes a MT model trainer, two machine translators, several crawlers, a similarity calculator, and a corpus truncator.

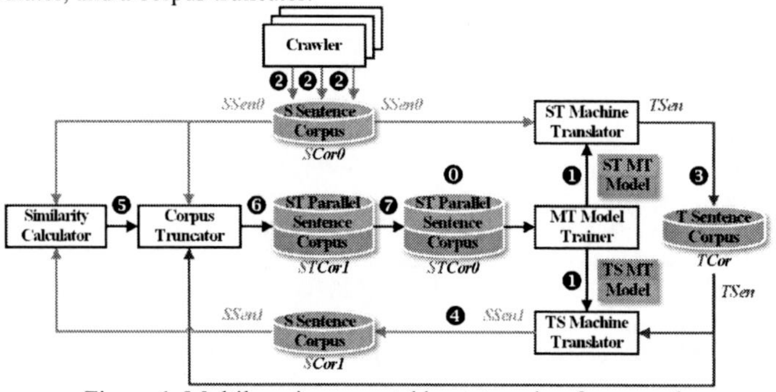

Figure 1. Multiloop incremental bootstrapping framework.

The MIB route is made up of multiple improvement loops. **Step⓿**: We need to prepare a ST (source language to target language) parallel sentence corpus named as *STCor0*. **Step❶**: The MT model trainer receives the *STCor0*, and trains out two MT models respectively from language S to language T and from language T to language S. **Step❷**: A group of parallel crawlers continuously crawl language S texts from the Internet, and build a super-large-scale language S sentence corpus (*SCor0*). **Step❸**: The ST machine translator translates each language S sentence (*SSen0*) in *SCor0* into the corresponding language T sentence (*TSen*) according to the ST MT model, and collects them to form a language T sentence corpus (*TCor*). **Step❹**: The TS machine translator translates the language T sentence (*TSen*) in *TCor* back into the language S sentence (*SSen1*) according to the TS MT model, and collects them to form a language S sentence corpus (*SCor1*). **Step❺**: The similarity calculator calculates the similarity between the source sentence *SSen0* and the result sentence *SSen1* flowing through the two machine translators. **Step❻**: The corpus truncator sorts the corresponding sentence pair <*SSen0*, *TSen*> according to the similarity between *SSen0* and *SSen1*, and truncate the TopN sentence pairs with the highest similarity to form a new ST parallel sentence corpus (*STCor1*). **Step❼**: The *STCor1* is merged into the *STCor0*. The first closed loop is completed from the Step⓿ to the Step❼, and then the second loop is started from the Step⓿ again, and so on. The above multiple loops are used together to implement the complete MIB framework.

Our MIB framework gives a novel idea of semi-supervised low-resource MT based on pseudo-corpus incremental learning. It has three significant features: **(1)** The framework is a very flexible meta-framework. On the one hand, it is independent of both specific MT model training algorithms and sentence similarity calculating algorithms. On the other hand, if a domain-independent universal parallel sentence corpus is used as the *STCor0*, and a directionally-crawled domain-dependent language S sentence corpus is used as the *SCR0*, it can quickly and conveniently implement precise MT systems adapting to various domains. **(2)** Although the working of the crawlers is a step contained in the loop, the preparation of the corresponding language S sentence corpus can also be separated out to establish an individual module. Because the scale of the language S sentence corpus affects the effectiveness of incremental learning, it is necessary to implement functions such as uninterrupted crawling, sentence segmentation, and sentence deduplication. We can use parallel computing technology to maximize the scale of the language S sentence corpus, use NLP technology to segment the language S sentences, and use information retrieval technology to delete the language S sentences contained in *STCor0*. **(3)** Two prior parameters need to be set. Where, the TopN parameter indicates the increment of sentence pairs in each loop, which determines the delta effect of each loop learning. The parameter of the total number of loops not only represents the MIB termination condition, but also determines the total learning time overhead. The two parameters together determine the depth of the whole learning.

3.2. Algorithm

According to the MIB idea, we design a multiloop incremental bootstrapping machine translation (MIBMT) algorithm as shown in the pseudo-code in Figure 2 to specifically implement the above MIB framework. The MIBMT algorithm mainly includes two main functions of MIB training (MTMODELS: ***train*** ()) and translating (STRING: ***translate*** ()), and a specific model training function (MTMODEL: ***modeltrain*** ()), a crawling function (SCOR: ***crawl*** ()), and so on.

```
// Multiloop Incremental Bootstrapping Machine Translation (MIBMT) Algorithm
// MIB Training
// n: total number of loops
// topn: increment of sentence pairs
// stcor0: parallel sentence corpus
Main Function MTMODELS: train(n, topn, stcor0)
MTMODELS mtmodels ← MTMODELS.new();
For 0 To n Do
    mtmodels.st ← modeltrain(stcor0, 's', 't');
    mtmodels.ts ← modeltrain(stcor0, 't', 's');
    SCOR scor0 ← crawl(stcor0.get('s'), 's');
    STCOR stcor1 ← STCOR.new();
    For STRING ssen0 : scor0 Do
        STRING tsen ← translate(mtmodels.st, ssen0, 's');
        STRING ssen1 ← translate(mtmodels.ts, tsen, 't');
        FLOAT sim ← similaritycalculate(ssen0, ssen1);
        stcor1← corpustruncate(stcor1, ssen0, tsen, sim, topn);
    End For
    stcor0.merge(stcor1);
    mtmodels ← MTMODELS.new();
End For
Return mtmodels.
// Specific Model Training
// stcor0: parallel sentence corpus
// ls: source language id
// lt: target language id
Function MTMODEL: modeltrain(stcor0, ls, lt)
SCOR newscor ← mpt.tokenize(stcor0.get(ls), ls);
TCOR newtcor ← mpt.tokenize(stcor0.get(lt), lt);
MTMODEL mtmodel ← specificmodeltrain(newscor, newtcor);
Return mtmodel.
// Crawling
// scor: sentence corpus
// l: language id
Function SCOR: crawl(scor, l)
SCOR scor0 ← SCOR.new();
SCOR crawledscor ← mpt.sensplit(crawledtxt, l);
For STRING sen : crawledscor Do
    If (!scor.contain(sen)) Then scor0.add(sen);
End For
Return scor0.
// MIB Translating
// mtmodel: machine translation model
// inputtxt: input text
// ls: source language id
Main Function STRING: translate(mtmodel, inputtxt, ls)
STRING outputtxt ← STRING.new();
SCOR inputscor ← mpt.sensplit(inputtxt, ls);
For STRING sen : inputscor Do
    outputtxt ← outputtxt + mtmodel.specifictranslate(sen) + separator;
End For
Return outputtxt.
```

Figure 2. Multiloop incremental bootstrapping machine translation algorithm.

In the main function of MIB training (Function MTMODELS: *train* ()), the inputs are the preset total number of loops (*n*), increment of sentence pairs (*topn*), and initial parallel sentence corpus (*stcor0*), while the output is a pair of MT models (*mtmodels*). The outermost loop is run *n*+1 times based on the preset total number of loops *n* (lines 8 to 21 in Figure 2). In each loop, firstly, perform bidirectional translation model training (lines 9 and 10 in Figure 2), then crawl the monolingual sentence corpus (line 11 in Figure 2), then perform bidirectional translation on the sentences in the monolingual sentence corpus one by one, and obtain the pseudo bilingual sentence corpus according to the similarity (lines 13 to 18 in Figure 2). Finally, merge the pseudo corpus into the initial parallel sentence corpus.

In the main function of MIB translating (**Function** STRING: ***translate*** ()), the inputs are MT model (*mtmodel*), source language text (*inputtxt*), and source language identifier (*ls*), while the output is target language text (*outputtxt*). Firstly, the input source language text is segmented into sentences (line 48 in Figure 2), then translated one by one according to the translation model (line 50 in Figure 2), and the translated sentences are connected and assembled by the target sentence separator (loop between lines 49 and 51 in Figure 2), finally the target language text is output.

The inputs of the specific model training function (**Function** MTMODEL: ***modeltrain*** ()) are a parallel sentence sorpus (*stcor0*), a source language identifier (*ls*), and a target language identifier (*lt*). The output is a translation model (*mtmodel*). In addition to the need for token feature representations based on language (lines 28 and 29 in Figure 2), the most important step is the specific training step for MT models (line 30 in Figure 2), which is an end-to-end training process for NMT models.

The inputs of the crawling function (**Function** SCOR: ***crawl*** ()) is the existing monolingual sentence corpus (*scor*) and language identifier (*l*), while the output is the newly added monolingual sentence corpus (*scor0*). In addition to sentence segmentation for the crawled text (line 37 in Figure 2), it is necessary to perform a repeat judgment operation (line 39 in Figure 2) to ensure that the new sentence is not in the existing monolingual sentence corpus.

3.3. Algorithm Analysis

Inheriting the meta-framework characteristic of the MIB framework, the MIBMT algorithm is also a general meta-algorithm. Any high-performance MT algorithm can be embedded in the meta-algorithm to implement specific functions of model training and translating. This meta-algorithm uses repetitive hardware multi-process and multi-threading to implement the efficient crawling (***crawl***), and uses sentence fingerprint indexing and retrieval to implement the Boolean judgment (***contain***). There are three characteristics that need special attention in practical use: (i) The scale and quality of the initial parallel sentence corpus *stcor0* must meet the requirements of specific model training to ensure that the MT model trained in the first loop has high translation precision. Just as "no powerful First Impulse, no more and more precise celestial orbits". (ii) The MIBMT bias is controlled by the crawled super-large-scale sentence corpus *scor0*. If *scor0* comes from open domain contents, a universal MT model is eventually produced, while from narrow domain contents, a domain MT model is produced. "What foods he feeds, what eggs hen will lay." (iii) For each source language or target language, a dedicated morphological processing tool (***mpt***) is required. For instance, during specific model training, the tokenize tool (***tokenize***) represents each single Chinese character as a token, while it represents the lowercase form of each English word separated by spaces as a token. For another instance, both the crawled text (*crawledtxt*) and input text (*inputtxt*) need to execute a sentence splitting tool (***sensplit***) according to the corresponding language to obtain a sentence sequence. We have to customize the morphological processing tool for each language because different languages have different morphological representation systems. That is "different shoes for different feet".

The time overhead of the MIBMT algorithm is mainly used for the learning process of the training function, which is directly proportional to the total number of loops and the training time of the specific MT model. For instance, the total number of loops is n, the time cost of training a specific model using a NMT algorithm is m, and the bidirectional models are trained in parallel (line 9, 10 of Figure 2), then the main time complexity will be $\boldsymbol{O}(nm)$. The space overhead of the MIBMT algorithm is not only related to the increment of sentence pairs (TopN) and the size of the initial parallel sentence corpus, but also to the space cost of the specific MT model. Since the training corpus is processed in batches during model training, this relationship is only a positive correlation and not a simple direct proportional relationship. If a NMT model is specifically used, and the source language vocabulary size is S and the target language vocabulary size is T, then the main spatial complexity is $\boldsymbol{O}(ST)$. Of course, the above-mentioned space-time complexity is still very huge. Fortunately, the learning process of the training function is an offline processing, and it is learned once and used multiple times. While the online processing of the translating function is efficient in time and space. In order to achieve excellent MT results in practical applications, longer learning time and larger storage space are worthwhile and acceptable. We can also increase the GPU and memory to reduce actual space-time overhead.

4. Experiment

In order to verify that the MIB can be effectively used for low-resource MT, we first implement a MIBMT meta-algorithm by embedding an open source sequence-to-sequence NMT model[1]. The hparams of the NMT model mainly include the number of neurons (*num_units* = 512), the number of encoding and decoding layers (*num_encoder_layers* = *num_decoder_layers* = 4), the batch size (*batch_size* = 512), and the beam search width (*beam_width* = 10), while others remain the default values. Next, the 15 languages of Indonesian (ind), Malay (msa), Vietnamese (vie), Thai (tha), Khmer (khm), Lao (lao), Filipino (fil), Myanmar (mya), Italian (ita), Kazakh (kaz), Kyrgyz (kir), Ukrainian (ukr), Polish (pol), Czech (ces), and Slovak (slk), which are relatively scarce in parallel sentence pair resources to Chinese (zho), are selected and their morphological processing tools are implemented respectively. Finally, a prototype system for MT experiments from these 15 languages to Chinese was built.

A total of 15 NMT models need to be trained to support MT from the 15 low-resource languages to Chinese in the experimental prototype system, which have been successfully deployed as web application systems at present[2]. During the training of these models, we fixed the total number of loops and the increment of sentence pairs (TopN) to 11 and 1,000,000 respectively. The parallel sentence corpus (*STCor0*) for each language and Chinese, that is, the initial training set, contains 5,000,000 sentence pairs, while the final training set will contain 15,000,000 sentence pairs after the 11 loop executions. At the same time, in order to train specific sequence-to-sequence NMT models, we also equip an additional 100,000 sentence-pair development set and 100,000 sentence-pair test set for each language. For each language, the initial training set is exactly the same distribution as the development set and the test set, which are divided from the same corpus by simple random sampling. While the crawler captures from open domain to form the monolingual sentence corpus (*SCor0*), which is independent of the initial training set. In order to ensure the high availability of the Top1,000,000 pseudo-corpus, monolingual sentences at least 10 times TopN is captured in each loop, and then the Top1,000,000 sentence pairs are truncated based on the Levenshtein similarity.

---

[1] https://github.com/tensorflow/nmt

[2] http://nmt.cpolar.cn

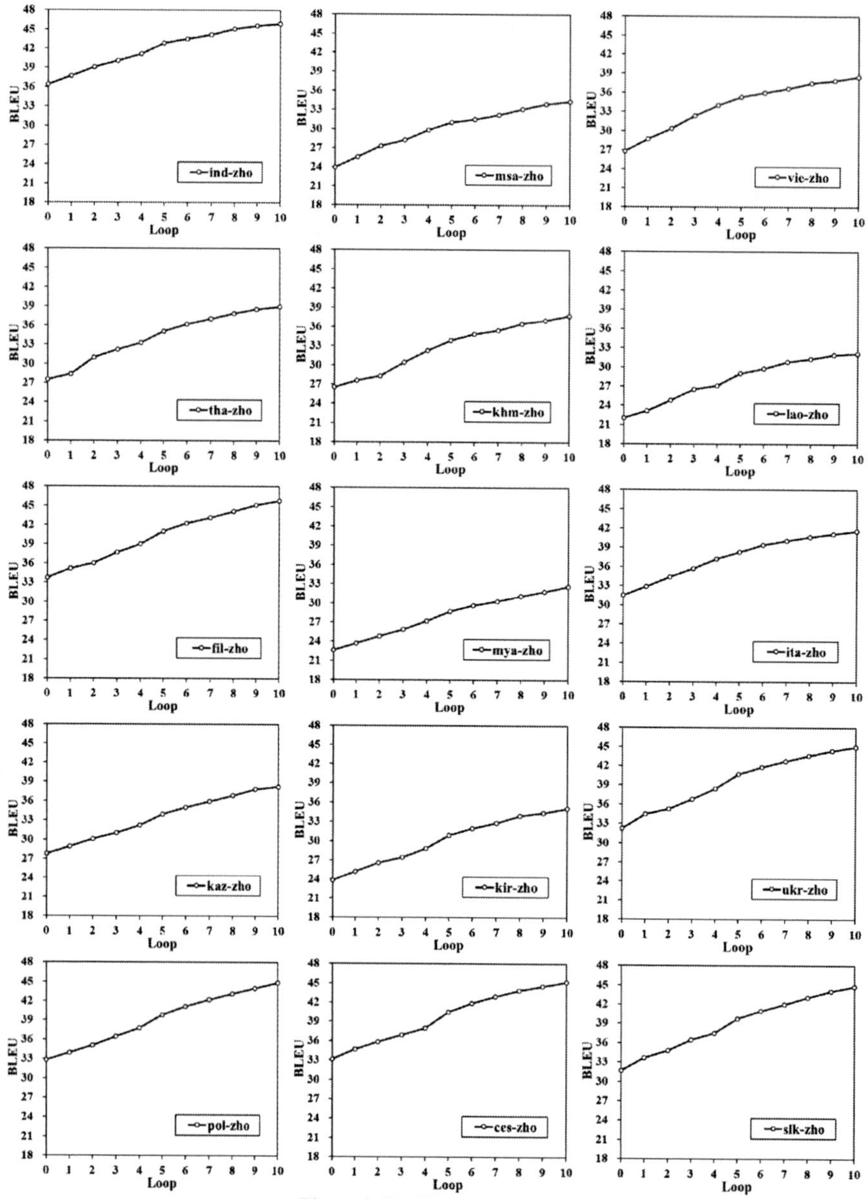

Figure 3. BLEU trend curves.

After 15 months of training, the BLEU trend curves of the above 15 MT models are shown in Figure 3. Where, the abscissa axis represents the loop ordinal, and the ordinate axis represents the BLEU value. Among them, Loop=0 represents the sequence to sequence NMT model obtained from the initial training set of 5,000,000 sentence pairs without pseudo corpus, which is used as the benchmark model for the following effect comparison. We find from the curves in Figure 3: (i) The BLEU value of each curve increases approximately linearly with the number of loops (increment of 1,000,000 sentence pairs per loop). This shows that the MIB has a general promotion effect on low-resource MT lack of bilingual sentence pair resources. The reason is that with the extension of the corpus, the vocabulary space is more complete and the model is more generalized. (ii) Almost the linear growth rate of each curve around the Loop=5 point will change slightly, and the linear growth rate in the first half is greater than that in the second half. Among them, the vie-zho curve is the most obvious. This shows that when the scale of real corpus is larger than that of pseudo-corpus, the enhancement effect of pseudo-corpus is more significant. Because the fixed test set often has the best fit model, when the proportion of the pseudo-corpus is too large, it may cause overfitting. (iii) There is a significant difference among the BLEU values of the initial model Loop=0 in different languages, with a maximum difference of over 10, while the BLEU increment (ΔBLEU) between the final model and the initial model is basically maintained at around 10. This is because different languages have different entropy, so the information contained in the same scale corpus is not equal, resulting in uneven performance of the initial model trained by sentence pairs of the same scale.

Source-Target Language	Vocabulary Size of Source Language of Loop 10	Vocabulary Size of Target Language of Loop 10	BLEU of Loop 10	ΔBLEU between Loop 10 and Loop 0
ind-zho	604,869	8,960	**45.90**	9.55
msa-zho	357,264	8,168	34.32	10.38
vie-zho	66,242	8,293	38.51	11.71
tha-zho	8,110	6,980	38.95	11.45
khm-zho	128,930	6,995	37.77	11.22
lao-zho	149,478	6,913	32.12	10.07
fil-zho	201,835	6,393	**45.74**	12.01
mya-zho	24,384	6,907	32.60	9.93
ita-zho	884,503	9,759	41.57	10.11
kaz-zho	699,425	7,017	38.26	10.44
kir-zho	740,651	7,007	35.03	11.18
ukr-zho	627,365	7,023	44.94	12.69
pol-zho	541,620	6,929	44.85	12.04
ces-zho	550,807	6,931	**45.14**	12.02
slk-zho	576,679	6,930	44.79	**13.11**

Table 1. Final vocabulary size and BLEU values.

The final vocabulary size and corresponding BLEU values are shown in Table 1. Where, the Chinese vocabulary size is relatively fixed, with value ranging from 6,000 to 10,000. Each "word" in the Chinese vocabulary is a single Chinese character or other token. But there are two forms of uppercase and lowercase in Latin, Cyrillic or other alphabet languages, which use a lowercase vocabulary for MT to Chinese. Observing the final BLEU values, we found that the BLEU value of the NMT model from Indonesian, Filipino and Czech to Chinese exceeded 45. Among them, the BLEU value of Indonesian-Chinese NMT model reaches the highest of 45.90. Observing the ΔBLEU values between Loop=10 model and Loop=0 model, it is found that the BLEU values of 15 low-resource languages to Chinese NMT models can be improved between 9.55 and 13.11 by using the proposed method. The BLEU value of the Slovak-Chinese NMT model increased the most, while that of the Indonesian-Chinese NMT model increased the least. It can be seen that the higher the performance of Loop=0 model, the higher the final performance can be obtained by adopting the MIB method. In summary, the experimental results prove that our proposed MIB is effective for low-resource MT.

5. Conclusion

The incremental pseudo-corpus in the MIB of this paper is derived from the newly trained MT models, while the MT models are trained from the training set enhanced by newly produced pseudo-corpus, which is a closed-loop self-lifting idea based on the homogeneous MT models. The experimental results on multiple languages prove that the language resources expanded by this idea can effectively improve the performance of low-resource MT.

The next research will concern an open-loop mutual-lifting idea based on heterogeneous MT models. That is, the source and output MT models of incremental pseudo-corpus are two different excellent MT models. It is hoped that an excellent MT model will enhance another one through the produced corpus transmission. In addition, we also hope to transfer the general MIB framework of this paper to low-resource MT in other languages and precise domain MT.

Acknowledgments

The research is supported by the New Liberal Arts Research and Reform Practice Project of Ministry of Education of China (No. 2021060049), the Postgraduate Education and Teaching Reform Research Project of Shandong (No. SDYJG21185), the Key Project of Undergraduate Teaching Reform Research of Shandong (No. Z2021323), the Science and Technology Program of Guangzhou (No. 202201010061), the Humanity and Social Science Research Project of Ministry of Education of China (No. 20YJAZH069, No. 20YJC740062), and the Social Science Foundation of Shanghai (No. 2019BYY028).

References

Garg, A. and Agarwal, M. (2018). Machine Translation: A Literature Review. arXiv:1901.01122v1.

Tan, Z., Wang, S., Yang, Z., Chen, G., Huang, X., Sun, M., and Liu, Y. (2020). Neural Machine Translation: A Review of Methods, Resources, and Tools. *AI Open*, 1:5–21.

Stahlberg, F. (2020). Neural Machine Translation: A Review. *Journal of Artificial Intelligence Research*, 69:343–418.

Ranathunga, S., Lee, E. A., Skenduli, M. P., Shekhar, R., Alam, M., and Kaur, R. (2021). Neural Machine Translation for Low-Resource Languages: A Survey. arXiv:2106.15115v1.

Sennrich, R., Haddow, B., and Birch, A. (2016). Improving Neural Machine Translation Models with Monolingual Data. In *Proceedings of the 54th Annual Meeting of the Association for Computational Linguistics*, pages 86–96, Berlin, Germany.

Hoang, V. C. D., Koehn, P., Haffari, G., and Cohn, T. (2018). Iterative Back-Translation for Neural Machine Translation. In *Proceedings of the 2nd Workshop on Neural Machine Translation and Generation*, pages 18–24, Melbourne, Australia.

Artetxe, M., Labaka, G., and Agirre, E. (2019). Bilingual Lexicon Induction through Unsupervised Machine Translation. In *Proceedings of the 57th Annual Meeting of the Association for Computational Linguistics*, pages 5002–5007, Florence, Italy.

Zoph, B., Yuret, D., May, J., and Knight, K. (2016). Transfer Learning for Low-Resource Neural Machine Translation. In *Proceedings of the 2016 Conference on Empirical Methods in Natural Language Processing*, pages 1568–1575, Austin, USA.

Kim, Y., Gao, Y., and Ney, H. (2019). Effective Cross-lingual Transfer of Neural Machine Translation Models without Shared Vocabularies. In *Proceedings of the 57th Annual Meeting of the Association for Computational Linguistics*, pages 1246–1257, Florence, Italy.

Liu, W., Xiao, L., Jiang, S., and Wang, L. (2018). Language Resource Extension for Indonesian-Chinese Machine Translation. In *Proceedings of the 22nd International Conference on Asian Language Processing*, pages 221–225, Bandung, Indonesia.

Maimaiti, M., Liu, Y., Luan, H., and Sun, M. (2019). Multi-Round Transfer Learning for Low-Resource NMT Using Multiple High-Resource Languages. *ACM Transactions on Asian and Low-Resource Language Information Processing*, 18(4):1–26.

Dabre, R., Fujita, A., and Chu, C. (2019). Exploiting Multilingualism through Multistage Fine-Tuning for Low-Resource Neural Machine Translation. In *Proceedings of the 2019 Conference on Empirical Methods in Natural Language Processing and the 9th International Joint Conference on Natural Language Processing*, pages 1410–1416, Hong Kong, China.

Wu, N., Hou, H., Guo, Z., and Zheng, W. (2021). Low-Resource Neural Machine Translation Using XLNet Pre-training Model. In *Proceedings of the 30th International Conference on Artificial Neural Networks and Machine Learning*, pages 503–514, Bratislava, Slovakia.

Khatri, J., Murthy, R., and Bhattacharyya, P. (2021). Language Model Pretraining and Transfer Learning for Very Low Resource Languages. In *Proceedings of the 6th Conference on Machine Translation*, pages 995–998, Online.

Artetxe, M., Labaka, G., Agirre, E., and Cho, K. (2018). Unsupervised Neural Machine Translation. In *Proceedings of the 6th International Conference on Learning Representations*, Vancouver, Canada.

Sun, H., Wang, R., Chen, K., Utiyama, M., Sumita, E., and Zhao, T. (2020). Knowledge Distillation for Multilingual Unsupervised Neural Machine Translation. In *Proceedings of the 58th Annual Meeting of the Association for Computational Linguistics*, pages 3525–3535, Online.

Üstün, A., Berard, A., Besacier, L., and Gallé, M. (2021). Multilingual Unsupervised Neural Machine Translation with Denoising Adapters. In *Proceedings of the 2021 Conference on Empirical Methods in Natural Language Processing*, pages 6650–6662, Online and Punta Cana, Dominican Republic.

Yang, Z., Chen, W., Wang, F., and Xu, B. (2018). Generative Adversarial Training for Neural Machine Translation. *Neurocomputing*, 321:146–155.

Joint Dropout: Improving Generalizability in Low-Resource Neural Machine Translation through Phrase Pair Variables

Ali Araabi a.araabi@uva.nl
Vlad Niculae v.niculae@uva.nl
Christof Monz c.monz@uva.nl
Informatics Institute, University of Amsterdam, Amsterdam, The Netherlands

Abstract

Despite the tremendous success of Neural Machine Translation (NMT), its performance on low-resource language pairs still remains subpar, partly due to the limited ability to handle previously unseen inputs, i.e., generalization. In this paper, we propose a method called *Joint Dropout*, that addresses the challenge of low-resource neural machine translation by substituting phrases with variables, resulting in significant enhancement of compositionality, which is a key aspect of generalization. We observe a substantial improvement in translation quality for language pairs with minimal resources, as seen in BLEU and Direct Assessment scores. Furthermore, we conduct an error analysis, and find Joint Dropout to also enhance generalizability of low-resource NMT in terms of robustness and adaptability across different domains.

1 Introduction

Although Neural Machine Translation (NMT) has made remarkable advances (Vaswani et al., 2017), it still requires large amounts of data to induce correct generalizations that characterize human intelligence (Lake et al., 2017). However, such a vast amount of data to make robust, reliable, and fair predictions is not available for low-resource NMT (Koehn and Knowles, 2017).

The generalizability of NMT has been extensively studied in prior research, revealing the volatile behaviour of translation outputs when even a single token in the source sentence is modified (Belinkov and Bisk, 2018; Fadaee and Monz, 2020; Li et al., 2021). For instance, in the sentence "*smallpox killed billions of people on this planet*" from our IWSLT test set, when replacing the noun "*smallpox*" with another acute disease like "*tuberculosis*", the model should ideally generate a correct translation by only modifying the relevant part while keeping the rest of the sentence unchanged. However, in many instances, such a small perturbation adversely affects the translation of the entire sentence, highlighting the limited generalization and robustness of existing NMT models (Fadaee and Monz, 2020).

Compositionality is regarded as the most prominent form of generalization that embodies the ability of human intelligence to generalize to new data, tasks, and domains (Schmidhuber, 1990; Lake and Baroni, 2018), while other types mostly focus on the practical considerations across domains, tasks, and languages, model robustness, and structural generalization (Hupkes et al., 2022). Research in compositional generalization has two main aspects: evaluating the current models' compositional abilities as well as improving them.

Proceedings of Machine Translation Summit XIX, Vol. 1: Research Track, pages 12–25
September 4–8, 2023, Macau SAR, China.

In terms of evaluation, some studies use artificially created test sets that mimic arithmetic-like compositionality (Lake and Baroni, 2018), while others evaluate compositionality in a more natural way (Keysers et al., 2020; Kim and Linzen, 2020; Dankers et al., 2022). In terms of improvement, earlier work aimed to enhance the models' compositional abilities on tasks such as semantic parsing datasets (Qiu et al., 2022), math word problem solving (Lan et al., 2022), data-to-text generation (Mehta et al., 2022), and classification (Kim et al., 2021). As for NMT, previous work has shown shortcomings in systematic compositional skills Lake and Baroni (2018); Li et al. (2021), particularly for low-resource languages Dankers et al. (2022), yet no direct improvements have been proposed.

We aim to improve compositionality in NMT, with a focus on low-resource scenarios that necessitate more robustness to form new combinations of previously seen smaller units. To achieve this, we introduce Joint Dropout (JD), a simple and effective method that jointly replaces translation-equivalent phrase pairs in the source and target sentences with variables, encouraging the model to maintain the translation of the remaining sentence, regardless of the dropped phrases. JD is orthogonal to and compatible with other methods for improving NMT performance. Specifically, it is designed to be data-centric and model-agnostic, allowing it to be easily combined with existing techniques that focus on different aspects of the NMT pipeline.

Our analysis on simulated and real low-resource data demonstrates JD's ability to significantly improve compositional generalization and translation quality.

2 Methodology

Generalization has been a longstanding concern in the field of machine translation. In the past, Statistical MT utilized phrases as the fundamental translation units in order to consider contextual information, such as in Phrase-Based Statistical Machine Translation (Zens et al., 2002, PBSMT). To increase generalization, Hierarchical PBSMT proposed by Chiang (2005) builds upon the bilingual phrase pairs of PBSMT to learn hierarchical rules, capturing discontinuous translation equivalences and therefore allowing for better generalization.

Similarly, JD leverages bilingual phrases to make the rest of the translation not dependent on a specific phrase pair. However, the main idea behind JD originates from compositionality: the meaning of a sentence is a function of the meanings of its known atoms and how they are systematically and syntactically combined (Partee et al., 1984). By substituting *meaning* with *translation* in this definition, we come up with a rule of compositionality for translation systems:

$$\tau(P \circ Q) = \tau(P) \circ \tau(Q) \tag{1}$$

in which τ is the translation function, P and Q are the constituents of the sentence, and $\circ$ is a combiner. JD aims to transfer the principle of compositionality to the translation model in order to improve generalization and robustness of NMT by replacing joint phrases with variables. To exemplify, given the De-En sentence pair $\langle$*Sie hat Rom besucht, She visited Rome*$\rangle$, we replace nouns with variables: $\langle X_1$ *hat* X_2 *besucht,* Y_1 *visited* $Y_2\rangle$. Per Equation1:

$$\begin{aligned}
&\tau(\text{Sie hat Rom besucht}) \\
&= \tau(((X_1 \text{ hat } X_2 \text{ besucht}) \circ_{X_1} \text{ Sie}) \circ_{X_2} \text{Rom}) \\
&= \tau((X_1 \text{ hat } X_2 \text{ besucht}) \circ_{X_1} \text{Sie}) \circ_{\tau(X_2)} \tau(\text{Rom}) \\
&= (\tau(X_1 \text{ hat } X_2 \text{ besucht}) \circ_{\tau(X_1)} \tau(\text{Sie})) \circ_{\tau(X_2)} \tau(\text{Rom}) \\
&= ((Y_1 \text{ visited } Y_2) \circ_{Y_1} \text{ She}) \circ_{Y_2} \text{Rome} \\
&= \text{She visited Rome}
\end{aligned} \tag{2}$$

where $\tau(X_i) = Y_i$, and $\sigma \circ_X \gamma = \sigma[X_i \backslash \gamma]$, i.e., $\circ_X$ performs the replacement of γ in the position X_i in the sentence σ. In the above sketch, we disregard any potential dependencies within the sentence. However, the variables are independent of the rest of the sentence in any manner. Therefore, our goal is to enable the model to translate the entire sentence without being affected by the specific words or phrases at position X_i. Hence, if the model learns the rules of composition properly, changing one or more lexical units will not hurt the rest of the translation. To this end, inspired by hierarchical PBSMT, we make use of bilingual phrases to improve generalization in low-resource NMT. However, since NMT has a strong capability to learn ordering through the cross-attention mechanism (Toral and Sánchez-Cartagena, 2017), our aim is not to directly apply hierarchical PBSMT to NMT, but to propose an approximation as a lightweight and efficient regularization method.

First, using Eflomal (Östling and Tiedemann, 2016), an efficient word alignment tool, we generate symmetrized word alignments for the parallel training corpus to find the correspondences between source and target words in each pair of training sentences. Then, we use alignments as the input to generate the phrase translation table by decomposing the source and target sentences into a set of dozens of bilingual phrase pairs that are consistent with the word alignment (Koehn et al., 2003). In the next step, we select phrase pairs from the phrase table for each pair of training sentences and replace them with joint variables of (X_i,Y_i). More specifically, given a pair of sentences $S = \{w_1, w_2, ...w_n\}$ and $T = \{w'_1, w'_2, ...w'_m\}$, after substitution the sentences are $S = \{w_1, ..., X_i, ..., w_l, ..., X_j, ..., w_n\}$ and $T = \{w'_1, ..., Y_i, ..., w'_k, ..., Y_j, ..., w'_m\}$, where X and Y are variables corresponding to the source and target phrases, respectively. We discuss different criteria to replace phrases with variables in §3.2.[1] Finally, we add the variable-induced corpus to the original training set, effectively doubling its size.[2]

3 Experiments

In this section, we present a comprehensive overview of our experiments. We begin by providing details regarding the datasets used and the training systems employed. Next, we delve into the specific criteria we considered when replacing phrases with variables. Subsequently, we discuss the significant improvements achieved by our proposed method, JD, across various aspects, including compositional generalization, translation performance, robustness, and the ability to generalize across domains.

3.1 Experimental setup

Data. For the preliminary experiments, we use the TED data from the IWSLT 2014 German-English (De-En) shared translation task (Cettolo et al., 2014) and randomly sample from the training data to represent various low-resource settings. In order to evaluate the models trained on IWSLT subsets, we use the concatenation of the IWLST 2014 dev sets (tst2010–2012, dev2010, dev2012) as our test set, which consists of 6,750 sentence pairs.

We further evaluate JD on multiple actual low-resource language pairs: Belarusian (Be), Galician (Gl), and Slovak (Sk) TED talks (Qi et al., 2018) and Slovenian (Sl) from IWSLT2014 (Cettolo et al., 2014) with training sets ranging from 4.5k to 55k sentence pairs.

In order to evaluate the compositional ability of JD, following Dankers et al. (2022), we use an English-Dutch (En-Nl) training set from OPUS [3] (Tiedemann and Thottingal, 2020) and randomly sample to create low-resource sets. To evaluate these models, we use both the 'dev' and the 'devtest' sets from FLORES-101 (Goyal et al., 2022) as the validation and test data.

[1]The code is available at `https://github.com/aliaraabi/Joint_Dropout`

[2]We ensure all models undergo the same maximum number of updates during training, allowing a fair evaluation.

[3]Available on `https://github.com/Helsinki-NLP/Tatoeba-Challenge/blob/master/data/README-v2020-07-28.md`

Setup	#Phrases	BLEU
T-base	0	12.2
T-opt.	0	18.0
T-opt. + JD_PP	8013	18.6
T-opt. + JD_VP	8013	18.8
T-opt. + JD_NP	8013	18.7
T-opt. + JD_Mix	8013	18.8

Table 1: Results of Transformer-base, Transformer-optimized and Joint Dropout with various phrase types on 10K De-En training samples. Noun Phrases (NP), Prepositional Phrases (PP), Verb Phrases (VP), and mixture (Mix) of all the above.

Setup	BLEU
T-opt.	18.0
T-opt. + JD	19.9
T-opt. + target variables only	15.5
T-opt. + source variables only	17.3
T-opt. + not aligned variables	17.8

Table 2: Importance of jointly dropping aligned phrases for model trained on 10K De-En samples.

Pre-processing. We apply punctuation normalization, tokenization, data cleaning, and truecasing using the Moses scripts (Koehn et al., 2007). The sentence length is limited to a maximum of 175 tokens during training. After replacing phrases with variables, we also apply BPE segmentation (Sennrich et al., 2016b) with the parameter tailored to the low-resource training data (Araabi and Monz, 2020). We ensure that variables are not split into smaller segments.

Data annotation. To generate a realistic test set for evaluating robustness against sentence perturbation, we first randomly select 300 translation outputs from the inference stage of baseline systems trained using optimized parameters on 20k samples. These outputs are then ranked using the Direct Assessment (DA) method by engaging native annotators. The top 100 outputs are then selected and the corresponding outputs from the model trained with JD are extracted and ranked using DA. Next, the input sentences are modified by replacing specific phrases or words while ensuring their syntactic and semantic accuracy. After obtaining the outputs for both the baseline and JD systems on the perturbed sentences, we conduct a DA on them.

Training system. To conduct our experiments, we employ two different models: Transformer-optimized (Araabi and Monz, 2020), specifically tailored to low-resource NMT and Transformer-base with its default hyper-parameters (Vaswani et al., 2017). This choice allows us to demonstrate that the improvements achieved are consistent and independent of the specific model settings. We use the Fairseq library (Ott et al., 2019) for our experiments and average sacreBLEU[4] (Post, 2018) over three runs as the evaluation metric. All of the models are trained on a single GPU for a few hours with the model parameters ranging from 28M to 47M.

3.2 Joint Dropout parameters

The following conditions are considered in replacing phrases with variables. First, we do not allow two adjacent phrases to be replaced with variables. Although phrases can vary in length, we consider all phrases as potential candidates for substitution with variables, irrespective of their length. After conducting initial experiments, we have determined that setting the maximum number of variables allowed in each sentence to 10 yields satisfactory results.

Since noun phrases are the most cross-linguistically common phrases, we hypothesize that they are good candidates to be replaced. Therefore, in a set of experiments we investigate the choice of phrase types. We consider four different scenarios: replacing 1) only Noun

[4] sacreBLEU parameters: nrefs:1|case:mixed|eff:no|tok:13a|smooth:exp|version:2.0.0

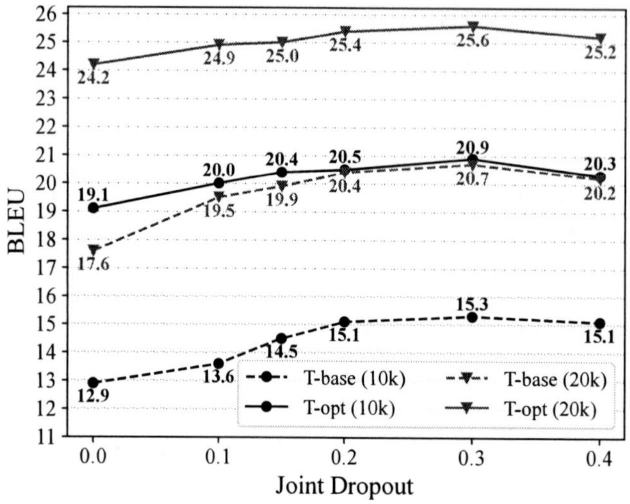

Figure 1: Effect of different Joint Dropout rates on Transformer-base and Transformer-optimized, on the validation sets of two De-En training subsets.

Phrases (NP), 2) only Prepositional Phrases (PP), 3) only Verb Phrases (VP), and 4) mixtures of all the above. We train four systems on 10k samples from the TED talks dataset with four different substitution scenarios yet the same number of variables (8013).[5] We use the constituency parser from Stanford CoreNLP (Manning et al., 2014).

It is important to note that our selection of phrase pairs in both languages is solely based on English constituency parse trees. We do not rely on the use of a constituency parser, which is often not available for many low-resource languages. The results presented in Table 1 demonstrate that the choice of different phrase types does not lead to significant differences in our method. Therefore, our approach eliminates the need for a constituency parser, making it applicable to a wider range of low-resource languages. For the rest of the experiments, we substitute phrases regardless of their types.

To make JD independent of a phrase translation table, we consider not-aligned phrases in both or either translation sides. The importance of using aligned phrases is demonstrated in Table 2, where it is observed that utilizing not-aligned phrases results in a degradation of performance by 2.5 BLEU points. This finding highlights the significance of incorporating aligned phrases in the JD method.

To maintain control over the number of variables across the entire training corpus, we introduce a concept called the *Joint Dropout rate*. This rate is determined by calculating the proportion of dropped tokens, specifically from within phrases, in relation to the total length of both the source and target sentences. By utilizing this Joint Dropout rate, we can effectively regulate and manage the presence of variables throughout the training process. Figure 1 illustrates the improvements achieved by two distinct systems as the Joint Dropout rate increases. Notably, JD consistently improves the performance of both the Transformer-base and Transformer optimized models. Specifically, on a dataset of 110k samples, JD yields a notable increase of +2.4 BLEU points for the Transformer-base model and +1.8 BLEU points for the

[5]8013 is the number of all possible substitutions for PPs.

	BLEU		Consistency	
#Samples	T-opt.	T.opt.+JD	T-opt.	T.opt.+JD
$5k$	4.2	**6.1**	2.0	**4.0***
$20k$	10.4	**10.7**	8.1	**11.0***
$40k$	12.8	**13.4**	13.1	**15.6***
$80k$	**16.4**	**16.4**	37.1	**43.8***
$200k$	**19.2**	18.7	58.2	**65.4***

Table 3: BLEU and consistency scores (En $\rightarrow$ Nl) when replacing a noun in the subject position with a different noun. Significant improvements on compositionality of JD over the strong baseline are marked with $*$ (approximate randomization, p $<$ 0.01).

Transformer-optimized model. Moreover, when evaluating a larger dataset of 20k samples, JD further improves translation quality by $+3.1$ BLEU points for the Transformer-base model and $+1.4$ BLEU points for the Transformer-optimized model.

We see that the Joint Dropout rate of 0.3 is a good choice, while more noise in the training set hurts performance. We use this rate for the remainder of the experiments.

3.3 Compositional generalization

Unlike phenomena such as idioms, which require a more global understanding, JD concentrates on improving compositionality at the local level. In this section, we aim to evaluate our method on local compositionality. Here, we take advantage of the most relevant theoretically grounded test from Hupkes et al. (2020) which is *systematicity*, a notion frequently used in the context of compositionality. This attribute of the model concerns the recombination of known parts and rules, ensuring that the model's ability to grasp novel inputs is systematically tied to their aptitude to comprehend related inputs. For instance, understanding "smallpox killed billions of people on this planet" and "tuberculosis", also implies understanding "tuberculosis killed billions of people on this planet".

Given that there are an infinite number of potential novel combinations that can be derived from known parts in natural data, we concentrate on a sentence-level, context-free rule: S $\rightarrow$ NP VP, as proposed by Dankers et al. (2022), where a noun from the NP in the subject position is replaced with a different noun, while maintaining number agreement with the VP. Additionally, they highlight that a systematic system necessitates consistency. We assess this systematicity of translations based on their consistency across various contexts when presenting words or phrases. Consistency is measured by evaluating the equality between two translations while taking into account anticipated modifications. In S $\rightarrow$ NP VP setup, after replacement, translations are deemed consistent if there is only one word difference between them. Table 3 illustrates that JD consistently enhances the consistency scores for various low-resource data conditions.

3.4 Translation performance

In this section, we conduct a comprehensive evaluation of translation quality across multiple language pairs to assess the effectiveness of JD. The results presented in Table 4 highlight the significant improvements in translation quality achieved by JD for actual low-resource language pairs. Importantly, these improvements also hold true for the reverse language direction.

Furthermore, we compare JD to three comparable methods for dropping tokens: Zero-Out, where the embedding of a token is set to zero (Sennrich et al., 2016a), Token Drop, which replaces tokens with the `<dropped>` tag Zhang et al. (2020), and SwitchOut, where words are replaced with random words from their corresponding vocabularies Wang et al. (2018). The

Method	Be-En	Gl-En	Sl-En	Sk-En	En-Be	En-Gl	En-Sl	En-Sk
T-base	4.6	13.4	8.9	24.0	3.5	10.1	6.8	19.0
T-base + JD	**6.5**	**15.8**	**10.2**	**25.0**	**4.5**	**12.9**	**7.8**	**19.2**
T-opt.	8.0	21.8	15.2	28.9	5.5	18.3	12.3	23.1
T-opt. + JD	**9.9**	**22.8**	**16.1**	**29.8**	**7.3**	**18.9**	**12.7**	**23.5**

Table 4: BLEU scores for actual extremely low-resource languages: Be, Gl, Sl, and Sk with 4.5k, 10k, 13k, and 55k training samples, respectively.

Method	5k	10k	20k
T-opt.	13.4	18.0	23.0
T-opt. + ZO	13.6	18.3	22.8
T-opt. + TD	9.5	16.8	23.9
T-opt. + SW	13.4	18.4	24.0
T-opt. + JD	**15.2**	**19.9**	**24.4**

(a) Transformer-optimized

Method	5k	10k	20k
T-base	8.6	12.1	16.6
T-base + ZO	8.9	13.3	18.3
T-base + TD	5.3	8.9	14.6
T-base + SW	5.5	9.8	14.5
T-base + JD	**9.8**	**14.5**	**19.1**

(b) Transformer-base

Table 5: Comparing BLEU scores for Joint Dropout (JD) and the reimplementations of Token Drop (TD), Zero Out (ZO), and SwitchOut (SW) on 5k, 10k and 20k training samples from IWSLT De-En.

results in Table 5a demonstrate that Zero-Out only provides marginal improvements. Moreover, both Token Drop and SwitchOut methods prove to be ineffective in low-resource scenarios. In contrast, JD consistently outperforms these methods, particularly in extreme low-resource cases. As shown in Table 5a, Zero-Out only provides marginal improvements. In addition, while Token Drop and SwitchOut methods prove to be ineffective in low-resource situations, JD consistently yields the largest improvements, especially for extreme low-resource cases. In addition, Table 5b provides additional evidence supporting the superiority of JD over similar methods, even when optimized parameters for the Transformer model are not specifically chosen.

3.5 NMT Robustness

Recent work has shown that trivial modifications to the source sentence can cause unexpected changes in the translation (Fadaee and Monz, 2020). Furthermore, models with stronger compositional abilities are anticipated to generate more robust translations Dankers et al. (2022). To evaluate the robustness of JD against such modifications, we differ from previous methods that automatically introduce noise to the test set (Michel and Neubig, 2018; Cheng et al., 2019) which is prone to creating semantic and syntactic errors in the input. Instead, we manually develop a more realistic test set.

First, based on Direct Assessment (DA) on a 100-point scale (Graham et al., 2013), we select the top 100 sentences out of randomly selected 300 translation outputs generated by a Transformer-optimized model trained on 20k samples. We then alter the input sentences by replacing a specific phrase or word, while ensuring that they remain syntactically and semantically accurate. Table 6 illustrates that perturbing the original sentences results in a smaller performance decrease for the model trained with JD, when compared to the baseline. This means that our proposed method significantly decreases the volatile behavior of low-resource NMT.

Table 7 shows an example of perturbing a sentence. After replacing "*ein Kind in Indien*" in

Method	Metric	Orig.	Per.	Δ
T-base	DA	62.1	49.3	−12.8
	BLEU	28.5	26.0	−2.5
T-base + JD	DA	69.8	59.3	**−10.5**
	BLEU	30.7	30.4	**−0.3**
T-opt.	DA	79.9	56.6	−23.3
	BLEU	37.4	31.8	−5.6
T-opt. + JD	DA	83.7	77.4	**−6.3**
	BLEU	41.8	39.9	**−1.9**

Table 6: Direct assessment and BLEU scores, pre and post input perturbation on random samples from De-En test set.

	Original test sentence	Test sentence after perturbation
Src	[**ein Kind in Indien**] sagt: "heute habe ich einen Affen gesehen".	{**meine Oma in China**} sagt: "heute habe ich einen Affen gesehen".
Ref.	[a child in India] says , "I saw a monkey today ."	{my grandmother in China} says, "I saw a monkey today ."
T-opt.	[a child in India] says, "today I've seen a monkeys."	{my grandmother's mother in China} says, "Look today."
T-opt. + JD	[a kid in India] says, "I've seen a monkeys today."	{my grandmother in China} says, "today I've seen a monkeys."

Table 7: By replacing the German noun phrase ***ein Kind in Indien*** [a child in India] with ***meine Oma in China*** [my grandmother in China], there is no undesirable behavior in the rest of the translation when using Joint Dropout. Underlined text means the rest of the translation is approximately the same with the reference, while the wavy underline means it has changed. Bracket shows the phrase that we perturb, while the curly bracket is the perturbed phrase

the source sentence with "*meine Oma in China*", while the rest of the translation is negatively affected using the baseline model, the JD shows more robustness against the input perturbation and does not exhibit any negative behavior.

3.6 Generalization across domains

In low-resource language settings, NMT systems frequently encounter challenges when it comes to achieving effective translation across distinct domains. This is primarily attributed to their tendency to prioritize the idiosyncrasies of the training domain, rather than capturing the broader linguistic characteristics shared by the language pairs. Therefore, in addition to evaluating generalization in terms of compositionality and robustness, it is also crucial to assess generalization concerning distributional shift and uncertainty estimation (Hupkes et al., 2022). While the definition of a domain is not precisely defined (van der Wees et al., 2015),for our evaluation, we consider TED talks and news as belonging to different domains.

Table 8 provides insights into the behavior of JD when there is a domain shift between the training domain (TED talks) and the test domain (news from WMT). The results demonstrate that JD exhibits greater robustness in such scenarios, showcasing its ability to better handle

Method	10k	20k	40k
T-base	2.4	3.9	7.1
T-base + JD	**3.2**	**5.4**	**9.8**
T-opt.	6.2	8.7	13.9
T-opt. + JD	**7.5**	**10.9**	**14.6**

Table 8: Results of training on different subsamples of TED talks and testing on a domain with different distribution (Newstest2020).

distributional shifts and improve translation quality across different domains. This highlights the effectiveness of JD in mitigating the negative effects of domain-specific training and enhancing the generalizability of NMT systems in low-resource language pairs.

4 Conclusion

Despite the fact that NMT's success is closely tied to having large amounts of training data, it is still beneficial to explore methods that can help improve generalization when working with limited data. In this paper, we introduce Joint Dropout as a straightforward yet effective approach to enhancing the compositional generalization and translation quality of low-resource NMT. Specifically, we demonstrate that jointly replacing phrases with variables has a regularizing effect that mitigates overfitting by enabling the system to translate sentences regardless of the specific phrases present at the variable positions.

5 Future work

We only focus on improving generalizability of low-resource NMT, while higher-resource settings might also gain from joint variables. Additionally, we demonstrate the effectiveness of our proposed method using multiple low-resource language pairs, whereas there are many other language pairs with limited data. Furthermore, since JD tries to capture the rules of compositionality in translation, we expect more benefit to the language pairs with less similarity. Additionally, our approach is data-centric and model-agnostic, applicable to various models and tasks beyond the methods evaluated in this paper. Therefore, it has the potential to improve existing pre-trained models such as mBART (Liu et al., 2020), when fine-tuning on low-resource languages, but further experimentation is needed to confirm its effectiveness. We leave these investigations to future work.

6 Broader Impact

The implementation of NMT has brought about significant progress in the translation field, however, it also poses potential challenges such as liability for mistakes made by using NMT and mistranslation, which could be more of a concern when dealing with limited data. Furthermore, the high ability of NMT to generalize well presents a potential risk of difficulty in identifying errors, specifically those related to compositionality. This can be a concern in safety-critical domains where a single error can have severe consequences. Moreover, the ability of NMT to produce more coherent and fluent translations may impede the identification of where the system is malfunctioning, thus hindering the correction of errors or biases in the model.

References

Araabi, A. and Monz, C. (2020). Optimizing transformer for low-resource neural machine translation. In Scott, D., Bel, N., and Zong, C., editors, *Proceedings of the 28th International Conference on Computational Linguistics, COLING 2020, Barcelona, Spain (Online), December 8-13, 2020*, pages 3429–3435. International Committee on Computational Linguistics.

Belinkov, Y. and Bisk, Y. (2018). Synthetic and natural noise both break neural machine translation. In *6th International Conference on Learning Representations, ICLR 2018, Vancouver, BC, Canada, April 30 - May 3, 2018, Conference Track Proceedings*. OpenReview.net.

Cettolo, M., Niehues, J., Stüker, S., Bentivogli, L., and Federico, M. (2014). Report on the 11th IWSLT evaluation campaign. In Federico, M., Stüker, S., and Yvon, F., editors, *Proceedings of the 11th International Workshop on Spoken Language Translation: Evaluation Campaign@IWSLT 2014, Lake Tahoe, CA, USA, December 4-5, 2014*.

Cheng, Y., Jiang, L., and Macherey, W. (2019). Robust neural machine translation with doubly adversarial inputs. In Korhonen, A., Traum, D. R., and Màrquez, L., editors, *Proceedings of the 57th Conference of the Association for Computational Linguistics, ACL 2019, Florence, Italy, July 28- August 2, 2019, Volume 1: Long Papers*, pages 4324–4333. Association for Computational Linguistics.

Chiang, D. (2005). A hierarchical phrase-based model for statistical machine translation. In Knight, K., Ng, H. T., and Oflazer, K., editors, *ACL 2005, 43rd Annual Meeting of the Association for Computational Linguistics, Proceedings of the Conference, 25-30 June 2005, University of Michigan, USA*, pages 263–270. The Association for Computer Linguistics.

Dankers, V., Bruni, E., and Hupkes, D. (2022). The paradox of the compositionality of natural language: A neural machine translation case study. In Muresan, S., Nakov, P., and Villavicencio, A., editors, *Proceedings of the 60th Annual Meeting of the Association for Computational Linguistics (Volume 1: Long Papers), ACL 2022, Dublin, Ireland, May 22-27, 2022*, pages 4154–4175. Association for Computational Linguistics.

Fadaee, M. and Monz, C. (2020). The unreasonable volatility of neural machine translation models. In Birch, A., Finch, A. M., Hayashi, H., Heafield, K., Junczys-Dowmunt, M., Konstas, I., Li, X., Neubig, G., and Oda, Y., editors, *Proceedings of the Fourth Workshop on Neural Generation and Translation, NGT@ACL 2020, Online, July 5-10, 2020*, pages 88–96. Association for Computational Linguistics.

Goyal, N., Gao, C., Chaudhary, V., Chen, P., Wenzek, G., Ju, D., Krishnan, S., Ranzato, M., Guzmán, F., and Fan, A. (2022). The flores-101 evaluation benchmark for low-resource and multilingual machine translation. *Trans. Assoc. Comput. Linguistics*, 10:522–538.

Graham, Y., Baldwin, T., Moffat, A., and Zobel, J. (2013). Continuous measurement scales in human evaluation of machine translation. In Dipper, S., Liakata, M., and Pareja-Lora, A., editors, *Proceedings of the 7th Linguistic Annotation Workshop and Interoperability with Discourse, LAW-ID@ACL 2013, August 8-9, 2013, Sofia, Bulgaria*, pages 33–41. The Association for Computer Linguistics.

Hupkes, D., Dankers, V., Mul, M., and Bruni, E. (2020). Compositionality decomposed: How do neural networks generalise? *J. Artif. Intell. Res.*, 67:757–795.

Hupkes, D., Giulianelli, M., Dankers, V., Artetxe, M., Elazar, Y., Pimentel, T., Christodoulopoulos, C., Lasri, K., Saphra, N., Sinclair, A., Ulmer, D., Schottmann, F., Batsuren, K., Sun, K., Sinha, K., Khalatbari, L., Ryskina, M., Frieske, R., Cotterell, R., and Jin, Z. (2022). State-of-the-art generalisation research in NLP: a taxonomy and review. *CoRR*, abs/2210.03050.

Keysers, D., Schärli, N., Scales, N., Buisman, H., Furrer, D., Kashubin, S., Momchev, N., Sinopalnikov, D., Stafiniak, L., Tihon, T., Tsarkov, D., Wang, X., van Zee, M., and Bousquet, O. (2020). Measuring compositional generalization: A comprehensive method on realistic data. In *8th International Conference on Learning Representations, ICLR 2020, Addis Ababa, Ethiopia, April 26-30, 2020*. OpenReview.net.

Kim, J., Ravikumar, P., Ainslie, J., and Ontañón, S. (2021). Improving compositional generalization in classification tasks via structure annotations. In Zong, C., Xia, F., Li, W., and Navigli, R., editors, *Proceedings of the 59th Annual Meeting of the Association for Computational Linguistics and the 11th International Joint Conference on Natural Language Processing, ACL/IJCNLP 2021, (Volume 2: Short Papers), Virtual Event, August 1-6, 2021*, pages 637–645. Association for Computational Linguistics.

Kim, N. and Linzen, T. (2020). COGS: A compositional generalization challenge based on semantic interpretation. In Webber, B., Cohn, T., He, Y., and Liu, Y., editors, *Proceedings of the 2020 Conference on Empirical Methods in Natural Language Processing, EMNLP 2020, Online, November 16-20, 2020*, pages 9087–9105. Association for Computational Linguistics.

Koehn, P., Hoang, H., Birch, A., Callison-Burch, C., Federico, M., Bertoldi, N., Cowan, B., Shen, W., Moran, C., Zens, R., Dyer, C., Bojar, O., Constantin, A., and Herbst, E. (2007). Moses: Open source toolkit for statistical machine translation. In Carroll, J. A., van den Bosch, A., and Zaenen, A., editors, *ACL 2007, Proceedings of the 45th Annual Meeting of the Association for Computational Linguistics, June 23-30, 2007, Prague, Czech Republic*. The Association for Computational Linguistics.

Koehn, P. and Knowles, R. (2017). Six challenges for neural machine translation. In Luong, T., Birch, A., Neubig, G., and Finch, A. M., editors, *Proceedings of the First Workshop on Neural Machine Translation, NMT@ACL 2017, Vancouver, Canada, August 4, 2017*, pages 28–39. Association for Computational Linguistics.

Koehn, P., Och, F. J., and Marcu, D. (2003). Statistical phrase-based translation. In Hearst, M. A. and Ostendorf, M., editors, *Human Language Technology Conference of the North American Chapter of the Association for Computational Linguistics, HLT-NAACL 2003, Edmonton, Canada, May 27 - June 1, 2003*. The Association for Computational Linguistics.

Lake, B. M. and Baroni, M. (2018). Generalization without systematicity: On the compositional skills of sequence-to-sequence recurrent networks. In Dy, J. G. and Krause, A., editors, *Proceedings of the 35th International Conference on Machine Learning, ICML 2018, Stockholmsmässan, Stockholm, Sweden, July 10-15, 2018*, volume 80 of *Proceedings of Machine Learning Research*, pages 2879–2888. PMLR.

Lake, B. M., Ullman, T. D., Tenenbaum, J. B., and Gershman, S. J. (2017). Building machines that learn and think like people. *Behavioral and Brain Sciences*, 40:e253.

Lan, Y., Wang, L., Jiang, J., and Lim, E. (2022). Improving compositional generalization in math word problem solving. *CoRR*, abs/2209.01352.

Li, Y., Yin, Y., Chen, Y., and Zhang, Y. (2021). On compositional generalization of neural machine translation. In Zong, C., Xia, F., Li, W., and Navigli, R., editors, *Proceedings of the 59th Annual Meeting of the Association for Computational Linguistics and the 11th International Joint Conference on Natural Language Processing, ACL/IJCNLP 2021, (Volume 1: Long Papers), Virtual Event, August 1-6, 2021*, pages 4767–4780. Association for Computational Linguistics.

Liu, Y., Gu, J., Goyal, N., Li, X., Edunov, S., Ghazvininejad, M., Lewis, M., and Zettlemoyer, L. (2020). Multilingual denoising pre-training for neural machine translation. *Trans. Assoc. Comput. Linguistics*, 8:726–742.

Manning, C. D., Surdeanu, M., Bauer, J., Finkel, J., Bethard, S. J., and McClosky, D. (2014). The Stanford CoreNLP natural language processing toolkit. In *Association for Computational Linguistics (ACL) System Demonstrations*, pages 55–60.

Mehta, S. V., Rao, J., Tay, Y., Kale, M., Parikh, A., and Strubell, E. (2022). Improving compositional generalization with self-training for data-to-text generation. In Muresan, S., Nakov, P., and Villavicencio, A., editors, *Proceedings of the 60th Annual Meeting of the Association for Computational Linguistics (Volume 1: Long Papers), ACL 2022, Dublin, Ireland, May 22-27, 2022*, pages 4205–4219. Association for Computational Linguistics.

Michel, P. and Neubig, G. (2018). MTNT: A testbed for machine translation of noisy text. In Riloff, E., Chiang, D., Hockenmaier, J., and Tsujii, J., editors, *Proceedings of the 2018 Conference on Empirical Methods in Natural Language Processing, Brussels, Belgium, October 31 - November 4, 2018*, pages 543–553. Association for Computational Linguistics.

Östling, R. and Tiedemann, J. (2016). Efficient word alignment with markov chain monte carlo. *Prague Bull. Math. Linguistics*, 106:125–146.

Ott, M., Edunov, S., Baevski, A., Fan, A., Gross, S., Ng, N., Grangier, D., and Auli, M. (2019). fairseq: A fast, extensible toolkit for sequence modeling. In Ammar, W., Louis, A., and Mostafazadeh, N., editors, *Proceedings of the 2019 Conference of the North American Chapter of the Association for Computational Linguistics: Human Language Technologies, NAACL-HLT 2019, Minneapolis, MN, USA, June 2-7, 2019, Demonstrations*, pages 48–53. Association for Computational Linguistics.

Partee, B. et al. (1984). Compositionality. *Varieties of formal semantics*, 3:281–311.

Post, M. (2018). A call for clarity in reporting BLEU scores. In Bojar, O., Chatterjee, R., Federmann, C., Fishel, M., Graham, Y., Haddow, B., Huck, M., Jimeno-Yepes, A., Koehn, P., Monz, C., Negri, M., Névéol, A., Neves, M. L., Post, M., Specia, L., Turchi, M., and Verspoor, K., editors, *Proceedings of the Third Conference on Machine Translation: Research Papers, WMT 2018, Belgium, Brussels, October 31 - November 1, 2018*, pages 186–191. Association for Computational Linguistics.

Qi, Y., Sachan, D. S., Felix, M., Padmanabhan, S., and Neubig, G. (2018). When and why are pre-trained word embeddings useful for neural machine translation? In Walker, M. A., Ji, H., and Stent, A., editors, *Proceedings of the 2018 Conference of the North American Chapter of the Association for Computational Linguistics: Human Language Technologies, NAACL-HLT, New Orleans, Louisiana, USA, June 1-6, 2018, Volume 2 (Short Papers)*, pages 529–535. Association for Computational Linguistics.

Qiu, L., Shaw, P., Pasupat, P., Nowak, P. K., Linzen, T., Sha, F., and Toutanova, K. (2022). Improving compositional generalization with latent structure and data augmentation. In Carpuat, M., de Marneffe, M., and Ruíz, I. V. M., editors, *Proceedings of the 2022 Conference of the North American Chapter of the Association for Computational Linguistics: Human Language Technologies, NAACL 2022, Seattle, WA, United States, July 10-15, 2022*, pages 4341–4362. Association for Computational Linguistics.

Schmidhuber, J. (1990). Towards compositional learning in dynamic networks.

Sennrich, R., Haddow, B., and Birch, A. (2016a). Edinburgh neural machine translation systems for WMT 16. In *Proceedings of the First Conference on Machine Translation, WMT 2016, colocated with ACL 2016, August 11-12, Berlin, Germany*, pages 371–376. The Association for Computer Linguistics.

Sennrich, R., Haddow, B., and Birch, A. (2016b). Neural machine translation of rare words with subword units. In *Proceedings of the 54th Annual Meeting of the Association for Computational Linguistics, ACL 2016, August 7-12, 2016, Berlin, Germany, Volume 1: Long Papers*. The Association for Computer Linguistics.

Tiedemann, J. and Thottingal, S. (2020). OPUS-MT - building open translation services for the world. In Forcada, M. L., Martins, A., Moniz, H., Turchi, M., Bisazza, A., Moorkens, J., Arenas, A. G., Nurminen, M., Marg, L., Fumega, S., Martins, B., Batista, F., Coheur, L., Escartín, C. P., and Trancoso, I., editors, *Proceedings of the 22nd Annual Conference of the European Association for Machine Translation, EAMT 2020, Lisboa, Portugal, November 3-5, 2020*, pages 479–480. European Association for Machine Translation.

Toral, A. and Sánchez-Cartagena, V. M. (2017). A multifaceted evaluation of neural versus phrase-based machine translation for 9 language directions. In Lapata, M., Blunsom, P., and Koller, A., editors, *Proceedings of the 15th Conference of the European Chapter of the Association for Computational Linguistics, EACL 2017, Valencia, Spain, April 3-7, 2017, Volume 1: Long Papers*, pages 1063–1073. Association for Computational Linguistics.

van der Wees, M., Bisazza, A., Weerkamp, W., and Monz, C. (2015). What's in a domain? analyzing genre and topic differences in statistical machine translation. In *Proceedings of the 53rd Annual Meeting of the Association for Computational Linguistics and the 7th International Joint Conference on Natural Language Processing of the Asian Federation of Natural Language Processing, ACL 2015, July 26-31, 2015, Beijing, China, Volume 2: Short Papers*, pages 560–566. The Association for Computer Linguistics.

Vaswani, A., Shazeer, N., Parmar, N., Uszkoreit, J., Jones, L., Gomez, A. N., Kaiser, L., and Polosukhin, I. (2017). Attention is all you need. In Guyon, I., von Luxburg, U., Bengio, S., Wallach, H. M., Fergus, R., Vishwanathan, S. V. N., and Garnett, R., editors, *Advances in Neural Information Processing Systems 30: Annual Conference on Neural Information Processing Systems 2017, December 4-9, 2017, Long Beach, CA, USA*, pages 5998–6008.

Wang, X., Pham, H., Dai, Z., and Neubig, G. (2018). Switchout: an efficient data augmentation algorithm for neural machine translation. In Riloff, E., Chiang, D., Hockenmaier, J., and Tsujii, J., editors, *Proceedings of the 2018 Conference on Empirical Methods in Natural Language Processing, Brussels, Belgium, October 31 - November 4, 2018*, pages 856–861. Association for Computational Linguistics.

Zens, R., Och, F. J., and Ney, H. (2002). Phrase-based statistical machine translation. In Jarke, M., Koehler, J., and Lakemeyer, G., editors, *KI 2002: Advances in Artificial Intelligence,*

25th Annual German Conference on AI, KI 2002, Aachen, Germany, September 16-20, 2002, Proceedings, volume 2479 of *Lecture Notes in Computer Science*, pages 18–32. Springer.

Zhang, H., Qiu, S., Duan, X., and Zhang, M. (2020). Token drop mechanism for neural machine translation. In Scott, D., Bel, N., and Zong, C., editors, *Proceedings of the 28th International Conference on Computational Linguistics, COLING 2020, Barcelona, Spain (Online), December 8-13, 2020*, pages 4298–4303. International Committee on Computational Linguistics.

A Study of Multilingual versus Meta-Learning for Language Model Pre-Training for Adaptation to Unseen Low Resource Languages

Jyotsana Khatri jyotsanak@cse.iitb.ac.in
Department of Computer Science and Engineering, IIT Bombay, India.
Rudra Murthy rmurthyv@in.ibm.com
IBM Research India
Amar Prakash Azad amarazad@in.ibm.com
IBM Research India
Pushpak Bhattacharyya pb@cse.iitb.ac.in
Department of Computer Science and Engineering, IIT Bombay, India.

Abstract

In this paper, we compare two approaches to train a multilingual language model: (i) simple multilingual learning using data-mixing, and (ii) meta-learning. We examine the performance of these models by extending them to unseen language pairs and further finetune them for the task of unsupervised NMT. We perform several experiments with varying amounts of data and give a comparative analysis of the approaches. We observe that both approaches give a comparable performance, and meta-learning gives slightly better results in a few cases of low amounts of data. For *Oriya-Punjabi* language pair, meta-learning performs better than multilingual learning when using 2M, and 3M sentences.

1 Introduction

Neural Machine Translation (NMT) works well with large amounts of parallel data (Vaswani et al., 2017). For many language pairs, such data is not available. Unsupervised NMT has achieved performance comparable to supervised NMT for a few European language pairs; however, it only works well for languages that have a good amount of monolingual data available. The current state-of-the-art approaches of unsupervised NMT have a language model pre-training phase and a finetuning phase based on iterative back-translation (Conneau and Lample, 2019; Song et al., 2019a; Lewis et al., 2019).

Translation involving low-resource languages (for which monolingual data is also scarce) is very difficult. The current state-of-the-art approaches of unsupervised NMT perform poorly for such language pairs (Kim et al., 2020; Marchisio et al., 2020). To utilize the benefit of high-resource language pairs, multilingual language model pre-training has been utilized (Lewis et al., 2020; Siddhant et al., 2020). Chronopoulou et al. (2020) proposed to train a language model for high-resource language pair and then use it as initialization for the low-resource language pair.

Dou et al. (2019) explored the use of meta-learning after pretraining with high-resource languages for low resource natural language understanding tasks. They claim that multi-task

Proceedings of Machine Translation Summit XIX, Vol. 1: Research Track, pages 26–34
September 4–8, 2023, Macau SAR, China.

learning might favor high-resource tasks, while meta-learning learns a good initialization that can be adapted to any task with a small number of iterations.

In this paper, we use a meta-learning framework for multilingual language model pretraining and compare it with a multilingual learning paradigm based on data-mixing and finetuning it for unseen language pairs. We use these finetuned models to further training for the task of unsupervised NMT. Specifically, we utilize MAML (Model Agnostic Meta-Learning) Finn et al. (2017) which is a meta-learning algorithm based on gradient descent and is used to get good generalizations for multiple tasks. When using meta-learning, each language is considered a task in the pretraining phase. Our goal is to find a method to efficiently learn parameters in a shared parameter space across multiple languages in the language model pretraining, which works as good initialization for the language model training for unseen language pairs and improves the performance of unsupervised NMT. A good pretrained multilingual language model should be able to adjust to newer language pairs (unseen languages) using a limited amount of training data. Our contributions are:

- Comparison of two approaches of multilingual language model pre-training: (i) simple multilingual learning using data-mixing, and (ii) meta-learning. We compare these two approaches by extending them for unseen language pairs and further finetuning them for unsupervised NMT.
- We perform experiments with varying amounts of data for unseen language pairs and analyze the impact of different pretraining mechanisms.

2 Related Work

2.1 Unsupervised NMT

The initial works on unsupervised MT were based on statistical decipherment (Ravi and Knight, 2011; Dou and Knight, 2012, 2013; Dou et al., 2015, 2014). Decipherment assumes one language as cipher text and tries to generate the text in other languages.

Unsupervised NMT gained popularity after the initial proposals of Artetxe et al. (2018) and Lample et al. (2018) to train an NMT system without using any parallel data. These systems are majorly based on three things: unsupervised bilingual embeddings, denoising auto-encoders, and iterative back-translation. The first step is to learn bilingual embeddings in an unsupervised way by training two pretrained monolingual embedding spaces and aligning them using a linear transformation based on Procrustes refinement. Denoising auto-encoder aims to make the decoder learn to generate sentences. The Back-translation step involves generating synthetic parallel sentences using the current state of the machine translation model and using them to train the model in the opposite direction. This process of generation of synthetic parallel corpus and training is performed iteratively.

Current state-of-the-art approaches to unsupervised NMT involve a language model pretraining and a finetuning phase based on iterative back-translation. Different kinds of language modeling objectives have been proposed for the pretraining (Conneau and Lample, 2019; Song et al., 2019a; Lewis et al., 2019). Conneau and Lample (2019) (XLM) uses the Masked Language Modeling (MLM) objective, whereas Song et al. (2019b) (MASS) uses the Masked Sequence Generation objective. Lewis et al. (2020) proposed a language modeling objective similar to Song et al. (2019b), but it predicts the entire sentence on the decoder side and uses a different masking strategy. The architecture is based on a shared encoder and a shared decoder.

The success of unsupervised NMT depends on the model's capability to learn effective multilingual representations in the pretraining stage. Existing unsupervised NMT approaches fail for distant languages and languages with low amounts of data (Marchisio et al., 2020). Recently, many multilingual pretraining mechanisms have been proposed using similar masking objec-

tives but involving multiple languages, which were shown to perform better for low-resource languages (Liu et al., 2020; Conneau et al., 2019; Siddhant et al., 2020).
Recently few papers have also explored the use of in-context learning, instruction tuning with large language models (Chowdhery et al., 2022; Brown et al., 2020; Zhang et al., 2023; Moslem et al., 2023; Lyu et al., 2023; Peng et al., 2023; Karpinska and Iyyer, 2023; Wang et al., 2023; Jiao et al., 2023a; Zhu et al., 2023; Hendy et al., 2023; Garcia et al., 2023; Pilault et al., 2023; Vilar et al., 2022; Jiao et al., 2023b; Agrawal et al., 2022). Our work is not in the direction of in-context learning rather we are trying to find an optimal way of training a multilingual model based on its capabilities to be able to extend to unseen languages.

2.2 Meta-learning

Meta-learning solves the problem of fast adaptation to new training data. Gu et al. (2018) proposed an approach to apply meta-learning in NMT for low-resource language pairs. They use MAML (model agnostic meta-learning) to train a multilingual model that can be finetuned for new language pairs, this finetuning requires very few numbers of iterations, which is referred to as fast-adaptation. Sharaf et al. (2020) proposed an approach for domain adaptation based on a meta-learning framework, they use MAML and reptile for meta-learning. Qian and Yu (2019) propose to use meta-learning for domain adaptation. Nooralahzadeh et al. (2020) proposed to introduce MAML for cross-lingual language understanding tasks to effectively utilize training data of high resource and other auxiliary languages. The approach is to first train XLM using a high-resource language, followed by meta-learning using the low-resource languages, and final few-shot finetuning using low resource target language for the target task. Dou et al. (2019) explores the use of MAML for low-resource natural language understanding tasks.

3 Approach

We compare two multilingual language model pretraining approaches: (i) multilingual learning based on simple data mixing and (ii) other based on a meta-learning framework. We try to find a good set of initialization for language model pretraining for unseen language pairs using many high-resource languages. In multilingual learning, the training simply iterates between different languages. For meta-learning, we utilize MAML together with MASS Song et al. (2019b) objective to train a multilingual language model. The main aim of MAML is to find a good initialization from which a target task learning requires fewer iterations. It uses many other source tasks related to the target task to learn this initialization. We try to meta-learn using the source tasks and then continue to learn for the target tasks. This process is different than a simple multilingual learning framework. Algorithm 1 shows the training algorithm for the meta-learning framework. We extend both the models to finetune them for unseen language pairs and use the vocabulary extension method proposed in Chronopoulou et al. (2020) to extend the vocabulary of the multilingual model.

$$\theta = \theta - \alpha \sum_{T_i} \nabla L_i(f_{\theta_i^k}) \tag{1}$$

α is a hyperparameter, which represents the learning rate. The model is represented by a function f_θ with parameters θ. θ_i^k represents the state of the parameters when adapting to task T_i and here gradient update is performed using k examples. L represents the loss function.

4 Experiments

We experiment with *Hindi*, *Bengali*, *Gujarati* as our high resource languages to train a multilingual model using masked sequence to sequence pretraining objective. We use *Oriya-Punjabi*

Algorithm 1 Multilingual LM pretraining with MAML

Source tasks: L_1,L_2,...L_n
Target tasks: T_1,T_2
while true **do**
  for all Source tasks L_i **do**
    Compute θ_i^k using MASS objective
  end for
  Update θ as per MAML objective as per equation 1
end while

and *Assamese-Nepali* as our unseen language pairs. The details of the data are given in Section 4.1.

4.1 Dataset

We experimented using monolingual data provided by the AI4Bharat Kunchukuttan et al. (2020) dataset for the Indic languages, *viz, Hindi, Bengali, Gujarati, Punjabi*, and *Assamese*. We use *Nepali* monolingual dataset from common crawl corpus [1] Wenzek et al. (2020), and use the same amount of sentences equal to *Assamese*. The size of the data is given in Table 1. Our test data is taken from WAT2021 multi-indic-nmt shared task. The details of the dev and test data in Table 2. The dev and test data of *as-ne* is taken from FLORES-2021 dataset (Guzmán et al., 2019; Goyal et al., 2022). We convert all language data to same script (we choose devnagri as the common script which is an arbitrary choice) to reduce the vocabulary mismatch and have same lexical representations (Khatri et al., 2021).

Language	Number of Sentences
Bengali (bn)	7.21 M
Gujarati (gu)	7.89 M
Hindi (hi)	63.00 M
Oriya (or)	3.59 M
Punjabi (pa)	6.55 M
Assamese (as)	1.38M
Nepali (ne)	1.38M

Table 1: Monolingual data

4.2 Results

We train 3 types of models:

- **Bilingual**: Bilingual language model pretraining using only monolingual data of target language pair, followed by finetuning using iterative back-translation.
- **Multilingual**: Multilingual pretraining using masked sequence to sequence pretraining using high resource languages, followed by training for unseen language pair using same language modeling objective and then final finetuning using iterative back-translation.

[1] `https://metatext.io/redirect/cc100-nepali`

Language pair	Validation data	Test data
or-pa	1000	2390
as-ne	997	1012

Table 2: Validation and Test data

Data Size	Bilingual		Multilingual		Meta-learning	
	or → pa	**pa → or**	**or → pa**	**pa → or**	**or → pa**	**pa → or**
1M	1.2 ± 0.2	0.6 ± 0.1	6.9 ± 0.4	**3.3 ± 0.3**	**7.1 ± 0.4**	3.2 ± 0.3
2M	3.5 ± 0.3	2.3 ± 0.3	7.7 ± 0.4	4.1 ± 0.4	**8.5 ± 0.4**	**4.4 ± 0.4**
3M	4.6 ± 0.3	3.4 ± 0.3	8.3 ± 0.4	4.4 ± 0.4	**9.0 ± 0.5**	**4.9 ± 0.4**
Full data	5.2 ± 0.4	4.2 ± 0.4	9.8 ± 0.5	5.3 ± 0.4	9.8 ± 0.5	5.3 ± 0.5
Data Size	**Bilingual**		**Multilingual**		**Meta-learning**	
	as → ne	**ne → as**	**as → ne**	**ne → as**	**as → ne**	**ne → as**
0.5M	1.1 ± 0.3	1.0 ± 0.3	**2.2 ± 0.3**	**2.2 ± 0.3**	2.0 ± 0.4	2.1 ± 0.3
1M	2.5 ± 0.4	2.4 ± 0.4	3.0 ± 0.4	**3.0 ± 0.4**	3.0 ± 0.4	2.9 ± 0.4
Full data	2.6 ± 0.4	2.5 ± 0.4	3.0 ± 0.4	3.2 ± 0.4	**3.1 ± 0.4**	3.2 ± 0.4

Table 3: Test set BLEU scores for *Oriya-Punjabi* and *Assamese-Nepali* using Bilingual, Multilingual and Meta-learning approaches for language model pretraining

- **Meta-learning**: Multilingual pretraining using masked sequence to sequence pretraining with meta-learning framework explained in Algorithm 1, followed by the same process described in multilingual learning.

Our multilingual models are trained using *Hindi*, *Bengali*, and *Gujarati* for two approaches of multilingual language model pretraining one is based on data-mixing, and another one utilizes meta-learning. We use six layers in the transformer encoder and decoder, which is shared across all languages. The number of attention heads is 8. We use the toolkit provided by Song et al. (2019a) [2], and modify it for using MAML in the language model pretraining phase.

We also modify the codebase for vocabulary extension when finetuning a pretrained multilingual model for unseen languages. We use IndicNLP [3] library for tokenization and script conversion. The multilingual models are trained for 150 epochs, where epoch size is 0.2M sentences. The multilingual model is finetuned for 100 epochs using the data of unseen low resource language pair for MASS objective and then finetuned for 50 epochs using iterative back-translation. We report results in the form of BLEU score for our experiments in Table 3. The BLEU score is calculated using sacreBLEU (Post, 2018).

5 Discussion

Pretrained multilingual models help in improving the performance for unseen languages, which is clear from Table 3; all bilingual models have lower BLEU scores compared to models which have been initialized using multilingual pretrained models. When we use 2M, and 3M sentences for *or-pa*, we see minor improvements when using meta-learning over our baseline model.

[2]`https://github.com/microsoft/MASS`

[3]`https://github.com/anoopkunchukuttan/indic_nlp_library`

When we utilize full available data of *Oriya* and *Punjabi*, meta-learning performs similar to multilingual learning. But when we use 0.5M sentences, multilingual learning is working better than meta-learning for *or-pa*. For *as-ne* multilingual learning and meta-learning both give similar performance.
For *or-pa*, after the language model pretraining phase is complete for the unseen language pair, the cross-lingual perplexity is higher for meta-learning than the multilingual model but the BLEU score is better, which indicates that fluency is not getting better but the translation is getting improved indicating better learning of shared representations. We also observe that the ratio of source words is 3.27% for multilingual and 4.27% for meta-learning when experimenting with 2M sentences for *or* to *pa* translation even without finetuning it for iterative back-translation.

6 Conclusion and Future Work

In this paper, we perform a comparison of two approaches to train a multilingual language model: (i) simple multilingual learning, and (ii) meta-learning. We conduct experiments to extend these models for unseen language-pair and then finetune them for unsupervised NMT to compare the performance. We observe that both approaches give a comparable performance. In a few cases of low amounts of data, meta-learning gives slightly better results. In the future, we would like to explore the performance of both approaches to train the multilingual language model for other tasks.

References

Agrawal, S., Zhou, C., Lewis, M., Zettlemoyer, L., and Ghazvininejad, M. (2022). In-context examples selection for machine translation. *arXiv preprint arXiv:2212.02437*.

Artetxe, M., Labaka, G., Agirre, E., and Cho, K. (2018). Unsupervised neural machine translation. In *ICLR 2018, Proceedings of the Sixth International Conference on Learning Representations*, Vancouver, Canada. 12pp.

Brown, T., Mann, B., Ryder, N., Subbiah, M., Kaplan, J. D., Dhariwal, P., Neelakantan, A., Shyam, P., Sastry, G., Askell, A., et al. (2020). Language models are few-shot learners. *Advances in neural information processing systems*, 33:1877–1901.

Chowdhery, A., Narang, S., Devlin, J., Bosma, M., Mishra, G., Roberts, A., Barham, P., Chung, H. W., Sutton, C., Gehrmann, S., et al. (2022). Palm: Scaling language modeling with pathways.

Chronopoulou, A., Stojanovski, D., and Fraser, A. (2020). Reusing a Pretrained Language Model on Languages with Limited Corpora for Unsupervised NMT. In *Proceedings of the 2020 Conference on Empirical Methods in Natural Language Processing (EMNLP)*, pages 2703–2711, Online. Association for Computational Linguistics.

Conneau, A., Khandelwal, K., Goyal, N., Chaudhary, V., Wenzek, G., Guzmán, F., Grave, E., Ott, M., Zettlemoyer, L., and Stoyanov, V. (2019). Unsupervised cross-lingual representation learning at scale. *arXiv preprint arXiv:1911.02116*.

Conneau, A. and Lample, G. (2019). Cross-lingual language model pretraining. In *Advances in Neural Information Processing Systems, Proceedings*, pages 7057–7067, Vancouver, Canada.

Dou, Q. and Knight, K. (2012). Large scale decipherment for out-of-domain machine translation. In *Proceedings of the 2012 Joint Conference on Empirical Methods in Natural Language Processing and Computational Natural Language Learning*, pages 266–275, Jeju Island, Korea. Association for Computational Linguistics.

Dou, Q. and Knight, K. (2013). Dependency-based decipherment for resource-limited machine translation. In *Proceedings of the 2013 Conference on Empirical Methods in Natural Language Processing*, pages 1668–1676, Seattle, Washington, USA. Association for Computational Linguistics.

Dou, Q., Vaswani, A., and Knight, K. (2014). Beyond parallel data: Joint word alignment and decipherment improves machine translation. In *Proceedings of the 2014 Conference on Empirical Methods in Natural Language Processing (EMNLP)*, pages 557–565, Doha, Qatar. Association for Computational Linguistics.

Dou, Q., Vaswani, A., Knight, K., and Dyer, C. (2015). Unifying Bayesian inference and vector space models for improved decipherment. In *Proceedings of the 53rd Annual Meeting of the Association for Computational Linguistics and the 7th International Joint Conference on Natural Language Processing (Volume 1: Long Papers)*, pages 836–845, Beijing, China. Association for Computational Linguistics.

Dou, Z.-Y., Yu, K., and Anastasopoulos, A. (2019). Investigating meta-learning algorithms for low-resource natural language understanding tasks. In *Proceedings of the 2019 Conference on Empirical Methods in Natural Language Processing and the 9th International Joint Conference on Natural Language Processing (EMNLP-IJCNLP)*, pages 1192–1197.

Finn, C., Abbeel, P., and Levine, S. (2017). Model-agnostic meta-learning for fast adaptation of deep networks. In *International conference on machine learning*, pages 1126–1135. PMLR.

Garcia, X., Bansal, Y., Cherry, C., Foster, G., Krikun, M., Feng, F., Johnson, M., and Firat, O. (2023). The unreasonable effectiveness of few-shot learning for machine translation. *arXiv preprint arXiv:2302.01398*.

Goyal, N., Gao, C., Chaudhary, V., Chen, P.-J., Wenzek, G., Ju, D., Krishnan, S., Ranzato, M., Guzmán, F., and Fan, A. (2022). The flores-101 evaluation benchmark for low-resource and multilingual machine translation. *Transactions of the Association for Computational Linguistics*, 10:522–538.

Gu, J., Wang, Y., Chen, Y., Li, V. O., and Cho, K. (2018). Meta-learning for low-resource neural machine translation. In *Proceedings of the 2018 Conference on Empirical Methods in Natural Language Processing*, pages 3622–3631.

Guzmán, F., Chen, P., Ott, M., Pino, J., Lample, G., Koehn, P., Chaudhary, V., and Ranzato, M. (2019). Two new evaluation datasets for low-resource machine translation: Nepali-english and sinhala-english. arxiv 2019. *arXiv preprint arXiv:1902.01382*.

Hendy, A., Abdelrehim, M., Sharaf, A., Raunak, V., Gabr, M., Matsushita, H., Kim, Y. J., Afify, M., and Awadalla, H. H. (2023). How good are gpt models at machine translation? a comprehensive evaluation. *arXiv preprint arXiv:2302.09210*.

Jiao, W., Huang, J.-t., Wang, W., Wang, X., Shi, S., and Tu, Z. (2023a). Parrot: Translating during chat using large language models. *arXiv preprint arXiv:2304.02426*.

Jiao, W., Wang, W., Huang, J.-t., Wang, X., and Tu, Z. (2023b). Is chatgpt a good translator? a preliminary study. *arXiv preprint arXiv:2301.08745*.

Karpinska, M. and Iyyer, M. (2023). Large language models effectively leverage document-level context for literary translation, but critical errors persist. *arXiv preprint arXiv:2304.03245*.

Khatri, J., Murthy, R., Banerjee, T., and Bhattacharyya, P. (2021). Simple measures of bridging lexical divergence help unsupervised neural machine translation for low-resource languages. *Machine Translation*, 35(4):711–744.

Kim, Y., Graça, M., and Ney, H. (2020). When and why is unsupervised neural machine translation useless? *arXiv preprint arXiv:2004.10581*.

Kunchukuttan, A., Kakwani, D., Golla, S., N.C., G., Bhattacharyya, A., Khapra, M. M., and Kumar, P. (2020). AI4Bharat-IndicNLP Corpus: Monolingual Corpora and Word Embeddings for Indic Languages. In *5th Workshop on Representation Learning for NLP (RepL4NLP-2020)*, Online. 7pp.

Lample, G., Conneau, A., Denoyer, L., and Ranzato, M. (2018). Unsupervised machine translation using monolingual corpora only. In *Proceedings of the Sixth International Conference on Learning Representations*, Vancouver, Canada. 14pp.

Lewis, M., Liu, Y., Goyal, N., Ghazvininejad, M., Mohamed, A., Levy, O., Stoyanov, V., and Zettlemoyer, L. (2019). Bart: Denoising sequence-to-sequence pre-training for natural language generation, translation, and comprehension. *arXiv preprint arXiv:1910.13461*.

Lewis, M., Liu, Y., Goyal, N., Ghazvininejad, M., Mohamed, A., Levy, O., Stoyanov, V., and Zettlemoyer, L. (2020). BART: Denoising sequence-to-sequence pre-training for natural language generation, translation, and comprehension. In *Proceedings of the 58th Annual Meeting of the Association for Computational Linguistics*, pages 7871–7880, Online. Association for Computational Linguistics.

Liu, Y., Gu, J., Goyal, N., Li, X., Edunov, S., Ghazvininejad, M., Lewis, M., and Zettlemoyer, L. (2020). Multilingual denoising pre-training for neural machine translation. *Transactions of the Association for Computational Linguistics*, 8:726–742.

Lyu, C., Xu, J., and Wang, L. (2023). New trends in machine translation using large language models: Case examples with chatgpt. *arXiv preprint arXiv:2305.01181*.

Marchisio, K., Duh, K., and Koehn, P. (2020). When does unsupervised machine translation work? In *Proceedings of the Fifth Conference on Machine Translation*, pages 571–583, Online. Association for Computational Linguistics.

Moslem, Y., Haque, R., and Way, A. (2023). Adaptive machine translation with large language models. *arXiv preprint arXiv:2301.13294*.

Nooralahzadeh, F., Bekoulis, G., Bjerva, J., and Augenstein, I. (2020). Zero-shot cross-lingual transfer with meta learning. In *Proceedings of the 2020 Conference on Empirical Methods in Natural Language Processing (EMNLP)*, pages 4547–4562.

Peng, K., Ding, L., Zhong, Q., Shen, L., Liu, X., Zhang, M., Ouyang, Y., and Tao, D. (2023). Towards making the most of chatgpt for machine translation. *arXiv preprint arXiv:2303.13780*.

Pilault, J., Garcia, X., Bražinskas, A., and Firat, O. (2023). Interactive-chain-prompting: Ambiguity resolution for crosslingual conditional generation with interaction. *arXiv preprint arXiv:2301.10309*.

Post, M. (2018). A call for clarity in reporting bleu scores. In *Proceedings of the Third Conference on Machine Translation: Research Papers*, pages 186–191.

Qian, K. and Yu, Z. (2019). Domain adaptive dialog generation via meta learning. In *Proceedings of the 57th Annual Meeting of the Association for Computational Linguistics*, pages 2639–2649.

Ravi, S. and Knight, K. (2011). Deciphering foreign language. In *Proceedings of the 49th Annual Meeting of the Association for Computational Linguistics: Human Language Technologies*, pages 12–21, Portland, Oregon, USA. Association for Computational Linguistics.

Sharaf, A., Hassan, H., and Daumé III, H. (2020). Meta-learning for few-shot nmt adaptation. In *Proceedings of the Fourth Workshop on Neural Generation and Translation*, pages 43–53.

Siddhant, A., Bapna, A., Cao, Y., Firat, O., Chen, M. X., Kudugunta, S., Arivazhagan, N., and Wu, Y. (2020). Leveraging monolingual data with self-supervision for multilingual neural machine translation. In *Proceedings of the 58th Annual Meeting of the Association for Computational Linguistics*, pages 2827–2835.

Song, K., Tan, X., Qin, T., Lu, J., and Liu, T.-Y. (2019a). Mass: Masked sequence to sequence pre-training for language generation. In *International Conference on Machine Learning*, pages 5926–5936.

Song, K., Tan, X., Qin, T., Lu, J., and Liu, T.-Y. (2019b). MASS: Masked Sequence to Sequence Pre-training for Language Generation. In *ICML 2019, Thirty-sixth International Conference on Machine Learning, Proceedings*, pages 5926–5936, Long Beach, California, USA.

Vaswani, A., Shazeer, N., Parmar, N., Uszkoreit, J., Jones, L., Gomez, A. N., Kaiser, Ł., and Polosukhin, I. (2017). Attention is all you need. *Advances in neural information processing systems*, 30.

Vilar, D., Freitag, M., Cherry, C., Luo, J., Ratnakar, V., and Foster, G. (2022). Prompting palm for translation: Assessing strategies and performance. *arXiv preprint arXiv:2211.09102.*

Wang, L., Lyu, C., Ji, T., Zhang, Z., Yu, D., Shi, S., and Tu, Z. (2023). Document-level machine translation with large language models. *arXiv preprint arXiv:2304.02210.*

Wenzek, G., Lachaux, M.-A., Conneau, A., Chaudhary, V., Guzmán, F., Joulin, A., and Grave, É. (2020). Ccnet: Extracting high quality monolingual datasets from web crawl data. In *Proceedings of the 12th Language Resources and Evaluation Conference*, pages 4003–4012.

Zhang, B., Haddow, B., and Birch, A. (2023). Prompting large language model for machine translation: A case study. *arXiv preprint arXiv:2301.07069.*

Zhu, W., Liu, H., Dong, Q., Xu, J., Kong, L., Chen, J., Li, L., and Huang, S. (2023). Multilingual machine translation with large language models: Empirical results and analysis. *arXiv preprint arXiv:2304.04675.*

Data Augmentation with Diversified Rephrasing for Low-Resource Neural Machine Translation

Yuan Gao y.gao1@massey.ac.nz
Feng Hou* f.hou@massey.ac.nz
Huia Jahnke h.t.jahnke@massey.ac.nz
Ruili Wang ruili.wang@massey.ac.nz
SMCS, Massey University, Auckland, 0632, New Zealand

Abstract

Data augmentation is an effective way to enhance the performance of neural machine translation models, especially for low-resource languages. Existing data augmentation methods are either at a token level or a sentence level. The data augmented using token level methods lack syntactic diversity and may alter original meanings. Sentence level methods usually generate low-quality source sentences that are not semantically paired with the original target sentences. In this paper, we propose a novel data augmentation method to generate diverse, high-quality and meaning-preserved new instances. Our method leverages high-quality translation models trained with high-resource languages to rephrase an original sentence by translating it into an intermediate language and then back to the original language. Through this process, the high-performing translation models guarantee the quality of the rephrased sentences, and the syntactic knowledge from the intermediate language can bring syntactic diversity to the rephrased sentences. Experimental results show our method can enhance the performance in various low-resource machine translation tasks. Moreover, by combining our method with other techniques that facilitate NMT, we can yield even better results.

1 Introduction

Current neural machine translation (NMT) (Ng et al., 2019; Wang et al., 2021; Wei et al., 2022; Shao and Feng, 2022) systems, especially those based on Transformer (Vaswani et al., 2017), have achieved human-level performance in translation quality (Hassan et al., 2018; Popel et al., 2020). These systems are trained using hundreds of millions of sentence pairs to ensure that they can generalize to unseen instances. However, large-scale parallel data is scarce and only available for a few high-resource language pairs (Lample et al., 2018; Haddow et al., 2022). Thus, the generalization of low-resource NMT models is far below an acceptable standard.

Recently, data augmentation (Sennrich et al., 2016a; Gao et al., 2019; Provilkov et al., 2020; Nguyen et al., 2020; Wei et al., 2022) has shown to be an effective way to improve the generalization of NMT models, especially for low-resource languages (Currey et al., 2017). Existing data augmentation methods for NMT can be categorized into token level or sentence level methods. Token level methods randomly replace words with rare words in both source and target sides to enhance the translation of rare words (Fadaee et al., 2017), or introduce

*Corresponding author

Proceedings of Machine Translation Summit XIX, Vol. 1: Research Track, pages 35–47
September 4–8, 2023, Macau SAR, China.

token level noises in the source side (Sennrich et al., 2016a; Lample et al., 2018; Artetxe et al., 2018; Wang et al., 2018; Gao et al., 2019; Provilkov et al., 2020) to improve the robustness of models (Khayrallah and Koehn, 2018). Sentence level methods are mainly based on back-translation (Sennrich et al., 2016b; Edunov et al., 2018), which uses target side monolingual data to synthesize pseudo-parallel data. Variants of back-translation include iterative back-translation (Hoang et al., 2018; Sánchez-Martínez et al., 2020), data diversification (Nguyen et al., 2020) and meta back-translation (Pham et al., 2021).

We argue that existing data augmentation methods for low-resource translations have two major limitations: (i) Token level methods perform token level manipulations (e.g., drop, re-order, replace) to generate new training data; thus, the generated sentences lack syntactic diversity; moreover, the token level manipulations may change the original meanings (Wei et al., 2022); (ii) Sentence level methods take natural sentences as input and generate synthetic corresponding translations using pre-trained low-quality models that are susceptible to errors (Edunov et al., 2018; Kambhatla et al., 2022), hence the augmented sentences often struggle to capture the complete semantics in the original sentences, resulting in the failure to semantically align with the target sentences. Pham et al. (2021) also noted the importance of the quality of augmented sentences.

In this paper, we propose a simple yet effective data augmentation method, **Bi**directional **T**ranslation-based **D**ata **A**ugmentation (BiTDA), to generate meaning-preserved and syntactic-diverse new training data for NMT. BiTDA uses pairs of high-quality translation models to rephrase the original sentences for low-resource translation. For example, for the Māori$\rightleftharpoons$English translation, the original English translation/sentence of a Māori sentence is first translated into an intermediate high-resource language (e.g., German or French) and then translated back into English. In this way, we obtain one more English translation for the Māori sentence. Instead of applying the translation models trained on the original low-resource data as back-translation does, we use the high-quality translation models trained with high-resource languages to generate new sentences. High-resource models generally yield higher-quality translations compared to low-resource translation models, leading to an enhancement in the quality of generated sentences. On the other hand, the knowledge of an intermediate language learned by the high-resource models can be injected into the generated sentences and resulting in syntactic diversity.

To evaluate the effectiveness of BiTDA, we conduct experiments on eight low-resource translation tasks. Experimental results show that our method significantly and consistently improves the translation performance for low-resource machine translation. We further combine our proposed method with other techniques that facilitate NMT, and the results demonstrate that BiTDA works well with the other techniques that facilitate NMT and achieves better results.

2 Methodology

2.1 BiTDA

Let $\mathcal{D} = (\mathcal{S}, \mathcal{T})$ be the original parallel training data for a low-resource translation, where $\mathcal{S}$ and $\mathcal{T}$ denotes the source and target side data, respectively; $\mathcal{M}_{\mathcal{S}\rightarrow\mathcal{I}}$ is a pre-trained translation model, which is used to translate sentences from source language $\mathcal{L}_\mathcal{S}$ to an intermediate high-resource language $\mathcal{L}_\mathcal{I}$. Given the source side data $\mathcal{S}$ from the training data and a pre-trained translation model $\mathcal{M}_{\mathcal{S}\rightarrow\mathcal{I}}$, we can obtain the translated sentences $\mathcal{I}$ in an intermediate language. This process introduces the linguistic knowledge of the intermediate language, and $\mathcal{I}$ exhibits a syntactic structure that is biased towards the intermediate language. Such diverse syntactic variants are beneficial for improving generalization.

Then, we use a reverse model $\mathcal{M}_{\mathcal{I}\rightarrow\mathcal{S}}$ to translate $\mathcal{I}$ back to the source language, the generated data is denoted as $\hat{\mathcal{S}}$. Although the generated sentences are still in language $\mathcal{L}_\mathcal{S}$ and

Algorithm 1 BiTDA

Inputs: Original dataset $\mathcal{D} = (\mathcal{S}, \mathcal{T})$,
Pre-trained translation models $\mathcal{M} \in \{\ldots, \mathcal{M}_{\mathcal{S}\to\mathcal{I}_i}, \mathcal{M}_{\mathcal{I}_i\to\mathcal{S}}, \ldots\}$

Output: A new training set $\hat{\mathcal{D}}$

procedure BiTDA($\mathcal{D} = (\mathcal{S}, \mathcal{T}), \mathcal{M}$)
  $\mathcal{D}_0 \leftarrow \mathcal{D}$
  for each $i \in 1, \ldots, N$ **do**
    $\mathcal{I}_i \leftarrow$ Inference($\mathcal{M}_{\mathcal{S}\to\mathcal{I}_i}, \mathcal{S}$) ▷ Translate $\mathcal{S}$ to an intermediate language $\mathcal{L}_{\mathcal{I}i}$
    $\hat{\mathcal{S}}_i \leftarrow$ Inference($\mathcal{M}_{\mathcal{I}_i\to\mathcal{S}}, \mathcal{I}_i$) ▷ Translate $\mathcal{I}_i$ back to the source language $\mathcal{L}_\mathcal{S}$
    $\mathcal{D}_x \leftarrow \mathcal{D}_{x-1} \cup \left(\hat{\mathcal{S}}_i, \mathcal{T}\right)$ ▷ Merge original data and augmented data
  end for
  return $\hat{\mathcal{D}} \leftarrow \mathcal{D}_x$

largely hold the same meaning, the linguistic knowledge learned by translation models $\mathcal{M}_{\mathcal{S}\to\mathcal{I}}$ and $\mathcal{M}_{\mathcal{I}\to\mathcal{S}}$ have been injected into, and the rephrased sentences $\hat{\mathcal{S}}$ show syntactic diversity following the intermediate language. To describe our method clearly, we summarize the overall process in Algorithm 1.

As a result, we obtain multiple source sentences for one target sentence in this case. These rephrased sentences are directly paired with the corresponding target sentences from the original training data, and then we combine the synthetic data $(\hat{\mathcal{S}}, \mathcal{T})$ with the original training data as a larger training set to train our final translation model. The combined training set allows the model to learn from both the original data and the rephrased data, and the increased diversity provides the translation model with powerful generalization capabilities that can be applied to accurately translate a wider range of (unseen) sentences.

Our method can utilize multiple paired translation models with different intermediate languages to produce a more diverse set of augmented data. In practice, we only rephrase the sentences in English for low-resource translation tasks since the performance of low-resource translation models is consistently inadequate. In our research, we employ two high-resource languages, German and French, as intermediate languages to implement our method. As for the pre-trained translation models, we use the checkpoints shared by Facebook (Ng et al., 2019) instead of training them from scratch.

2.2 Relations with Existing Methods

Back Translation (BT) and **Data Diversification** BT is a widely used data augmentation method that generates new parallel data from monolingual data of the target side language using a backward translation model (i.e., target-to-source translation). Data diversification (Nguyen et al., 2020) generates a diverse set of synthetic training data from both lingual sides (in the parallel data) using multiple models trained for both forward and backward translation tasks. Similar to data diversification, our method uses the original bilingual data and multiple auxiliary translation models to generate sentence level new examples. However, data diversification is still based on back-translation and the generated source side is of low-quality (Wei et al., 2022). In contrast, we use pre-trained translation models of high-resource languages to generate high-quality sentences without requiring any monolingual data.

Knowledge Distillation Knowledge distillation is a technique that is frequently used in resource-limited scenarios (Kim and Rush, 2016; Wang et al., 2021). It uses the predictions of a pre-trained complex teacher model as soft targets to train a simple student model.

As a result, the student model is able to achieve comparable performance to the teacher model under limited resources. In our method, we use pre-trained models of high-resource languages to generate diverse training data that enhances the robustness of low-resource models. The knowledge acquired by the pre-trained models is also distilled into the augmented data.

Pivot Translation Pivot translation is particularly useful in scenarios where direct translation between the source and target languages is challenging due to limited training data. It works by incorporating a (relatively) high-resource *pivot* language to establish a bridge between the source and target languages and then translating sentences via the pivot language. Typically, the pivot language is required to be highly related to the low-resource side language and has a large amount of training data with the high-resource side language (Xia et al., 2019). Our method does not necessitate a strong relationship between the pivot language and the low-resource languages, making it more applicable to independent low-resource languages.

3 Experiments

In this section, we conduct experiments in a wide range of low-resource translation directions with different corpora sizes and languages to demonstrate the effectiveness of our method. In addition to the main experiments, we combine our method with other techniques to further improve the performance of translation models.

3.1 Datasets

To comprehensively evaluate BiTDA, we conduct experiments on both WMT and IWSLT tasks. For WMT[*] tasks, we conduct experiments on WMT2016 Romanian → English, Russian → English, WMT2017 Finnish → English, Latvian → English and WMT2018 Turkish → English. For IWSLT tasks[†], we use IWSLT2014 Hebrew → English and IWSLT2015 Vietnamese → English. Besides, we also apply a tiny size dataset, Korean Parallel Dataset, from Google site[‡]. We use the officially provided training sets, development sets and test sets for all of these translation tasks.

Before performing translations, we use the standard Moses toolkit[§] to preprocess all datasets and we use extra scripts from Sennrich et al. (2016a) to further process Romanian side data. To tackle unknown and rare words effectively, we use Byte Pair Encoding (BPE) (Sennrich et al., 2016c) to segment words with 4k merge operations for Vietnamese, Turkish and Korean → English. For Hebrew → English translation, we follow the set-up as Gao et al. (2019) with 10k merge operations; we also follow Sennrich et al. (2016a) which learns 89,500 merge operations for Romanian → English. As for Russian and Finnish → English, we adopt 40k merge operations. In our experiments, we build joint dictionaries for all tasks.

3.2 Training Settings

In our experiments, we adopt Transformer (Vaswani et al., 2017) as our translation model with a configuration that consists of 6 encoder and decoder layers with 4 attention heads. The dimensionalities of all sub-layers in the model are set to 512, and the inner layers of feed-forward networks have 1024 dimensions. Dropout is applied to all sub-layers, and the rate is set to 0.1. We train our models by using Adam (Kingma and Ba, 2015) as an optimizer with $(\beta_1, \beta_2) = (0.9, 0.98)$ and using cross-entropy as criterion with *label smoothing* $= 0.1$. The

[*] `https://www.statmt.org/`
[†] `https://wit3.fbk.eu/`
[‡] `https://sites.google.com/site/koreanparalleldata`
[§] `https://github.com/moses-smt/mosesdecoder`

	Vi→En	He→En	Tr→En	Ro→En
Baseline	31.64	36.52	21.86	34.08
+ WordDropout	31.62	36.67	21.92	34.16
+ Swap	31.63	36.56	21.94	34.22
+ SwitchOut	32.35	36.93	22.28	33.86
+ BPEDropout	32.73	37.66	22.95	34.83
+ BiTDA-de	32.33	37.20	22.72	**35.07**
+ BiTDA-fr	32.37	37.23	22.63	34.75
+ BiTDA-double	**32.96**	**37.72**	**23.56**	34.63
+ BiTDA-de + BPEDropout	**33.49**	**38.47**	23.40	**35.20**
+ BiTDA-de + MLS	33.19	37.38	22.90	34.38
	Ru→En	**Fi→En**	**Lv→En**	**Ko→En**
Baseline	28.69	28.01	17.20	5.26
+ WordDropout	28.15	28.12	17.32	5.46
+ Swap	28.92	28.31	17.52	5.37
+ SwitchOut	28.13	28.33	17.10	5.00
+ BPEDropout	28.94	27.55	17.61	5.86
+ BiTDA-de	**30.01**	**28.57**	**17.75**	5.63
+ BiTDA-fr	28.95	27.24	16.95	5.54
+ BiTDA-double	29.87	28.22	17.42	**5.89**
+ BiTDA-de + BPEDropout	29.98	**29.01**	**17.98**	**6.21**
+ BiTDA-de + MLS	29.64	28.74	17.82	5.02

Table 1: SacreBLEU scores on various translation tasks. The baseline denotes a Transformer model trained without any data augmentation.

initial learning rate is set to $1e^{-7}$, then gradually increases till $1e^{-4}$ within 4,000 warm-up updates. The batch size for a single GPU is set to 4k. During inference, we average the last five models before early stopping as the final model to decode where beam search is applied with the beam size 12. We calculate the BLEU (Papineni et al., 2002) score to evaluate the performance of models. Considering the discrepancy among different tokenization processes, we apply the SacreBLEU score (Post, 2018) for all experiments.

3.3 Results

The results are presented in Table 1. For our experiments, we utilize German and French as intermediate languages, and the methods employed with these languages are named BiTDA-de and BiTDA-fr, respectively. As we can see, for all translation tasks, our method consistently outperforms the baseline (Transformer without data augmentation) with up to +1.32 SacreBLEU points. In addition to using the data augmented by BiTDA-de and BiTDA-fr alone, we also combine the new training data obtained from both methods with the original data to train

Method	|D|	***test2016***	***test2018***
Baseline	1×	20.53	21.86
+ BiTDA-de	2×	20.99	22.72
+ BT	11×	22.90	24.83
+ BT+ BiTDA-de	12×	23.44	25.17

Table 2: SacreBLEU scores in the Tr-En task with BT and BiTDA. |D| denotes the training sample size for each method

% of training data	**AVG**	***test2016***	***test2017***	***test2018***
0% BiTDA + 100% original	20.81	20.53	20.03	21.86
25% BiTDA + 75% original	20.58	20.42	19.73	21.58
50% BiTDA + 50% original	20.48	20.25	19.57	21.63
75% BiTDA + 25% original	20.35	20.02	19.56	21.46
100% BiTDA + 0% original	20.01	19.80	19.40	20.84

Table 3: SacreBLEU scores degradation as the proportion of synthetic data used.

translation models, named BiTDA-double. We find that the performance gains achieved by BiTDA-double are roughly equivalent to the combined performance gains achieved by BiTDA-de and BiTDA-fr when compared with the model trained only with natural text data. This shows that the improvements achieved through BiTDA-de and BiTDA-fr are largely independent of each other. Further, our finding encourages augmenting the training data with an intermediate language that has a distinctive syntactic structure from the target language.

Moreover, we compare our method with existing data augmentation methods, including WordDropout (Sennrich et al., 2016a), Swap (Lample et al., 2018), SwitchOut (Wang et al., 2018) and BPEDropout (Provilkov et al., 2020). For WordDropout and BPEDropout, we follow their (Sennrich et al., 2016a; Provilkov et al., 2020) configurations with a dropout rate of 0.1 and 0.1, respectively. We adopt a window size of 3 (Gao et al., 2019) to implement Swap. For SwitchOut, we reuse the hyperparameters in their repository[¶]. For all these methods, we merge the synthetic data with the original training set to train translation models together. Our proposed method also has demonstrated superior performance compared to the other data augmentation methods, which provides empirical evidence of the effectiveness of our method.

3.4 Analysis

Complements Existing Methods. We combine BiTDA with other methods that facilitate NMT, including BPEDropout (Provilkov et al., 2020) and MLS (Chen et al., 2022), which are data augmentation and label smoothing decoding techniques, respectively. BPEDropout works by randomly omitting some merge steps of BPE, which is able to generate diverse subword sequences and is a subword-level data augmentation method. MLS is a parameter-free label smoothing method, designed to ensure that soft probabilities are not assigned to words exclusive to the source side sentences during decoding. As shown in the bottom rows of Table 1, BiTDA-de demonstrates consistent improvements across 7 datasets when combined with each of the two methods separately. The results demonstrate the potential of synergising our

[¶]https://github.com/nsapru/SwitchOut

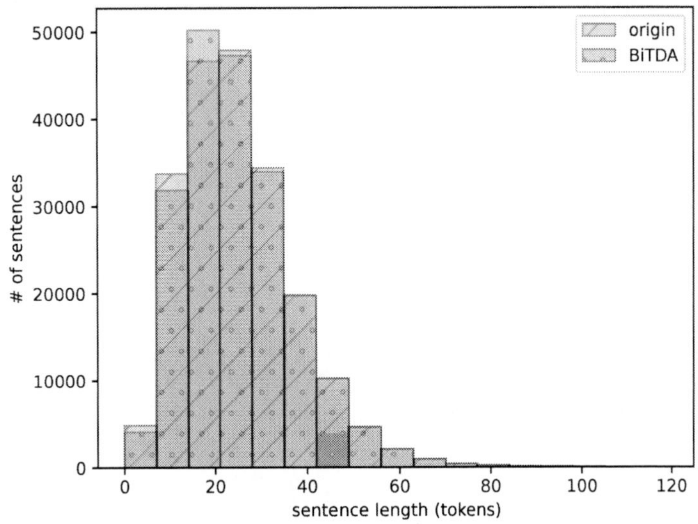

Figure 1: Distributions of sentence lengths in the English part of the original training set and the augmented training set in WMT2018 Tr-En.

	Baseline	**BiTDA-de**	**BiTDA-de**	**BiTDA-double**
Tr-orig	17.17	17.96	17.80	18.51
En-orig	25.90	27.57	27.23	28.21

Table 4: SacreBLEU scores for WMT18 Tr-En. Test sets are divided by their original source language.

method with others to further improve the performance of NMT models in partial translation directions.

Complements Back-Translation. We also combine our method with back-translation and find out the performance when they work together. To implement BT, we select WMT2018 Turkish $\rightarrow$ English (which contains 206K sentence pairs) as an example and extract 2,000,000 monolingual English sentences from News Crawl 2010. Thus, we obtain around 11 times more training examples after implementing back-translation. We conduct experiments on two test sets, *newstest2016* and *newstest2018*, both of which contain around $3,000$ sentence pairs. As shown in Table 2, BT outperforms baseline with 2.37 and 2.97 BLEU points on two sets, respectively. While BT has already achieved significant gains in performance, integrating the data generated by BiTDA results in an additional improvement of 0.34-0.54 points. The results demonstrate that BiTDA complements well with BT. It is worth noting that BiTDA does not utilize external monolingual data like BT, but rather relies solely on the original training data. Therefore, a direct comparison between BiTDA and BT based on the same amount of data was

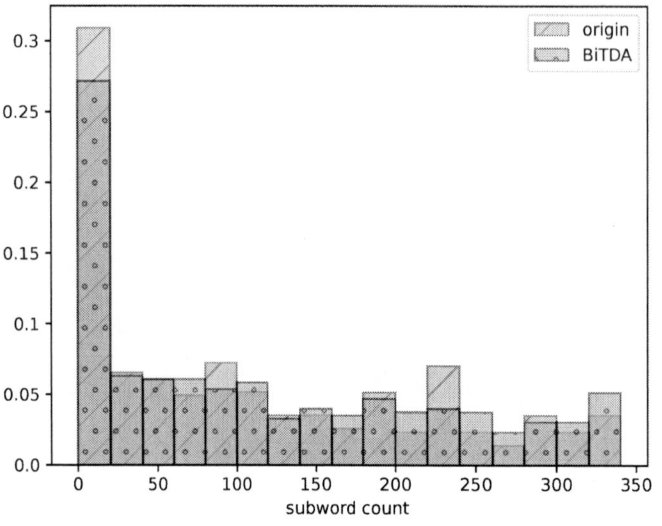

Figure 2: Distributions of top rare tokens, only 10% of the rarest words are shown. The range of numbers from 0 to 350 represents the count of subwords that appear in the whole set.

not conducted.

No Translationese Effects. Recently, Edunov et al. (2020) reveal that BT has the drawback of *translationese effect* (Gellerstam, 1986), i.e., an NMT model trained with back-translated data performs better on translated texts (simpler and shorter) than on natural texts (Marie et al., 2020). Thus, we conduct experiments to verify whether our method also suffers from this *translationese effect*. We first replace the original training data with the syntactic data in various proportions to train a translation model from scratch. We conduct experiments on the WMT2018 Turkish → English translation and present the results in Table 3. The results show that using the synthetic data as a part of training data can not directly improve the translation quality of a translation model and even does not impact the quality seriously (SacreBLEU only drops 0.8 on average when using 100% synthetic data). We then plot the distribution of sentence lengths in the English part of the original training set and the augmented training set in Figure 1. Note that the sentence lengths are counted in tokens instead of subwords from BPE encoding. As we can see, the lengths of the two sets show almost identical distributions. This finding supports the previously mentioned experimental results and underscores that our method can generate high-quality paraphrases that closely resemble natural sentences. We also follow the work of Freitag et al. (2019) in splitting each test set according to its original language. As illustrated in Table 4, BiTDA improves both the Tr-orig and En-orig test sets, further confirming our analysis.

Effect on Rare Subwords We conjecture that reducing the impact of rare subwords (encoded by BPE) is one of the reasons why BiTDA performs well. We argue that the syntactic diversity of the synthetic sentences provides a more comprehensive context for rare words, which can

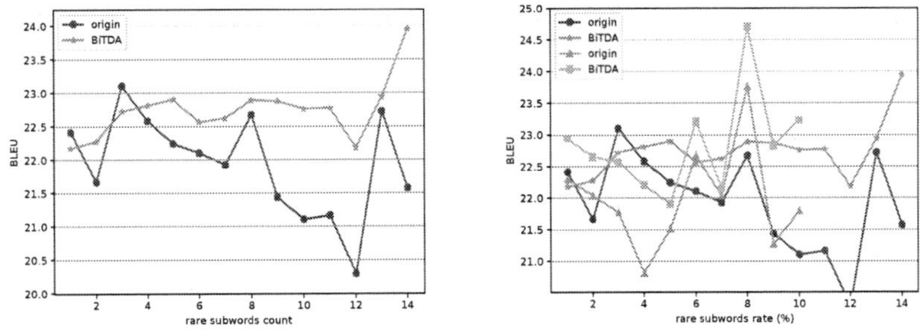

(a) (b)

Figure 3: SacreBLEU score for sentences containing rare subwords. The range of numbers from 1 to 14 in (a) represents the count of rare subwords in a single sentence, and the range of numbers from 1 to 10 in (b) represents the proportion of rare subwords in a single sentence.

effectively enhance the model's ability to understand rare words. To verify this, we select the 10% rarest subwords as samples to illustrate the distribution of word frequencies. Specifically, we have selected the Turkish $\rightarrow$ English translation dataset from WMT2018 as an illustrative example. Figure 2 displays the distributions of subword frequencies in both the original set and the synthetic set by BiTDA (contains the same number of sentences as the original set). Comparing the subword distributions of the original set and the synthetic set, we observe that the synthetic set contains fewer rare subwords and increases the number of relatively common subwords. In other words, the number of partially rare subwords is increased, which enables more information to be shared between sentences. This advantage is crucial in contexts with limited resources. To provide a more intuitive demonstration of the enhanced performance of the BiTDA-augmented model, we have organized the sentences containing rare subwords and evaluated them separately. Two grouping methods have been employed in this study: grouping by the number of rare subwords in a single sentence, and grouping by the proportion of rare subwords in a single sentence. It is important to note that we have excluded results from groups with extremely small sample sizes, such as those with a proportion of rare words exceeding 10%. The results are presented in Figure 3. The model augmented by BiTDA exhibits superior performance when it comes to sentences containing rare subwords, providing further support for our conjecture.

3.5 Case Study

We present several examples generated by BiTDA in Table 5. We observe that BiTDA can reasonably adjust the syntactic structure of the original sentences, and some words are replaced with contextually appropriate alternatives. While word replacement is not the primary objective of our method, it does provide additional benefits for training NMT models.

4 Limitations

The limitations of our method are as follows: (i) It is restricted to the high-resource language side (e.g., English) of low-resource parallel data. While it is possible to use pairs of pre-trained low-resource translation models like BT can rephrase Non-English sentences, the quality of the generated sentences would be too low. (ii) It can be affected by domain shift (Deheeger et al., 2022) of the translation models we use. As seen in Table 1, using French translation models can

Original:	Ten years ago, when a local bank launched its first credit card, only one shop in Bucharest's downtown was able to accept electronic payments.
BiTDA-de:	When a local bank introduced its first credit card ten years ago, only one shop in downtown Bucharest could accept electronic payments.
BiTDA-fr:	Ten years ago, when a local bank started its first credit card, a single store in Bucharest, in the center-city was able to accept electronic payments.
Original:	Some foresee a growth of up to 500 per cent by the end of the year for transactions originating in Romania.
BiTDA-de:	Some expect up to 500 percent growth in transactions originating in Romania by the end of the year.
BiTDA-fr:	Some are forecasting a growth rate of up to 500%, at the end of the year for transactions from Romania.

Table 5: A case study on BiTDA.

be much worse than using German translation models. We conjecture that domain shift causes the sentences generated by French models to be of relatively low quality. Using high-resource translation models trained on multi-domain large-scale datasets would be better. (iii) With the same consideration as mentioned in (i), it cannot be used for the direct translation between two low-resource languages, e.g., Māori⇌Tongan.

5 Conclusion

In this work, we proposed BiTDA, a simple yet effective data augmentation method for low-resource NMT. Our method rephrases the original sentences using pairs of pre-trained high-resource translation models in opposite directions. Experiments validate the consistent effectiveness of our method across various low-resource translation tasks. Further experiments and analysis show that our method complements existing methods well.

In future work, we will explore using more pre-trained high-resource translation models and exploiting similarities (Mikolov et al., 2013) between the intermediate language and the language to be augmented.

Ethics Statement

We use public datasets and models that permit academic research. The preprocessing tools and model training toolkit are open-sourced without copyright conflicts.

Acknowledgements

We would like to thank the anonymous reviewers for their helpful comments. This work is supported by the 2020 Catalyst: Strategic New Zealand - Singapore Data Science Research Programme Fund by Ministry of Business, Innovation and Employment (MBIE), New Zealand.

References

Artetxe, M., Labaka, G., Agirre, E., and Cho, K. (2018). Unsupervised neural machine translation. In *International Conference on Learning Representations*.

Chen, L., Xu, R., and Chang, B. (2022). Focus on the target's vocabulary: Masked label smoothing for machine translation. In *Proceedings of the 60th Annual Meeting of the Association for Computational Linguistics*.

Currey, A., Miceli-Barone, A. V., and Heafield, K. (2017). Copied monolingual data improves low-resource neural machine translation. In *Proceedings of the Second Conference on Machine Translation*.

Deheeger, F., MOUGEOT, M., Vayatis, N., et al. (2022). Discrepancy-based active learning for domain adaptation. In *International Conference on Learning Representations*.

Edunov, S., Ott, M., Auli, M., and Grangier, D. (2018). Understanding back-translation at scale. In *Proceedings of the 2018 Conference on Empirical Methods in Natural Language Processing*.

Edunov, S., Ott, M., Ranzato, M., and Auli, M. (2020). On the evaluation of machine translation systems trained with back-translation. In *Proceedings of the 58th Annual Meeting of the Association for Computational Linguistics*.

Fadaee, M., Bisazza, A., and Monz, C. (2017). Data augmentation for low-resource neural machine translation. In *Proceedings of the 55th Annual Meeting of the Association for Computational Linguistics*.

Freitag, M., Caswell, I., and Roy, S. (2019). Ape at scale and its implications on mt evaluation biases. In *Proceedings of the Fourth Conference on Machine Translation*.

Gao, F., Zhu, J., Wu, L., Xia, Y., Qin, T., Cheng, X., Zhou, W., and Liu, T.-Y. (2019). Soft contextual data augmentation for neural machine translation. In *Proceedings of the 57th Annual Meeting of the Association for Computational Linguistics*.

Gellerstam, M. (1986). Translationese in swedish novels translated from english. *Translation studies in Scandinavia*.

Haddow, B., Bawden, R., Barone, A. V. M., Helcl, J., and Birch, A. (2022). Survey of low-resource machine translation. *Computational Linguistics*.

Hassan, H., Aue, A., Chen, C., Chowdhary, V., Clark, J., Federmann, C., Huang, X., Junczys-Dowmunt, M., Lewis, W., Li, M., et al. (2018). Achieving human parity on automatic chinese to english news translation. *arXiv preprint arXiv:1803.05567*.

Hoang, V. C. D., Koehn, P., Haffari, G., and Cohn, T. (2018). Iterative back-translation for neural machine translation. In *Proceedings of the 2nd Workshop on Neural Machine Translation and Generation*.

Kambhatla, N., Born, L., and Sarkar, A. (2022). Cipherdaug: Ciphertext based data augmentation for neural machine translation. In *Proceedings of the 60th Annual Meeting of the Association for Computational Linguistics)*.

Khayrallah, H. and Koehn, P. (2018). On the impact of various types of noise on neural machine translation. In *Proceedings of the 2nd Workshop on Neural Machine Translation and Generation*.

Kim, Y. and Rush, A. M. (2016). Sequence-level knowledge distillation. In *Proceedings of the 2016 Conference on Empirical Methods in Natural Language Processing*.

Kingma, D. P. and Ba, J. (2015). Adam: A method for stochastic optimization. In *Proceedings of the 3rd International Conference for Learning Representations*.

Lample, G., Conneau, A., Denoyer, L., and Ranzato, M. (2018). Unsupervised machine translation using monolingual corpora only. In *International Conference on Learning Representations*.

Marie, B., Rubino, R., and Fujita, A. (2020). Tagged back-translation revisited: Why does it really work? In *Proceedings of the 58th Annual Meeting of the Association for Computational Linguistics*.

Mikolov, T., Le, Q. V., and Sutskever, I. (2013). Exploiting similarities among languages for machine translation. *arXiv preprint arXiv:1309.4168*.

Ng, N., Yee, K., Baevski, A., Ott, M., Auli, M., and Edunov, S. (2019). Facebook fair's wmt19 news translation task submission. In *Proceedings of the Fourth Conference on Machine Translation*.

Nguyen, X.-P., Joty, S., Kui, W., and Aw, A. T. (2020). Data diversification: a simple strategy for neural machine translation. In *Proceedings of the 34th International Conference on Neural Information Processing Systems*.

Papineni, K., Roukos, S., Ward, T., and Zhu, W.-J. (2002). Bleu: a method for automatic evaluation of machine translation. In *Proceedings of the 40th annual meeting of the Association for Computational Linguistics*.

Pham, H., Wang, X., Yang, Y., and Neubig, G. (2021). Meta back-translation. In *International Conference on Learning Representations*.

Popel, M., Tomkova, M., Tomek, J., Kaiser, Ł., Uszkoreit, J., Bojar, O., and Žabokrtský, Z. (2020). Transforming machine translation: a deep learning system reaches news translation quality comparable to human professionals. *Nature communications*.

Post, M. (2018). A call for clarity in reporting bleu scores. In *Proceedings of the Third Conference on Machine Translation: Research Papers*.

Provilkov, I., Emelianenko, D., and Voita, E. (2020). Bpe-dropout: Simple and effective subword regularization. In *Proceedings of the 58th Annual Meeting of the Association for Computational Linguistics*.

Sánchez-Martínez, F., Sánchez-Cartagena, V. M., Pérez-Ortiz, J. A., Forcada, M. L., Espla-Gomis, M., Secker, A., Coleman, S., and Wall, J. (2020). An english-swahili parallel corpus and its use for neural machine translation in the news domain. In *Proceedings of the 22nd Annual Conference of the European Association for Machine Translation*.

Sennrich, R., Haddow, B., and Birch, A. (2016a). Edinburgh neural machine translation systems for wmt 16. In *Proceedings of the First Conference on Machine Translation*.

Sennrich, R., Haddow, B., and Birch, A. (2016b). Improving neural machine translation models with monolingual data. In *Proceedings of the 54th Annual Meeting of the Association for Computational Linguistics*.

Sennrich, R., Haddow, B., and Birch, A. (2016c). Neural machine translation of rare words with subword units. In *Proceedings of the 54th Annual Meeting of the Association for Computational Linguistics*.

Shao, C. and Feng, Y. (2022). Overcoming catastrophic forgetting beyond continual learning: Balanced training for neural machine translation. In *Proceedings of the 60th Annual Meeting of the Association for Computational Linguistics*.

Vaswani, A., Shazeer, N., Parmar, N., Uszkoreit, J., Jones, L., Gomez, A. N., Kaiser, Ł., and Polosukhin, I. (2017). Attention is all you need. In *Proceedings of the 31st International Conference on Neural Information Processing Systems*.

Wang, F., Yan, J., Meng, F., and Zhou, J. (2021). Selective knowledge distillation for neural machine translation. In *Proceedings of the 59th Annual Meeting of the Association for Computational Linguistics and the 11th International Joint Conference on Natural Language Processing*.

Wang, X., Pham, H., Dai, Z., and Neubig, G. (2018). Switchout: an efficient data augmentation algorithm for neural machine translation. In *Proceedings of the 2018 Conference on Empirical Methods in Natural Language Processing*.

Wei, X., Yu, H., Hu, Y., Weng, R., Luo, W., and Jin, R. (2022). Learning to generalize to more: Continuous semantic augmentation for neural machine translation. In *Proceedings of the 60th Annual Meeting of the Association for Computational Linguistics*.

Xia, M., Kong, X., Anastasopoulos, A., and Neubig, G. (2019). Generalized data augmentation for low-resource translation. In *Proceedings of the 57th Annual Meeting of the Association for Computational Linguistics*.

A Dual Reinforcement Method for Data Augmentation using Middle Sentences for Machine Translation

Wenyi Tang tang@akane.waseda.jp
Yves Lepage yves.lepage@waseda.jp
Graduate School of IPS, Waseda University, Kitakyushu, Japan

Abstract

This paper presents an approach to enhance the quality of machine translation by leveraging middle sentences as pivot points and employing dual reinforcement learning. Conventional methods for generating parallel sentence pairs for machine translation rely on parallel corpora, which may be scarce, resulting in limitations in translation quality. In contrast, our proposed method entails training two machine translation models in opposite directions, utilizing the middle sentence as a bridge for a virtuous feedback loop between the two models. This feedback loop resembles reinforcement learning, facilitating the models to make informed decisions based on mutual feedback. Experimental results substantiate that our proposed method significantly improves machine translation quality.

1 Introduction

The accuracy of neural machine translation is limited by the quantity of available training data (Wang et al., 2022; Sennrich et al., 2016), leading to the development of various techniques for data augmentation. In this paper, we propose a novel method that leverages middle sentences (Wang et al., 2021) as pivot points and uses dual reinforcement learning (Zhou et al., 2019) for data augmentation in machine translation.

Dual learning (He et al., 2016; Yi et al., 2017; Zhou et al., 2019) entails the concurrent training of two neural networks, to enhance translation accuracy by leveraging the reconstruction model's ability to generate synthetic parallel sentence pairs. Data augmentation involves artificially augmenting the size of the training data by generating additional sentence pairs through diverse techniques, such as back-translation (Brislin, 1970; Douglas and Craig, 2007; Edunov et al., 2018). These techniques offer potential solutions to mitigate the scarcity of parallel corpora and improve the quality of machine translation models by providing supplementary training data.

In our proposal, we aim to combine the strengths of dual learning and data augmentation with the use of middle sentences as pivot points to reinforce the training process and further enhance the accuracy of the machine translation model. We start by presenting our dual reinforcement method in Section 2. We present our experiment setup in Section 3 and results in Section 4.

Proceedings of Machine Translation Summit XIX, Vol. 1: Research Track, pages 48–58
September 4–8, 2023, Macau SAR, China.

2 Methods

Our method combines the use of a dual learning framework with data augmentation techniques, leveraging the middle sentences of parallel sentence pairs as pivot points. The general process involves generating additional parallel sentence pairs through middle sentence generation, using the middle sentences to create new sentence pairs and refining the translations using a machine translation model. This process is repeated iteratively, forming a reinforcement loop that enhances the quality of the translation model through synthetic data, i.e., middle sentences. In the following subsections, we provide a detailed explanation of each step in our method.

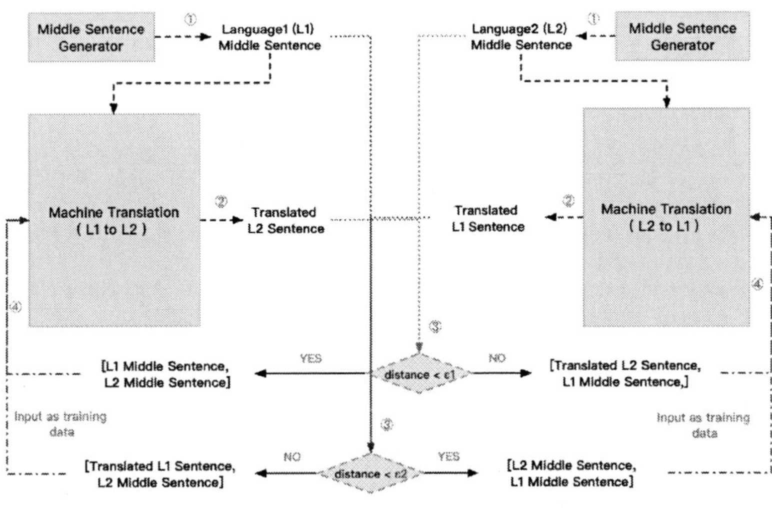

Figure 1: Framework of dual reinforcement method

2.1 Middle Sentence Generation

A middle sentence refers to a sentence that is generated or identified as an intermediate sentence between two given sentences, namely the start sentence and the end sentence (Wang et al., 2021). They suggest computing the middle sentences using Formula 1.

$$m = \frac{1}{2} \times (s + e) \tag{1}$$

Our method uses the semantic representations of the input sentences, i.e., their embedding vectors obtained using a pre-trained language model. Specifically, we use the following formula to calculate the embedding vector of the middle sentence:

$$m = \frac{1}{2} \times \frac{\|s\| + \|e\|}{\|s + e\|}(s + e) \tag{2}$$

where s and e represent the embedding vectors of the start and end sentences, respectively. The resulting embedding vector m represents the semantic midpoint between the two input sentences.

The inclusion of normalization terms in the Formula 2 takes into account the lengths of the input vectors. This ensures that the resulting midpoint vector has a relatively similar length as the input vectors, regardless of their initial lengths. By considering the magnitudes of the vectors, the equation provides a better suited representation of the semantic center between the start and end sentences.

Once the embedding vector of the middle sentence is obtained, we utilize it as input to a decoder model to generate an actual sentence.

By using the aforesaid technique, we create middle sentences for two languages, L_1 and L_2, by entering two parallel sentence pairs in each language. The problem is to check whether this pair of middle sentences is parallel and suitable for use as training data to enhance machine translation quality.

Let us take Chinese and English as examples. We randomly select a pair of start and end sentences in Chinese, such as '我爱吃苹果' (I love eating apples) and '我想学习' (I want to study). The generated intermediate sentence is '我爱学习' (I love study). Similarly, in English, we generated 'i like study' as the middle sentence.

2.2 Generation of Corresponding Translations

Once the middle sentences in two languages are generated, they can be used as input to their respective machine translation models to obtain corresponding translations. For instance, the middle sentences of L_1 can be fed into the machine translation model for translation in the direction L_1 to L_2, resulting in the translated sentences in L_2. And similarity for sentences in L_2, resulting in translations in L_1.

For the same example as above, we can translate the Chinese middle sentence '我爱学习' into English as 'I love study,' and the translation of the English middle sentence 'i like study' would be '我喜欢学习' in Chinese.

2.3 Selection of Sentence Pairs

We begin by measuring the distance between the L_1 middle sentence and the translated L_1 sentence obtained through the L_2 to L_1 machine translation model using the $L2$ middle sentence. For that, we use euclidean distance with a pre-set threshold. If the L_1 middle sentence bears significant resemblance to the translated L_1 sentence, indicating that the middle sentence in L_1 aligns closely with the L_1 sentence obtained through machine translation of the L_2 middle sentence, then we consider the L_1 middle sentence to be both middle and parallel to the L_2 middle sentence. They can be regarded as a pair of parallel sentences and utilized as training data for machine translation. Similarly, in the other direction with L_2 and L_1.

If the L_1 middle sentence and the translated L_1 sentence exceed the distance threshold, then we consider the L_1 middle sentence and the L_2 middle sentence to be middle but not parallel. As we aim to have parallel sentences that can improve machine translation model accuracy, we treat the L_1 middle sentence and its L_2 translation obtained through machine translation as a pair of parallel sentences. These parallel sentences can be utilized for training the L_2 to L_1 machine translation model. Similarly, in the other direction.

We continue the aforementioned process and calculate the distance between the Chinese middle sentence '我爱学习' and the translation of the English middle sentence, '我喜欢学习' It is evident that these two sentences are very similar, indicating that we can determine that the Chinese middle sentence '我爱学习' and the English middle sentence 'i like study' is a pair of parallel middle sentences. The same applies to the English middle sentence in the other translation direction.

However, if the Chinese middle sentence is '我爱学习' (I love studying), and the English middle sentence is 'i want to sleep,' which translates to '我想睡觉', it is evident that these two sentences are not similar. Therefore, the Chinese middle sentence and the English middle sentence, despite both being middle sentences, are not parallel to each other. In this case, we would replace the Chinese middle sentence with the translation of the English middle sentence and consider 'i want to sleep' and '我想睡觉' as a pair of data to be included in the training set of the Chinese-to-English machine translation model.

2.4 Reinforcement Loop

The iterative process of utilizing dual learning and middle sentences is repeated in a reinforcement loop. The use of distance to determine sentence similarity and facilitate sentence substitution can be likened to the reward function employed in traditional reinforcement learning approaches. The refined translations from the machine translation model are used to generate additional augmented sentence pairs, which are incorporated into the training data. This loop enables continuous refinement of the model, allowing for further improvement of its accuracy over successive iterations.

3 Experimental Setup

The experimental setup for this study uses a neural machine translation (NMT) model avaiable in the OpenNMT tool (Klein et al., 2017). The selected architecture is a transformer encoder and decoder, with a word vector size of 512, 6 layers, and 8 heads, alongside an RNN size of 512. The transformer feed-forward network has a size of 2048. During training, gradients are accumulated over 8 batches, and the model is optimized using the Adam optimizer with beta1 set to 0.9, beta2 set to 0.998, and a learning rate of 0.001. Batch sizes are set to 4096, utilizing token batch type, with token normalization and a dropout rate of 0.1, while label smoothing was set to 0.1.

We employ a parallel dataset in English and Chinese extracted from Tatoeba [1]. The statistics of the dataset are presented in Table 1.

Language	Sentences	Tokens	Types	Avg. length of sentences (in char)
English	67,333	556,529	16,248	8.27
Chinese	67,333	888,743	24,864	13.20

Table 1: Statistics on Tatoeba corpus

To evaluate our system's performance, we use three standard metrics: BLEU (Bilingual Evaluation Understudy), CHRF (CHaRacter-level F-score), and TER (Translation Error Rate). BLEU (Papineni et al., 2002) quantifies the n-gram overlap between the generated text and the reference text. CHRF (Popović, 2015) calculates the character n-gram F-score between the generated and reference text. Finally, TER (Snover et al., 2006) measures the minimum edit distance between the generated and reference text, accounting for insertions, deletions, and substitutions. Furthermore, we use SacreBLEU (Post, 2018) to conduct significance testing, and highlight the experimental outcomes that exhibited a significant improvement by bolding them.

4 Results

4.1 Different Data Sizes

We conduct experiments to analyze the impact of dataset size on our results. We partition the dataset into subsets ranging from 10k to 50k, with increments of 10k. The data is then divided into training, validation, and test sets in an 8:1:1 ratio.

[1]https://tatoeba.org

Figures 2a and 2b present the BLEU scores obtained by training on datasets of varying sizes. The general trend observed is an increase in score as the dataset size increases. When the dataset is less than 24 thousand, our proposed method outperforms the other two methods. However, as the dataset size increases, our method does not surpass the model trained on the original data. Nevertheless, our method does consistently outperform the method with data augmentation without dual learning on all dataset sizes.

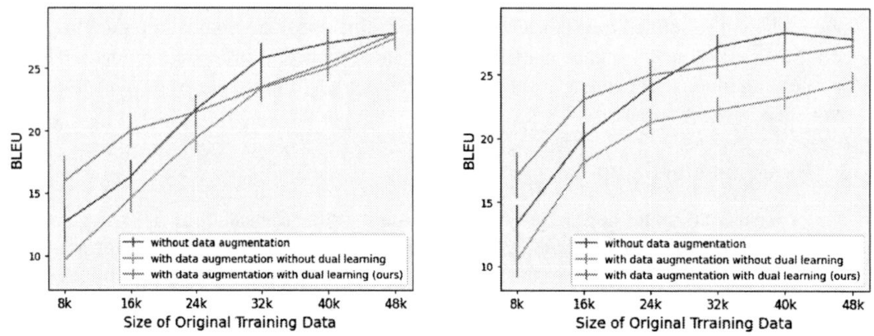

(a) English to Chinese machine translation model (b) Chinese to English machine translation model

Figure 2: BLEU scores across different data sizes. The model without data augmentation uses the original data size. The models with data augmentation add up data to the original training data, three times as model data, which makes these models learn from a four times larger training data.

Considering that our experimental outcomes show superior performance when the training dataset consists of 8 thousand data points, we conduct an analysis of the original 8 thousand sentence pair data compared with the method with data augmentation without dual learning with our own data augmentation method.

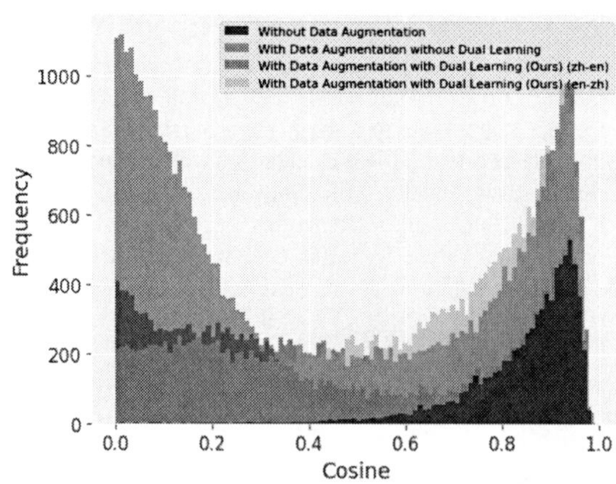

Figure 3: Distributions of training data and augmented data

The analysis of the distribution of the generated data using our method compared to the method with data augmentation without dual learning shows that our method generates data with a distribution more similar to that of the original data, as most of the generated data has a cosine similarity in the range of 0.8–1.0. In contrast, the method with data augmentation without dual learning generates data mostly in the range of 0–0.2, which may indicate lower alignment quality of the generated data. However, it is noted that our method also generates some sentence pairs with cosine similarity in the range of 0–0.4, which may explain why our method performs better with a smaller amount of raw data. It seems that when the original data is small, our method generates more high-quality sentence pairs, which can be beneficial for improving translation accuracy. However, when the dataset is large, our method may generate low-quality pairs, which potentially has a negative impact on models that have already been trained on a substantial amount of parallel data.

4.2 Impact of Parallel and Nonparallel Start-End Sentence Pairs on Machine Translation Models

To ensure the reliability and effectiveness of our proposed method, we conducted an extensive experiment to evaluate its robustness in handling both parallel and non-parallel start and end sentence pairs, which are selected at random. By examining the impact of data parallelism on the machine translation model, we aimed to investigate the performance of our proposed method under different input conditions.

Parallel	cosine similarity	Euclidean distance
Yes	0.84	0.60
No	0.08	1.79

Table 2: Similarity and distance of parallel and non-parallel sentence pairs

As observed from Figure 4, the model trained on parallel sentence pairs (dark blue bar) achieved a significantly higher BLEU score compared to the model trained on non-parallel sentence pairs (medium-dark blue bar) . This suggests that the utilization of non-parallel sentence pairs as input for machine translation models can adversely affect their accuracy. Nonetheless, it shows that our method can enhance the performance of machine translation models, even when non-parallel sentence pairs are used as input. While the use of non-parallel sentence pairs does result in a decrease in accuracy compared to parallel sentence pairs, the performance is still improved compared to the original model (medium-light blue bar) without data augmentation.

4.3 Different Euclidean Distance Threshold to Select Sentence Pairs

Given that we have a threshold for determining the degree of parallelism between the middle and translated sentences, this threshold directly impacts the quality and quantity of the training data utilized. Consequently, we perform experiments with various euclidean distance thresholds to evaluate this impact.

Figure 5 illustrates that the model reaches its best performance at a euclidean distance threshold of 0.3, after which its efficacy decreases. This observation implies that setting the threshold at 0.3 enables us to effectively eliminate non-parallel sentence pairs, while retaining an adequate number of high-quality parallel sentence pairs for training the machine translation model.

5 Conclusion

This paper presented a novel data augmentation method for enhancing machine translation performance by using middle sentences and dual learning. Our approach aims to overcome the

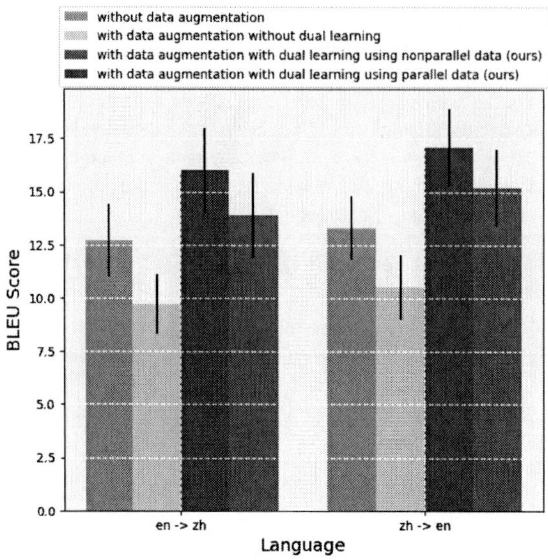

Figure 4: BLEU score across different methods

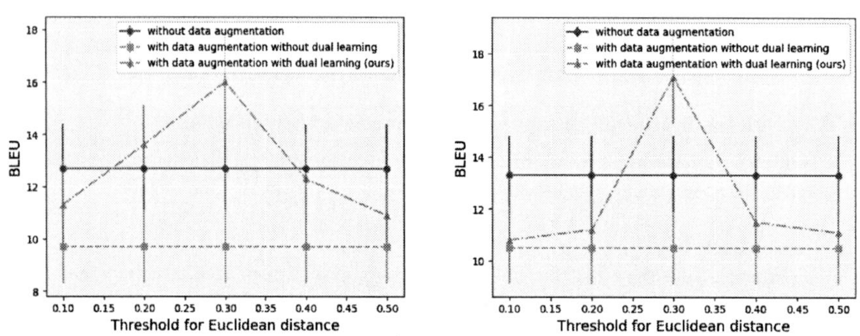

(a) en-zh machine translation model

(b) zh-en machine translation model

Figure 5: BLEU scores for various thresholds of Euclidean distance challenge of availability and quality of parallel corpora, which can substantially impair the accuracy of machine translation systems. By utilizing middle sentences as pivot points and integrating dual learning with data augmentation techniques, we generated a considerable number of high-quality parallel sentence pairs to train machine translation models. The experimental results substantiate the superiority of our proposed method over two baseline methods.

Similar to any research, there exist potential challenges and opportunities for future work. One promising direction is to examine the adaptability of our proposed method for other languages, particularly those with limited available training data. Additionally, it would be worthwhile to investigate the applicability of our method in other natural language processing tasks beyond machine translation, such as text summarization or sentiment analysis. Moreover, future research could investigate the use of more sophisticated similarity metrics to determine parallel sentence pairs.

References

Brislin, R. W. (1970). Back-translation for cross-cultural research. *Journal of cross-cultural psychology*, 1(3):185–216.

Douglas, S. P. and Craig, C. S. (2007). Collaborative and iterative translation: An alternative approach to back translation. *Journal of International Marketing*, 15(1):30–43.

Edunov, S., Ott, M., Auli, M., and Grangier, D. (2018). Understanding back-translation at scale. In *Proceedings of the 2018 Conference on Empirical Methods in Natural Language Processing*, pages 489–500.

He, D., Xia, Y., Qin, T., Wang, L., Yu, N., Liu, T.-Y., and Ma, W.-Y. (2016). Dual learning for machine translation. In *Proceedings of the 30th International Conference on Neural Information Processing Systems*, pages 820–828.

Klein, G., Kim, Y., Deng, Y., Senellart, J., and Rush, A. (2017). OpenNMT: Open-source toolkit for neural machine translation. In *Proceedings of ACL 2017, System Demonstrations*, pages 67–72, Vancouver, Canada. Association for Computational Linguistics.

Papineni, K., Roukos, S., Ward, T., and Zhu, W.-J. (2002). Bleu: a method for automatic evaluation of machine translation. In *Proceedings of the 40th Annual Meeting of the Association for Computational Linguistics*, pages 311–318, Philadelphia, Pennsylvania, USA. Association for Computational Linguistics.

Popović, M. (2015). chrF: character n-gram F-score for automatic MT evaluation. In *Proceedings of the Tenth Workshop on Statistical Machine Translation*, pages 392–395, Lisbon, Portugal. Association for Computational Linguistics.

Post, M. (2018). A call for clarity in reporting BLEU scores. In *Proceedings of the Third Conference on Machine Translation: Research Papers*, pages 186–191, Belgium, Brussels. Association for Computational Linguistics.

Sennrich, R., Haddow, B., and Birch, A. (2016). Neural machine translation of rare words with subword units. In *Proceedings of the 54th Annual Meeting of the Association for Computational Linguistics (Volume 1: Long Papers)*, pages 1715–1725.

Snover, M., Dorr, B., Schwartz, R., Micciulla, L., and Makhoul, J. (2006). A study of translation edit rate with targeted human annotation. In *Proceedings of the 7th Conference of the Association for Machine Translation in the Americas: Technical Papers*, pages 223–231, Cambridge, Massachusetts, USA. Association for Machine Translation in the Americas.

Wang, H., Wu, H., He, Z., Huang, L., and Church, K. W. (2022). Progress in machine translation. *Engineering*, 18:143–153.

Wang, P., Wang, L., and Lepage, Y. (2021). Generating the middle sentence of two sentences using pre-trained models: a first step for text morphing. In *Proceedings of the 27th annual meeting of the Association for Natural Language Processing*, pages 1481–1485.

Yi, Z., Zhang, H., Tan, P., and Gong, M. (2017). Dualgan: Unsupervised dual learning for image-to-image translation. In *Proceedings of the IEEE international conference on computer vision*, pages 2849–2857.

Zhou, J. T., Zhang, H., Jin, D., Zhu, H., Fang, M., Goh, R. S. M., and Kwok, K. (2019). Dual adversarial neural transfer for low-resource named entity recognition. In *Proceedings of the 57th Annual Meeting of the Association for Computational Linguistics*, pages 3461–3471.

A Table of Experiment Results

A.1 Different Data Sizes

Data size	Language Pairs	Data augmentation	Dual laerning	BLEU	chrF	TER
8k	en ->zh	without	without	12.7 $\pm$ 1.7	16.1 $\pm$ 1.3	67.6 $\pm$ 1.8
		with	without	9.7 $\pm$ 1.4	12.3 $\pm$ 1.1	72.4 $\pm$ 1.6
		with	with (ours)	**16.0 $\pm$ 2.0**	**17.7 $\pm$ 1.6**	**66.5 $\pm$ 1.9**
	zh ->en	without	without	13.3 $\pm$ 1.5	28.3 $\pm$ 1.4	68.5 $\pm$ 1.9
		with	without	10.5 $\pm$ 1.4	23.5 $\pm$ 1.3	75.6 $\pm$ 1.8
		with	with (ours)	**17.1 $\pm$ 1.8**	**32.0 $\pm$ 1.7**	**62.9 $\pm$ 1.8**
16k	en ->zh	without	without	16.3 $\pm$ 1.3	19.2 $\pm$ 1.0	64.4 $\pm$ 1.4
		with	without	14.6 $\pm$ 1.2	16.2 $\pm$ 1.0	70.2 $\pm$ 1.6
		with	with (ours)	**20.0 $\pm$ 1.4**	**23.6 $\pm$ 1.2**	63.8 $\pm$ 2.3
	zh ->en	without	without	20.1 $\pm$ 1.2	35.8 $\pm$ 1.1	60.3 $\pm$ 1.3
		with	without	18.1 $\pm$ 1.2	32.3 $\pm$ 1.1	62.1 $\pm$ 1.2
		with	with (ours)	**23.1 $\pm$ 1.3**	**40.0 $\pm$ 1.3**	**56.0 $\pm$ 1.4**
24k	en ->zh	without	without	21.7 $\pm$ 1.2	22.0 $\pm$ 1.0	63.4 $\pm$ 1.2
		with	without	19.4 $\pm$ 1.2	20.7 $\pm$ 1.0	67.3 $\pm$ 1.3
		with	with (ours)	21.5 $\pm$ 1.2	22.7 $\pm$ 1.0	58.5 $\pm$ 1.2
	zh ->en	without	without	24.1 $\pm$ 1.1	37.6 $\pm$ 1.0	59.3 $\pm$ 1.1
		with	without	21.3 $\pm$ 1.0	37.2 $\pm$ 1.0	62.3 $\pm$ 1.1
		with	with (ours)	**25.0 $\pm$ 1.2**	**41.0 $\pm$ 1.0**	**55.0 $\pm$ 1.1**
32k	en ->zh	without	without	25.8 $\pm$ 1.2	28.9 $\pm$ 1.0	53.9 $\pm$ 1.1
		with	without	23.4 $\pm$ 1.1	25.0 $\pm$ 1.0	58.1 $\pm$ 1.2
		with	with (ours)	23.5 $\pm$ 1.2	27.6 $\pm$ 1.0	54.7 $\pm$ 1.1
	zh ->en	without	without	27.2 $\pm$ 1.0	44.2 $\pm$ 0.9	51.6 $\pm$ 1.0
		with	without	22.3 $\pm$ 1.0	37.4 $\pm$ 0.9	56.5 $\pm$ 0.9
		with	with (ours)	25.7 $\pm$ 1.0	40.9 $\pm$ 1.0	55.1 $\pm$ 1.0
40k	en ->zh	without	without	27.0 $\pm$ 1.1	29.4 $\pm$ 0.9	52.7 $\pm$ 1.0
		with	without	25.0 $\pm$ 1.0	26.5 $\pm$ 0.9	56.0 $\pm$ 0.9
		with	with (ours)	25.4 $\pm$ 1.0	27.3 $\pm$ 1.0	54.6 $\pm$ 1.0
	zh ->en	without	without	28.3 $\pm$ 0.9	44.8 $\pm$ 0.8	51.0 $\pm$ 0.9
		with	without	23.2 $\pm$ 0.9	40.8 $\pm$ 0.8	55.4 $\pm$ 0.9
		with	with (ours)	26.5 $\pm$ 0.9	41.9 $\pm$ 0.9	54.7 $\pm$ 0.9
48k	en ->zh	without	without	27.8 $\pm$ 1.0	30.7 $\pm$ 0.9	52.2 $\pm$ 0.9
		with	without	27.4 $\pm$ 1.0	29.2 $\pm$ 0.9	54.1 $\pm$ 0.9
		with	with (ours)	27.8 $\pm$ 1.0	30.1 $\pm$ 0.9	53.7 $\pm$ 0.9
	zh ->en	without	without	27.8 $\pm$ 1.0	45.3 $\pm$ 0.7	64.2 $\pm$ 0.9
		with	without	24.5 $\pm$ 0.8	40.7 $\pm$ 0.8	59.3 $\pm$ 1.1
		with	with (ours)	27.3 $\pm$ 0.9	42.9 $\pm$ 0.8	54.3 $\pm$ 0.9

Table 3: Translation results of different sizes of dataset

A.2 Different Euclidean Distance Thresholds to Select Sentence Pairs

Data augmentation	Dual learning	Euclidean dis.	Language Pairs	BLEU	chrF	TER
without	without	/	en ->zh	12.7 ± 1.7	16.1 ± 1.3	67.6 ± 1.8
			zh ->en	13.3 ± 1.5	28.3 ± 1.4	68.5 ± 1.9
with	without	/	en ->zh	9.7 ± 1.4	12.3 ± 1.1	72.4 ± 1.6
			zh ->en	10.5 ± 1.4	23.5 ± 1.3	75.6 ± 1.8
with	with (ours)	0.1	en - >zh	11.3 ± 1.7	13.2 ± 1.5	70.3 ± 1.7
			zh ->en	10.8 ± 1.3	24.0 ± 1.5	69.2 ± 1.5
		0.2	en - >zh	13.6 ± 1.5	18.3 ± 1.3	65.7 ± 1.7
			zh ->en	11.2 ± 1.3	26.7 ± 1.3	65.9 ± 1.5
		0.3	en - >zh	**16.0 ± 2.0**	**17.7 ± 1.6**	**66.5 ± 1.9**
			zh ->en	**17.1 ± 1.8**	**32.0 ± 1.7**	**62.9 ± 1.8**
		0.4	en - >zh	12.3 ± 1.7	14.8 ± 1.4	65.7 ± 1.7
			zh ->en	11.5 ± 1.2	25.1 ± 1.3	70.3 ± 1.8
		0.5	en - >zh	10.9 ± 1.4	13.9 ± 1.1	72.4 ± 1.8
			zh ->en	11.1 ± 1.3	26.1 ± 1.1	75.3 ± 2.0

Table 4: Translation results of using different euclidean distance for selecting sentence pairs

A.3 Impact of Parallel and Nonparallel Start-End Sentence Pairs on Machine Translation Models

Language Pairs	Parallel	Cos similarity	Euclidean distance	BLEU	CHRF	TER
en ->zh	Yes	0.84	0.60	**16.0 ± 2.0**	**17.7 ± 1.6**	**66.5 ± 1.9**
	No	0.08	1.79	13.9 ± 1.8	16.1 ± 1.5	70.8 ± 2.0
zh ->en	Yes	0.84	0.60	**17.1 ± 1.8**	**32.0 ± 1.7**	**62.9 ± 1.8**
	No	0.08	1.79	15.2 ± 1.7	30.1 ± 1.5	64.6 ± 1.7

Table 5: Translation results starting from parallel and nonparallel start-end sentence pairs

Perturbation-based QE: An Explainable, Unsupervised Word-level Quality Estimation Method for Blackbox Machine Translation

Tu Anh Dinh tu.dinh@kit.edu
Karlsruhe Institute of Technology, Germany

Jan Niehues jan.niehues@kit.edu
Karlsruhe Institute of Technology, Germany

Abstract

Quality Estimation (QE) is the task of predicting the quality of Machine Translation (MT) system output, without using any gold-standard translation references. State-of-the-art QE models are supervised: they require human-labeled quality of some MT system output on some datasets for training, making them domain-dependent and MT-system-dependent. There has been research on unsupervised QE, which requires glass-box access to the MT systems, or parallel MT data to generate synthetic errors for training QE models. In this paper, we present *Perturbation-based QE* - a word-level Quality Estimation approach that works simply by analyzing MT system output on perturbed input source sentences. Our approach is unsupervised, explainable, and can evaluate any type of blackbox MT systems, including the currently prominent large language models (LLMs) with opaque internal processes. For language directions with no labeled QE data, our approach has similar or better performance than the zero-shot supervised approach on the WMT21 shared task. Our approach is better at detecting gender bias and word-sense-disambiguation errors in translation than supervised QE, indicating its robustness to out-of-domain usage. The performance gap is larger when detecting errors on a nontraditional translation-prompting LLM, indicating that our approach is more generalizable to different MT systems. We give examples demonstrating our approach's explainability power, where it shows which input source words have influence on a certain MT output word.

1 Introduction

Machine Translation (MT), with the aim of translating text from a source language to a target language, has been increasingly adopted in different real-world scenarios, ranging from translations in healthcare areas to translations in the legal domains (Vieira et al., 2021). In many of these applications, errors in translation output could cause serious harm to the users, e.g., translation errors leading to wrong medical diagnoses in healthcare or wrong judgment in court. Therefore, it is important to let the users know how much they can trust a translation, by providing them with some quality assessment of the MT output. This is not always straightforward due to the lack of gold-standard human translations, or the mismatch between evaluation data and real-world usage. As a result, researchers have been looking into Quality Estimation.

Quality Estimation (QE) is the task of predicting the quality of MT system output without access to reference translations. State-of-the-art QE systems are built in a supervised manner,

Proceedings of Machine Translation Summit XIX, Vol. 1: Research Track, pages 59–71
September 4–8, 2023, Macau SAR, China.

where they require human-labeled quality assessment on MT output for training (Rei et al., 2022). This approach has 2 drawbacks: the labeled QE data is costly to obtain, and the trained QE models would only know about the types of error that are presented in the training data. Supervised QE models are likely to underperform in unfamiliar settings (Kocyigit et al., 2022), e.g., when evaluating the output of a new MT system on a new dataset from a different domain. Consequently, there has been research into unsupervised QE, where the human-labeled assessment data is no longer required (Fomicheva et al., 2020b; Tuan et al., 2021). These works either require glass-box information of the MT system (e.g., output log probabilities or attention scores), or a large amount of parallel MT data to create synthetic QE data for training. This is problematic for language pairs with low-resourced MT data, or when the MT system is kept blackbox, which is the current trend of some widely-discussed API-only large language models.

In this paper, we propose an **unsupervised** word-level QE approach to evaluate **blackbox** MT systems, termed Perturbation-based QE. Our motivation is inspired by a known problem: when uncertain, MT systems rely on spurious correlations learnt from the training data to generate translation (Emelin et al., 2020; Savoldi et al., 2021). We assume that, when outputting a translation token, if the MT system relies on too many parts of the source sentence, it is likely that the system is exploiting irrelevant correlations, thus the output token is unreliable. Consider the English → German example: *"My friend has a Ph.D. degree, and now she is a professor."* → *"Meine Freundin hat einen Doktortitel, und sie ist jetzt eine Professorin."*. The translation word *"Freundin"* should only depends on *"friend"* and *"she"*, where *"friend"* indicates the meaning and *"she"* indicates the gender form. The output word being influenced by more source words would indicate that the MT system is focusing on the wrong part of the input sentence.

Broadly speaking, in Perturbation-based QE, we perturb words in the source sentences one by one to find out which source words influence a single output word. If an output word is influenced by too many source words, then it is predicted as a bad translation. Due to its simplicity, our approach does not require human-labeled QE data, nor parallel MT data, nor glass-box access to the evaluated MT system. Additionally, our QE approach comes with explainability power: it shows which source words affect each output word in the translation, thus can be used as an indication of the wrong correlations that is inherent in the MT system.

To summarize, our contributions are as follows:

- Proposing Perturbation-based QE[1]: a simple word-level Quality Estimation approach that is explainable, unsupervised and works with any type of blackbox MT systems, including the API-only large language models (i.e., MT-system-agnostic).
- Experiments showing the advantages of Perturbation-based QE: (1) it has similar or better performance than zero-shot QE, without making use of labeled data of auxiliary language pairs and (2) it is domain-independent and MT-system-independent compared to supervised QE methods: it can better capture out-of-domain gender errors and word-sense-disambiguation errors, especially from an unseen, nontraditional translation-prompting large language model and (3) it is not sensitive to hyperparameters.
- Analysis showing an example use of the explainability power of Perturbation-based QE.

2 Related work

Quality Estimation (QE) aims to predict the quality of Machine Translation (MT) output, either at the sentence level or word level. For word-level QE, the goal is to predict whether each word in the translation is correct. State-of-the-art word-level QE methods are supervised (Kim et al., 2017a; Specia et al., 2021b), i.e., requiring labeled data for training, which is costly to obtain.

[1]Implementation available at `https://github.com/TuAnh23/Perturbation-basedQE`.

Additionally, supervised QE is likely to be domain-dependent and MT-system-dependent, as they do not aware of errors not occurring in the training data (Kocyigit et al., 2022).

Unsupervised QE overcomes the need for labeled data. Several works perform unsupervised QE by using glass-box features from the MT systems (Popović, 2012; Moreau and Vogel, 2012; Etchegoyhen et al., 2018; Niehues and Pham, 2019; Fomicheva et al., 2020b). As an example, Fomicheva et al. (2020b) proposed unsupervised QE using the output probability distribution and the attention mechanism from encoder-decoder MT models. Therefore, their methods are model-specific. Tuan et al. (2021) excludes the need for human-labeled data and MT glass-box access by creating synthetic data to train QE models. The synthetic data is generated by aligning candidate MT translations to the target references to find errors, or rewriting target reference sentences using a masked language model to introduce errors. These methods require a large and diverse amount of parallel MT data (i.e., source sentences and the gold-standard translations), which is not always available for different domains and language pairs. Additionally, these methods are also likely to be domain-dependent and MT-system-dependent, as the QE model is trained on the output of pre-selected MT systems on pre-selected MT data.

Researchers also focus on Quality Estimation from the explainability perspective. He et al. (2019) propose using integrated gradients from MT models (i.e., glass-box information) to quantify how important each source word is to the output translated words. The method is then used for QE by detecting under-translated source words that have low importance to the output translation. Ferrando et al. (2022) also quantify the contribution of each source word on the output translation using glass-box information from transformer-based MT models, which is the layer-wise tokens attributions. Here the source words' contribution can also be used to detect under-translated source words, or to assess the quality of the whole translation. Another line of research is on explainable sentence-level QE, where the word-level error scores are provided as the explanation for the predicted sentence-level score (Fomicheva et al., 2021). Explanations can be extracted by using methods such as LIME (Ribeiro et al., 2016) or SHAP (Lundberg and Lee, 2017) on top of sentence-level QE models, or building interpretable models that output both sentence-level quality and word-level explanations (Fomicheva et al., 2021).

In contrast to the previous works on Quality Estimation, Perturbation-based QE does not require labeled QE data, parallel MT data, nor glass-box access to the evaluated MT system. From the explainability perspective, our approach provides a new type of explanation for target-side word-level QE, i.e., the information on which source words affect each translated word.

3 Perturbation-based Quality Estimation

In this section, we describe Perturbation-based QE. Recall our motivation: if the MT system relies on too many tokens in the source sentence to output a translation token, it is likely that the system is exploiting irrelevant correlations, thus the translation token is unreliable.

Perturbation generation (Step I Figure 1): We first perform perturbation to the source sentence. The subset of source words to perturb, which is a hyperparameter choice, is one of the following: (1) content words, i.e., noun, verb, adjective, adverb, pronoun, determined by NLTK part-of-speech tagging (Bird et al., 2009); (2) all words including functional words such as "a", "an", "the"; or (3) all tokens including non-word tokens such as punctuation marks. For each perturbed source word s_i, we mask it out from the source sentence and use a language model to generate n best replacements. The language masking model can be BERT (Devlin et al., 2019), RoBERTa (Liu et al., 2019) or DistilBERT (Sanh et al., 2019) (choice of the language masking model is a hyperparameter).

Translation (Step II Figure 1): We use the MT system to translate all perturbed versions.

Alignment (Step III Figure 1): We align at word level all the perturbed translations with the original translation. Two possible alignment methods are (1) Levenshtein (Levenshtein et al.,

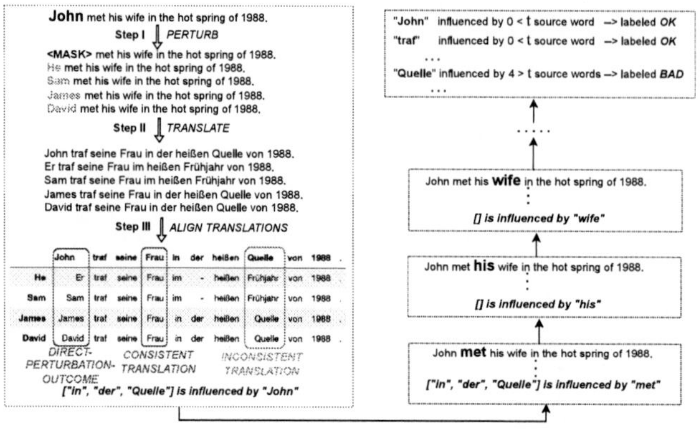

Figure 1: Perturbation-based QE. Words in the source sentence are perturbed one by one to find out their influence on the output words. If an output word h_j is influenced by more than t source words (excluding the source word directly translated to h_j), it is predicted as a BAD translation.

1966), which is the standard edit-distance alignment method that minimizes the number of insertion, deletion and substitution operations; and (2) Tercom (Snover et al., 2006), which additionally considers the shift operation. In Figure 1, the alignment outcome is shown in a table, where the column titles are the tokenized original translation, the row titles are the replacements of the perturbed source word, and each row is the aligned translation of the perturbed source sentence. Note that sometimes the alignments are not one-to-one. Some words in the original translation could have no aligned version in the perturbed translation. In this case, we align the original word with an empty token. Similarly, some words in the perturbed translation might not be aligned with any word in the original translation. In this case, we discard the words in the perturbed translation, since we only evaluate the consistency of the original words.

Consistency evaluation (Step III Figure 1): An MT-output word h_j is considered either a consistent translation, an inconsistent translation, or a direct-perturbation-outcome w.r.t. each perturbed source word s_i.

- Consistent translation is a translation that remains the same across perturbations. For example, in Figure 1, *"Frau"* is a consistent translation w.r.t perturbing *"John"*. To account for possible noise in alignment, we mark a translation as consistent if it remains the same across more than $c\%$ out of n perturbations w.r.t s_i. The threshold c is a hyperparameter.

- Direct-perturbation-outcome is the translation of the perturbed word, thus should vary in all perturbations. For example, in Figure 1, *"John"* is a direct-perturbation-outcome translation w.r.t perturbing *"John"*. To account for possible noise in translation and alignment, we mark a translation as direct-perturbation-outcome if the number of unique versions over the total n perturbations is larger than $p\%$. The threshold p is a hyperparameter.

- Inconsistent translation is a translation that has a few versions of it across n perturbations (i.e., the remaining cases). In Figure 1, *"Quelle"* is an inconsistent translation w.r.t perturbing *"John"*. When an MT-output word h_j is inconsistent due to perturbing a source word s_i, we say that h_j is influenced by s_i. Here *"Quelle"* is influenced by *"John"*.

Quality label prediction (Last block Figure 1): If the number of source words influencing h_j (excluding the one directly translated to h_j) is higher than a threshold t, then h_j is predicted as a BAD translation, otherwise predicted as OK[2]. The threshold t is a hyperparameter.

Our approach comes with several advantages. First, it is unsupervised. The method does not rely on any labeled QE data or parallel MT data for training. This potentially makes the approach domain-independent and MT-system-independent. In other words, the approach would be robust to discover errors not presented in previous datasets, such as errors from a new MT system on a different domain. A small amount of labeled QE data can be used for hyperparameter tuning. However, our experiments show that the approach is not sensitive to hyperparameter choices, and that hyperparameters can be transferred across languages. Second, our approach is MT-system-agnostic and works for blackbox MT systems, as it only uses the MT system to generate translations. Third, our approach comes with explainability power. For each MT output word, our method shows which source words affect the generation of the considered output word. In this way, one can find wrong correlations inherent in the MT systems.

In terms of computational cost, Perturbation-based QE does not involve any training process. However, it requires computational power when using the evaluated MT system to generate translations of different perturbed versions of the source sentence. This can be considered as the trade-off between our approach and the previous QE approaches.

4 Experimental setup

4.1 Overall evaluation

Dataset: We use the word-level part of the MLQE-PE dataset (Fomicheva et al., 2020a), which is the benchmark in the WMT21 QE shared task (Specia et al., 2021b). The dataset consists of source sentences, the machine translation output and the word-level *OK/BAD* labels. We conduct experiments on four language pairs: English-German (*en-de*), English-Chinese(*en-zh*), English-Japanese (*en-ja*) and English-Czech (*en-cs*). In this dataset, *en-de* and *en-zh* directions are supervised, while *en-ja* and *en-cs* directions are zero-shot. However, we only use the development split for *en-de* and *en-zh* to perform hyperparameter tuning.

Evaluated MT systems: We use the to-be-evaluated encoder-decoder MT systems from WMT21, i.e., the fairseq Transformer (Ott et al., 2019) bilingual models for *en-de* and *en-zh*; and the ML50 fairseq multilingual Transformer model (Tang et al., 2020) for *en-cs* and *en-ja*.

Metrics: Following the WMT21 shared task, we use the Matthews correlation coefficient (MCC) (Matthews, 1975) as the evaluation metric for word-level QE in our experiments.

Hyperparameters: Hyperparameters for our approach, as explained in Section 3, are the number of unmasking replacements n, thresholds c, p, t, choices of source word subset for perturbation, language masking models to generate perturbation replacements and alignment tools. We use grid search to find the hyperparameter setting that yields the highest MCC score on development data. The best setting for *en-de* (which is then applied on *en-cs*) is $n = 30$, $c = 0.95$, $p = 0.9$, $t = 2$, perturbing content words, Tercom alignment and RoBERTa unmasking. The best setting for *en-zh* (which is then applied on *en-ja*) is $n = 30$, $c = 0.95$, $p = 0.8$, $t = 4$, perturbing all tokens, Tercom alignment and RoBERTa unmasking. We transfer the hyperparameters across languages in such a way since we expect more language-similarity between *de/cs* (alphabetic writing systems) and *zh/ja* (logographic writing systems).

Unsupervised QE baselines: For unsupervised baseline, we use the word-level log probabilities generated by the MT system. If the log probability of an output word is larger than a certain threshold l, then it is marked as OK, otherwise it is marked as BAD. The threshold l is a hyperparameter. Here we also use the development split to find the best l for *en-de* and *en-zh*. We apply the best value of l for *en-de* (which is $log_2 0.45$) on *en-cs* and the best value of l for

[2]We focus on evaluating the translation words that were output by the MT system. Our approach is not suitable to evaluate the gap between words or to detect untranslated parts of the source sentence.

en-zh (which is $log_2 0.60$) on *en-ja*. We choose this baseline since it has the same data usage as our approach, and it requires little information from the MT system (although here we no longer treat the MT system completely as blackbox).

Supervised QE baselines: We use the supervised baseline from the WMT21 QE shared task (Specia et al., 2021a). The baseline is a multilingual transformer-based Predictor-Estimator (Kim et al., 2017b), trained on labeled data for all available seven language directions. The model is trained multi-tasked, requiring both word-level and sentence-level labeled data.

4.2 Out-of-domain, unseen-MT-system evaluation

Common in-domain, known-MT-system setup: The common evaluation setup for QE approaches, e.g., in the WMT21 shared task, are in-domain and on known MT systems. That is, the QE test data is generated in the same way as the QE training data, and the to-be-evaluated MT system is the same as the one used to create the QE training data. However, in order to be useful in real-world applications, QE approaches should be capable of out-of-domain evaluation on unseen MT systems. That is, QE approaches should be able to evaluate different types of MT systems on different types of datasets. Therefore, we design experiments using QE approaches in an out-of-domain, unknown-MT-system setting, described as follows.

Evaluated MT systems: We test the QE approaches on evaluating two MT systems, one known and one unseen. The known MT system is the one that was used to create the WMT21 QE training and test data: the Fairseq encoder-decoder MT model. The unseen system is Flan-UL2 (available on HuggingFace) - a recent prompt-based large language model (LLM). We generate MT output from this LLM by prompting the system with "*Translate this into German: <English_input>*:". We choose this system as LLMs have been gaining a lot of attention and are more and more widely used (Vilar et al., 2022; Zhang et al., 2023; Bawden and Yvon, 2023). Going beyond the conventional encoder-decoder MT systems, we attempt to show that our approach is applicable to prompt-based translation using these prominent decoder-only LLMs.

Out-of-domain test data: We use two challenge sets on *en-de*. The first one is WinoMT (Stanovsky et al., 2019), used to evaluate gender bias from MT systems. WinoMT contains English input sentences with marked gender roles (e.g., "The **doctor** asked the nurse to help her in the operation") and evaluation protocol to identify whether the MT system outputs the correct gender form. The second challenge set is MuCoW (WMT 2019 translation test suite version) (Raganato et al., 2019), used to evaluate word-sense-disambiguation ability of MT systems. MuCoW contains English input sentences with ambiguous words and evaluation protocol to identify whether the MT system outputs the correct sense translations of the ambiguous words.

On WinoMT, the correct-gender accuracy is 69.4% for the Fairseq encoder-decoder MT system and 47.5% for the Prompt-based LLM Flan-UL2 system. On MuCoW, the correct-disambiguation accuracy is 47.59% for the Fairseq encoder-decoder MT system and 22.95% for the Prompt-based LLM Flan-UL2 system. Both MT systems do not perform well in outputting the correct gender form nor outputting the correct sense for ambiguous words. Therefore, it would be interesting to see whether QE methods can detect these mistakes.

Out-of-domain error detection: We test whether QE approaches can detect gender errors (which we refer to as GenderBAD tokens) and word-sense-disambiguation errors (which we refer to as WSD-BAD tokens). Given an MT system, we first generate translations for the WinoMT/MuCoW English sentences. Then we run WinoMT/MuCoW evaluation protocol to mark the GenderBAD/WSD-BAD tokens. An ideal QE approach should be able to detect all the GenderBAD/WSD-BAD tokens, i.e., correctly labeling them as BAD translations.

Metrics: We report on the GenderBAD-recall and WSD-BAD-recall, i.e., the percentage of GenderBAD/WSD-BAD tokens (marked by WinoMT/MuCoW) that are successfully predicted as BAD by the QE methods. We do not report on the GenderBAD/WSD-BAD accuracy, since tokens with correct gender form or correct disambiguated sense are not necessarily OK translations. They could contain some other types of errors such as tense or singular/plural forms. Note that the recall metric could favor QE methods that are overly harsh (e.g., predicting everything as BAD would result in perfect GenderBAD/WSD-BAD recall). Therefore, we additionally report on the GenderBAD-precision and WSD-BAD-precision. Precision scores only serve as an indication of whether a QE model is too harsh. The reason is that, GenderBAD and WSD-BAD are not the only types of BAD error, thus it is not correct to always punish the QE model for predicting a non-GenderBAD or non-WSD-BAD token as BAD.

4.3 Robustness w.r.t hyperparameter choices

Recall that, in the previous experiments, we use the WMT21 development data of *en-de* and *en-zh* to perform hyperparameter tuning for Perturbation-based QE. The best hyperparameters for *en-de* are then also used for *en-cs*, and the ones for *en-zh* are used for *en-ja*, since we assumed more language similarity between *de/cs* and *zh/ja*. We refer to this as *"ideal hyperparameters"*.

The aim of this experiment is to test the robustness of our approach w.r.t hyperparameter choices, i.e., how much our approach relies on labeled development data. Similar to the experiment in Section 4.1, we report the MCC scores on in-domain setting, i.e., WMT21 test data. Here we apply the hyperparameter settings in an opposite way compared to previous experiment, i.e., (1) applying the best hyperparameter setting of *en-de* on *en-zh* and *en-ja*, and (2) applying the best hyperparameter setting of *en-zh* on *en-de* and *en-cs*. We refer to this as *"suboptimal hyperparameters"*. The MCC scores reducing significantly would indicate that our approach is sensitive to hyperparameters and vice versa. Additionally, we provide ablation experiments on the discrete hyperparameters to see their effects on the QE performance.

5 Results and Discussion

5.1 Overall QE performance

	Supervised/Tuned		Zero-shot/Un-tuned	
	en-de	en-zh	en-ja	en-cs
Log probability QE	0.241	0.149	0.112	0.257
WMT21 QE baseline	**0.370**	**0.247**	0.131	0.273
Perturbation-based QE	0.287	0.180	**0.218**	0.270

Table 1: Performance (in MCC score) of word-level QE approaches on WMT21 test data.

The performance of our Perturbation-based QE on the WMT21 test data, in comparison to other baselines, is shown in Table 1. Our approach outperforms the log-probability baseline over all language pairs. The largest gap is on *en-ja*, where our approach obtains 0.106 points higher. For *en-de* and *en-zh*, the gain from our approach is around 0.040 points. The smallest gain is on *en-cs*, where our approach outperforms the log-probability baseline by 0.013 points.

Compared to the WMT21 QE baseline, on *en-de* and *en-zh*, our approach falls behind by 0.083 and 0.067 points respectively. Recall that for these language pairs, the WMT21 QE is supervised, requiring labeled word-level data, and additionally uses sentence-level data for multi-task training. In contrast, our approach only uses the development split of word-level data for hyperparameter tuning. It can be concluded that our approach is not competitive to the supervised approaches that make use of more labeled data for training.

On *en-ja* and *en-cs*, our approach is competitive to the WMT21 QE baseline. Our approach outperforms the baseline by 0.087 points on *en-ja*, while having similar performance on *en-cs*. Recall that on these language pairs, both approaches do not use any labeled data of the language pairs in consideration. The WMT21 baseline is zero-shot: it uses labeled training data of 7 other language pairs. In contrast, our approach only uses the development split of 2 other language pairs for hyperparameter tuning. It can be concluded that, when there is no direct labeled data for the language pair of interest, our approach has competitive performance while being more data efficient compared to the zero-shot approach. Additionally, observe that the performance of the WMT21 zero-shot baseline on *en-ja* is low compared to *en-cs*. This is possibly due to the low similarity between *ja* and other languages in the training data. This indicates that the zero-shot approach is more data-dependent, while this is not an issue for our approach.

5.2 Out-of-domain, unseen-system evaluation

The QE approaches' performance on detecting out-of-domain errors from known/unseen evaluated MT-system is shown in Table 2. As can be seen, our Perturbation-based QE approach has the best performance. When the task is to detect gender errors, our GenderBAD-recall is significantly higher than the second-best QE approach by over 0.200 points. When the task is to detect word sense disambiguation errors, our WSD-BAD-recall is higher than the second-best QE approach by over 0.049 points. At the same time, our GenderBAD-precision and WSD-BAD-precision scores are similar to the other methods, indicating that we are not overly predicting tokens as BAD to cheat for a higher GenderBAD-recall and WSD-BAD-recall.

	Known MT system (Encoder-Decoder MT)		Unseen MT system (Prompt-based LLM)	
	GenderBAD recall	GenderBAD precision	GenderBAD recall	GenderBAD precision
Log probability QE	0.175	0.036	0.429	0.047
WMT21 QE (supervised)	0.021	0.031	0.065	0.036
Perturbation-based QE	**0.391**	0.045	**0.658**	0.042
	Known MT system (Encoder-Decoder MT)		Unseen MT system (Prompt-based LLM)	
	WSD-BAD recall	WSD-BAD precision	WSD-BAD recall	WSD-BAD precision
Log probability QE	0.137	0.007	0.347	0.005
WMT21 QE (supervised)	0.290	0.028	0.177	0.004
Perturbation-based QE	**0.339**	0.009	**0.709**	0.005

Table 2: Results on detecting out-of-domain errors by different QE methods. The top half indicates results on WinoMT. The bottom half indicates results on MuCoW.

Another observation is that, the supervised WMT21 QE model performs poorly on detecting GenderBAD tokens from MT outputs on WinoMT. Its GenderBAD-recall is very low, at 0.021 for known MT system and at 0.065 for unseen MT system. This performance is even worse than that of the naive Log probability QE, whose GenderBAD-recall is 0.175 on known MT system output and 0.429 on unseen MT system output. A possible explanation is that, the WMT21 QE model does not aware of gender errors since this type of error does not present in the training data. This indicates the data-dependent issue inherent to supervised QE approaches.

The performance gap between our Perturbation-based QE approach and the supervised WMT21 QE model is larger on the unseen MT system than the known MT system. On the unseen MT system, our GenderBAD-recall is higher than the WMT21 QE model by +0.593 points, which is larger than the corresponding gap of +0.370 when evaluating the known MT system. Similarly, the WSD-recall gap is +0.532 on the unseen MT system, which is larger than the gap of +0.049 on the known MT system. Additionally, when detecting word sense disambiguation errors from the unseen MT system, the performance of the WMT21 QE model is once again worse than the naive Log probability QE approach, where its WSD-BAD-recall is lower by -0.170 points. This indicates the MT-system-dependent issue inherent to supervised QE approaches, where they are not able to perform as well on evaluating unseen MT systems.

Overall, the supervised QE models, while performing better in a similar setting as their training process, fail behind Perturbation-based QE in out-of-domain and unseen-system settings. This strengthens the domain-independent and system-independent power of our approach: it can better detect errors from a new MT system on a new domain usage.

5.3 Robustness w.r.t hyperparameter choices

The difference in performance when using different hyperparameter settings in our approach is shown in Table 3. As can be seen, the MCC scores only deviate by around 0.010 points when using ideal versus suboptimal hyperparameter values. The difference in performance when using different values for the discrete hyperparameters is shown in Table 4. We consider 3 hyperparameters, in the top-to-bottom order displayed in Table 4: sets of perturbed source words, unmasking models and alignment methods. It can be seen that, the MCC scores generally deviate by only around 0.010 points. Overall, different choices of hyperparameters do not significantly affect our QE performance. This shows that our approach is not sensitive to hyperparameter choices, which is useful since we are not dependent on labeled data for hyperparameter tuning.

	en-de	en-zh	en-ja	en-cs
Ideal hyperparameters	0.287	0.180	0.218	0.270
Suboptimal hyperparameters	0.274	0.167	0.206	0.284

Table 3: Perturbation-based QE performance in MCC using ideal/suboptimal hyperparameters.

	en-de		en-zh	
	Best val MCC	Test MCC	Best val MCC	Test MCC
content words	0.282 ± 0.004	0.287 ± 0.005	0.196 ± 0.003	0.169 ± 0.005
all words	0.267 ± 0.004	0.277 ± 0.003	0.196 ± 0.002	0.162 ± 0.004
all tokens	0.270 ± 0.002	0.269 ± 0.006	0.208 ± 0.003	0.177 ± 0.004
BERT large	0.272 ± 0.006	0.278 ± 0.011	0.198 ± 0.006	0.174 ± 0.006
BERT base	0.272 ± 0.006	0.279 ± 0.009	0.199 ± 0.005	0.166 ± 0.006
DistilBERT	0.269 ± 0.008	0.272 ± 0.008	0.198 ± 0.008	0.168 ± 0.009
RoBERTa	0.277 ± 0.007	0.278 ± 0.008	0.203 ± 0.007	0.169 ± 0.007
Levenshtein	0.272 ± 0.006	0.275 ± 0.008	0.199 ± 0.006	0.170 ± 0.007
Tercom	0.274 ± 0.009	0.280 ± 0.009	0.200 ± 0.007	0.168 ± 0.007

Table 4: Ablation experiments on discrete hyperparameter settings for Perturbation-based QE. The performance of a setting in a specific group is averaged over all settings of the other groups.

5.4 Perturbation-based QE for explainable MT

We investigate some examples of using Perturbation-based QE for explaining the MT output gender errors on WinoMT and the word sense disambiguation errors on MuCoW. One gender error example is shown in Figure 2a. The MT system outputs the female form for *"housekeeper"*, while the form should be male, indicated by the word *"he"*. In an ideal scenario, the gender form of *"housekeeper"* (*"Haushälterin/Haushalter"*) should only depend on *"he"*. However, our approach shows that, when perturbing the source word *"he"*, the output word *"Haushälterin"* does not change. Instead, when perturbing *["chief", "gave", "tip", "was", "helpful"]*, the output varies between *"Haushälterin"* and *"Haushalter"*, showing that the MT model is focusing on the wrong part of the sentence to determine the gender form.

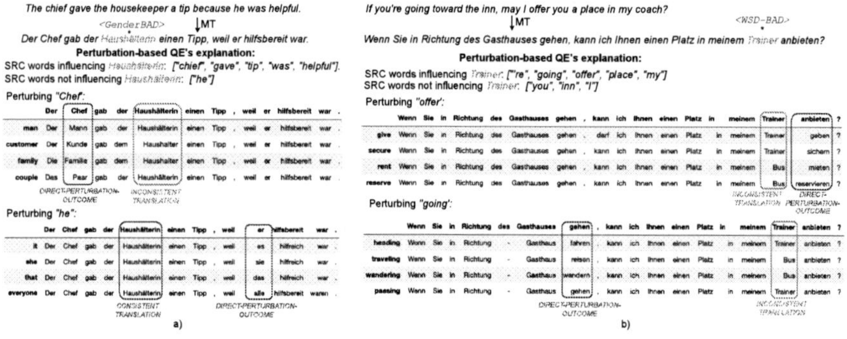

Figure 2: Example of Perturbation-based QE's explanation on WinoMT (a) and MuCoW (b).

One word sense disambiguation error example is shown in Figure 2b. The MT system outputs the wrong sense for *"coach"*. It outputs *"Trainer"*, which means the sports trainer. However, given the context, *"coach"* should mean the vehicle, thus the correct output should be *"Bus"*. Ideally, the MT system should only look at the context source words indicating movements to decide on the sense of *"coach"*. Nevertheless, our approach shows that the MT output translation for *"coach"* varies when perturbing multiple source words. For example, replacing *"offer"* with *"rent"* or *"reserve"* makes the system outputs the correct sense *"Bus"*, while for other replacements it still outputs *"Trainer"*. Similarly, when replacing *"going"* with other words that indicate movements, only *"traveling"* and *"wandering"* make the system outputs the correct sense *"Bus"*. This explanation provides an insight into the MT system: the sense *"Bus"* is only correlated to a few context words. Therefore, when the source sentence does not contain those specific words, the MT system fails to output the correct sense.

6 Conclusion

We proposed an unsupervised word-level Quality Estimation method, termed Perturbation-based QE. Our method does not rely on labeled QE data nor parallel MT data, masking it more domain-independent and system-independent to find MT errors that cannot be foreseen. This advantage is supported by our experiment on finding gender bias and word-sense-disambiguation erroneous translation from a nontraditional translation-prompting LLM. Our approach is not sensitive to hyperparameter settings, thus less dependent on labeled data for hyperparameter tuning. Our approach is also explainable: it shows which source words affect an output translated word. Additionally, our approach is MT-system-agnostic and works for black-box systems. Overall, Perturbation-based QE, as an unsupervised method, still falls behind supervised QE on in-domain and known-MT-system settings, but outperforms supervised QE on zero-shot settings and on out-domain and unseen-MT-system settings. As future work, it can be extended to assess the quality of other tasks, such as question answering or summarization, in the same manner: minimally perturb the input and analyze changes in the output.

References

Bawden, R. and Yvon, F. (2023). Investigating the translation performance of a large multilingual language model: the case of bloom. *arXiv preprint arXiv:2303.01911*.

Bird, S., Klein, E., and Loper, E. (2009). *Natural language processing with Python: analyzing text with the natural language toolkit*. " O'Reilly Media, Inc.".

Devlin, J., Chang, M.-W., Lee, K., and Toutanova, K. (2019). BERT: Pre-training of deep bidirectional transformers for language understanding. In *Proceedings of the 2019 Conference of the North American Chapter of the Association for Computational Linguistics: Human Language Technologies, Volume 1 (Long and Short Papers)*, pages 4171–4186, Minneapolis, Minnesota. Association for Computational Linguistics.

Emelin, D., Titov, I., and Sennrich, R. (2020). Detecting word sense disambiguation biases in machine translation for model-agnostic adversarial attacks. In *Proceedings of the 2020 Conference on Empirical Methods in Natural Language Processing (EMNLP)*, pages 7635–7653, Online. Association for Computational Linguistics.

Etchegoyhen, T., Martínez Garcia, E., and Azpeitia, A. (2018). Supervised and unsupervised minimalist quality estimators: Vicomtech's participation in the WMT 2018 quality estimation task. In *Proceedings of the Third Conference on Machine Translation: Shared Task Papers*, pages 782–787, Belgium, Brussels. Association for Computational Linguistics.

Ferrando, J., Gállego, G. I., Alastruey, B., Escolano, C., and Costa-jussà, M. R. (2022). Towards opening the black box of neural machine translation: Source and target interpretations of the transformer. In *Proceedings of the 2022 Conference on Empirical Methods in Natural Language Processing*, pages 8756–8769, Abu Dhabi, United Arab Emirates. Association for Computational Linguistics.

Fomicheva, M., Lertvittayakumjorn, P., Zhao, W., Eger, S., and Gao, Y. (2021). The Eval4NLP shared task on explainable quality estimation: Overview and results. In *Proceedings of the 2nd Workshop on Evaluation and Comparison of NLP Systems*, pages 165–178, Punta Cana, Dominican Republic. Association for Computational Linguistics.

Fomicheva, M., Sun, S., Fonseca, E., Zerva, C., Blain, F., Chaudhary, V., Guzmán, F., Lopatina, N., Specia, L., and Martins, A. F. (2020a). Mlqe-pe: A multilingual quality estimation and post-editing dataset. *arXiv preprint arXiv:2010.04480*.

Fomicheva, M., Sun, S., Yankovskaya, L., Blain, F., Guzmán, F., Fishel, M., Aletras, N., Chaudhary, V., and Specia, L. (2020b). Unsupervised quality estimation for neural machine translation. *Transactions of the Association for Computational Linguistics*, 8:539–555.

He, S., Tu, Z., Wang, X., Wang, L., Lyu, M., and Shi, S. (2019). Towards understanding neural machine translation with word importance. In *Proceedings of the 2019 Conference on Empirical Methods in Natural Language Processing and the 9th International Joint Conference on Natural Language Processing (EMNLP-IJCNLP)*, pages 953–962, Hong Kong, China. Association for Computational Linguistics.

Kim, H., Lee, J.-H., and Na, S.-H. (2017a). Predictor-estimator using multilevel task learning with stack propagation for neural quality estimation. In *Proceedings of the Second Conference on Machine Translation*, pages 562–568.

Kim, H., Lee, J.-H., and Na, S.-H. (2017b). Predictor-estimator using multilevel task learning with stack propagation for neural quality estimation. In *Proceedings of the Second Conference on Machine Translation*, pages 562–568, Copenhagen, Denmark. Association for Computational Linguistics.

Kocyigit, M., Lee, J., and Wijaya, D. (2022). Better quality estimation for low resource corpus mining. In *Findings of the Association for Computational Linguistics: ACL 2022*, pages 533–543, Dublin, Ireland. Association for Computational Linguistics.

Levenshtein, V. I. et al. (1966). Binary codes capable of correcting deletions, insertions, and reversals. In *Soviet physics doklady*, volume 10, pages 707–710. Soviet Union.

Liu, Y., Ott, M., Goyal, N., Du, J., Joshi, M., Chen, D., Levy, O., Lewis, M., Zettlemoyer, L., and Stoyanov, V. (2019). Roberta: A robustly optimized bert pretraining approach. *arXiv preprint arXiv:1907.11692*.

Lundberg, S. M. and Lee, S.-I. (2017). A unified approach to interpreting model predictions. *Advances in neural information processing systems*, 30.

Matthews, B. W. (1975). Comparison of the predicted and observed secondary structure of t4 phage lysozyme. *Biochimica et Biophysica Acta (BBA)-Protein Structure*, 405(2):442–451.

Moreau, E. and Vogel, C. (2012). Quality estimation: an experimental study using unsupervised similarity measures. In *Proceedings of the Seventh Workshop on Statistical Machine Translation*, pages 120–126, Montréal, Canada. Association for Computational Linguistics.

Niehues, J. and Pham, N.-Q. (2019). Modeling confidence in sequence-to-sequence models. In *Proceedings of the 12th International Conference on Natural Language Generation*, pages 575–583, Tokyo, Japan. Association for Computational Linguistics.

Ott, M., Edunov, S., Baevski, A., Fan, A., Gross, S., Ng, N., Grangier, D., and Auli, M. (2019). fairseq: A fast, extensible toolkit for sequence modeling. In *Proceedings of the 2019 Conference of the North American Chapter of the Association for Computational Linguistics (Demonstrations)*, pages 48–53, Minneapolis, Minnesota. Association for Computational Linguistics.

Popović, M. (2012). Morpheme- and POS-based IBM1 and language model scores for translation quality estimation. In *Proceedings of the Seventh Workshop on Statistical Machine Translation*, pages 133–137, Montréal, Canada. Association for Computational Linguistics.

Raganato, A., Scherrer, Y., and Tiedemann, J. (2019). The MuCoW test suite at WMT 2019: Automatically harvested multilingual contrastive word sense disambiguation test sets for machine translation. In *Proceedings of the Fourth Conference on Machine Translation (Volume 2: Shared Task Papers, Day 1)*, pages 470–480, Florence, Italy. Association for Computational Linguistics.

Rei, R., Treviso, M., Guerreiro, N. M., Zerva, C., Farinha, A. C., Maroti, C., de Souza, J. G., Glushkova, T., Alves, D. M., Lavie, A., et al. (2022). Cometkiwi: Ist-unbabel 2022 submission for the quality estimation shared task. *arXiv preprint arXiv:2209.06243*.

Ribeiro, M. T., Singh, S., and Guestrin, C. (2016). " why should i trust you?" explaining the predictions of any classifier. In *Proceedings of the 22nd ACM SIGKDD international conference on knowledge discovery and data mining*, pages 1135–1144.

Sanh, V., Debut, L., Chaumond, J., and Wolf, T. (2019). Distilbert, a distilled version of bert: smaller, faster, cheaper and lighter. *arXiv preprint arXiv:1910.01108*.

Savoldi, B., Gaido, M., Bentivogli, L., Negri, M., and Turchi, M. (2021). Gender bias in machine translation. *Transactions of the Association for Computational Linguistics*, 9:845–874.

Snover, M., Dorr, B., Schwartz, R., Micciulla, L., and Makhoul, J. (2006). A study of translation edit rate with targeted human annotation. In *Proceedings of the 7th Conference of the Association for Machine Translation in the Americas: Technical Papers*, pages 223–231.

Specia, L., Blain, F., Fomicheva, M., Zerva, C., Li, Z., Chaudhary, V., and Martins, A. F. (2021a). Findings of the wmt 2021 shared task on quality estimation. In *Proceedings of the Sixth Conference on Machine Translation*, pages 684–725.

Specia, L., Blain, F., Fomicheva, M., Zerva, C., Li, Z., Chaudhary, V., and Martins, A. F. T. (2021b). Findings of the WMT 2021 shared task on quality estimation. In *Proceedings of the Sixth Conference on Machine Translation*, pages 684–725, Online. Association for Computational Linguistics.

Stanovsky, G., Smith, N. A., and Zettlemoyer, L. (2019). Evaluating gender bias in machine translation. In *Proceedings of the 57th Annual Meeting of the Association for Computational Linguistics*, pages 1679–1684, Florence, Italy. Association for Computational Linguistics.

Tang, Y., Tran, C., Li, X., Chen, P.-J., Goyal, N., Chaudhary, V., Gu, J., and Fan, A. (2020). Multilingual translation with extensible multilingual pretraining and finetuning. *arXiv preprint arXiv:2008.00401*.

Tuan, Y.-L., El-Kishky, A., Renduchintala, A., Chaudhary, V., Guzmán, F., and Specia, L. (2021). Quality estimation without human-labeled data. In *Proceedings of the 16th Conference of the European Chapter of the Association for Computational Linguistics: Main Volume*, pages 619–625, Online. Association for Computational Linguistics.

Vieira, L. N., O'Hagan, M., and O'Sullivan, C. (2021). Understanding the societal impacts of machine translation: a critical review of the literature on medical and legal use cases. *Information, Communication & Society*, 24(11):1515–1532.

Vilar, D., Freitag, M., Cherry, C., Luo, J., Ratnakar, V., and Foster, G. (2022). Prompting palm for translation: Assessing strategies and performance. *arXiv preprint arXiv:2211.09102*.

Zhang, B., Haddow, B., and Birch, A. (2023). Prompting large language model for machine translation: A case study. *arXiv preprint arXiv:2301.07069*.

Semi-supervised Learning for Quality Estimation of Machine Translation

Tarun Bhatia tarunbhatia.ind@gmail.com
Technische Universität Berlin, Berlin, Germany and SAP SE

Martin Krämer martin.kraemer@sap.com
Eduardo Vellasques eduardo.vellasques@sap.com
SAP SE

Eleftherios Avramidis eleftherios.avramidis@dfki.de
German Research Center for Artificial Intelligence (DFKI), Berlin, Germany

Abstract

We investigate whether using semi-supervised learning (SSL) methods can be beneficial for the task of word-level Quality Estimation of Machine Translation in low-resource conditions. We show that the Mean Teacher network can provide equal or significantly better MCC scores (up to +12%) than supervised methods when a limited amount of labeled data is available. Additionally, following previous work on SSL, we investigate Pseudo-Labeling in combination with SSL, which nevertheless does not provide consistent improvements.

1 Introduction

Through the recent development of Machine Translation (MT), Quality Estimation (QE) has come to serve the need to predict the quality of translation provided by MT systems when no reference translations are available. QE has been mostly treated as a supervised learning problem, where supervised models can be trained on the source and translated text along with their respective quality labels. For example, QE at the word level includes the source and translated sentences as the data and their label sequence includes an OK or BAD label for each translated word in the sentence, which can determine if the word is correctly translated or not and potential errors in the translations can be flagged. In order to train supervised models for such problems, a large amount of labeled data is needed. However, such data is expensive to create as it involves human annotators to post-edit or generate labels for the given translations. Whereas the unavailability of labeled data is a problem, there is an abundance of unlabeled data for such a task, i.e. source sentences and the corresponding translations generated by MT systems. Semi-supervised learning (SSL) methods could be utilized to train QE models with few labeled data available along with unlabeled data that can be generated in abundance.

While the prominent SSL approach of Mean Teacher has shown good performance in computer vision (Tarvainen and Valpola, 2017), there has been little experimentation in NLP. Until now, no research has followed SSL to fine-tune pre-trained language models (LMs) for the task of QE of MT. This work focuses on implementing the aforementioned SSL strategies for word-level QE and tries to answer the following questions:

Proceedings of Machine Translation Summit XIX, Vol. 1: Research Track, pages 72–83
September 4–8, 2023, Macau SAR, China.

```
anschließend wird in jeder Methode die übergeordnete Superclass-Version von selbst
aufgerufen .

anschließend wird in jeder Methode die Superclass-Version dieser Methode
aufgerufen .

OK OK OK OK OK OK OK OK OK OK OK OK OK BAD OK OK OK BAD OK BAD OK OK OK OK OK
```

Figure 1: Example of German translation by a MT system and its human post-edited version with labels of gaps and target words for the example translated text. Tags for Gap tokens are highlighted in yellow and tags for words in sequence are highlighted in blue (Specia et al., 2021)

1. Can the SSL method of Mean Teacher perform equal or better than supervised methods on low-resource conditions?
2. Is it possible to utilize the Pseudo-Labeling approach on top of the Mean Teacher architecture to improve the results?

One should note that our research does not aim to achieve the highest MCC scores as compared to SoTA, but to test if SSL techniques can be useful in low resource conditions. Hence, our baseline here are the models created with a fully supervised setup under low resource conditions, which are then compared against our proposed models trained with SSL.

2 Related work

There has been few previous works on SSL methods for NLP. Liang et al. (2020) showed improvement on models trained with labeled data through Pseudo-Labeling for Named Entity Recognition. Wang et al. (2022) suggest a noise-injected consistency training with entropy-constrained pseudo labeling for labeling extractive summarization data. Such approaches have not been investigated for other NLP problems involving token level classification.

State-of-the art QE methods (Rei et al., 2020, 2022) employ fine-tuning of pre-trained LMs, but they don't take into consideration low-resource conditions. Concerning non-supervised methods, Fomicheva et al. (2020) perform unsupervised QE by utilizing internal decoding features of the MT models. With regards to low-resource conditions, Ranasinghe et al. (2021) demonstrate that it is possible to accurately predict word-level quality for any given new language pair from models trained on other language pairs. In an effort to address low resource conditions, Tuan et al. (2021) train off-the-shelf architectures for supervised QE using synthetic data from parallel corpora. To the best of our knowledge, none of the related work in QE of MT has used semi-supervised methods to address low resource conditions.

3 Methods

We focus on the task of QE of MT at the word level, as specified at the Shared Task of QE of WMT (Zerva et al., 2022), which aims at flagging potential errors in the translations generated by any MT system. The word-level task requires assigning binary tags of OK/BAD to determine the correctness of each word in source and target/translated sentences. The following types of labels are used:

Source side Each word in the source sentence is assigned a label (OK/BAD) which determines if the respective word is correctly translated in the target language or not.

Target side Each word in the target sentence is assigned a label (OK/BAD) which determines if the word is a correct translation for the respective word in the source sentence. Additionally,

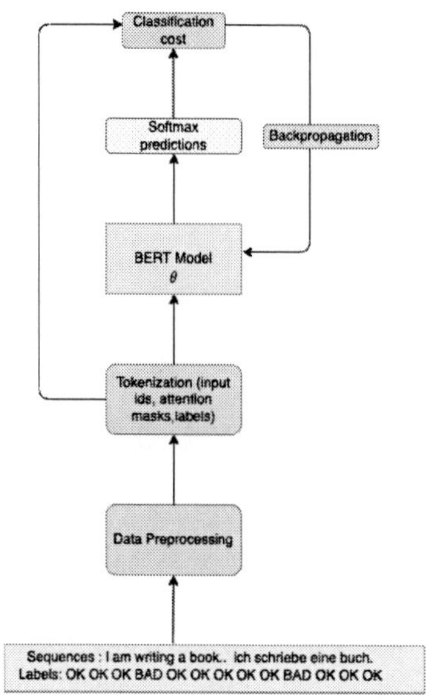

Figure 2: Training flow diagram of supervised fine-tuning methodology

gap tokens are also considered in the beginning, at the end, and between two words of the target sentence. Each gap token is assigned the label BAD if a word or more than a word is missing in the position of the gap token, and it is tagged OK otherwise. An example of the gap tokens can be seen in figure 1.

The proposed methods involve the training of models with Supervised and SSL methods. The fine-tuning of a large LM is done by utilizing three strategies i.e. 1) Supervised Learning, 2) SSL using the Mean Teacher approach., 3) SSL using a Mean Teacher with the Pseudo-Labeling approach.

3.1 Supervised Fine-tuning

Our baseline method is based on supervised fine tuning of a large language model. Here, the pre-trained LM is fine-tuned with only the labeled data for the problem to perform classification of the word sequence. The architecture for fine-tuning of the supervised model is shown in figure 2. As it can be seen, the data is first loaded from files preprocessed to remove the non-useful sequence from the train data. The simple fine-tuning involves utilizing the tokenized data as input to the model. As part of our problem, the input to the model is a sequence of two sentences. The first sentence is the sentence in the source language and the second is the sentence in the translated language.

3.2 Mean Teacher fine-tuning

The Mean Teacher approach (Tarvainen and Valpola, 2017) involves the usage of both labeled and unlabeled data to train the models in this setup. In this architecture (figure 3), two models are initialized, namely Teacher and Student, and weights for both the models are updated differently. The Student is trained using the mainstream method of minimizing the loss, whereas the Teacher is not trained but its weights are updated using an exponential moving average of the Student's weights after processing each batch of data. This behaves as an ensemble technique because eventually, Teacher model weights are the mean of Student model weights from

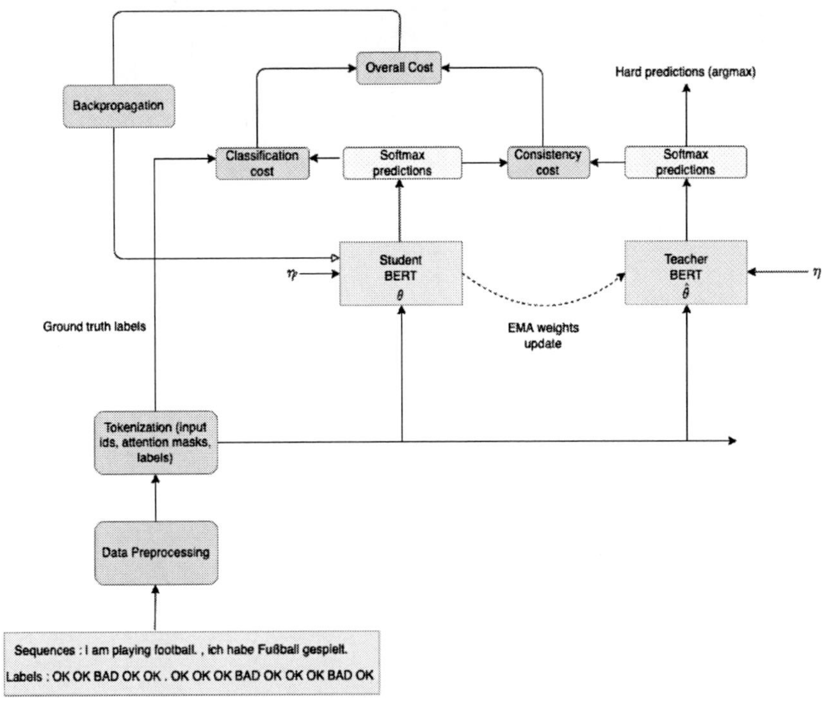

Figure 3: Training flow diagram of proposed fine-tuning methodology with Mean Teacher approach.

previous training iterations, therefore this method is known as *Mean Teacher*.

As shown in figure 3, the data is first preprocessed, and then tokenized using the BERT tokenizer or respective LM tokenizer, which converts the text data into numerical data by mapping each token to a numerical id. The tokenization also involves creating other tensors such as an attention mask, that is passed to convey the model information about the padded tokens. Also, another tensor for the label is passed that contains an actual label for the labeled data and default values for unlabeled data. The data loader, therefore, wraps both labeled and unlabeled data for each training batch, and then the data is passed through the network in batches. The input tensors for each batch are passed through both Teacher BERT and Student BERT models. The models utilize the same structure as defined for the supervised model in the previous section 3.1. An additional noising layer is added to the model which adds random Gaussian noise to the word embeddings generated by the LM. The noising strategy is based on one of the strategies of Zhang and Yang (2018). This noise is controlled by the standard deviation parameter while initializing the respective model, therefore this parameter has to be set to different values while initializing the Teacher and Student model. The noise is added to the models to ensure that both models' classifiers eventually receive a different perturbed version of the same input data. Figure 3 indicates how different loss functions play a crucial role while back-propagating.

The consistency cost ($C(\theta)$) is calculated between the soft predictions of Teacher and Student models so that models eventually learns to predict the same label for the tokens for two perturb version of the same data. Using this consistency cost, the model can effectively utilize

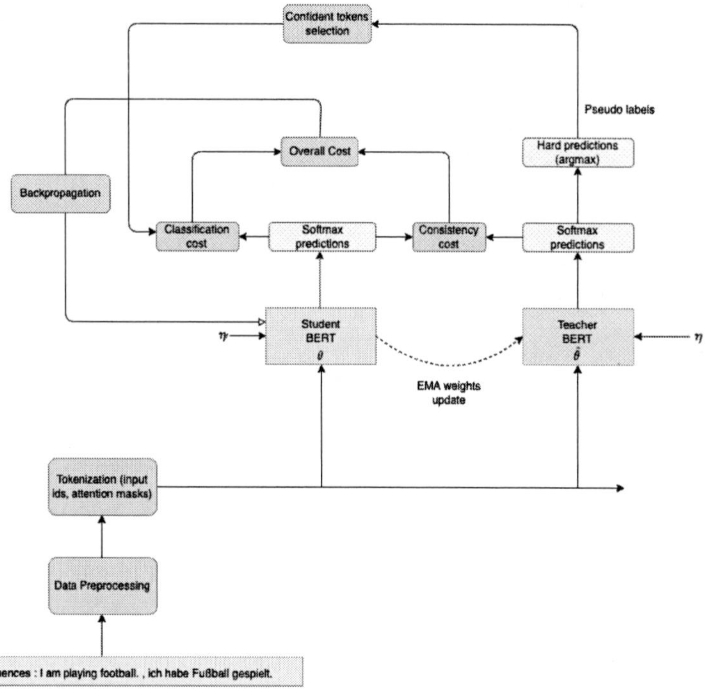

Figure 4: Training flow diagram of proposed PL fine-tuning methodology for stage II

unlabeled data as well to learn the patterns as this cost does not require ground truth labels.

3.3 Pseudo-Labeling fine-tuning

This proposed method calls for using the similar architecture as described in the previous section 3.2 for fine tuning the LMs but using a different methodology, called Pseudo-Labeling. The method is closely related to the work of Liang et al. (2020) and utilizes both labeled and unlabeled data during training. This SSL approach follows a two-stage framework, where in the first stage a baseline supervised model is trained using the limited labeled data and in the second stage, Pseudo-Labeling is used to improve the model fitting using unlabeled data.

In the first stage, the model is trained in supervised setup following the same strategy as for supervised fine-tuning (section 3.1). Figure 2 shows the model training in the initial step, on purely labeled data. The trained models using the first approach of supervised fine tuning could be utilized for implementation of this methodology. Model trained in this first stage is then used to initialize Teacher and Student models in second stage of the implementation.

The second stage (figure 4) is similar to the Mean Teacher fine-tuning (section 3.2) but here no labeled data is used, as all the data given to the Teacher and Student models is unlabeled. The Teacher provides predictions for its respective input sequence and the hard labels generated by Teacher model are then utilized as pseudo labels for the Student model to train on. The classification cost is only calculated for the tokens that are above a certain confidence threshold. In case of a two-class classification problem, the model will predict probabilities for both the classes for each token, the class with the higher probability is selected as the final prediction and the higher probability value is the confidence of prediction. Therefore confidence is the

Labeled	Unlabeled	Validation	Test
250	1750	500	1000
500	1500	500	1000
750	1250	500	1000
1000	1000	500	1000
1250	750	500	1000
1500	500	500	1000
1750	250	500	1000

Table 1: Labeled/Unlabeled split

probability with which the model predicted the label for the token. This high confidence tokens selection ensures the Student model to fit the tokens with high confidence better and thereby improves the robustness of the model for low confidence tokens.

4 Experiment Setup

4.1 Dataset

The experiments are performed using the dataset of Fomicheva et al. (2022) provided by the WMT 2021 shared task (Specia et al., 2021). The original dataset consisted of 7000 train, 1000 test and 1000 dev data for all language pairs. From that dataset, in order to simulate a low-resource setting, we sampled 2000 training sentence pairs along with 500 validation and 1000 test sentences to train the models for Mean Teacher, Pseudo-Labeling, and supervised set ups and evaluate their performances. The ratio of labeled and unlabeled data was varied keeping the amount of training sentences fixed at 2000 as shown in Table 1, in order to test the performance of SSL methods under different ratios, with the labeled data gradually increasing between 250 and 1750 sentences. For each given ratio in the table 1, a supervised model was trained on the number of labeled samples mentioned for the ratio, and SSL models were trained using the same labeled data and additional unlabeled data. The performance metrics for each model in the experiments were evaluated on the fixed 1000 test dataset provided in Fomicheva et al. (2022). In all cases, one joined model was trained including all language pairs of the dataset.

The supervised models are shown as a baseline for SSL methods using the same amount of labeled data. The performance of both the supervised and SSL models was compared in order to check if SSL algorithms provided better performance due to the presence of additional unlabeled data while training.

4.2 Model implementation

The experiments were performed with $\text{XLMRoBERTa}_{\text{Base}}$ by adding a feed-forward layer on top of the model.[1] For model training, AWS Sagemaker is used. The model is fine-tuned with early stopping on the evaluation metric on validation data. It is trained in batches and while training, the loss is calculated using weighted binary cross-entropy (Ho and Wookey, 2019) loss to tackle the issue of the imbalanced dataset in our case. The hyperparameters where initiated based on previous research involving LMs, and were optimized after multiple preliminary experiments to the ones shown in table 2. The Loss ratio (r) was found best to have the rampup value from 0 to 1 on steps. The ratio was kept very low in the begining of the training so that the models could adjust the weights according to actual labeled data provided and the loss of unlabeled

[1]The code and the data of the experiment are be publicly available with an open source license at `https://github.com/DFKI-NLP/semisupervised-mt-qe`

Hyper parameter	Values
Classification cost ($C(\theta)$)	Weighted Binary Cross Entropy
Batch Size	8
Learning rate	$2e-5$
Dropout	0.3
Optimizer	Adam
Consistency cost ($J(\theta)$)	Mean Squared Error
Max length	128
Epochs	25
Early stopping	8
Loss Ratio (r)	Rampup from 0 to 1.0 till 2 epochs (on steps)
Alpha (α)	0.99

Table 2: Hyperparameter Details

data have almost no contribution in the begining of the learning steps. This value is ramped up till the number of steps involved in two epochs. A reason for choosing the rampup period till two epochs was that LMs usually need around two epochs to fine tune for any problem. The maximum value of ratio after rampup is set to 1 as higher values resulted into large deviations of the learned weights and sudden increase in the validation errors. In order to determine the value of alpha (α), that controls the amount of weights being transferred to Teacher models from the Student models, various experiments were performed. The rampup of the EMA decay, as suggested in previous works related to computer vision (Tarvainen and Valpola, 2017; Laine and Aila, 2017) did not lead to good performance for our problem and hence we tried to determine the value of the parameter by testing the values from the set [0.99, 0.995, 0.999], concluding that the value of 0.99 performed relatively best amongst the values experimented and also gave consistent results.

4.3 Training strategies

For each given ratio of labeled/unlabeled data in table 1, models were trained with these strategies:

Supervised is the model trained on the amount of labeled data in a fully supervised fashion as described in 3.1. For example, for labeled data 250, the Supervised model is trained on 250 labeled data, and performance metrics of the model are calculated on the fixed 1000 test dataset. So, one supervised model was trained for each set of ratio labeled/unlabeled data mentioned in the table 1.

Mean Teacher: Teacher & Student are trained using the Mean Teacher network (Section 3.2). For each amount of labeled data, one Teacher and one Student model is trained. Apart from the labeled data in the given ratio, the rest of the data is utilized as unlabeled data, which is used in training the models with the Mean Teacher approach. The performance metrics for the models trained by utilizing the different ratios of labeled and unlabeled data are reported in the table with learning strategies as Mean Teacher Teacher and Mean Teacher Student. So, two models were generated for each ratio of labeled/unlabeled data by using this SSL strategy of fine-tuning.

Mean Teacher with Pseudo-Labeling: Teacher & Student are trained using the Pseudo-Labeling network (Section 3.3). For each amount of labeled data, one Teacher and one Student model is trained. Apart from the labeled data in the given ratio, the rest of the data is used as unlabeled data, for training the models with the Pseudo-Labeling approach. So, two models

lab'd	supervised	Student	Teacher	relative improvement (%)	
				Student	Teacher(%)
250	0.252	0.280	***0.283**	11.11	12.30
500	0.288	0.299	***0.300**	3.82	4.17
750	0.313	**0.317**	0.312	1.28	0.00
1000	0.320	0.344	***0.346**	7.50	8.13
1250	0.335	0.340	**0.344**	1.49	2.69
1500	0.333	***0.350**	***0.350**	5.11	5.11
1750	0.328	0.355	***0.361**	8.23	10.06

Table 3: MCC scores for Supervised and Mean Teacher experiments; * indicates significantly better scores based on bootstrap re-sampling, as compared to the supervised baseline

were generated for each ratio of labeled/unlabeled data by using this SSL strategy of fine-tuning. We repeated the experiments with confidence thresholds of 0,6 and 0,8, and the latter was chosen due to the higher performance. Additionally, we repeated the experiments without a consistency cost, but results are not reported, as no significant difference was observed.

4.4 Evaluation

For evaluating the systems generated with fully supervised approach or SSL approaches, the metric used is Matthews correlation coefficient (MCC; Matthews, 1975), as per WMT (Zerva et al., 2022) along with F1-scores for OK/BAD classes. In the first part of our experiments, contrary to WMT calculating MCC scores for source, target and gap tokens, we focused on the MCC score for the whole sequence, to ensure that our models can produce good labels for all the tokens of the sequence, as MCC for whole sequence consolidates classification and misclassification errors for all the tokens. In the second part of our experiments, we present disjoint MCC results, following the official WMT calculation.

In order to test the significance of the results with the Mean Teacher, we tested these models using paired bootstrap resampling method (Koehn, 2004). For this, 250 sentence sequences were sampled out of 1000 test dataset with replacement to form 100 virtual test sets of 250 sentences each.

5 Results

5.1 Mean Teacher fine-tuning

The performance of models trained with Mean Teacher vs. supervised learning are shown in table 3. Teacher models outperform the Student and supervised models significantly for every ratio of labeled to unlabeled data, apart from two cases where they don't show a significant improvement. In the best case, where a very little amount of training data is available, the Teacher model gives a relative improvement of 12.3% over the supervised baseline. It is also noticed that the average relative improvement for all experiments with different ratios of labeled/unlabeled data is approximately 6% for Teacher and 5.5% for Student models. Confirming previous work (Tarvainen and Valpola, 2017), the Teacher is more robust and performs better than the Student after certain iterations of training.

5.2 Pseudo-Labeling

As seen in Table 4, the approach of Pseudo-Labeling gave small improvements for some experiments but for most experiments it didn't perform as expected. There could be several reasons for this. One of them is models suffer from confirmation bias (Arazo et al., 2020), i.e mod-

lab'd	supervised	Student	Teacher	relative improvement (%)	
				Student	Teacher(%)
250	0.250	0.280	**0.283**	12.0	13.20
500	0.288	0.287	0.287	0.0	0.00
750	0.313	0.294	0.302	0.0	0.00
1000	0.320	0.306	0.310	0.0	0.00
1250	0.335	0.335	**0.337**	0.0	0.60
1500	0.333	0.314	0.331	0.0	0.00
1750	0.328	0.327	**0.332**	0.0	1.22

Table 4: MCC scores for Pseudo-Labeling

els relying on its own predictions. Additionally, despite experimenting with various confidence thresholds and the consistency cost, we generally used the same hyperparameters as in the Mean Teacher setup, so it is not possible to exclude the case that better results occur after a broader hyperparameter search.

5.3 Disjoint comparative analysis

More detailed results, following the disjoined calculations of all metrics as per WMT can be seen in Table 5. Here we present the MCC and the F1-scores for BAD/OK labels, measured for the source and target sentence with and without gaps, for every ratio of labeled/unlabeled data. It can be seen that in all cases, the MCC score and and the F1 score for BAD labels outperform the ones of the supervised baseline. In some cases there is no improvement shown for the F1 score for OK labels, but one should consider that the amount of OK labels in the dataset is overly high, and the F1 score is affected by the big amount of true positives.

6 Conclusion

This research focused on the Quality Estimation of Machine Translation at the word level. The goal is to generate a binary label of OK/BAD for each word and gap in the translations, by predicting if the word is correctly translated or not. We investigated two approaches of Semi-Supervised Learining that have not been explored yet for the given problem: The first utilized the well-known Mean Teacher approach that involves a Student and a Teacher model while training, initialized with the default weights of a pretrained LM. The second proposed architecture extends the former, by involving Pseudo-Labeling and follows a two-stage learning approach. In the first stage, the model is trained with limited labeled data available, through supervised learning. In the second stage, the Teacher and Student model are initialized with the model learned in the first stage, and are further trained using only unlabeled data.

It was experimentally shown that in low-resource settings the Mean Teacher architecture performed better or (in one case) comparably to the supervised models, achieving an improvement of up to 12%. The second proposed architecture of using Pseudo-Labeling with Mean Teacher framework did not behave as expected, when tested with various values of thresholds. Further work could focus on the implication of the improvements on various language pairs, as well as architectural improvements and data augmentation techniques.

Acknowledgments

This work was supported by the Deutsche Forschungsgemeinschaft (DFG) through the project TextQ, and by the German Federal Ministry of Education and Research (BMBF) through the project SocialWear (grant no. 01IW20002).

items	model_words	MCC	F1 BAD	F1 OK
250	supervised source	0.207	0.331	0.874
	supervised target and gaps	0.282	0.374	0.906
	supervised target	0.240	0.391	0.845
	Mean Teacher source	**0.240**	**0.373**	0.828
	Mean Teacher target and gaps	**0.309**	**0.384**	0.804
	Mean Teacher target	**0.248**	**0.411**	0.759
500	supervised source	0.240	0.373	0.811
	supervised target and gaps	0.319	0.401	0.840
	supervised target	0.252	0.411	0.703
	Mean Teacher source	**0.249**	**0.379**	0.816
	Mean Teacher target and gaps	**0.325**	**0.413**	0.909
	Mean Teacher target	**0.276**	**0.430**	0.768
750	supervised source	0.267	0.393	0.826
	supervised target and gaps	0.341	0.427	0.878
	supervised target	0.289	0.440	0.785
	Mean Teacher source	**0.276**	**0.399**	0.826
	Mean Teacher target and gaps	**0.343**	**0.427**	0.875
	Mean Teacher target	**0.291**	**0.440**	0.780
1000	supervised source	0.278	0.393	0.773
	supervised target and gaps	0.345	0.423	0.854
	supervised target	0.288	0.434	0.736
	Mean Teacher source	**0.300**	**0.418**	0.858
	Mean Teacher target and gaps	**0.375**	**0.458**	0.899
	Mean Teacher target	**0.336**	**0.473**	0.826
1250	supervised source	0.295	0.414	0.858
	supervised target and gaps	0.360	0.445	0.903
	supervised target	0.323	0.463	0.839
	Mean Teacher source	**0.304**	**0.421**	0.863
	Mean Teacher target and gaps	**0.369**	**0.453**	0.902
	Mean Teacher target	**0.330**	**0.469**	0.834
1500	supervised source	0.291	0.403	0.782
	supervised target and gaps	0.354	0.433	0.858
	supervised target	0.305	0.445	0.742
	Mean Teacher source	**0.312**	**0.427**	0.854
	Mean Teacher target and gaps	**0.374**	**0.456**	0.898
	Mean Teacher target	**0.334**	**0.472**	0.826
1750	supervised source	0.288	0.407	0.820
	supervised target and gaps	0.347	0.352	0.435
	supervised target	0.304	0.446	0.786
	Mean Teacher source	**0.320**	**0.433**	0.851
	Mean Teacher target and gaps	**0.387**	**0.466**	0.895
	Mean Teacher target	**0.347**	**0.480**	0.819

Table 5: Comparative analysis of Supervised and MT models on disjoint performance of tokens in source and target sentence.

References

Arazo, E., Ortego, D., Albert, P., O'Connor, N. E., and McGuinness, K. (2020). Pseudo-labeling and confirmation bias in deep semi-supervised learning. In *2020 International Joint Conference on Neural Networks (IJCNN)*, pages 1–8. IEEE.

Fomicheva, M., Sun, S., Fonseca, E., Zerva, C., Blain, F., Chaudhary, V., Guzmán, F., Lopatina, N., Specia, L., and Martins, A. F. T. (2022). MLQE-PE: A multilingual quality estimation and post-editing dataset. In *Proceedings of the Thirteenth Language Resources and Evaluation Conference*, pages 4963–4974, Marseille, France. European Language Resources Association.

Fomicheva, M., Sun, S., Yankovskaya, L., Blain, F., Guzmán, F., Fishel, M., Aletras, N., Chaudhary, V., and Specia, L. (2020). Unsupervised Quality Estimation for Neural Machine Translation. *Transactions of the Association for Computational Linguistics*, 8:539–555.

Ho, Y. and Wookey, S. (2019). The real-world-weight cross-entropy loss function: Modeling the costs of mislabeling. *IEEE Access*, 8:4806–4813.

Koehn, P. (2004). Statistical significance tests for machine translation evaluation. In *Proceedings of the 2004 conference on empirical methods in natural language processing*, pages 388–395.

Laine, S. and Aila, T. (2017). Temporal ensembling for semi-supervised learning. In *Proceedings of the 5th International Conference on Learning Representations, ICLR 2017, Toulon, France, April 24-26, 2017, Conference Track Proceedings*.

Liang, C., Yu, Y., Jiang, H., Er, S., Wang, R., Zhao, T., and Zhang, C. (2020). Bond: Bert-assisted open-domain named entity recognition with distant supervision. In *Proceedings of the 26th ACM SIGKDD International Conference on Knowledge Discovery & Data Mining*, pages 1054–1064.

Matthews, B. W. (1975). Comparison of the predicted and observed secondary structure of t4 phage lysozyme. *Biochimica et Biophysica Acta (BBA)-Protein Structure*, 405(2):442–451.

Ranasinghe, T., Orasan, C., and Mitkov, R. (2021). An Exploratory Analysis of Multilingual Word-Level Quality Estimation with Cross-Lingual Transformers. In *Proceedings of the 59th Annual Meeting of the Association for Computational Linguistics and the 11th International Joint Conference on Natural Language Processing (Volume 2: Short Papers)*, pages 434–440, Online. Association for Computational Linguistics.

Rei, R., Stewart, C., Farinha, A. C., and Lavie, A. (2020). COMET: A Neural Framework for MT Evaluation. In *Proceedings of the 2020 Conference on Empirical Methods in Natural Language Processing (EMNLP)*, pages 2685–2702, Online. Association for Computational Linguistics.

Rei, R., Treviso, M., Guerreiro, N. M., Zerva, C., Farinha, A. C., Maroti, C., C. de Souza, J. G., Glushkova, T., Alves, D., Coheur, L., Lavie, A., and Martins, A. F. T. (2022). CometKiwi: IST-Unbabel 2022 submission for the quality estimation shared task. In *Proceedings of the Seventh Conference on Machine Translation*, pages 634–645, Abu Dhabi. Association for Computational Linguistics.

Specia, L., Blain, F., Fomicheva, M., Zerva, C., Li, Z., Chaudhary, V., and Martins, A. (2021). Findings of the wmt 2021 shared task on quality estimation. Association for Computational Linguistics.

Tarvainen, A. and Valpola, H. (2017). Mean teachers are better role models: Weight-averaged consistency targets improve semi-supervised deep learning results. *Advances in neural information processing systems*, 30.

Tuan, Y.-L., El-Kishky, A., Renduchintala, A., Chaudhary, V., Guzmán, F., and Specia, L. (2021). Quality Estimation without Human-labeled Data. In *Proceedings of the 16th Conference of the European Chapter of the Association for Computational Linguistics: Main Volume*, pages 619–625, Online. Association for Computational Linguistics.

Wang, Y., Mao, Q., Liu, J., Jiang, W., Zhu, H., and Li, J. (2022). Noise-injected consistency training and entropy-constrained pseudo labeling for semi-supervised extractive summarization. In *Proceedings of the 29th International Conference on Computational Linguistics*, pages 6447–6456, Gyeongju, Republic of Korea. International Committee on Computational Linguistics.

Zerva, C., Blain, F., Rei, R., Lertvittayakumjorn, P., C. de Souza, J. G., Eger, S., Kanojia, D., Alves, D., Orăsan, C., Fomicheva, M., Martins, A. F. T., and Specia, L. (2022). Findings of the WMT 2022 shared task on quality estimation. In *Proceedings of the Seventh Conference on Machine Translation (WMT)*, pages 69–99, Abu Dhabi, United Arab Emirates (Hybrid). Association for Computational Linguistics.

Zhang, D. and Yang, Z. (2018). Word embedding perturbation for sentence classification. *arXiv preprint arXiv:1804.08166*.

Learning from Past Mistakes: Quality Estimation from Monolingual Corpora and Machine Translation Learning Stages

Thierry Etchegoyhen[1] tetchegoyhen@vicomtech.org
David Ponce[1,2] adponce@vicomtech.org

[1] Vicomtech Foundation, Basque Research and Technology Alliance (BRTA)
[2] University of the Basque Country - UPV/EHU

Abstract

Quality Estimation (QE) of Machine Translation output suffers from the lack of annotated data to train supervised models across domains and language pairs. In this work, we describe a method to generate synthetic QE data based on Neural Machine Translation (NMT) models at different learning stages. Our approach consists in training QE models on the errors produced by different NMT model checkpoints, obtained during the course of model training, under the assumption that gradual learning will induce errors that more closely resemble those produced by NMT models in adverse conditions. We test this approach on English-German and Romanian-English WMT QE test sets, demonstrating that pairing translations from earlier checkpoints with translations of converged models outperforms the use of reference human translations and can achieve competitive results against human-labelled data. We also show that combining post-edited data with our synthetic data yields to significant improvements across the board. Our approach thus opens new possibilities for an efficient use of monolingual corpora to generate quality synthetic QE data, thereby mitigating the data bottleneck.

1 Introduction

Significant improvements have been achieved in Machine Translation (MT) in recent years, in particular with the advent of Neural Machine Translation (NMT) (Sutskever et al., 2014; Bahdanau et al., 2015; Vaswani et al., 2017). However, the quality of automated translations can vary significantly depending on training data volumes, domain of application, language pairs or the complexity of specific source segments. Machine translation errors can significantly increase the risks and costs of using MT and the automatic estimation of MT quality becomes increasingly necessary to pinpoint or discard erroneous automatic translations.

Traditionally, the quality of MT output has been assessed against human references, via automated metrics such as BLEU (Papineni et al., 2002) or TER (Snover et al., 2006). However, such references are not always available and are costly to produce, which has led to the development of Quality Estimation (QE) approaches based on the sole properties of the source and machine-translated sentences (Blatz et al., 2004; Specia et al., 2010). Most approaches to QE are based on supervised learning, traditionally via feature engineering (Specia et al., 2013), and, in recent years via neural models (Kim and Lee, 2016; Kim et al., 2017; Fonseca et al., 2019;

Proceedings of Machine Translation Summit XIX, Vol. 1: Research Track, pages 84–98
September 4–8, 2023, Macau SAR, China.

Specia et al., 2021). Although they provide the most accurate estimates to date, supervised methods depend on human annotations or post-edited translations to perform the task. The cost of producing quality QE training datasets hinders the development of QE models for the large number of possible domains and language pairs.

Two main alternatives address the lack of training QE data. On the one hand, unsupervised and self-supervised approaches (Moreau and Vogel, 2012; Popović, 2012; Etchegoyhen et al., 2018; Fomicheva et al., 2020; Zheng et al., 2021) discard the need for QE training data altogether, but typically fail to consistently meet the accuracy of supervised alternatives or may require access to additional information such as internal states of the MT model. On the other hand, methods that exploit synthetic training data have also been proposed in recent years, leveraging parallel dataset references. Under this approach, parallel training data can be exploited, for instance, by taking a target reference translation as the approximated post-edited version of a machine-translated source segment and generating artificial QE labels (Lee, 2020). The two may differ significantly however, thereby introducing noise in the QE training data. Alternatively, synthetic data can be generated by devising QE error generation pipelines from the parallel data (Baek et al., 2020; Tuan et al., 2021), although this requires approximating errors that may not correspond to actual MT ones.

In this work, we describe and evaluate a novel approach to synthetic QE data generation by exploiting the actual errors committed by NMT models at different learning stages. The hypothesis underlying this approach is that this type of errors might resemble more closely the errors produced by MT systems in scenarios where they typically fail, such as language pairs for which parallel training data are insufficient, or domains that deviate from those represented in the training sets. To test this hypothesis, we train NMT models on generic parallel data and select model checkpoints of varying quality to contrast their translations with either human reference translations or translations from the best converged NMT models. The generated synthetic data are then used to train neural QE estimators, either in isolation or in combination with human-generated data. We demonstrate the potential of this novel approach on WMT 2021 datasets in English-German and Romanian-English. We notably show that it outperforms the use of human reference translations, directly or via self-supervised learning, is competitive with the use of human post-edited data, and can complement the latter to achieve further gains in QE accuracy. Additionally, contrasting checkpoint translations with those of converged NMT models allows for a direct exploitation of monolingual data, thus opening new possibilities for the effective generation of synthetic QE data across languages and domains.

2 Related Work

Machine translation quality estimation has been standardly tackled via supervised approaches, with annotated or post-edited machine-translated segments being used to train machine learning classifiers (Blatz et al., 2004; Quirk, 2004) or regressors (Specia et al., 2009). Several approaches have been explored using different feature sets or underlying learning models such as Support Vector Machines or Gaussian Processes (Callison-Burch et al., 2012; Bojar et al., 2014; Specia et al., 2013; Felice and Specia, 2012; Forcada et al., 2017).

In recent years, approaches based on artificial neural networks have been successfully applied to the task as well, either as additional features (Shah et al., 2015, 2016) or as end-to-end quality estimation systems (Kim and Lee, 2016; Martins et al., 2017; Ive et al., 2018; Fan et al., 2019). The Predictor-Estimator framework proposed by Kim et al. (2017) can be considered the current standard, since it outperformed alternatives in recent WMT QE tasks (Bojar et al., 2017; Specia et al., 2018) and now serves as baseline in the latest editions of the task (Specia et al., 2020, 2021; Zerva et al., 2022). In this framework, a contextual word Predictor component acts as a feature extractor and an Estimator exploits the extracted features to predict QE labels. A neural word prediction model can be trained on the parallel data (Kim et al., 2017; Zhou et al., 2019), though in recent years, pretrained large language models, such as BERT (Devlin et al., 2019) and XLM-R (Conneau et al., 2020), have also been successfully employed for this task (Kim et al., 2019; Kepler et al., 2019a; Specia et al., 2020).

As previously noted, supervised approaches depend on the availability of annotated datasets, typically HTER scores obtained from post-edited machine translation output, quality values on a predefined quality scale, or OK/BAD annotations at the word-level. Creating quality annotated datasets is a costly process, hindering the development of quality supervised QE models. To date, most publicly available QE datasets are those prepared for the WMT shared tasks, which are only available for a limited number of language pairs and domains.

To address this data bottleneck, alternatives to supervised modelling have been explored for the QE task. Thus, Moreau and Vogel (2012) tackled weakly supervised and single-feature unsupervised methods, as a means to minimise the dependency on annotated data. Popović (2012) describes an unsupervised method based on combining IBM1 models with language models over morphemes and part-of-speech tags, with a dependence on external tagging tools. In Etchegoyhen et al. (2018), unsupervised quality estimation is performed via lexical translation overlaps and n-gram language model scores, outperforming some feature-based supervised models but falling short against more sophisticated neural QE models. An unsupervised glass-box approach, based on the confidence of NMT models, was proposed by Fomicheva et al. (2020), achieving promising results, though it requires access to the NMT models that generate the evaluated translations. Recently, Zheng et al. (2021) proposed a self-supervised approach based on target token masking in parallel data, outperforming other methods based on unsupervised modelling or synthetic data generation.

Another approach to the lack of human-annotated training QE data is to leverage existing parallel corpora, similarly to what was suggested for automated post-editing (Negri et al., 2018). Thus, Lee (2020) and Tuan et al. (2021) explored the use of target reference translations as post-edited versions of machine-translated source sentences, showing that it can provide a basis for supervised QE models. In this type of approach, however, target references may differ significantly from MT output and therefore introduce noisy training tuples in the QE data. Alternatively, synthetic data can be generated by devising QE error generation pipelines from the parallel data (Baek et al., 2020; Tuan et al., 2021), although this requires approximating errors that may not correspond to the actual ones produced by MT models.

The study most related to ours is that of Ding et al. (2021), who evaluated their Levenshtein Transformer approach to word-level quality estimation using synthetic data, part of which was generated by using the output from a weaker MT model and contrasting it with the output of another MT model of higher quality, taken as reference translator. Although the idea of contrasting weaker and stronger MT models is similar, this differs from our approach in important respects: their synthetic data results are only established for their proposed QE framework based on the Levenshtein Transformer, only for word-level QE, and, most importantly, they use the output of unrelated converged translation models, instead of the related learning stages of the same model which we explore in this work.

3 Methodology

As previously indicated, our approach is based on the assumption that NMT models at different training stages might produce errors that resemble those committed by fully trained MT systems, in scenarios where they fail to properly translate such as domain shifts or insufficient training data. The methodology can be summarised as follows:

1. Train an NMT model on parallel data from language L_1 to language L_2.

Corpus	Type	English-German Sentences	English-German Tokens	Romanian-English Sentences	Romanian-English Tokens
WMT21-QE train	Post-edited	7,000	114,980	7,000	120,247
WMT21-QE dev	Post-edited	1,000	16,519	1,000	17,279
WMT21-QE test	Post-edited	1,000	16,371	1,000	17,359
WikiMatrix	Comparable	696,880	15,386,735	102,106	2,120,383
WMT21-MT	Parallel	22,782,867	490,297,937	3,080,304	72,004,236
WikiDump	Monolingual	1,923,782	38,456,268	1,392,034	25,320,444

Table 1: Corpora statistics (number of tokens computed over source sentences)

2. Select model checkpoints at different stages of training. We used three different checkpoints in our experiments, though more could be defined as needed:
   - *b50*: the checkpoint whose development set BLEU score is the closest to 50% of the score of the converged NMT model.
   - *b75*: the checkpoint whose development set BLEU score is the closest to 75% of the score of the converged NMT model.
   - *best*: the checkpoint corresponding to the converged NMT model.
3. Translate a source corpus in L_1 using the selected checkpoints.
4. Extract tuples <*src*, *mt*, *ref*>, where *src* is the source sentence, *mt* is the translation generated by a given checkpoint, and *ref* is either a human reference translation (*hrt*), or the output of the *best* model when *b50* and/or *b75* are used to generate the translations.
5. Train the estimator of a Predictor-Estimator QE model (Kim et al., 2017) on the generated tuples.

Under this approach, synthetic QE data can be generated from monolingual or parallel source data, in any domain or language pair for which an NMT model was trained. Several aspects need to be examined to determine an optimal setup for this method, mainly the impact of: (i) using *best* model translations as opposed to an existing reference in parallel data; (ii) using different volumes of synthetic data; (iii) creating synthetic data from different domains; (iv) combining synthetic data from different model checkpoints; and (v) combing synthetic data and human post-edited translations. In the next sections, we describe the experimental protocols to tackle these aspects and evaluate the potential of our approach.

4 Experimental Setup

Our experiments centred on two language pairs, English-German (EN-DE) and Romanian-English (RO-EN), and the datasets of the WMT 2021 shared QE task (Specia et al., 2021) . The selected datasets and models for our experiments are described in turn below.

4.1 Data

We selected the WMT 2021 datasets from the quality estimation task[1] (hereafter, WMT21-QE) as development and test data for our QE models, on the translation pairs English-German and Romanian-English. For the experiments described in Section 7, we also merged our synthetic

[1] https://www.statmt.org/wmt21/quality-estimation-task.html

data with the human post-edited train dataset from the task. Our choice of datasets was mainly motivated by the balanced datasets introduced for the 2020 shared task, following work by Sun et al. (2020). English-German was selected as representative of a language pair with significant volumes of parallel data to train NMT models; Romanian-English features lower volumes of such data and was also selected to represent translation from a different source language.

To train the NMT models from which we extract the different checkpoints, we used the parallel training and development data provided in the 2021 QE shared task (WMT21-MT) for the two selected language pairs. To generate synthetic QE data, we used the following datasets:[2]

- *WikiMatrix*: since the domain for the selected language pairs in the WMT 2021 QE shared task was Wikipedia, we used the WikiMatrix dataset (Schwenk et al., 2021), selecting the top pairs with a LASER score (Artetxe and Schwenk, 2019) above a 1.06 threshold, following Tuan et al. (2021). With this dataset, either the aligned comparable target sentences or the *best* model translations were used as references, depending on the method at hand.

- *WMT21-MT*: to assess the impact of synthetic QE data generated from a different domain, we used a subset of the WMT21-MT data, selecting 2M sentence pairs via uniform sampling. As with the previous dataset, we evaluated the use of either the parallel translation or the *best* model translation as reference.

- WikiDump: this dataset is strictly monolingual and was only used for the experiments reported in Section 7, as there are no reference translations to perform the full set of experiments. We used Wikipedia dumps in both English and Romanian[3], as an additional monolingual test case, translating the source with model checkpoints and using *best* model translations as references.

The data were tokenised and truecased, using scripts from the Moses tookit (Koehn et al., 2007). Truecasing models were trained on the WMT21-MT datasets, and only applied on the QE datasets; for the NMT models, we used inline casing (Berard et al., 2019; Etchegoyhen and Gete, 2020), where all words are lowercased and casing information, if any, is prepended as symbols. The output of the NMT models was then recased and subsequently truecased for QE training and inference. For NMT training, subwords were generated via Byte Pair Encoding (Sennrich et al., 2016), training BPE models on WMT21-MT data with 32K operations.

4.2 Models

To compare different approaches to QE without human-labeled data, we selected the models described below.

Baseline. As a QE baseline, we followed the setup in the WMT 2021 QE shared task and trained Predictor-Estimator models on WMT21-QE data with OpenKiwi v2.1.0 (Kepler et al., 2019b), using XLM-R (Conneau et al., 2020) as Predictor. The baselines were trained separately for each language pair on the selected data.

Checkpoint-based QE. For our approach, we used MarianNMT (Junczys-Dowmunt et al., 2018) to train Transformer-base NMT models (Vaswani et al., 2017), with 6 encoder layers, 6 decoder layers, and 8 attention heads. We saved checkpoints every 5000 steps and translated the selected source datasets with a beam search of 6. The converged models obtained BLEU scores of 39.4 and 41.0 on the EN-DE and RO-EN WMT21-MT devsets, respectively. The QE models trained on data translated with checkpoint NMT models followed the setup of the baseline.

[2]In all cases, we filtered sentences containing more than 100 tokens, empty lines and duplicates.
[3]https://dumps.wikimedia.org/. Accessed 2022/12.

NMT QE. In this approach, the output of the NMT models is contrasted with the target references in the comparable or parallel dataset. This is similar to the approach denoted as NMT in Tuan et al. (2021), which obtained better results overall than their synthetic error generation method, with further gains obtained when both were used in combination. QE models based on this approach also followed the same setup as the baseline. Note that this approach is also similar, in a sense, to the use of unrelated contrastive NMT models as in Ding et al. (2021): in our case, the weaker model would be the NMT model, and the stronger model would be represented by the human translator, who can be assumed to provide the highest possible translation quality. Differences may arise from contrasting the output of the weaker model with human translations instead of the output of a strong MT model, although the results in Ding et al. (2021) indicate only minor differences in this respect.

Self-supervised QE. We selected the approach of Zheng et al. (2021), which is based on retrieving masked target words considering the source and target context, as it outperformed alternatives such as synthetic error generation (Tuan et al., 2021) in their experiments. We trained self-supervised models on the selected datasets where reference translations were available, i.e. WMT21-MT and WikiMatrix, using the publicly available code with default parameters.[4]

All models were trained until convergence. To evaluate their performance, we used the setup of the WMT 2021 QE shared task for Task 2, which measures word and sentence level post-editing effort. At the word level, targets are word level OK/BAD tags to signify the correctness of words and gaps in the source and translated sentences. The primary metric in this case is the Matthews correlation coefficient (MCC) (Matthews, 1975). For comparison purposes, we only report MCC results over the translated tags, as these are the only word-level predictions generated by the self-supervised approach. At the sentence-level, the targets are the HTER scores contrasting the machine translated output against the human reference, and the primary metric is the Pearson r correlation score. We used the evaluation scripts provided for the shared task to compute the results.

4.3 Checkpoint-based Variants

Under our approach, synthetic data may be generated via different configurations, in terms of data combination, type of data and volumes of data used to train the QE models. We describe our experimental setup for each one of these aspects below.

Checkpoint combination. Since our method allows for any model checkpoint to be used for synthetic data generation, different combinations may be exploited. We trained QE models that merged datasets generated by the following combinations of the selected checkpoints described in Section 3, using as reference either the parallel or comparable human reference (*hrt*) or the translation from the converged model (*best*): *<b50, hrt>*, *<b50, best>*, *<b75, hrt>*, *<b75, best>*, *<b50+b75, hrt>*, *<b50+b75, best>*, *<b50+b75+best, hrt>*.[5] We also indicate the results obtained with *<best, hrt>*, which corresponds to the NMT QE model described above.

Data type. Synthetic data may be generated from source data close to, or differing from, the domain of interest in a given QE task. As domain proximity may impact the usefulness of the synthetic data, we applied our method to the WikiMatrix data, closer in nature to the Wikipedia data used in the QE task, and the parallel data from the WMT 2021 MT task, which merges data from different domains.

Data size. The amount of potential synthetic data for a given language pair, under our approach, is only limited by the availability of monolingual source data, which may be available

[4]https://github.com/THUNLP-MT/SelfSupervisedQE.

[5]The notation + indicates concatenation of the data translated with each indicated checkpoint model.

in large quantities. However, synthetic data might differ significantly from human-labelled data and may feature noisy data. Therefore, adding large quantities of synthetic data might be detrimental to the quality of QE models. To determine the impact of synthetic data volumes, we trained different QE models based on: 7K synthetic data (*small* dataset), matching the amount of human post-edited data used in the WMT 2021 QE task; 70K (*medium*) to increase the initial size by an order of magnitude; and, finally, the maximum amount of data (*large*) available in the WikiMatrix dataset, using the same amount for the WMT 2021 MT training data.

5 Checkpoint-based QE Results

		English-German			Romanian-English		
Model	Dataset	Small	Medium	Large	Small	Medium	Large
<best, hrt>	WMT21-MT	0.213	0.277	0.207	0.576	0.598	0.609
<b50, hrt>	WMT21-MT	0.304	0.394	0.366	0.622	0.660	0.608
<b75, hrt>	WMT21-MT	0.355	0.397	0.385	0.557	0.611	0.604
<b50+b75+best, hrt>	WMT21-MT	0.369	0.435	0.427	0.541	0.628	0.610
<b50, best>	WMT21-MT	0.383	0.425	0.419	0.724	0.746	0.765
<b75, best>	WMT21-MT	0.366	**0.464**	0.424	0.731	0.787	0.786
<b50+b75, best>	WMT21-MT	0.431	0.421	0.462	0.767	0.783	**0.798**
<best, hrt>	WikiMatrix	0.259	0.306	0.089	0.774	0.803	0.791
<b50, hrt>	WikiMatrix	0.341	0.343	0.158	0.752	0.736	0.745
<b75, hrt>	WikiMatrix	0.352	0.370	0.159	0.747	0.777	0.784
<b50+b75+best, hrt>	WikiMatrix	0.370	0.400	0.143	0.786	0.781	0.788
<b50, best>	WikiMatrix	0.403	0.374	0.345	0.781	0.774	0.776
<b75, best>	WikiMatrix	0.411	0.436	0.390	0.801	**0.829**	0.828
<b50+b75, best>	WikiMatrix	**0.448**	0.425	0.413	0.808	0.814	0.809

Table 2: Pearson correlation results on WMT21-QE test sets for Task2 Sentence-level HTER prediction, using *small, medium* and *large* synthetic datasets. Best results across dataset splits are indicated in bold; best results per dataset split are underlined.

We first evaluated the impact of using different combinations of synthetic data, and either the human reference translation or the *best* model translation as references. The results at the sentence-level, for the two domains where comparable or parallel references were available, are shown in Table 2. The most notable result is that contrasting checkpoint translations with the output of the converged model markedly outperformed the alternatives in both language pairs and across datasets. In particular, these models obtained significantly better results than the NMT QE approach based on <best, hrt> coupling. These results at the sentence level thus indicate that directly exploiting monolingual source data via checkpoint and converged model translations can provide a better basis for QE than unrelated parallel or comparable references. Among models that used human reference translations, the checkpoint-based variants performed better than <best, hrt> in all cases and datasets for EN-DE. For RO-EN, the results featured less differences in scores, although <best, hrt> performed slightly better overall.

In terms of data size, in three out of four cases, the checkpoint-based models that relied on *best* translations as references obtained the best results with small (7K) or medium samples (70K). The larger datasets led to the best performance only in RO-EN on WMT21-MT and was competitive overall, but smaller data volumes seemed sufficient for the most part to reach the highest Pearson correlations on the test sets.

		English-German		Romanian-English	
Model	Dataset	Pearson	MCC	Pearson	MCC
Baseline	WMT21-QE	**0.541**	**0.374**	**0.829**	**0.575**
NMT QE	WMT21-MT	0.277	0.213	0.609	0.180
Self-supervised QE	WMT21-MT	0.238	0.253	0.565	0.386
<b50, best>	WMT21-MT	0.425	0.320	0.765	0.489
<b75, best>	WMT21-MT	0.464	0.336	0.787	0.450
<b50+b75, best>	WMT21-MT	0.462	0.335	0.798	0.423
NMT QE	WikiMatrix	0.306	0.272	0.803	0.445
Self-supervised QE	WikiMatrix	0.286	0.283	0.731	0.500
<b50, best>	WikiMatrix	0.403	0.314	0.781	0.469
<b75, best>	WikiMatrix	0.436	0.343	**0.829**	0.543
<b50+b75, best>	WikiMatrix	0.448	0.325	0.814	0.520

Table 3: Comparative results on the WMT 2021 Task2 test sets for the Pearson (sentence-level) and MCC (word-level on MT tags) primary metrics. Baselines trained on human post-edited (PE) data. Best results overall are indicated in bold; best results among methods that do not rely on PE data are underlined.

Among the top-performing methods, *<b75, best>* and *<b50+b75, best>* outperformed *<b50, best>* overall, and the best results were distributed among the two depending on the dataset and language pair: *<b75, best>* was optimal in EN-DE with WMT21-MT and RO-EN with WikiMatrix using medium sized datasets, whereas *<b50+b75, best>* was optimal on WikiMatrix with the small dataset for EN-DE and on WMT21-MT with the large dataset for RO-EN. Either method might thus be a reasonable choice to generate synthetic QE data, and future experiments would be needed to further distinguish between the two options.

Finally, although the QE test sets were based on data from Wikipedia for these language pairs, using synthetic data generated from a different domain like WMT21-MT did not seem significantly detrimental, as it even led to better scores than WikiMatrix-based synthetic data in EN-DE on the medium and large datasets. The best scores in most cases for the two top-performing variants were nonetheless still achieved with synthetic data generated from the WikiMatrix datasets, which is closer in nature to the QE test data.

6 Comparative Results

In this Section, we compare our results with the selected alternative approaches, namely: baselines trained on the 7K post-edited data of the WMT-QE-Train datasets; Self-supervised models trained on the available parallel and comparable corpora, as these models require aligned data; the NMT QE model based on contrasting the NMT translation and the parallel or comparable target human reference (*<best, hrt>*); and the best variants of our approach as determined in the previous Section, all based on checkpoint translations of the source data and translations of the converged NMT models as references. In Table 3, we present the comparative results at the sentence and word levels, according to the primary metric in each case.[6]

The baselines obtained the best results overall, at both the sentence and word levels, which is not unexpected as they were trained on the post-edited data from the task. However, our best

[6]For each method, we indicate the best score obtained at the sentence and word level independently, irrespective of QE training data partition size.

		English-German		Romanian-English	
Model	Dataset	Pearson	MCC	Pearson	MCC
Baseline	WMT21-QE	0.541	0.374	0.829	0.575
WMT21-QE 7K + Synthetic 7K	WikiDump	0.583	0.407	0.815	0.571
WMT21-QE 7K + Synthetic 70K	WikiDump	0.567	0.399	<u>0.836</u>	0.551
WMT21-QE 70K + Synthetic 70K	WikiDump	<u>**0.594**</u>	<u>**0.429**</u>	0.827	<u>0.579</u>
WMT21-QE 7K + Synthetic 7K	WikiMatrix	0.563	0.398	0.842	0.570
WMT21-QE 7K + Synthetic 70K	WikiMatrix	0.552	0.390	0.838	0.555
WMT21-QE 70K + Synthetic 70K	WikiMatrix	<u>0.588</u>	<u>0.414</u>	<u>**0.844**</u>	<u>**0.578**</u>
WMT21-QE 7K + Synthetic 7K	WMT21-MT	0.558	0.387	<u>0.838</u>	0.556
WMT21-QE 7K + Synthetic 70K	WMT21-MT	0.573	0.403	0.825	0.522
WMT21-QE 70K + Synthetic 70K	WMT21-MT	<u>0.591</u>	<u>0.409</u>	0.831	<u>0.560</u>

Table 4: Sentence and word level results on the WMT 2021 Task2 test sets for QE models trained on combined human post-edited data and synthetic data generated from different datasets. Best results overall are indicated in bold; best results per dataset are underlined.

variant matched the best sentence-level score in RO-EN and obtained competitive results in all other cases at both sentence and word level. Considering that the training data were randomly sampled monolingual source sentences from datasets differing from the shared task post-edited training data, these results confirm the potential of the checkpoint-based approach to create synthetic QE data that can match or approximate the usefulness of human post-edited data.

Across metrics, both the NMT QE and the Self-supervised QE approaches were markedly outperformed by all variants of our approach, except for RO-EN on the WikiMatrix dataset, where NMT QE obtained better results than the least accurate <b50, best> variant at the sentence level. Self-supervised QE performed better than NMT QE on word-level accuracy in all cases, with opposite results at the sentence level. Note that the use of *unrelated* contrastive translations, at least in the form of NMT QE with high quality human translations contrasted with translations from a baseline NMT model, was outperformed by the use of translations from related NMT stages overall.

7 Natural and Synthetic Data Combination

Synthetic data can be used to fully train QE models when no human-labelled data are available, thus alleviating the training data bottleneck for supervised models. When human post-edited data are available however, it remains to be determined if checkpoint-based synthetic data can be used in a complementary manner to further improve the accuracy of QE models.

To study this question, we trained QE models on datasets that merged the QE training data of the WMT shared task with synthetic data generated from a separate dataset. For both English and Romanian, we thus randomly sampled sentences from the selected source monolingual datasets and generated synthetic data with the *<b75, best>* variant, which provided robust results across the board.[7] Since the shared task training datasets consist of 7K data points, we considered three different merged data partitions: (i) merging the 7K WMT QE training data with 7K tuples from the synthetic data; (ii) merging the WMT QE 7K with 70K synthetic tuples, corresponding to our medium datasets in the previous experiments; and (iii) upsampling the QE

[7]For the WikiMatrix and WMT21-MT datasets, the selected source sentences were the same as in the previous experiments.

training data to 70K and merging them with 70K synthetic tuples. There were thus two balanced datasets, and one unbalanced with an order of magnitude more synthetic data points.

The results of these experiments are shown in Table 4. At the sentence level, combinations of synthetic and human data outperformed the baseline in all cases for EN-DE and in 6 out of 9 combinations in RO-EN. At the word level, in RO-EN the baseline was outperformed by the balanced 70K models trained on WikiDump and WikiMatrix data, but obtained better results in the other configurations. In EN-DE, all combinations outperformed the baseline at the word level as well. Regarding data combination volumes, balancing the amount of human and synthetic data proved optimal on all three datasets. Slight improvements were obtained with the larger datasets, although the impact of upsampling the human QE data should be further analysed to measure eventual overfitting side-effects with this data augmentation approach. Finally, the top-performing variants were obtained by mixing the post-edited Wikipedia data with the synthetic data from WikiMatrix and WikiDump, but, as was the case in the previous experiments, the results obtained with the WMT21-MT corpus were competitive overall.

The synthetic data generated via checkpoint translation can thus provide additional accuracy to QE models based on human post-edited data, at both word and sentence levels. We left further experimentation for future research, notably the combination of natural data with mixed synthetic data sampled from different domains.

8 Conclusions

In this work, we described a novel approach to synthetic data generation for translation quality estimation, based on translation models at different learning stages. We exploited NMT model checkpoints, derived from standard training processes, to generate faulty translations that can be contrasted with either human references in parallel datasets, or the translations produced by the converged NMT model. We showed that the latter approach outperformed the use of human references by a significant margin, demonstrating the effectiveness of our method to directly exploit monolingual corpora for synthetic QE data generation. We also showed that checkpoint-based QE performed markedly better than both self-supervised QE and contrasting MT output with human references on parallel data.

The synthetic data generated under our approach was shown to match, or be competitive with, human post-edited data, with a relatively minor impact of domain relatedness between the synthetic training data and the test data in our experiments. We also demonstrated that combining human-generated and synthetic data led to significant improvements on the QE tasks, showing the potential of our approach as both a standalone solution when no human-labelled data are available, and as a complementary option when such data are available.

The main drawback of the checkpoint-based approach is the need to train a separate NMT model for synthetic data generation. However, since the goal of these models is to generate pairs of translations of differing relative quality, there is no requirement for them to be trained on large volumes of data to achieve high translation quality. As shown by our results in Romanian-English, using a relatively small MT training corpus can lead to quality QE synthetic datasets.

Our approach could be further explored along different lines. In this work, we only selected two arbitrary checkpoint models for our experiments, based on their distance to the converged model in terms of BLEU. Additional checkpoints could be used to enrich the synthetic datasets, exploiting earlier or later training stages. The relative distances between checkpoints, or alternative selection metrics beyond BLEU, could also be used to determine optimal checkpoints for QE data generation. Further experimentation will also be relevant to assess optimal data sampling and combination strategies, for specific domains in particular. Finally, determining if the errors learned from checkpoints may bias the QE system towards model-specific error types would require a dedicated analysis as well. We leave these research questions for future work.

References

Artetxe, M. and Schwenk, H. (2019). Massively multilingual sentence embeddings for zero-shot cross-lingual transfer and beyond. *Transactions of the Association for Computational Linguistics*, 7:597–610.

Baek, Y., Kim, Z. M., Moon, J., Kim, H., and Park, E. (2020). PATQUEST: Papago translation quality estimation. In *Proceedings of the Fifth Conference on Machine Translation*, pages 991–998, Online. Association for Computational Linguistics.

Bahdanau, D., Cho, K., and Bengio, Y. (2015). Neural machine translation by jointly learning to align and translate. In *3rd International Conference on Learning Representations, ICLR 2015, San Diego, CA, USA, May 7-9, 2015, Conference Track Proceedings*.

Berard, A., Calapodescu, I., and Roux, C. (2019). Naver Labs Europe's Systems for the WMT19 Machine Translation Robustness Task. In *Proceedings of the Fourth Conference on Machine Translation (Volume 2: Shared Task Papers, Day 1)*, pages 526–532, Florence, Italy. Association for Computational Linguistics.

Blatz, J., Fitzgerald, E., Foster, G., Gandrabur, S., Goutte, C., Kulesza, A., Sanchis, A., and Ueffing, N. (2004). Confidence estimation for machine translation. In *COLING 2004: Proceedings of the 20th International Conference on Computational Linguistics*, pages 315–321, Geneva, Switzerland. COLING.

Bojar, O., Buck, C., Federmann, C., Haddow, B., Koehn, P., Leveling, J., Monz, C., Pecina, P., Post, M., Saint-Amand, H., Soricut, R., Specia, L., and Tamchyna, A. (2014). Findings of the 2014 workshop on statistical machine translation. In *Proceedings of the Ninth Workshop on Statistical Machine Translation*, pages 12–58, Baltimore, Maryland, USA. Association for Computational Linguistics.

Bojar, O., Chatterjee, R., Federmann, C., Graham, Y., Haddow, B., Huang, S., Huck, M., Koehn, P., Liu, Q., Logacheva, V., Monz, C., Negri, M., Post, M., Rubino, R., Specia, L., and Turchi, M. (2017). Findings of the 2017 conference on machine translation (WMT17). In *Proceedings of the Second Conference on Machine Translation*, pages 169–214, Copenhagen, Denmark. Association for Computational Linguistics.

Callison-Burch, C., Koehn, P., Monz, C., Post, M., Soricut, R., and Specia, L. (2012). Findings of the 2012 workshop on statistical machine translation. In *Proceedings of the Seventh Workshop on Statistical Machine Translation*, pages 10–51, Montréal, Canada. Association for Computational Linguistics.

Conneau, A., Khandelwal, K., Goyal, N., Chaudhary, V., Wenzek, G., Guzmán, F., Grave, E., Ott, M., Zettlemoyer, L., and Stoyanov, V. (2020). Unsupervised cross-lingual representation learning at scale. In *Proceedings of the 58th Annual Meeting of the Association for Computational Linguistics*, pages 8440–8451, Online. Association for Computational Linguistics.

Devlin, J., Chang, M.-W., Lee, K., and Toutanova, K. (2019). BERT: Pre-training of deep bidirectional transformers for language understanding. In *Proceedings of the 2019 Conference of the North American Chapter of the Association for Computational Linguistics: Human Language Technologies, Volume 1 (Long and Short Papers)*, pages 4171–4186, Minneapolis, Minnesota. Association for Computational Linguistics.

Ding, S., Junczys-Dowmunt, M., Post, M., and Koehn, P. (2021). Levenshtein training for word-level quality estimation. In *Proceedings of the 2021 Conference on Empirical Methods in Natural Language Processing*, pages 6724–6733, Online and Punta Cana, Dominican Republic. Association for Computational Linguistics.

Etchegoyhen, T. and Gete, H. (2020). To case or not to case: Evaluating casing methods for neural machine translation. In *Proceedings of the Twelfth Language Resources and Evaluation Conference*, pages 3752–3760, Marseille, France. European Language Resources Association.

Etchegoyhen, T., Martínez Garcia, E., and Azpeitia, A. (2018). Supervised and unsupervised minimalist quality estimators: Vicomtech's participation in the WMT 2018 quality estimation task. In *Proceedings of the Third Conference on Machine Translation: Shared Task Papers*, pages 782–787, Belgium, Brussels. Association for Computational Linguistics.

Fan, K., Wang, J., Li, B., Zhou, F., Chen, B., and Si, L. (2019). "bilingual expert" can find translation errors. In *Proceedings of the Thirty-Third AAAI Conference on Artificial Intelligence and Thirty-First Innovative Applications of Artificial Intelligence Conference and Ninth AAAI Symposium on Educational Advances in Artificial Intelligence*, AAAI'19/IAAI'19/EAAI'19. AAAI Press.

Felice, M. and Specia, L. (2012). Linguistic features for quality estimation. In *Proceedings of the Seventh Workshop on Statistical Machine Translation*, pages 96–103, Montréal, Canada. Association for Computational Linguistics.

Fomicheva, M., Sun, S., Yankovskaya, L., Blain, F., Guzmán, F., Fishel, M., Aletras, N., Chaudhary, V., and Specia, L. (2020). Unsupervised quality estimation for neural machine translation. *Transactions of the Association for Computational Linguistics*, 8:539–555.

Fonseca, E., Yankovskaya, L., Martins, A. F. T., Fishel, M., and Federmann, C. (2019). Findings of the WMT 2019 shared tasks on quality estimation. In *Proceedings of the Fourth Conference on Machine Translation (Volume 3: Shared Task Papers, Day 2)*, pages 1–10, Florence, Italy. Association for Computational Linguistics.

Forcada, M. L., Esplà-Gomis, M., Sánchez-Martínez, F., and Specia, L. (2017). One-parameter models for sentence-level post-editing effort estimation. In *Proceedings of Machine Translation Summit XVI: Research Track*, pages 132–143, Nagoya Japan.

Ive, J., Blain, F., and Specia, L. (2018). deepQuest: A framework for neural-based quality estimation. In *Proceedings of the 27th International Conference on Computational Linguistics*, pages 3146–3157, Santa Fe, New Mexico, USA. Association for Computational Linguistics.

Junczys-Dowmunt, M., Grundkiewicz, R., Dwojak, T., Hoang, H., Heafield, K., Neckermann, T., Seide, F., Germann, U., Aji, A. F., Bogoychev, N., Martins, A. F. T., and Birch, A. (2018). Marian: Fast neural machine translation in C++. In *Proceedings of ACL 2018, System Demonstrations*, pages 116–121, Melbourne, Australia. Association for Computational Linguistics.

Kepler, F., Trénous, J., Treviso, M., Vera, M., Góis, A., Farajian, M. A., Lopes, A. V., and Martins, A. F. T. (2019a). Unbabel's participation in the WMT19 translation quality estimation shared task. In *Proceedings of the Fourth Conference on Machine Translation (Volume 3: Shared Task Papers, Day 2)*, pages 78–84, Florence, Italy. Association for Computational Linguistics.

Kepler, F., Trénous, J., Treviso, M., Vera, M., and Martins, A. F. T. (2019b). OpenKiwi: An open source framework for quality estimation. In *Proceedings of the 57th Annual Meeting of the Association for Computational Linguistics: System Demonstrations*, pages 117–122, Florence, Italy. Association for Computational Linguistics.

Kim, H. and Lee, J.-H. (2016). Recurrent neural network based translation quality estimation. In *Proceedings of the First Conference on Machine Translation: Volume 2, Shared Task Papers*, pages 787–792, Berlin, Germany. Association for Computational Linguistics.

Kim, H., Lee, J.-H., and Na, S.-H. (2017). Predictor-estimator using multilevel task learning with stack propagation for neural quality estimation. In *Proceedings of the Second Conference on Machine Translation*, pages 562–568, Copenhagen, Denmark. Association for Computational Linguistics.

Kim, H., Lim, J.-H., Kim, H.-K., and Na, S.-H. (2019). QE BERT: Bilingual BERT using multi-task learning for neural quality estimation. In *Proceedings of the Fourth Conference on Machine Translation (Volume 3: Shared Task Papers, Day 2)*, pages 85–89, Florence, Italy. Association for Computational Linguistics.

Koehn, P., Hoang, H., Birch, A., Callison-Burch, C., Federico, M., Bertoldi, N., Cowan, B., Shen, W., Moran, C., Zens, R., Dyer, C., Bojar, O., Constantin, A., and Herbst, E. (2007). Moses: Open source toolkit for statistical machine translation. In *Proceedings of the 45th Annual Meeting of the Association for Computational Linguistics Companion Volume Proceedings of the Demo and Poster Sessions*, pages 177–180, Prague, Czech Republic. Association for Computational Linguistics.

Lee, D. (2020). Two-phase cross-lingual language model fine-tuning for machine translation quality estimation. In *Proceedings of the Fifth Conference on Machine Translation*, pages 1024–1028, Online. Association for Computational Linguistics.

Martins, A. F. T., Kepler, F., and Monteiro, J. (2017). Unbabel's participation in the WMT17 translation quality estimation shared task. In *Proceedings of the Second Conference on Machine Translation*, pages 569–574, Copenhagen, Denmark. Association for Computational Linguistics.

Matthews, B. W. (1975). Comparison of the predicted and observed secondary structure of t4 phage lysozyme. *Biochimica et Biophysica Acta (BBA)-Protein Structure*, 405(2):442–451.

Moreau, E. and Vogel, C. (2012). Quality estimation: an experimental study using unsupervised similarity measures. In *Proceedings of the Seventh Workshop on Statistical Machine Translation*, pages 120–126, Montréal, Canada. Association for Computational Linguistics.

Negri, M., Turchi, M., Chatterjee, R., and Bertoldi, N. (2018). ESCAPE: a large-scale synthetic corpus for automatic post-editing. In *Proceedings of the Eleventh International Conference on Language Resources and Evaluation (LREC 2018)*, Miyazaki, Japan. European Language Resources Association (ELRA).

Papineni, K., Roukos, S., Ward, T., and Zhu, W.-J. (2002). Bleu: a method for automatic evaluation of machine translation. In *Proceedings of the 40th Annual Meeting of the Association for Computational Linguistics*, pages 311–318, Philadelphia, Pennsylvania, USA. Association for Computational Linguistics.

Popović, M. (2012). Morpheme- and POS-based IBM1 and language model scores for translation quality estimation. In *Proceedings of the Seventh Workshop on Statistical Machine Translation*, pages 133–137, Montréal, Canada. Association for Computational Linguistics.

Quirk, C. B. (2004). Training a sentence-level machine translation confidence measure. In *Proceedings of the Fourth International Conference on Language Resources and Evaluation (LREC'04)*, Lisbon, Portugal. European Language Resources Association (ELRA).

Schwenk, H., Chaudhary, V., Sun, S., Gong, H., and Guzmán, F. (2021). WikiMatrix: Mining 135M parallel sentences in 1620 language pairs from Wikipedia. In *Proceedings of the 16th Conference of the European Chapter of the Association for Compuational Linguistics: Main Volume*, pages 1351–1361, Online. Association for Computational Linguistics.

Sennrich, R., Haddow, B., and Birch, A. (2016). Neural machine translation of rare words with subword units. In *Proceedings of the 54th Annual Meeting of the Association for Computational Linguistics (Volume 1: Long Papers)*, pages 1715–1725, Berlin, Germany. Association for Computational Linguistics.

Shah, K., Bougares, F., Barrault, L., and Specia, L. (2016). SHEF-LIUM-NN: Sentence level quality estimation with neural network features. In *Proceedings of the First Conference on Machine Translation: Volume 2, Shared Task Papers*, pages 838–842, Berlin, Germany. Association for Computational Linguistics.

Shah, K., Logacheva, V., Paetzold, G., Blain, F., Beck, D., Bougares, F., and Specia, L. (2015). SHEF-NN: Translation quality estimation with neural networks. In *Proceedings of the Tenth Workshop on Statistical Machine Translation*, pages 342–347, Lisbon, Portugal. Association for Computational Linguistics.

Snover, M., Dorr, B., Schwartz, R., Micciulla, L., and Makhoul, J. (2006). A study of translation edit rate with targeted human annotation. In *Proceedings of the 7th Conference of the Association for Machine Translation in the Americas: Technical Papers*, pages 223–231, Cambridge, Massachusetts, USA. Association for Machine Translation in the Americas.

Specia, L., Blain, F., Fomicheva, M., Fonseca, E., Chaudhary, V., Guzmán, F., and Martins, A. F. T. (2020). Findings of the WMT 2020 shared task on quality estimation. In *Proceedings of the Fifth Conference on Machine Translation*, pages 743–764, Online. Association for Computational Linguistics.

Specia, L., Blain, F., Fomicheva, M., Zerva, C., Li, Z., Chaudhary, V., and Martins, A. F. T. (2021). Findings of the WMT 2021 shared task on quality estimation. In *Proceedings of the Sixth Conference on Machine Translation*, pages 684–725, Online. Association for Computational Linguistics.

Specia, L., Blain, F., Logacheva, V., F. Astudillo, R., and Martins, A. F. T. (2018). Findings of the WMT 2018 shared task on quality estimation. In *Proceedings of the Third Conference on Machine Translation: Shared Task Papers*, pages 689–709, Belgium, Brussels. Association for Computational Linguistics.

Specia, L., Raj, D., and Turchi, M. (2010). Machine translation evaluation versus quality estimation. *Machine translation*, 24:39–50.

Specia, L., Shah, K., de Souza, J. G., and Cohn, T. (2013). QuEst - a translation quality estimation framework. In *Proceedings of the 51st Annual Meeting of the Association for Computational Linguistics: System Demonstrations*, pages 79–84, Sofia, Bulgaria. Association for Computational Linguistics.

Specia, L., Turchi, M., Cancedda, N., Cristianini, N., and Dymetman, M. (2009). Estimating the sentence-level quality of machine translation systems. In *Proceedings of the 13th Annual conference of the European Association for Machine Translation*, Barcelona, Spain. European Association for Machine Translation.

Sun, S., Guzmán, F., and Specia, L. (2020). Are we estimating or guesstimating translation quality? In *Proceedings of the 58th Annual Meeting of the Association for Computational Linguistics*, pages 6262–6267, Online. Association for Computational Linguistics.

Sutskever, I., Vinyals, O., and Le, Q. V. (2014). Sequence to sequence learning with neural networks. In *Advances in neural information processing systems*, pages 3104–3112.

Tuan, Y.-L., El-Kishky, A., Renduchintala, A., Chaudhary, V., Guzmán, F., and Specia, L. (2021). Quality estimation without human-labeled data. In *Proceedings of the 16th Conference of the European Chapter of the Association for Computational Linguistics: Main Volume*, pages 619–625, Online. Association for Computational Linguistics.

Vaswani, A., Shazeer, N., Parmar, N., Uszkoreit, J., Jones, L., Gomez, A. N., Kaiser, L., and Polosukhin, I. (2017). Attention is all you need. In *Advances in Neural Information Processing Systems 30: Annual Conference on Neural Information Processing Systems 2017, December 4-9, 2017, Long Beach, CA, USA*, pages 5998–6008.

Zerva, C., Blain, F., Rei, R., Lertvittayakumjorn, P., C. De Souza, J. G., Eger, S., Kanojia, D., Alves, D., Orăsan, C., Fomicheva, M., Martins, A. F. T., and Specia, L. (2022). Findings of the WMT 2022 shared task on quality estimation. In *Proceedings of the Seventh Conference on Machine Translation (WMT)*, pages 69–99, Abu Dhabi, United Arab Emirates (Hybrid). Association for Computational Linguistics.

Zheng, Y., Tan, Z., Zhang, M., Maimaiti, M., Luan, H., Sun, M., Liu, Q., and Liu, Y. (2021). Self-supervised quality estimation for machine translation. In *Proceedings of the 2021 Conference on Empirical Methods in Natural Language Processing*, pages 3322–3334, Online and Punta Cana, Dominican Republic. Association for Computational Linguistics.

Zhou, J., Zhang, Z., and Hu, Z. (2019). SOURCE: SOURce-conditional elmo-style model for machine translation quality estimation. In *Proceedings of the Fourth Conference on Machine Translation (Volume 3: Shared Task Papers, Day 2)*, pages 106–111, Florence, Italy. Association for Computational Linguistics.

Exploring Domain-shared and Domain-specific Knowledge in Multi-Domain Neural Machine Translation

Zhibo Man zhiboman@bjtu.edu.cn
Yujie Zhang* yjzhang@bjtu.edu.cn
Yuanmeng Chen yuanmengchen@bjtu.edu.cn
Yufeng Chen yfchen@bjtu.edu.cn
Jinan Xu jaxu@bjtu.edu.cn
School of Computer and Information Technology, Beijing Jiaotong University, Beijing, China

Abstract

Currently, multi-domain neural machine translation (NMT) has become a significant research topic in domain adaptation machine translation, which trains a single model by mixing data from multiple domains. Multi-domain NMT aims to improve the performance of the low-resources domain through data augmentation. However, mixed domain data brings more translation ambiguity. Previous work focused on domain-general or domain-context knowledge learning, respectively. Therefore, there is a challenge for acquiring domain-general or domain-context knowledge simultaneously. To this end, we propose a unified framework for learning simultaneously domain-general and domain-specific knowledge, we are the first to apply parameter differentiation in multi-domain NMT. Specifically, we design the differentiation criterion and differentiation granularity to obtain domain-specific parameters. Experimental results on multi-domain UM-corpus English-to-Chinese and OPUS German-to-English datasets show that the average BLEU scores of the proposed method exceed the strong baseline by 1.22 and 1.87, respectively. In addition, we investigate the case study to illustrate the effectiveness of the proposed method in acquiring domain knowledge.

1 Introduction

In recent years, Neural Machine Translation (NMT) has shown excellent performance in various translation tasks, as evidenced by state-of-the-art (SOTA) results reported in studies such as (Bahdanau et al., 2015; Wu et al., 2016; Vaswani et al., 2017; Liu et al., 2021; Fernandes et al., 2022), among which Multi-domain NMT aims to construct a single NMT model with the ability to translate sentences across different domains (Wang et al., 2020). Mixed-domain data can improve cross-domain knowledge on low-resource domains by data augmentation. However, word ambiguity increases when we mix data from multiple domains. Therefore, a challenge remains in how to learn the domain-shared and domain-specific knowledge for multi-domain NMT.

To address the above problem, researchers design domain-shared (Zeng et al., 2018, 2019; Pham et al., 2019; Wang et al., 2020) and domain-specific knowledge learning mechanisms

Proceedings of Machine Translation Summit XIX, Vol. 1: Research Track, pages 99–110
September 4–8, 2023, Macau SAR, China.

Example 1 : Translation based on domain-shared knowledge learning	
Input (*Law*)	promotion centers and technology enterprise incubation base
Reference	促进中心和科技企业孵化✓基地
Mixed	促进中心和技术企业孵化✓基地
Single	促进中心和技术企业潜伏×基地
MDNMT (Jiang et al., 2020)	促进中心和技术企业培养×基地
Mixed data (*Education*)	incubation (孵化✓) lasts anywhere from 24-28 days.
Example 2 : Translation based on domain-specific knowledge learning	
Input (*Science*)	output power can never equal the input power for there always losses.
Reference	输出功率决不可能等于输入功率✓因为总有损耗。
Mixed	输出电力×从来不等于输入电力×由于常有损耗。
Single	输出功率从来不等于输入功率✓因为总有损耗。
MDNMT (Jiang et al., 2020)	输出功率从不等于输入功率✓由于总有损耗。
Mixed data (*News*)	which is also the source of most of Beijing's power (电力×) supply.

Table 1: Two English-Chinese translations of "incubation" and "power" with different models.

(Kobus et al., 2016; Britz et al., 2017; Jiang et al., 2020; Lee et al., 2022). Nevertheless, these strategies have inherent limitations, such as Example 1 in Table 1 shows that the word "incubation" is incorrectly translated to "潜伏" and "培养" by the Single and Jiang et al. (2020), respectively. On the one hand, this suggests that domain-specific data only has the translation "潜伏" in the Law domain. On the other hand, MDNMT (Jiang et al. (2020)) learns domain-specific features using a domain discriminator, resulting in translations relying on the results of the domain discriminator. In addition, the word is translated to "孵化" by Mixed, illustrating that mixing multiple domains' data can improve domain-shared knowledge. In contrast, Example 2 in Table 1 shows that "power" is incorrectly translated to "电力" by Mixed, showing that this model introduces the ambiguity of "电力" from the News domain, demonstrating the importance of domain-specific knowledge learning. Therefore, effectively representing domain-shared and domain-specific knowledge has become a key issue in multi-domain NMT.

To tackle the above issues, we found that some research work has proven that parameters play a key role in Multilingual NMT (Wang and Zhang, 2022; Sachan and Neubig, 2018) and Multilingual Speech Translation (Wang et al., 2022). In our work, we calculate the gradient from different domains based on cosine similarity as domain-specific parameters, and then obtain the domain-shared and domain-specific parameters of the model to represent the corresponding knowledge.

To summarize, our contributions are three-fold:

- To the best of our knowledge, our model is the first to explore domain-shared and domain-specific parameters of multi-domain NMT.
- We design different mechanisms to dynamically acquire domain-shared and domain-specific knowledge, respectively.
- Experimental results and analyses on multiple language pairs show that the proposed model improves over several baselines, then we further analyze the approach insights into its actual contributions in multi-domain NMT.

2 Related Work

According to the domain representation learning strategy, we divide it into domain-shared and domain-specific knowledge methods: **Domain-shared knowledge learning**: Mixed domain data is a simple and convenient method to obtain domain-shared knowledge. Additionally, Zeng et al. (2018) designed the domain-shared discriminator to learn cross-domain features. Pham et al. (2019) proposed isolating domain-agnostic from domain-specific lexical representations while sharing most of the network across domains. Furthermore, Wang et al. (2020) proposed two complementary supervision signals by leveraging the power of knowledge distillation and adversarial learning. **Domain-specific knowledge learning**: From a sentence-level perspective, training a discriminator to detect and embed the domain tag for a sentence has become the mainstream approach (Kobus et al., 2016; Britz et al., 2017; Tars and Fishel, 2018; Aharoni and Goldberg, 2020; Lee et al., 2022). Both Zeng et al. (2018) and Su et al. (2021) propose a maximum weighted likelihood estimation method, where the weight is obtained by masking the domain-aware word level to encourage the model to pay more attention to the domain-specific representation of words. Recent work proposes Domain Proportion to improve the adaptability of each word (Jiang et al., 2020; Lai et al., 2021; Zhang et al., 2021). Some works propose the domain proportion of words for MDNMT, where each word in the sentence has a corresponding proportion in each domain (Jiang et al., 2020; Zhang et al., 2021; Lai et al., 2021). However, this approach may also affect the performance of the domain discriminator in the target language to some extent, potentially leading to translation ambiguity.

Compared with the previous approaches, there are two salient features in our methods: (1) Our method can capture domain-shared and domain-specific knowledge simultaneously within the framework of multi-domain NMT instead of separately. (2) Our method learns domain-shared and domain-specific knowledge from the perspective of parameter learning, rather than utilizing domain discriminators.

3 Our model

Multi-domain NMT task: The objective of this task is to create a unified model using mixed-domain data, aiming to maximize performance across all domains (Wang et al., 2020). Specifically, there are J subsets, denoted as $\mathcal{D}_1, \mathcal{D}_2, ..., \mathcal{D}_J$. Each subset $\mathcal{D}_j$ consists of pairs of input-output sequences, represented as $\mathcal{D}_j = \{[\mathbf{x}_j^m, \mathbf{y}_j^m]\}_{m=1}^{M_j}$, where j indicates the domain and m denotes the index within the domain, M_j represents the number of all sentences in the j-th domain. The training objective can be formulated as follows:

$$\mathcal{L}_{MDNMT}(\theta) = \arg\max_{\theta} \frac{1}{J} \sum_{j=1}^{J} \mathcal{L}_j(\theta) \quad (1)$$

where θ represents the learnable parameters in the model, and $\mathcal{L}_j$ denotes the training objective for each specific domain.

3.1 Parameter Differentiation

Figure 1 gives the process of parameter differentiation (Wang and Zhang, 2022). This method enables the model to identify language-specific parameters during the training of multi-lingual NMT task. Shared parameters in this approach have the ability to dynamically specialize into different types, akin to cellular differentiation. Moreover, Wang and Zhang (2022) define the differentiation criterion as inter-task gradient cosine similarity (Yu et al., 2020; Wang et al., 2021). Consequently, parameters exhibiting conflicting inter-task gradients are more likely to be language-specific. As the key problem of multi-domain NMT is how to learn domain-shared and domain-specific knowledge. Inspired by the parameter differentiation of multi-lingual NMT. In our work, we consider domain-specific knowledge learning as the process of parameter differentiation, the model determines which parameters should be domain-specific during training, and other parameters are domain-shared knowledge.

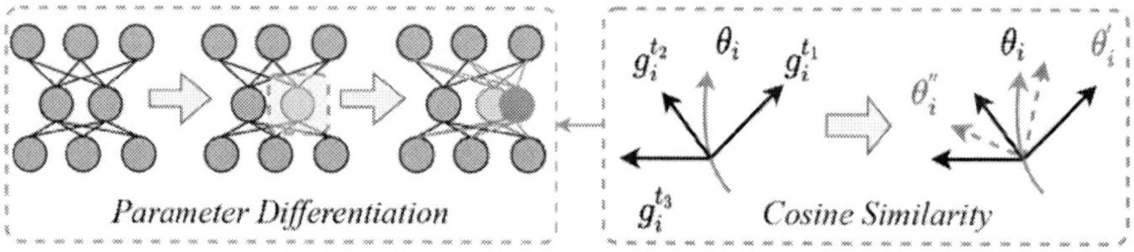

Figure 1: The process of Parameter Differentiation

3.2 The Framework of Our Model

As shown in Figure 2, we design a model consisting of an encoder-decoder based on Transformer (Vaswani et al., 2017). The blue box in Figure 2 represents domain-shared and domain-specific parameters in the encoder and decoder, respectively. Specifically, we obtain domain-shared and domain-specific parameters in the following ways: **(1) Domain-shared Knowledge Learning:** We design a unified multi-domain NMT framework that allows parameter sharing for each domain translation. Shared parameters of different layers in the encoder and decoder of Transformer are updated to exploit commonalities and differences across tasks. **(2) Domain-specific Knowledge Learning:** We calculate the gradient conflict of parameters in different layers of Transformer between different domains as the basis for domain-specific knowledge.

3.3 Domain-shared Knowledge Learning

Parameter sharing strategies are mainly used in multilingual *one-to-many* or *many-to-many* scenarios (Sachan and Neubig, 2018; Wang and Zhang, 2022; Wang et al., 2022). To be precise, all subtasks are passed through individual encoders and decoders simultaneously. As shown in Figure 2, we migrate parameter strategies from multilingual translation to multi-domain NMT. The parameters are described below:

Encoder Parameter Setting Individual encoder and decoder are set for source domain and target domain, respectively. The source domain parameters θ_{enc}=$\{W^{\text{enc}}_{\text{K}}, W^{\text{enc}}_{\text{Q}}, W^{\text{enc}}_{\text{V}}, W^{\text{enc}}_{\text{F}}, W^{\text{enc}}_{\text{L}_1}, W^{\text{enc}}_{\text{L}_2}\}$ are shared among different source domains, where $W^{\text{enc}}_{\text{K}}$, $W^{\text{enc}}_{\text{Q}}$, $W^{\text{enc}}_{\text{V}}$, $W^{\text{enc}}_{\text{F}}$ are the self-attention weights, $W^{\text{enc}}_{\text{L}_1}$, $W^{\text{enc}}_{\text{L}_2}$ are the FFN sublayer parameters.

Decoder Parameter Setting Regarding decoding stage, θ_{enc}, θ_{dec}=$\{W^{\text{dec}}_{\text{K}_1}, W^{\text{dec}}_{\text{Q}_1}, W^{\text{dec}}_{\text{V}_1}, W^{\text{dec}}_{\text{F}_1}, W^{\text{dec}}_{\text{K}_2}, W^{\text{dec}}_{\text{Q}_2}, W^{\text{dec}}_{\text{V}_2}, W^{\text{dec}}_{\text{F}_2}, W^{\text{dec}}_{\text{L}_1}, W^{\text{dec}}_{\text{L}_2}\}$ are shared for different target domains, where $W^{\text{dec}}_{\text{K}_1}$, $W^{\text{dec}}_{\text{Q}_1}$, $W^{\text{dec}}_{\text{V}_1}$, $W^{\text{dec}}_{\text{F}_1}$ are the self-attention weights of the decoder, θ_{enc}, $W^{\text{dec}}_{\text{K}_2}$, $W^{\text{dec}}_{\text{Q}_2}$, $W^{\text{dec}}_{\text{V}_2}$, $W^{\text{dec}}_{\text{F}_2}$ are parameters in the encoder-decoder attention sublayer, and $W^{\text{dec}}_{\text{L}_1}$, $W^{\text{dec}}_{\text{L}_2}$ are the feed-forward parameters shared in each decoder block.

3.4 Domain-specific Knowledge Learning

The main challenge in parameter differentiation is to define the criterion for differentiation, which assists in identifying shared parameters that should be specialized into specific types. Our approach defines the differentiation criterion using inter-task gradient cosine similarity, allowing us to identify parameters that encounter conflicting gradients and are likely domain-specific. Therefore, we first build the model as completely shared and initialize the parameters with a pre-trained model. Following prior work (Wang and Zhang, 2022), parameter differentiation consists of differentiation criterion and differentiation granularity.

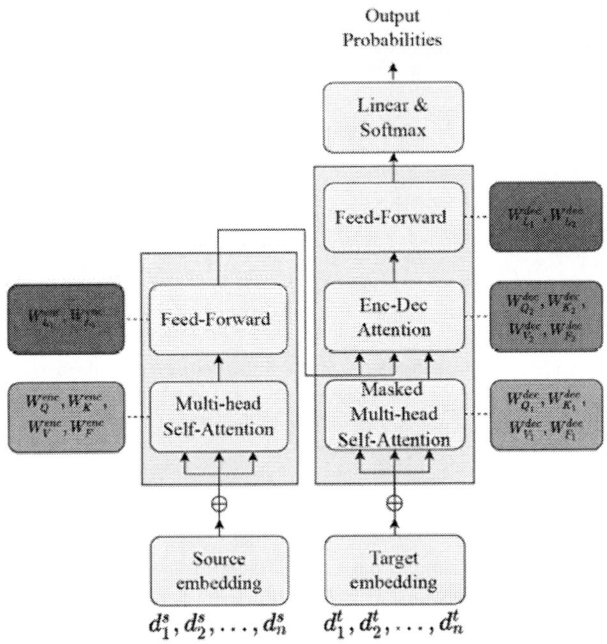

Figure 2: The Framework of Our Model

Differentiation Criterion: To assess the level of specialization for a shared parameter, we quantify its interference degree across three tasks using inter-task gradient cosine similarity. The i-th parameter θ_i in an multi-domain NMT model is shared by a set of tasks T_i, the interference degree $\mathcal{I}$ of the parameter θ_i is defined by:

$$\mathcal{I}(\theta_i, T_i) = \max_{t_j, t_k \in T_i} -\frac{g_i^{t_j} \cdot g_i^{t_k}}{\| g_i^{t_j} \| \| g_i^{t_k} \|} \tag{2}$$

where $g_i^{t_j}$ and $g_i^{t_k}$ are the gradients of task t_j and t_k respectively on the parameter .

Differentiation Granularity contains Layer{encoder layer, decoder layer}, Module{self-attention, FFN, Enc-Dec attention}, and Operation{linear projection, layer normalization}, "Layer granularity" refers to distinct layers within the model, while "Module granularity" refers to individual modules within a layer. On the other hand, "Operation granularity" encompasses the fundamental transformations in the model that possess trainable parameters. Each granularity level groups parameters into separate units for differentiation. For instance, at Layer level granularity, parameters within a layer are combined into a vector and differentiated as a single entity, which is known as a differentiation unit.

3.5 Training Method

In our method, we incorporate dynamic changes to the model architecture, resulting in distinct computational graphs for each task. To achieve this, we construct batches from multi-domain data, ensuring that each batch exclusively contains samples from a single task. This approach differs from training a conventional completely shared multi-domain NMT model, thus we train the model of each domain from $\mathcal{D}_1, \mathcal{D}_2, ..., \mathcal{D}_J$. Specifically, to stabilize the training of θ_i on task t_i, we reinitialize the optimizer states by performing a warm-up update for those differentiated parameters(Wang and Zhang, 2022):

$$m_t^{'} = \beta_1 m_t + (1 - \beta_1)(g_i^{t_i}) \tag{3}$$

$$v_t^{'} = \beta_2 m_t + (1 - \beta_2)(g_i^{t_i})^2 \tag{4}$$

where m_t and v_t are the Adam states of θ_i, and $g_i^{t_1}$ is the gradient of task t_1 on the held-out validation data.

4 Experiments

In our experiments, we aim to investigate the following research problems: (1) What is the improved performance of our method against previous work? (3) Can our model learn the more effective domain-shared and domain-specific knowledge?

4.1 Datasets

In our experiments, we use the following datasets for two machine translation tasks: **(1) English-to-Chinese**: We select UM-Corpus as multi-domain dataset [1] containing five domains: News, Spoken, Science, Education, and Laws. **(2) German-to-English**: We also choose OPUS [2] as multi-domain dataset containing five domains: Law, It, Koran, Medical, and Subtitles.

English-to-Chinese				German-to-English			
Domain	**Train**	**Dev**	**Test**	**Domain**	**Train**	**Dev**	**Test**
Education	444,608	1,996	462	It	222,297	1,888	2,000
Law	207,195	1,979	456	Koran	17,982	1,872	2,000
News	443,778	1,997	1,500	Law	467,309	1,861	2,000
Science	263,031	1,992	503	Medcial	248,099	1,861	2,000
Spoken	216,521	1,985	455	Subtitles	14,458,058	1,899	2,000

Table 2: The numbers of sentences in UM-Corpus and OPUS datasets.

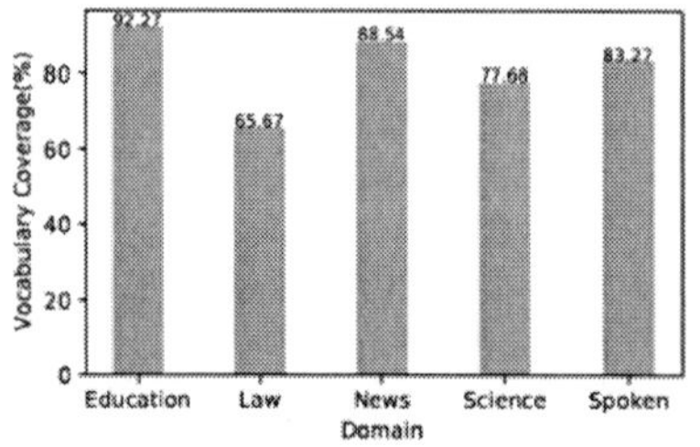

(a) Vocabulary Coverage

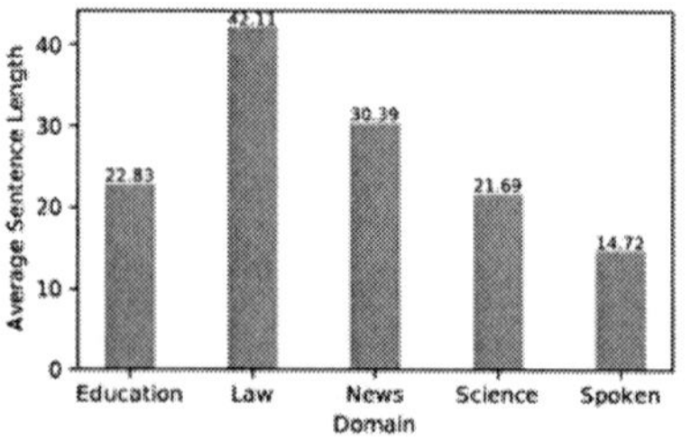

(b) Average Sentence Length

Figure 3: Statistics of English-to-Chinese dataset

[1] http://nlp2ct.cis.umac.mo/um-corpus/

[2] https://github.com/ZurichNLP/domain-robustness

Table 2 provides an overview of the dataset partition, and Figure 3 (a) and (b) shows the statistics of vocabulary coverage and average sentence length on English-to-Chinese dataset. We adopt the same pre-processing as the baseline model (Jiang et al., 2020). To process the English and German sentences, we employ the MOSES script (Koehn et al., 2007) for tokenization. For Chinese sentences, we utilize the Stanford Segmenter (Tseng et al., 2005) for word segmentation. To encode all sentences, we apply byte-pair encoding (BPE) (Sennrich et al., 2016). Specifically, for the German-to-English task, we train a joint BPE vocabulary with 32k merge operations. On the other hand, for the English-to-Chinese task, we separately train BPE vocabularies with a size of 32k for each language.

4.2 Comparative Models

We select seven models to compare the performance of results. Specifically, (1)-(2) are the strategy of domain data and (3)-(7) are the strategy of multi-domain NMT methods: **(1) Single**: This method only uses single domain data. **(2) Mixed**: This method uses mixed domain data. **(3) Disc**: Kobus et al. (2016) uses a sentence-level domain discriminator for domain representation learning. **(4) AdvL**: Britz et al. (2017) This approach is similar to Disc, except that when back-propagating from the discriminator to the encoder, gradients are reversed by multiplying. **(5) PAdvL**: Britz et al. (2017) is a combination of Disc and AdvL, spliting the embedding into half of Disc part and Adv part. **(6) WDCD**: Zeng et al. (2018) integrate Multi-Task Learning (MTL) and AdvL approaches by incorporating word-level domain contexts. **(7) WALDM**: Jiang et al. (2020) uses the domain proportion to learn the representation of each word. In addition, we reproduce the above comparison model based on the same parameter settings with fairseq[3] framework. Table 3 shows that the detailed hyperparameter settings.

Hyperparameter	Value
Epoch	50
Optimizer	Adam
(β_1, β_2)	(0.9, 0.98)
Beam Size	5
dropout rate	0.3
Learning Rate	5×10^{-4}
Tokens Per Batch	4096
Minimumm Learning Rate	10^{-9}
Feed-Forward Hidden State	1024
Encoder and Decoder Layers	6
Warmup Initial Learning Rate	5×10^{-4}
Word Embedding Dimensions	512

Table 3: Hyperparameter Settings

4.3 Main Results

The Results of English-to-Chinese Translation Task As shown at the top of Table 4. The BLEU scores of the *Single* on Law and News domains are 74.86 and 35.18, respectively, reaching the highest level compared to other models, reflecting that training on a single domain data avoids introducing noise. However, due to the limited data volume and complexity of content in the Science and Spoken domains, using solely the data from a single domain does not lead

[3]https://github.com/facebookresearch/fairseq

Task	Models	Domain					Avg↑	#Param↓
		Edu	Law	New	Sci	Spo		
English-to-Chinese	Single	30.03	**74.86**	**35.18**	17.93	28.11	37.22	-
	Mixed	35.13	62.76	32.07	27.43	28.14	37.11	145M
	Disc	34.87	62.90	31.92	27.44	28.70	37.17	145M
	AdvL	34.29	63.39	31.73	27.64	28.70	37.15	146M
	PAdvL	34.29	62.82	32.15	27.47	28.32	37.01	145M
	WDCD	33.15	60.87	33.17	27.03	28.40	36.62	211M
	WALDM	**35.87**	67.17	32.50	27.71	28.30	38.31	252M
	Ours	34.72	72.63	33.34	**28.06**	**28.89**	**39.53**	158M
Task	**Models**	**Domain**					**Avg↑**	**#Param↓**
		IT	**Kor**	**Law**	**Med**	**Sub**		
German-to-English	Single	66.58	20.07	**76.98**	71.76	**50.98**	57.27	-
	Mixed	64.65	40.03	74.04	69.16	49.77	59.77	70M
	Disc	64.54	40.29	74.62	67.45	49.09	59.20	177M
	AdvL	63.92	41.41	74.42	67.89	49.42	59.41	177M
	PAdvL	63.88	41.32	74.12	67.99	49.84	59.43	177M
	WDCD	63.89	41.11	74.03	67.97	49.68	59.34	204M
	WALDM	64.34	41.19	74.98	67.99	49.94	59.69	220M
	Ours	**67.02**	**42.51**	75.48	**71.92**	50.87	**61.56**	83M

Table 4: BLEU scores on the English-to-Chinese and German-to-English translation task. We bold the best performance results.

to optimal performance. Despite the Law domain having a data volume comparable to both domains, as shown in Figure 3 (a), Law domain data have longer text lengths than other domains, resulting in better performance when training the translation model separately (Chu and Wang, 2018). *Mixed* is a fundamental framework for multi-domain NMT, and it exhibits improvement compared to Single in Education, Science, and Spoken domains, suggesting that employing a mixed data training approach can enhance model performance in these particular domains. *Disc*, *Advl*, and *WADLM* bring+0.06,+0.04, and+1.20 on average BLEU scores compared to *Mixed*, indicating that multi-domain methods have improved with sentence-level or word-level domain discriminators. In addition, our method exceeds *WADLM*+1.22 BLEU scores. Among all the methods, our method is closest to the performance of Law and News domains of *Single*.

The Results of German-to-English Translation Task We further validate the effectiveness of our method on English-to-German datasets. From the bottom section of Table 4, it can be observed that our model achieves the highest average BLEU score of 61.56. These results provide further validation of the robustness and versatility of our model in the task of German-to-English translation. It should be noted that Single obtained the highest BLEU scores of 76.98 and 50.98 in the Law and Subtitles domains, respectively. Our method is closest to the performance of the Law and Subtitles domains of *Single*. In conclusion, the proposed method effectively learns domain-shared and domain-specific knowledge through parameter learning. It is expected to bring improvements when applied to other language translation tasks.

5 Analysis and Discussion

In this section, we first examine the effectiveness of differentiation. Then, we visualize the domain distribution and analyze the case study. It is worth noting that we mainly verify the English-to-Chinese translation task.

5.1 The effectiveness of Differentiation Granularity

Models	Edu	Law	News	Sci	Spo	Avg	Δ
Mixed	**35.13**	62.76	32.07	27.43	28.14	37.11	-
Domain-specific w *Layer*	34.54	72.01	33.11	28.01	28.54	39.09	+1.98
Domain-specific w *Module*	34.32	72.43	33.02	27.89	28.23	39.18	+2.07
Domain-specific w *Operation*	34.72	72.63	**33.34**	**28.06**	**28.89**	**39.53**	**+2.42**

Table 5: Ablation study on English-to-Chinese, "w" represents with. "Domain-specific" represents domain-specific knowledge learning

We show the effectiveness of differentiation granularity in Table 5. From the average BLEU, "Domain-specific w *Operation*" has the highest improvement on Mixed compared to other granularity, indicating that the finer-grained parameter differentiation can learn more domain-specific knowledge, which is consistent with previous research (Wang and Zhang, 2022; Wang et al., 2022). Moreover, "Domain-specific w *Layer*" exceeds "Domain-specific w *Module*" +0.22, +0.09, and +0.12 on Education, News, and Spoken domains, respectively, indicating that coarse-grained method can obtain more domain knowledge in these domains than fine-grained method.

5.2 Visualization of Domain Distribution

To conduct the effectiveness of our proposed method in domain-specific knowledge learning, we utilize t-SNE (Van der Maaten and Hinton, 2008) to project representations of source sentences. The Visualization of *Mixed*, *WADLM* (Jiang et al., 2020), and Ours are shown in Figure 4 (a), (b), and (c), respectively.

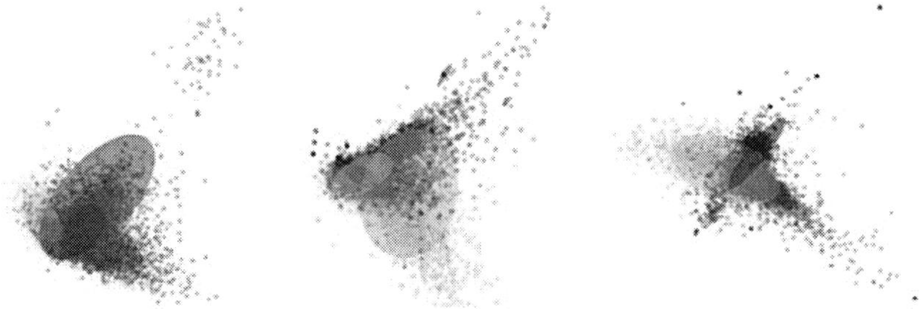

(a) Mixed (b) WADLM (Jiang et al., 2020) (c) Ours

Figure 4: Green, Red, Pink, Orange, and Blue represents Education, Law, News, Science, and Spoken domains, respectively.

As shown in Figure 4, we can observe that *Mixed* does not effectively distinguish the sentences from different domains compared to and *WADLM* and Ours, as the clusters appear more mixed and overlapping, showing that domain representation learning can improve the source sentences representation. In addition, our approach demonstrates a significant improvement as it successfully organizes the sentences into separate domain clusters with clear and distinct boundaries. This improvement shows that the domain-specific weight parameters of Ours enhances the encoder's ability to disambiguate and translate sentences accurately.

5.3 Case Study

We provide a case study to visually demonstrate the improvements made by our proposal. Example 1 of Table 6 shows the case from the Law domain on *Single*, *Mixed*, Jiang et al. (2020), and our model, respectively. When we mix domain data the word ambiguity introduced at the same time, Jiang et al. (2020) erroneously translates the word "incubation" to "培养", showing that the domain-shared knowledge always be ignored because of the domain discriminator. We can find that in this case, the proposed method corrects the ambiguous translation error, showing that our model can better capture domain-shared knowledge. In addition, Example 2 of Table 6 from the Science domain shows that the word "power" correctly translation into "功率" by *Single*, *Mixed*, Jiang et al. (2020) and our model. It further shows that our method can effectively learn domain-specific knowledge through parameter differentiation to obtain the correct domain when translating words.

Example 1 : Translation based on domain-shared knowledge learning	
Input (*Law*)	promotion centers and technology enterprise incubation base
Reference	促进中心和科技企业孵化✓基地
Mixed	促进中心和技术企业孵化✓基地
Single	促进中心和技术企业潜伏×基地
MDNMT (Jiang et al., 2020)	促进中心和技术企业培养×基地
Ours	促进中心和技术企业孵化✓基地
Example 2 : Translation based on domain-specific knowledge learning	
Input (*Science*)	output power can never equal the input power for there always losses.
Reference	输出功率决不可能等于输入功率✓因为总有损耗。
Mixed	输出电力×从来不等于输入电力×由于常有损耗。
Single	输出功率从来不等于输入功率✓因为总有损耗。
MDNMT (Jiang et al., 2020)	输出功率从不等于输入功率✓由于总有损耗。
Ours	输出功率从不等于输入功率✓因为总有损耗。

Table 6: Case Study

6 Conclusion and Future work

In this paper, we explore domain-shared and domain-specific knowledge in multi-domain NMT. Our method can simultaneously learn domain-shared and domain-specific parameters to resolve word ambiguity. Experimental results on two translation tasks show that our method can bring significant improvements. Further analyses confirm that our method can improve word ambiguity between domains. In future work, we will improve the gradient similarity method to further improve the accuracy of domain-specific parameters.

7 Acknowledgements

The present research was supported by the National Nature Science Foundation of China (No. 61876198, 61976015, 61976016). Yujie Zhang is is the corresponding author. We would like thank the anonymous reviewers for their constructive suggestions and insightful comments.

References

Aharoni, R. and Goldberg, Y. (2020). Unsupervised domain clusters in pretrained language models. In *ACL*.

Bahdanau, D., Cho, K. H., and Bengio, Y. (2015). Neural machine translation by jointly learning to align and translate. In *3rd International Conference on Learning Representations, ICLR 2015*.

Britz, D., Le, Q., and Pryzant, R. (2017). Effective domain mixing for neural machine translation. In *Proceedings of the Second Conference on Machine Translation*, pages 118–126.

Chu, C. and Wang, R. (2018). A survey of domain adaptation for neural machine translation. In *Proceedings of the 27th International Conference on Computational Linguistics*, pages 1304–1319.

Fernandes, P., Farinhas, A., Rei, R., De Souza, J., Ogayo, P., Neubig, G., and Martins, A. (2022). Quality-aware decoding for neural machine translation. In *Proceedings of the 2022 Conference of the North American Chapter of the Association for Computational Linguistics: Human Language Technologies*, pages 1396–1412, Seattle, United States. Association for Computational Linguistics.

Jiang, H., Liang, C., Wang, C., and Zhao, T. (2020). Multi-domain neural machine translation with word-level adaptive layer-wise domain mixing. In *Proceedings of the 58th Annual Meeting of the Association for Computational Linguistics*, pages 1823–1834.

Kobus, C., Crego, J., and Senellart, J. (2016). Domain control for neural machine translation. *arXiv preprint arXiv:1612.06140*.

Koehn, P., Federico, M., Shen, W., Bertoldi, N., Bojar, O., Callison-Burch, C., Cowan, B., Dyer, C., Hoang, H., Zens, R., et al. (2007). Open source toolkit for statistical machine translation: Factored translation models and confusion network decoding. In *CLSP Summer Workshop Final Report WS-2006, Johns Hopkins University*.

Lai, W., Libovický, J., and Fraser, A. (2021). Improving both domain robustness and domain adaptability in machine translation. *arXiv preprint arXiv:2112.08288*.

Lee, J., Kim, H., Cho, H., Choi, E., and Park, C. (2022). Specializing multi-domain nmt via penalizing low mutual information. *arXiv preprint arXiv:2210.12910*.

Liu, M., Yang, E., Xiong, D., Zhang, Y., Sheng, C., Hu, C., Xu, J., and Chen, Y. (2021). Exploring bilingual parallel corpora for syntactically controllable paraphrase generation. In *Proceedings of the Twenty-Ninth International Conference on International Joint Conferences on Artificial Intelligence*, pages 3955–3961.

Pham, M. Q., Crego, J.-M., Yvon, F., and Senellart, J. (2019). Generic and specialized word embeddings for multi-domain machine translation. In *International Workshop on Spoken Language Translation*.

Sachan, D. and Neubig, G. (2018). Parameter sharing methods for multilingual self-attentional translation models. In *Proceedings of the Third Conference on Machine Translation: Research Papers*, pages 261–271.

Sennrich, R., Haddow, B., and Birch, A. (2016). Neural machine translation of rare words with subword units. In *Proceedings of the 54th Annual Meeting of the Association for Computational Linguistics (Volume 1: Long Papers)*, pages 1715–1725.

Su, J., Zeng, J., Xie, J., Wen, H., Yin, Y., and Liu, Y. (2021). Exploring discriminative word-level domain contexts for multi-domain neural machine translation. *IEEE Transactions on Pattern Analysis and Machine Intelligence*, 43(5):1530–1545.

Tars, S. and Fishel, M. (2018). Multi-domain neural machine translation. *arXiv preprint arXiv:1805.02282*.

Tseng, H., Chang, P.-C., Andrew, G., Jurafsky, D., and Manning, C. D. (2005). A conditional random field word segmenter for sighan bakeoff 2005. In *Proceedings of the fourth SIGHAN workshop on Chinese language Processing*.

Van der Maaten, L. and Hinton, G. (2008). Visualizing data using t-sne. *Journal of machine learning research*, 9(11).

Vaswani, A., Shazeer, N., Parmar, N., Uszkoreit, J., Jones, L., Gomez, A. N., Kaiser, Ł., and Polosukhin, I. (2017). Attention is all you need. In *Advances in neural information processing systems*, pages 5998–6008.

Wang, Q., Wang, C., and Zhang, J. (2022). Investigating parameter sharing in multilingual speech translation. *Proc. Interspeech 2022*, pages 1731–1735.

Wang, Q. and Zhang, J. (2022). Parameter differentiation based multilingual neural machine translation. In *Proceedings of the AAAI Conference on Artificial Intelligence*, volume 36, pages 11440–11448.

Wang, Y., Wang, L., Shi, S., Li, V. O., and Tu, Z. (2020). Go from the general to the particular: Multi-domain translation with domain transformation networks. In *Proceedings of the AAAI Conference on Artificial Intelligence*, volume 34, pages 9233–9241.

Wang, Z., Tsvetkov, Y., Firat, O., and Cao, Y. (2021). Gradient vaccine: Investigating and improving multi-task optimization in massively multilingual models. In *International Conference on Learning Representations*.

Wu, Y., Schuster, M., Chen, Z., Le, Q. V., Norouzi, M., Macherey, W., Krikun, M., Cao, Y., Gao, Q., Macherey, K., et al. (2016). Google's neural machine translation system: Bridging the gap between human and machine translation. *arXiv preprint arXiv:1609.08144*.

Yu, T., Kumar, S., Gupta, A., Levine, S., Hausman, K., and Finn, C. (2020). Gradient surgery for multi-task learning. *Advances in Neural Information Processing Systems*, 33:5824–5836.

Zeng, J., Liu, Y., Su, J., Ge, Y., Lu, Y., Yin, Y., and Luo, J. (2019). Iterative dual domain adaptation for neural machine translation. In *Proceedings of the 2019 Conference on Empirical Methods in Natural Language Processing and the 9th International Joint Conference on Natural Language Processing (EMNLP-IJCNLP)*, pages 845–855.

Zeng, J., Su, J., Wen, H., Liu, Y., Xie, J., Yin, Y., and Zhao, J. (2018). Multi-domain neural machine translation with word-level domain context discrimination. In *Proceedings of the 2018 Conference on Empirical Methods in Natural Language Processing*, pages 447–457.

Zhang, S., Liu, Y., Xiong, D., Zhang, P., and Chen, B. (2021). Domain-aware self-attention for multi-domain neural machine translation. *Proc. Interspeech 2021*, pages 2047–2051.

Enhancing Translation of Myanmar Sign Language by Transfer Learning and Self-Training

Hlaing Myat Nwe hlaingmyatnwe@jaist.ac.jp
Kiyoaki Shirai kshirai@jaist.ac.jp
Natthawut Kertkeidkachorn natt@jaist.ac.jp
Japan Advanced Institute of Science and Technology, Nomi, Ishikawa, Japan

Thanaruk Theeramunkong tthanaruk@gmail.com
Sirindhorn International Institute of Technology, Thammasat University, Thailand

Ye Kyaw Thu yekyaw.thu@nectec.or.th
Thepchai Supnithi thepchai@nectec.or.th
National Electronic & Computer Technology Center (NECTEC), Thailand

Natsuda Kaothanthong natsuda@siit.tu.ac.th
Sirindhorn International Institute of Technology, Thammasat University, Thailand

Abstract

This paper proposes a method to develop a machine translation (MT) system from Myanmar Sign Language (MSL) to Myanmar Written Language (MWL) and vice versa for the deaf community. Translation of MSL is a difficult task since only a small amount of a parallel corpus between MSL and MWL is available. To address the challenge for MT of its being a low-resource language, transfer learning is applied. An MT model is trained first for a high-resource language pair, American Sign Language (ASL) and English, then it is used as an initial model to train an MT model between MSL and MWL. The mT5 model is used as a base MT model in this transfer learning. Additionally, a self-training technique is applied to generate synthetic translation pairs of MSL and MWL from a large monolingual MWL corpus. Furthermore, since the segmentation of a sentence is required as preprocessing of MT for the Myanmar language, several segmentation schemes are empirically compared. Experiments show that both transfer learning and self-training can enhance the performance of the translation between MSL and MWL compared with a baseline model fine-tuned from a small MSL–MWL parallel corpus only.

1 Introduction

In Myanmar, approximately 1.1 M of the population is deaf or has a hearing impairment.[1] Hard-of-hearing people have difficulty comprehending spoken languages because they cannot distinguish sounds. They mostly rely on Myanmar Sign Language (MSL) for communication instead of voice. Since the structure of the grammar, syntax, and lexicon of MSL are different from Myanmar Written Language (MWL), both deaf and hearing people find it rather difficult

[1]https://themimu.info/disabilities-dashboard

Proceedings of Machine Translation Summit XIX, Vol. 1: Research Track, pages 111–122
September 4–8, 2023, Macau SAR, China.

to learn. In 2010, the Myanmar government launched a project to establish a standard sign language with the aid of the Japanese Federation of the Deaf (Swe, 2010). This highlights the importance of supporting and promoting MSL to ensure the deaf community has equal access to education and opportunities in Myanmar. Currently, a relatively small number, 0.006% of deaf people have a university education. This percentage is significantly smaller than that for the general population of Myanmar. However, there are few (and limited) assistive technologies available for them. Therefore, deaf people require appropriate ways or tools to enhance communication with hearing people as well as to support their education.

Nowadays, machine translation (MT) plays a role in breaking down language barriers and improving communication between people from various cultures and backgrounds. However, translating low-resource languages is still challenging. One of the solutions to this problem is transfer learning. Transfer learning in MT allows models to use knowledge acquired from other languages to enhance their performance in the target language. It can reduce the costs of the construction of large parallel corpora, enabling the development of high-quality MT systems for low-resource languages. Another technique to tackle the sparseness of the data is semi-supervised learning with self-training, which can construct a parallel corpus automatically.

The goal of this paper is to develop a system to translate MSL to MWL and vice versa. This is a difficult task since the available parallel corpora are very limited. To address the challenge of translating this low-resource language, we propose an approach that combines transfer learning and self-training. Although a few studies have so far been made of the translation of MSL as will be reported in subsection 2.2, there has not been any previous attempt to apply those two techniques to the translation of MSL. We also carry out several experiments to empirically investigate how effective the transfer learning and self-training are.

2 Related Work

2.1 Machine Translation for Low-Resource Languages Using Transfer Learning

Many researchers have explored the use of transfer learning for MT, particularly in low-resource scenarios. Zoph et al. (2016) prove that transfer learning significantly improves BLEU scores for low-resource languages in neural machine translation (NMT). Their method involves training an MT model for a high-resource language pair (the parent model) and transferring some information from it to an MT model for a low-resource language pair (the child model) by using the parameters of the parent model as the initial parameters of the child model. Experimental results show that the performance of the baseline NMT models is improved by an average of 5.6 BLEU on four low-resource language pairs. Dabre et al. (2017) present how the selection of a parent model influences the performance of child models in transfer learning for NMT. The authors analytically show that the use of a parent model with a source language that is the same or linguistically similar to that of a child model yields the best achievement.

Kocmi and Bojar (2018) propose a simple transfer learning method for NMT under low-resource conditions, where a parent model for a high-resource language pair is first trained and then the training is continued by replacing a training corpus with a low-resource language pair. Unlike the method of (Zoph et al., 2016) where the target language of the parent model is supposed to be the same as that of the child model, any language pairs can be used to train the parent model in their method. The child model performs significantly better than the baseline trained on the parallel corpus of low-resource pairs only, even when unrelated languages with different alphabets are used for training the parent model. The authors claim that it is the first attempt to apply this method to various languages.

Maimaiti et al. (2022) propose a language-independent Hybrid Transfer Learning (HTL) method for improving the quality of the translation in NMT for low-resource languages. They point out that the quality of the translation of NMT for morphologically rich languages tends

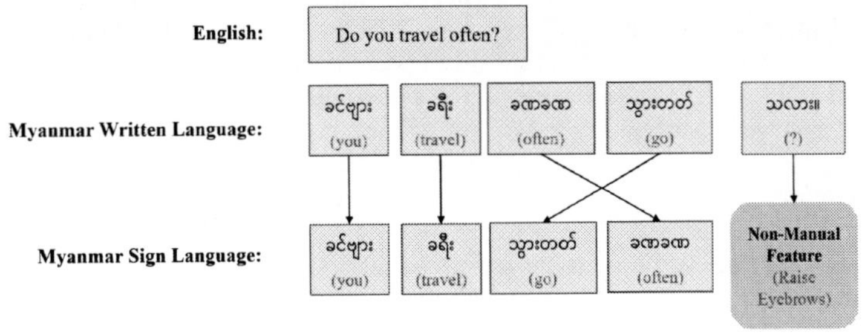

Figure 1: Difference of Grammatical Structure between Myanmar Sign and Written Languages.

to be insufficient due to the sparseness of the data. The suggested HTL approach shares lexicon embeddings between the parent and child languages without using back translation or adding noise manually. According to experimental results, the model trained by the proposed HTL technique consistently exceeds five state-of-the-art methods in the translation of two low-resource languages, namely, Azerbaijani and Uzbek.

2.2 Machine Translation for Myanmar Sign Language

Translation of MSL has been a challenging research topic due to the limited amount of available parallel data, which is difficult to construct. Thus, there are few previous studies on MT for MSL. Moe et al. (2018a) evaluate the quality of automatic translation between MSL and MWL using three different statistical machine translation (SMT) approaches and three distinct segmentation schemes and report that Operation Sequence Model and Hierarchical Phrase-based SMT with the syllable-based segmentation achieve the highest performance for translation of MSL $\rightarrow$ MWL and MWL $\rightarrow$ MSL, respectively. The same authors explore NMT approaches and four different segmentation schemes (Moe et al., 2018b). The model based on Transformer (Vaswani et al., 2017) outperforms the Convolutional Neural Network and Recurrent Neural Network in their experiments. They also investigate the utility of unsupervised neural machine translation (U-NMT) on low-resource language pairs, specifically MSL and MWL (Moe et al., 2020). Several monolingual corpora are used and compared for training the NMT model. The highest BLEU score is obtained when the myPOS corpus (Hlaing et al., 2022) is used.

3 Myanmar Sign Language

This section briefly introduces the characteristics of MSL, which is the primary communication language for deaf people in Myanmar. To convey meaning, there are two types of features: manual features and non-manual features. The manual features can be categorized into three types: hand shape, hand location, and orientation, which represent words and concepts. To convey additional meanings, MSL also incorporates non-manual features such as movements of the head, eyes, eyebrows, mouth, shoulders, and facial expressions. The facial expressions represent questions, negation, relative clauses, boundaries between sentences, and the argument structure of some verbs. For example, MSL uses non-manual marking, similar to American Sign Language (ASL), to convey yes-or-no questions. That is done by raising the eyebrows and moving the head forward (Boundreault and Mayberry, 2006).

MSL is a natural language with a diverse variety of linguistic features such as grammar, vocabulary, word order, and so on. Such linguistic features are distinct from those of the written language of Myanmar. The Myanmar language is tonal and syllable-based, whereas MSL relies on visual-spatial elements to convey meaning. Additionally, the grammar of MSL and MWL is different. For instance, the grammatical structures of the sentence "Do you travel often?" of MSL and MWL are shown in Figure 1. The word order of MWL is "you," "travel," "often," and "go" followed by the question mark. In contrast, in MSL, the words "often" and "go" are switched reflecting the visual-spatial nature of the sign language. In addition, the question mark is omitted from the word sequence and indicated by a non-manual gesture. That is, they raise their eyebrows to indicate that the sentence is a question.

This study focuses on translating word sequences from MSL to MWL and vice versa. Sentences in MSL are conveyed using glosses, which serve as textual representations of signs. As such, this endeavor can be categorized as a text-to-text translation task, akin to conventional machine translation tasks. Our research may pave the way for a comprehensive system that facilitates seamless conversion between MSL and MWL. However, it's worth noting that while our current approach can convert an MSL gloss into a sign or gesture, it doesn't account for non-manual features – only the manual features represented by words are considered. Expanding the translation process to encompass both manual and non-manual features of MSL remains a challenge for future endeavors.

4 Proposed Method

This section describes our proposed method for translation between Myanmar sign and written languages. We use Multilingual Pre-trained Text-to-Text Transfer Transformer (mT5) (Xue et al., 2021) as a base translation system, which is multilingual extension of the Text-to-Text Transfer Transformer (T5) (Raffel et al., 2020). Figure 2 shows a flowchart to train our MT model. Our method consists of two basic methodologies. The first is transfer learning. Firstly, the parent MT model is obtained by fine-tuning the mT5 model using a parallel corpus of high-resource languages, ASL and English. Then the child MT model is trained by fine-tuning the parent model using a relatively small amount of a parallel corpus of the source and target languages. The other basic method is self-training. A new parallel corpus of MSL and MWL is obtained by translating sentences in a monolingual corpus using the initial child MT model. The final MT model is obtained by fine-tuning the parent MT model using the enlarged parallel corpus.

4.1 Preprocessing

For preprocessing, sentences in MSL and MWL are segmented into a sequence of tokens. In this study, the following three segmentation schemes are used to split both MSL and MWL sentences and compared in the experiments.

Word-based Segmentation A sentence is divided into a word sequence by using spaces. In this study, we manually segment the sentences of MWL using the word-based segmentation rules defined in the previous work (Win et al., 2015). For MSL sentences, segmentation is also manually carried out based on the meaningful MSL word units.

Syllable-based Segmentation Myanmar words consist of multiple syllables that usually comprise two or more characters. These syllables are also considered as the basic units for pronouncing Myanmar words. To effectively segment Myanmar syllables, rule-based approaches such as a context-free grammar (Tin, 2012) or regular expressions (RE) can be used. We use the RE-based Myanmar syllable segmentation tool called sylbreak.[2] By syllable-based segmentation, the pronunciation of Myanmar words can be accurately represented and effectively used in the machine learning process.

[2]https://github.com/ye-kyaw-thu/sylbreak

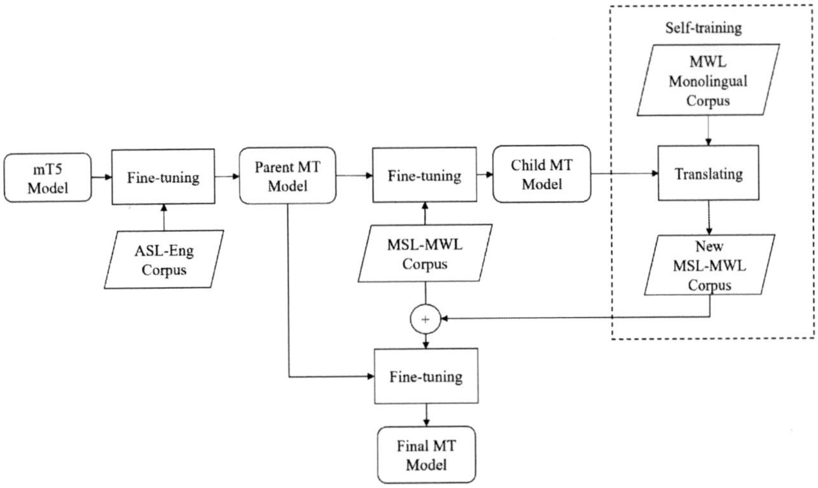

Figure 2: Overview of Proposed Method.

Byte-pair Encoding (BPE)-based Segmentation BPE is a method to segment a sentence into subword units. It is particularly effective for handling out-of-vocabulary words, which are words that are not present in the training data. Since BPE builds up a subword vocabulary by merging the most frequently occurring characters, it can handle rare or unknown words by representing them as a combination of common subword units (Sennrich et al., 2016). This study builds the BPE model for segmentation using the subword Neural Machine Translation (subword-nmt)[3] library from the large monolingual corpus of MWL, myPOS corpus, of which the details are described in 5.1.3.

Although the mT5 model has its own tokenizer, in our method, the sentences are split into words, syllables, or BPE by a space and fed into the mT5 model. They are re-tokenized by the mT5 model.

4.2 Transfer Learning

Two methods of transfer learning are applied. The first one is to transfer the knowledge obtained from the general pre-trained language model to the task-specific model. Specifically, we use the pre-trained mT5 model, which is applicable to any text-to-text task, for various languages. Among the available five pre-trained mT5 models with different sizes, we choose mT5-Base, which has 580 million parameters.[4] This model is fine-tuned for MT using several parallel corpora.

Another method of transfer learning is a two-step fine-tuning of the mT5 model. First, the parallel corpus of ASL and English is used for fine-tuning the parent MT model. Although the source and target languages are not the Myanmar languages, a relatively large amount of parallel corpus is available. Furthermore, it is supposed that the characteristics of translating between ASL and English and that between MSL and MWL are similar. In other words, the parent MT model can capture some general knowledge about the translation between sign and written languages. Next, the parent MT model is fine-tuned again using a parallel corpus of

[3]https://github.com/rsennrich/subword-nmt
[4]https://github.com/google-research/multilingual-t5

Table 1: Statistics of the Datasets.

	Parallel				Mono	Parallel*
	ASL–Eng		MSL–MWL		MWL	MSL–MWL
	Training	Test	Training	Test		
Sentence	85,710	2,000	2,836	300	43,196	10,000
Word	2,131,033	50,072	36,164	3,999	537,272	92,336
Character	11,828,933	278,499	472,044	51,905	7,534,916	1,085,076

* automatically constructed by self-training.

MSL and MWL to obtain the child MT model. The knowledge in the parent MT model is transferred to the child MT model, which can compensate for the sparseness of the data of any Myanmar parallel corpus.

4.3 Self-Training

A semi-supervised learning approach is applied to improve the MT model between MSL and MWL. We suppose that a small amount of an initial parallel corpus and a large amount of monolingual MWL corpus is available. First, the MT model is trained by transfer learning using the initial parallel corpus as well as the ASL-English parallel corpus. Then, the sentences in the monolingual corpus are translated into MSL sentences using the trained MT model. The pairs of the original and translated sentences form a new parallel corpus. Although it is common to synthesize parallel sentences by back-translation from a parallel corpus, our method generates new samples from a monolingual corpus.

The translated sentences are not always correct, especially when the original sentence is long. To improve the quality of the automatically constructed parallel corpus, unreliable translations are filtered out. To do this, the score of the translated sentence s is calculated using Equation (1),

$$score(s) = \log P(s) \simeq \sum_{w_i \in s} \log P_{mT5}(w_i), \quad (1)$$

where w_i is the i-th token in s and $P(s)$ is the probability of generating s, while $P_{mT5}(w_i)$ is the probability of generating w_i estimated by the fine-tuned mT5 model. Specifically, at each generation step in the decoder, the distribution of the logits of the mT5 model for all tokens in the vocabulary is converted to the probabilistic distribution by the softmax function. The top N translations with the highest scores are kept to make the new parallel corpus.[5]

5 Experiment

5.1 Dataset

Three datasets or corpora are used for the experiment. The number of sentences, words and characters of the datasets are summarized in Table 1.

5.1.1 Parallel Corpus of English

The English–ASL Gloss Parallel Corpus 2012 (ASLG-PC12) has been used for training the parent MT model. Due to the absence of a large parallel corpus of sign and written languages in this field, Othman and Tmar (2013) proposed a novel rule-based approach that transformed English part-of-speech (POS) tagged sentences into ASL glosses. This ASLG-PC12 project provided a large parallel corpus consisting of more than one hundred million pairs of sentences

[5]Note that shorter sentences tend to have higher scores and are more likely chosen.

between English and ASL. It includes both manual and non-manual features, where non-manual features are represented by special tokens. The aslg_pc12 dataset[6], which is a part of ASLG-PC12, is used in this experiment. For training the parent model, 85,710 sentences were used as the training data, and 2,000 sentences were used as the test data. Note that the size of the parallel corpus is much larger than the parallel corpus of MSL and MWL reported in 5.1.2.

5.1.2 Parallel Corpus of Myanmar Language

There is only one parallel corpus of MSL and MWL, which was collected from 30 sign language trainers and deaf people. There are 3,136 parallel sentences, from basic conversations in daily life. For our experiment, 2,836 sentences are used for training and 300 for evaluation.

5.1.3 Monolingual Corpus of Myanmar Language

The myPOS corpus[7] was used for self-training. This corpus, also known as the Myanmar POS Tag Corpus, consists of 43,196 sentences that have been manually word-segmented and POS-tagged for the purpose of NLP research and development (Hlaing et al., 2022). The initial child MT model with the word-based segmentation scheme was used to translate the sentences in the myPOS corpus to MSL. In this experiment, the 10,000 sentences that have the highest scores are selected. When training the MT model with the syllable-based and BPE-based segmentation strategies, the sentences in the newly constructed parallel corpus, which are segmented by words, are automatically segmented again by the same strategy.

5.2 Experimental Setup

The MT models for both directions, i.e., the models translating from MSL to MWL as well as from MWL to MSL, are trained. Furthermore, several MT models are trained and compared. First, three segmentation schemes (word, syllable, BPE) are used. Second, the models trained with and without transfer learning are compared. Third, the models trained with and without the enlarged parallel corpus obtained by self-training are evaluated.

Two evaluation criteria are used. One is the Bilingual Evaluation Understudy (BLEU) score (Papineni et al., 2002). The bleukit-NTCIR7 Scoring tools[8] is used to calculate the BLEU score. Here, BLEU is measured by counting the overlap of character n-gram to compare MT systems using different segmentation schemes. That is, regardless of the segmentation schemes, the hypothesis and reference sentences are treated as character sequences when BLEU is measured. The other is the Word Error Rate (WER), which is defined by

$$WER = \frac{S + D + I}{N} \tag{2}$$

where S, D, and I are the number of substitution, deletion, and insertion errors calculated by the alignment between hypothesis and reference sentences, while N is the total number of tokens in the reference. We used the SCLITE[9] (Score Lite) program to get WER.

As already described, the mT5 Base model was utilized as the pre-trained language model. During its fine-tuning, the batch size was set to 20 sentences, and the maximum sequence length was set to 96 tokens so as to handle reasonably long texts. We chose eight hidden layers and six head attention layers, with a hidden layer size of 512. The dropout rate was set to 0.1. The training epochs for the child MT models were set to 500. The number of epochs for training the parent MT model was 10. Servers with NVIDIA A40 and A100 GPUs were used for this experiment.

[6]https://huggingface.co/datasets/aslg

[7]https://github.com/ye-kyaw-thu/myPOS

[8]http://www.nlp.mibel.cs.tsukuba.ac.jp/bleu_kit/

[9]https://github.com/usnistgov/SCTK

Table 2: BLEU Scores and WER of MT Models.

(a) BLEU score (↑)

Model	MSL→MWL			MWL→MSL		
	word	syllable	BPE	word	syllable	BPE
mT5	47.77 [43.95,50.70]	50.67 [46.14,54.06]	46.30 [43.26,50.11]	52.79 [48.80,55.94]	51.23 [47.51,54.44]	49.62 [45.56,53.00]
mT5+T	49.62 [45.83,52.58]	51.29 [41.89,54.77]	46.42 [43.29,49.11]	52.01 [47.46,55.22]	56.29 [51.80,59.03]	50.73 [40.77,54.58]
mT5+S	50.19 [45.99,54.27]	52.26 [48.60,55.89]	48.00 [44.47,50.25]	49.40 [45.96,52.54]	55.93 [52.31,59.37]	49.61 [45.94,52.96]
mT5+T+S	51.65 [47.71,55.29]	**56.60** [52.72,59.76]	53.48 [49.98,56.91]	56.53 [52.92,59.84]	**57.11** [52.61,60.62]	51.02 [47.79,52.54]

(b) WER(%) (↓)

Model	MSL→MWL			MWL→MSL		
	word	syllable	BPE	word	syllable	BPE
mT5	53.5	50.3	52.8	57.4	51.8	51.2
mT5+T	53.1	49.2	51.6	56.5	48.3	52.6
mT5+S	53.9	49.7	51.2	55.9	47.9	50.8
mT5+T+S	51.1	**48.2**	50.4	55.2	**46.5**	49.2

5.3 Results and Discussion

Table 2 (a) shows the BLEU scores with confidence interval values at the significant level of 0.95 of the different MT models. The suffix "+T" in the model name indicates that the MT model is trained by transfer learning with the ASL–English parent MT model. The suffix "+S" indicates that self-training is applied to enlarge the parallel corpus of MSL and MWL. Boldface indicates the best result among the 4 models × 3 segmentation schemes = 12 MT models.

Among the three segmentation schemes, syllable-based segmentation performs better than the others. The syllable, which represents the pronunciation of a word, might be an appropriate linguistic unit for the translation between MSL and MWL.

Comparing the models mT5 and mT5+T, the use of the parent MT model can improve the BLEU score in most cases. An improvement of 0.62 points in MSL → MWL and 5.06 points in MWL → MSL with the syllable-based segmentation is found. Transfer learning using the ASL–English parallel corpus is especially effective for translating from written to sign languages. In addition, the quality of the parent MT model has been evaluated. The BLEU scores of the translation of ASL → English and English → ASL are 85.46 and 98.20 respectively, which are sufficiently high for transfer learning.

Comparing models mT5 and mT5+S, self-training can also boost the BLEU score. The maximum improvement is 4.7 points of the MT model for MWL → MSL with the syllable-based segmentation. Self-training is more effective than transfer learning for the translation from MSL to MWL since the BLEU score of mT5+S is better than mT5+T. As for the translation from MWL to MSL, however, transfer learning can improve the performance more as mT5+T is better than mT5+S. Anyway, the contributions of transfer learning and self-training seem comparable, since no significant difference is found between the BLEU scores of mT5+T and mT5+S.

Combining transfer learning and self-training can further boost MT performance since the model mT5+T+S achieves the best BLEU score for all segmentation schemes and translation directions. The highest BLEU scores are 56.60 and 57.11 for MSL → MWL and MWL → MSL, which are 5.93 and 5.88 points higher than the baseline (the model mT5).

Table 3: Rough Comparison of BLEU Score Between Previous Work and This Study.

Method		MSL→MWL	MWL→MSL
mT5+T+S	syllable	37.83	39.97
(Moe et al., 2018a)	Supervised, SMT	34.78	35.11
(Moe et al., 2018b)	Supervised, NMT	38.21	32.92
(Moe et al., 2020)	Unsupervised, NMT	10.47	29.53

Table 2 (b) shows the WER of the MT models. The lowest WER is obtained by mT5+T+S with the syllable segmentation scheme. However, since nearly half of the words in translated sentences are errors, there is much room to improve the translation quality. As for the comparison of the models, the results of WER are similar to BLEU, that is, (1) the syllable segmentation is the best, (2) both transfer learning and self-training are effective, and (3) the contributions of those two techniques are comparable.

Table 3 shows the best BLEU scores reported in the previous papers for comparison with our model (mT5+T+S). BLEU score of our method is measured between the hypothesis and reference sentences that are sequences of not characters but syllables, since the previous papers mostly achieved the best results using the syllable segmentation scheme. It is confirmed that the performance of our method is better than or comparable to three previous studies. Note that it is not a fair comparison since the datasets used for the evaluation are different.

5.4 Error Analysis

We investigate the errors of the model mT5+T+S for translating from MSL to MWL with the syllable segmentation scheme. In the calculation of WER, three types of errors are considered: a substitution error S (tokens in the reference and output of the MT model are different), a deletion error D (a token in the reference is omitted in the output) and an insertion error I (an extra token is added to the output). The ratios of these errors to the total number of the tokens in the reference are shown in Table 4.

Table 4: Word Error Ratio of Each Type of Error

S (Substitution)	D (Deletion)	I (Insertion)
20.5%	22.8%	4.9%

The most frequent error is a deletion error. This indicates that the word order or grammatical structure is wrong. Example E1 in Figure 3 shows an example of deletion and insertion errors, as well as substitution errors. However, for the purpose of this discussion, we will primarily focus on the deletion and insertion errors. The word "they" is generated as the first word, even though it is the sixth word in the reference. The translation of this example highlights the inability of the model to capture the difference in the grammatical structure between MSL and MWL.

Substitution errors are also often found. This means that the word order is correct, but the word selection is inappropriate. In Example E2, the word "she" in the reference is replaced with "he," causing an inconsistency in the gender with "girl." Besides, some of the substitution errors are not problematic. In Example E3, the Myanmar word "you$_1$" is replaced with the other word "you$_2$." Both words have almost the same meaning but are used in different situations. Specifically, "you$_1$" is used in a business conversation and is never used to talk with family, whereas "you$_2$" is an informal word. Thus, the output is acceptable, although it is different from the reference.

E1:	Input:	သူ တို့ (they) နောက် (next) ရာ သီ (weather) နွေ (summer) လက် ထပ် (marry) ။ (end word)
	Output:	**သူ တို့** (they) က (preposition) နွေ (summer) ရာ သီ (weather) မှာ (PPM-TIME$_1$) လက် ထပ် (marry) တယ် (PPM-FUTURE) ။ (end word)
	Reference:	နောက် (next) လာ မယ့် (coming) နွေ (summer) ရာ သီ (weather) ဆို (PPM-TIME$_2$) **သူ တို့** (they) လက် ထပ် (marry) တော့ မှာ (PPM-PAST) ။ (end word)
	English:	They will get married next summer.
E2:	Input:	ဟင့် အင်း (no) အ ပျို (single girl) ။ (end word)
	Output:	ဟင့် အင်း (no) **ကျွန် တော်** (he) အ ပျို (single girl) ပါ (am) ။ (end word)
	Reference:	ဟင့် အင်း (no) **ကျွန် မ** (she) အ ပျို (single girl) ပါ (am) ။ (end word)
	English:	No, I am a single girl.
E3:	Input:	ခင် ဗျား (you$_1$) လက် (hand) လှုပ် (move) ရ (can) လား (?) ။ (end word)
	Output:	**မင်း** (you$_2$) လက် (hand) လှုပ် (move) တတ် (can) လား (can ?) ။ (end word)
	Reference:	**ခင် ဗျား** (you$_1$) လက်(hand) လှုပ် (move) လို့ ရ (can) သေး (still) လား (?) ။ (end word)
	English:	Can you move your hand?

PPM: Post-Positional Marker

Figure 3: Example of Errors in Translation from MSL to MWL.

6 Conclusion

This paper proposed a novel method to train a machine translation (MT) model for translating between Myanmar Sign Language (MSL) and Myanmar Written Language (MWL). To tackle the problem posed by the fact that MSL is an extremely low-resource language, an mT5 pre-trained model was used as the backbone, and then transfer learning and self-training were applied to improve the quality of the MT system. The contribution of this paper is summarized as follows.

- Transfer learning was first applied for the translation between MSL and MWL. The data of the high-resource language, i.e., the parallel corpus of American Sign Language (ASL) and English, was used to train the parent MT model, and then the knowledge in it was transferred to the child MT model for MSL and MWL.

- Self-training was additionally used to extend the parallel corpus of MSL and MWL that was used for training the child MT model.

- Via the experiments, it was empirically confirmed that both transfer learning and self-training contributed to improving the translation in both directions (MSL $\rightarrow$ MWL and MWL $\rightarrow$ MSL).

In the near future, we will extend our method for the translation of MSL to include both manual and non-manual features. We will also evaluate our MT model from the practical point of view when it is applied for downstream tasks such as cross-lingual information extraction.

References

Boundreault, P. and Mayberry, R. I. (2006). Grammatical processing in American Sign Language: Age of first-language acquisition effects in relation to syntactic structure. *Language and Cognitive Processes*, 21(5):608–635.

Dabre, R., Nakagawa, T., and Kazawa, H. (2017). An empirical study of language relatedness for transfer learning in neural machine translation. In *Proceedings of the 31st Pacific Asia Conference on Language, Information and Computation*, pages 282–286. The National University (Philipines).

Hlaing, Z. Z., Thu, Y. K., Supnithi, T., and Netisopakul, P. (2022). Improving neural machine translation with POS-tag features for low-resource language pairs. *Heliyon Journal*, 8(8).

Kocmi, T. and Bojar, O. (2018). Trivial transfer learning for low-resource neural machine translation. In *Proceedings of the Third Conference on Machine Translation: Research Papers*, pages 244–252, Brussels, Belgium.

Maimaiti, M., Liu, Y., Luan, H., and Sun, M. (2022). Enriching the transfer learning with pre-trained lexicon embedding for low-resource neural machine translation. *Tsinghua Science and Technology*, 27(1):150–163.

Moe, S. Z., Thu, Y. K., Hlaing, H. W. W., Nwe, H. M., Aung, N. H., Thant, H. A., and Min, N. W. (2018a). Statistical machine translation between Myanmar sign language and Myanmar written text. In *16th International Conference on Computer Applications*, Yangon, Myanmar.

Moe, S. Z., Thu, Y. K., Thant, H. A., and Min, N. W. (2018b). Neural machine translation between Myanmar sign language and Myanmar written text. In *The Second Regional Conference on Optical Character Recognition and Natural Language Processing Technologies for ASEAN Languages 2018 (ONA 2018)*, Phnom Penh, Cambodia.

Moe, S. Z., Thu, Y. K., Thant, H. A., Min, N. W., and Supnithi, T. (2020). Unsupervised neural machine translation between Myanmar sign language and Myanmar language. *Journal of Intelligent Informatics and Smart Technology*, 1(1):53–61.

Othman, A. and Tmar, Z. (2013). English–ASL gloss parallel corpus 2012: ASLG-PC12, the second release. In *Fourth International Conference On Information and Communication Technology and Accessibility ICTA13*, Hammamet, Tunisia.

Papineni, K., Roukos, S., Ward, T., and Zhu, W.-J. (2002). BLEU: a method for automatic evaluation of machine translation. In *Proceedings of the 40th Annual Meeting of the Association for Computational Linguistics*, pages 311–318, Philadelphia, PA, USA.

Raffel, C., Shazeer, N., Roberts, A., Lee, K., Narang, S., Matena, M., Zhou, Y., Li, W., and Liu, P. J. (2020). Exploring the Limits of Transfer Learning with a Unified Text-to-Text Transformer. *Journal of Machine Learning Research*, 21(140):1–67.

Sennrich, R., Haddow, B., and Birch, A. (2016). Neural machine translation of rare words with subword units. In *Proceedings of the 54th Annual Meeting of the Association for Computational Linguistics (Volume 1: Long Papers)*, pages 1715–1725, Berlin, Germany.

Swe, D. Y. Y. (2010). *Myanmar Sign Language Basic Conversation Book.* Ministry of Social Welfare, Relief and Resettlement, Department of Social Welfare, Japan International Cooperation Agency.

Tin, H. H. (2012). Manually constructed context-free grammar for Myanmar syllable structure. In *Proceedings of the Student Research Workshop at the 13th Conference of the European Chapter of the Association for Computational Linguistics (EACL12), Association for Computational Linguistics*, pages 32–37, Stroudsburg, PA, USA.

Vaswani, A., Shazeer, N., Parmar, N., Uszkoreit, J., Jones, L., Gomez, A. N., Kaiser, L., and Polosukhin, I. (2017). Attention is all you need. In *Proceedings of the Advances in Neural Information Processing Systems*, page 5998–6008, Long Beach, CA, USA.

Win, P. P., Ye, K. T., Finch, A., and Sumita, E. (2015). Word boundary identification for Myanmar text using conditional random fields. In *Proceedings of the Ninth International Conference on Genetic and Evolutionary Computing*, pages 447–456, Long Beach, CA, USA.

Xue, L., Constant, N., Roberts, A., Kale, M., Al-Rfou, R., Siddhant, A., Barua, A., and Raffel, C. (2021). mT5: A massively multilingual pre-trained text-to-text transformer. In *Proceedings of the 2021 Conference of the North American Chapter of the Association for Computational Linguistics: Human Language Technologies*, pages 483–498. Association for Computational Linguistics.

Zoph, B., Yuret, D., May, J., and Knight, K. (2016). Transfer learning for low-resource neural machine translation. In *Proceedings of the 2016 Conference on Empirical Methods in Natural Language Processing*, pages 1568–1575, Austin, TX, USA. Association for Computational Linguistics.

Improving Embedding Transfer for Low-Resource Machine Translation

Van-Hien Tran tran.vanhien@nict.go.jp
Chenchen Ding chenchen.ding@nict.go.jp
Hideki Tanaka hideki.tanaka@nict.go.jp
Masao Utiyama mutiyama@nict.go.jp
National Institute of Information and Communications Technology,
3-5 Hikaridai, Seika-cho, Soraku-gun, Kyoto, 619-0289, Japan

Abstract

Low-resource machine translation (LRMT) poses a substantial challenge due to the scarcity of parallel training data. This paper introduces a new method to improve the transfer of the embedding layer from the Parent model to the Child model in LRMT, utilizing trained token embeddings in the Parent model's high-resource vocabulary. Our approach involves projecting all tokens into a shared semantic space and measuring the semantic similarity between tokens in the low-resource and high-resource languages. These measures are then utilized to initialize token representations in the Child model's low-resource vocabulary. We evaluated our approach on three benchmark datasets of low-resource language pairs: Myanmar-English, Indonesian-English, and Turkish-English. The experimental results demonstrate that our method outperforms previous methods regarding translation quality. Additionally, our approach is computationally efficient, leading to reduced training time compared to prior works.

1 Introduction

Neural machine translation (NMT) systems have revolutionized the field of natural language processing (NLP), offering remarkable performance gains. Extensive studies (Sutskever et al., 2014; Bahdanau et al., 2015; Vaswani et al., 2017) have consistently demonstrated that NMT systems trained on substantial parallel corpora yield exceptional results. However, low-resource machine translation (LRMT) remains a significant obstacle in the NLP domain. The need for more training data presents a formidable hurdle in training accurate and robust machine translation systems, particularly for languages with limited resources. Unfortunately, many languages fall into this category and require increased availability of parallel corpora for practical machine translation training. As a result, researchers have dedicated their efforts to developing innovative methods to enhance machine translation quality for low-resource languages.

The challenge of LRMT has sparked considerable research interest in recent years (Aji et al., 2020; Xu and Hong, 2022; Li et al., 2022), leading to innovative approaches to tackle the issue. Transfer learning, unsupervised learning, and active learning techniques are some of the methods that have been explored, all showing promising results in enhancing translation quality for low-resource languages. In particular, transfer learning has emerged as a highly effective and straightforward approach for the LRMT task. It has significantly improved translation model performance by leveraging pre-trained high-resource language models. In essence,

Proceedings of Machine Translation Summit XIX, Vol. 1: Research Track, pages 123–134
September 4–8, 2023, Macau SAR, China.

this approach involves transferring knowledge from a high-resource parent model to a low-resource child model, resulting in a remarkable enhancement in the latter's efficacy. Overall, transfer learning is a highly efficacious and practical technique that holds immense potential in improving machine translation for low-resource languages.

The Parent-Child transfer learning framework, initially introduced by Zoph et al. (2016), has been a vital breakthrough in improving the LRMT task. Several studies have optimized the technique's effectiveness by transferring additional information from the parent model's embedding layer through different means. For instance, Kocmi and Bojar (2018) and Gheini and May (2019) proposed using a shared vocabulary, while Kim et al. (2019) suggested a cross-lingual token mapping method. Aji et al. (2020) emphasized the importance of aligning the vocabulary before embedding transfer, which led to notable improvements. Recently, Xu and Hong (2022) have taken this work a step further by duplicating aligned sub-word embeddings, improving transferable Parent-Child NMT. These techniques have improved the transfer learning effect and enhanced the LRMT task's performance.

This study introduces a new method to enhance the parent-child transfer framework by transferring the embedding layer from the parent to child models. The previous work by Aji et al. (2020) only partially transferred word embeddings from the parent model for words with identical forms. Meanwhile, Xu and Hong (2022) used both aligned multilingual and morphologically-identical sub-words for embedding transfer, which may lead to inconsistencies. Our new approach overcomes the existing limitations in earlier works (Aji et al., 2020; Xu and Hong, 2022) and tends to optimize the embedding transfer process. Specifically, it involves projecting tokens from parent and child models into a shared semantic space, then computing their semantic similarity measure. This way, each token in the embedding layer of the child model can be represented using the relevant pre-trained embeddings of the related tokens in the parent model, leading to enhanced embedding transfer accuracy.

We validated our approach by conducting comprehensive experiments on three benchmark datasets, Myanmar-English, Indonesian-English, and Turkish-English. The results from the experiments showed that our approach not only outperformed the existing state-of-the-art methods but also reduced the training effort, thus proving its effectiveness and efficiency. In short, our contributions revolve around two key points: introducing a new approach to transferring token embeddings from the Parent to Child model by measuring their semantic similarity within the same semantic space and validating its effectiveness and efficiency through meticulous experiments on benchmark datasets.

2 Related Work

Transfer learning has been proven effective for NMT under low-resource conditions. Zoph et al. (2016) pioneered the transferable Parent-Child framework, significantly improving BLEU scores across various low-resource languages. Their method involved training a high-resource language pair as a parent model and using the trained weights to initialize a child model. The Child model was then trained on a limited parallel corpus of a low-resource language pair. However, this approach overlooked a significant challenge: the vocabulary mismatch between parent and child models. Subsequent research endeavors have tackled this challenge with determination and perseverance.

Kocmi and Bojar (2018) advocated for using a shared vocabulary between Parent and Child models, as it has proven advantageous. However, it comes with a catch: the Parent model needs prior knowledge of the Child's language during training. This can be limiting and may only sometimes be feasible. To overcome this obstacle, Gheini and May (2019) proposed a universal vocabulary strategy for transfer learning. This approach involves simultaneously training sub-word tokens across multiple languages and using Romanisation for languages with non-Latin scripts. While this method is promising, it may only work for some languages in real-world scenarios. Additionally, it could result in overly aggressive and sub-optimal subword segmentation for unseen languages.

In another direction, several studies (Kim et al., 2018; Lample et al., 2018; Artetxe et al., 2018; Kim et al., 2019) have utilized bilingual word embedding alignment as an approach to initialize the embedding layer. Kim et al. (2018) proposed a simple yet effective method that improves word-by-word translation of cross-lingual embeddings using only monolingual corpora without resorting to back-translation. Lample et al. (2018), on the other hand, utilized careful parameter initialization, denoising effects of language models, and automatic generation of parallel data through iterative back-translation. Kim et al. (2019) demonstrated effective techniques for transferring a pre-trained NMT model to a new, unrelated language that lacks shared vocabularies. Their approach involved mitigating vocabulary mismatches through cross-lingual word embeddings, training a more language-agnostic encoder through artificial noise injection, and generating synthetic data from pretraining data without back-translation.

Recently, Aji et al. (2020) conducted a study to investigate the effects of various strategies for transferring token embeddings between Parent and Child models. The study found that aligning the vocabulary before transferring the embeddings is essential for practical performance improvements. However, their approach only involved partial token matching, where morphologically-identical tokens were duplicated embeddings while the rest were randomly assigned embeddings. Subsequently, Xu and Hong (2022) attempted to address this limitation by copying token embeddings among aligned multilingual tokens, enabling the transfer of embeddings for morphologically-identical and elaborately-aligned tokens. However, duplicating embeddings for the same token across different languages may only sometimes be appropriate as it could result in different meanings (Vernikos and Popescu-Belis, 2021). Furthermore, using distinct techniques to transfer embeddings for morphologically-similar and morphologically-dissimilar token types may lead to inconsistency.

Therefore, this paper presents a unified and comprehensive approach to transfer embeddings by projecting all tokens in the same semantic space and considering their relationships. By doing so, we can overcome the existing limitations of previous approaches and ensure consistency in transferring embeddings for morphologically-similar and morphologically-dissimilar token types.

3 Our Approach

3.1 Basic Parent-Child Transfer Framework

Following the research conducted by Aji et al. (2020) and Xu and Hong (2022), we also construct NMT models utilizing the 12-layer base transformer architecture proposed by Vaswani et al. (2017). As elucidated by Vaswani et al. (2017), this architecture composes the first six layers in the encoder and the subsequent six layers in the decoder, forming a total of 12 layers. The encoder is often coupled with a trainable embedding layer, which retains a fixed bilingual vocabulary and trainable subword embeddings. Also, each embedding is designated as a 512-dimensional real-valued vector.

Taking inspiration from the pioneering work of Zoph et al. (2016), we conduct Parent-Child transfer learning. For the Parent model, we have selected an off-the-self transformer-based NMT model[1], similar to the approach taken by Xu and Hong (2022), which was adequately trained on a substantial amount of De→En (German→English) parallel sentence pairs

[1]`https://github.com/Helsinki-NLP/OPUS-MT-train/blob/master/models/de-en/README.md`

(approximately 351.7 million pairs) from the OPUS dataset[2] (Tiedemann, 2012). We treat this NMT model as the Parent. Meanwhile, the Child model also uses the 12-layer base transformer architecture like the Parent, and it will be trained on the low-resource X→En language pairs after completing the transfer process. Specifically, we first transfer all inner parameters (non-embedding) of the 12-layer transformers from the Parent to the Child. Toward embedding transfer, it is not straightforward since different languages have distinct vocabularies. Thus, we make an effort to perform the embedding transfer more effectively.

3.2 Embedding Transfer

Let V_h denote the high-resource bilingual vocabulary (e.g., the aforementioned De-En) in the Parent model with the tokenizer T_h and the corresponding token embeddings $\mathbf{E}_h \in \mathbb{R}^{|V_h| \times d}$. Specifically, $\mathbf{E}_h$ maps each token v in the vocabulary V_h to its vector representation $\boldsymbol{v} \in \mathbb{R}^d$ with the hidden size of d (e.g., $d = 512$).

To handle the low-resource X→En language pair for the Child model, we employ two separate vocabularies for the source language X and the target language English. For the English target language side, we directly reuse the vocabulary V_h and its corresponding token embeddings $\mathbf{E}_h$. However, for the X source language X side, we use a low-resource vocabulary V_l with a tokenizer T_l and corresponding token embeddings $\mathbf{E}_l \in \mathbb{R}^{|V_l| \times d}$. Our primary objective is to initialize the token embeddings $\mathbf{E}_l$ effectively using the trained token embeddings $\mathbf{E}_h$. To achieve this, we follow these steps.

Train Subword Tokenizer Following Xu and Hong (2022), we train a subword tokenizer, denoted as T_l, for the low-resource source language X in the Child model (e.g., X is Myanmar, Indonesian, or Turkish). Specifically, we use the unigram model of SentencePiece[3] to train T_l. We collect monolingual plain texts from Wikipedia dumps[4] and use the toolkit Wikiextractor[5] to extract them from the semi-structured data. The statistics of the training data are presented in Table 1.

X	Doc.	Sent.	Token
Myanmar (My)	113K	1.1M	17.4M
Indonesian (Id)	1.1M	8.3M	156.2M
Turkish (Tr)	705K	5.8M	128.2M

Table 1: Statistics of the monolingual Wikipedia data for each low-resource language X.

We uniformly set the low-resource vocabulary size $|V_l|$ in the Child model to 50K when training the tokenizer T_l. Meanwhile, the size of the mixed De-En high-resource vocabulary $|V_h|$ in the trained Parent NMT model is 58K. For the training and inference phases of the Child model with the low-resource language pair X→En, we use T_l to tokenize only the source language X while T_h to tokenize the target language English.

Obtain Token Representation To accurately measure the semantic similarity between the vocabularies of V_h and V_l, it is crucial to obtain the representation of each token first. This important step allows us to thoroughly analyze and evaluate the tokens in the vocabulary sets, giving us a deeper understanding of their interconnectedness. This understanding then enhances our knowledge of the relationship between the two vocabularies and enables us to unlock their

[2] `https://opus.nlpl.eu`
[3] `https://github.com/google/sentencepiece`
[4] `https://dumps.wikimedia.org/`
[5] `https://github.com/attardi/wikiextractor`

full potential, creating more meaningful connections. Thus, obtaining token representation is a top priority in understanding semantic similarity comprehensively.

Following the work by Vernikos and Popescu-Belis (2021), we obtain token representations in V_l by utilizing the corresponding pre-trained FastText embeddings[6] for the low-resource language X. In particular, regarding tokens that are subwords in V_l, the FastText embeddings of the language X also create the corresponding representations by decomposing each subword into n-grams of characters and taking the average of the embeddings of all occurring these n-grams. It is equivalent to how creating embeddings for out-of-vocabulary words is introduced in FastText (Bojanowski et al., 2017). Similarly, we also obtain token representations in V_h using the pre-trained FastText embeddings for English.

Find A Rotation Matrix After utilizing the static pre-trained FastText embeddings in the previous step, we obtained representation vectors for the tokens in both V_h and V_l. However, it is essential to note that these token embeddings are located in two separate semantic spaces; one for the English language and the other for the X language. To properly analyze their semantic relationship, unifying these token embeddings into a shared semantic space is necessary. To achieve this, we need to find a rotation matrix.

In the quest for accurate estimations of semantic similarities between tokens, the use of optimal rotation matrices can be highly effective. Let $\mathbf{F}_h \in \mathbb{R}^{|V_h| \times 300}$ and $\mathbf{F}_l \in \mathbb{R}^{|V_l| \times 300}$ denote the obtained embedding matrices of the tokens in V_h and V_l by using FastText, respectively, after which we strive to find the optimal rotation matrix $\mathbf{M}$ that transforms $\mathbf{F}_h$ onto $\mathbf{F}_l$. This transformation paves the way for calculating semantic similarities between tokens in the same semantic space.

To achieve this matrix, the first step is to acquire the given train set of the low-resource (X-En) parallel pairs, which we then run through Eflomal[7], a powerful tool that enables us to acquire a bilingual word alignment list. Armed with the obtained X-En alignment list, we proceed to get two corresponding embedding matrices, one containing English word embeddings and the other containing embeddings for words in the X language, using the static pre-trained FastText. Following this, we treat the obtained bilingual alignment list as the supervised signal and leverage the Orthogonal Procrustes method (Schönemann, 1966; Artetxe et al., 2016), a highly effective learning method, to derive the rotation matrix $\mathbf{M}$.

Initialize the Token Embeddings $\mathbf{E}_l$ Using the trained matrix $\mathbf{M}$, we project $\mathbf{F}_h$ to the semantic space of $\mathbf{F}_l$. Through this transformation, we can easily calculate the cosine similarity of each token within V_l to each token in V_h. By doing so, we can establish meaningful connections between these two semantic spaces, allowing for heightened understanding. The cosine similarity between two tokens x and y is defined as follows:

$$sim(x, y) = \frac{\boldsymbol{x}\boldsymbol{y}^T}{\|\boldsymbol{x}\| * \|\boldsymbol{y}\|}$$

, where $\boldsymbol{x}$ and $\boldsymbol{y}$ are the vectors of the tokens $x \in V_l$ and $y \in V_h$, respectively, in the shared semantic space of $\mathbf{F}_l$; $\|\boldsymbol{x}\|$ and $\|\boldsymbol{y}\|$ are the Euclidean norms of the two vectors $\boldsymbol{x}$ and $\boldsymbol{y}$, respectively.

Through the above formulation, we can achieve results by attaining the cosine similarity of every individual token in V_l with all tokens in V_h. These similarities are subsequently ranked in descending order, creating a comprehensive and insightful view of our data. To transform this data into even more valuable insights, we consider two methods for creating embedding vectors for each token x in V_l in $\mathbf{E}_l$.

The first method is called the Top-1 method. For each token $x \in V_l$, we only keep the

[6] `https://fasttext.cc/docs/en/crawl-vectors.html`
[7] `https://github.com/robertostling/eflomal`

single token $y \in V_h$ with the highest cosine similarity to x and duplicate its embedding in $\mathbf{E}_h$ to the token embedding of x in $\mathbf{E}_l$, resulting in a highly effective and intuitive system.

On the other hand, the second method, known as the Softmax method, is equally compelling. For each token $x \in V_l$, we create the corresponding set S_x, including the K nearest tokens of V_h to the given token x. The Softmax function is then applied to these similarity measures, producing a highly weighted token embedding of x in $\mathbf{E}_l$ as follows:

$$\mathbf{E}_l(x) = \sum_{y \in S_x} \frac{\exp\left(sim(x, y)\right)}{\sum_{y' \in S_x} \exp\left(sim(x, y')\right)} \cdot \mathbf{E}_h(y)$$

Once we have acquired the token embeddings $\mathbf{E}_l$ for the Child model's vocabulary, it is time to train the Child model using the provided X-En low-resource parallel train set. Our careful embedding transfer is expected to improve the system's performance and decrease the training time for the model.

4 Experiments

4.1 Datasets and Evaluation Metric

Following the previous work by Xu and Hong (2022), we use the same benchmark datasets and similar experimental settings. Specifically, we evaluate the transferable NMT models for three different source languages, including Myanmar (My), Indonesian (Id), and Turkish (Tr). In addition, English is fixed as the target language.

We use three low-resource parallel datasets for training the Child NMT model, including Asian Language Treebank (ALT) (Ding et al., 2018), PAN Localization BPPT[8], and the corpus of WMT17 news translation task (Bojar et al., 2017). The statistics in the training, validation, and test sets are shown in Table 2. Also, we evaluate all the considered NMT models with SacreBLEU (Post, 2018).

4.2 Experimental Settings

As introduced in Section 3.1, we used an off-the-shelf NMT model as Parent whose state variables (i.e., hyperparameters and transformer parameters) and embedding layer are all set. This Parent NMT model was adequately trained on high-resource De→En (German→English) language pairs.

We adopt the following hyperparameters to transfer the embedding layer and train the Child NMT model. We set K nearest tokens to 15 in the Softmax technique for our embedding transfer method. Also, each source language was tokenized using SentencePiece (Kudo and Richardson, 2018) with a 50K vocabulary size. The training process was carried out with HuggingFace Transformers library (Wolf et al., 2020) using the Adam optimizer with 0.1 weight decay rate. The maximum sentence length was set to 128 and the batch size to 64 sentences.

[8] `http://www.panl10n.net/english/OutputsIndonesia2.htm`

Dataset	**Train.**	**Val.**	**Test**
My-En (ALT)	18K	1K	1K
Id-En (BPPT)	22K	1K	1K
Tr-En (WMT17)	207K	3K	3K

Table 2: Statistics for low-resource parallel datasets.

The learning rate was set to $5e-5$ and checkpoint frequency to 500 updates. For each model, we chose the checkpoint with the lowest perplexity on the validation set for testing.

4.3 Results and Analysis

In this section, we perform extensive experiments and analysis results to evaluate our approach for the low-resource NMT task.

Baseline Models We compare our approach to three previous Parent-Child (PC) transfer NMT models. Our model and all the baseline models duplicate non-embedding parameters from the same Parent model, which we introduced in Section 3.1. However, these models differ in how they transfer the embedding layer. The first baseline Child model is named Random-PC, in which the embedding layer is randomly initialized with a Gaussian distribution. Meanwhile, the second baseline Child model, called MI-PC, uses the embedding transfer method by Aji et al. (2020), which only transfers the embeddings of morphologically-identical tokens. The last baseline Child model, Mean-PC (Xu and Hong, 2022), extends Aji et al. (2020)'s work by leveraging embedding duplication between aligned sub-words.

Main Results Table 3 presents the test results of various PC transfer models on three benchmark datasets, utilizing the SentencePiece tokenizer. From the analysis, it is evident that the Random-PC model performs the worst among all the models. This is because it overlooks the embedding transfer from the Parent model and randomly initializes all token embeddings for the embedding layer. As a result, the Random-PC model fails to comprehend the meaning of low-resource tokens, particularly in the low-resource NMT scenario, where the training set is limited. Therefore, leveraging embedding transfer from the Parent to the Child model is crucial in enabling low-resource models to understand the meaning of tokens and improve translation quality.

Our approach has proven more effective than the Random-PC baseline model, exhibiting a stable increase in the BLEU score across all three benchmark datasets. We significantly improve 3.1 BLEU points on the Id-En set. Additionally, our method surpasses the state-of-the-art work by Xu and Hong (2022) and consistently improves results on all three low-resource datasets. The most notable improvement is observed in the Id-En dataset, with an increase of up to 1.1 BLEU scores. Our approach effectively transfers the embedding layer, enhancing system performance in the LRMT task.

In our approach, we have analyzed and compared two techniques, namely Top-1 and Softmax, which have been discussed in Section 3.2. As shown in Table 3, the Softmax technique brings the best performance, while the remaining technique results in performance degradation. One possible reason is that using a single token for embedding duplication in the Top-1 technique does not express fully and precisely the meaning of each token in the Child model's vocabulary, especially when tokens are subwords in different languages (i.e., between high-resource and low-resource languages). Therefore, aggregating and normalizing embeddings of

Model		My-En	Id-En	Tr-En
Random-PC		20.5	26.0	17.0
MI-PC (Aji et al., 2020)		21.0	27.5	17.6
Mean-PC (Xu and Hong, 2022)		22.5	28.0	18.1
Ours	Top-1	22.1	28.0	18.4
	Softmax	**23.3***	**29.1***	**19.0***

Table 3: Results using **SentencePiece** tokenizer. The symbol * denotes statistically significant ($p < 0.02$) improvement (Koehn, 2004), compared to the Mean-PC model.

Model		My-En	Id-En	Tr-En
Random-PC		20.2	24.5	16.5
MI-PC (Aji et al., 2020)		20.4	24.2	16.8
Mean-PC (Xu and Hong, 2022)		21.9	27.1	16.9
Ours	Top-1	22.4	27.8	18.0
	Softmax	**23.2**†	**28.5**†	**18.2**†

Table 4: Results using **BPE** tokenizer. The symbol † denotes statistically significant ($p < 0.02$) improvement (Koehn, 2004), compared to the Mean-PC model.

the top K nearest tokens via the Softmax technique helps to overcome the existing problem and create token representations more comprehensively and accurately.

We further check the effectiveness of all the PC transfer models when using BPE tokenizer (Sennrich et al., 2016) instead of SentencePiece tokenizer (Kudo and Richardson, 2018). Table 4 shows all models' experimental results. Compared to all remaining models, our approach performs best when using a BPE tokenizer. In particular, compared to the Random-PC baseline model, our model substantially improves the system performance by 3.0, 4.0, and 1.7 BLEU scores on the My-En, Id-En, and Tr-en benchmark datasets, respectively. Additionally, our model outperforms the state-of-the-art work by Xu and Hong (2022) by over 1.0 BLEU scores on all three datasets. In our approach, the Softmax technique performs better than the Top-1 technique when using a BPE tokenizer.

In summary, the experimental findings presented in Tables 3 and 4 provide strong evidence supporting the efficacy of our proposed method for transferring the embedding layer. Our approach demonstrates the potential to effectively enhance system performance in the low-resource NMT task, indicating the effectiveness of our method. Additionally, our findings suggest that the Softmax technique is a more suitable and practical approach for creating an effective embedding layer initialization for the transfer PC model, compared to the Top-1 technique.

Training Time It has been speculated that the initialization of token embeddings through embedding transfer not only enhances the BLEU score of the system but also has the potential to reduce the training time of the Child model. Therefore, we delved into this matter and conducted a comprehensive investigation of the training time for each model. We used mixed precision to train the Child NMT model to achieve optimal results. Furthermore, all experiments were conducted on a single Tesla V100-SXM2-32GB GPU. Our findings are reported in Table 5.

Our model with the Softmax technique consumes less time during the training phase than other models. In particular, in the case of the Tr-En dataset, the training duration is even shortened from 4.51 hours in the Random-PC model to 2.06 hours in our model. Besides, compared to the method by Xu and Hong (2022), the training time of our approach is also competitive or slightly better. These advantages come from avoiding redundant learning over token embed-

Model		My-En	Id-En	Tr-En
Random-PC		1.78	1.50	4.51
MI-PC (Aji et al., 2020)		1.64	1.26	4.35
Mean-PC (Xu and Hong, 2022)		1.09	1.06	2.19
Ours	Top-1	1.05	0.95	2.07
	Softmax	**0.95**	**0.85**	**2.06**

Table 5: The training time (in hour) of the different NMT models on three benchmark datasets.

dings once they are initialized well before starting the training phase.

To sum up, initializing a good embedding layer in the PC transfer models is vital in enhancing the system's effectiveness and efficiency. Our embedding transfer method helps initialize the embedding layer of the Child model productively, thereby improving the BLEU scores as shown in Tables 3 and 4 and decreasing the training time as shown in Table 5.

Impact of the Hyperparameter K As outlined in Section 3.2, our proposed approach utilizing the Softmax technique searches for the top K nearest tokens in the Parent model's vocabulary for each token in the Child model's vocabulary. This process is instrumental in creating the initialization embedding of the given token. It is necessary to understand how the hyperparameter K affects the embedding quality, which has a certain impact on the overall system performance. Therefore, we fine-tune K in [1, 5, 15, 30, 45, 60] to investigate how the value K affects to the quality translation. In the special case of $K = 1$, the Softmax technique becomes the Top-1 technique in our approach. All experimental results on three low-resource benchmark datasets are visually represented in Figure 1.

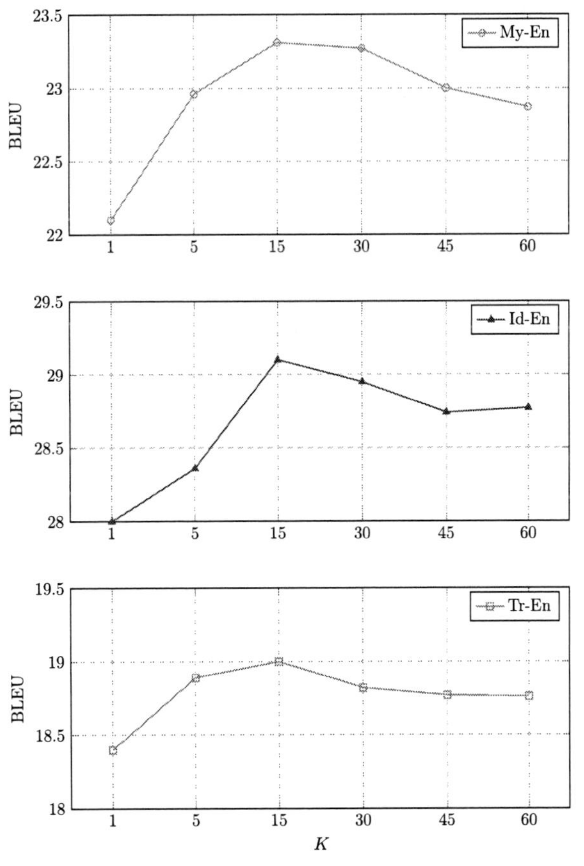

Figure 1: Impact of the Hyperparameter K to the performance of our model on the test set.

The importance of the hyperparameter K cannot be underestimated, as it plays an essential role in our approach to determining the quality of the embedding layer initialization and, ultimately, the overall system performance. The experimental findings demonstrate that a K value of 1 results in the lowest BLEU score across all three benchmark datasets compared to all other cases of $K > 1$. Meanwhile, our model outperforms all others when the K value is set to 15 across all three low-resource datasets. However, the system's performance deteriorates when K exceeds 15. Therefore, selecting the appropriate value of K is necessary for our approach since it affects achieving the most optimal token representation for the embedding layer of the Child model.

5 Conclusion

This paper introduced a new method to improve embedding transfer for the Child model in the LRMT task by leveraging trained token embeddings in the Parent model's high-resource vocabulary. By projecting all tokens of the Child and Parent models into a shared semantic space, it helps easily calculate the semantic similarity measure between tokens, thereby creating high-quality embeddings of the tokens in the Child model's low-resource vocabulary with the Softmax technique. Our approach is then thoroughly evaluated on the three benchmark low-resource datasets: Myanmar-English, Indonesian-English, and Turkish-English. The experimental results indicate that our method yields stable improvements in translation quality on all the datasets. Our approach is also computationally efficient, resulting in a reduction in training time consumption compared to baseline models. In future work, we will continue to enhance the embedding transfer technique since it is vital to improving the LRMT task in terms of effectiveness and efficiency.

References

Aji, A. F., Bogoychev, N., Heafield, K., and Sennrich, R. (2020). In neural machine translation, what does transfer learning transfer? In *Proceedings of the 58th Annual Meeting of the Association for Computational Linguistics*, pages 7701–7710, Online. Association for Computational Linguistics.

Artetxe, M., Labaka, G., and Agirre, E. (2016). Learning principled bilingual mappings of word embeddings while preserving monolingual invariance. In *Proceedings of the 2016 Conference on Empirical Methods in Natural Language Processing*, pages 2289–2294, Austin, Texas. Association for Computational Linguistics.

Artetxe, M., Labaka, G., and Agirre, E. (2018). Unsupervised statistical machine translation. In *Proceedings of the 2018 Conference on Empirical Methods in Natural Language Processing*, pages 3632–3642, Brussels, Belgium. Association for Computational Linguistics.

Bahdanau, D., Cho, K., and Bengio, Y. (2015). Neural machine translation by jointly learning to align and translate. In Bengio, Y. and LeCun, Y., editors, *3rd International Conference on Learning Representations, ICLR 2015, San Diego, CA, USA, May 7-9, 2015, Conference Track Proceedings*.

Bojanowski, P., Grave, E., Joulin, A., and Mikolov, T. (2017). Enriching word vectors with subword information. *Transactions of the Association for Computational Linguistics*, 5:135–146.

Bojar, O., Chatterjee, R., Federmann, C., Graham, Y., Haddow, B., Huang, S., Huck, M., Koehn, P., Liu, Q., Logacheva, V., Monz, C., Negri, M., Post, M., Rubino, R., Specia, L., and Turchi,

M. (2017). Findings of the 2017 conference on machine translation (WMT17). In *Proceedings of the Second Conference on Machine Translation*, pages 169–214, Copenhagen, Denmark. Association for Computational Linguistics.

Ding, C., Utiyama, M., and Sumita, E. (2018). Nova: A feasible and flexible annotation system for joint tokenization and part-of-speech tagging. *ACM Trans. Asian Low-Resour. Lang. Inf. Process.*, 18(2).

Gheini, M. and May, J. (2019). A universal parent model for low-resource neural machine translation transfer. *ArXiv*, abs/1909.06516.

Kim, Y., Gao, Y., and Ney, H. (2019). Effective cross-lingual transfer of neural machine translation models without shared vocabularies. In *Proceedings of the 57th Annual Meeting of the Association for Computational Linguistics*, pages 1246–1257, Florence, Italy. Association for Computational Linguistics.

Kim, Y., Geng, J., and Ney, H. (2018). Improving unsupervised word-by-word translation with language model and denoising autoencoder. In *Proceedings of the 2018 Conference on Empirical Methods in Natural Language Processing*, pages 862–868, Brussels, Belgium. Association for Computational Linguistics.

Kocmi, T. and Bojar, O. (2018). Trivial transfer learning for low-resource neural machine translation. In *Proceedings of the Third Conference on Machine Translation: Research Papers*, pages 244–252, Brussels, Belgium. Association for Computational Linguistics.

Koehn, P. (2004). Statistical significance tests for machine translation evaluation. In *Proceedings of the 2004 Conference on Empirical Methods in Natural Language Processing*, pages 388–395, Barcelona, Spain. Association for Computational Linguistics.

Kudo, T. and Richardson, J. (2018). SentencePiece: A simple and language independent subword tokenizer and detokenizer for neural text processing. In *Proceedings of the 2018 Conference on Empirical Methods in Natural Language Processing: System Demonstrations*, pages 66–71, Brussels, Belgium. Association for Computational Linguistics.

Lample, G., Ott, M., Conneau, A., Denoyer, L., and Ranzato, M. (2018). Phrase-based & neural unsupervised machine translation. In *Proceedings of the 2018 Conference on Empirical Methods in Natural Language Processing*, pages 5039–5049, Brussels, Belgium. Association for Computational Linguistics.

Li, Z., Liu, X., Wong, D. F., Chao, L. S., and Zhang, M. (2022). ConsistTL: Modeling consistency in transfer learning for low-resource neural machine translation. In *Proceedings of the 2022 Conference on Empirical Methods in Natural Language Processing*, pages 8383–8394, Abu Dhabi, United Arab Emirates. Association for Computational Linguistics.

Post, M. (2018). A call for clarity in reporting BLEU scores. In *Proceedings of the Third Conference on Machine Translation: Research Papers*, pages 186–191, Brussels, Belgium. Association for Computational Linguistics.

Schönemann, P. H. (1966). A generalized solution of the orthogonal procrustes problem. *Psychometrika*, 31:1–10.

Sennrich, R., Haddow, B., and Birch, A. (2016). Neural machine translation of rare words with subword units. In *Proceedings of the 54th Annual Meeting of the Association for Computational Linguistics (Volume 1: Long Papers)*, pages 1715–1725, Berlin, Germany. Association for Computational Linguistics.

Sutskever, I., Vinyals, O., and Le, Q. V. (2014). Sequence to sequence learning with neural networks. In Ghahramani, Z., Welling, M., Cortes, C., Lawrence, N., and Weinberger, K., editors, *Advances in Neural Information Processing Systems*, volume 27. Curran Associates, Inc.

Tiedemann, J. (2012). Parallel data, tools and interfaces in opus. In *International Conference on Language Resources and Evaluation*.

Vaswani, A., Shazeer, N., Parmar, N., Uszkoreit, J., Jones, L., Gomez, A. N., Kaiser, L., and Polosukhin, I. (2017). Attention is all you need. In Guyon, I., von Luxburg, U., Bengio, S., Wallach, H. M., Fergus, R., Vishwanathan, S. V. N., and Garnett, R., editors, *Advances in Neural Information Processing Systems 30: Annual Conference on Neural Information Processing Systems 2017, December 4-9, 2017, Long Beach, CA, USA*, pages 5998–6008.

Vernikos, G. and Popescu-Belis, A. (2021). Subword mapping and anchoring across languages. In *Findings of the Association for Computational Linguistics: EMNLP 2021*, pages 2633–2647, Punta Cana, Dominican Republic. Association for Computational Linguistics.

Wolf, T., Debut, L., Sanh, V., Chaumond, J., Delangue, C., Moi, A., Cistac, P., Rault, T., Louf, R., Funtowicz, M., Davison, J., Shleifer, S., von Platen, P., Ma, C., Jernite, Y., Plu, J., Xu, C., Le Scao, T., Gugger, S., Drame, M., Lhoest, Q., and Rush, A. (2020). Transformers: State-of-the-art natural language processing. In *Proceedings of the 2020 Conference on Empirical Methods in Natural Language Processing: System Demonstrations*, pages 38–45, Online. Association for Computational Linguistics.

Xu, M. and Hong, Y. (2022). Sub-word alignment is still useful: A vest-pocket method for enhancing low-resource machine translation. In *Proceedings of the 60th Annual Meeting of the Association for Computational Linguistics (Volume 2: Short Papers)*, pages 613–619, Dublin, Ireland. Association for Computational Linguistics.

Zoph, B., Yuret, D., May, J., and Knight, K. (2016). Transfer learning for low-resource neural machine translation. In *Proceedings of the 2016 Conference on Empirical Methods in Natural Language Processing*, pages 1568–1575, Austin, Texas. Association for Computational Linguistics.

Boosting Unsupervised Machine Translation with Pseudo-Parallel Data

Ivana Kvapilíková kvapilikova@ufal.mff.cuni.cz
Ondřej Bojar bojar@ufal.mff.cuni.cz
Charles University, Faculty of Mathematics and Physics, Institute of Formal and Applied Linguistics, Prague, 118 00, Czechia

Abstract

Even with the latest developments in deep learning and large-scale language modeling, the task of machine translation (MT) of low-resource languages remains a challenge. Neural MT systems can be trained in an unsupervised way without any translation resources but the quality lags behind, especially in truly low-resource conditions. We propose a training strategy that relies on pseudo-parallel sentence pairs mined from monolingual corpora in addition to synthetic sentence pairs back-translated from monolingual corpora. We experiment with different training schedules and reach an improvement of up to 14.5 BLEU points (English to Ukrainian) over a baseline trained on back-translated data only.

1 Introduction

After the great advancements in machine translation (MT) quality brought by neural MT (NMT; Bahdanau et al., 2015; Vaswani et al., 2017) trained on millions of pre-translated sentence pairs, there came a realization that parallel data is expensive and surely not available for most language pairs in the world. Researchers started focusing their attention on methods leveraging monolingual data for machine translation (Sennrich et al., 2016b) and even explored the extreme scenario of training a translation system in a completely unsupervised way with no parallel data at all (Artetxe et al., 2018b; Lample et al., 2018a).

The recent impressive progress in language modeling did not leave the area of machine translation intact. However, the translation capabilities of large language models such as the latest GPT models (Brown et al., 2020) are weak for underrepresented languages (Hendy et al., 2023) and unsupervised MT aimed at low-resource languages still deserves special attention.

There are two ways to approach machine translation trained exclusively on monolingual data. In the absence of parallel texts, the monolingual training sentences can either be coupled with their synthetic counterparts which are automatically generated through back-translation (Artetxe et al., 2018b; Lample et al., 2018a), or with authentic counterparts which are automatically selected from existing monolingual texts to be as close translations as possible (Ruiter et al., 2019). Researchers have successfully explored both of these avenues with the conclusion that it is indeed possible to train a functional MT system on monolingual texts only. However, little attention has been paid to combining the two approaches together.

In this paper, we work with the standard framework for training unsupervised MT but we incorporate an additional training step where sentence pairs mined from monolingual corpora are used to train the model with a standard supervised MT objective. We consider the mined

Proceedings of Machine Translation Summit XIX, Vol. 1: Research Track, pages 135–147
September 4–8, 2023, Macau SAR, China.

sentence pairs as *pseudo-parallel* as they should ideally be identical in meaning but in practice only share a certain degree of similarity. We show that they improve the translation quality nonetheless. We experiment with different training schedules to determine when to incorporate the pseudo-parallel data and when to remove it from the training.

In Section 2, we summarize the related work on the topics of unsupervised MT and parallel corpus mining. In Section 3, we introduce our method, focusing on how we obtain the pseudo-parallel sentences and how we incorporate them into the unsupervised MT training. Section 4 gives the results of our experiments which are discussed in Section 5.

2 Related Work

We separate two lines of work in the area of low-resource MT: unsupervised training on monolingual data where the research focuses on the training techniques (*unsupervised MT*) and supervised training on mined parallel sentences where the research focuses on how to create the training corpus (*parallel corpus mining*).

2.1 Unsupervised MT

Unsupervised MT was first tackled by Artetxe et al. (2018b) and Lample et al. (2018a) who introduced a neural model with shared encoder parameters for both language directions that was capable of translating without being trained on parallel data. The authors relied on pre-trained embeddings to ignite the learning process and then trained the model using denoising (Vincent et al., 2008) and back-translation (Sennrich et al., 2016a). Artetxe et al. (2018a) and Lample et al. (2018a) also explored the possibilities of unsupervised phrase-based MT where the initial phrase table is induced from a cross-lingual embedding space.

A significant improvement in neural models was brought by splitting the training of the entire model into a pre-training phase where the weights are first trained on an auxiliary task aimed at language understanding (e.g. masked language modeling, denoising) and a fine-tuning phase where the model is trained for translation. Conneau and Lample (2019) train a cross-lingual BERT-like (Devlin et al., 2018) language model on the concatenation of the monolingual corpora and copy its weights to initialize the parameters of both the encoder and the decoder. Song et al. (2019) reach slightly better translation quality by pre-training the entire sequence-to-sequence model to reconstruct a missing piece of a sentence given the surrounding tokens.

Liu et al. (2020) explore the benefits of multilingual pre-training of the entire translation model on the task of multilingual denoising (mBART) and reach state-of-the-art results in unsupervised MT. Üstün et al. (2021) extend the pre-trained mBART model with denoising adapters and fine-tune on auxiliary parallel language pairs without the need for back-translation. Garcia et al. (2020, 2021) train a multilingual translation system and combine back-translation from monolingual data with cross-translation of auxiliary parallel data in high-resource language pairs.

Unsupervised MT has been influenced by the latest advancements in large-scale multilingual language modeling (Costa-jussà et al., 2022). The GPT-3 model (Brown et al., 2020) is capable of translation without being trained on an explicit translation objective and its performance increases considerably with one-shot or few-shot fine-tuning. However, its ability to handle low-resource and non-English-centric language pairs lags behind (Hendy et al., 2023).

2.2 Parallel Corpus Mining for MT

Using mined sentence pairs for MT training was heavily explored by Schwenk (2018) and Artetxe and Schwenk (2019b) who introduced LASER, a multilingual sentence encoder that is able to find translation equivalents in 93 languages with high precision. Costa-jussà et al. (2022) extend the approach to cover 200 languages by student-teacher training. However, the training of the teacher model is heavily supervised by millions of parallel sentence pairs and its distillation also requires at least some parallel sentences.

Ruiter et al. (2019) introduce self-supervised translation where the model used for selecting translation examples is the emergent NMT model itself. The authors search for the nearest neighbors in a sentence embedding space extracted from an NMT system and apply a strong filter to only select meaningful candidates for training. Tran et al. (2020) use self-supervised training of a pre-trained multilingual model (mBART) which iteratively selects parallel sentence pairs and trains itself on the mined examples. They show an improvement over the mBART model fine-tuned on back-translated data only.

Similar to our work, Ruiter et al. (2021) incorporate a training step using denoising and back-translation into their self-supervised MT system. We take the opposite direction to reach a similar goal when we start from an unsupervised MT system and incorporate a training step supervised by the mined sentence pairs extracted outside of the NMT model. Kvapilíková and Bojar (2022) observed a positive role of pseudo-parallel data in an unsupervised MT shared task but the most effective way to integrate this type of data into the training is yet to be established.

3 Unsupervised MT with Pseudo-Parallel Data

It was demonstrated by Artetxe et al. (2018b) and Lample et al. (2018a) that the key elements of an unsupervised neural MT are shared model parameters, good initialization, and iterative learning on back-translated data. We build upon the existing work in unsupervised MT and extend the training procedure with a training step leveraging pseudo-parallel sentence pairs obtained from monolingual training corpora.

3.1 Search for Pseudo-Parallel Data

A multilingual language model trained on monolingual data only can be used to create language-neutral sentence representations (Libovický et al., 2020) in an unsupervised way. Pseudo-parallel sentence pairs are retrieved as closest neighbors in the multilingual space (Artetxe and Schwenk, 2019a).

Sentence Encoder

Multilingual masked language models (MLMs) such as mBERT (Devlin et al., 2018), XLM (Conneau and Lample, 2019) and XLM-R (Conneau et al., 2019) are Transformer (Vaswani et al., 2017) encoders trained with a masked language modeling (MLM) objective (Devlin et al., 2018) where random tokens from the input text stream are masked and the model is trained to predict them back. MLM models create representations where each token carries information about its left and right context. Sentence embeddings can be retrieved from any layer of the model but the per-token encoder outputs need to first be aggregated, e.g. by taking their mean or their element-wise maximum over the sentence tokens.

Pires et al. (2019) and Libovický et al. (2020) studied the language neutrality of the representations produced by multilingual language models and Kvapilíková et al. (2020) showed that with minimal fine-tuning, the sentence embeddings extracted from the mid-layers of the model by mean-pooling per-token encoder outputs can be used for parallel corpus mining. They also observed that fine-tuning an MLM sentence encoder on a small synthetic parallel corpus increases both precision and recall on the task of parallel sentence mining even for unrelated language pairs.

Parallel Sentence Search

To perform the search for parallel sentence pairs, all sentences from the two monolingual corpora are encoded and all possible sentence combinations are scored to select the most similar sentence pairs. The scoring is performed by a margin-based similarity metric (Artetxe and Schwenk, 2019a)

$$\text{xsim}(x, y) = \text{margin}\Big(\cos(x, y), \sum_{z \in \text{NN}_k(x)} \frac{\cos(x, z)}{2k} + \sum_{z \in \text{NN}_k(y)} \frac{\cos(y, z)}{2k}\Big) \tag{1}$$

where $\text{margin}(a, b) = \frac{a}{b}$, $\text{NN}_k(x)$ is the set of k nearest neighbors of x. The method for scoring involves cosine similarity which is comparatively evaluated against the average cosine similarity of a given sentence with its nearest neighbors to eliminate the "hubs". When the score surpasses a designated threshold T, two sentences are deemed to be parallel:

$$\text{xsim}(x, y) > T \tag{2}$$

3.2 Unsupervised MT Architecture

The design of an NMT system needs to meet several requirements to be functional for unsupervised translation. Firstly, a significant number of parameters needs to be shared among the languages in order to allow the model to generate a shared latent space where meaning is represented regardless of the language it is expressed in (Lample et al., 2018b). Secondly, the initialization of the model weights is vital to produce an initial solution and kick-start the training process (Conneau and Lample, 2019).

The configuration of our unsupervised MT system follows that of Conneau and Lample (2019) and consists of a Transformer encoder and decoder, both of which are shared between the two languages. The tokenized input in both languages is processed by a single BPE (Sennrich et al., 2016b) model learned on the concatenation of the two monolingual corpora and the joint vocabulary enables both languages to use a shared embedding matrix.

3.3 Unsupervised Pre-Training

The model is initialized with weights from a masked language model pre-trained on the monolingual corpora and copied into both the encoder and the decoder as in Conneau and Lample (2019). The initialized model is further pre-trained as a bilingual denoising autoencoder (Liu et al., 2020). The fine-tuning of the pre-trained model is scheduled in stages which are discussed in Section 3.4.

3.4 Fine-Tuning for Translation

The pre-trained model is fine-tuned on both back-translated and pseudo-parallel data which are combined into different training schedules to determine their role at a given point in training. Intuitively, non-equivalent sentence pairs with some translation information should be useful at the beginning of the training when the model has minimal or no cross-lingual information. However, as the training progresses, it starts to produce synthetic translations of increasing quality which at a certain point surpass the quality of the pseudo-parallel corpus. We hypothesize that the most effective approach is to train the model on both synthetic and pseudo-parallel data until a certain breaking point, and from that point on, continue training solely on synthetic data.

3.4.1 Fine-Tuning on Pseudo-Parallel Data

To fine-tune the model on pseudo-parallel data, the standard supervised MT objective is used. In every step of the training, a mini-batch of pseudo-parallel sentences is added and the model is trained to minimize the loss function

$$L_{PPMT}(\theta_{\text{enc}}, \theta_{\text{dec}}) = E_{(x,y)\sim \textit{PseudoPar}, \hat{y}\sim \text{dec}(\text{enc}(x))} \Delta(\hat{y}, y) \tag{3}$$

	de-hsb	en-ka	en-kk	en-uk
train (mono)	29.4M/0.9M	17.1M/6.6M	17.1M/7.7M	17.1M/17.3M
train (pseudo-parallel)	770K	230K	169K	496K

Table 1: Number of sentences in the monolingual corpora and mined pseudo-parallel corpora.

where $(\theta_{\text{enc}}, \theta_{\text{dec}})$ is the trained model, (x, y) is a sentence pair sampled from the pseudo-parallel data set $PseudoPar$, and Δ is the cross-entropy loss.

3.4.2 Fine-Tuning on Iteratively Back-Translated Data

In the back-translation step, the model is first set to the inference mode and used to translate a batch of sentences. The synthetic translations serve as source sentences fed into the model while the original sentences serve as the ground truth for the cross-entropy loss computation. The back-translation loss for translation from language $Lsrc$ to $Ltgt$ is defined as

$$L_{IBT}(\theta_{\text{enc}}, \theta_{\text{dec}}, Ltgt) = E_{x \sim D_{Ltgt}, \hat{x} \sim \text{dec}(\text{enc}(T(x)))}(\Delta(\hat{x}, x)) \tag{4}$$

where x is a sentence sampled from the target corpus D_{Ltgt}, $T(x)$ is the translation model which generates a synthetic translation of x, and Δ is the cross-entropy loss.

4 Experimental Details

4.1 Data

We train translation models for the following language pairs: German-Upper Sorbian (de-hsb), English-Georgian (en-ka), English-Kazakh (en-kk) and English-Ukrainian (en-uk). The German and Upper Sorbian monolingual training data as well as the parallel validation and test sets were provided in the WMT22 unsupervised shared task (Weller-Di Marco and Fraser, 2022). The monolingual training data for the other languages come from the Oscar[1] corpus. The training data summary is given in Table 1. The English-centric validation and test sets were taken from the Flores Evaluation Benchmark (Costa-jussà et al., 2022). In addition, the legal test sets from the MT4All shared task (de Gibert Bonet et al., 2022) were used for evaluation.

The data was tokenized and split into BPE units using the fastText (Joulin et al., 2016) library. We shared one BPE vocabulary of 55k entries for en-ka-kk-uk and another vocabulary of 18k entries for de-hsb.

4.2 Training Details

4.2.1 Model Architecture

All our translation models have a dual character to translate in both translation directions. They have the same 6-layer Transformer architecture with 8 attention heads and the hidden size of 1024, language embeddings, GELU (Hendrycks and Gimpel, 2017) activations and a dropout rate of 0.1. For language model pre-training, we use mini-batches of 64 text streams (256 tokens per stream) per GPU and Adam (Kingma and Ba, 2015) optimization with `lr=0.0001`. For denoising and MT fine-tuning, we use mini-batches of 3400 tokens per GPU and Adam optimization with a linear warm-up `(beta1=0.9,beta2=0.98,lr=0.0001)`. The models are trained on 8 GPUs. We use the XLM[2] toolkit for training.

4.2.2 Sentence Encoder

We use the XLM-100 model (Conneau and Lample, 2019) fine-tuned on English-German synthetic sentence pairs according to Kvapilíková et al. (2020) as our sentence encoder. To mea-

[1] `https://oscar-project.org/`
[2] `https://github.com/facebookresearch/XLM`

	de-hsb	en-ka	en-kk	en-uk
Precision	87.08	44.8	49.3	67.4
Recall	76.15	44.4	42.4	74.2
F1	81.25	44.6	45.6	70.6
Threshold	1.034	1.023	1.022	1.026

Table 2: The evaluation metrics on the PSM task and the respective mining thresholds.

sure its ability to create representations with a high level of multilingualism, we evaluate its performance of an auxiliary task of parallel sentence mining (PSM). For each language pair, we randomly select 200k sentences from the monolingual data, mix in the parallel validation set, and measure the precision and recall of the model when trying to reconstruct it.

Since XLM-100 was trained on 100 languages and Upper Sorbian is not one of them, we fine-tune the model on German and Upper Sorbian sentences before using it to mine parallel sentence pairs. We stop fine-tuning when the quality of the mined corpus starts deteriorating. We determine the optimal length of fine-tuning on the PSM task and observe that both precision and recall start slowly decreasing after the model had seen 500k sentences.

To retrieve sentence embeddings from the trained model, we mean-pool the encoder outputs from the fifth-to-last layer across sentence tokens (the layer and aggregation choice follow Kvapilíková et al. (2020)). We search the embedding space as described in Equation (1) and Equation (2). We select a threshold T that maximizes the F1 score on the PSM task. Table 2 lists the precision and recall of all sentence encoders used for mining together with the optimal mining threshold. The amount of mined parallel sentences used for unsupervised MT training is given in Table 1.

4.2.3 Pre-Training

We pre-train one multilingual language model for en+ka+kk+uk and one bilingual language model for de+hsb. In one training step, the model sees a minibatch of text streams in all languages. The weights from the pre-trained language models are copied into both the encoder and the decoder of the respective bilingual NMT models. The initialized NMT model for each language pair is then further pre-trained with the denoising auto-encoding loss on the two languages until convergence. The details of the denoising task are identical to Lample et al. (2018a).

4.2.4 Fine-Tuning

We experiment with different fine-tuning strategies for unsupervised machine translation. For each language pair, all translation models are initialized with the same weights obtained in the pre-training stage described in the previous paragraph.

IBT (baseline) models are fine-tuned solely with the iterative back-translation loss.

PseudoPar models are fine-tuned with the standard supervised MT loss on our pseudo-parallel corpora.

IBT+PseudoPar models are fine-tuned simultaneously with the iterative back-translation loss on the monolingual sentences and with the standard MT loss on the pseudo-parallel sentence pairs.

IBT+PseudoPar↦IBT models are a continuation from different checkpoints of the *IBT+PseudoPar* models where the supervised MT objective is dropped and the training continues with iterative back-translation only. We experiment with different checkpoints to find the optimal point to switch the training.

	de-hsb	hsb-de	en-ka	ka-en	en-kk	kk-en	en-uk	uk-en
WMT22 best	17.9	18.0	-	-	-	-	-	-
ChatGPT	6.4	-	3.9	-	5.2	-	**25.8**	-
IBT (baseline)	29.5	35.6	3.6	5.2	0.8	1.0	8.4	12.9
PseudoPar	11.3	12.0	1.9	4.8	1.0	3.1	4.6	8.6
IBT+PseudoPar	32.18	36.13	6.8	12.7	5.9	11.3	12.2	20.8
↦IBT	**34.94**	**39.63**	**7.7**	**14.0**	**7.2**	**12.1**	**15.7**	**23.7**

	de-hsb	hsb-de	en-ka	ka-en	en-kk	kk-en	en-uk	uk-en
de Gibert Bonet (2022)	-	-	12.0	-	6.4	-	20.8	-
IBT (baseline)	-	-	9.0	12.7	0.3	0.3	14.9	12.6
PseudoPar	-	-	2.1	6.8	8.0	11.6	14.6	13.1
IBT+PseudoPar	-	-	11.5	22.0	**16.3**	**18.6**	**29.3**	21.7
↦IBT	-	-	**15.0**	**23.5**	9.3	12.7	27.5	**21.8**

Table 3: MT performance of our systems measured by BLEU scores on the general test set (top) and the legal test set (bottom). Compared to the WMT22 winner (Shapiro et al., 2022), ChatGPT, and the system trained by de Gibert Bonet et al. (2022).

4.2.5 Evaluation

The baseline for our approach is an improved model of Conneau and Lample (2019) with an extra pre-training step on the denoising task for better performance. We initialize the baseline model with the weights of a cross-lingual language model, further pre-train as a denoising autoencoder and fine-tune with iterative back-translation.

We benchmark our results against MT systems of de Gibert Bonet et al. (2022) trained as a baseline for the MT4All shared task according to the methodology of Artetxe et al. (2019), and against Shapiro et al. (2022) who won the WMT22 de-hsb unsupervised task with a multilingual system that was pre-trained according to the mBART (Liu et al., 2020) methodology and fine-tuned on synthetic texts generated by a phrase-based system.

To challenge the relevance of unsupervised MT in the world of large language models, we also translate our test sets by the GPT-3.5 Turbo model[3] using the ChatGPT API and compare to our results.

We measure translation quality by BLEU score using sacreBLEU[4] (Post, 2018).

5 Results & Discussion

5.1 Results

We observed a significant improvement in translation quality over the baseline for all translation pairs. Table 3 shows that the baseline *IBT* system falls short of our proposed method by between 4.7 BLEU points (en→kk) and 10.7 BLEU points (uk→en) on the general test set. The differences on the legal test set are even more pronounced: we observe an increase of up to 14.5 BLEU over the baseline (en→uk). Our de→hsb system outperforms the WMT22 winner by 17 BLEU points. When translating from English to Kazakh, our approach reaches a BLEU score of 16.3 while the baseline which solely relies on iterative back-translation does not receive enough cross-lingual signal to start learning at all. The hybrid system by de Gibert Bonet et al. (2022) which uses additional translation information from an unsupervised phrase-based system falls behind with a BLEU score of 6.4.

[3]`https://platform.openai.com/docs/models/gpt-3-5`

[4]`sacrebleu -tok '13a' -s 'exp'`

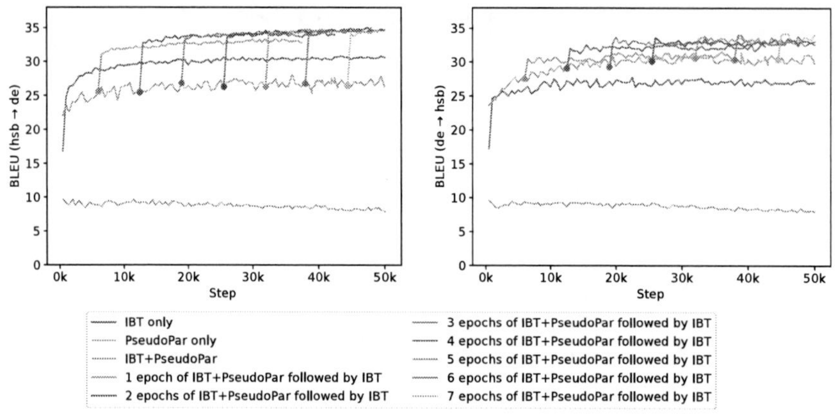

Figure 1: The development of validation BLEU scores during training. Any parallel resources were prohibited.

The results of translation by ChatGPT from English or German into truly low-resource languages (hsb, ka, kk) are significantly worse than our results. However, after manually evaluating several translations with a zero BLEU score, we believe that the automatic metric puts ChatGPT's less literal translations at a disadvantage. ChatGPT definitely favors fluency over accuracy, but it gets zero BLEU credit even in situations when it conveys the same information in different words. Nonetheless, the en→uk translation by ChatGPT is better than all unsupervised MT systems. It must be noted that the systems cannot be directly compared to ChatGPT since its training corpus is larger and might include parallel texts.

5.2 Training Schedules

Figure 1 shows training curves with validation BLEU scores of all our de↔hsb systems. We see that the *IBT+PseudoPar* system trained simultaneously on back-translated and pseudo-parallel data without any special schedule outperforms the baseline for de→hsb but not in the opposite direction. For hsb→de, the baseline performance is surpassed as soon as we remove the pseudo-parallel corpus from the training.

We trained several de-hsb models starting from *IBT+PseudoPar* after each completed epoch of 770k pseudo-parallel sentences. Upon examination of the training curves in Figure 1, we see an immediate increase in validation BLEU score of ~0.9–4.9 BLEU points which occurred within the first 500 training steps after removing the pseudo-parallel corpus from the training. This observation confirms our hypothesis that pseudo-parallel sentence pairs aid the training in the beginning but the quality of the corpus itself poses an upper bound on the performance of the system. However, removing the corpus too early (after one or two epochs) leads to a lower final BLEU score. Therefore, we recommend to keep training the *IBT+PseudoPar* model until convergence and only then switch to iterative back-translation alone *IBT+PseudoPar*↦*IBT*.

The flat *PseudoPar* training curves indicate that the quality of the pseudo-parallel corpus alone is inadequate for training a functional MT system without back-translation.

5.3 Domain-specific MT

Interestingly, removing the pseudo-parallel corpus from the training harms the translation quality measured on the legal test sets where the best performance for en→kk, kk→en and en→uk

#	Upper Sorbian	German	Score
1	Thomas de Maizière	Thomas de Maizière	1.286
2	Es ist ein harter Kampf, die Konkurrenz ist groß.	To bě napjata hra, a konkurenca bě wulka.	1.185
3	Der Roman hat *1200* Seiten.	Kniha ma *300* stronow.	1.178
4	Er passt zu diesem Team wie der Deckel auf den Topf.	Wón so k mustwu hodźi kaž wěko na hornc.	1.161
5	Die größte misst über *fünf Meter, die kleinste wenige Milli*meter.	Najkrótša měri *10 cm*, najdlěša *1 meter.*	1.101
6	Wer Wohlstand will, braucht Wissenschaft.	Štóž chce *něšto změnić, trjeba sylnu wolu.*	1.063
7	*Auch für Apple ist das iPhone wichtig.*	*Tež aleje su jara wažne.*	1.037

Table 4: A sample from the de-hsb mined parallel corpus. Non-matching words in italics.

is achieved by *IBT+PseudoPar*. We suspect that this is the result of the repeating terminology in the domain-specific test sets which is better handled by the *IBT+PseudoPar* for some language pairs. This is consistent with the fact that the *PseudoPar* system trained exclusively on pseudo-parallel data performs quite well on the en-kk and en-uk legal test set (8.0 on en→kk, 11.6 on kk→en and 14.6 on en→uk) while having poor results on the general test set (1.0 on en→kk, 3.1 on kk→en and 4.6 on en→uk). Based on our findings, we believe that utilizing pseudo-parallel sentences extracted from domain-specific monolingual corpora has the potential to enhance the training of domain-specific MT in general. However, further experiments are out of the scope of this paper.

5.4 Data quality

The sentence pairs in the pseudo-parallel corpus are far from equivalent in meaning. As illustrated in Table 4, many of the sentences are paired because they share a named entity, a numeral (not necessarily identical), a punctuation mark, or one distinctive word. Others have a similar sentence structure, they contain a similar segment or they contain words that are somehow related, e.g. Apple/alleys (*"aleje"*), although the word Apple is not the fruit in this context. On the other hand, synthetic sentences in the first training iterations are also extremely noisy, and even later they contain artifacts such as non-translated words or mistranslated named entities.

Table 5 shows what the back-translated and pseudo-parallel data can look like. We observed how the back-translated version of one sentence changes as the training progresses and witnessed several types of error, e.g. the German word *"laufend"* is not translated at all in the initial iterations; the word "April" remains mistranslated as "March" (*"měrc"*) throughout the entire training. On the other hand, the pseudo-parallel sentence matched based on its distance from the source sentence has a similar meaning but is factually inaccurate.

We see that many of the pseudo-parallel translations are far from equivalent but it is difficult to measure the quality of the entire corpus. We measure it indirectly by the increase in BLEU score associated with introducing the corpus into the unsupervised MT training or by measuring the quality of the sentence encoder used for creating the corpus. To be able to evaluate the precision/recall of the sentence encoder, we have to control the number of parallel sentences hidden in the input corpora. However, in real-life scenarios, the level of comparability of two monolingual corpora is never known precisely. If the monolingual corpora provided for unsupervised translation come from a different domain and contain dissimilar sentences, the model has no good candidates to find. This poses a challenge especially when setting the correct mining threshold for the monolingual corpora at hand.

It is not clear what are the attributes of the pseudo-parallel corpus that the unsupervised

SRC	Ich musste mich laufend weiterbilden, und so legte ich im April 1952 die erste und ein Jahr darauf die zweite Lehramtsprüfung ab.
REF	Dyrbjach so běžnje dale kwalifikować, a tak złožich w aprylu 1952 prěnje a lěto po tym druhe wučerske pruwowanje.
PseudoPar	*Hańža Winarjec-Orsesowa* wotpołoži prěnje wučerske pruwowanje *w lěće 1949 a druhe w lěće* 1952.
IBT @ 500	Dyrbjach so *laufend* dale *kubłać*, a tak *legte w měrcu* 1952 *prěnje a lěto na to druhe Lejnjanske pruwowanje ab.*
IBT @ 3000	Dyrbjach so běžnje dale *kubłać*, a tak w *měrcu* 1952 prěnju a lěto na to druhu *lektoratu serbšćiny wotpołožichmy.*
IBT @ 10000	Dyrbjach so běžnje dale *kubłać*, a tak wotpołožich w *měrcu* 1952 prěnju a lěto *na* to druhu *lektoratu.*

Table 5: A sample sentence translated by the IBT model after 500, 3,000 and 10,000 training steps compared to the closest neighbor of such sentence from the bilingual sentence space (PseudoPar). The mistranslated words are indicated in italics.

MT training benefits from the most. We believe that the benefits of training on such noisy data are twofold: 1) the perfect matches are a valuable source of correct supervision, and 2) the abundant less-than-perfect matches still introduce a new translation signal which can help the model leave a suboptimal situation which we often observe during back-translation when the model learns to mistranslate a word and never forgets it.

6 Conclusion

We have demonstrated the benefits of MT training on pseudo-parallel data in situations when true parallel data is not available. While the pseudo-parallel corpus alone does not reach sufficient quality for standard supervised MT training, it works well in combination with iterative back-translation. It is optimal to train the model until convergence on both pseudo-parallel and synthetic sentence pairs, remove the pseudo-parallel corpus and continue training with iterative back-translation only.

Incorporating similar sentence pairs into the standard unsupervised MT training increases translation quality across all evaluated language pairs with an improvement of up to 14.5 BLEU over the baseline trained without pseudo-parallel data and 8.5 BLEU over a hybrid unsupervised system (en→uk). Furthermore, we observed that in some situations (en↔kk), the iterative back-translation becomes trapped in a suboptimal state where no learning occurs. Introducing pseudo-parallel data can rescue the model from this state and trigger the learning process.

After evaluating our approach on a legal test set, we believe that training on pseudo-parallel sentences could be particularly useful for domain-specific unsupervised MT. If we have two in-domain monolingual corpora at hand, parallel corpus mining is an efficient strategy to retrieve translation information.

The pseudo-parallel corpus helps the training despite being noisy. We hypothesize that while exact translations help the model find correct correspondences, also the noise can introduce new information and prevent the model from memorizing some of the artifacts of back-translated sentences. We leave it up to future research to evaluate whether a cleaner but smaller corpus would bring even larger gains.

Acknowledgements

This research was partially supported by the grant 19-26934X (NEUREM3) of the Czech Science Foundation and by the SVV project number 260 698 of the Charles University.

References

Artetxe, M., Labaka, G., and Agirre, E. (2018a). Unsupervised statistical machine translation. In *Proceedings of the 2018 Conference on EMNLP*, Brussels. Association for Computational Linguistics.

Artetxe, M., Labaka, G., and Agirre, E. (2019). An effective approach to unsupervised machine translation. In *Proceedings of the 57th Annual Meeting of the Association for Computational Linguistics*, pages 194–203, Florence. Association for Computational Linguistics.

Artetxe, M., Labaka, G., Agirre, E., and Cho, K. (2018b). Unsupervised neural machine translation. In *Proceedings of the Sixth International Conference on Learning Representations.*

Artetxe, M. and Schwenk, H. (2019a). Margin-based parallel corpus mining with multilingual sentence embeddings. *Proceedings of the 57th Annual Meeting of the Association for Computational Linguistics.*

Artetxe, M. and Schwenk, H. (2019b). Massively multilingual sentence embeddings for zero-shot cross-lingual transfer and beyond. *Transactions of the Association for Computational Linguistics*, 7:597–610.

Bahdanau, D., Cho, K., and Bengio, Y. (2015). Neural machine translation by jointly learning to align and translate. In *3rd International Conference on Learning Representations, ICLR 2015, San Diego, CA, USA, May 7-9, 2015, Conference Track Proceedings.*

Brown, T., Mann, B., Ryder, N., Subbiah, M., Kaplan, J. D., Dhariwal, P., Neelakantan, A., Shyam, P., Sastry, G., Askell, A., Agarwal, S., Herbert-Voss, A., Krueger, G., Henighan, T., Child, R., Ramesh, A., Ziegler, D., Wu, J., Winter, C., Hesse, C., Chen, M., Sigler, E., Litwin, M., Gray, S., Chess, B., Clark, J., Berner, C., McCandlish, S., Radford, A., Sutskever, I., and Amodei, D. (2020). Language models are few-shot learners. In Larochelle, H., Ranzato, M., Hadsell, R., Balcan, M., and Lin, H., editors, *Advances in Neural Information Processing Systems*, volume 33, pages 1877–1901. Curran Associates, Inc.

Conneau, A., Khandelwal, K., Goyal, N., Chaudhary, V., Wenzek, G., Guzmán, F., Grave, E., Ott, M., Zettlemoyer, L., and Stoyanov, V. (2019). Unsupervised cross-lingual representation learning at scale.

Conneau, A. and Lample, G. (2019). Cross-lingual language model pretraining. In Wallach, H., Larochelle, H., Beygelzimer, A., d'Alché-Buc, F., Fox, E., and Garnett, R., editors, *Advances in Neural Information Processing Systems 32*, pages 7059–7069. Curran Associates, Inc.

Costa-jussà, M. R., Cross, J., Çelebi, O., Elbayad, M., Heafield, K., Heffernan, K., Kalbassi, E., Lam, J., Licht, D., Maillard, J., Sun, A., Wang, S., Wenzek, G., Youngblood, A., Akula, B., Barrault, L., Gonzalez, G. M., Hansanti, P., Hoffman, J., Jarrett, S., Sadagopan, K. R., Rowe, D., Spruit, S., Tran, C., Andrews, P., Ayan, N. F., Bhosale, S., Edunov, S., Fan, A., Gao, C., Goswami, V., Guzmán, F., Koehn, P., Mourachko, A., Ropers, C., Saleem, S., Schwenk, H., and Wang, J. (2022). No language left behind: Scaling human-centered machine translation.

de Gibert Bonet, O., Goenaga, I., Armengol-Estapé, J., Perez-de Viñaspre, O., Parra Escartín, C., Sanchez, M., Pinnis, M., Labaka, G., and Melero, M. (2022). Unsupervised machine translation in real-world scenarios. In *Proceedings of the Thirteenth Language Resources and Evaluation Conference*, pages 3038–3047, Marseille, France. European Language Resources Association.

Devlin, J., Chang, M., Lee, K., and Toutanova, K. (2018). BERT: pre-training of deep bidirectional transformers for language understanding. *arXiv [e-Print archive]*, abs/1810.04805.

Garcia, X., Foret, P., Sellam, T., and Parikh, A. P. (2020). A multilingual view of unsupervised machine translation.

Garcia, X., Siddhant, A., Firat, O., and Parikh, A. (2021). Harnessing multilinguality in unsupervised machine translation for rare languages. In *Proceedings of the 2021 Conference of the North American Chapter of the Association for Computational Linguistics: Human Language Technologies*, pages 1126–1137, Online. Association for Computational Linguistics.

Hendrycks, D. and Gimpel, K. (2017). Bridging nonlinearities and stochastic regularizers with gaussian error linear units. *CoRR*, abs/1606.08415.

Hendy, A., Abdelrehim, M., Sharaf, A., Raunak, V., Gabr, M., Matsushita, H., Kim, Y. J., Afify, M., and Awadalla, H. H. (2023). How good are gpt models at machine translation? a comprehensive evaluation.

Joulin, A., Grave, E., Bojanowski, P., Douze, M., Jégou, H., and Mikolov, T. (2016). Fasttext.zip: Compressing text classification models. *arXiv preprint arXiv:1612.03651*.

Kingma, D. P. and Ba, J. (2015). Adam: A method for stochastic optimization. In *Proceedings of the 3rd International Conference for Learning Representations*.

Kvapilíková, I., Artetxe, M., Labaka, G., Agirre, E., and Bojar, O. (2020). Unsupervised multilingual sentence embeddings for parallel corpus mining. In *Proceedings of the 58th Annual Meeting of the Association for Computational Linguistics: Student Research Workshop*, pages 255–262, Online. Association for Computational Linguistics.

Kvapilíková, I. and Bojar, O. (2022). CUNI submission to MT4All shared task. In *Proceedings of the 1st Annual Meeting of the ELRA/ISCA Special Interest Group on Under-Resourced Languages*, pages 78–82, Marseille, France. European Language Resources Association.

Lample, G., Denoyer, L., and Ranzato, M. (2018a). Unsupervised machine translation using monolingual corpora only. In *Proceedings of the 6th International Conference on Learning Representations*.

Lample, G., Ott, M., Conneau, A., Denoyer, L., and Ranzato, M. (2018b). Phrase-based & neural unsupervised machine translation. In *Proceedings of the 2018 Conference on EMNLP*, pages 5039–5049.

Libovický, J., Rosa, R., and Fraser, A. (2020). On the language neutrality of pre-trained multilingual representations. In *Findings of the Association for Computational Linguistics: EMNLP 2020*, pages 1663–1674, Online. Association for Computational Linguistics.

Liu, Y., Gu, J., Goyal, N., Li, X., Edunov, S., Ghazvininejad, M., Lewis, M., and Zettlemoyer, L. (2020). Multilingual denoising pre-training for neural machine translation. *Transactions of the Association for Computational Linguistics*, 8:726–742.

Pires, T., Schlinger, E., and Garrette, D. (2019). How multilingual is multilingual BERT? In *Proceedings of the 57th Annual Meeting of the Association for Computational Linguistics*, pages 4996–5001, Florence. Association for Computational Linguistics.

Post, M. (2018). A call for clarity in reporting BLEU scores. In *Proceedings of the Third Conference on Machine Translation: Research Papers*, pages 186–191, Brussels, Belgium. Association for Computational Linguistics.

Ruiter, D., España-Bonet, C., and van Genabith, J. (2019). Self-supervised neural machine translation. In *Proceedings of the 57th Annual Meeting of the Association for Computational Linguistics*, pages 1828–1834, Florence, Italy. Association for Computational Linguistics.

Ruiter, D., Klakow, D., van Genabith, J., and España-Bonet, C. (2021). Integrating unsupervised data generation into self-supervised neural machine translation for low-resource languages. In *Proceedings of Machine Translation Summit XVIII: Research Track*, pages 76–91, Virtual. Association for Machine Translation in the Americas.

Schwenk, H. (2018). Filtering and mining parallel data in a joint multilingual space. In *Proceedings of the 56th Annual Meeting of the Association for Computational Linguistics*, pages 228–234, Melbourne, Australia. Association for Computational Linguistics.

Sennrich, R., Haddow, B., and Birch, A. (2016a). Improving neural machine translation models with monolingual data. In *Proceedings of the 54th Annual Meeting of the Association for Computational Linguistics (Volume 1: Long Papers)*, pages 86–96, Berlin, Germany. Association for Computational Linguistics.

Sennrich, R., Haddow, B., and Birch, A. (2016b). Neural machine translation of rare words with subword units. In *Proceedings of the 54th Annual Meeting of the Association for Computational Linguistics*, pages 1715–1725, Berlin. Association for Computational Linguistics.

Shapiro, A., Salama, M., Abdelhakim, O., Fayed, M., Khalafallah, A., and Adly, N. (2022). The AIC system for the WMT 2022 unsupervised MT and very low resource supervised MT task. In *Proceedings of the Seventh Conference on Machine Translation (WMT)*, pages 1117–1121, Abu Dhabi, United Arab Emirates (Hybrid). Association for Computational Linguistics.

Song, K., Tan, X., Qin, T., Lu, J., and Liu, T. (2019). MASS: masked sequence to sequence pre-training for language generation. *CoRR*, abs/1905.02450.

Tran, C., Tang, Y., Li, X., and Gu, J. (2020). Cross-lingual retrieval for iterative self-supervised training. *CoRR*, abs/2006.09526.

Üstün, A., Berard, A., Besacier, L., and Gallé, M. (2021). Multilingual unsupervised neural machine translation with denoising adapters. In *Proceedings of the 2021 Conference on Empirical Methods in Natural Language Processing*, pages 6650–6662, Online and Punta Cana, Dominican Republic. Association for Computational Linguistics.

Vaswani, A., Shazeer, N., Parmar, N., Uszkoreit, J., Jones, L., Gomez, A. N., Kaiser, L., and Polosukhin, I. (2017). Attention is all you need. *CoRR*, abs/1706.03762.

Vincent, P., Larochelle, H., Bengio, Y., and Manzagol, P.-A. (2008). Extracting and composing robust features with denoising autoencoders. pages 1096–1103.

Weller-Di Marco, M. and Fraser, A. (2022). Findings of the wmt 2022 shared tasks in unsupervised mt and very low resource supervised mt. In *Proceedings of the Seventh Conference on Machine Translation*, pages 801–805, Abu Dhabi. Association for Computational Linguistics.

A Study on the Effectiveness of Large Language Models for Translation with Markup

Raj Dabre raj.dabre@nict.go.jp
Hideki Tanaka hideki.tanaka@nict.go.jp
National Institute of Information and Communications Technology, Japan

Bianka Buschbeck bianka.buschbeck@sap.com
Miriam Exel miriam.exel@sap.com
SAP SE, Walldorf, Germany

Abstract

In this paper we evaluate the utility of large language models (LLMs) for translation of text with markup in which the most important and challenging aspect is to correctly transfer markup tags while ensuring that the content, both, inside and outside tags is correctly translated. While LLMs have been shown to be effective for plain text translation, their effectiveness for structured document translation is not well understood. To this end, we experiment with BLOOM and BLOOMZ, which are open-source multilingual LLMs, using zero, one and few-shot prompting, and compare with a domain-specific in-house NMT system using a detag-and-project approach for markup tags. We observe that LLMs with in-context learning exhibit poorer translation quality compared to the domain-specific NMT system, however, they are effective in transferring markup tags, especially the large BLOOM model (176 billion parameters). This is further confirmed by our human evaluation which also reveals the types of errors of the different tag transfer techniques. While LLM-based approaches come with the risk of losing, hallucinating and corrupting tags, they excel at placing them correctly in the translation.

1 Introduction

Recent work involving Large Language Models (LLMs) has shown impressive performance in various Natural Language Processing (NLP) tasks. These models have the ability to perform few-shot (or in-context) learning based on prompts, an alternative to fine-tuning, requiring only a forward pass of the neural network (Brown et al., 2020). Prompts are instructions in natural language given as input to LLMs along with a test sequence, allowing a few examples (i.e. few-shot) to be fed to the model at test time. Researchers have shown that LLMs via prompting can be effective as Machine Translation (MT) systems (Brown et al., 2020; Wei et al., 2022; Chowdhery et al., 2022; Zhang et al., 2023; Hendy et al., 2023; Bawden and Yvon, 2023), whose quality approaches that of traditional encoder-decoder neural MT (NMT) systems trained or fine-tuned on parallel corpora. The majority of the aforementioned research has been conducted on plain text, neglecting the practical application of MT for text containing markup, see Table 1, where the challenge is to properly transfer markup tags *within* the translatable content from the source to the target language. Given that a significant portion of web-based content and proprietary or business documents requiring translation comes in structured for-

Proceedings of Machine Translation Summit XIX, Vol. 1: Research Track, pages 148–159
September 4–8, 2023, Macau SAR, China.

en	Click <uicontrol>Prepayment</uicontrol>.
ja	<uicontrol>前払</uicontrol>をクリックします。

Table 1: Example with inline markup (in gray), taken from Buschbeck et al. (2022).

mats like HTML pages or Microsoft Office files, it is important to understand the effectiveness of LLMs in handling this task.

In this paper, we conduct the first of its kind study on the use of LLMs for translation of text with markup where the transfer of markup tags, or tag placement, is as important as the translation of the content inside and outside the tags. We use SAP's Asian language dataset (Buschbeck et al., 2022) focusing on translation involving Japanese, Chinese, Korean and English and experiment with zero, one and few-shot prompting of the open-source multilingual BLOOM and BLOOMZ LLMs (Le Scao et al., 2022; Muennighoff et al., 2022). We compare our results against those obtained via a general-domain MT system, M2M[1] (Fan et al., 2021), as well as a domain-specific in-house NMT system that handles markup tags via a detag-and-project approach. Our multi-metric evaluations using BLEU, chrF and COMET reveal that while LLMs exhibit relatively poorer translation quality compared to the domain-specific NMT system, they are often competitive with a general-domain MT system, and that the degree to which LLMs are able to transfer markup tags out-of-the-box depends on the prompting strategy and the model size. This is further confirmed by our human evaluation that reveals the various error types associated with different tag transfer approaches. Notably, the 176 billion parameter model employing few-shot prompting outperforms the detag-and-project strategy in terms of tag positioning, demonstrating its strong potential. Our study focuses on the impact of example retrieval approaches, number of shots and their ordering. It provides insights for MT practitioners, and should encourage further research in this area.

2 Related Work

This paper focuses on an evaluation of LLMs for the translation of text with markup. We briefly review the related work in this area.

2.1 Structured Document Translation

Hashimoto et al. (2019) present a data set from the IT domain that features structure via inline markup, and corresponding MT results using a constrained beam search approach for decoding. Further, Hanneman and Dinu (2020) compare different data augmentation methods with a detag-and-project approach, and evaluate on data from legal documents from the European Union. The methods for tag transfer in Zenkel et al. (2021) are also related, even though they focus on inserting the tags into a fixed human translation. In contrast to these works, Buschbeck et al. (2022), who also release an evaluation dataset for structured document translation of Asian languages, propose to use existing multilingual pre-trained NMT models as black-boxes for translating texts with inline elements directly. They show that these models perform surprisingly well at transferring markup tags during translation despite not being explicitly trained to handle structured content. In this paper, we further investigate black-box approaches for structured document translation, focusing specifically on LLMs.

2.2 Language Model Prompting

Ever since the intoduction of GPT-3 (Brown et al., 2020), which showed that LLMs are excellent zero and few-shot text learners, there has been a lot of interest in using LLMs for various NLP tasks. GPT-3 has been followed by models like BLOOM (Le Scao et al., 2022) and XGLM (Lin

[1]M2M is not explicitly trained to handle markup tags.

et al., 2022) which are multilingual supporting between 40 and 120 languages. These LLMs have shown that by providing them with some examples of a downstream task, in what is known as prompting, they are able to produce outputs of reasonably high quality. We specifically focus on their ability to handle structured content, something that has not been explored so far. Muennighoff et al. (2022) have shown that multi-task fine-tuning of LLMs can improve their performance, especially in a zero-shot setting, which we also study with BLOOMZ which is an extension of BLOOM.

3 Methodology

The methodology employed in this work focuses on prompting approaches, namely, the template or format of instructions fed to the LLMs along with input sequences to be translated, as well as example retrieval techniques.

3.1 Prompting Approach

For our experiments, we use an N-shot approach, selecting N translation pairs (S_i, T_i) from an example pool. We then use these examples (or shots) in a templated form to prompt the LLM. The template is of the following form for all experiments in this paper:

> "Translate the following sentence from E to F: $[\ S_1\ ]\ [\ T_1\ ] \cdots$ Translate the following sentence from E to F: $[\ S_N\ ]\ [\ T_N\ ]$ Translate the following sentence from E to F: $[\ S_t\ ]$"

where E is the source language, F is the target language, and S_t is the test example for which we want to obtain a translation. We use structure-aware prompting, where we retrieve examples containing markup tags for test sentences with tags, and examples without markup tags for test sentences without tags. Unless explicitly mentioned, few-shot results are reported with 4 examples. Note that in the template each source and target language sentence is wrapped in opening and closing square brackets ([,]). After the model produces outputs, we remove the prompted prefix and retain the first segment produced by the model within the [and] brackets as the model's translation.

3.2 Example Retrieval

In this paper, we primarily use LABSE-based embedding similarity[2] (Feng et al., 2022) to extract fitting examples from the example pool. We compute cosine similarity between the LABSE representations of the test sentence and the source side of the example set, and retrieve N pairs such that their sources have the highest similarity. We employ the LABSE model because it is a multilingual model capable of calculating the similarity between sentences in any language. In our analyses, we also use BM25[3] (Robertson et al., 1995) and the chrF metric (Popović, 2015) for retrieval. BM25 is a bag-of-words[4] based retrieval algorithm which is widely used for information retrieval. It is a probabilistic model which computes the similarity between a query and a document as a function of the term frequencies in the document and the query. In our case, the query is the test sentence and the document is the source side of the example set. chrF is a character level n-gram based metric which is used for machine translation evaluation. We calculate it between the test sentence and the source sides of the example set, and extract examples that maximize chrF. We would like to investigate whether leveraging chrF for example retrieval can improve the translations' chrF scores.

[2] https://huggingface.co/setu4993/LaBSE

[3] https://github.com/dorianbrown/rank_bm25

[4] Since Japanese, Chinese and Korean are unsegmented, for simplicity we treat each character as a word.

4 Experimental Setup

In this section, we describe the datasets, language models and baselines used in our experiments to evaluate the utility of LLMs for structured document translation.

4.1 Datasets

We experiment with the Software Documentation Data Set (Buschbeck et al., 2022), henceforth the SAP dataset, which covers Japanese, Chinese, Korean translation from/to English.[5] It belongs to the domain of enterprise software documentation and consists of high-quality, n-way parallel structured documents in form of XML or XLIFF files. Using this dataset allows us to show how LLMs perform on domain-specific technical data, and whether LLMs can preserve the structural markup during translation. For the experiments, we use the data in the provided `text-dita-translatables` format, with 2,011 and 2,002 segments as development and test data respectively. We use the development set as example pool for example retrieval and report results on the test set.

4.2 Language Models

Our main results focus on the BLOOM model and its multi-task fine-tuned variant BLOOMZ, both of which support 46 languages and contain around 7.1 billion parameters. We also employ the BLOOM model with 176 billion parameters for analysis focusing on model size and translation quality. Note that BLOOM is not officially trained for Japanese and Korean but it is still able to handle them potentially due to unintentional inclusion of these languages. We use the Transformers library (version 4.27.0.dev0) by HuggingFace which supports decoding using BLOOM and BLOOMZ. We apply 32-bit floating point precision for greedy search with batch sizes of 2 and generate 128 additional tokens on a 40GB-A100 GPU. For the 176 billion parameter model, we use a batch size of 1 and 8 GPUs. 8-bit decoding is employed via Transformers' integration of the bitsandbytes[6] library (Dettmers et al., 2022).

4.3 Baseline and Upperbound

We compare against two MT baselines: one that is publicly available but markup-agnostic, and another that is an in-house system that can be considered in-domain for software documentation and thus serves as an upper bound for the performance achievable with current NMT systems. The publicly available system is the M2M 1.2 billion parameter model, and we use a beam of size 4 for decoding. The in-house system is a corporate MT engine by SAP that uses the Transformer architecture and that is trained on a multitude of data sources including the contents of company-internal translation memories. These comprise parallel texts from the test domain of software documentation; however, note that it is a multi-domain system that has not been fine-tuned to the test domain specifically. For the tag transfer, a detag-and-project approach along the lines of Hanneman and Dinu (2020) is used.

4.4 Evaluation Metrics

We follow the evaluation method which encompasses both lexical and structural content, as presented in Buschbeck et al. (2022), wherein the MT output and its reference are decomposed into lexical content (sequences are stripped from XML tags, noted *lex*) and structural content (sequences are stripped from lexical content, noted *tag*) before running the automatic metrics. We also compute automatic scores for the unmodified translations (mix of lexical and structural content, noted *raw*). The automatic metrics we report in this paper are BLEU (Papineni et al.,

[5]`https://github.com/SAP/software-documentation-data-set-for-machine-translation`

[6]`https://github.com/TimDettmers/bitsandbytes`

2002) and chrF[7] (Popović, 2015) obtained using the SacreBLEU toolkit (Post, 2018). We apply appropriate tokenization for *raw*, *lex* and *tag*[8] BLEU. The *raw* and *lex* tokenizations depend on the target language and are chosen correspondingly for English[9], Japanese[10], Chinese[11] and Korean[12]. We also report COMET (Rei et al., 2020) using the WMT'22[13] model for the *lex* content as it is the current best practice in MT evaluation.

5 Results and Analysis

We now present our results for translation with markup for the experimental setup lined out in Section 4. We provide a detailed analysis of the impact of various factors on the performance of LLMs on this task. A human evaluation will follow in Section 6.

5.1 Main Results

Table 2 contains the main results of translating text with markup, comparing the LLMs BLOOM and BLOOMZ with and without in-context learning with the multilingual translation model M2M and the corporate in-house MT model. Overall, across the metrics and language pairs, zero-shot configurations lead to poor results, with BLOOMZ, being multilingually fine-tuned, having an advantage over BLOOM. However, including one and four translation examples with the model input (one-shot and few-shot) consistently improves the performances of both BLOOM and BLOOMZ. Both lexical and structural scores improve, showing that the LLMs learn from the provided examples. Note that the relative improvements as well as absolute scores observed with BLOOM in one- and few-shot configurations are larger compared to those obtained with BLOOMZ for all translation directions. See also Section 5.2 for further discussion of this phenomenon. Interestingly, although BLOOM is not officially trained for Japanese and Korean, it still performs well on these languages, especially in the few-shot configuration.

When comparing to the baselines, we can observe that few-shot BLOOM, on average, seems to be roughly on par with M2M according to the reported metrics, with M2M performing better for some language pairs (e.g. en↔ko) and BLOOM for others (e.g. en↔zh). The in-house MT model, that has likely seen more in-domain training data than the other models, outperforms all other models across all metrics and translation directions.

With regards to the metrics themselves, we can see that *lex* BLEU, chrF and COMET are roughly correlated with each other. However, note that the difference in translation quality between the LLMs and the in-house system looks a lot larger with the string-based metrics than with COMET. Given that COMET is known to have the highest correlation with human annotations, BLEU and chrF can be used as reasonable approximates, at least in this paper, which is why we rely mainly on BLEU for the rest of the paper.

5.2 Analysis: Impact of the number of examples

We observed that increasing the number of examples from 1 to 4 had a positive impact on the results of both BLOOM and BLOOMZ. Therefore, taking Japanese to English and English to Japanese translation as a case study, we explore the impact of an increasing number of examples. Specifically, we consider up to 16 retrieved examples when prompting the models, the results for which are shown in Figure 1. We observe that, for both translation directions,

[7] `nrefs:1|case:mixed|eff:yes|nc:6|nw:0|space:no|version:2.3.1`

[8] `nrefs:1|case:mixed|eff:no|tok:none|smooth:exp|version:2.3.1`

[9] `nrefs:1|case:mixed|eff:no|tok:13a|smooth:exp|version:2.3.1`

[10] `nrefs:1|case:mixed|eff:no|tok:ja-mecab-0.996-IPA|smooth:exp|version:2.3.1`

[11] `nrefs:1|case:mixed|eff:no|tok:zh|smooth:exp|version:2.3.1`

[12] `nrefs:1|case:mixed|eff:no|tok:ko-mecab-0.996/ko-0.9.2-KO|smooth:exp|version:2.3.1`

[13] https://huggingface.co/Unbabel/wmt22-comet-da

	en→ja	en→ko	en→zh	ja→en	ko→en	zh→en
M2M	42.1 (35.3, 76.8)	34.6 (27.1, 75.2)	49.2 (43.4, 79.5)	29.0 (24.8, 13.1)	37.0 (25.9, 61.3)	40.2 (29.8, 61.1)
In-house	73.8 (71.3, 91.5)	69.6 (64.8, 90.5)	80.4 (78.2, 93.8)	60.8 (47.4, 80.2)	56.2 (43.0, 71.9)	63.9 (51.2, 77.4)
			zero-shot			
BLOOM	3.0 (0.2, 13.9)	2.9 (0.3, 18.7)	3.0 (0.3, 16.4)	3.0 (0.9, 15.0)	5.8 (1.1, 34.5)	8.0 (1.3, 53.4)
BLOOMZ	12.6 (6.9, 47.5)	7.2 (2.6, 30.4)	30.8 (28.0, 42.4)	15.7 (13.5, 7.8)	11.8 (7.9, 8.8)	25.6 (24.0, 17.7)
			one-shot			
BLOOM	31.3 (21.8, 75.4)	20.7 (11.4, 66.7)	49.7 (42.6, 88.6)	30.5 (18.2, 66.6)	24.4 (12.4, 51.7)	41.9 (30.6, 76.5)
BLOOMZ	22.3 (14.6, 64.2)	10.1 (5.5, 27.9)	45.1 (38.4, 84.1)	24.8 (15.4, 50.8)	14.6 (8.0, 30.2)	37.8 (28.1, 70.3)
			few-shot			
BLOOM	36.0 (26.3, 79.1)	24.1 (13.9, 67.0)	53.8 (46.6, 94.1)	33.5 (20.3, 69.2)	27.4 (14.2, 56.8)	44.4 (31.7, 76.2)
BLOOMZ	27.3 (19.6, 62.4)	17.1 (8.8, 56.0)	47.8 (41.6, 81.1)	27.9 (17.8, 51.5)	20.3 (11.2, 37.2)	41.1 (30.7, 71.2)
M2M	53.2 (40.2, 92.1)	50.3 (34.2, 95.8)	57.5 (37.5, 93.5)	56.1 (53.8, 45.7)	60.2 (54.7, 89.7)	63.6 (58.4, 91.5)
In-house	81.4 (75.8, 99.9)	78.5 (69.2, 99.9)	82.6 (72.9, 99.9)	80.1 (77.2, 98.1)	77.4 (74.2, 97.5)	81.9 (79.4, 98.1)
			zero-shot			
BLOOM	10.0 (0.7, 54.2)	10.6 (1.0, 57.0)	11.8 (0.7, 57.5)	16.1 (12.5, 34.9)	18.5 (12.1, 58.0)	19.0 (10.8, 72.9)
BLOOMZ	22.9 (11.0, 60.7)	15.9 (4.3, 48.9)	35.4 (24.8, 56.3)	37.9 (39.0, 31.4)	28.2 (27.0, 34.1)	49.2 (50.5, 42.9)
			one-shot			
BLOOM	43.6 (27.9, 89.1)	34.5 (16.5, 80.7)	58.7 (37.5, 93.9)	51.8 (45.7, 84.3)	42.1 (35.0, 79.6)	63.7 (58.6, 90.9)
BLOOMZ	33.4 (18.8, 77.5)	19.7 (8.0, 51.5)	54.2 (33.6, 89.7)	45.4 (40.6, 72.6)	30.4 (26.4, 53.6)	59.2 (54.6, 85.3)
			few-shot			
BLOOM	47.9 (32.2, 91.4)	39.0 (20.1, 84.6)	62.4 (41.0, 97.1)	54.5 (48.1, 88.4)	45.4 (38.0, 83.9)	65.7 (60.2, 94.1)
BLOOMZ	38.2 (24.3, 78.9)	28.1 (11.3, 74.7)	55.4 (36.3, 87.6)	49.1 (44.7, 73.6)	36.9 (31.9, 64.1)	63.0 (58.6, 86.3)
M2M	0.846	0.799	0.844	0.795	0.802	0.806
In-house	0.945	0.919	0.923	0.901	0.886	0.895
			zero-shot			
BLOOM	0.435	0.438	0.436	0.531	0.575	0.546
BLOOMZ	0.681	0.604	0.775	0.745	0.650	0.780
			one-shot			
BLOOM	0.796	0.679	0.854	0.810	0.747	0.851
BLOOMZ	0.756	0.592	0.837	0.771	0.684	0.828
			few-shot			
BLOOM	0.817	0.712	0.867	0.823	0.765	0.859
BLOOMZ	0.783	0.653	0.849	0.806	0.731	0.850

Table 2: BLEU (top), chrF (middle) and COMET (bottom) scores obtained with BLOOM and BLOOMZ pretrained models in zero-, one- and few-shot (4) configurations, compared to the pretrained M2M model and the in-house MT engine. Scores are presented as *raw* (*lex*, *tag*) following the metrics presented in Section 4.4. COMET scores are only computed for *lex*.

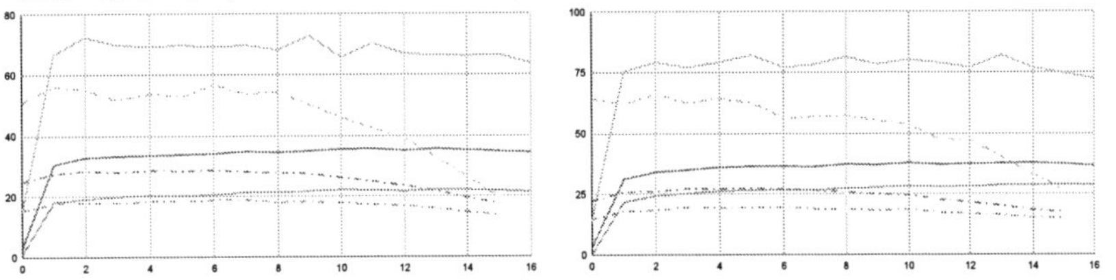

Figure 1: Impact of the number of examples/shots (0 to 16) on the *raw*, *lex* and *tag* BLEU scores of translations obtained by BLOOM and BLOOMZ for ja→en (left) and en→ja (right).

while increasing the number of examples beyond 4 results in a slight improvement in translation quality using BLOOM, the opposite happens with BLOOMZ. Specifically, beyond 5 to 6 examples the quality of BLOOMZ starts dropping with lowest scores for 16 examples. Note

Model	zero-shot	one-shot	few-shot
BLOOM 7b1	3.0 (0.2, 13.9)	31.3 (21.8, 75.4)	36.0 (26.3, 79.1)
BLOOM 176b	3.6 (0.3, 14.1)	41.4 (32.3, 85.9)	45.3 (35.9, 91.9)
M2M		42.1 (35.3, 76.8)	
In-house		73.8 (71.3, 91.5)	

Table 3: *raw*, *lex* and *tag* BLEU scores for the 7.1 billion (7b1) and 176 billion (176b) parameter BLOOM models in comparison to the baselines for en→ja.

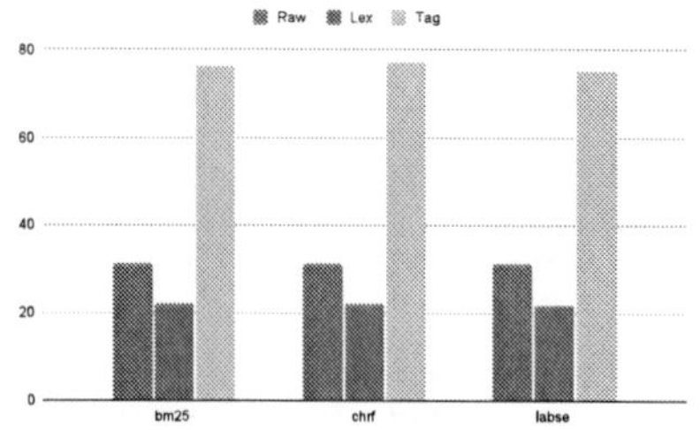

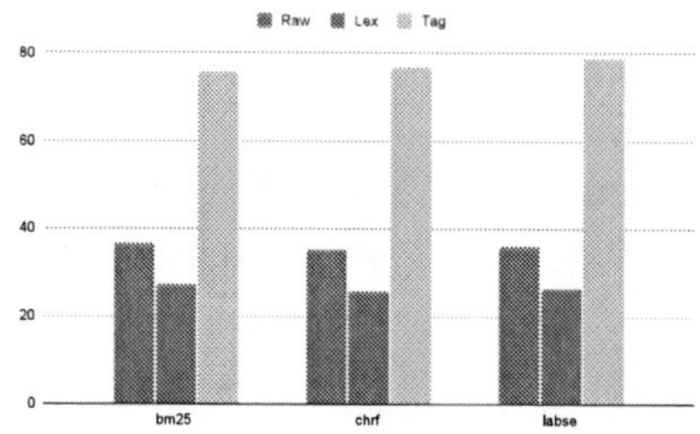

Figure 2: Impact of the example retrieval approach on the *raw*, *lex* and *tag* BLEU scores of English to Japanese translations obtained by BLOOM, for 1-shot (left) and 4-shot (right).

that the BLOOMZ model is a fine-tuned version of BLOOM on xP3 (Muennighoff et al., 2022) which is a multilingual multitask dataset. There is a key difference between the training styles of BLOOM and BLOOMZ, namely that BLOOM is trained on long documents with no specific task in mind, whereas BLOOMZ is trained on supervised task-specific data. Therefore, the latter is not well suited for handling increasing lengths of inputs since the fine-tuning step causes it to forget how to rely on longer context. Although BLOOMZ is superior to BLOOM in a zero-shot setting, it is not suitable for use when large number of examples are available.

5.3 Analysis: Impact of model size

All aforementioned results use BLOOM(Z) models of 7.1 billion parameters, but the largest BLOOM model contains 176 billion parameters and we now study the impact of increasing the model size. We evaluate again for 0, 1 and 4 shots, focusing only on English to Japanese translation due to computational constraints. We present the results in Table 3. It is clear that using the large BLOOM model brings about a large jump in the *raw*, *lex* and *tag* scores as compared to the small BLOOM model. By using four examples, the large model is able to surpass the M2M model; however, it falls far behind the in-house model in terms of *raw* and *lex* BLEU. This is not much of a surprise as BLOOM and M2M are general-domain models, whereas the corporate in-house model has seen substantial training data from the software documentation domain and related domains. Note that in terms of *tag* BLEU the large few-shot BLOOM model can well compete with the detag-and-project approach of the corporate in-house model, indicating that it has the ability to transfer structure effectively from the source to the translation. A more fine-grained analysis for exactly the four presented models will follow in Section 6.

5.4 Analysis: Impact of the example retrieval approach

For the results presented so far, we used LABSE to select the examples for one- and few-shot translation. We now compare to BM25 and chrF (cf. Section 3.2) for English to Japanese translation. See Figure 2 for the results. Overall, we observe minor differences between the retrieval approaches. However, in a few-shot setting, LABSE tends to give the best *tag* BLEU scores.

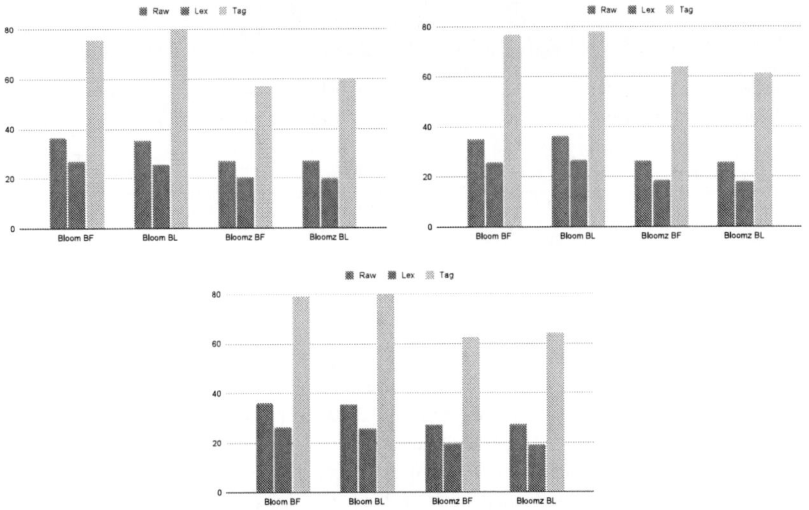

Figure 3: Impact of the order of examples on the *raw*, *lex* and *tag* BLEU scores of English to Japanese few-shot translations obtained by BLOOM and BLOOMZ, for different example retrieval approaches: BM25 (top-left), chrF (top-right) and LABSE (bottom).

5.5 Analysis: Impact of the order of examples

In the few-shot experiments presented thus far, the examples were always ordered *best first* (BF), meaning the best examples (according to the example retrieval approach) are at the beginning of the prompt and the worse example at the end. We now explore the impact of this ordering. Specifically, we reverse this order for few-shot translation for English to Japanese, which we call *best last* (BL). We report the results in Figure 3. We observe that while the *raw* BLEU scores are not largely affected, the *lex* BLEU scores are often reduced by keeping the best examples closest to the test sentence being translated. However, an opposite effect is observed on the *tag* BLEU scores. For BM25 for example, we observe that the *tag* BLEU scores for BL are higher than BF by 6.1 points for translation with BLOOM. Therefore, we recommend that the appropriate ordering be used depending on what evaluation metric is most important for the task at hand. However, further investigation is required to understand why this ordering has such a large impact on the *tag* BLEU scores.

6 Human Evaluation

As the automatic lexical matching metrics used in this paper have their limitations in measuring MT quality (Freitag et al., 2022), and evaluating tag placement automatically is a non-trivial task without a standardized methodology, we perform human evaluation to assess the correctness of translation and tag placement. We focus on the language pair English to Japanese, for which translations of BLOOM 7b1 and BLOOM 176b both few-shot, M2M and the in-house NMT system (see Table 3) were assessed regarding translation quality (Section 6.1) and tag placement (Section 6.2). From the test set, we randomly selected 200 source sentences containing tags and their corresponding translations of the four selected systems. For translation quality assessment, the tags were removed, as tag placement was evaluated separately. Assessing text quality and tag handling separately enables a more accurate understanding.

Model	Tester 1 CharacTER	Tester 1 TER	Tester 2 CharacTER	Tester 2 TER	Average CharacTER	Average TER
BLOOM 7b1 few-shot	41.65	61.14	43.03	63.36	42.34	62.25
BLOOM 176b few-shot	26.56	48.02	28.86	52.49	27.71	50.26
M2M	44.12	58.55	45.42	62.59	44.77	60.57
In-house	8.15	13.86	10.17	20.33	**9.16**	**17.09**

Table 4: Results of minimal post-editing of 200 sentences by two translators for English to Japanese measured in CharacTER ↓ and TER ↓

6.1 Post-editing evaluation

MT quality can be efficiently measured using minimal post-editing. It is more reliable than rating as translators are required to edit the translations, which at the same time reveals the encountered problems. By measuring the edit distance between the MT and its post-edited version – a common praxis in the translation industry – the quality of different models can be ranked. We report two metrics: TER (translation edit rate) (Snover et al., 2006) that measures the post-editing effort on the token level and CharacTER (Wang et al., 2016) for character-level edit distance. For TER, the implementation of the SacreBLEU toolkit (Post, 2018)[14] is used. The four sets of 200 translations were post-edited by two professional translators specialized in the domain. Segments were presented in random order. Table 4 shows the outcome.

Assessing the post-editing effort, there is a consensus among testers, with tester 2 being marginally stricter. The inter-annotator agreement, calculated as the Pearson correlation coefficient, yields 0.83 for TER and 0.86 for CharacTER. Both edit distance metrics confirm that the smaller BLOOM model and M2M require significantly more post-editing than the large BLOOM model. The least edits were required for the in-house model, our upperbound baseline. As post-edition was performed on the text without tags, these result could be related to the *lex* BLEU scores of the four selected models in Table 3. Knowing that the data selected for human evaluation is only a subset of the test data, it is still surprising that M2M, being of comparable quality to few-shot BLOOM 176b according to BLEU, was found on the same quality level of few-shot BLOOM 7b1. For both models, M2M and BLOOM 7b1, post-editing effort is massive. Although translations from BLOOM 176b necessitate significantly less post-editing, they cannot be considered practically valuable translations.

6.2 Tag placement evaluation

To assess tag placement independently from translation quality, we also chose post-editing as evaluation method, but this time only tags could be added, moved, renamed, or removed by the testers. The instructions included to never modify any target text so that the editing was restricted to opening and closing tags, their names and syntax. If the translation did not contain the content where the tags should be placed, the testers were instructed to skip the segment. Additionally, testers were asked to indicate whether the content inside tag pairs was indeed translated or just copied from the source. Tag placement was evaluated by 5 testers, but each segment was only evaluated once, as the task was rather deterministic and did not allow the variance one would expect in translation.

The results of the tag placement evaluation of the four systems are shown in Table 5. We report the percentage of tags that were not modified during the post-editing task (*correct*), tags that the testers could not place because the translation did not allow for it (*skipped*), and tags

[14]Signature: `nrefs:1|case:lc|tok:tercom|norm:yes|punct:yes|asian:yes|version:2.3.1`

Model	%Tags						Untranslated
	Correct	Skipped	Wrong				
			Missing	Position	Tag	Hallucinated	
BLOOM 7b1	81.73	14.19	2.28	0.49	1.31	3.43	3.5
BLOOM 176b	**92.66**	6.53	**0.00**	**0.33**	0.49	1.96	3.5
M2M	85.64	8.81	0.65	1.14	3.75	0.16	74.0
In-house	86.46	**2.28**	**0.00**	11.26	**0.00**	**0.00**	**1.5**

Table 5: Results of human tag placement evaluation for English to Japanese

that were modified by the testers (*wrong*). For the latter, we further analyse the post-editing modifications, and report in which way the tags are problematic: tags can be missing in the MT output (*missing*), they can be placed in the wrong position (*position*), the tag itself can be corrupted in some way and/or have the wrong name (*tag*), and the tag can be hallucinated in the MT output (*hallucinated*). We furthermore report the percentage of segments that contain *untranslated* (copied) content between tag pairs.

The results reveal that the large few-shot BLOOM model effectively transfers and accurately places markup tags in translations. However, it may occasionally hallucinate tags or use incorrect tag names. These effects are more pronounced with the small BLOOM model, which looses some tags, while being quite accurate for the transferred tags. In contrast, the in-house MT model's detag-and-project method avoids losing, hallucinating, or corrupting tags but is less precise in placing them accurately in the translation. M2M struggles to perform translation and tag transfer simultaneously, often failing to translate content between markup tags and just copying the source. This issue affects 74% of M2M translations. We should also note the number of tags in skipped translations, which correspond directly to the translation quality, see Section 6.1. As testers could not place tags in translations due to low quality and missing content, we assume that the system's tag placement was rather off.

This tag post-editing study is complementary to the automatic evaluation scores presented in Section 5. In contrast to the *raw* metrics, it evaluates tag transfer and placement independent of translation quality. The *tag* metrics only cover the transfer of tags to the translation and their order to some extend, but not their placement within the translation. This detailed human analysis provides valuable insights into the specific shortcomings of each approach, from which improvement measures or fall-back strategies can be derived.

7 Conclusion

We explored various LLMs and a specialized MT system to assess their ability to translate structured documents in the software documentation domain, focusing on both the translation quality and the transfer of markup elements. The investigation of different prompting approaches showed that LLMs learn from in-domain examples and are capable to produce correct text markup in the target language. With this respect, the foundation model BLOOM is more responsive to prompting than its fine-tuned variant BLOOMZ. We also observed that the large-scale BLOOM model with few-shot prompting largely outperforms its smaller cousins in both translation quality and tag placement. However, this comes at a higher price and with sub-par performance, which raises doubts about its practical usefulness for commercial translation purposes. While LLMs excel at transferring structural markup, most likely because they were trained on it, none of the investigated models achieve the translation accuracy of a dedicated machine translation system. Nevertheless, this opens up interesting possibilities for future research, such as the combination of LLMs and MT systems to achieve the best of both worlds.

References

Bawden, R. and Yvon, F. (2023). Investigating the translation performance of a large multilingual language model: the case of BLOOM. In *Proceedings of the 24th Annual Conference of the European Association for Machine Translation*.

Brown, T., Mann, B., Ryder, N., Subbiah, M., Kaplan, J. D., Dhariwal, P., Neelakantan, A., Shyam, P., Sastry, G., Askell, A., et al. (2020). Language models are few-shot learners. *Advances in neural information processing systems*, 33:1877–1901.

Buschbeck, B., Dabre, R., Exel, M., Huck, M., Huy, P., Rubino, R., and Tanaka, H. (2022). A multilingual multiway evaluation data set for structured document translation of Asian languages. In *Findings of the Association for Computational Linguistics: AACL-IJCNLP 2022*, pages 237–245.

Chowdhery, A., Narang, S., Devlin, J., Bosma, M., Mishra, G., Roberts, A., Barham, P., Chung, H. W., Sutton, C., Gehrmann, S., et al. (2022). PaLM: Scaling language modeling with pathways. *arXiv preprint arXiv:2204.02311*.

Dettmers, T., Lewis, M., Belkada, Y., and Zettlemoyer, L. (2022). Llm.int8(): 8-bit matrix multiplication for transformers at scale. *arXiv preprint arXiv:2208.07339*.

Fan, A., Bhosale, S., Schwenk, H., Ma, Z., El-Kishky, A., Goyal, S., Baines, M., Celebi, O., Wenzek, G., Chaudhary, V., Goyal, N., Birch, T., Liptchinsky, V., Edunov, S., Grave, E., Auli, M., and Joulin, A. (2021). Beyond English-centric multilingual machine translation. *J. Mach. Learn. Res.*, 22(1).

Feng, F., Yang, Y., Cer, D., Arivazhagan, N., and Wang, W. (2022). Language-agnostic BERT sentence embedding. In *Proceedings of the 60th Annual Meeting of the Association for Computational Linguistics (Volume 1: Long Papers)*, pages 878–891.

Freitag, M., Rei, R., Mathur, N., Lo, C.-k., Stewart, C., Avramidis, E., Kocmi, T., Foster, G., Lavie, A., and Martins, A. F. (2022). Results of WMT22 Metrics shared task: Stop using BLEU–neural metrics are better and more robust. In *Proceedings of the Seventh Conference on Machine Translation (WMT)*, pages 46–68.

Hanneman, G. and Dinu, G. (2020). How should markup tags be translated? In *Proceedings of the Fifth Conference on Machine Translation*, pages 1160–1173.

Hashimoto, K., Buschiazzo, R., Bradbury, J., Marshall, T., Socher, R., and Xiong, C. (2019). A high-quality multilingual dataset for structured documentation translation. In *Proceedings of the Fourth Conference on Machine Translation (Volume 1: Research Papers)*, pages 116–127.

Hendy, A., Abdelrehim, M., Sharaf, A., Raunak, V., Gabr, M., Matsushita, H., Kim, Y. J., Afify, M., and Awadalla, H. H. (2023). How good are GPT models at machine translation? A comprehensive evaluation. *arXiv preprint arXiv:2302.09210*.

Le Scao, T., Fan, A., Akiki, C., Pavlick, E., Ilić, S., Hesslow, D., Castagné, R., Luccioni, A. S., Yvon, F., Gallé, M., et al. (2022). BLOOM: A 176b-parameter open-access multilingual language model. *arXiv preprint arXiv:2211.05100*.

Lin, X. V., Mihaylov, T., Artetxe, M., Wang, T., Chen, S., Simig, D., Ott, M., Goyal, N., Bhosale, S., Du, J., Pasunuru, R., Shleifer, S., Koura, P. S., Chaudhary, V., O'Horo, B.,

Wang, J., Zettlemoyer, L., Kozareva, Z., Diab, M., Stoyanov, V., and Li, X. (2022). Few-shot learning with multilingual generative language models. In *Proceedings of the 2022 Conference on Empirical Methods in Natural Language Processing*, pages 9019–9052, Abu Dhabi, United Arab Emirates. Association for Computational Linguistics.

Muennighoff, N., Wang, T., Sutawika, L., Roberts, A., Biderman, S., Scao, T. L., Bari, M. S., Shen, S., Yong, Z.-X., Schoelkopf, H., et al. (2022). Crosslingual generalization through multitask finetuning. *arXiv preprint arXiv:2211.01786.*

Papineni, K., Roukos, S., Ward, T., and Zhu, W.-J. (2002). BLEU: a method for automatic evaluation of machine translation. In *Proceedings of the 40th annual meeting of the Association for Computational Linguistics*, pages 311–318.

Popović, M. (2015). chrF: character n-gram F-score for automatic MT evaluation. In *Proceedings of the tenth workshop on statistical machine translation*, pages 392–395.

Post, M. (2018). A call for clarity in reporting BLEU scores. In *Proceedings of the Third Conference on Machine Translation: Research Papers*, pages 186–191.

Rei, R., Stewart, C., Farinha, A. C., and Lavie, A. (2020). COMET: A neural framework for MT evaluation. In *Proceedings of the 2020 Conference on Empirical Methods in Natural Language Processing (EMNLP)*, pages 2685–2702.

Robertson, S. E., Walker, S., and Hancock-Beaulieu, M. M. (1995). Large test collection experiments on an operational, interactive system: Okapi at TREC. *Information Processing & Management*, 31(3):345–360.

Snover, M., Dorr, B., Schwartz, R., Micciulla, L., and Makhoul, J. (2006). A study of translation edit rate with targeted human annotation. In *Proceedings of the 7th Conference of the Association for Machine Translation in the Americas: Technical Papers*, pages 223–231.

Wang, W., Peter, J.-T., Rosendahl, H., and Ney, H. (2016). CharacTer: Translation edit rate on character level. In *Proceedings of the First Conference on Machine Translation: Volume 2, Shared Task Papers*, pages 505–510, Berlin, Germany. Association for Computational Linguistics.

Wei, J., Bosma, M., Zhao, V., Guu, K., Yu, A. W., Lester, B., Du, N., Dai, A. M., and Le, Q. V. (2022). Finetuned language models are zero-shot learners. In *International Conference on Learning Representations.*

Zenkel, T., Wuebker, J., and DeNero, J. (2021). Automatic bilingual markup transfer. In *Findings of the Association for Computational Linguistics: EMNLP 2021*, pages 3524–3533.

Zhang, B., Haddow, B., and Birch, A. (2023). Prompting large language model for machine translation: A case study. *arXiv preprint arXiv:2301.07069.*

A Case Study on Context Encoding in Multi-Encoder based Document-Level Neural Machine Translation

Ramakrishna Appicharla appicharla_2021cs01@iitp.ac.in
Baban Gain gainbaban@gmail.com
Department of Computer Science and Engineering,
Indian Institute of Technology Patna, Patna, India

Santanu Pal santanu.pal.ju@gmail.com
Wipro AI, Lab45, London, UK

Asif Ekbal asif@iitp.ac.in
Department of Computer Science and Engineering,
Indian Institute of Technology Patna, Patna, India

Abstract

Recent studies have shown that the multi-encoder models are agnostic to the choice of context, and the context encoder generates noise which helps improve the models in terms of BLEU score. In this paper, we further explore this idea by evaluating with context-aware pronoun translation test set by training multi-encoder models trained on three different context settings *viz,* previous two sentences, random two sentences, and a mix of both as context. Specifically, we evaluate the models on the ContraPro test set to study how different contexts affect pronoun translation accuracy. The results show that the model can perform well on the ContraPro test set even when the context is random. We also analyze the source representations to study whether the context encoder generates noise. Our analysis shows that the context encoder provides sufficient information to learn discourse-level information. Additionally, we observe that mixing the selected context (the previous two sentences in this case) and the random context is generally better than the other settings.

1 Introduction

Document-level neural machine translation (DocNMT) has gained a lot of attention due to the ability to incorporate context through different paradigms such as single encoder (Tiedemann and Scherrer, 2017; Agrawal et al., 2018), multiple encoders (Zhang et al., 2018; Li et al., 2020; Huo et al., 2020), memory networks (Maruf and Haffari, 2018) and pre-trained language models (Donato et al., 2021). This additional context helps to produce more consistent translations (Bawden et al., 2018; Voita et al., 2019) than sentence-level models. Two of the most followed approaches to incorporating context are the concatenation-based and multi-encoder-based approaches. In the concatenation-based method, by concatenating context and current input sentence, a context-aware input sentence is generated (Tiedemann and Scherrer, 2017; Agrawal et al., 2018; Junczys-Dowmunt, 2019; Zhang et al., 2020) and use it as the input to the

Proceedings of Machine Translation Summit XIX, Vol. 1: Research Track, pages 160–172
September 4–8, 2023, Macau SAR, China.

encoder. In the multi-encoder approach, to encode the source or target context, an additional encoder is used (Zhang et al., 2018; Voita et al., 2018; Kim et al., 2019; Ma et al., 2020) and the entire model is jointly optimized. Typically, the current sentence's neighboring sentences (previous or next) are used as the context, whereas models consist of multiple encoders and a single decoder.

Recent studies on Multi-Encoder (MultiEnc) based DocNMT models (Li et al., 2020; Wang et al., 2020; Gain et al., 2022) have shown that the context-encoder is acting as noise generator which improves the robustness of the model and makes the model agnostic to the choice of context. However, the improvement is in terms of BLEU (Papineni et al., 2002), which might not capture the discourse-level phenomenon effectively (Müller et al., 2018). This phenomenon is not studied well in the existing literature. The context encoder might not generate noise if the model can effectively capture any discourse phenomenon, such as pronoun translation from the source to the target language. Modeling the relation between sentences in a given document is essential to capture any discourse phenomenon (Voita et al., 2018). To this end, we hypothesize that, during the training phase, if the model can learn the similarities between all the sentences in a given document given in the form of *(context, source)* pairs, the context encoder might not be generating noise since all the sentences in the given document are connected via the context.

In this work, we aim to study the effect of the context in MultiEnc-based DocNMT models and the models' behavior in random context settings but not to introduce a novel technique. We use the 'Outside Attention Multi-Encoder' model (Li et al., 2020) with four different context settings to study the effect of the context. We conduct experiments on News-commentary v14 and TED corpora from English–German direction. We report the results on the ContraPro test set (Müller et al., 2018), a contrastive test set to evaluate models' performance in translating pronouns. We also report sentence-BLEU (s-BLEU) (Papineni et al., 2002), document-BLEU (d-BLEU) (Liu et al., 2020b; Bao et al., 2021), and COMET (Rei et al., 2020) scores.

To summarize, the specific attributes of our current work are as follows:

- We conduct experiments on multi-encoder based DocNMT models to study if the context encoder is generating noise or not by evaluating the model with ContraPro (Müller et al., 2018) test set.
- We empirically show that the model can learn discourse-level information even when trained with random context.

2 Related Work

The performance of document-level NMT is better than that of sentence-level NMT models due to the encoding of context (Sim Smith, 2017; Voita et al., 2018). Towards this goal to represent context, Tiedemann and Scherrer (2017) concatenate consecutive sentences and use them as input to the single-encoder-based DocNMT model. Agrawal et al. (2018) conducted experiments on varying neighboring contexts and then tied them with the current sentence as input to their model. However, this approach introduced a lot of long-range dependencies. This problem can be alleviated by introducing an additional encoder to encode the context. Towards this, Zhang et al. (2018) and Voita et al. (2018) proposed transformer-based multi-encoder NMT models where the other encoder is used to encode the context. While Miculicich et al. (2018) proposed a hierarchical attention network to encode the context and a more recent approach Kang et al. (2020) proposed a reinforcement learning-based dynamic context selection module for DocNMT. Recent studies (Kim et al., 2019; Li et al., 2020; Wang et al., 2020) have shown that the improvement in the performance of multi-encoder DocNMT models is not due to context encoding but rather the context encoder acting as a noise generator, which improves the robustness of the DocNMT model. Other approaches such as pre-training (Junczys-Dowmunt, 2019; Donato et al., 2021) and memory-based approaches (Feng et al., 2022) are shown to have improved the performance of DocNMT models. Recent studies (Sun et al., 2022; Post and Junczys-Dowmunt, 2023) have demonstrated that single encoder-decoder models can capture long-range dependencies. Still, special care must be taken to break a large document into smaller fragments for training. Along with document-level translation, multi-encoder models are also commonly used in automatic post-editing (Pal et al., 2019, 2018; Junczys-Dowmunt and Grundkiewicz, 2018; Shin and Lee, 2018), multimodal translation (Libovický et al., 2018; Liu et al., 2020a) and multitask learning (Luong et al., 2015; Zhang et al., 2017; Anastasopoulos and Chiang, 2018) scenarios.

In this work, we study the effect of context in the multi-encoder (Li et al., 2020) based approach. Specifically, we verify if the context encoder is generating noise or not. If the context encoder is generating noise, then the model may not be able to effectively capture the discourse-level phenomenon, such as pronoun translation accuracy, even when the model can perform well on other automatic metrics, such as BLEU.

3 Methodology

3.1 Outside Context Multi-Encoder Model

We conduct all experiments on the 'Outside Attention Multi-Encoder' (Li et al., 2020) model. The model (cf. Fig 1) consists of two encoders and one decoder. Both source and context are encoded through two encoders, and the output of these encoders is passed through an attention layer. An element-wise addition is performed on the outputs of the source encoder and the attention layer before passing it to the decoder.

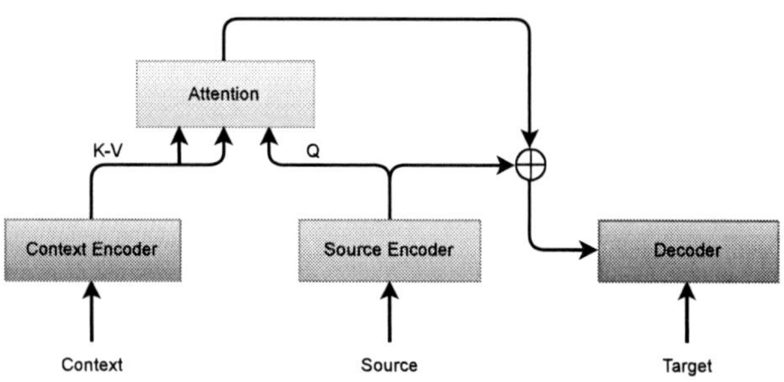

Figure 1: The overview of the Outside Context Multi-Encoder DocNMT architecture. The input to the model consists of (*Context*, *Source*, *Target*, *Label*). Both the encoders are encoding *Context* and *Source*. The Context and Source encoder outputs are passed through the Attention layer. Here, '*K-V*' represents Key-Value pairs from the Context encoder, and '*Q*' represents Query from the Source encoder. The output of the Attention layer is element-wise summed with the output of the Source encoder before passing to the Decoder. None of the layers are shared.

3.2 Context-Aware Models

We train context-aware models in four different settings. They are,

1. **MultiEnc-Prev@2**: In this setting, the context consists of the previous two sentences concatenated, with respect to the current source sentence (Zhang et al., 2018), and the

model is trained in this context setting. The same sentence is used as context if the sentence is the first or second sentence in the document.

2. **MultiEnc-Random@2**: In this setting, the context consists of two random sentences sampled from the complete training set.

3. **MultiEnc-Mix@2**: In this setting, 50% of the training set consists of context from '*MultiEnc-Prev@2*' setting and the remaining 50% consists of context from '*MultiEnc-Random@2*' setting. Essentially, this setting combines the context settings from the above two approaches.

4. **MultiEnc-Mix-Adapt@2**: This setting is similar to the '*MultiEnc-Mix@2*' setting but the loss during the training is modified as follows:

$$\mathcal{L} = \alpha \times \mathcal{L} \tag{1}$$

   Where 'α' is a scaling factor which is the fraction of source sentences having the previous two sentences as context over all the sentences in the current batch, and '$\mathcal{L}$' is the loss for the current batch. During the training, we also provide the labels list to facilitate this counting, with 0 indicating random context and 1 indicating the previous two sentences as context. Our motivation in this approach is to penalize the model [1] based on the number of random context inputs per batch and force the model not to learn from random context.

The validation set consists of the previous two sentences as the context in all four settings.

4 Experimental Setup

This section describes the data sets and the experimental setup used in the experiments.

4.1 Data Statistics

We conduct experiments on English–German corpus obtained from combining [2] WMT news-commentary, IWSLT'17 TED, and Europarl-v7 corpora. For the WMT news-commentary, we use news-commentary v14[3] as the train set and newstest2018 as the test set. For IWSLT'17 TED and Europarl-v7 corpora, we follow the train and test set splits mentioned in the previous work (Maruf et al., 2019)[4]. We use newstest2017 as the validation set for all the models. The models are trained from English to German. Table 1 shows data statistics of the train, validation, and test sets.

4.2 NMT Model Setups

We conduct all the experiments on transformer architecture (Vaswani et al., 2017). All the models are implemented in PyTorch[5]. The models consist of 6-layer encoder-decoder stacks, 8 attention heads, and a 2048-cell feed-forward layer. Positional and token embedding sizes are set to 512. Adam optimizer (Kingma and Ba, 2015) is used for training with a noam learning rate scheduler (Vaswani et al., 2017) and the initial learning rate set to 0.2. The dropout and warmup steps are set to 0.3 (Li et al., 2020; Sun et al., 2022) and 16,000 (Popel and Bojar, 2018) respectively, and we used a mini-batch of 30 sentences. We create joint subword vocabularies of

[1] If the entire batch consists of random context, then the loss for that batch will be 0 and vice versa.

[2] We combine corpora from all three sources into a single corpus and train our models on this corpus.

[3] `https://data.statmt.org/news-commentary/v14/training/`

[4] `https://github.com/sameenmaruf/selective-attn/tree/master/data`

[5] `https://pytorch.org/`

Data	Corpus	# Sentences	# Documents
Train	News	329,041	8,462
	TED	206,112	1,698
	Europarl	1,666,904	117,855
	Total	2,202,057	128,015
Validation	newstest2017	3,004	130
Test	News	2,998	122
	TED	2,271	23
	Europarl	5,134	360

Table 1: Data statistics of corpora. **# Sentences, # Documents** represent the number of sentences and documents, respectively. The train set consists of the corpus obtained by combining News, TED, and Europarl corpora. The models are tested on each test set separately.

size 40,000 by combing source and target parts of the training corpus into a single joint corpus. We use the BPE (Sennrich et al., 2016) to create subword vocabularies with SentencePiece (Kudo and Richardson, 2018) implementation. We also learn the positional encoding of tokens (Devlin et al., 2019), and the maximum sequence length is set to 140 tokens for all models. All models are trained till convergence, and we use perplexity on the validation set as early stopping criteria with the patience of 7 (Popel and Bojar, 2018).

5 Results and Analysis

We test context-aware models with two different contexts *viz.* previous two and random sentences as context. Table 2 shows the s-BLEU (Papineni et al., 2002; Post, 2018)[6], d-BLEU (Liu et al., 2020b; Bao et al., 2021), and COMET (Rei et al., 2020)[7] scores. Overall, *MultiEnc-Mix@2* and *MultiEnc-Mix-Adapt@2* models achieve the best overall scores on all test sets. The *MultiEnc-Mix@2* model achieves 23.1 s-BLEU and 25.3 d-BLEU on the News test set in *Prev@2* setting. For Ted test set, *MultiEnc-Mix-Adapt@2* model achieving 20.8 s-BLEU and 24.6 d-BLEU in *Prev@2* setting. For the Europarl test set, *MultiEnc-Mix@2* and *MultiEnc-Mix-Adapt@2* models are achieving 26.5 s-BLEU and the *MultiEnc-Prev@2* model achieving 28.8 d-BLEU on *Random@2* setting. However, the results from *Prev@2* and *Random@2* settings are very similar and not statistically significant when compared to each other.

The COMET scores are also similar in the settings of both *Prev@2* and *Random@2*. On the News test set, *MultiEnc-Mix@2* model achieves a score of 65.8 in *Prev@2* setting. On the Ted test set, *MultiEnc-Mix-Adapt@2* model obtains a score of 71.4 in *Random@2* setting. Similarly, on the Europarl test set, *MultiEnc-Mix@2* model achieves 82.1 in *Prev@2* setting. All the results indicate that the random context might not be random as the performance of the models is similar across both the context setting in terms of BLEU and COMET scores. To verify this, we conduct experiments on the ContraPro test set (Müller et al., 2018) to study the effects of random context and context encoder on pronoun translation accuracy.

5.1 Results on the ContraPro test set

ContraPro test set (Müller et al., 2018) is a test set for contrastive evaluation of models' performance on translating German pronouns *es*, *er* and *sie*. Contrastive tests test the model's ability

[6] sacreBLEU signature: nrefs:1|case:mixed|eff:no|tok:13a|smooth:exp|version:2.3.1
[7] COMET model: wmt22-comet-da

Model	s-BLEU			d-BLEU			COMET		
	News	TED	Europarl	News	TED	Europarl	News	TED	Europarl
Prev@2									
MultiEnc-Prev@2	22.9	20.4	26.3	25.2	24.3	28.6	65.3	71.3	81.9
MultiEnc-Random@2	22.7	19.9	26.4	25.0	23.8	28.7	65.4	70.7	81.9
MultiEnc-Mix@2	**23.1**	20.3	26.4	**25.3**	24.2	28.7	**65.8**	71.1	**82.1**
MultiEnc-Mix-Adapt@2	22.9	**20.8**	26.4	25.1	**24.6**	28.7	65.5	71.3	82.0
Random@2									
MultiEnc-Prev@2	22.9	20.5	26.4	25.2	24.4	**28.8**	65.1	71.3	81.8
MultiEnc-Random@2	22.7	19.9	26.4	25.0	23.8	28.7	65.4	70.7	81.9
MultiEnc-Mix@2	23.0	20.5	**26.5**	25.2	24.4	28.7	65.6	71.1	82.0
MultiEnc-Mix-Adapt@2	22.7	20.6	**26.5**	25.0	24.5	28.7	65.7	**71.4**	82.0

Table 2: s-BLEU, d-BLEU, and COMET scores of the Outside Context DocNMT models, tested with correct and random context. **Prev@2** and **Random@2** denote the previous two and random two-sentence context during the testing. The best scores are shown in bold.

to discriminate between correct and incorrect outputs. In the ContraPro test set, the models' performance is measured in terms of the model's accuracy regarding reference pronoun, antecedent location, and antecedent distance. Similar to the training phase, we use the previous two sentences as context for the ContraPro test set, and Table 3 shows the performance of the trained context-aware models. All the models' performance is similar to reference pronoun translation accuracy, with *MultiEnc-Mix@2* and *MultiEnc-Mix-Adapt@2* achieving a best overall score of 0.47. However, in terms of specific pronouns, *MultiEnc-Random@2*, *MultiEnc-Mix@2*, and *MultiEnc-Mix-Adapt@2* achieved best scores of 0.87, 0.25, and 0.35 for pronouns *es*, *er* and *sie* respectively. This shows that all the models can capture discourse information to translate pronouns, even the model trained with random context (*MultiEnc-Random@2*).

Model	reference pronoun				antecedent location		antecedent distance				
	total	*es*	*er*	*sie*	intrasegmental	external	0	1	2	3	>3
MultiEnc-Prev@2	0.46	0.81	0.21	0.34	0.71	0.39	0.71	0.36	0.45	0.48	0.62
MultiEnc-Random@2	0.46	**0.87**	0.18	0.33	0.70	0.40	0.70	0.36	0.46	**0.49**	**0.68**
MultiEnc-Mix@2	**0.47**	0.85	**0.25**	0.31	0.71	**0.41**	0.71	0.38	**0.47**	0.48	**0.68**
MultiEnc-Mix-Adapt@2	**0.47**	0.83	0.24	**0.35**	**0.73**	**0.41**	**0.73**	0.38	0.46	**0.50**	0.64

Table 3: Accuracy on ContraPro test set for Outside Context DocNMT models regarding reference pronoun, antecedent location (within segment vs. outside segment), and antecedent distance of antecedent (in sentences). The best scores are shown in bold.

The results regarding antecedent location show that the *MultiEnc-Mix-Adapt@2* model can perform well when the antecedent occurs in the current segment (intrasegmental). The *MultiEnc-Prev@2* model can perform well when the antecedent is happening within the segment but poorly when the antecedent is outside (external). Similarly, *MultiEnc-Random@2* model is able when the antecedent occurs outside the segment but poorly when the antecedent is within. However, both models *viz.* *MultiEnc-Mix@2* and *MultiEnc-Mix-Adapt@2* perform well in both settings. The results show that mixing some random context is beneficial for the model to learn this discourse phenomenon effectively.

Similarly, the results regarding antecedent distance show that both the *MultiEnc-Mix@2* and *MultiEnc-Mix-Adapt@2* models achieve the best overall performance. Interestingly, the *MultiEnc-Prev@2* model's performance is good when the antecedent distance is <3 but drops when the distance is >3, but *MultiEnc-Random@2* model is achieving best score when the distance is >3 but slightly less in other settings than the *MultiEnc-Prev@2* model. The results from *antecedent distance* indicate that the model trained with random context can learn the long distant discourse properties better than the model trained with fixed context (previous two sentences). Based on this, we conclude that the random context might not be random as the model can learn discourse-level information well. These results also indicate that the context encoder might not generate noise as the discourse information outside the current source can only be learned if the context encoder can encode the context well. We further investigate this by analyzing the source sentence embeddings.

5.2 t-SNE Visualization of Source and Target Embeddings

Since the relation between the sentences in a given document is learned through context, the context encoder should be trained sufficiently to capture this aspect. To study this, we take a document and visualize the source sentence representations obtained after performing attention over context and source encoder outputs and combining the resulting output with source encoder output via element-wise addition (cf. Fig 1). Figure 2 shows t-SNE visualization (Van der Maaten and Hinton, 2008)[8] of the source representations. The document is taken from the train set of *News-commentary v14* corpus and contains 30 sentences. We obtain the source representations in two settings similar to the testing phase *viz.* previous two sentences and randomly sampled two sentences as context.

Figure 2(a) shows the representation when the context consists of the previous two sentences. Interestingly the representations from *MultiEnc-Prev@2* and *MultiEnc-Mix@2* models spread out more than the other two models. The reason might be that the model requires more context to encode the sentences effectively for these two models. The *MultiEnc-Random@2* model can encode the sentences better than the *MultiEnc-Prev@2* model. This might be why the models trained with random context can perform well, as the model can learn sufficient information even from the random context. This shows that the random context might not be random, and it is helping the model to encode sentences well enough to capture the discourse-level information. The *MultiEnc-Mix-Adapt@2* model can learn the source representation better than other models as the sentences are projected in a smaller zone. This shows that the *MultiEnc-Mix-Adapt@2* model can perform well even when the context is limited.

Similarly, Figure 2(c) shows the representation when the context consists of two random sentences. The representation of *MultiEnc-Prev@2* model is adversely affected by the random context, but all other models can learn the representations of sentences well. Interestingly, the spread of *MultiEnc-Mix@2* model is smaller than the spread when the context consists of the previous two sentences. This indicates that the model can learn better representations from random context even though the model is trained by mixing 50% of previous sentence context and 50% of random context. The same is true for the *MultiEnc-Random@2* model also. The representations of the *MultiEnc-Mix-Adapt@2* model are the same as the model trained with the previous sentence context and show that this model is consistent even when the type of context changes.

We also analyze how different types of context affect the decoder. Figure 2(b) and Figure 2(d) shows the target representations when the context consists of the previous two and random two sentences, respectively. We observe that the source context is insufficient to project the target embeddings closer even though the sentences are from the same document. Interestingly, in the random context setting (cf. Figure 2(d)), the representations are projected closer than the correct context setting (cf. Figure 2(b)), indicating that the decoder is mainly unaffected by the choice of the context. This might be due to the context being chosen from the source side and

[8] https://scikit-learn.org/stable/modules/generated/sklearn.manifold.TSNE.html

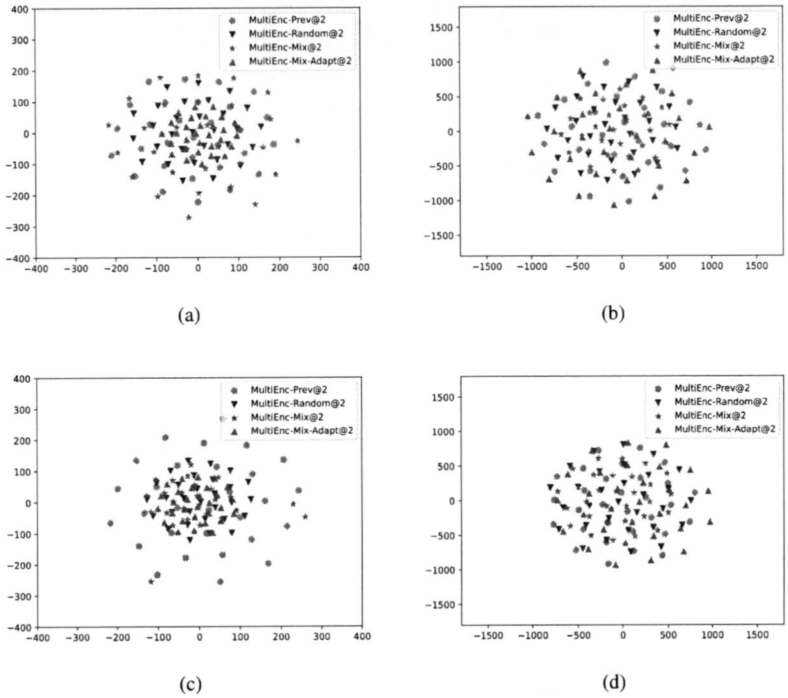

Figure 2: t-SNE visualization of the source and target representations of the Outside Context Multi-Encoder DocNMT models with different context settings. (a) and (b) show when the previous two sentences are used as context, (c) and (d) show When two random sentences are used as context. (a) and (c) show the source representations, (b) and (d) shows the target representations. Each point represents a sentence.

leading to the sub-optimal encoding of target sentences. We hypothesize that the model can learn better target representation if trained with target-side context.

Based on the analysis, the model can learn discourse-level properties even when the context is random, indicating that the random context might not adversely affect the context-aware model. This also shows that the context encoder might not be generating noise; instead, it can generate sufficient information to capture discourse-level properties based on the type of context the model is trained with. The t-SNE visualization shows that the source representations are affected by the choice of context, and the target representations are mainly unaffected. This suggests that metrics such as BLEU might not be enough to measure the discourse-level information the system can learn and requires unique discourse-level test sets to evaluate.

5.3 Results of Multi-Encoder models with identical Source and Context

We further study whether the context encoder generates noise by feeding the same source sentence as the context. If the context encoder is generating noise, then the models' performance should be similar, as the inputs are identical to every model. Table 4 shows the s-BLEU scores of the models tested in this setting. Interestingly *MultiEnc-Random@2* models' performance

Model	News	TED	Europarl
MultiEnc-Prev@2	16.9	16.1	22.8
MultiEnc-Random@2	14.1	15.7	20.1
MultiEnc-Mix@2	20.5	19.0	24.4
MultiEnc-Mix-Adapt@2	**23.0**	**20.5**	**26.5**

Table 4: s-BLEU scores of the Outside Context DocNMT models, tested with the same source sentences as the context. The best scores are shown in bold.

is lowest than the other models. This indicates that the context encoder might generate noise when the context is random. Similarly, *MultiEnc-Mix@2* and *MultiEnc-Mix-Adapt@2* models' performance is better than the other models. Results indicate that mixing the random context with the correct context makes the model robust and results in better-quality translations.

6 Conclusion and Future Work

In this work, we conducted experiments on multi-encoder-based DocNMT systems to study how different types of contexts affect context-aware pronoun translation. Specifically, we consider three different types of context settings *viz,* previous two sentences, random two sentences, and a mix of both these settings. We use the ContraPro test set as the context-aware test set to analyze the pronoun translation accuracy. Our analysis shows that the multi-encoder models can perform well on pronoun translation even when the context is random. We further conduct experiments to study whether the context encoder is generating noise or not by projecting the sentence representations from a single document using t-SNE. The analysis shows that the context encoder can encode the context sufficiently enough to capture the relation between the sentences, as these sentences are connected only via context. Based on the analysis, we conclude that the random context might not adversely affect the performance of multi-encoder-based DocNMT models. Choosing context is essential for effectively capturing any discourse phenomenon. The context encoder might not be generating noise. Instead, the encoding from the context encoder is dependent on the choice of context. As we observed that mixing selected context (previous two sentences in this case) and random context is performing better than the other settings, we plan to explore effective context encoding through contrastive learning (Hwang et al., 2021) and dynamic context generation based on the source and target pairs which can help during the inference in round-trip-translation (Tu et al., 2017) method.

Acknowledgements

We gratefully acknowledge the support from "NLTM: VIDYAAPATI" project, sponsored by Electronics and IT, Ministry of Electronics and Information Technology (MeitY), Government of India. We also thank the anonymous reviewers for their insightful comments.

References

Agrawal, R. R., Turchi, M., and Negri, M. (2018). Contextual handling in neural machine translation: Look behind, ahead and on both sides. In *21st Annual Conference of the European Association for Machine Translation*, pages 11–20.

Anastasopoulos, A. and Chiang, D. (2018). Tied multitask learning for neural speech translation. In *Proceedings of the 2018 Conference of the North American Chapter of the Association for Computational Linguistics: Human Language Technologies, Volume 1 (Long Papers)*, pages 82–91, New Orleans, Louisiana. Association for Computational Linguistics.

Bao, G., Zhang, Y., Teng, Z., Chen, B., and Luo, W. (2021). G-transformer for document-level machine translation. In *Proceedings of the 59th Annual Meeting of the Association for Computational Linguistics and the 11th International Joint Conference on Natural Language Processing (Volume 1: Long Papers)*, pages 3442–3455, Online. Association for Computational Linguistics.

Bawden, R., Sennrich, R., Birch, A., and Haddow, B. (2018). Evaluating discourse phenomena in neural machine translation. In *Proceedings of the 2018 Conference of the North American Chapter of the Association for Computational Linguistics: Human Language Technologies, Volume 1 (Long Papers)*, pages 1304–1313, New Orleans, Louisiana. Association for Computational Linguistics.

Devlin, J., Chang, M.-W., Lee, K., and Toutanova, K. (2019). BERT: Pre-training of deep bidirectional transformers for language understanding. In *Proceedings of the 2019 Conference of the North American Chapter of the Association for Computational Linguistics: Human Language Technologies, Volume 1 (Long and Short Papers)*, pages 4171–4186, Minneapolis, Minnesota. Association for Computational Linguistics.

Donato, D., Yu, L., and Dyer, C. (2021). Diverse pretrained context encodings improve document translation. In *Proceedings of the 59th Annual Meeting of the Association for Computational Linguistics and the 11th International Joint Conference on Natural Language Processing (Volume 1: Long Papers)*, pages 1299–1311, Online. Association for Computational Linguistics.

Feng, Y., Li, F., Song, Z., Zheng, B., and Koehn, P. (2022). Learn to remember: Transformer with recurrent memory for document-level machine translation. In *Findings of the Association for Computational Linguistics: NAACL 2022*, pages 1409–1420, Seattle, United States. Association for Computational Linguistics.

Gain, B., Appicharla, R., Chennabasavaraj, S., Garera, N., Ekbal, A., and Chelliah, M. (2022). Investigating effectiveness of multi-encoder for conversational neural machine translation. In *Proceedings of the Seventh Conference on Machine Translation (WMT)*, pages 949–954, Abu Dhabi, United Arab Emirates (Hybrid). Association for Computational Linguistics.

Huo, J., Herold, C., Gao, Y., Dahlmann, L., Khadivi, S., and Ney, H. (2020). Diving deep into context-aware neural machine translation. In *Proceedings of the Fifth Conference on Machine Translation*, pages 604–616, Online. Association for Computational Linguistics.

Hwang, Y., Yun, H., and Jung, K. (2021). Contrastive learning for context-aware neural machine translation using coreference information. In *Proceedings of the Sixth Conference on Machine Translation*, pages 1135–1144, Online. Association for Computational Linguistics.

Junczys-Dowmunt, M. (2019). Microsoft translator at WMT 2019: Towards large-scale document-level neural machine translation. In *Proceedings of the Fourth Conference on Machine Translation (Volume 2: Shared Task Papers, Day 1)*, pages 225–233, Florence, Italy. Association for Computational Linguistics.

Junczys-Dowmunt, M. and Grundkiewicz, R. (2018). MS-UEdin submission to the WMT2018 APE shared task: Dual-source transformer for automatic post-editing. In *Proceedings of the Third Conference on Machine Translation: Shared Task Papers*, pages 822–826, Belgium, Brussels. Association for Computational Linguistics.

Kang, X., Zhao, Y., Zhang, J., and Zong, C. (2020). Dynamic context selection for document-level neural machine translation via reinforcement learning. In *Proceedings of the 2020 Conference on Empirical Methods in Natural Language Processing (EMNLP)*, pages 2242–2254, Online. Association for Computational Linguistics.

Kim, Y., Tran, D. T., and Ney, H. (2019). When and why is document-level context useful in neural machine translation? In *Proceedings of the Fourth Workshop on Discourse in Machine Translation (DiscoMT 2019)*, pages 24–34, Hong Kong, China. Association for Computational Linguistics.

Kingma, D. P. and Ba, J. (2015). Adam: A method for stochastic optimization. In Bengio, Y. and LeCun, Y., editors, *3rd International Conference on Learning Representations, ICLR 2015, San Diego, CA, USA, May 7-9, 2015, Conference Track Proceedings*.

Kudo, T. and Richardson, J. (2018). SentencePiece: A simple and language independent subword tokenizer and detokenizer for neural text processing. In *Proceedings of the 2018 Conference on Empirical Methods in Natural Language Processing: System Demonstrations*, pages 66–71, Brussels, Belgium. Association for Computational Linguistics.

Li, B., Liu, H., Wang, Z., Jiang, Y., Xiao, T., Zhu, J., Liu, T., and Li, C. (2020). Does multi-encoder help? a case study on context-aware neural machine translation. In *Proceedings of the 58th Annual Meeting of the Association for Computational Linguistics*, pages 3512–3518, Online. Association for Computational Linguistics.

Libovický, J., Helcl, J., and Mareček, D. (2018). Input combination strategies for multi-source transformer decoder. In *Proceedings of the Third Conference on Machine Translation: Research Papers*, pages 253–260, Brussels, Belgium. Association for Computational Linguistics.

Liu, J., Luo, L., Ao, X., Song, Y., Xu, H., and Ye, J. (2020a). Meet changes with constancy: Learning invariance in multi-source translation. In *Proceedings of the 28th International Conference on Computational Linguistics*, pages 1122–1132, Barcelona, Spain (Online). International Committee on Computational Linguistics.

Liu, Y., Gu, J., Goyal, N., Li, X., Edunov, S., Ghazvininejad, M., Lewis, M., and Zettlemoyer, L. (2020b). Multilingual denoising pre-training for neural machine translation. *Transactions of the Association for Computational Linguistics*, 8:726–742.

Luong, M.-T., Le, Q. V., Sutskever, I., Vinyals, O., and Kaiser, L. (2015). Multi-task sequence to sequence learning. *arXiv preprint arXiv:1511.06114*.

Ma, S., Zhang, D., and Zhou, M. (2020). A simple and effective unified encoder for document-level machine translation. In *Proceedings of the 58th Annual Meeting of the Association for Computational Linguistics*, pages 3505–3511, Online. Association for Computational Linguistics.

Maruf, S. and Haffari, G. (2018). Document context neural machine translation with memory networks. In *Proceedings of the 56th Annual Meeting of the Association for Computational Linguistics (Volume 1: Long Papers)*, pages 1275–1284, Melbourne, Australia. Association for Computational Linguistics.

Maruf, S., Martins, A. F. T., and Haffari, G. (2019). Selective attention for context-aware neural machine translation. In *Proceedings of the 2019 Conference of the North American Chapter of the Association for Computational Linguistics: Human Language Technologies, Volume 1 (Long and Short Papers)*, pages 3092–3102, Minneapolis, Minnesota. Association for Computational Linguistics.

Miculicich, L., Ram, D., Pappas, N., and Henderson, J. (2018). Document-level neural machine translation with hierarchical attention networks. In *Proceedings of the 2018 Conference on Empirical Methods in Natural Language Processing*, pages 2947–2954, Brussels, Belgium. Association for Computational Linguistics.

Müller, M., Rios, A., Voita, E., and Sennrich, R. (2018). A large-scale test set for the evaluation of context-aware pronoun translation in neural machine translation. In *Proceedings of the Third Conference on Machine Translation: Research Papers*, pages 61–72, Brussels, Belgium. Association for Computational Linguistics.

Pal, S., Herbig, N., Krüger, A., and van Genabith, J. (2018). A transformer-based multi-source automatic post-editing system. In *Proceedings of the Third Conference on Machine Translation: Shared Task Papers*, pages 827–835, Belgium, Brussels. Association for Computational Linguistics.

Pal, S., Xu, H., Herbig, N., Krüger, A., and van Genabith, J. (2019). USAAR-DFKI – the transference architecture for English–German automatic post-editing. In *Proceedings of the Fourth Conference on Machine Translation (Volume 3: Shared Task Papers, Day 2)*, pages 124–131, Florence, Italy. Association for Computational Linguistics.

Papineni, K., Roukos, S., Ward, T., and Zhu, W.-J. (2002). Bleu: a method for automatic evaluation of machine translation. In *Proceedings of the 40th Annual Meeting of the Association for Computational Linguistics*, pages 311–318, Philadelphia, Pennsylvania, USA. Association for Computational Linguistics.

Popel, M. and Bojar, O. (2018). Training tips for the transformer model. *arXiv preprint arXiv:1804.00247*.

Post, M. (2018). A call for clarity in reporting BLEU scores. In *Proceedings of the Third Conference on Machine Translation: Research Papers*, pages 186–191, Brussels, Belgium. Association for Computational Linguistics.

Post, M. and Junczys-Dowmunt, M. (2023). Escaping the sentence-level paradigm in machine translation.

Rei, R., Stewart, C., Farinha, A. C., and Lavie, A. (2020). COMET: A neural framework for MT evaluation. In *Proceedings of the 2020 Conference on Empirical Methods in Natural Language Processing (EMNLP)*, pages 2685–2702, Online. Association for Computational Linguistics.

Sennrich, R., Haddow, B., and Birch, A. (2016). Neural machine translation of rare words with subword units. In *Proceedings of the 54th Annual Meeting of the Association for Computational Linguistics (Volume 1: Long Papers)*, pages 1715–1725, Berlin, Germany. Association for Computational Linguistics.

Shin, J. and Lee, J.-H. (2018). Multi-encoder transformer network for automatic post-editing. In *Proceedings of the Third Conference on Machine Translation: Shared Task Papers*, pages 840–845, Belgium, Brussels. Association for Computational Linguistics.

Sim Smith, K. (2017). On integrating discourse in machine translation. In *Proceedings of the Third Workshop on Discourse in Machine Translation*, pages 110–121, Copenhagen, Denmark. Association for Computational Linguistics.

Sun, Z., Wang, M., Zhou, H., Zhao, C., Huang, S., Chen, J., and Li, L. (2022). Rethinking document-level neural machine translation. In *Findings of the Association for Computational Linguistics: ACL 2022*, pages 3537–3548, Dublin, Ireland. Association for Computational Linguistics.

Tiedemann, J. and Scherrer, Y. (2017). Neural machine translation with extended context. In *Proceedings of the Third Workshop on Discourse in Machine Translation*, pages 82–92, Copenhagen, Denmark. Association for Computational Linguistics.

Tu, Z., Liu, Y., Shang, L., Liu, X., and Li, H. (2017). Neural machine translation with reconstruction. In *Proceedings of the AAAI Conference on Artificial Intelligence*, volume 31.

Van der Maaten, L. and Hinton, G. (2008). Visualizing data using t-sne. *Journal of machine learning research*, 9(11).

Vaswani, A., Shazeer, N., Parmar, N., Uszkoreit, J., Jones, L., Gomez, A. N., Kaiser, Ł., and Polosukhin, I. (2017). Attention is all you need. In *Advances in neural information processing systems*, pages 5998–6008.

Voita, E., Sennrich, R., and Titov, I. (2019). When a good translation is wrong in context: Context-aware machine translation improves on deixis, ellipsis, and lexical cohesion. In *Proceedings of the 57th Annual Meeting of the Association for Computational Linguistics*, pages 1198–1212, Florence, Italy. Association for Computational Linguistics.

Voita, E., Serdyukov, P., Sennrich, R., and Titov, I. (2018). Context-aware neural machine translation learns anaphora resolution. In *Proceedings of the 56th Annual Meeting of the Association for Computational Linguistics (Volume 1: Long Papers)*, pages 1264–1274, Melbourne, Australia. Association for Computational Linguistics.

Wang, L., Tu, Z., Wang, X., Ding, L., Ding, L., and Shi, S. (2020). Tencent AI lab machine translation systems for WMT20 chat translation task. In *Proceedings of the Fifth Conference on Machine Translation*, pages 483–491, Online. Association for Computational Linguistics.

Zhang, J., Liu, Q., and Zhou, J. (2017). Me-md: An effective framework for neural machine translation with multiple encoders and decoders. In *Proceedings of the 26th International Joint Conference on Artificial Intelligence*, pages 3392–3398.

Zhang, J., Luan, H., Sun, M., Zhai, F., Xu, J., Zhang, M., and Liu, Y. (2018). Improving the transformer translation model with document-level context. In *Proceedings of the 2018 Conference on Empirical Methods in Natural Language Processing*, pages 533–542, Brussels, Belgium. Association for Computational Linguistics.

Zhang, P., Chen, B., Ge, N., and Fan, K. (2020). Long-short term masking transformer: A simple but effective baseline for document-level neural machine translation. In *Proceedings of the 2020 Conference on Empirical Methods in Natural Language Processing (EMNLP)*, pages 1081–1087, Online. Association for Computational Linguistics.

In-context Learning as Maintaining Coherency: A Study of On-the-fly Machine Translation Using Large Language Models

Suzanna Sia ssia1@jh.edu
Kevin Duh kevinduh@cs.jhu.edu
Johns Hopkins University

Abstract

The phenomena of in-context learning has typically been thought of as "learning from examples". In this work which focuses on Machine Translation, we present a perspective of in-context learning as the desired generation task maintaining coherency with its context, i.e., the prompt examples. We first investigate randomly sampled prompts across 4 domains, and find that translation performance improves when shown in-domain prompts. Next, we investigate coherency for the in-domain setting, which uses prompt examples from a moving window. We study this with respect to other factors that have previously been identified in the literature such as length, surface similarity and sentence embedding similarity. Our results across 3 models (GPTNeo2.7B, Bloom3B, XGLM2.9B), and three translation directions (`en`→{`pt`, `de`, `fr`}) suggest that the long-term coherency of the prompts and the test sentence is a good indicator of downstream translation performance. In doing so, we demonstrate the efficacy of in-context Machine Translation for on-the-fly adaptation. Code for this paper is available at `https://github.com/suzyahyah/icl_coherence_mt`.

1 Introduction

The in-context learning paradigm describes a phenomena where large autoregressive language models perform a task when shown examples (known as prompts) in the prefix (Brown et al., 2020; Bommasani et al., 2021). In-context Machine Translation is a relatively new paradigm that uses large autoregressive Language Models to carry out the task of Machine Translation (MT) by being shown translation pairs in the prefix. From a practitioner's viewpoint, in-context learning presents itself as an attractive approach for rapidly adapting a translation model on-the-fly. Previous strategies for adapting a pre-trained MT model still require additional engineering or training of the model, e.g fine-tuning with in-domain data using adaptor layers (Philip et al., 2020). Instead, simply changing the inputs to the model might be an effective way to adapt on-the-fly without any model modification.

Previous work assumes that the role of the prompt context is to allow the model to "learn by examples". This has led to formulating the task of prompt selection as selecting examples that are similar to the source sentence being translated. Semantic similarity based on sentence embeddings (Liu et al., 2021) and BM25 have been proposed to select examples to present as "demonstrations" (Rubin et al., 2021). This approach was further expanded by Agrawal et al. (2022) who use a heuristic version optimizing for word coverage.

Proceedings of Machine Translation Summit XIX, Vol. 1: Research Track, pages 173–185
September 4–8, 2023, Macau SAR, China.

Translate English to French.		
English: A discomfort which lasts ..	French:	Un malaise qui dure
English: HTML is a language for formatting	French:	HTML est un langage de formatage
...		...
English: After you become comfortable with formatting ..	French:	

Table 1: A single continuous input sequence presented to the model for decoding a single test source sentence "After you become comfortable with formatting..". Given the entire sequence as input, the model proceeds to generate the target sequence.

We focus on Machine Translation as a complex conditional generation task and offer an alternate perspective: **the in-context paradigm depends on maintaining *coherency*.** Coherence is an aspect of natural language that reflects the overall semantic and syntatic consistency in a body of text (Flowerdew and Mahlberg, 2009). We investigate this by first exploring the model's behavior when showing matching and mismatching domains in the context and the test sentence. Next we consider a stricter notion of coherency using a moving window of previous gold translations directly preceding the test source sentence to be next translated. Our experiments compare the coherence factor with similarity based factors for prompt selection, additionally controlling for length (Xie et al., 2021) which is typically overlooked but is important to consider for performance and available labeling (translation) budget. The contributions of this work are

- We identify coherency of prompt examples with respect to test sentence as a critical factor for translation performance. Experiments across 3 models (GPTNeo2.7B, Bloom3B, XGLM2.9B) and 4 domains (Medical, Social Media, Wikipedia, and TED Talks) suggest that models perform better when prompts are randomly drawn from the same domain.
- Within the TED talks domain, we investigate local coherence using document-level translation experiments, by adopting a moving window directly preceding the test source sentence to be translated. Overall, our results across the 3 models and three translation directions (`en`→{`pt, de, fr`}) suggest that the coherency of the prompts with regard to the test sentence is a good indicator of translation performance.

2 Preliminaries

2.1 In-context Machine Translation

In an in-context learning setup, several formatting decisions need to be made on how to present the prompt examples to the model. We adopt the following commonly used prompt format where the instructions are straightforwardly provided as in the following (Table 1).[1] In this work, we consider both sentence level translation (Section 5.1) and an on-the-fly document-level setting (Section 5.3).

2.2 Coherence in Natural Language Text

The computational linguistics literature holds many competing definitions of coherence in text (Wang and Guo, 2014). We consider two aspects of coherence, first from a more global level where we investigate domain effects, and also from a local sentence level, where we consider a coherent context as a moving window of previous (gold) translations which directly precede

[1]We also experiment with a different separator "=" used in (Lin et al., 2021) (instead of "English" and "French"), but find that this does not perform significantly better.

a test sentence. A similar working definition of coherence has been used in discrimination tasks that require a model to identify the right order of (shuffled) sentences (Elsner et al., 2007; Barzilay and Lapata, 2008; Laban et al., 2021).

3 Factors which affect In-context MT

We outline several factors studied in this paper related to example selection for in-context MT in Figure 1. While we emphasise the notion of *Coherence* (Section 2.2), by studying the domain factor (Section 3.4) and local coherence (Section 3.5), our experiments seek to compare this against other factors that have been highlighted in previous literature. Namely, length (Section 3.1), surface similarity (Section 3.2) and semantic similarity (Section 3.3). To demonstrate, in Table 1, the first sentence is semantically similar and the second sentence has surface similarity with the test sentence.

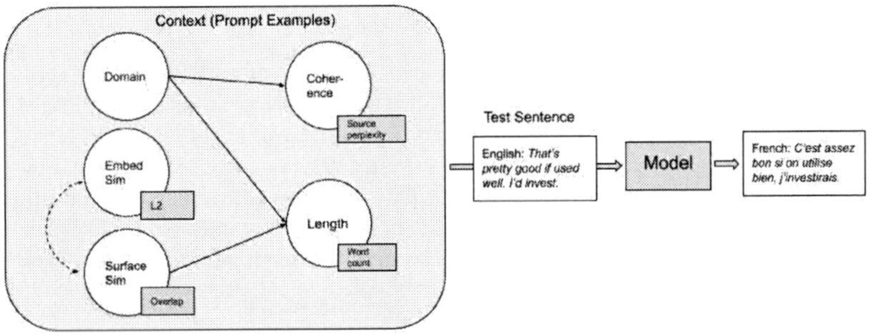

Figure 1: Factors identified and studied in this paper. Each domain has different length distributions (Section 5.2). Surface similarity and embedding similarity are associated (Table 4). Surface similarity selection also results in longer sentences (Section 5.4) Rectangle boxes next to the node are measures of these factors.

3.1 Length (Translation Budget)

One previously overlooked factor is the length (number of words) of prompt examples. The perspective of in-context Learning as implicit Bayesian Inference argues that longer examples provide more evidence to the model on the desired task pattern (Xie et al., 2021). Longer examples are also more likely to contain non-trivial translation exemplars, although it is not clear whether this affects downstream performance. We find example length to be correlated with the domain (Figure 2), and it may thus be a confounding factor for in-context MT.

Controlling for Length We adopt the notion of a "Translation Budget" which is the total word count of all the prompt examples provided (excluding the test sentence). Examples can be selected as long as they satisfy the budget constraint. A generalized algorithm is provided in Section 4.3. From a resource perspective, this reflects the work of the human annotator in providing example translations.

3.2 Surface Similarity

3.2.1 BM25

BM25 (Robertson et al., 2009) is a bag-of-words unsupervised retrieval function that ranks a set of documents based on the query terms appearing in the documents. Agrawal et al. (2022) report that using BM25 to retrieve similar prompt examples outperforms random selection. They also advocate for a variant of BM25 with increased coverage of test sentence source words although with marginal gains ($<$ 1 BLEU point) increase. Following Agrawal et al. (2022), we order the examples according to their similarity to the source, with the most similar examples on the left in all our experiments.

3.2.2 Maximising Surface Similarity Coverage

To maximise word overlap across all prompts and the source sentence, we adopt Submodular optimisation by Maximal Marginal Relevance (Carbonell and Goldstein, 1998; Lin and Bilmes, 2010). Formally we are given a finite size set of objects U (the size of the prompt bank). A valuation function $f : 2^U \rightarrow R_+$ returns a non-negative real value for any subset $X \subset U$. The function f is said to be submodular if it satisfies the property of "diminishing returns", namely, for all $X \subset Z$ and $Z \notin U$, we have $f(X \cup u) - f(X) \geq f(Z \cup u) - f(Z)$. The algorithm optimises for sentences with maximal word overlap weighted by the BM25 score.

3.3 Semantic Similarity (Nearest Neighbors)

The semantic similarity of prompts based on their sentence embeddings has also been advocated for selecting good in-context examples. Liu et al. (2021) apply a pre-trained Roberta-large sentence encoder to the test sentence, and query for its nearest neighbors to use as in-context demonstrations. In our experiments we apply a similar strategy using MPNet base (Song et al., 2020) which achieved highest scores on HuggingFace sentence embedding and semantic search benchmarks.[2] We do not consider training a prompt retriever (Rubin et al., 2021) or fine-tuning the sentence encoder (Liu et al., 2021) in this study, as these are no longer "light-weight" retrieval methods that are comparable with the other unsupervised strategies.

3.4 Domain Coherence

GPT is able to do style transfer just from instructions or from being shown surface prompt examples (Reif et al., 2022). Simply providing demonstrations from the same domain may induce the large language model (LLM) to generate a similar style which is coherent with the target text. Another possibility is that particular lexical translation exemplars which match the source sentence may be present. However, due to the very high dimensionality of the raw vocabulary, this is less likely if translation examples are randomly sampled.

Domain may also present spurious correlations which are confounded by the training data of LLMs. For instance, there may be certain domains which are better at eliciting Translation behavior from the model, regardless of what the test domain is.

3.5 Local Coherence (Moving Window)

We hypothesise that the local coherence (Section 2.2) of the context to the test sentence to be translated may be an important factor for performance. To test this, we adopt a moving context window of the previously translated gold sentence pairs as the prompt examples. To our knowledge, Section 3.4 and Section 3.5 are previously unexplored for in-context MT.

4 Experiments

4.1 Data

Domain Coherence We organise our experiments investigating four `en`$\rightarrow$`fr` domains, WMT19 Biomedical (MED) (Bawden et al., 2019), a social media dataset, MTNT (Michel and Neubig, 2018), multilingual TED Talks, and Wikipedia-based FLORES (Goyal et al., 2021).

[2] `https://www.sbert.net/docs/pretrained_models.html`

Algorithm 1: Generalised greedy (submodular) algorithm with length budget

Input: (Submodular) function $f : 2^U \rightarrow R_+$, cost function m, budget b, finite prompt bank U

Output: X_k where k is the number of iterations/prompts.

Set $X_0 \leftarrow$; $i \leftarrow 0$;

while $m(X_i) < b$ **do**

  $u_i = \text{argmax}_{u \in U \setminus X_i} f(\{u\} \mid X_i)$

  $X_{i+1} \leftarrow X_i \cup u_i$;

  $i \leftarrow i + 1$

Except for MED, all other datasets have a wide range of topics in the train (prompt bank) and test set which are shuffled in random sampling, and thus the domain experiments are more focused on the writing style of the text. We use standard train-test splits, with the trainset being used as the prompt bank. Scores are reported using SacreBLEU (Post, 2018).[3]

Local Coherence (document level) We use the Multitarget TED Talks dataset from Duh (2018). The original dataset has 30 documents in the test set, where each document corresponds to a 10-20 minute TED talk. To increase the size of the test set, we partition the "original" trainset into a train (prompt bank) and test split, where talks with a minimum of 100 lines were used as the test and talks with less than 100 lines were used as the "out-of-document" prompt bank. We used 120 test documents that had a minimum of 100 lines, and we evaluated each up to 120 lines, where each TED talk is a document. The document level BLEU scores are reported for three language directions `en`$\rightarrow$\{`fr`, `pt`, `de`\}. We do not use a dev set as there is no training or any tuning of any hyperparameters.

Since this is a non-standardised data split, we provide the numbers in the following table.

	Talks (Docs)	Lines per doc	Total Lines
"Outside-doc" Prompt Bank	450	<100	26000+
"Within-doc" Prompt Bank	1	100-120	120
Test	120	100-120	12000+

4.2 Models

We use three models, GPTNeo2.7B (Black et al., 2021), XGLM2.9B (Lin et al., 2021), and Bloom3B (Scao et al., 2022) which are open access LLMs available on HuggingFace (Wolf et al., 2020). The later two have been advertised as "Multilingual Language Models". We also experimented with OPT2.7B, but find that its incontext MT abilities were nearly twice as poor as GPTNeo2.7B. GPTNeo2.7B is a GPT3 replicate pretrained on The Pile (Gao et al., 2020), while XGLM adopts a similar architecture trained on a multilingual corpus (CC100-XL). Bloom3B has been trained on the ROOTS Corpus (Laurençon et al., 2022), a collection of huggingface datasets of 1.6 TB of text. To our knowledge, there has not been any reports of sentence level parallel corpora in the training datasets of these models.

4.3 Algorithm for Greedy selection with Length Constraint

In our experiments, we investigate `BM25` (Section 3.2.1), `BM25` with submodular optimisation (`BM25-s`; Section 3.2.2), and semantic similarity (`nn`; Section 3.3). To control for length effects, we employ an algorithm for selection with length constraints (algorithm 1) which closely

[3] nrefs:1 | case:lower | eff:no | tok:13a | smooth:exp | version:2.0.0

Prompt / Test	GPTNeo2.7B FLORES	MED	MTNT	TED	Bloom3B FLORES	MED	MTNT	TED	XGLM2.9B FLORES	MED	MTNT	TED
FLORES	**24.6**	**19.7**	**23.1**	**24.6**	**36.7**	28.5	28.5	31.1	**29.3**	20.9	24.7	**25.7**
MED	23.0	19.2	21.1	23.2	34.5	**28.7**	26.2	29.5	27.5	**21.4**	22.9	24.4
MTNT	23.7	18.6	22.4	23.7	35.5	27.7	**29.1**	30.6	27.9	21.2	**25.0**	25.4
TED	23.2	18.6	22.1	23.6	36.1	27.9	**29.1**	**31.2**	27.8	21.1	24.2	24.8

Table 2: Crosstable of BLEU scores from sampling and testing in different domains. We present the average BLEU scores across 5 randomly sampled prompt sets. The size of the prompt sets (number of translation pair examples) is 5. We bold the largest value column-wise.

follows greedy submodular algorithms (Krause and Guestrin, 2008). Retrieval methods adopts a utility function: f, which is used to retrieve highest scoring sentences. For `BM25` and `BM25-s`, $f$is `BM25`, while u_i is selected by $f(\{u\})$, and $f(\{u\}|X_i)$ respectively. While for `nn`, f is the L2 embedding similarity between prompt sentence and test query.

5 Analysis of Factors

5.1 Domain Coherence [Table 2]

Does coherence of domain allow models to adapt on the fly? If models are adapting to the domain shown in the context, sampling and testing within the same domain should result in the highest translation performance, as compared to being shown examples out of domain. For example, if we are testing on the TED domain, is it important that the prompt be also drawn from TED or is it sufficient to have sentence pairs from any domain illustrating the translation task? To account for prompt selection and ordering effects, all inference runs were repeated with 5 randomly sampled prompt sets from the training data. We focus on `en` $\rightarrow$ `fr` which is common across datasets.

Results and Discussion

- Multilingual GPT models namely Bloom and XGLM appear to be doing domain adaptation, as sampling and testing within the same domain (e.g., sample from MED test with MED) mostly results in the highest performance column-wise.

- For GPTNeo, sampling from FLORES results in the best translation performance across all test sentences even with domain mismatch. This suggests that translation performance in GPTNeo is best induced using FLORES and is less adaptive to the domain. Note that the second best column wise result for GPTNeo tends to occur when there is matching prompt and test domain.

5.2 Domain controlling for Length

How does length of prompts affect translation across different domains? In Figure 2, we randomly sample 1000 sentences from each domain's training set. Randomly sampled sentences from different domains show distinct length effects. We study the impact of these length effects by selecting either a 5-10 word or 15-20 word long sentences for translation examples, and compare the differences in scores for the non-filtered scenario (Table 3).

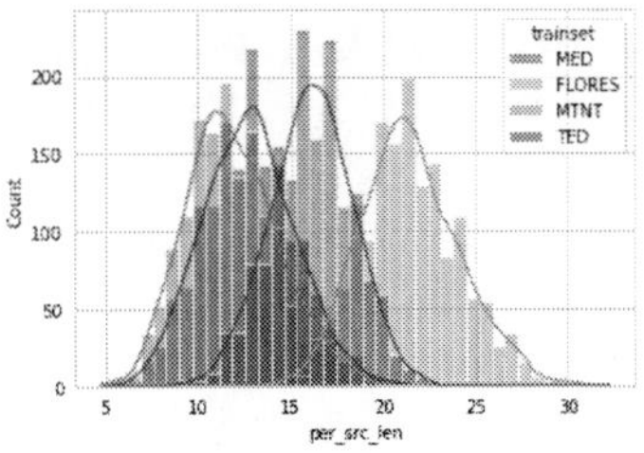

Figure 2: Histograms of sentence lengths (word counts) randomly sampled from different domains, which has implications for the total prompt length when sampling from these domains. FLORES sentences tend to be nearly twice as long as MTNT and TED sentences.

Prompt / Test	FLORES	MED	MTNT	TED
FLORES	-	-	-	-
MED	⇓22.4	⇓18.5	↓20.8	⇓22.5
MTNT	⇓23.2	↓18.3	⇓21.9	↓23.5
TED	⇓21.7	⇓17.6	⇓20.1	⇓22.3
5-10 words long sentences; GPTNeo 2.7B				
FLORES	24.2↓	19.6	22.7↓	24.3↓
MED	22.9	19.3	21.1	22.8 ↓
MTNT	24.0 ↑	18.9↑	22.5	24.3⇑
TED	23.8⇑	19.0↑	22.9⇑	23.8
15-20 words long sentences; GPTNeo 2.7B				

Table 3: Selecting for short source sentences (5-10 words) vs longer source sentences (15-20 words) as translation examples. ↓and ↑refers to differences > 0.3, and ⇓and ⇑refers to differences > 0.5 when compared to the no-length filter scenario in Table 2.

Results and Discussion

- When source prompt sentences are 5-10 words, all BLEU scores decrease. For 15-20 words sentences which is "long" for MTNT and TED, but "short" for FLORES, the BLEU score of the former increases while the latter decreases. BLEU scores are similar for MED as 15-20 words is close to the mean of MED length distribution.
- We inspect the length of generation under different prompt lengths, and find that average differences in generation length are marginal (only 1-2 words difference) indicating that poorer performance is not simply due to a difference in generation lengths.

5.3 Local Coherence [Table 4]

How important is a coherent context (as compared to other prompt selection methods?) Section 5.1 showed that models are able to adapt when shown prompts from a matching domain. We hypothesise that coherence of the prompts with respect to the test source sentence (Section 2.2) is an important factor for performance.

We use the TED talks dataset (data preparation described in Section 4.1), and consider a moving window of previous gold translations (`window`) as a coherent context for the model.[4] We compare this against the baselines of (`BM25`; Section 3.2.1), (`BM25-s`; Section 3.2.2), and Nearest Neighbor retrieval of sentence embeddings (`nn`; Section 3.3) from a large prompt bank outside the document. We use a prompt set of 5 examples for all experiments, and randomly sample from outside of the document if the available window is smaller than 5. Document level BLEU scores are averaged across 120 documents and reported in Table 4.

Quantifying Similarity We report the ROUGE1-precision (`coverage`; Lin (2004)) and the L2 Euclidean distance (`L2`) of the source sentences in the prompt set, with the test source sentence to be translated. If translation performance is due to word overlap or embedding similarity, then we expect that having a higher `coverage` or lower `L2` would have better performance than `window`. Note that all similarity based retrieval methods depend only on the

[4]Preliminary experiments using model generated instead of gold translations performed worse than random.

		GPTNeo2.7B(BLEU)			Bloom3B(BLEU)			XGLM2.9B(BLEU)			L2	coverage
	In/outdoc	en→fr	en→pt	en→de	en→fr	en→pt	en→de	en→fr	en→pt	en→de	-	-
random	out	26.3	27.1	16.6	35.2	35.5	7.9	24.9	26.7	18.9	1.35	0.31
nn	out	26.8	26.9	16.9	35.1	35.1	8.2	25.4	26.6	18.3	0.98	0.49
BM25	out	27.1	27.4	17.3	35.1	35.3	**9.4**	25.9	27.0	18.4	1.21	0.75
BM25-s	out	27.2	27.5	17.4	34.8	34.9	9.1	25.4	27.4	18.7	1.25	0.80
random	within	27.4	27.3	17.3	35.9	35.8	7.8	26.6	28.8	19.6	1.28	0.34
window	within	**28.1**	**28.3**	**17.9**	**36.9**	**37.0**	8.8	**26.7**	**31.6**	**21.2**	1.22	0.40

Table 4: BLEU score comparison of similarity-based retrieval methods from out of document, and moving window (window) from within the document. Coverage (Rouge1-precision) refers to the word overlap between prompt source sentences and test source sentence. L2 refers to the average L2 Euclidean distance between source prompt sentence embeddings and the test sentence embedding.

source sentences, and is model and target language independent. i.e., the single coverage and L2 value applies for all results columns in Table 4.

Results and Discussion

- The moving window (window) outperforms all other baselines across the 3 models and 3 language directions, with the exception of Bloom3B on en→de direction. The gains are from 0.5 to 2.6 BLEU points from the next best performing retrieval method. Importantly, coverage and L2 shows that the performance is not due to similarity or word overlap.
- Interestingly, randomly sampling sentences from within the document (talk) performs well compared to other similarity based retrieval methods from outside of the document. This further highlights that coherence is a critical factor for In-context Machine Translation. Our results are consistent with concurrent work by Karpinska and Iyyer (2023) who show that translating an entire document is more effective than sentence by sentence translation.
- Similarity based retrieval mostly does better than randomly sampled prompt sets, which is consistent with existing literature which did not consider the factor of coherence. A notable exception is XGLM en→fr results, where similarity based methods are doing poorly compared to that reported by (Agrawal et al., 2022).

Crucially, this set of experiments show that *similarity based methods are not as critical for translation as compared to coherency*, a new factor that we identify in this work.

5.4 Similarity based Retrieval within the Document

How well do similarity based retrieval methods perform for previous on-the-fly translations? In Section 5.3, we established that using a moving window (local coherence) outperforms retrieval from outside the document with similarity-based retrieval methods. Here we apply BM25, BM25-s, nn for retrieval *within* the document. We consider the more realistic on-the-fly or computer-aided translation scenario, where the human translator works with MT systems, and translation examples in the document can only be selected prior to the test sentence (Alabau et al., 2014).

Controlling for Length When doing retrieval based methods within the document for an on-the-fly setting, length factors in and longer sentences are retrieved on average. We thus investigate budgeting for the length constraint to be same as the moving window (window). For every test sentence, we compute the budget used by it's own moving window, and apply it as a length constraint to for the other retrieval based methods as described in Section 4.3. Results are presented in Figure 3.

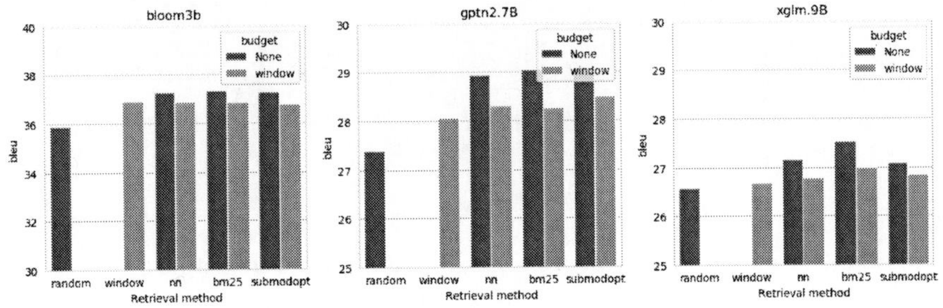

Figure 3: Comparison of Retrieval methods controlling for length budget: No budget or same budget as moving window. `random` is sampled within the document.

Results and Discussion

- We observe similar performance for all retrieval methods, with `BM25-s` doing slightly better than `BM25` and nearest neighbors (`nn`).
- Without any budget restriction, performance of retrieval methods outperforms `window`. However when restricted to the same budget as `window`, we find that the performance is within 0.1-0.5 BLEU score difference. Furthermore, the `coverage` is only 0.01-0.03 less if not using similarity based retrieval, indicating that most of the differences in contributions could be coming from the length effect and not because of similarity.

6 Further Analysis and Discussion

In this section, we focus on GPTNeo2.7B and in the `en`→`fr` direction.

6.1 Perplexity and Coverage

One natural question that arises is the relationship between `Coverage`, Coherence, and translation performance. Although there is no widely accepted measure of *general coherence*, we can formulate this with respect to the particular model being studied. We consider the model's conditional perplexity of the test sentence given the context. Perplexity is a widely used measure of suprisal in text and has also been used as a measure in topic coherence (Newman et al., 2010). Concurrent work by Gonen et al. (2022) argue that total perplexity of the input sequence is related to in-context performance.

In Figure 4, we produce scatterplots of Sentence BLEU scores, source perplexity and `Coverage` (word overlap). We observe that there is a negative relationship between source perplexity and Sentence BLEU (-0.22 Pearson's r), but very noisy relationship between Sentence BLEU and word overlap, and word overlap and source perplexity.

6.2 Studying Local Coherence [Table 5]

We compare the `window` with other baselines which may give some indication of what is important in the document in terms of local coherence.

- `Shuffle` simulates whether the model is affected by the the local coherence by shuffling sentences within `window`.
- `Static` refers to the first k (window size) translation sentences of the document which is then held fix throughout when translating the rest of the document.

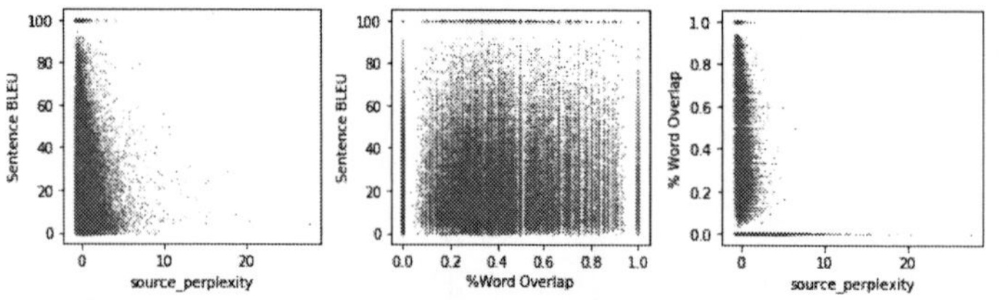

Figure 4: Scatterplots of Sentence BLEU Scores, with Source Perplexity and Word Overlap

retrieval	bleu	L2	Coverage	ppl_s
static	26.6	1.22	0.41	16.8
random	27.4	1.28	0.31	14.9
window	28.1	1.22	0.40	11.1
shuffle	28.3	1.22	0.40	12.0

Table 5: Ordering effects within document. All retrieval methods are within documnent.

Interestingly, shuffling the set of prompts within the moving window which breaks the natural ordering of the document "coherence" does not deteriorate in-context translation performance. The ordering of the document does affect source perplexity, with perplexity increasing from 11.1 $\rightarrow$ to 12.0, however this does not negatively affect translation performance. This suggests that the relationship between coherence and translation is indirect or non-linear, and the way models use context might be counter-intuitive; a view increasingly advocated by recent research (Webson and Pavlick, 2021; Min et al., 2022). Overall this suggests we may benefit from methods which perform selection from within the document which we leave to future work.

7 Conclusion

In-context Learning has typically been thought of as learning from examples. In this work, we introduce a different perspective of coherency of the context with the test sentence. We found that 2 out of 3 models are able to adapt to different writing styles when the prompt bank and test set are matching/consistent in domain. Experiments across 3 models and 3 languages show that a moving window is up to 2.6 BLEU points better than previously reported similarity based retrieval methods from outside the document. From this perspective, the problem of prompt selection for in-context MT is one of maintaining a coherency for text generation. Preliminary analysis on local coherence effects, and the presence of negative interference compared to the zero-shot setting, suggests avenues for future work on investigating more careful mechanisms for controlling in-context Machine Translation.

8 Limitations

While we have identified coherency of domain and document as a factor for in-context MT, we expect there should be other factors that could be more predictive of downstream performance, such as activation of attention patterns from source to target sentence during generation. We studied GPTNeo, Bloom and XGLM which have different training data but similar sizes. Due to GPU memory limitations we did not study larger models and it is not clear whether findings generalise to even larger models.

References

Agrawal, S., Zhou, C., Lewis, M., Zettlemoyer, L., and Ghazvininejad, M. (2022). In-context examples selection for machine translation. *arXiv preprint arXiv:2212.02437*.

Alabau, V., Buck, C., Carl, M., Casacuberta, F., García-Martínez, M., Germann, U., González-Rubio, J., Hill, R. L., Koehn, P., Leiva, L. A., et al. (2014). Casmacat: A computer-assisted translation workbench. In *Proceedings of the Demonstrations at the 14th Conference of the European Chapter of the Association for Computational Linguistics*, pages 25–28.

Barzilay, R. and Lapata, M. (2008). Modeling local coherence: An entity-based approach. *Computational Linguistics*, 34(1):1–34.

Bawden, R., Bretonnel Cohen, K., Grozea, C., Jimeno Yepes, A., Kittner, M., Krallinger, M., Mah, N., Neveol, A., Neves, M., Soares, F., Siu, A., Verspoor, K., and Vicente Navarro, M. (2019). Findings of the WMT 2019 biomedical translation shared task: Evaluation for MEDLINE abstracts and biomedical terminologies. In *Proceedings of the Fourth Conference on Machine Translation (Volume 3: Shared Task Papers, Day 2)*, pages 29–53, Florence, Italy. Association for Computational Linguistics.

Black, S., Leo, G., Wang, P., Leahy, C., and Biderman, S. (2021). GPT-Neo: Large scale autoregressive language modeling with Mesh-Tensorflow.

Bommasani, R., Hudson, D. A., Adeli, E., Altman, R., Arora, S., von Arx, S., Bernstein, M. S., Bohg, J., Bosselut, A., Brunskill, E., et al. (2021). On the opportunities and risks of foundation models. *arXiv preprint arXiv:2108.07258*.

Brown, T., Mann, B., Ryder, N., Subbiah, M., Kaplan, J. D., Dhariwal, P., Neelakantan, A., Shyam, P., Sastry, G., Askell, A., et al. (2020). Language models are few-shot learners. *Advances in neural information processing systems*, 33:1877–1901.

Carbonell, J. and Goldstein, J. (1998). The use of mmr, diversity-based reranking for reordering documents and producing summaries. In *Proceedings of the 21st annual international ACM SIGIR conference on Research and development in information retrieval*, pages 335–336.

Duh, K. (2018). The multitarget ted talks task. `http://www.cs.jhu.edu/~kevinduh/a/multitarget-tedtalks/`.

Elsner, M., Austerweil, J., and Charniak, E. (2007). A unified local and global model for discourse coherence. In *Human Language Technologies 2007: The Conference of the North American Chapter of the Association for Computational Linguistics; Proceedings of the Main Conference*, pages 436–443.

Flowerdew, J. and Mahlberg, M. (2009). *Lexical cohesion and corpus linguistics*, volume 17. John Benjamins Publishing.

Gao, L., Biderman, S., Black, S., Golding, L., Hoppe, T., Foster, C., Phang, J., He, H., Thite, A., Nabeshima, N., et al. (2020). The Pile: An 800GB dataset of diverse text for language modeling. *arXiv preprint arXiv:2101.00027*.

Gonen, H., Iyer, S., Blevins, T., Smith, N. A., and Zettlemoyer, L. (2022). Demystifying prompts in language models via perplexity estimation. *arXiv preprint arXiv:2212.04037*.

Goyal, N., Gao, C., Chaudhary, V., Chen, P.-J., Wenzek, G., Ju, D., Krishnan, S., Ranzato, M., Guzmán, F., and Fan, A. (2021). The flores-101 evaluation benchmark for low-resource and multilingual machine translation.

Karpinska, M. and Iyyer, M. (2023). Large language models effectively leverage document-level context for literary translation, but critical errors persist. *arXiv preprint arXiv:2304.03245*.

Krause, A. and Guestrin, C. (2008). Beyond convexity: Submodularity in machine learning. *ICML Tutorials*.

Laban, P., Dai, L., Bandarkar, L., and Hearst, M. A. (2021). Can transformer models measure coherence in text? re-thinking the shuffle test. *arXiv preprint arXiv:2107.03448*.

Laurençon, H., Saulnier, L., Wang, T., Akiki, C., del Moral, A. V., Le Scao, T., Von Werra, L., Mou, C., Ponferrada, E. G., Nguyen, H., et al. (2022). The bigscience roots corpus: A 1.6 tb composite multilingual dataset. In *Thirty-sixth Conference on Neural Information Processing Systems Datasets and Benchmarks Track*.

Lin, C.-Y. (2004). Rouge: A package for automatic evaluation of summaries. In *Text summarization branches out*, pages 74–81.

Lin, H. and Bilmes, J. (2010). Multi-document summarization via budgeted maximization of submodular functions. In *Human Language Technologies: The 2010 Annual Conference of the North American Chapter of the Association for Computational Linguistics*, pages 912–920.

Lin, X. V., Mihaylov, T., Artetxe, M., Wang, T., Chen, S., Simig, D., Ott, M., Goyal, N., Bhosale, S., Du, J., et al. (2021). Few-shot learning with multilingual language models. *arXiv preprint arXiv:2112.10668*.

Liu, J., Shen, D., Zhang, Y., Dolan, B., Carin, L., and Chen, W. (2021). What makes good in-context examples for gpt-3? *arXiv preprint arXiv:2101.06804*.

Michel, P. and Neubig, G. (2018). MTNT: A testbed for machine translation of noisy text. *arXiv preprint arXiv:1809.00388*.

Min, S., Lyu, X., Holtzman, A., Artetxe, M., Lewis, M., Hajishirzi, H., and Zettlemoyer, L. (2022). Rethinking the role of demonstrations: What makes in-context learning work? *arXiv preprint arXiv:2202.12837*.

Newman, D., Lau, J. H., Grieser, K., and Baldwin, T. (2010). Automatic evaluation of topic coherence. In *Human language technologies: The 2010 annual conference of the North American chapter of the association for computational linguistics*, pages 100–108.

Philip, J., Berard, A., Gallé, M., and Besacier, L. (2020). Monolingual adapters for zero-shot neural machine translation. In *Proceedings of the 2020 Conference on Empirical Methods in Natural Language Processing (EMNLP)*, pages 4465–4470, Online. Association for Computational Linguistics.

Post, M. (2018). A call for clarity in reporting BLEU scores. In *Proceedings of the Third Conference on Machine Translation: Research Papers*, pages 186–191, Brussels, Belgium. Association for Computational Linguistics.

Reif, E., Ippolito, D., Yuan, A., Coenen, A., Callison-Burch, C., and Wei, J. (2022). A recipe for arbitrary text style transfer with large language models. In *Proceedings of the 60th Annual Meeting of the Association for Computational Linguistics (Volume 2: Short Papers)*, pages 837–848, Dublin, Ireland. Association for Computational Linguistics.

Robertson, S., Zaragoza, H., et al. (2009). The probabilistic relevance framework: Bm25 and beyond. *Foundations and Trends® in Information Retrieval*, 3(4):333–389.

Rubin, O., Herzig, J., and Berant, J. (2021). Learning to retrieve prompts for in-context learning. *arXiv preprint arXiv:2112.08633*.

Scao, T. L., Fan, A., Akiki, C., Pavlick, E., Ilić, S., Hesslow, D., Castagné, R., Luccioni, A. S., Yvon, F., Gallé, M., et al. (2022). Bloom: A 176b-parameter open-access multilingual language model. *arXiv preprint arXiv:2211.05100*.

Song, K., Tan, X., Qin, T., Lu, J., and Liu, T.-Y. (2020). Mpnet: Masked and permuted pre-training for language understanding. *Advances in Neural Information Processing Systems*, 33:16857–16867.

Wang, Y. and Guo, M. (2014). A short analysis of discourse coherence. *Journal of Language Teaching and Research*, 5(2):460.

Webson, A. and Pavlick, E. (2021). Do prompt-based models really understand the meaning of their prompts? *arXiv preprint arXiv:2109.01247*.

Wolf, T., Debut, L., Sanh, V., Chaumond, J., Delangue, C., Moi, A., Cistac, P., Rault, T., Louf, R., Funtowicz, M., Davison, J., Shleifer, S., von Platen, P., Ma, C., Jernite, Y., Plu, J., Xu, C., Le Scao, T., Gugger, S., Drame, M., Lhoest, Q., and Rush, A. (2020). Transformers: State-of-the-art natural language processing. In *Proceedings of the 2020 Conference on Empirical Methods in Natural Language Processing: System Demonstrations*, pages 38–45, Online. Association for Computational Linguistics.

Xie, S. M., Raghunathan, A., Liang, P., and Ma, T. (2021). An explanation of in-context learning as implicit bayesian inference. In *International Conference on Learning Representations*.

Beyond Correlation: Making Sense of the Score Differences of New MT Evaluation Metrics

Chi-kiu Lo 羅致翹 chikiu.lo@nrc-cnrc.gc.ca
Rebecca Knowles rebecca.knowles@nrc-cnrc.gc.ca
Cyril Goutte cyril.goutte@nrc-cnrc.gc.ca
National Research Council Canada (NRC-CNRC)

Abstract

While many new automatic metrics for machine translation evaluation have been proposed in recent years, BLEU scores are still used as the primary metric in the vast majority of MT research papers. There are many reasons that researchers may be reluctant to switch to new metrics, from external pressures (reviewers, prior work) to the ease of use of metric toolkits. Another reason is a lack of intuition about the meaning of novel metric scores. In this work, we examine "rules of thumb" about metric score differences and how they do (and do not) correspond to human judgments of statistically significant differences between systems. In particular, we show that common rules of thumb about BLEU score differences do not in fact guarantee that human annotators will find significant differences between systems. We also show ways in which these rules of thumb fail to generalize across translation directions or domains.

1 Introduction

Despite mounting evidence over the course of many years (Akiba et al., 2003; Callison-Burch et al., 2006; Chiang et al., 2008; Tan et al., 2015; Mathur et al., 2020a, i.a.) demonstrating that BLEU (Papineni et al., 2002) has fundamental flaws in accurately reflecting translation quality, it has remained the de facto standard automatic MT evaluation metric for both scientific research and practical deployment (Marie et al., 2021). Numerous research efforts (Callison-Burch et al., 2007; Przybocki et al., 2009; Bojar et al., 2017; Freitag et al., 2021b, 2022, i.a.) have focused on the correlations between human judgments of translation quality and automatic metric scores; year after year, these have shown new metrics correlating better with human judgments than BLEU does. There are certainly some other obstacles beyond correlation with human judgment on translation quality that hinder the adoption of newer and better human-correlating automatic MT evaluation metrics in practice.

Przybocki et al. (2009) outlined four objectives in the search for new and improved automatic MT evaluation metrics: 1) "high correlation with human assessments of translation quality"; 2) "applicable to multiple target languages"; 3) "ability to differentiate between systems of varying quality" and finally, 4) "intuitive interpretation", i.e. whether the scores are meaningful and easy to understand on their own, with values and differences that are interpretable and clear in practice. As the first three objectives can be addressed by the correlation analysis of MT metrics with human judgment on translation quality but not the last one, we believe that gaining an intuitive understanding of the properties and behavior of the metrics is one

Proceedings of Machine Translation Summit XIX, Vol. 1: Research Track, pages 186–199
September 4–8, 2023, Macau SAR, China.

of the remaining challenges that MT researchers are facing when they are considering adopting a new metric. One way to do this is by designing metrics to be easily interpretable; another way is to examine whether we can build up reliable and useful intuitions about existing metrics. In order for metrics to be widely adopted, a combination of these—making new metrics that are more interpretable and simple to understand or debug,[1] as well as forming intuitions about them—may be necessary. Our focus in this work is on the latter, examining existing metrics to understand the meaning of the score differences they present.

In this work, we focus in particular on whether it is possible to get a sense of what kinds of metric score differences may correspond to significant improvements as judged by human annotators.[2] We examine whether this is consistent across target languages and across translation domains, within a specific metric. We do not suggest that this means that MT researchers can forego running significance tests or doing the appropriate human evaluation; as Marie (2022) notes, "A rule of thumb may yield correct results but can't be scientifically credible." However, having these rules of thumb and intuitive senses of metric score meanings may indeed be necessary to encourage broader adoption, so we present this work solely focusing on whether it is possible to build such rules of thumb about some of the modern metrics.

2 Related work

Mathur et al. (2020a) demonstrated that even statistically significant BLEU score differences of 0-3 BLEU points do not reliably correspond to human judgments of significant differences between systems. With a focus on pairwise ranking of systems, Kocmi et al. (2021) argued for evaluating metrics primarily based on whether the metric's pairwise rankings of two systems agrees with human pairwise rankings. They found that among the system pairs that were deemed statistically significant by humans, but where BLEU produced a flipped ranking compared to humans, the median BLEU difference is 1.3 BLEU. They found this result concerning as "BLEU differences higher than 1 or 2 BLEU are commonly and historically considered to be reliable by the field" (Kocmi et al., 2021) and their result showed otherwise. They further encouraged the use of paired statistical significance tests for more reliable conclusions on MT quality improvement. Subsequently, Marie (2022) examined the Conference on Machine Translation (WMT) 2021 and 2022 data to see what thresholds of metric score difference magnitudes corresponded reliably to statistically significant differences in metric scores (at p-values < 0.05, < 0.01, and < 0.001). They found that to claim a significant improvement in metric scores with p-value < 0.001, statistical significance testing should be done for differences lower that 2 BLEU. However, they only focused on significance in metric scores improvement but did not consider whether such thresholds correspond to significance in human judgments.

Nevertheless, there remain some common "gut feelings" among researchers and reviewers about what constitutes "significant" improvement on the basis of metric score differences alone, without running human evaluation or significance tests. As Marie et al. (2021) note, the majority of MT papers since 2018 do not use significance tests and instead rely on score differences. One number commonly tossed about informally is that a score difference of around 2 BLEU points can typically be expected to be significant. But where does this assumption come from, and does it hold? One possible source for this is Koehn (2004), which found, specific to the particular test scenario that "Even for small test sets of size 300 sentences (about 9000 words), we can reliably draw the right conclusion, if the true BLEU score difference is at least 2-3%."[3] In that setting,

[1]Another reason, beyond the scope of this work, that researchers may be hesitant to adopt new, complex metrics, is the possibility that they may have unexpected failure modes (see, e.g., Yan et al., 2023).

[2]Concurrent work, Deutsch et al. (2023), provides another way to examine score differences and their relation to human annotation.

[3]Note that this refers to a score difference of 2 or 3 BLEU points, not relative improvement.

the "right conclusion" is the one that matches the conclusion drawn from a very large test set (30,000 sentences) about which of two systems is better, based on automatic metric scores. The goal of that work is to identify how small of a dataset can still be reliably used (along with bootstrap resampling for statistical significance) to draw conclusions about the automatically measured differences between two systems. However, sometimes this kind of BLEU difference is used informally as a proxy for whether a *human* annotator will find the difference notable, something that does not follow from that particular paper. Marie (2022) found that for systems from WMT21 and 22, almost all system pairs with a BLEU difference greater than 2.0 were significantly different with p-value < 0.001, though this significance judgment relates only to the metric scores and not to any human annotation. In this work, we focus on a question more closely related to this and to Mathur et al. (2020a), rather than Marie (2022): whether there exist rules of thumb about metric score differences and their correspondence to significant differences in *human judgments*. Regardless of the exact source of these rules of thumb (which may never be known) or the exact BLEU score difference (or exact relative improvement) of a particular rule of thumb, some researchers feel that they have a sense of metric score differences, and we examine how that may correspond (or not) to judgments of MT quality across a range of metrics in this work.

Similar to Mathur et al. (2020a), we are interested in the relationship between metric score differences and significant differences in human scores. That work is interested both in Type I errors (where an insignificant metric difference might correspond to an actually significant difference under human evaluation) and Type II errors (where the metric score difference is significant, but the human evaluation does not find a significant difference). We take a related but slightly different approach to examining this relationship. We examine the "rules of thumb" about which metric score differences are meaningful. Using the large number of system pairs from WMT evaluations, we look at how the metric difference between two systems is related to the probability that the human annotations find the systems to be statistically significantly different. We select a threshold for this probability and examine the metric difference that corresponds. We then examine whether this is consistent across different test sets, domains, and target languages. That is, *are* there consistent rules of thumb about metric score differences? Or is there too much variation?

3 Do BLEU score rules of thumb correspond to human judgments?

In casual discussion and sometimes even formal work or reviewing, there is often a conflation of several (somewhat) orthogonal topics, which may be the source of these intuitions and rules of thumb. Sometimes "significant" is used simply to mean some value of "large", unrelated to precise definitions of statistical significance testing. Marie et al. (2021) note the use of this convention and suggest that it indicates some level of consensus among researchers on BLEU differences, albeit a consensus that is not necessarily well-founded; they address a number of other pitfalls in MT evaluation as well. In particular, in their meta-evaluation of 769 MT papers, they note that the majority of recent papers do not perform statistical significance tests, relying instead just on the "amplitude of the differences between metric scores to state whether they are significant or not"; in fact they note that even a BLEU score difference of around 1 may be used by most MT papers as "*significant* evidence of the superiority of an MT system and as an improvement in translation quality" (Marie et al., 2021). These are assumptions that sufficiently large metric score differences guarantee significant differences in *metric* scores; when combined with the assumption that metric scores and human scores are well-correlated, this often leads to the assumption that a certain metric score difference guarantees a statistically significant difference in *human scores*. We examine this relationship between statistically significant differences in human scores and the magnitude of metric differences in this work.

First, we investigate whether the more generous rule of thumb surrounding the significance of 2 BLEU improvement has a basis in fact. While Marie (2022) has shown that (at least for WMT21 and 22) such a BLEU difference tends to be a significant difference ($p < 0.001$) in metrics score, does that mean that human annotators will judge the pair of systems to be meaningfully different? That is to say, we assess the probability that an MT system pair would be judged by humans as having a statistically significant difference in quality, if BLEU showed a difference of 2 or more points for that pair.

3.1 Data

We use the human direct assessment (DA) and direct assessment with scalar quality metric (DA+SQM, which we refer to in figures as SQM for conciseness) scores collected at the WMT News/General shared tasks from 2019 to 2022 (Barrault et al., 2019, 2020; Akhbardeh et al., 2021; Kocmi et al., 2022) and organized in the MT Metrics Eval package.[4] The MT Metrics Eval package includes all scores from baseline and participating MT evaluation metrics in the Metrics shared task (Ma et al., 2019; Mathur et al., 2020b; Freitag et al., 2021b, 2022), covering all segments of all MT systems in WMT News/General shared tasks. It also contains complete information about which segments of each MT system were annotated by human evaluators on translation quality, allowing us to run paired t-test for each system pair on their sentence-level human DA/SQM (normalized) scores.

3.2 DA/SQM

In DA (Graham et al., 2017) at WMT, human annotators are asked to rate translations compared to the corresponding source/reference sentence on a slider of continuous scale between 0 and 100. The difference between DA and the DA+SQM performed at WMT22 (Kocmi et al., 2022) is that, for the latter, the slider is marked with seven tick marks where four of them are labeled with quality guidelines. The sentence-level human scores are standardized using z-scores.

3.3 Automatic MT evaluation metrics

The automatic MT evaluation metrics chosen for this study are the baselines and the high-performing participants in the WMT19-22 Metrics shared tasks. **BLEU** (Papineni et al., 2002) is the (clipped) precision of word n-grams between the MT output and its reference weighted by a brevity penalty. **spBLEU** (Team et al., 2022) is BLEU computed with subword tokenization done by standardized Sentencepiece Models (Kudo and Richardson, 2018). **chrF** (Popović, 2015) uses character n-gram to compare the MT output with the reference and it is a balance of precision and recall. **BERTScore** (Zhang et al., 2020) uses cosine similarity of contextual embeddings from pretrained transformers to compute F-score of sentence level similarity. **BLEURT-20** (Sellam et al., 2020) is fine-tuning RemBERT to predict DA score for a MT-reference pair. **COMET-20** (Rei et al., 2020) is fine-tuning XLM-R to predict DA score for a MT-source-reference tuple. **YiSi-1** (Lo, 2019) measures the semantic similarity between the MT output and reference by the IDF-weighted cosine similarity of contextual embeddings extracted from pretrained language models, e.g. RoBERTa, CamemBERT, XLM-R, etc., depending on the target language in evaluation. **COMET-22** (Rei et al., 2022) is an ensemble of two models: COMET-20 and a multitask model jointly predicting sentence-level MQM and word-level translation quality annotation. **metricX XXL** is the MQM prediction from a massive multi-task metric fine-tuned 30B mT5 using a variety of human feedback data such as, DA, MQM, QE, NLI and Summarization Eval. **UniTE** (Wan et al., 2022) is a learnt metric that unified

[4] `https://github.com/google-research/mt-metrics-eval`

commit: bdda529ce4fae9cec8156ea8a0abd94fe1b85988

ΔBLEU	2.0	5.0	10.0
$Pr(p < 0.05 \mid \Delta\text{BLEU})$	0.56	0.70	0.91

Table 1: Probability of significant human score difference at $p < 0.05$ given Δ BLEU of 2.0, 5.0 and 10.0 respectively.

the reference-based, reference-free and MT-source-reference way of evaluation trained on data with synthetic translation quality label.

3.4 Statistical significance test on human scores and isotonic regression

To ensure enough statistical power in the paired t-test on the sentence-level human DA/SQM (normalized) scores, we first filter out system pairs that have fewer than 250 sentences in common annotated by the human evaluators. Since we are running the significance test on the normalized human scores with the sign of the human score differences known, we run the one-sided t-test with the equal variance assumption.

After collecting the metric score difference and p-value of the t-test on the human scores for each system pair, we fit the data to an isotonic regression (Robertson et al., 1988) that predicts whether the human score difference will be significant given the metric's score difference. Isotonic regression produces a non-decreasing function where the classifier output is interpretable as a confidence level.[5] We set p<0.05 as the significance level of human scores. Thus, the output of our isotonic regression function can be viewed as $Pr(p < 0.05|\Delta M)$ where p is the p-value of the t-test on the human scores for each system pair and ΔM is the metric score difference.

3.5 Results

Figure 1 and 2 show the (log) p-value of one-sided paired t-test on human DA/SQM z-scores[6] for each metric score difference of each system pair in WMT19-22, across all translation directions and domains. Note that each system is only compared against other systems within its same language pair and direction (and for which there is an overlap of at least 250 common human-annotated segments for the pair of systems).

For all the metrics, we can choose metric score difference cutoffs (i.e., a point along the x-axis) to give a particular level of confidence that this metric difference genuinely reflects significant human score differences. Drawing a line up from the metric difference to the red line enables us to say that the metric difference at that x-value corresponds to a confidence level at corresponding y-value on the red line (for example, as seen in Table 1, a BLEU score difference of 2.0 corresponds to a 56% chance of the corresponding human evaluation finding a significant difference between the two systems). However, in the sub-figure of BLEU, we can see that data points are more spread out to the top-center of the graph. This indicates even where the BLEU differences are high human evaluators are not always finding the two systems to be significantly different; these are areas where the conclusion drawn from BLEU would be incorrect from the perspective of human evaluation. More data points spread out to the top-center also means having to make a tradeoff in the rule of thumb: either a very high score difference for high confidence of human judgment significance, or a smaller score difference but a lower confidence that the difference will be judged to be significant by human annotators.

More importantly, table 1 shows the probabilities of significant human score difference at p<0.05 given BLEU differences of 2.0, 5.0 and 10.0 respectively. For 2 BLEU difference, the probability that human evaluators find the MT output significant different is as low as 56%, i.e.

[5]https://scikit-learn.org/stable/modules/isotonic.html

[6]Points with lower y-axis values have smaller p-values and are "more" statistically significant.

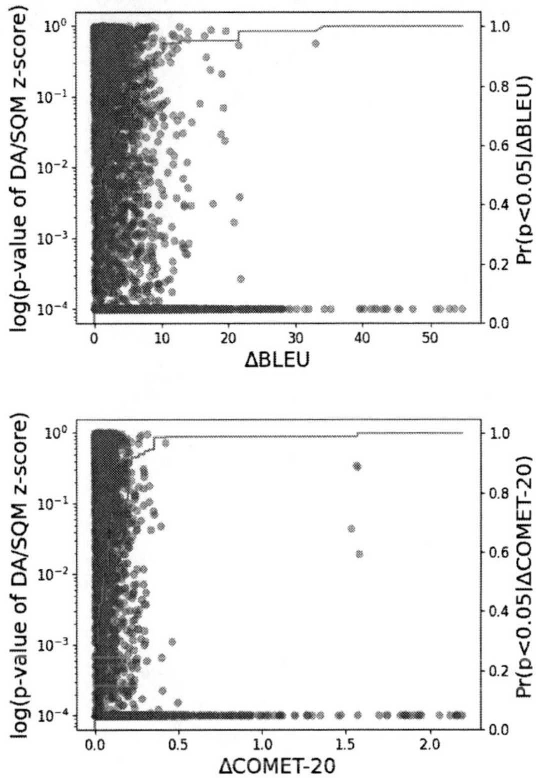

Figure 1: Log p-value of one-sided paired t-test on human DA/SQM z-scores for each metric (top: BLEU, bottom: COMET-20) score difference of each system pair in WMT19-22, all translation directions/domains. Red line is the isotonic regression fit to all data points, representing $Pr(p < 0.05|\Delta M)$. Note: for readability, p-values of $p \leq 0.0001$ are rounded up to 0.0001.

nearly one in every two times when we observe 2 BLEU improvement, it does not correspond to a significant human difference. A wider BLEU improvement margin (5 or 10 points) is needed for higher confidence that translation quality improvement will be judged to be significant by human annotators. This indicates that these rule of thumb intuitions about what kind of BLEU score differences are meaningful (or statistically significant) appear to be overstated and inaccurate, at least when it comes to significant differences in *human* judgment, which is generally considered to be the gold standard and what metric scores are seeking to replicate.

Finally, table 2 shows the cutoff of metrics' score differences for human notable difference at 50%, 80% and 95% confidence level. This table serves as a lookup between BLEU differences and differences in some of the modern metrics. For example, we see that a BLEU score difference of 1.2 corresponds to 50% confidence that human annotators will agree with the metric's ranking of the two systems and do so with a significant difference. Meanwhile, a COMET-20 score difference of 0.05 would have the same 50% chance of human-judged significant difference.

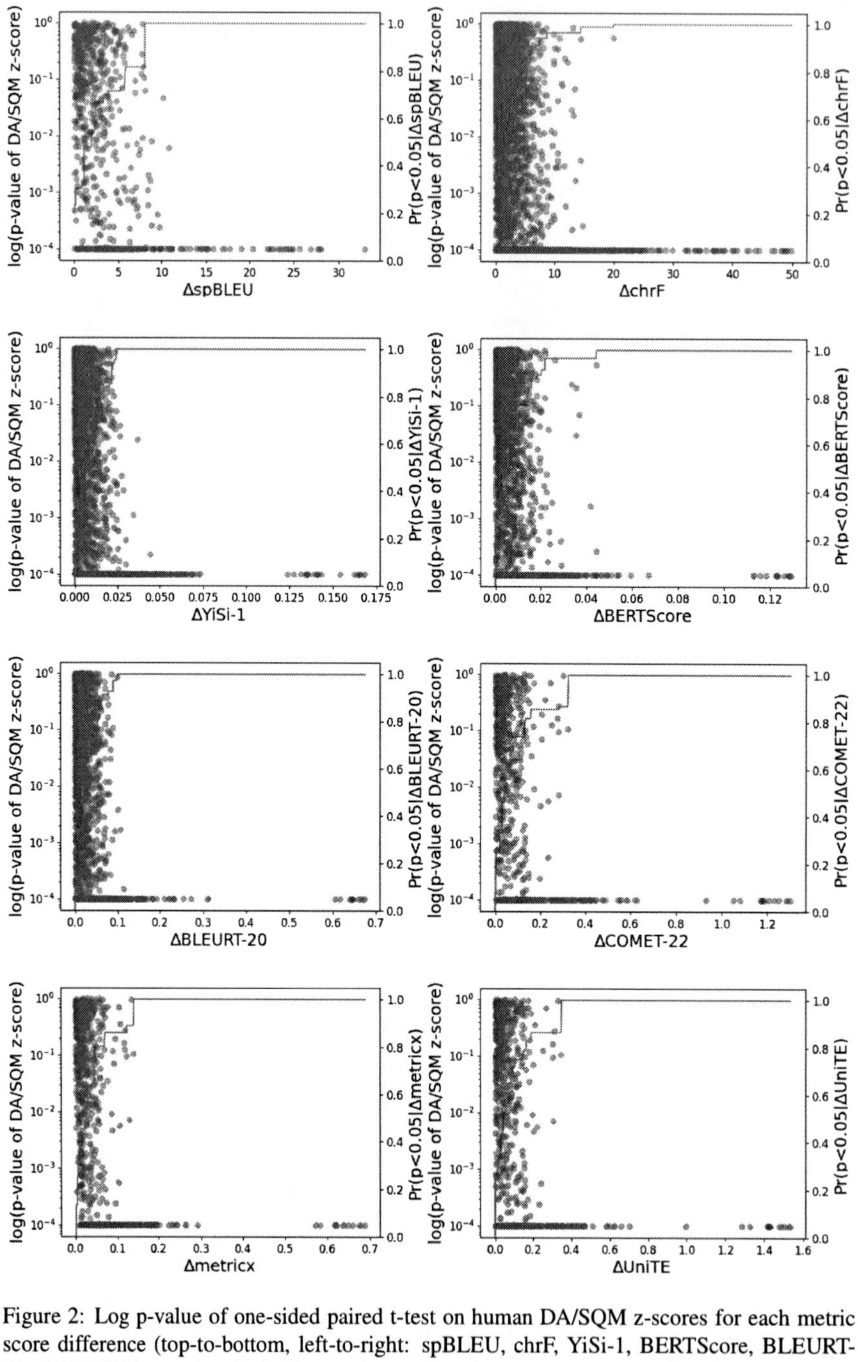

Figure 2: Log p-value of one-sided paired t-test on human DA/SQM z-scores for each metric score difference (top-to-bottom, left-to-right: spBLEU, chrF, YiSi-1, BERTScore, BLEURT-20, COMET-22, metricx, UniTE) of each system pair in WMT19-22 all translation directions and domains. The red line is the isotonic regression fit to all the data points, representing $Pr(p < 0.05|\Delta M)$. Note: for readability, p-values of $p \leq 0.0001$ are rounded up to 0.0001.

$Pr(p < 0.05 \mid \Delta M)$	0.5	0.8	0.95
surface matching			
ΔBLEU	1.2	5.5	12.9
ΔspBLEU	1.9	5.8	8.1
ΔchrF	1.6	5.4	8.7
neural (before 2022)			
ΔBERTScore	0.005	0.014	0.022
ΔBLEURT-20	0.018	0.052	0.088
ΔCOMET-20	0.05	0.20	0.35
ΔYiSi-1	0.003	0.015	0.023
neural (in 2022)			
ΔCOMET-22	0.04	0.13	0.33
Δmetricx	0.02	0.05	0.14
ΔUniTE	0.04	0.16	0.35

Table 2: Cutoff of metrics' score differences for significant human difference at 50%, 80% and 95% confidence level.

4 Discussion

Another unaddressed problem of the rules of thumb is that the MT community may sometimes treat them as though they are language and domain independent, applying rules of thumb across different target languages and domains without considering their differences. This is the case despite the fact that it is widely known that language typology affects BLEU scores (for example, highly inflected languages may see their BLEU scores penalized due to single-character differences in affixes). In addition, recent WMT Metrics shared tasks (Freitag et al., 2021b, 2022) has moved on to using multidimensional quality metric (MQM) (Lommel et al., 2014) as the human annotation method for translation quality for more consistent and reliable annotations (Freitag et al., 2021a). We now investigate into the consistency of the cutoff of metrics' score differences at 80% confidence level for different target languages, evaluation domains and human annotation methods.

4.1 Consistency across target languages

We divide the target languages into several groups: we examine all target languages together, English (the most common target language), and three groups of other target languages. These remaining groups are split into languages that use alphabetical/abugida writing systems (which we call group I: Bengali, Czech, German, French, Hausa, Croatian, Icelandic, Kazakh, Lithuanian, Polish, Russian and Ukrainian), those that use logographic writing systems (which we call group II: Chinese and Japanese), and then separately Inuktitut (which uses an abugida but is also the most morphologically complex of the target languages at WMT, in addition to being low-resource as compared to many of the other language pairs, and being covered by a smaller set of the metrics). For simplicity and space-related reasons, we select a single threshold: 80% confidence that the score difference will correspond to a significant ($p < 0.05$) human score difference. The resulting thresholds are shown in Table 3.

Beginning with BLEU, we observe a fairly stark difference between the groups of languages, with English requiring an 8.0 BLEU difference and group I languages requiring a 3.6 BLEU difference for this confidence level, with Inuktitut falling between the two. This pattern is repeated across the other metrics, though it varies by metric whether the group II languages are more similar to English or to the group I languages (in some of the pre-2022 neural metrics, the group II languages require an even smaller metric score difference than English).

target lang.	all	English	I	II	Inuktitut
surface matching					
ΔBLEU	5.5	8.0	3.6	8.0	4.5
ΔspBLEU	5.8	8.1	2.4	6.2	—
ΔchrF	5.4	6.2	3.0	3.8	6.2
neural (before 2022)					
ΔBERTScore	0.014	0.016	0.011	0.009	—
ΔBLEURT-20	0.052	0.063	0.033	0.018	—
ΔCOMET-20	0.20	0.20	0.10	0.08	0.05
ΔYiSi-1	0.015	0.022	0.005	0.010	0.023
neural (in 2022)					
ΔCOMET-22	0.13	0.33	0.07	0.08	—
Δmetricx	0.05	0.15	0.03	0.05	—
ΔUniTE	0.16	0.35	0.06	0.09	—

Table 3: Comparison of thresholds of ΔM when $Pr(p < 0.05|\Delta M) = 0.8$ for different target languages. Language group I contains system pairs translating into Bengali, Czech, German, French, Hausa, Croatian, Icelandic, Kazakh, Lithuanian, Polish, Russian and Ukrainian. Language group II contains system pairs translating into Chinese and Japanese.

In addition to highlighting the difference between languages, this also highlights another challenge: that variations on metrics have different thresholds. This should come as little surprise; even simple differences in preprocessing are known to produce differences in the same metric scores (Post, 2018). For example, we observe some inconsistency in the thresholds for BLEU and spBLEU.

BERTScore has the most consistent threshold where human annotators agree that the translation quality improvements are significant. This perhaps is because it is an untrained metric based on one multilingual pretrained transformer model so that it avoids having inconsistent implications like YiSi-1, a metric with language specific models or BLEURT-20, COMET-22 and UniTE, metrics that may be overfit to predict human scores for higher correlation.

4.2 Consistency across domains

We perform a similar comparison of thresholds for 80% confidence in human evaluation statistical significance (at $p < 0.05$) in Table 4 across domains. This analysis is restricted to 2022, where the evaluation was multi-domain. Here we combine all target languages. We again observe inconsistency across metrics, though some metrics show smaller relative threshold differences. For example, it requires double the BLEU score difference margin to be confident that translation quality of systems in the ecommerce and conversational domains significantly improved according to human evaluators, as compared to the news and social domains. For this analysis, COMET-22 has the most consistent cutoff across different domains.

4.3 Do human annotation methods matter?

Similar to the previous analyses, we perform a comparison of thresholds for 80% confidence in human evaluation statistical significance (at $p < 0.05$) in Table 5 for different human annotation protocols. Some metrics, like BLEU and chrF, show much higher score differences required for 80% confidence under MQM evaluation, while others like BLEURT-20, COMET-20, and UniTE show the opposite. More study would be required to understand these differences across human evaluation protocols and determine how to compare across different annotation methods.

domain	news	social	ecommerce	conversational
surface matching				
ΔBLEU	10.0	12.0	23.0	22.0
ΔspBLEU	10.0	13.0	14.0	10.0
ΔchrF	8.5	12.0	6.5	19.0
neural (before 2022)				
ΔBERTScore	0.013	0.016	0.009	0.025
ΔBLEURT-20	0.058	0.100	0.073	0.070
ΔCOMET-20	0.20	0.40	0.26	0.25
ΔYiSi-1	0.035	0.003	0.002	0.025
neural (in 2022)				
ΔCOMET-22	0.14	0.15	0.18	0.11
Δmetricx	0.10	0.18	0.13	0.10
ΔUniTE	0.17	0.45	0.31	0.28

Table 4: Comparison of thresholds of ΔM when $Pr(p < 0.05|\Delta M) = 0.8$ across domains.

annotation	DA/SQM	MQM
surface matching		
ΔBLEU	5.5	12.9
ΔspBLEU	5.8	5.7
ΔchrF	5.4	10.0
neural (before 2022)		
ΔBERTScore	0.014	0.012
ΔBLEURT-20	0.052	0.028
ΔCOMET-20	0.20	0.13
ΔYiSi-1	0.015	0.011
neural (in 2022)		
ΔCOMET-22	0.13	0.11
Δmetricx	0.05	0.03
ΔUniTE	0.16	0.06

Table 5: Comparison of thresholds of ΔM when $Pr(p < 0.05|\Delta M) = 0.8$ for different human annotation methods.

5 Conclusions

We presented an empirical study of the relationship between statistically significant differences in human scores and the magnitude of metric differences. We showed that the rules of thumb surrounding the significance of BLEU improvement does not hold according to human judgment on translation quality (regardless of whether the rule of thumb is exactly 1 or 2 or even slightly larger BLEU differences). We provided an intuitive interpretation between BLEU differences and the differences in some of the modern metrics. However, we found that for some metrics, the score differences corresponding to significant improvements as judged by human annotators may not be transferable across target languages or translation domains. We have to emphasize again that we do not suggest that this means that MT researchers can forego running significance tests or doing the appropriate human evaluation. This work only supports an intuitive senses of metric score meanings to encourages broader adoption of new automatic MT evaluation metrics.

References

Akhbardeh, F., Arkhangorodsky, A., Biesialska, M., Bojar, O., Chatterjee, R., Chaudhary, V., Costa-jussa, M. R., España-Bonet, C., Fan, A., Federmann, C., Freitag, M., Graham, Y., Grundkiewicz, R., Haddow, B., Harter, L., Heafield, K., Homan, C., Huck, M., Amponsah-Kaakyire, K., Kasai, J., Khashabi, D., Knight, K., Kocmi, T., Koehn, P., Lourie, N., Monz, C., Morishita, M., Nagata, M., Nagesh, A., Nakazawa, T., Negri, M., Pal, S., Tapo, A. A., Turchi, M., Vydrin, V., and Zampieri, M. (2021). Findings of the 2021 conference on machine translation (WMT21). In *Proceedings of the Sixth Conference on Machine Translation*, pages 1–88, Online. Association for Computational Linguistics.

Akiba, Y., Sumita, E., Nakaiwa, H., Yamamoto, S., and Okuno, H. G. (2003). Experimental comparison of MT evaluation methods: RED vs.BLEU. In *Proceedings of Machine Translation Summit IX: Papers*, New Orleans, USA.

Barrault, L., Biesialska, M., Bojar, O., Costa-jussà, M. R., Federmann, C., Graham, Y., Grundkiewicz, R., Haddow, B., Huck, M., Joanis, E., Kocmi, T., Koehn, P., Lo, C.-k., Ljubešić, N., Monz, C., Morishita, M., Nagata, M., Nakazawa, T., Pal, S., Post, M., and Zampieri, M. (2020). Findings of the 2020 conference on machine translation (WMT20). In *Proceedings of the Fifth Conference on Machine Translation*, pages 1–55, Online. Association for Computational Linguistics.

Barrault, L., Bojar, O., Costa-jussà, M. R., Federmann, C., Fishel, M., Graham, Y., Haddow, B., Huck, M., Koehn, P., Malmasi, S., Monz, C., Müller, M., Pal, S., Post, M., and Zampieri, M. (2019). Findings of the 2019 conference on machine translation (WMT19). In *Proceedings of the Fourth Conference on Machine Translation (Volume 2: Shared Task Papers, Day 1)*, pages 1–61, Florence, Italy. Association for Computational Linguistics.

Bojar, O., Graham, Y., and Kamran, A. (2017). Results of the WMT17 metrics shared task. In *Proceedings of the Second Conference on Machine Translation*, pages 489–513, Copenhagen, Denmark. Association for Computational Linguistics.

Callison-Burch, C., Fordyce, C., Koehn, P., Monz, C., and Schroeder, J. (2007). (meta-) evaluation of machine translation. In *Proceedings of the Second Workshop on Statistical Machine Translation*, pages 136–158, Prague, Czech Republic. Association for Computational Linguistics.

Callison-Burch, C., Osborne, M., and Koehn, P. (2006). Re-evaluating the role of Bleu in machine translation research. In *11th Conference of the European Chapter of the Association for Computational Linguistics*, pages 249–256, Trento, Italy. Association for Computational Linguistics.

Chiang, D., DeNeefe, S., Chan, Y. S., and Ng, H. T. (2008). Decomposability of translation metrics for improved evaluation and efficient algorithms. In *Proceedings of the 2008 Conference on Empirical Methods in Natural Language Processing*, pages 610–619, Honolulu, Hawaii. Association for Computational Linguistics.

Deutsch, D., Foster, G., and Freitag, M. (2023). Ties matter: Modifying kendall's tau for modern metric meta-evaluation.

Freitag, M., Foster, G., Grangier, D., Ratnakar, V., Tan, Q., and Macherey, W. (2021a). Experts, errors, and context: A large-scale study of human evaluation for machine translation. *Transactions of the Association for Computational Linguistics*, 9:1460–1474.

Freitag, M., Rei, R., Mathur, N., Lo, C.-k., Stewart, C., Avramidis, E., Kocmi, T., Foster, G., Lavie, A., and Martins, A. F. T. (2022). Results of WMT22 metrics shared task: Stop using BLEU – neural metrics are better and more robust. In *Proceedings of the Seventh Conference on Machine Translation (WMT)*, pages 46–68, Abu Dhabi, United Arab Emirates (Hybrid). Association for Computational Linguistics.

Freitag, M., Rei, R., Mathur, N., Lo, C.-k., Stewart, C., Foster, G., Lavie, A., and Bojar, O. (2021b). Results of the WMT21 metrics shared task: Evaluating metrics with expert-based human evaluations on TED and news domain. In *Proceedings of the Sixth Conference on Machine Translation*, pages 733–774, Online. Association for Computational Linguistics.

Graham, Y., Baldwin, T., Moffat, A., and Zobel, J. (2017). Can machine translation systems be evaluated by the crowd alone. *Nat. Lang. Eng.*, 23(1):3–30.

Kocmi, T., Bawden, R., Bojar, O., Dvorkovich, A., Federmann, C., Fishel, M., Gowda, T., Graham, Y., Grundkiewicz, R., Haddow, B., Knowles, R., Koehn, P., Monz, C., Morishita, M., Nagata, M., Nakazawa, T., Novák, M., Popel, M., and Popović, M. (2022). Findings of the 2022 conference on machine translation (WMT22). In *Proceedings of the Seventh Conference on Machine Translation (WMT)*, pages 1–45, Abu Dhabi, United Arab Emirates (Hybrid). Association for Computational Linguistics.

Kocmi, T., Federmann, C., Grundkiewicz, R., Junczys-Dowmunt, M., Matsushita, H., and Menezes, A. (2021). To ship or not to ship: An extensive evaluation of automatic metrics for machine translation. In *Proceedings of the Sixth Conference on Machine Translation*, pages 478–494, Online. Association for Computational Linguistics.

Koehn, P. (2004). Statistical significance tests for machine translation evaluation. In *Proceedings of the 2004 Conference on Empirical Methods in Natural Language Processing*, pages 388–395, Barcelona, Spain. Association for Computational Linguistics.

Kudo, T. and Richardson, J. (2018). SentencePiece: A simple and language independent subword tokenizer and detokenizer for neural text processing. In *Proceedings of the 2018 Conference on Empirical Methods in Natural Language Processing: System Demonstrations*, pages 66–71, Brussels, Belgium. Association for Computational Linguistics.

Lo, C.-k. (2019). YiSi - a unified semantic MT quality evaluation and estimation metric for languages with different levels of available resources. In *Proceedings of the Fourth Conference on Machine Translation (Volume 2: Shared Task Papers, Day 1)*, pages 507–513, Florence, Italy. Association for Computational Linguistics.

Lommel, A., Uszkoreit, H., and Burchardt, A. (2014). Multidimensional quality metrics (mqm): A framework for declaring and describing translation quality metrics. *Tradumàtica*, (12):0455–463.

Ma, Q., Wei, J., Bojar, O., and Graham, Y. (2019). Results of the WMT19 metrics shared task: Segment-level and strong MT systems pose big challenges. In *Proceedings of the Fourth Conference on Machine Translation (Volume 2: Shared Task Papers, Day 1)*, pages 62–90, Florence, Italy. Association for Computational Linguistics.

Marie, B. (2022). Yes, we need statistical significance testing. https://pub.towardsai.net/yes-we-need-statistical-significance-testing-927a8d21f9f0.

Marie, B., Fujita, A., and Rubino, R. (2021). Scientific credibility of machine translation research: A meta-evaluation of 769 papers. In *Proceedings of the 59th Annual Meeting of the Association for Computational Linguistics and the 11th International Joint Conference on Natural Language Processing (Volume 1: Long Papers)*, pages 7297–7306, Online. Association for Computational Linguistics.

Mathur, N., Baldwin, T., and Cohn, T. (2020a). Tangled up in BLEU: Reevaluating the evaluation of automatic machine translation evaluation metrics. In *Proceedings of the 58th Annual Meeting of the Association for Computational Linguistics*, pages 4984–4997, Online. Association for Computational Linguistics.

Mathur, N., Wei, J., Freitag, M., Ma, Q., and Bojar, O. (2020b). Results of the WMT20 metrics shared task. In *Proceedings of the Fifth Conference on Machine Translation*, pages 688–725, Online. Association for Computational Linguistics.

Papineni, K., Roukos, S., Ward, T., and Zhu, W.-J. (2002). Bleu: a method for automatic evaluation of machine translation. In *Proceedings of the 40th Annual Meeting of the Association for Computational Linguistics*, pages 311–318, Philadelphia, Pennsylvania, USA. Association for Computational Linguistics.

Popović, M. (2015). chrF: character n-gram F-score for automatic MT evaluation. In *Proceedings of the Tenth Workshop on Statistical Machine Translation*, pages 392–395, Lisbon, Portugal. Association for Computational Linguistics.

Post, M. (2018). A call for clarity in reporting BLEU scores. In *Proceedings of the Third Conference on Machine Translation: Research Papers*, pages 186–191, Brussels, Belgium. Association for Computational Linguistics.

Przybocki, M., Peterson, K., Bronsart, S., and Sanders, G. (2009). The nist 2008 metrics for machine translation challenge—overview, methodology, metrics, and results. *Machine Translation*, 23(2/3):71–103.

Rei, R., C. de Souza, J. G., Alves, D., Zerva, C., Farinha, A. C., Glushkova, T., Lavie, A., Coheur, L., and Martins, A. F. T. (2022). COMET-22: Unbabel-IST 2022 submission for the metrics shared task. In *Proceedings of the Seventh Conference on Machine Translation (WMT)*, pages 578–585, Abu Dhabi, United Arab Emirates (Hybrid). Association for Computational Linguistics.

Rei, R., Stewart, C., Farinha, A. C., and Lavie, A. (2020). COMET: A neural framework for MT evaluation. In *Proceedings of the 2020 Conference on Empirical Methods in Natural Language Processing (EMNLP)*, pages 2685–2702, Online. Association for Computational Linguistics.

Robertson, T., Wright, F., and Dykstra, R. (1988). *Order Restricted Statistical Inference*. Probability and Statistics Series. Wiley.

Sellam, T., Das, D., and Parikh, A. (2020). BLEURT: Learning robust metrics for text generation. In *Proceedings of the 58th Annual Meeting of the Association for Computational Linguistics*, pages 7881–7892, Online. Association for Computational Linguistics.

Tan, L., Dehdari, J., and van Genabith, J. (2015). An awkward disparity between BLEU / RIBES scores and human judgements in machine translation. In *Proceedings of the 2nd Workshop on Asian Translation (WAT2015)*, pages 74–81, Kyoto, Japan. Workshop on Asian Translation.

Team, N., Costa-jussà, M. R., Cross, J., Çelebi, O., Elbayad, M., Heafield, K., Heffernan, K., Kalbassi, E., Lam, J., Licht, D., Maillard, J., Sun, A., Wang, S., Wenzek, G., Youngblood, A., Akula, B., Barrault, L., Gonzalez, G. M., Hansanti, P., Hoffman, J., Jarrett, S., Sadagopan, K. R., Rowe, D., Spruit, S., Tran, C., Andrews, P., Ayan, N. F., Bhosale, S., Edunov, S., Fan, A., Gao, C., Goswami, V., Guzmán, F., Koehn, P., Mourachko, A., Ropers, C., Saleem, S., Schwenk, H., and Wang, J. (2022). No language left behind: Scaling human-centered machine translation.

Wan, Y., Liu, D., Yang, B., Zhang, H., Chen, B., Wong, D., and Chao, L. (2022). UniTE: Unified translation evaluation. In *Proceedings of the 60th Annual Meeting of the Association for Computational Linguistics (Volume 1: Long Papers)*, pages 8117–8127, Dublin, Ireland. Association for Computational Linguistics.

Yan, Y., Wang, T., Zhao, C., Huang, S., Chen, J., and Wang, M. (2023). BLEURT has universal translations: An analysis of automatic metrics by minimum risk training. In *Proceedings of the 61st Annual Meeting of the Association for Computational Linguistics (Volume 1: Long Papers)*, pages 5428–5443, Toronto, Canada. Association for Computational Linguistics.

Zhang, T., Kishore, V., Wu, F., Weinberger, K. Q., and Artzi, Y. (2020). Bertscore: Evaluating text generation with BERT. In *8th International Conference on Learning Representations, ICLR 2020, Addis Ababa, Ethiopia, April 26-30, 2020*. OpenReview.net.

Bad MT Systems are Good for Quality Estimation

Iryna Tryhubyshyn[⋆] tryhubyshyn@gmail.com
Aleš Tamchyna[†] ales.tamchyna@phrase.com
Ondřej Bojar[⋆] bojar@ufal.mff.cuni.cz
Charles University, Faculty of Mathematics and Physics, Institute of Formal and Applied Linguistics, Prague, Czech Republic[⋆]
Phrase a.s., Václavské náměstí 2132/47, 110 00 Prague, Czech Republic[†]

Abstract

Quality estimation (QE) is the task of predicting quality of outputs produced by machine translation (MT) systems. Currently, the highest-performing QE systems are supervised and require training on data with golden quality scores. In this paper, we investigate the impact of the quality of the underlying MT outputs on the performance of QE systems. We find that QE models trained on datasets with lower-quality translations often outperform those trained on higher-quality data. We also demonstrate that good performance can be achieved by using a mix of data from different MT systems.

1 Introduction

Quality Estimation (QE) involves predicting the quality of a machine-translated text based on the original text and the machine translation (MT) output (Blatz et al., 2004; Specia et al., 2009). This can be done at the word, sentence, or document level.

In this paper, we focus on sentence-level QE, where the goal is to predict a score that a human assessor would attribute to the sentence. Depending on the manual evaluation process used to gather data, we can talk about different variations of the task. These include Direct Assessment QE (Graham et al., 2015), which aims to estimate the perceived quality of translation, Post-editing QE, which measures the effort required to edit the translation, and MQM QE (Lommel et al., 2014), which identifies critical errors in the translation.

Evaluating a QE system means checking how closely its predictions match manual scores on a held-out set. QE systems are closely tied to MT systems in many ways. Their performance can vary greatly depending on the MT system on which they are being evaluated. The current high-performing solutions for quality estimation are based on supervised methods, which in turn makes these QE systems dependent on the specifics of the MT systems used to create the training data. It is not clear which MT system should be used to create a QE system with the best performance. The contributions of this experimental work are as follows:

1. We examine the relationship between MT system quality and QE system performance by training QE models on datasets that consist of the same source data but different translations produced by MT of varying quality.

2. We evaluate the models on evaluation datasets from different domains and show that the QE system trained on translations from low-quality MT systems outperforms the QE system trained on translations from high-quality MT systems.

Proceedings of Machine Translation Summit XIX, Vol. 1: Research Track, pages 200–208
September 4–8, 2023, Macau SAR, China.

3. We demonstrate that QE systems trained on a mix of translations from different MT models also show good performance but do not necessarily outperform the best-performing system that is trained on the translations from one MT system.

2 Proposed approach

We investigate the impact of MT system quality on QE system performance by training QE models on datasets consisting of a fixed set of source sentences and differing in the target side which is translated by MT systems of varying quality. As there are no existing QE datasets that have the same source sentences translated by different MT systems of known performance, we create our own datasets by training MT systems and translating the same source sentences. Due to the lack of human annotators and a large amount of work required, we approximate the manual quality scores, i.e. our targets for QE are assigned automatically. The scores are assigned by calculating the similarity between the translations and reference translations available in a parallel dataset. Note that for QE itself, reference translations are not needed, only the quality judgments.

We explore the use of two automatic reference-based metrics of MT quality, namely TER (Snover et al., 2006a) and COMET (Rei et al., 2020), as the golden truth for QE training. We select these metrics because they mimic the manual targets typically used in QE tasks, and each highlights a distinct aspect of translation quality. Specifically, COMET has been trained to predict sentence-level Direct Assessment scores, while TER is a proxy for HTER (Snover et al., 2006b), which measures post-editing effort. Additionally, we conduct the evaluation of the models trained on COMET scores on available data with Direct Assessment scores to demonstrate that the relationship that holds for proxy targets also applies to real targets.

COMET is a metric based on sentence embeddings and designed to predict the quality score that a human annotator would assign. This leads us to believe that COMET reflects the overall meaning match. As a pre-trained metric, it has a high correlation with human-based scores. However, its training to directly predict DA scores is also a limitation. COMET may contain a bias towards the MT systems on which it was trained, which is the exact bias that we are trying to evaluate in our QE systems. While COMET is available in QE mode with multiple releases, it is not suitable for our purposes, since they differ in various aspects like training procedures, source data, and MTs used in training. Our focus, however, is solely on understanding the impact of the MT used in translation and using QE COMET models would not allow us to separate the MT's impact from other factors affecting the QE evaluation.

TER, on the other hand, is focused on string editing, which means a rather superficial similarity of the candidate and the reference translation. It uses the same mechanism of string comparison as HTER, so we use it as a proxy for HTER-measured post-editing effort. TER is known for having a lower correlation with translation targets. However, it is not trained on translations of any kind, so the risk of any bias towards some training data is avoided.

3 Experiments

Our experimental approach involves training QE systems on translations of varying quality, and then evaluating their performance on datasets with different target types, namely COMET and TER targets, as well as DA targets. In this section, we provide a detailed description of our experimental setup, including information on how we trained the MT and QE systems, as well as the datasets used for training and evaluation.

3.1 Setup

For our experiments, we need MT systems of varying performance. We achieve this by adjusting the amount of training data used, with one MT system trained on 10 million sentence pairs

Dataset	Domain	Sentences	Words	Distinct words
CzEng	Mixed: Europarl, News commentary, Wikititles, etc.	10 000	124 481	26 466
WMT18	News	2983	55 920	12 548
Antrecorp	Student presentations by non-native English speakers	571	7 893	1 532
SAO	Presentations by officers of two supreme audit institutions	654	13 158	1 897
Khan Academy	Subtitles to math educational videos	538	4 470	871

Table 1: Datasets used in evaluation: domain, sentence and word count, vocabulary size. We report the statistics only for the source language (English). Antrecorp, SAO, and Khan Academy are parts of IWSLT dataset.

displaying superior quality compared to a second MT system trained on 1 million sentence pairs. Additionally, a mixed dataset is also created by utilizing the same source data, with translations randomly selected from both the high-quality and low-quality datasets at the 50:50 ratio.

Separate QE systems are trained for each type of target: one system is trained for direct assessment using COMET targets, and another system is trained for post-editing effort using TER targets. One system is trained on each dataset, resulting in a total of six QE systems (COMET and TER times low, high and mixed quality MT).

Training dataset. The experiments are performed on the English→Czech language pair. The MT and QE systems are trained on the authentic CzEng 2.0 dataset (Kocmi et al., 2020) using randomly selected non-overlapping parts: 10 million sentences for the MT training data and 500 thousand for the QE data.

MT systems. The MT systems trained are Transformers with base configuration in the Marian implementation (Junczys-Dowmunt et al., 2018). The default settings for the Transformer provided by the Marian package are used, only setting the pre-allocated memory space to 6500 MB for maximum possible batch size. Each system is trained on two GeForce GTX 1080 Ti GPUs. The dataset preprocessing includes normalization, tokenization, and truecasing using the Moses toolkit (Koehn et al., 2007), followed by BPE tokenization (Sennrich et al., 2016) with 32,000 merge operations.

QE systems. All our QE models use the Predictor-Estimator architecture (Kim et al., 2017) in the OpenKiwi implementation (Kepler et al., 2019) with XLM-R (Conneau et al., 2019) as the predictor. We follow the default settings for the XLM-R model adjusting certain parameters for the larger dataset size. These adjustments include setting the learning rate to 5e-6, using 1000 warm-up steps, and unfreezing the XLM-R predictor after 2000 steps. Additionally, the model is validated every 25 thousand sentences and the training process is stopped if the Pearson correlation of the predictions and the targets does not increase for 25 times in a row. The batch size of 4 with four gradient accumulation steps is used to fit the data into memory.

3.2 Evaluation datasets

The evaluation was carried out on three different datasets: one extracted from CzEng avoiding any overlap with the training data, an evaluation dataset from the WMT-2018 News Translation Task (Bojar et al., 2018), and a dataset used in the IWSLT 2020 Non-Native Speech Translation

Evaluation dataset	COMET models		TER models	
	Low-quality	High-quality	Low-quality	High-quality
CzEng	**0.638**	0.623	**0.524**	0.503
WMT18	**0.757**	0.744	**0.461**	0.435
IWSLT	**0.599**	0.594	**0.404**	0.357

Table 2: Evaluation of QE models trained on datasets generated by one MT (of a lower vs. higher quality), measured by Pearson correlation between predictions and targets. The winning model is denoted in bold. Results that are statistically significant at the 0.05 level are underlined.

Task (Ansari et al., 2020) that combines three sources of data: Antrecorp (Macháček et al., 2019), Khan Academy, and SAO. Table 1 provides information on the datasets, including the domain, size, and statistics such as the number of words and vocabulary size (distinct words) per dataset.

For the WMT-2018 dataset, we used translations obtained from MT systems that were entered into the competition. As an additional dataset, we use DA scores collected during the competition evaluations that are available only for a part of the dataset. IWSLT and CzEng were translated by various MT systems: the two explained in Section 3.1, Google Translate, and LINDAT Translation (sentence-level system).[1] Each QE evaluation dataset is then composed of translations combined from all MT systems, with two sets of targets computed using COMET and TER against the reference translations available for the respective test sets. We use the same test set for the evaluation of QE across all six QE settings.

4 Results

We evaluate the performance of our QE models by computing the Pearson correlation between their predictions and the corresponding targets. To determine whether there is a statistically significant difference in correlation between the models, we use a z-test on Fisher z-transformed correlation coefficients.

4.1 QE models derived from a single MT

Table 2 displays the evaluation results of QE models trained on translations from a single machine translation system. The "Low-Quality" column shows the results for QE models trained on the corpus with low-quality translations produced by the lower-quality MT, and the "High-Quality" column shows the results for QE models trained on the same corpus but with high-quality translations from the higher-quality MT.

On all datasets, the QE models trained on lower-quality translations perform better than those trained on higher-quality translations. This phenomenon is statistically significant for all datasets except IWSLT with COMET labels. These results indicate that choosing high-quality translations for training a QE system may actually result in an inferior performance compared to training on low-quality translations. This goes against conventional wisdom and suggests that opting for a mediocre MT instead of the best-performing one may be a wiser choice when selecting data to train a QE system.

4.2 How QE models' performance is affected by the evaluated MT system

This section focuses on analyzing how the performance of QE models varies depending on the MT system that is the subject of the quality estimation. We reused the data from the previous

[1] https://lindat.mff.cuni.cz/services/translation/

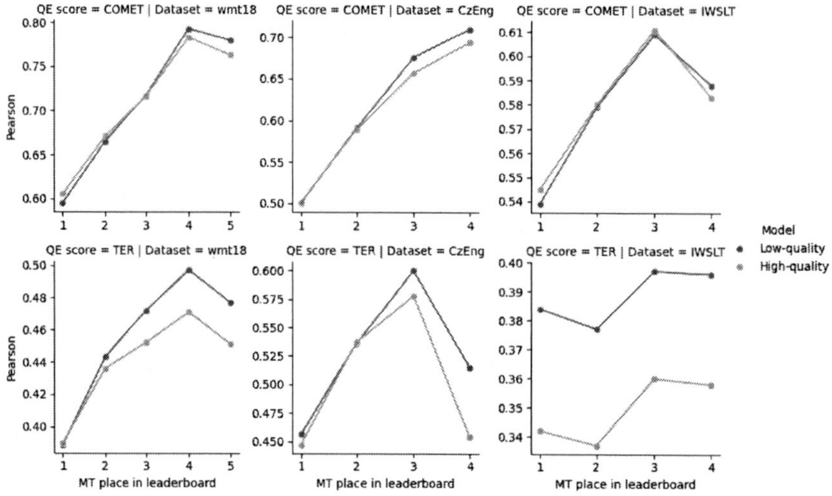

Figure 1: QE model performance for each translator separately measured by Pearson correlation between predictions and targets. On the x-axis, MT systems are sorted by their decreasing performance, with the MT that achieved the top position in the leaderboard labeled as 1, the second-best system as 2, and so on. The two lines correspond to lower and higher quality QE, i.e. QE trained on worse or better MT systems, resp.

section and evaluated the model's performance on test set translations produced by each MT system individually. We rank the evaluated MT systems by the quality of their translations using system-level COMET scores (MT evaluation results are available in Appendix A). Figure 1 shows how performance of the QE systems varies depending on the quality of the evaluated MT system. The results reveal a clear trend: the QE models' performance decreases as the quality of the evaluation dataset increases.

Interestingly, we also note that the low-quality and high-quality QE models exhibit different behaviors. The low-quality QE models (i.e. those trained on low-quality MT outputs) perform better on datasets lower on the leaderboard, but their performance deteriorates when they encounter more challenging translations of higher quality. We observe this behavior in all evaluation datasets, except for IWSLT with TER targets. On translations with higher quality, both high-quality and low-quality QE models perform on the same level, with high-quality models sometimes outperforming low-quality models. On translations with lower quality, low-quality translations QE models outperform high-quality translations QE models.

It is evident from these findings that the selection of optimal training data for QE models must take into account the intended application of the model, particularly the quality of the MT systems it will be operating on. Considering that the evaluation datasets were mostly constructed using MT systems that outperform the one used for generating translations to train lower-quality QE models, we suggest opting for data obtained from a slightly inferior translation system.

Evaluation dataset	COMET targets		DA targets	
	Low-quality	High-quality	Low-quality	High-quality
CUNI Transformer	0.570	**0.592**	0.349	**0.378**
UEDIN	0.645	**0.650**	0.427	**0.432**
online-B	**0.698**	0.693	**0.501**	0.493
online-A	**0.777**	0.767	**0.574**	0.567
online-G	**0.767**	0.754	**0.536**	0.523
Whole dataset	**0.743**	0.731	**0.524**	0.517

Table 3: Evaluation results for WMT-18 dataset with DA and COMET targets, measured by Pearson correlation between predictions and targets. For each type of target, the winning model is denoted in bold.

Evaluation dataset	COMET models		TER models	
	Best single MT	Mixed	Best single MT	Mixed
CzEng	0.638	**0.643**	**0.524**	0.518
WMT18	0.757	**0.764**	0.461	**0.471**
IWSLT	0.599	**0.605**	<u>**0.404**</u>	0.373

Table 4: Evaluation results comparing QE models trained on single-MT dataset with models trained on data mixed from different MTs. For better readability, we only show which model leads to better results.

4.3 Evaluation on DA scores

In the absence of a large-scale QE dataset labeled by humans, we have trained our QE models on proxy metrics, namely TER and COMET, and then evaluated them on datasets that also use these proxy metrics. In this section, we assess our QE models using DA scores that were generated for the WMT-18 competition to evaluate MT systems. However, these scores are only available for a subset of the data, so we compare them to results for the same subset of data with COMET targets. Table 3 shows that despite the overall lower performance on DA scores, the trend in the relationship between high-quality and low-quality QE models remains the same. The low-quality QE model performs better than the high-quality QE models, and just like with COMET labels, its performance deteriorates quicker than that of higher-performing models. As a result, high-quality models perform better only on translations from CUNI Transformer and UEDIN, which are the top MT systems in WMT-18. This evidence suggests that the relationship between lower-quality and higher-quality QE models is likely to be the same with actual human-based metrics: For standard quality MT outputs, it is safer to train QE on lower-quality MT.

4.4 QE models based on more MT systems

In this section, we investigate the effect of combining datasets created by MT systems of different qualities, compared to using datasets from a single MT (either lower or higher quality). The evaluation results are shown in Table 4. The column titled "Best single MT" displays the performance of the best QE systems trained on data from a single MT, namely the one that employs lower-quality translations. The column labeled "Mixed" presents the evaluation results for QE models trained on a combination of high-quality and low-quality translations.

Overall, the results suggest that combining stronger and weaker MT systems when preparing training data for QE may not necessarily improve QE performance. The outcome depends on the specific settings in which the models will be used. While the mixed setting shows better results, we would like to point out that adding more machine-translated datasets to the QE training data may come at a cost. If there are good translation data from one MT that yield good QE results, it may not be worth the effort to mix it with data from another MT.

5 Conclusion

Our study investigated the impact of MT quality used to train QE systems on the performance of the QE systems. We trained QE models on the datasets that consist of the same source data but different translations produced by MT systems of varying quality. The findings revealed that QE models trained on lower-quality MT translations tended to perform better than those trained on higher-quality MT outputs. Additionally, the study suggests that mixing the better and worse MT outputs for training QE models may not necessarily lead to improved QE performance, and the results may vary depending on the specific application or usage scenario.

Acknowledgement

This research was partially supported by the grant 19-26934X (NEUREM3) of the Czech Science Foundation.

References

Ansari, E., Axelrod, A., Bach, N., Bojar, O., Cattoni, R., Dalvi, F., Durrani, N., Federico, M., Federmann, C., Gu, J., Huang, F., Knight, K., Ma, X., Nagesh, A., Negri, M., Niehues, J., Pino, J., Salesky, E., Shi, X., Stüker, S., Turchi, M., Waibel, A., and Wang, C. (2020). FINDINGS OF THE IWSLT 2020 EVALUATION CAMPAIGN. In *Proceedings of the 17th International Conference on Spoken Language Translation*, pages 1–34, Online. Association for Computational Linguistics.

Blatz, J., Fitzgerald, E., Foster, G., Gandrabur, S., Goutte, C., Kulesza, A., Sanchis, A., and Ueffing, N. (2004). Confidence estimation for machine translation. In *COLING 2004: Proceedings of the 20th International Conference on Computational Linguistics*, pages 315–321, Geneva, Switzerland. COLING.

Bojar, O., Federmann, C., Fishel, M., Graham, Y., Haddow, B., Huck, M., Koehn, P., and Monz, C. (2018). Findings of the 2018 conference on machine translation (WMT18). In *Proceedings of the Third Conference on Machine Translation: Shared Task Papers*, pages 272–303, Belgium, Brussels. Association for Computational Linguistics.

Conneau, A., Khandelwal, K., Goyal, N., Chaudhary, V., Wenzek, G., Guzmán, F., Grave, E., Ott, M., Zettlemoyer, L., and Stoyanov, V. (2019). Unsupervised cross-lingual representation learning at scale. *arXiv preprint arXiv:1911.02116*.

Graham, Y., Baldwin, T., Moffat, A., and Zobel, J. (2015). Can machine translation systems be evaluated by the crowd alone. *Natural Language Engineering*, 23:3 – 30.

Junczys-Dowmunt, M., Grundkiewicz, R., Dwojak, T., Hoang, H., Heafield, K., Neckermann, T., Seide, F., Germann, U., Fikri Aji, A., Bogoychev, N., Martins, A. F. T., and Birch, A. (2018). Marian: Fast neural machine translation in C++. In *Proceedings of ACL 2018, System Demonstrations*, pages 116–121, Melbourne, Australia. Association for Computational Linguistics.

Kepler, F., Trénous, J., Treviso, M., Vera, M., and Martins, A. F. T. (2019). OpenKiwi: An open source framework for quality estimation. In *Proceedings of the 57th Annual Meeting of the Association for*

Computational Linguistics–System Demonstrations, pages 117–122, Florence, Italy. Association for Computational Linguistics.

Kim, H., Jung, H.-Y., Kwon, H., Lee, J.-H., and Na, S.-H. (2017). Predictor-estimator: Neural quality estimation based on target word prediction for machine translation. *ACM Transactions on Asian and Low-Resource Language Information Processing*, 17:1–22.

Kocmi, T., Popel, M., and Bojar, O. (2020). Announcing czeng 2.0 parallel corpus with over 2 gigawords. *arXiv preprint arXiv:2007.03006*.

Koehn, P., Hoang, H., Birch, A., Callison-Burch, C., Federico, M., Bertoldi, N., Cowan, B., Shen, W., Moran, C., Zens, R., Dyer, C., Bojar, O., Constantin, A., and Herbst, E. (2007). Moses: Open source toolkit for statistical machine translation. In *Proceedings of the 45th Annual Meeting of the Association for Computational Linguistics Companion Volume Proceedings of the Demo and Poster Sessions*, pages 177–180, Prague, Czech Republic. Association for Computational Linguistics.

Lommel, A., Burchardt, A., Popović, M., Harris, K., Avramidis, E., and Uszkoreit, H. (2014). Using a new analytic measure for the annotation and analysis of MT errors on real data. In *Proceedings of the 17th Annual conference of the European Association for Machine Translation*, pages 165–172, Dubrovnik, Croatia. European Association for Machine Translation.

Macháček, D., Kratochvíl, J., Vojtěchová, T., and Bojar, O. (2019). A speech test set of practice business presentations with additional relevant texts. In *Statistical Language and Speech Processing: 7th International Conference, SLSP 2019, Ljubljana, Slovenia, October 14–16, 2019, Proceedings*, page 151–161, Berlin, Heidelberg. Springer-Verlag.

Rei, R., Stewart, C., Farinha, A. C., and Lavie, A. (2020). COMET: A neural framework for MT evaluation. In *Proceedings of the 2020 Conference on Empirical Methods in Natural Language Processing (EMNLP)*, pages 2685–2702, Online. Association for Computational Linguistics.

Sennrich, R., Haddow, B., and Birch, A. (2016). Neural machine translation of rare words with subword units. In *Proceedings of the 54th Annual Meeting of the Association for Computational Linguistics (Volume 1: Long Papers)*, pages 1715–1725, Berlin, Germany. Association for Computational Linguistics.

Snover, M., Dorr, B., Schwartz, R., Micciulla, L., and Makhoul, J. (2006a). A study of translation edit rate with targeted human annotation. In *Proceedings of the 7th Conference of the Association for Machine Translation in the Americas: Technical Papers*, pages 223–231, Cambridge, Massachusetts, USA. Association for Machine Translation in the Americas.

Snover, M., Dorr, B., Schwartz, R., Micciulla, L., and Makhoul, J. (2006b). A study of translation edit rate with targeted human annotation. In *Proceedings of the 7th Conference of the Association for Machine Translation in the Americas: Technical Papers*, pages 223–231, Cambridge, Massachusetts, USA. Association for Machine Translation in the Americas.

Specia, L., Turchi, M., Cancedda, N., Cristianini, N., and Dymetman, M. (2009). Estimating the sentence-level quality of machine translation systems. In *Proceedings of the 13th Annual conference of the European Association for Machine Translation*, Barcelona, Spain. European Association for Machine Translation.

A MT systems evaluation

	MT	COMET
1	CUNI Transformer	0.800
2	UEDIN	0.720
3	online-B	0.587
4	online-A	0.321
5	online-G	0.191

Table 5: Evaluation of MT systems that compose WMT-18 dataset measured with COMET score

	MT	COMET
1	LINDAT	0.778
2	Our high-quality MT	0.729
3	Our low-quality MT	0.604
4	Google Translate	0.390

Table 6: Evaluation of MT systems that compose CzEng dataset measured with COMET score

	MT	COMET
1	LINDAT	0.629
2	Our high-quality MT	0.540
3	Google Translate	0.500
4	Our low-quality MT	0.437

Table 7: Evaluation of MT systems that compose IWSLT dataset measured with COMET score

Improving Domain Robustness in Neural Machine Translation with Fused Topic Knowledge Embeddings

Danai Xezonaki[1,2] danai.xezonaki1@huawei-partners.com
Talaat Khalil[1*] khalil.talaat@gmail.com
David Stap[2] d.stap@uva.nl
Brandon James Denis[1] brandon.james.denis@huawei.com
[1] Huawei Technologies R&D, Amsterdam, Netherlands
[2] Language Technology Lab, University of Amsterdam

Abstract

Domain robustness is a key challenge for Neural Machine Translation (NMT). Translating text from a different distribution than the training set requires the NMT models to generalize well to unseen domains. In this work we propose a novel way to address domain robustness, by fusing external topic knowledge into the NMT architecture. We employ a pretrained denoising autoencoder and fuse topic information into the system during continued pretraining, and finetuning of the model on the downstream NMT task. Our results show that incorporating external topic knowledge, as well as additional pretraining can improve the out-of-domain performance of NMT models. The proposed methodology meets state-of-the-art on out-of-domain performance. Our analysis shows that a low overlap between the pretraining and finetuning corpora, as well as the quality of topic representations help the NMT systems become more robust under domain shift.

1 Introduction

Neural Machine Translation (NMT) has achieved impressive performance over the last few years when trained on large-scale data (Bojar et al., 2018). This success relies heavily on the availability of such data. The use of deep neural models has become the dominant approach for translation systems. However, it is not always possible to obtain neither parallel nor monolingual domain-specific data.

Most approaches for improving domain robustness in NMT assume that the target domains are known in advance, and a significant amount of data is available from the target domain. In such cases, the dominant approach for addressing domain mismatch is domain adaptation. However, when building translation systems and, as in many real-life scenarios, the target domains cannot always be known a priori. Koehn and Knowles (2017) were the first to identify domain mismatch as one of the main challenges of NMT. It is important therefore to develop translation systems that can generalize to domains unseen during training and thus be robust even under domain shift, as no target-domain data can be seen during training.

*Work conducted while working in Huawei.

Proceedings of Machine Translation Summit XIX, Vol. 1: Research Track, pages 209–221
September 4–8, 2023, Macau SAR, China.

Furthermore, even if NMT systems are trained on large-scale data, it is always possible that new topics or domains will emerge over time. These new domains make it difficult to maintain large translation systems, since these would require additional training on the new domains. A typical example is the outbreak of COVID-19, which intruded into everyday life and affected millions of peoples' lives. Keeping translation models up-to-date with such emerging topics is practically difficult, due to the limited availability of parallel data (Mahdieh et al., 2020).

In this work we focus on the problem of improving robustness under domain shift in NMT. A domain is defined by a corpus extracted from a specific source, and may differ from other domains in terms of topic, genre, level of formality, etc. (Koehn and Knowles, 2017). To this end, we improve domain robustness by incorporating external topic knowledge into the NMT models. We employ a denoising autoencoder that has been pretrained on Masked Language Modeling (MLM) using monolingual data and thus has not been exposed to any parallel data of the unseen test domains during training. Moreover, we train a distributional topic model using monolingual source-side data and subsequently extract a topic feature vector for each token in the vocabulary. We incorporate this external topic information during continuing the autoencoder's monolingual pretraining, and also during finetuning it on the downstream task of NMT.

To the best of our knowledge, this is the first work studying the contribution of topic modeling for domain robustness in NMT. Our key contribution is that we integrate external topic information into the NMT models, meeting state-of-the-art results for both in- and out-of-domain performance. Our analysis shows that both the quality of topic vectors and also the overlap between the pretraining and finetuning corpora are key factors towards improving domain robustness. Our results show that the proposed methodology improves domain robustness across two of the five experiments we conducted.

2 Related Work

2.1 Domain Robustness in NMT

Domain robustness has been identified as one of the main challenges of NMT (Koehn and Knowles, 2017). Müller et al. (2020) experimented with subword regularization (Kudo, 2018), defensive distillation (Hinton et al., 2015), reconstruction (Tu et al., 2017) and neural noisy channel reranking (Li and Jurafsky, 2016), and showed that reconstruction, meaning training a reconstructor component to learn to reconstruct the source sentence from decoder states, is the most effective technique for improving out-of-domain robustness in NMT.

In addition, Wang and Sennrich (2020) correlated domain robustness with hallucinations and proposed Minimum Risk Training, a sentence-level training objective, in order to reduce hallucinations and thereby improve indirectly domain robustness. Müller and Sennrich (2021) further examined the role of Minimum Bayes Risk Decoding and showed that it can indeed increase the robustness against domain shift. Moreover, Berard et al. (2020) found that initializing the NMT encoder using pretrained embeddings from language models helped out-of-domain robustness, while Germann (2020) proposed improving robustness by adding noise to the output layers of the NMT systems.

2.2 Pretraining in NMT

Unsupervised pretraining has been widely used over the last years, in order to deal with scarcity of large parallel in-domain data. It has been shown that pretraining acts as a regularizer in deep neural networks, and thus allows better generalization (Erhan et al., 2010). During pretraining, large models are typically trained with a denoising objective using monolingual data, as Masked Language Modeling (MLM), and are subsequently finetuned on downstream NLP tasks.

Recent studies have shown that pretrained NLP models can further improve out-of-domain robustness in NMT (Hendrycks et al., 2020; Tu et al., 2020). However, Liu et al. (2021) claimed that MLM training teaches the decoder to copy tokens from the input to the output of the system, and addressed this limitation by proposing a copying penalty, which mitigates the copying behavior of NMT systems. Through their experiments, they showed that the proposed method was able to improve even out-of-domain robustness.

2.3 Topic Modeling

Topic modeling has also been employed in the context of NMT, in order to provide prior semantic knowledge to the models. Topic models are statistical tools which identify hidden patterns and semantic structure in text corpora (Blei et al., 2010). Despite the fact that it has been shown that topic models significantly improve translation performance when incorporated into NMT architectures (Zhang et al., 2016; Chen et al., 2016; Wang et al., 2021), it has been yet unexplored how they can contribute to domain robustness in NMT. In this work, we go a step further and show that external topic information can also improve the lexical selection of the NMT systems under domain shift and thus help them become more domain robust.

In contrast to statistical topic models, various works have proposed distributional topic algorithms that mix Latent Dirichlet Allocation (Blei et al., 2001) with word embeddings (Mikolov et al., 2013a,b). Dieng et al. (2020) proposed the Embedded Topic Model (ETM), which is used in this work. ETM is a generative probabilistic model which assumes that each word is modeled by a categorical distribution and each document is a mixture of topics. The words are represented by an embedding, and the topics are points in the same embedding space. The distribution of topics over words is then defined by the dot product between each word and each topic embedding.

3 MBARTOPIC

In this section we introduce MBARTOPIC, our proposed system in order to improve domain robustness in NMT. We employ a sequence-to-sequence system and initialize its weights using a pretrained model. We need to ensure that the pretrained model has not been exposed to any parallel data of the test domains. To this end, we use a multilingual denoising sequence autoencoder for initialization, and, in particular mBART (Liu et al., 2020), which has been trained on monolingual data only, and on a different task than NMT.

Assuming a corpus D consisting of sub-corpora D_j , where each D_j is a set of monolingual text samples $D_j = (X_1, X_2, ..., X_n)$, as well as a noising function g that corrupts text, the mBART model is trained to reconstruct X_i from $g(X_i)$. Therefore, during pretraining it learns to maximize the log-likelihood of predicting the input X, given a noisy variant of it, as follows:

$$L = \sum_{D_j \in D} \sum_{X_i \in D_j} \log p(X_i | g(X_i); \theta) \tag{1}$$

We employ this pretrained system and finetune it on the downstream NMT task. We feed the parallel domain-specific data to the encoder and the decoder, while also adding the special ID token of the source and target languages, respectively. During finetuning on NMT the model learns to minimize the cross-entropy loss function:

$$L_{CE} = -\sum_{t=1}^{n} \log p_\theta(y_t | y_{<t}, x), \tag{2}$$

where x is the input sequence, y is the generated output and y_t is the t-th generated token.

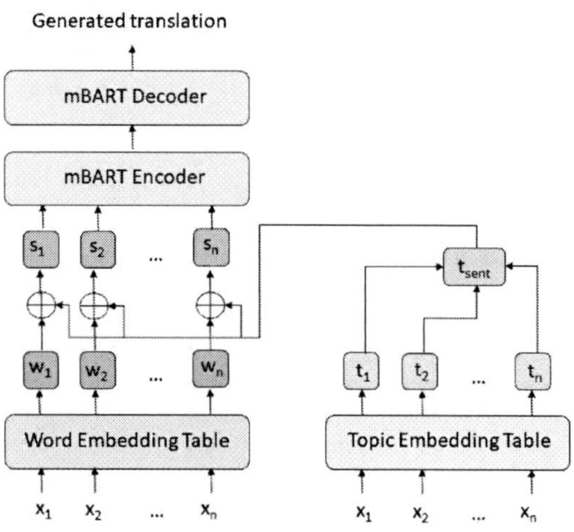

Figure 1: The illustration of the proposed MBARTOPIC architecture. The $\oplus$ is a sum operation. The t_{sent} is the sentence-level topic information obtained from the source tokens and the process of computation is given by Equation 3.

3.1 Integrating External Topic Information

A domain may differ from other domains in terms of topic, genre, level of formality, etc. (Koehn and Knowles, 2017). Based on this definition, we employ external topic information and incorporate it to the NMT models. The proposed system is shown in Figure 1.

We obtain the external topic knowledge by training a distributional topic model and extracting its topic embedding tables. Specifically, we employ the Embedded Topic Model (ETM, Dieng et al. (2020)) and train it on large monolingual corpora of the source language. Subsequently, we freeze the topic model and we use its trained topic embeddings. We extract one feature vector t_i for every term in the input sequence, which serves as an external context vector. We follow Wang et al. (2021) by employing their 'ENC_{pre}' topic integration method and propose an experimental setup where the extracted topic vectors can be utilized in the low-resource domain robustness scenario for NMT. As shown in Figure 1, we incorporate the topic vectors to the model architecture, by adding them to the embedding vector of each input token. In particular, we take the average of all the topic vectors of the source tokens and pass it through a projection layer. Through this projection we extract a sentence-level topic representation, t_{sent}, as follows:

$$t_{sent} = f\left(\frac{1}{n}\sum_{i=1}^{n} t_i\right), \tag{3}$$

where f is a learnable mapping.

The sentence-level topic information is then added to the word embeddings of the input tokens. Therefore, the final input representation for the i-th input token is given by:

$$s_i = w_i + t_{sent}, \tag{4}$$

where w_i is the embedding of the i-th input token. This combined input is finally fed to the encoder of mBART.

domains	corpora	size
IT	GNOME, KDE, PHP, Ubuntu, OpenOffice	222, 927
Law	JRC-Acquis	467, 309
Medical	EMEA	248, 099
Koran	Tanzil	17, 982
Subtitles	OpenSubtitles2018	500, 000

Table 1: Dataset overview. Size indicates number of sentence pairs after filtering.

We experiment with both continuing the pretraining of mBART, as well as finetuning it. During the continued pretraining, we train mBART on denoising source-language monolingual data. During finetuning, we finetune mBART on domain-specific parallel data. In both cases, we incorporate the external topic information to the source-side data as shown in Figure 1. The final model is then evaluated on translating out-of-domain data.

4 Experimental Setup

We compare five different systems:

1. **BASELINE**: As a weak baseline, we train a Transformer Base model (Vaswani et al., 2017).

2. **RANDOMINIT**: We train the mBART-large architecture from scratch, on domain-specific data. This experiment differs from MBART-FT as here we do not employ the pretrained weights of mBART, but instead initialize the network weights randomly. This model serves towards evaluating the contribution of pretraining.

3. **MBART-FT**: We employ the pretrained mBART-large system[1] and we do standard finetuning on our parallel data. Finetuning is performed on one domain at a time, and the models are evaluated on both seen and unseen domains.

4. **MBART-PT-FT**:We continue the pretraining and finetune mBART-large, but without adding any topic information at all. This experiment serves towards comparing against MBARTOPIC and thus discriminating the contribution of topics from the contribution of pretraining the model for more gradient updates.

5. **MBARTOPIC**: We augment the MBART-FT model with external topic knowledge, which is fed during additional pretraining of mBART and during finetuning on domain-specific data.

4.1 Datasets

We report experiments in the German → English (DE → EN) language direction. To verify the effectiveness of the proposed methods, we use corpora from five distant domains: IT, Medical, Law, Koran and Subtitles. For all experiments we make use of the same data as Müller et al. (2020); Wang and Sennrich (2020); Liu et al. (2021), as made available from the OPUS collection (Tiedemann, 2012). Each domain contains 2000 sentence pairs for evaluation and 2000 for testing. Additional details about the specific datasets of each domain and their sizes are shown in Table 1. For each experiment, we use one domain for pretraining/finetuning the models, and all five domains for testing both in- and out-of-domain performance.

[1] https://github.com/facebookresearch/fairseq/blob/main/examples/mbart/README.md

As monolingual source-side data for training the topic model and also for continuing the pretraining of mBART, we employ generic monolingual data from the news domain, and specifically the German News Dataset (Mi, 2020). This dataset is a collection of around $175k$ newspaper articles in German, where the articles are extracted from 15 news websites.

4.2 Preprocessing

For the BASELINE system, we use a joint BPE vocabulary (Sennrich et al., 2016) which is learnt with $32k$ merge operations over the entire corpus, taking both source and target samples into account. We preprocess the data by applying tokenization, normalizing punctuation, cleaning and removing non-printing characters using Moses (Koehn et al., 2007). For continuing the pretraining and finetuning, we do the same bpe processing as in the rest experiments, but we use the mBART pretrained sentencepiece tokenizer. We also use the same tokenizer to tokenize the monolingual data that we used to train the topic model.

4.3 Implementation Details

We implemented all experiments using FAIRSEQ (Ott et al., 2019). Our models use the Transformer architecture (Vaswani et al., 2017). Models are trained for a maximum of $100k$ steps with 1024 maximum tokens per GPU. All models are trained using 8 Nvidia Tesla-V100 GPUs. The continued pretraining, finetuning and topic model training required approximately 280, 470 and 210 GPU hours respectively. The Transformer Base systems consist of around $60M$ parameters and the mBART-based systems consist of approximately $610M$ parameters. We decode using beam search and a beam size of 5 and a length penalty of 1.4. Similar to the related works, we report case-sensitive BLEU (Papineni et al., 2002) scores on detokenized text using `sacrebleu` (Post, 2018).

We optimize all models with Adam (Kingma and Ba, 2015). We use early stopping to choose the model with the lowest loss on the validation set. For the baseline experiments, we use 5^{-4} maximum learning rate, 4000 warm-up steps and 0.2 dropout. For continuing the pretraining we mask 35% of the input words and train with 0.3 dropout. For finetuning, we train with 0.2 dropout. We also use 0.2 label smoothing, 2500 warm-up steps, polynomial decay and 3^{-5} maximum learning rate for both finetuning and continued pretraining.

For the topic model, we use the Embedded Topic Model (Dieng et al., 2020). We train the model for 500 epochs and set the number of topic clusters to 50 as in Wang et al. (2021). The embedding dimension of the trained topic vectors is set to 300.

5 Results

For each experiment, we train all systems on one domain at a time and evaluate them on the same (in-domain) and also on the rest four domains (out-of-domain). In Table 2 we compare the performance of the proposed models. In each sub-table of results, we report the train domains vertically and the test domains horizontally.

We observe that training the Transformer Base model (BASELINE) yields better results across almost all experiments, compared to training the mBART architecture from scratch (RANDOMINIT). This finding is expected given the large difference in the number of parameters between the two models and the relatively small amount of data we used to train the systems from scratch.

Moreover, initializing the network with pre-fitted weights (MBART-FT) is shown to achieve a significant gain in performance, compared to the results of RANDOMINIT and BASELINE, across all experiments, for both in- and out-of-domain translation. This observation stands in agreement with related literature indicating improvements in downstream NLP tasks when initializing the models with pretrained weights, due to transferring general knowledge to them (Liu et al., 2021), which contributes positively towards out-of-domain robustness.

System		Test domains IT	Law	Koran	Medical	Subtitles	**OOD p.d.**	**Avg. OOD**
	IT	42.5	9.7	2.3	16.9	8.4	9.3	
	Law	15.8	60.0	2.0	24.2	5.5	11.9	
BASELINE	Koran	0.2	0.2	14.6	0.1	1.0	0.4	7.5
	Medical	12.4	15.7	1.5	57.1	4.6	8.6	
	Subtitles	8.1	5.1	5.8	9.7	21.3	7.2	
	IT	34.8	4.6	1.5	5.6	6.3	4.5	
	Law	4.4	45.2	1.1	8.1	2.3	4.0	
RANDOMINIT	Koran	0.3	0.3	14.3	0.3	0.7	0.4	3.5
	Medical	4.1	9.3	1.2	47.7	2.2	4.2	
	Subtitles	5.6	3.0	4.6	4.6	23.9	4.5	
	IT	58.2	21.4	4.9	28.1	14.5	**17.2**	
	Law	28.3	76.3	2.6	30.9	7.5	17.3	
MBART-FT	Koran	0.8	1.2	19.2	1.1	3.1	**1.6**	14.3
	Medical	26.0	25.6	2.0	66.0	7.3	15.2	
	Subtitles	29.0	18.6	6.4	26.8	26.4	**20.2**	
	IT	59.3	20.1	4.5	26.8	13.4	16.2	
	Law	29.1	76.3	2.8	32.0	7.5	**17.9**	
MBART-PT-FT	Koran	0.4	1.0	18.9	0.9	2.7	1.3	14.6
	Medical	30.7	31.6	2.0	58.1	7.4	17.9	
	Subtitles	27.1	18.1	6.6	27.2	25.8	19.8	
	IT	59.6	20.3	4.6	27.4	13.3	16.4	
	Law	29.1	76.3	2.7	31.0	7.7	17.6	
MBARTOPIC	Koran	0.5	0.9	18.7	0.6	2.6	1.2	14.7
	Medical	30.7	31.4	2.3	58.0	8.4	**18.2**	
	Subtitles	27.2	18.3	6.7	28.0	26.1	20.1	

Table 2: Case-sensitive BLEU results of the 5 models for DE→EN. 'OOD p.d.' stands for the averaged out-of-domain score per domain-experiment. 'Avg. OOD' stands for the total average out-of-domain score, per system. We highlight the highest out-of-domain score per domain experiment in bold.

Comparing the MBART-PT-FT system to not performing any additional pretraining, as in MBART-FT, it becomes evident that the extra pretraining updates improve the domain robustness of the Law and Medical experiments. These models have a significant increase in their out-of-domain performance, while the Medical system seems to become more general after continuing the pretraining, given the decrease to its in-domain score. On the other hand, additional pretraining seems not to help the performance of the IT, Koran and Subtitles experiments. We argue in Section 6.1 that this finding is related to the overlap between the monolingual corpus used for pretraining and the finetuning domains.

Furthermore, we compare MBARTOPIC to MBART-PT-FT and observe that incorporating the topic knowledge to the system improves the out-of-domain translation for the IT, Medical and Subtitles experiments. On the other hand, the topic knowledge fusion has a slight decrease in the robustness of the Law and Koran experiments.

We would like to point out that for continuing the pretraining and for training the topic model, we used monolingual data from the news domain, which are relatively small and does not generalize well for all possible topics. These data are also biased towards specific domains, as per our overlap study in Section 6.2. We hypothesize that using large scale web crawled data for learning topic embeddings and continuing pretraining, e.g the mBART pre-training data, might help get rid of the side effect of knowledge overriding as suggested by the analysis, resulting in higher quality topic representations. We leave the investigation of this hypothesis to future work, since we were limited by computational constraints.

Finally, we provide some example translations of our systems in the out-of-domain setting [2].

System	Medical ID	Avg. Medical OOD
SMT (Müller et al., 2020)	58.4	11.8
NMT (Müller et al., 2020)	61.5	11.7
NMT+RC+SR+NC (Müller et al., 2020)	60.8	13.1
MLE w/ LS + MRT (Wang and Sennrich, 2020)	58.8	12.0
PRETRAINED (Liu et al., 2021)	63.1	17.6
PRETRAINED + CP (Liu et al., 2021)	**63.2**	**18.3**
MBART-FT	**66.0**	15.2
MBART-PT-FT	58.1	17.9
MBARTOPIC	58.0	**18.2**

Table 3: BLEU scores for the Medical experiment. We compare in-domain (ID) and out-of-domain (OOD) performance.

5.1 Comparison to Related Work

In Table 3 we compare our systems to the Related Work. These works employ the same corpora as we did, train their models on the Medical domain and evaluate them on all 5 domains. To this end, we compare our results of the Medical domain. We can see that our proposed systems perform comparably to the best systems in terms of out-of-domain performance, with Liu et al. (2021) achieving 18.3 and our MBARTOPIC model achieving 18.2 BLEU score. We also note that our proposed methodology might be orthogonal to the PRETRAINING + CP model of Liu et al. (2021); therefore combining them may lead to additional increases in quality.

Our MBART-FT model additionally achieves a high in-domain score. It should be noted that the PRETRAINED experiment (Liu et al., 2021) is the same experiment as our MBART-FT model. We attempted to replicate the results of PRETRAINED but unfortunately we were unable to do so. We were not able to determine the reason for the discrepancy. Overall, our most domain robust system for the Medical domain is MBARTOPIC, which achieves the biggest improvement in terms of out-of-domain performance.

6 Contributing Factors to Domain Robustness

To understand what contributes to the out-of-domain performance gains, we conduct an analysis of the results presented in Section 5.

6.1 N-gram Overlap between Pretraining and Finetuning Corpora

Recall that Table 2 shows that additional pretraining helps the Law and Medical domains achieve the most significant improvement in their out-of-domain scores. We hypothesize that

[2] https://gist.github.com/danaiksez/7cfe3463ebf43b188e37689c104075d2

Domains	Uni-grams (%)	Bi-grams (%)	Tri-grams (%)	Four-grams (%)
IT	96.58	4.74	0.98	0.18
Law	**84.65**	2.88	1.38	0.20
Koran	99.52	5.92	1.09	0.08
Medical	**91.18**	3.89	0.92	0.18
Subtitles	97.63	2.83	1.61	0.24

Table 4: Overlap of n-grams between the n-gram vocabularies of the German News monolingual dataset and each of the 5 domain corpora. The values are calculated using Equation 5.

this finding is related to the topic and style of the monolingual data used for additional pretraining. We investigate this by analyzing how much related is the pretraining to the finetuning datasets. To this end, we compute the overlap of n-grams between the German News Dataset and each of the five domain corpora. We particularly consider the uni-, bi-, tri- and four-gram vocabularies of the corpora we employ and calculate the percentage of the German News n-grams that co-exist in the finetuning domain vocabularies. Those n-gram overlaps are shown in Table 4. The values are calculated as the percentage of the following:

$$overlap_{ngram} = \frac{\#shared\_ngrams}{\#pretraining\_ngrams}, \tag{5}$$

where $\#shared\_ngrams$ is the number of shared entries between the pretraining and finetuning n-gram vocabularies, and $\#pretraining\_ngrams$ is the n-gram vocabulary size of the pretraining (German News) dataset.

We observe that the Law and Medical experiments, which improved their out-of-domain performance through additional pretraining, have the lowest overlap with the pretraining corpus. This finding suggests that during pretraining, the systems acquire extra general knowledge through the denoising of monolingual corpora. Therefore, during finetuning, when there is smaller n-gram overlap with the pretraining dataset, it is likely that the previously acquired general semantic knowledge helps the systems generalize well to unseen domains.

On the other hand, in the case of larger overlap, the models seem to 'erase' this general knowledge they aquired during pretraining, and instead overwrite it with the domain-specific context they are exposed to, during finetuning. To this end, these systems are likely to overfit on the finetuning domain and forget about the more general information. This in turn affects negatively their translation robustness under domain shift.

6.2 Topic Embeddings Analysis

We analyze the topic embedding vectors and their contribution when incorporated to the system architecture. We do that by measuring the distances between the intra-domain trained topic vectors.

We assume that the most important words per domain should lie closer to each other in the embedding space. In this case, fusing the topic representations to the network architecture should contribute towards discriminating the domains easier. We choose the top-n most 'categorical' words per domain. These are selected as the ones with the highest TF-IDF score. We then measure for each domain, the cosine distance between each possible pair of them. Since not all words are equally significant for a domain corpus, we want the final score to reflect the importance of the words. Therefore, we weigh the cosine distance of each word pair by the IDF scores of both words.

Given the top-n words of a specific domain, with n empirically selected to 10 in our case, and w_i being the i-th word of the top-n words, each entry of Table 5 is computed as follows:

$$\text{WCD} = \frac{1}{n^2}\sum_{i=1}^{n}\sum_{j=1}^{n}\cos_D(w_i, w_j)\text{IDF}(w_i)\text{IDF}(w_j) \quad (6)$$

Table 5 shows the averaged Weighted Cosine Distances (WCD) per domain. We notice that the WDC between the most important words of Law and Koran are the highest among the domains. As shown in Table 2, the Law and Koran experiments experience a decrease in performance when topics are added. On the other hand, the IT, Medical and Subtitles corpora, which have a smaller WCD among their most categorical words, have an increase in out-of-domain performance when fusing topic representations. These findings therefore seem to correlate with the behaviour of the experiments when fusing topic information, and highlight the need for a more concise topic embedding space.

	IT	Law	Koran	Medical	Subtitles
WCD	1.071	**1.202**	**1.347**	1.069	0.941

Table 5: Averaged Weighted Cosine Distances (WCD) between top-10 most categorical words per domain, weighted by their IDF score, as shown in Equation 6.

7 Conclusion

In this work we propose MBARTOPIC, a novel model for improving domain robustness in NMT with integrated external topic knowledge. This is the first work studying the contribution of topic information towards improving domain robustness in NMT. We use a sequence-to-sequence model, and specifically a pretrained multilingual denoising autoencoder. We train a distributional topic model on source-side monolingual data and integrate this topic knowledge to the encoder of the NMT system. We do that by extracting sentence-level topic features and subsequently combining them with the word embeddings of the each input token. In our approach we continue the pretraining of the denoising model using source-side monolingual corpora, and then finetune it on the downstream NMT task, using domain-specific parallel data. We incorporate the external topic features into both the additional pretraining and also during finetuning.

Our results show that the proposed method can improve the domain robustness of our experiments and meets state-of-the-art results in the out-of-domain performance. Our analysis suggests that additional self-supervised pretraining with a low overlap between the pretraining and finetuning corpora can be an important factor to the domain robustness of NMT systems. Finally, we show that smaller distances among the topic vectors of domain-specific words result in an increase in the out-of-domain performance.

In the future, we plan to investigate the contribution of topic knowledge when it is fused into both the encoder and decoder of the NMT system. We also plan to analyze the system performance on a leave-one-out scenario, when finetuned on multiple domains and evaluated on an unseen one.

Acknowledgements

We would like to thank Fokko Beekhof, Jun Luo and Nikolas Zygouras for their valuable suggestions and comments.

References

Berard, A., Calapodescu, I., Nikoulina, V., and Philip, J. (2020). Naver labs Europe's participation in the robustness, chat, and biomedical tasks at WMT 2020. In *Proceedings of the Fifth Conference on Machine Translation*, pages 462–472, Online. Association for Computational Linguistics.

Blei, D., Carin, L., and Dunson, D. (2010). Probabilistic topic models. *IEEE Signal Processing Magazine*, 27(6):55–65.

Blei, D., Ng, A., and Jordan, M. (2001). Latent dirichlet allocation. In Dietterich, T., Becker, S., and Ghahramani, Z., editors, *Advances in Neural Information Processing Systems*, volume 14. MIT Press.

Bojar, O., Federmann, C., Fishel, M., Graham, Y., Haddow, B., Koehn, P., and Monz, C. (2018). Findings of the 2018 conference on machine translation (WMT18). In *Proceedings of the Third Conference on Machine Translation: Shared Task Papers*, pages 272–303, Belgium, Brussels. Association for Computational Linguistics.

Chen, W., Matusov, E., Khadivi, S., and Peter, J.-T. (2016). Guided alignment training for topic-aware neural machine translation. In *Conferences of the Association for Machine Translation in the Americas: MT Researchers' Track*, pages 121–134, Austin, TX, USA. The Association for Machine Translation in the Americas.

Dieng, A. B., Ruiz, F. J. R., and Blei, D. M. (2020). Topic modeling in embedding spaces. *Transactions of the Association for Computational Linguistics*, 8:439–453.

Erhan, D., Bengio, Y., Courville, A., Manzagol, P.-A., Vincent, P., and Bengio, S. (2010). Why does unsupervised pre-training help deep learning? *Journal of Machine Learning Research*, 11(19):625–660.

Germann, U. (2020). The University of Edinburgh's submission to the German-to-English and English-to-German tracks in the WMT 2020 news translation and zero-shot translation robustness tasks. In *Proceedings of the Fifth Conference on Machine Translation*, pages 197–201, Online. Association for Computational Linguistics.

Hendrycks, D., Liu, X., Wallace, E., Dziedzic, A., Krishnan, R., and Song, D. (2020). Pretrained transformers improve out-of-distribution robustness. In *Proceedings of the 58th Annual Meeting of the Association for Computational Linguistics*, pages 2744–2751, Online. Association for Computational Linguistics.

Hinton, G., Vinyals, O., and Dean, J. (2015). Distilling the knowledge in a neural network. In *NIPS Deep Learning and Representation Learning Workshop*.

Kingma, D. P. and Ba, J. (2015). Adam: A method for stochastic optimization. In Bengio, Y. and LeCun, Y., editors, *3rd International Conference on Learning Representations, ICLR 2015, San Diego, CA, USA, May 7-9, 2015, Conference Track Proceedings*.

Koehn, P., Hoang, H., Birch, A., Callison-Burch, C., Federico, M., Bertoldi, N., Cowan, B., Shen, W., Moran, C., Zens, R., Dyer, C., Bojar, O., Constantin, A., and Herbst, E. (2007). Moses: Open source toolkit for statistical machine translation. In *Proceedings of the 45th Annual Meeting of the Association for Computational Linguistics Companion Volume Proceedings of the Demo and Poster Sessions*, pages 177–180, Prague, Czech Republic. Association for Computational Linguistics.

Koehn, P. and Knowles, R. (2017). Six challenges for neural machine translation. In *Proceedings of the First Workshop on Neural Machine Translation*, pages 28–39, Vancouver. Association for Computational Linguistics.

Kudo, T. (2018). Subword regularization: Improving neural network translation models with multiple subword candidates. In *Proceedings of the 56th Annual Meeting of the Association for Computational Linguistics (Volume 1: Long Papers)*, pages 66–75, Melbourne, Australia. Association for Computational Linguistics.

Li, J. and Jurafsky, D. (2016). Mutual information and diverse decoding improve neural machine translation.

Liu, X., Wang, L., Wong, D. F., Ding, L., Chao, L. S., Shi, S., and Tu, Z. (2021). On the copying behaviors of pre-training for neural machine translation. In *Findings of the Association for Computational Linguistics: ACL-IJCNLP 2021*, pages 4265–4275, Online. Association for Computational Linguistics.

Liu, Y., Gu, J., Goyal, N., Li, X., Edunov, S., Ghazvininejad, M., Lewis, M., and Zettlemoyer, L. (2020). Multilingual denoising pre-training for neural machine translation. *Transactions of the Association for Computational Linguistics*, 8:726–742.

Mahdieh, M., Chen, M. X., Cao, Y., and Firat, O. (2020). Rapid domain adaptation for machine translation with monolingual data. *ArXiv*, abs/2010.12652.

Mi, S. (2020). German news dataset.

Mikolov, T., Chen, K., Corrado, G., and Dean, J. (2013a). Efficient estimation of word representations in vector space.

Mikolov, T., Sutskever, I., Chen, K., Corrado, G. S., and Dean, J. (2013b). Distributed representations of words and phrases and their compositionality. In Burges, C., Bottou, L., Welling, M., Ghahramani, Z., and Weinberger, K., editors, *Advances in Neural Information Processing Systems*, volume 26. Curran Associates, Inc.

Müller, M., Rios, A., and Sennrich, R. (2020). Domain robustness in neural machine translation. In *14th Conference of the Association for Machine Translation in the Americas (AMTA 2020)*, Proceedings of the 14th Conference of the Association for Machine Translation in the Americas, pages 151–164. Association for Machine Translation in the Americas.

Müller, M. and Sennrich, R. (2021). Understanding the properties of minimum Bayes risk decoding in neural machine translation. In *Proceedings of the 59th Annual Meeting of the Association for Computational Linguistics and the 11th International Joint Conference on Natural Language Processing (Volume 1: Long Papers)*, pages 259–272, Online. Association for Computational Linguistics.

Ott, M., Edunov, S., Baevski, A., Fan, A., Gross, S., Ng, N., Grangier, D., and Auli, M. (2019). fairseq: A fast, extensible toolkit for sequence modeling. In *Proceedings of the 2019 Conference of the North American Chapter of the Association for Computational Linguistics (Demonstrations)*, pages 48–53, Minneapolis, Minnesota. Association for Computational Linguistics.

Papineni, K., Roukos, S., Ward, T., and Zhu, W.-J. (2002). Bleu: a method for automatic evaluation of machine translation. In *Proceedings of the 40th Annual Meeting of the Association for Computational Linguistics*, pages 311–318, Philadelphia, Pennsylvania, USA. Association for Computational Linguistics.

Post, M. (2018). A call for clarity in reporting BLEU scores. In *Proceedings of the Third Conference on Machine Translation: Research Papers*, pages 186–191, Brussels, Belgium. Association for Computational Linguistics.

Sennrich, R., Haddow, B., and Birch, A. (2016). Neural machine translation of rare words with subword units. In *Proceedings of the 54th Annual Meeting of the Association for Computational Linguistics (Volume 1: Long Papers)*, pages 1715–1725, Berlin, Germany. Association for Computational Linguistics.

Tiedemann, J. (2012). Parallel data, tools and interfaces in OPUS. In *Proceedings of the Eighth International Conference on Language Resources and Evaluation (LREC'12)*, pages 2214–2218, Istanbul, Turkey. European Language Resources Association (ELRA).

Tu, L., Lalwani, G., Gella, S., and He, H. (2020). An empirical study on robustness to spurious correlations using pre-trained language models. *Transactions of the Association for Computational Linguistics*, 8:621–633.

Tu, Z., Liu, Y., Shang, L., Liu, X., and Li, H. (2017). Neural machine translation with reconstruction. *Proceedings of the AAAI Conference on Artificial Intelligence*, 31(1).

Vaswani, A., Shazeer, N., Parmar, N., Uszkoreit, J., Jones, L., Gomez, A. N., Kaiser, L. u., and Polosukhin, I. (2017). Attention is all you need. In Guyon, I., Luxburg, U. V., Bengio, S., Wallach, H., Fergus, R., Vishwanathan, S., and Garnett, R., editors, *Advances in Neural Information Processing Systems*, volume 30. Curran Associates, Inc.

Wang, C. and Sennrich, R. (2020). On exposure bias, hallucination and domain shift in neural machine translation. In *Proceedings of the 58th Annual Meeting of the Association for Computational Linguistics*, pages 3544–3552, Online. Association for Computational Linguistics.

Wang, W., Peng, W., Zhang, M., and Liu, Q. (2021). Neural machine translation with heterogeneous topic knowledge embeddings. In *Proceedings of the 2021 Conference on Empirical Methods in Natural Language Processing*, pages 3197–3202, Online and Punta Cana, Dominican Republic. Association for Computational Linguistics.

Zhang, J., Li, L., Way, A., and Liu, Q. (2016). Topic-informed neural machine translation. In *Proceedings of COLING 2016, the 26th International Conference on Computational Linguistics: Technical Papers*, pages 1807–1817, Osaka, Japan. The COLING 2016 Organizing Committee.

Instance-Based Domain Adaptation for Improving Terminology Translation

Prashanth Nayak prashanth.nayak@adaptcentre.ie
School of Computing, Dublin City University, Dublin, Ireland

Rejwanul Haque rejwanul.haque@setu.ie
School of Computing, South East Technological University, Carlow, Ireland

John D. Kelleher john.kelleher@mu.ie
Department of Computer Science, Maynooth University, Dublin, Ireland

Andy Way andy.way@adaptcentre.ie
School of Computing, Dublin City University, Dublin, Ireland

Abstract

Terms are essential indicators of a domain, and domain term translation is dealt with priority in any translation workflow. Translation service providers who use machine translation (MT) expect term translation to be unambiguous and consistent with the context and domain in question. Although current state-of-the-art neural MT (NMT) models are able to produce high-quality translations for many languages, they are still not at the level required when it comes to translating domain-specific terms. This study presents a terminology-aware instance-based adaptation method for improving terminology translation in NMT. We conducted our experiments for French-to-English and found that our proposed approach achieves a statistically significant improvement over the baseline NMT system in translating domain-specific terms. Specifically, the translation of multi-word terms is improved by 6.7% over a strong baseline.

1 Introduction

NMT (Vaswani et al., 2017) has been the state-of-the-art in MT research and development for some time. Fine-tuning NMT models usually requires specialised domain data for translating domain text (Luong and Manning, 2015). In recent times, Large-scale pre-trained models (LPTMs) (Devlin et al., 2019; Brown et al., 2020; Liu et al., 2020) have gained significant attention due to their remarkable performance in various Natural Language Processing (NLP) tasks. These models have proven effective in diverse applications, from information extraction to text generation. As a result, the NLP community is increasingly focused on harnessing their potential. One of the key advantages of LPTMs is that they often require smaller amounts of data for domain adaptation compared to traditional machine learning models (Devlin et al., 2019). By leveraging pre-trained knowledge, LPTMs can be fine-tuned on specific domains with relatively limited data, making them a valuable resource for addressing domain-specific challenges in NLP. However, despite significant improvements in translation quality, NMT systems still struggle with translating terminology. Even domain-adapted models are found to have difficulty with accurately translating domain-specific terminology (Sato et al., 2020).

Proceedings of Machine Translation Summit XIX, Vol. 1: Research Track, pages 222–234
September 4–8, 2023, Macau SAR, China.

This paper proposes a simple yet effective instance-based fine-tuning approach based on terminology-aware mining. We tested our approach on the French-to-English terminology translation task [1] for COVID-19 domain data. Our findings show that the proposed approach helps improve terminology translation in COVID-19 domain data. Our in-depth analysis showed that adapting a single instance for a larger number of epochs helps improve the translation of domain-specific terms.

The rest of this paper is organised as follows. Section 2 discusses work related to our study. Section 3 gives details about the data we used in our experiments. We describe our methodology in Section 4. Our NMT model is explained in Section 5. Experiments and results are covered in Section 6. Finally, Section 7 summarises our work and discusses possible future research ideas.

2 Related Work

Although NMT models have shown significant improvement in many translation tasks, translating terms of specific domains, such as medical or technical (Ao and Acharya, 2021), still remains challenging for NMT. Numerous methods have been proposed to improve term translation in NMT. These include (i) fine-tuning with domain-specific data: these help NMT models understand and translate domain-specific terms more effectively (Nayak et al., 2020), (ii) data augmentation approaches, including generating synthetic data through back-translation or self-training: these methods expose the NMT model to a variety of examples, ultimately enhancing term recognition and translation (Fernando et al., 2020), (iii) incorporating external resources like glossaries, dictionaries, or terminology databases can assist NMT models in understanding and translating specialised terms more effectively (Scansani and Dugast, 2021), (iv) terminology injection during inference, using techniques like inline tags (Dinu et al., 2019), source-target alignments (Dougal and Lonsdale, 2020), or fixed source positions (Niehues, 2021) for reference terms, helps produce translations with accurate domain-specific terminology, and (v) introducing auxiliary objectives during training such as predicting masked source terms or generating domain-specific inflections (Michon et al., 2020) can handle domain-specific terms better during inference.

Standard NMT domain adaptation involves fine-tuning a generic NMT model using domain-specific data. Accordingly, it is essential to consider factors such as similarity or distinct domain features that characterise the specialised field to effectively select the appropriate data. In their study, Farajian et al. (2017) showed that fine-tuning a generic model using a sentence highly similar to the source-test sentence can improve the usage of domain-specific terminology after adaptation. Likewise, Li et al. (2018) conducted an experiment in which they fine-tuned a generic model on a small subset of bilingual training data acquired through a similarity search with the source test sentence. Their findings also indicated an improvement in translation performance. In their experiments, both Farajian et al. (2017) and Li et al. (2018) showed how only a small set of sentences based on similarity to that of the test sentence is sufficient to improve the quality of translation. However, it is crucial that the sentences used for fine-tuning exhibit considerable similarity to the sentence being translated; otherwise, this can lead to a deterioration in translation quality.

Unlike Farajian et al. (2017) and Li et al. (2018), who fine-tuned their models on fewer sentences for each test instance, Chen et al. (2020) took a different approach by employing n-gram matching for the entire test set. Their study focused on matching and selecting n-grams from the training data which are most relevant to the entire test set rather than just individual sentences. By doing so, they were able to create a more comprehensive fine-tuning dataset, which in turn led to improved terminology translation.

[1] https://www.statmt.org/wmt21/terminology-task.html

Numerous studies have investigated ways to better incorporate technical terms into MT systems during inference. For example, Dinu et al. (2019) added special tags to the source text sentence by identifying domain-specific terms. After translating, they found that these tags were correctly replaced with the appropriate terms in the target language. A similar approach was tried by Song et al. (2019), where they replaced specific phrases in the source text with pre-selected, domain-specific translations before translating. This made it easier for the system to use the correct domain-specific terms in the final translation. Michon et al. (2020) carried out a comparative analysis by experimenting with variations of inline terminology tags and discussed the optimal settings in the experiment that helped improve terminology translation. In their work, Dougal and Lonsdale (2020) added domain-specific terminology after the translation process as a post-processing step, replacing incorrect terms with approved ones using source-target alignments. This approach offers the benefit of not requiring the translation model to handle tags, so it could potentially be used to introduce terminology to MT system outputs. However, the effectiveness of this method relies on an effective alignment model. In their work, Chen et al. (2020) developed constraint-aware training data by randomly choosing phrases from the reference translation to serve as constraints and subsequently merging them into the source sentence with the help of a separation symbol. Their method does not require alignments and solely depends on bilingual dictionaries during translation. They inserted the reference terminology at a fixed location in the source text, facilitating the model's learning of proper alignment. Similarly, Niehues (2021) also placed the reference terminology at a fixed point within the source text. However, his primary focus was on using the lemma of the term, which encouraged the model to learn the appropriate inflections for the given terminology. In their experiments, Lee et al. (2021) presented a technique that estimates the range of masked source terms during MT training, facilitating the integration of multi-word domain-specific terms in the translation process. They found that their models produced performance similar to that of Chen et al. (2020) in terms of single-word accuracy but improved performance when it came to translating multi-word terms.

Nayak et al. (2020) conducted an experiment in which they mined sentences from a large general domain corpus based on the presence of domain-specific terms in the test data. They then utilised the extracted data to fine-tune the model and observed improvements in terminology translation. Similar experiments were carried out by Haque et al. (2020), with their approach also demonstrating improvements in terminology translation. In our experiment, we employ an approach similar to that used by Nayak et al. (2020) and Haque et al. (2020). However, we take it further by performing extraction and adaptation for each instance in the test data as in Farajian et al. (2017). This means that, instead of using a predetermined set of sentences containing domain-specific terms, we adapt our model on a per-instance basis, allowing the model to better handle the domain-specific terminology in each test sentence. Our proposed approach aims to provide a more tailored and flexible adaptation process, potentially resulting in more significant improvements in translation performance and domain-specific term management.

3 Dataset

In our experiment, we used French-to-English parallel data from WMT2021,[2] which includes sources such as Europarlv10, ParaCrawlv7.1, News Commentary v16, UN Parallel Corpus V1.0, CommonCrawl corpus, and 10^9French-English corpus. We combine these datasets, remove duplicates, and tokenise the text using Moses (Koehn et al., 2007)[3] tokeniser scripts. The resulting dataset consists of 44M unique sentence pairs. The terminologies for French-to-English

[2]https://www.statmt.org/wmt21/terminology-task.html

[3]https://github.com/moses-smt/mosesdecoder

translation were obtained from the TICO-19 project by Anastasopoulos et al. (2020),[4] focusing on the COVID-19 domain. There are 595 unique domain-specific terms, and the test set comprises a total of 2100 sentences.

4 Methodology

4.1 Domain adaptation using terminology-aware mining

Terms or phrases appearing in domain-specific data may encode meanings or usages different to those when they appear in generic data. In order to obtain correct translations for terms or phrases of a domain text, Translation Service Providers (TSPs) usually use domain-specific terminology or glossaries. Obtaining such terminological resources is challenging as this process can be very expensive in terms of both cost and time. Automatically identifying and extracting domain-specific terminology from training data or external resources and integrating them into industrial translation workflows can partly alleviate this problem (Haque et al., 2018; Mouratidis et al., 2022). A notable obstacle to these approaches could be the training itself. Since the NMT training process is a highly time-consuming task, integrating terminology at training or fine-tuning from scratch is not a feasible solution. In fact, this is unimaginable in an industrial setting where terminologies are often needed to be updated for translating newly arrived documents with particular styles. We could have certain situations where the training time may not be a concern, and the entire terminology is available at the training. However, an NMT system trained with added terminology or that uses terminology during inference does not guarantee to generate translations with expected terms. Adapting a generic NMT system to a specific domain and obtaining accurate translations for the domain-specific terms can be more challenging when one does not have domain-specific data. In this study, we investigate this specific scenario (i.e. unavailability of domain text) and systematically make use of large general-domain data in order to fine-tune our MT systems. First, we extract terms from the source sentence to be translated based on the named tags provided in the test data. Then we mine parallel sentences from the general domain parallel data based on the frequency of occurring the extracted domain-specific terms in the parallel sentences. The extracted sentences are then used to fine-tune our NMT models. Note that the entire process (term extraction from the test sentence to be translated and mining parallel sentences from large generic data) is characterised as *on-the-fly* instance-based adaptation by Farajian et al. (2017).

Algorithm 1 Algorithm for Instance-Based Adaptation Using Terminology-Aware Mining

for *src_sent* in *tst_set* **do**
  D_{Trm} = **Extract_trm**(*src_sent*)
  R_{Sent}= **Retrieve**(*max_trm*(Data,D_{Trm}))
  F_{MT}=**Finetune**(G_{MT},R_{Sent})
  Translate(F_{MT},*src_sent*)
end for

In Algorithm 1, we present our approach for instance-based adaptation using terminology-aware mining. The algorithm leverages domain-specific terminology to adapt the NMT system by fine-tuning it on relevant instances from the general-domain parallel data.

The algorithm picks a source sentence (*src_sent*) from the test set (*tst_set*) and performs the following steps:

- **Extract** domain-specific terminology (D_{Trm}) from the source sentence to be translated

[4]https://tico-19.github.io/

using the **Extract_trm** function. This function identifies terms that are specific to the given domain within the source text using the annotated tags provided in the test data.

- The **Retrieve** function, used with the max_trm parameter, mines sentences (R_{Sent}) matching most domain-specific terms D_{Trm} from general-domain data.

- Fine-tune the general-domain MT system (G_{MT},R_{Sent}) using the retrieved sentence (R_{Sent}). The **Finetune** function updates the model parameters based on the domain-specific instance, resulting in a fine-tuned MT system (F_{MT}).

- **Translate** the source text (*src_sent*) using the fine-tuned MT system (F_{MT}) to generate a domain-adapted translation.

5 Experimental Setup

5.1 NMT Model

The mBART (Multilingual BART) (Liu et al., 2020) model is a multilingual extension of the BART (Bidirectional and Auto-Regressive Transformers) (Lewis et al., 2020) model, a sequence-to-sequence pre-training framework for natural language understanding and generation tasks. mBART uses a standard sequence-to-sequence Transformer architecture with 12 layers of the encoder and 12 layers of the decoder, where each layer has 16 heads and a model dimension of 1024. The model is trained on large-scale multilingual data, enabling it to perform well across various languages and tasks. mBART is pre-trained using a combination of denoising auto-encoding and masked language modeling, involving reconstructing corrupted text or predicting masked tokens. One key feature of mBART is its shared vocabulary across languages, making it easier to fine-tune the model for downstream tasks, such as MT, summarisation, or sentiment analysis. Leveraging its pre-trained knowledge, mBART achieves state-of-the-art performance on various NLP tasks and languages.

In this study, we wanted to see how our proposed domain adaptation method of terminology-aware fine-tuning would work on mBART. We placed particular emphasis on terminology translation (cf. Section 4). Our experiment used mBart-50-many-to-many[5] MT, a strong checkpoint based on mBart, as our baseline model. In our experiment, we utilised the following hyperparameters: a learning rate of 2e-5, a weight decay of 0.01, a training batch size of 32, and an evaluation batch size of 32.

We apply the instance-based adaptation on mBART (see Algorithm 1). We expect that our terminology-aware mining techniques will be able to help adapt the baseline so that the model can correctly translate a larger number of domain-specific terms. In order to thoroughly assess how our proposed terminology-aware adaptation process works on terminology translation, we carried out experiments with a different number of instances (one, three, and five) and epochs (one, three, and five) for fine-tuning. By examining the impact of varying numbers of sentence and epoch combinations on the model's performance and its handling of domain-specific terms, we aimed to gain a deeper understanding of the potential benefits and limitations of the proposed approach.

6 Experiments and Results

We evaluated our MT systems using BLEU (Papineni et al., 2002), COMET (Rei et al., 2020), NIST (Przybocki et al., 2010) and Term Count as our evaluation metrics. Term Count (TC) measures the number of occurrences of domain-specific terms accurately translated by the MT system. Table 1 shows the results that we obtained through our experiments. It displays BLEU,

[5]https://huggingface.co/facebook/mbart-large-50-many-to-many-mmt

TC, NIST and COMET scores for each of the test scenarios described in Section 5. We can see from the table that TC improves in two cases over the baseline. In both cases, the improvement occurs for a single sentence with three and five epochs. We conducted statistical significance tests for two system comparisons using bootstrap resampling (Koehn, 2004) and found that the differences in scores were statistically significant.

Furthermore, the improvement in TC over the baseline MT system suggests that the proposed adaptation method effectively improves the generic NMT system's ability to handle domain-specific terminology. In order to further understand the results in Table 1, we visualise the results in Figures 1, 2, 3 and 4.

Sentence	Epoch	BLEU	Term Count	COMET	NIST
Base		27.63	2175	0.844	10.80
1	1	26.60	2155	0.825	09.75
1	3	27.21	2191	0.826	09.92
1	5	27.68	2190	0.822	10.06
3	1	26.12	2115	0.829	09.81
3	3	26.24	2111	0.832	10.08
3	5	26.43	2094	0.832	10.21
5	1	25.39	2119	0.817	09.38
5	3	26.18	2109	0.833	10.11
5	5	26.30	2089	0.835	10.23

Table 1: Results of instance-based adaptation using terminology-aware mining.

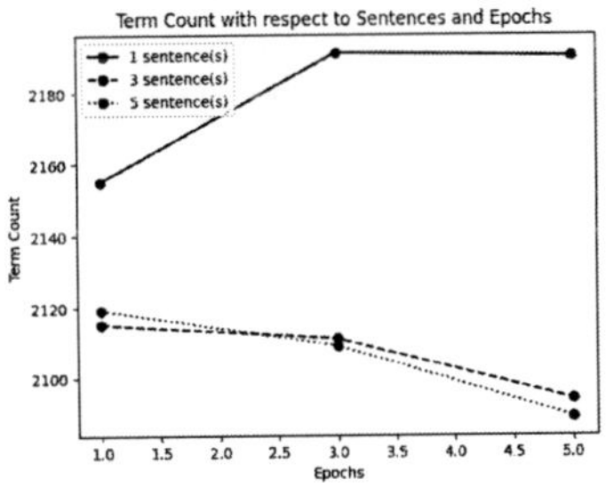

Figure 1: Term count scores in relation to the number of sentences and epochs used in the adapted model.

In Figure 1, we show the performance of our adapted MT systems for the French-to-English translation task using TC scores. The graph presents the results for different combinations of sentences (one, three, and five) and epochs (one, three, and five) in the fine-tuning process. The x-axis represents the number of epochs, and the y-axis represents TC. The lines with varying markers correspond to the different epoch combinations. In Figure 1, we observe that increasing the number of sentences used for fine-tuning does not contribute significantly to the improvement of terminology translation performance. Rather, we find that increasing the number of epochs for a single sentence is more beneficial. This finding suggests that the model may benefit from more focused training, concentrating its learning efforts on a smaller number of sentences for a longer period of time (i.e., more epochs). By doing so, the model can potentially gain a deeper understanding of the specific domain terminology, which in turn can lead to better translation performance with respect to the domain-specific terms.

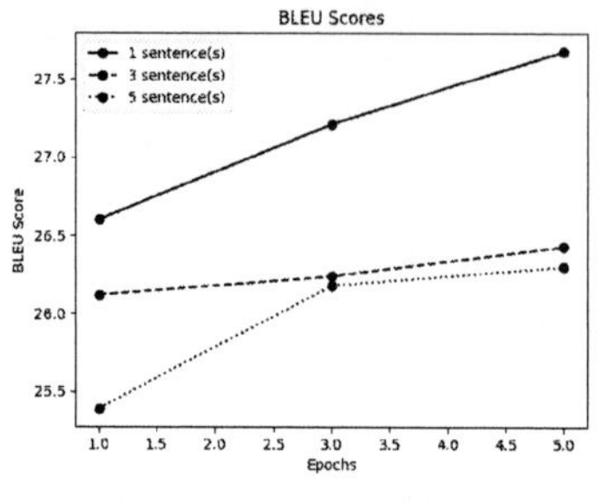

Figure 2: BLEU scores in relation to the number of sentences and epochs used in the adapted model.

In Figure 2, we have plotted the performance of our adapted MT systems using BLEU scores to analyze the relationship between the number of sentences, the number of epochs, and the translation quality. The x-axis represents the number of epochs, and the y-axis represents the BLEU scores. The lines with varying markers correspond to different sentence combinations. We observe that increasing the number of sentences does not proportionally improve the translation quality. This pattern resembles the findings in terms of TC (as in Figure 1), where adding more sentences offered no improvement. This suggests that adding more sentences to the fine-tuning data may not guarantee better translation outcomes.

While the graphs for TC and BLEU display a similar trend, it is crucial to understand that an increase in the BLEU score does not necessarily indicate an improvement in terminology. In fact, alterations made to the adapted model might have led to improvement in the meta-language without directly translating to substantial improvements in the translation of domain-specific terms.

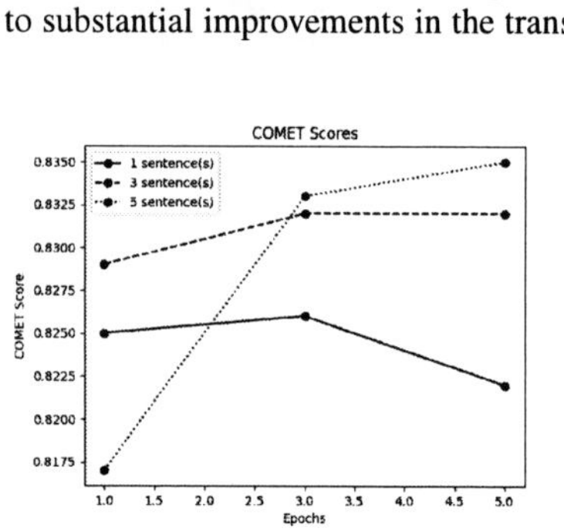

Figure 3: COMET scores in relation to the number of sentences and epochs used in the adapted model.

In Figure 3, we plotted our MT systems' performance based on COMET scores to analyse the relationship between the number of instances used for training and epochs. The x-axis represents the number of epochs, and the y-axis represents the COMET scores. The lines with varying markers correspond to different sentence combinations. We see that the COMET scores exhibit a different trend. When the number of sentences is increased, the translation quality measured by COMET scores appears to improve. This contrasts with the trends observed in terms of TC and BLEU. We also see that increasing the number of sentences did not consistently lead to betterment in translation quality.

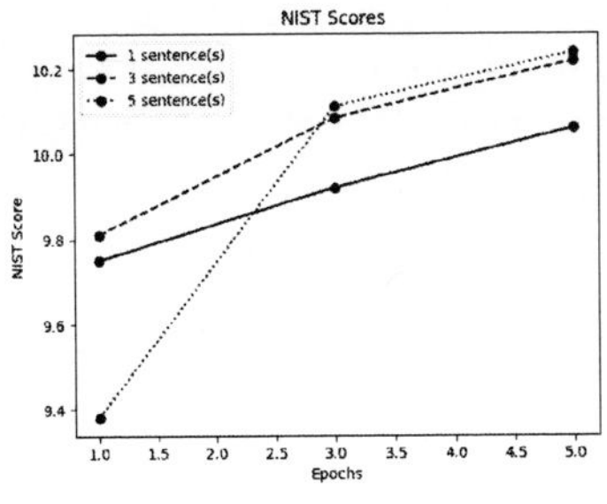

Figure 4: NIST scores in relation to the number of sentences and epochs used in the adapted model.

Similarly, in Figure 4, we plotted the performance of our MT systems based on NIST scores to analyse the relationship between the number of instances used for training and the number of epochs. We observe that increasing the number of epochs appears to benefit the quality of translation. Furthermore, we observed that training a model with more instances and epochs yields better results.

The discrepancy between the trends observed for three metrics (COMET, BLEU, NIST and TC) could be attributed to the differences in the evaluation metrics. While TC, NIST, and BLEU scores focus on specific aspects of translation quality, such as the handling of domain-specific terminology and *n*-gram overlaps between the reference and the translation, the COMET metric is designed to provide a more holistic assessment of translation quality by considering factors such as fluency, adequacy, and style.

6.1 Analysis of Terminology Improvements

Table 1 presents the results of our experiments aimed at improving terminology translation using instance-based adaptation. We discovered that the TC scores for the adapted MT system are found to be high in two cases (i.e. setup: a single sentence using three and five epochs). As for analysing translations produced by the MT systems, we choose the best-performing adapted MT system (i.e., one sentence and three epochs).

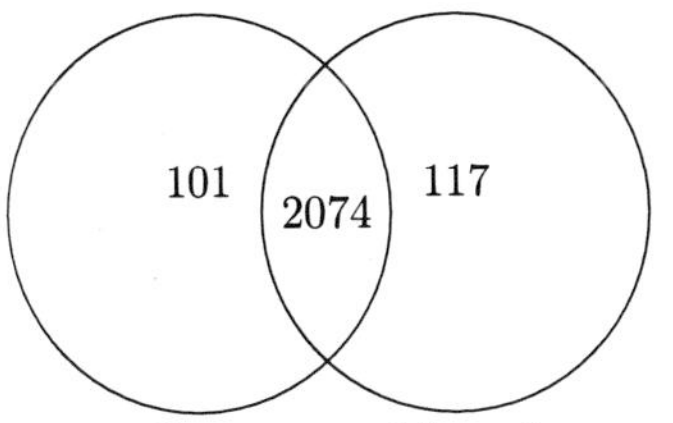

Figure 5: Venn diagram comparing terminology translation counts of the baseline and best domain-adapted MT system.

We produce a Venn diagram to visually compare and better understand how terms are translated by the baseline and the best domain-adapted MT systems. We show the Venn diagram in Figure 5. The diagram has two overlapping circles, showing the separate terminology counts produced by each of the MT models. The left circle, labeled "Base", represents the baseline

MT system and contains 101 terms. This area represents the unique terminology translation counts from the baseline model. The right circle, labelled "Adapted", represents the best domain-adapted model and contains 117 unique domain-specific terms. The area representing the overlap between both circles contains 2074 terms. This is shared terminology translation counts from both models.

Table 2: Example: adapted MT system correctly translates terminology.

Source	dans environ 14 % des cas , la COVID-19 entraîne une atteinte plus sévère nécessitant une hospitalisation , tandis que les 6% de cas restants développent une forme grave de la **maladie** nécessitant des soins intensifs .
Reference	in ca 14% cases , covid-19 develops into a more severe disease requiring hospitalisation while the remaining 6% cases experience critical **illness** requiring intensive care .
Baseline MT	in about 14% of cases, covid-19 causes a more severe condition requiring hospitalization, while the remaining 6% develop a serious form of the **disease** requiring intensive care.
Adapted MT	in about 14% of the cases, covid-19 leads to more severe illness requiring hospitalization, while 6% of the remaining cases develop a serious form of serious **illness** requiring intensive care

To further understand how the two models differ when it comes to the quality of terminology translation, we select an example sentence from the test set. In Table 2, we present translations of the sentence we picked by the baseline and adapted MT systems. We can see from the table that the adapted MT system demonstrates improvement over the baseline MT system, where the domain term "maladie" in the source sentence is accurately translated as "illness" by the adapted MT system. In contrast, the baseline system incorrectly translates it as "disease". However, it is essential to note that the baseline system still provides a decent translation. While it may not capture the exact terminology, the overall semantic content of the sentence is preserved, demonstrating the robustness of the baseline system.

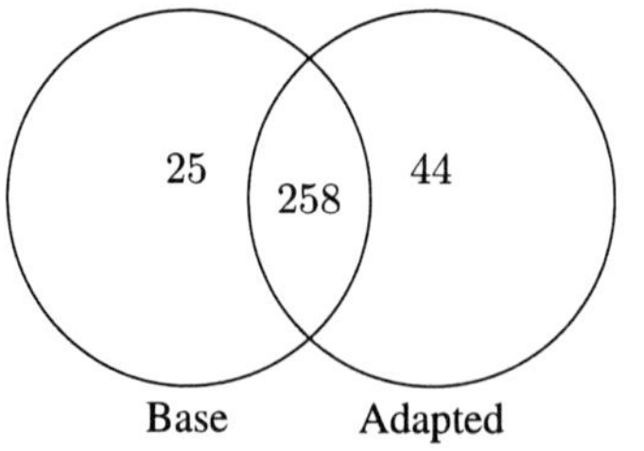

Figure 6: Venn diagram comparing multi-word terminology counts of the baseline and best domain-adapted MT system.

We observed that the adapted MT system better handles the translation of multi-word terms. We show a Venn diagram in Figure 6 where the left circle labelled as "Base" represents the baseline MT system and contains 25 multi-word terms. This indicates the unique terminology translation counts from the baseline model. The right circle labelled as "Adapted" represents the best domain-adapted model and contains 44 unique multi-word domain-specific terms. The area

Table 3: Example: adapted MT system correctly translates multi-word terminology.

Source	la ventilation mécanique devient plus complexe avec le développement du **syndrome de détresse respiratoire aiguë** (SDRA) au cours de la COVID-19 et l' oxygénation devient plus difficile .
Reference	mechanical ventilation becomes more complex as **acute respiratory distress syndrome** (ards) develops in covid-19 and oxygenation becomes increasingly difficult .
Baseline MT	mechanical ventilation becomes more complex with the development of **acute respiratory disorder syndrome** (sdra) during covid-19 and oxygenation becomes more difficult.
Adapted MT	mechanical ventilation becomes increasingly complex as **acute respiratory distress syndrome** (ards) develops in covid-19 and oxygenation becomes increasingly difficult.

representing the intersection between both circles contains 251 terms. This is shared terminology translation counts by both MT models. In Table 3, we show another example translation. This time, we chose a source sentence that contains a multi-word term. We see from the table that the adapted MT system shows improvement over the baseline MT system where the multi-word term "syndrome de détresse respiratoire aiguë" in the source sentence is accurately translated as "acute respiratory distress syndrome " by the adapted MT system. In contrast, the baseline system incorrectly translates it as "acute respiratory disorder syndrome".

7 Conclusion and Future Work

This study presents a terminology-aware instance-based domain adaptation method. We tested our method for English-to-French translation. Our results demonstrate that the proposed approach helps improve terminology translation. Furthermore, we discover that increasing the number of sentences used for fine-tuning does not significantly impact the improvement of terminology translation performance. Instead, a more efficient strategy appears to be one that considers a high number of epochs for a single sentence. This observation suggests that the model may benefit from more focused training, concentrating its learning efforts on a single sentence over an extended period (i.e., more epochs). We evaluated our MT systems using BLEU, NIST and COMET evaluation metrics. We observe that the BLEU metric correlates with the correct TC, while the COMET metric shows improvements for the adapted model with an increased number of sentences. NIST metric shows improvement for a higher number of instances and epochs. We also found that the adapted model outperformed the baseline when it comes to translating multi-word terms. Our current proposed approach fine-tunes all instances, irrespective of whether a test instance requires fine-tuning or not, which may lead to the deterioration of translation quality for some sentences. In the future, we plan to identify those sentences that require fine-tuning and adapt only to them.

Acknowledgments

This work was conducted with the financial support of the Science Foundation Ireland Centre for Research Training in Digitally-Enhanced Reality (d-real) under Grant No. 18/CRT/6224 and Microsoft Research Ireland.

References

Anastasopoulos, A., Cattelan, A., Dou, Z.-Y., Federico, M., Federmann, C., Genzel, D., Guzmán, F., Hu, J., Hughes, M., Koehn, P., Lazar, R., Lewis, W., Neubig, G., Niu, M., Öktem, A., Paquin, E., Tang, G., and Tur, S. (2020). TICO-19: the translation initiative for COvid-19. In *Proceedings of the 1st Workshop on NLP for COVID-19 (Part 2) at EMNLP 2020*, Online. Association for Computational Linguistics.

Ao, S. and Acharya, X. (2021). Learning ULMFiT and self-distillation with calibration for medical dialogue system. In *Proceedings of the 4th International Conference on Natural Language and Speech Processing (ICNLSP 2021)*, pages 196–203, Trento, Italy. Association for Computational Linguistics.

Brown, T., Mann, B., Ryder, N., Subbiah, M., Kaplan, J. D., Dhariwal, P., Neelakantan, A., Shyam, P., Sastry, G., Askell, A., Agarwal, S., Herbert-Voss, A., Krueger, G., Henighan, T., Child, R., Ramesh, A., Ziegler, D., Wu, J., Winter, C., Hesse, C., Chen, M., Sigler, E., Litwin, M., Gray, S., Chess, B., Clark, J., Berner, C., McCandlish, S., Radford, A., Sutskever, I., and Amodei, D. (2020). Language models are few-shot learners. In Larochelle, H., Ranzato, M., Hadsell, R., Balcan, M., and Lin, H., editors, *Advances in Neural Information Processing Systems*, volume 33, pages 1877–1901. Curran Associates, Inc.

Chen, G., Chen, Y., Wang, Y., and Li, V. O. (2020). Lexical-constraint-aware neural machine translation via data augmentation. In Bessiere, C., editor, *Proceedings of the Twenty-Ninth International Joint Conference on Artificial Intelligence, (IJCAI 2020a)*, pages 3587–3593. ijcai.org.

Devlin, J., Chang, M.-W., Lee, K., and Toutanova, K. (2019). BERT: Pre-training of deep bidirectional transformers for language understanding. In *Proceedings of the 2019 Conference of the North American Chapter of the Association for Computational Linguistics: Human Language Technologies, Volume 1 (Long and Short Papers)*, pages 4171–4186, Minneapolis, Minnesota. Association for Computational Linguistics.

Dinu, G., Mathur, P., Federico, M., and Al-Onaizan, Y. (2019). Training neural machine translation to apply terminology constraints. In *Proceedings of the 57th Annual Meeting of the Association for Computational Linguistics*, pages 3063–3068, Florence, Italy. Association for Computational Linguistics.

Dougal, D. K. and Lonsdale, D. (2020). Improving NMT quality using terminology injection. In *Proceedings of the Twelfth Language Resources and Evaluation Conference*, pages 4820–4827, Marseille, France. European Language Resources Association.

Farajian, M. A., Turchi, M., Negri, M., and Federico, M. (2017). Multi-domain neural machine translation through unsupervised adaptation. In *Proceedings of the Second Conference on Machine Translation*, pages 127–137, Copenhagen, Denmark. Association for Computational Linguistics.

Fernando, A., Ranathunga, S., and Dias, G. (2020). Data augmentation and terminology integration for domain-specific sinhala-english-tamil statistical machine translation. *ArXiv*, abs/2011.02821.

Haque, R., Moslem, Y., and Way, A. (2020). Terminology-aware sentence mining for NMT domain adaptation: ADAPT's submission to the adap-MT 2020 English-to-Hindi AI translation shared task. In *Proceedings of the 17th International Conference on Natural Language*

Processing (ICON): Adap-MT 2020 Shared Task, pages 17–23, Patna, India. NLP Association of India (NLPAI).

Haque, R., Penkale, S., and Way, A. (2018). Termfinder: log-likelihood comparison and phrase-based statistical machine translation models for bilingual terminology extraction. *Language Resources and Evaluation*, 52:365–400.

Koehn, P. (2004). Statistical significance tests for machine translation evaluation. In *Proceedings of the 2004 Conference on Empirical Methods in Natural Language Processing*, pages 388–395, Barcelona, Spain. Association for Computational Linguistics.

Koehn, P., Hoang, H., Birch, A., Callison-Burch, C., Federico, M., Bertoldi, N., Cowan, B., Shen, W., Moran, C., Zens, R., Dyer, C., Bojar, O., Constantin, A., and Herbst, E. (2007). Moses: Open source toolkit for statistical machine translation. In *Proceedings of the 45th Annual Meeting of the Association for Computational Linguistics Companion Volume Proceedings of the Demo and Poster Sessions*, pages 177–180, Prague, Czech Republic. Association for Computational Linguistics.

Lee, G., Yang, S., and Choi, E. (2021). Improving lexically constrained neural machine translation with source-conditioned masked span prediction. In *Proceedings of the 59th Annual Meeting of the Association for Computational Linguistics and the 11th International Joint Conference on Natural Language Processing (Volume 2: Short Papers)*, pages 743–753, Online. Association for Computational Linguistics.

Lewis, M., Liu, Y., Goyal, N., Ghazvininejad, M., Mohamed, A., Levy, O., Stoyanov, V., and Zettlemoyer, L. (2020). BART: Denoising sequence-to-sequence pre-training for natural language generation, translation, and comprehension. In *Proceedings of the 58th Annual Meeting of the Association for Computational Linguistics*, pages 7871–7880, Online. Association for Computational Linguistics.

Li, X., Zhang, J., and Zong, C. (2018). One sentence one model for neural machine translation. In *Proceedings of the Eleventh International Conference on Language Resources and Evaluation (LREC 2018)*, Miyazaki, Japan. European Language Resources Association (ELRA).

Liu, Y., Gu, J., Goyal, N., Li, X., Edunov, S., Ghazvininejad, M., Lewis, M., and Zettlemoyer, L. (2020). Multilingual denoising pre-training for neural machine translation. *Transactions of the Association for Computational Linguistics*, 8:726–742.

Luong, M.-T. and Manning, C. (2015). Stanford neural machine translation systems for spoken language domains. In *Proceedings of the 12th International Workshop on Spoken Language Translation: Evaluation Campaign*, pages 76–79, Da Nang, Vietnam.

Michon, E., Crego, J., and Senellart, J. (2020). Integrating domain terminology into neural machine translation. In *Proceedings of the 28th International Conference on Computational Linguistics*, pages 3925–3937, Barcelona, Spain (Online). International Committee on Computational Linguistics.

Mouratidis, D., Mathe, E., Voutos, Y., Stamou, K., Kermanidis, K. L., Mylonas, P., and Kanavos, A. (2022). Domain-specific term extraction: A case study on greek maritime legal texts. In *Proceedings of the 12th Hellenic Conference on Artificial Intelligence*, SETN '22, New York, NY, USA. Association for Computing Machinery.

Nayak, P., Haque, R., and Way, A. (2020). The ADAPT's submissions to the WMT20 biomedical translation task. In *Proceedings of the Fifth Conference on Machine Translation*, pages 841–848, Online. Association for Computational Linguistics.

Niehues, J. (2021). Continuous learning in neural machine translation using bilingual dictionaries. In *Proceedings of the 16th Conference of the European Chapter of the Association for Computational Linguistics: Main Volume*, pages 830–840, Online. Association for Computational Linguistics.

Papineni, K., Roukos, S., Ward, T., and Zhu, W.-J. (2002). Bleu: a method for automatic evaluation of machine translation. In *Proceedings of the 40th Annual Meeting of the Association for Computational Linguistics*, pages 311–318, Philadelphia, Pennsylvania, USA. Association for Computational Linguistics.

Przybocki, M., Peterson, K., Bronsart, P., and Sanders, G. (2010). The nist 2008 metrics for machine translation challenge - overview, methodology, metrics, and results.

Rei, R., Stewart, C., Farinha, A. C., and Lavie, A. (2020). COMET: A neural framework for MT evaluation. In *Proceedings of the 2020 Conference on Empirical Methods in Natural Language Processing (EMNLP)*, pages 2685–2702, Online. Association for Computational Linguistics.

Sato, S., Sakuma, J., Yoshinaga, N., Toyoda, M., and Kitsuregawa, M. (2020). Vocabulary adaptation for domain adaptation in neural machine translation. In *Findings of the Association for Computational Linguistics: EMNLP 2020*, pages 4269–4279, Online. Association for Computational Linguistics.

Scansani, R. and Dugast, L. (2021). Glossary functionality in commercial machine translation: does it help? a first step to identify best practices for a language service provider. In *Proceedings of Machine Translation Summit XVIII: Users and Providers Track*, pages 78–88, Virtual. Association for Machine Translation in the Americas.

Song, K., Zhang, Y., Yu, H., Luo, W., Wang, K., and Zhang, M. (2019). Code-switching for enhancing NMT with pre-specified translation. In *Proceedings of the 2019 Conference of the North American Chapter of the Association for Computational Linguistics: Human Language Technologies, Volume 1 (Long and Short Papers)*, pages 449–459, Minneapolis, Minnesota. Association for Computational Linguistics.

Vaswani, A., Shazeer, N., Parmar, N., Uszkoreit, J., Jones, L., Gomez, A. N., Kaiser, , and Polosukhin, I. (2017). Attention is all you need. In *Proceedings of the 31st Conference on Neural Information Processing Systems (NIPS 2017)*, pages 5998–6008, Long Beach, CA, USA. Curran Associates Inc.

Learning from Mistakes: Towards Robust Neural Machine Translation for Disfluent L2 Sentences

Shuyue Stella Li sli136@jhu.edu
Philipp Koehn phi@jhu.edu
Johns Hopkins University, Baltimore, MD 21218, USA

Abstract

We study the sentences written by second-language (L2) learners to improve the robustness of current neural machine translation (NMT) models on this type of data. Current large datasets used to train NMT systems are mostly Wikipedia or government documents written by highly competent speakers of that language, especially English. However, given that English is the most common second language, it is crucial that machine translation systems are robust against the large number of sentences written by L2 learners of English. By studying the difficulties faced by humans in their L2 acquisition process, we are able to transfer such insights to machine translation systems to recover from source-side fluency variations. In this work, we create additional training data with artificial errors similar to mistakes made by L2 learners of various fluency levels to improve the quality of the machine translation system. We test our method in zero-shot settings on the JFLEG-es (English→Spanish) dataset. The quality of our machine translation system on disfluent sentences outperforms the baseline by 1.8 BLEU scores.

1 Introduction

Neural machine translation (NMT) is a supervised learning problem that has been widely studied and achieved great success in numerous benchmarks (Koehn, 2020; Stahlberg, 2020; Bahdanau et al., 2014). Its power comes from learning high-level representations of meaning, which often relies on massive amounts of clean, parallel data. However, tiny perturbations of the data result in cascading degradation in the performance of the NMT model (Belinkov and Bisk, 2018; Cheng et al., 2018). Unlike humans who are able to ignore small discrepancies in trivial spelling and grammar errors, NMT systems still need to solve this crucial problem.

The noise in the data can come from various sources. The particular type of noise that we investigate in this work is when the source sentences of an NMT system are written by L2 learners of a language. Since the largest parallel corpora are mostly Wikipedia or government documents written by fluent speakers of that language, the L2 sentences are different from the ones seen by most machine translation models. Second, L2 learners come from different first language (L1) environments, bringing their own unique linguistic habits and cultural references into composing L2 sentences. Third, the collection and annotation of such data are difficult due to the linguistic diversity of the sentences. Therefore, the main challenges of translating L2 sentences are that they are not fluent, out-of-domain, and extremely low-resource.

When translating from low-flouency source sentences, NMT systems are especially prone to fail in the presence of highly noisy data. It might be trivial for humans to understand a sentence with grammar or spelling errors. But higher-level mistakes, such as unconventional usage of

Proceedings of Machine Translation Summit XIX, Vol. 1: Research Track, pages 235–247
September 4–8, 2023, Macau SAR, China.

phrases, could be hard to understand even for humans. As shown in Figure 1, a good NMT system should ideally learn such disfluencies and ambiguities so that it can help both the L2 speaker better express themselves and the listener better understand the output.

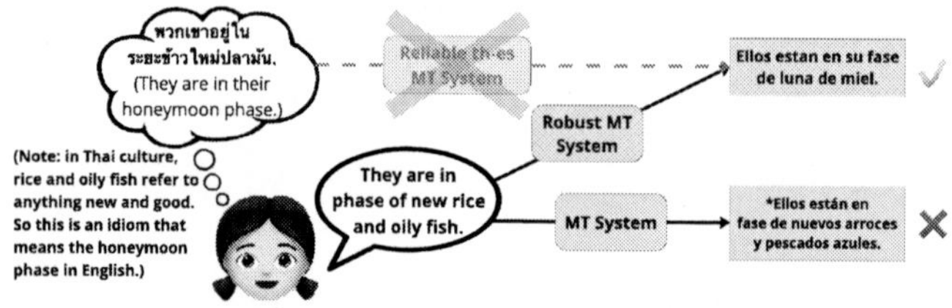

Figure 1: Robust NMT System from Disfluent English to Spanish. The L1 of the user is Thai. A robust English→Spanish NMT system is needed in the absence of a reliable Thai→Spanish system. The L2 English sentence she produces contains several L2 errors (e.g. missing article & phrase misuse). Thus, the goal of the robust NMT system is to recover the original meaning that the speaker *meant* to express.

We attempt to build an NMT model robust to disfluencies by first studying the mistakes made by the L2 learners on the word, phrase, and sentence levels. We compute detailed L2 error statistics that realistically resemble a cognitively-grounded second language acquisition (SLA) process. Then, we artificially inject the observed common errors into the clean training data to create a synthetic L2 training dataset. Our proposed artificial error augmentation method does not need any gold translations (except for the test set during evaluation) and can therefore be applied to extremely low-resource settings. In this work, our contributions include:

- We extensively analyze the writing errors produced by real L2 learners to study the second language acquisition process. We introduce a framework for creating written second language acquisition modeling that could be useful for a variety of applications.
- We propose a realistic error augmentation approach that incorporates low-level to high-level L2 errors and is target-language-agnostic. The data augmentation is able to improve the generalizability and robustness of the model even without labeled disfluent training data.
- Our experimental results show that error augmentation is extremely helpful. We observe an increase in the 1.8 BLEU score in the English→Spanish direction. We make our code and the generated silver dataset publicly available[1].

2 Related Work

2.1 Robust Machine Translation

Robust machine translation with noisy data has been a challenging research problem in the field of natural language processing (Belinkov and Bisk, 2018). The WMT Shared Tasks on Machine Translation Robustness (Li et al., 2019; Specia et al., 2020) aim to develop NMT models that can successfully handle real-world noises. One line of research focuses on using data augmentation techniques to generate additional training data. Some approaches add synthetic noise to the training data (Berard et al., 2019; Abdul Rauf et al., 2020). Several studies have explored the use of unsupervised and semi-supervised learning techniques for robust machine translation (Lample et al., 2018; Artetxe et al., 2018; Cheng and Cheng, 2019). Back-translation is commonly used as a bootstrapping method to augment training data and thus improve machine translation quality (Sennrich et al., 2015; Chauhan et al., 2022). Iterative methods can also be used to improve the quality of the back-translation (Hoang et al., 2018). Adversarial inputs have been widely used as a data augmentation approach for robust NMT and other NLP problems (Cheng et al., 2019; Hsu

[1] https://github.com/stellali7/L2MT

et al., 2022). These methods aim to leverage the vast amounts of unlabeled data available for machine translation and reduce the reliance on annotated data. However, one problem with many data augmentation methods is that it relies on an existing machine translation system, and might not be realistic and specific to the target domain of interest.

2.2 L2 Language Processing

Disfluent and ungrammatical sentences written by second-language learners can also be considered a source of noise. This is because most datasets do not contain sentences like these, and cannot generalize to irregular sentence formations that are determined by the L2 competency level and the L1 of the speakers. Existing work on disfluent sentences involves training parsing models on ungrammatical data (Hashemi and Hwa, 2016), or jointly training on a combination of clean and synthetic ungrammatical sentences (Anastasopoulos et al., 2019). Another approach incorporates the explicit syntactic and semantic structures into the NMT models to better handle disfluent sentences (Liu et al., 2021; Chen et al., 2017; Zhang et al., 2019a).

Most existing methods regarding disfluent or L2 data focus on creating low-level grammatical errors and have made minimal efforts on cognitive modeling of the actual SLA process. The Duolingo Second Language Acquisition Modeling Challenge (Settles et al., 2018) aims to combine knowledge of cognitive science, linguistics, and machine learning, but its scope is limited to token-level prediction and beginner-level language learner data. Even in the cognitive science literature, second language acquisition is largely studied in terms of spoken utterances rather than written sentences and focuses on individual case studies (Krashen, 1981). In our work, we propose cognitively-grounded errors to better model the SLA process.

2.3 Grammatical Error Correction

Grammatical error correction is closely related to disfluent sentence processing. Several robust machine translation approaches for disfluent sentences use a cascaded system to first correct the grammatical errors in the source sentence and then translate them into the target language (Anastasopoulos et al., 2019). There exist a number of publicly available corpora for grammatical error correction, including the NUCLE dataset of Singaporean English learners (Dahlmeier et al., 2013), the CoNLL-2014 GEC shared task dataset (Ng et al., 2014), and the ErAConD dialogue GEC dataset (Yuan et al., 2022). However, they mostly focus on error-coding rule-based grammatical errors.

In summary, unconstrained L2 generation and processing remain relatively underexplored, and our work attempts to study this topic in order to build a robust NMT system. Our work is inspired by the work done by Belinkov and Bisk (2018) and Anastasopoulos et al. (2019), but we focus on identifying more realistic and higher-level errors to model written SLA and thus create an artificial error augmentation corpus that closely resembles real L2 data.

3 Methods

3.1 Overview

With the main goal of training an NMT system robust to disfluent sentences, our work focuses on artificially generating data that are similar in distribution to the disfluent sentences. Through such artificial error augmentation, our NMT models can learn to be more robust to input sentences of various qualities. First, we study the types of mistakes and inconsistencies that contribute to disfluency. To do this, we manually annotate the fluency corrections that rewrite disfluent L2 sentences into native-sounding sentences. We learn an L2 error distribution from categorizing the corrections. Then we use this learned distribution to generate disfluent sentences from well-formed sentences by injecting syntactic, semantic, and sentence-level errors. Since the goal of the translation is to recover the speaker intent in the target language despite disfluency errors, we use the translation of the well-formed sentence as the pseudo-translation of the transformed erroneous sentence. Finally, we train an NMT system on a combination of the clean (fluent) parallel corpus and our artificial disfluent pseudo-parallel corpus.

3.2 Disfluency Error Analysis

We study the SLA process, including the common errors made by L2 learners, by analyzing the disfluent sentences and their correction references. We summarize the holistic fluency rewrites into different error types according to the underlying cognitive discontinuity in the L1-L2 switching process (e.g. grammar, semantic, or usage differences between L1 and L2). Figure 2 shows two real examples of disfluent L2 sentences, their revisions, and the errors contained in each sentence. By modeling the mapping of disfluent sentences to their corrections, we construct a written SLA model containing information and the likelihood of occurrence of each type of L2 error.

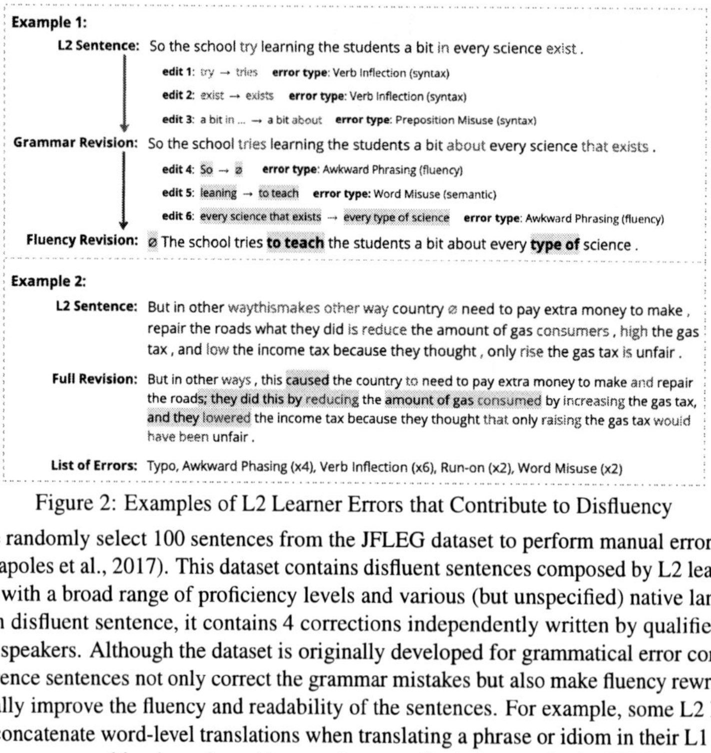

Figure 2: Examples of L2 Learner Errors that Contribute to Disfluency

We randomly select 100 sentences from the JFLEG dataset to perform manual error annotations (Napoles et al., 2017). This dataset contains disfluent sentences composed by L2 learners of English with a broad range of proficiency levels and various (but unspecified) native languages. For each disfluent sentence, it contains 4 corrections independently written by qualified fluent English speakers. Although the dataset is originally developed for grammatical error correction, the reference sentences not only correct the grammar mistakes but also make fluency rewrites that holistically improve the fluency and readability of the sentences. For example, some L2 learners tend to concatenate word-level translations when translating a phrase or idiom in their L1 into the target language, resulting in *awkward* (non-native-sounding) phrases. In the JFLEG annotations, the *awkward* words and phrases are rewritten to sound more *natural* (native-sounding) with the interpretation of the annotators. These annotations are extremely crucial in studying errors in the second language acquisition process, as it entails mistakes beyond being able to simply follow syntactic rules and grammar constructs.

Upon preliminary inspection, we summarize the major errors that contribute to the disfluency of sentences into the three main categories - *Grammar errors, Semantic errors and Fluency errors* - with subcategories for each type of error as shown in Table 1. First, grammar errors are low-level mistakes that violate grammatical rules. Beginner L2 learners tend to make these mistakes due to not being familiar with the grammar of the L2. Although the L1 of the writers of our dataset is various and unknown, this type of error is particularly common when the L1

Error Type	Subtype	Description
Grammar Errors	Verb Inflection	Incorrect tense/form or subject-verb agreement.
	Preposition Misuse	Wrong/missing preposition (typically in verb phrases).
	Article Misuse	Wrong or missing articles.
	Noun Form	Singular vs. Plural forms nouns, including special cases such as teeth→tooth.
Semantic Errors	Word Misuse	Made-up/wrong word or phrase, usually a synonym in their L1 but changes meaning in L2.
	Typo	Swapping of two adjacent letters; substitution of a letter with another; injection or deletion of a letter.
Fluency Errors	Awkward Phrasing	Uncommon usage that sounds unnatural to native speakers, but grammatically and semantically correct.
	Run-on/Long Sent.	Long and confusing sentences that would typically be broken into shorter sentences by native speakers.

Table 1: Common Error Types in Disfluent L2 Sentences.

of the learners is less *marked* ("easier") than the L2, resulting in a negative transfer (Eckman, 1977; Benson, 1986). For example, articles ('the', 'a', 'an') do not exist in Russian but exist in English, making articles less marked in Russian than in English. Therefore, it is difficult for Russian native speakers to use articles correctly when producing English sentences. Hence in our written SLA model, we attempt to determine the probability distribution of the grammar errors by approximating the markedness of the set of first languages of the L2 learners and English on four linguistic phenomena: verb inflection, preposition misuse, article misuse, and noun form.

The second category of errors is semantic errors, where the word or phrase of interest alters the meaning of the sentence. This is due to the lack of knowledge of the L2 language and its vocabulary usage. When there are multiple valid literal translations of a word from the source to the target language, the L2 learner might choose one arbitrarily without knowing the common combinations of phrases. Often, distinguishing which word to use out of a set of synonyms is a harder challenge than being familiar with the grammar rules, because it requires a more subtle understanding of the L2 language rather than a rigid memorization of rules. For example, such a word misuse, although grammatically acceptable, causes confusion even for humans (Edit 5 in Example 1 of Figure 2). Thus, we consider semantic errors higher-level than grammar errors. Additionally, we also classify typos as semantic errors. Although the cause of such errors is not the lack of semantic knowledge, typos can change the semantics of the sentence drastically for neural networks as it causes OOVs during tokenization (Belinkov and Bisk, 2018).

The last but arguably the most important category of errors is fluency errors. Although most grammatical error correction models can solve most of the above errors, revising fluency errors requires a more in-depth understanding of the language. During our annotation process, sentences with revisions that involve long-span word rearrangement or rewriting and sentences whose revisions differ largely from the source are labeled with "Awkward Phasing" errors. Note that awkward here means non-native sounding and is not related to the semantics of the sentence content. Furthermore, another common trend of the L2 sentences is that a number of the corrections broke down run-on or long sentences into shorter segments to make the sentence less confusing. To model the fluency errors, we compute the average number of sentences that each run-on or long L2 sentence breaks into shorter sentences and the percentage of lines marked with the Awkward Phrasing error.

3.2.1 Disfluency Error Analysis Results

Table 2 summarizes the error distributions by each subtype. 90% of the sentences have at least one error, and each sentence has 2.5 errors on average. The percentage of tokens for each error is used in the error augmentation process to create realistic error distributions, and the percentage of lines in which each error occurs is used to include multiple errors in one synthetic dataset by single-error mixture or in-line compounding (discussed in detail in Section 3.4).

Error Subtype	Total #	% of tokens*	% of lines
Verb Inflection	26	3.6	23
Preposition Misuse	19	4.4	18
Article Misuse	21	5.5	17
Noun Form	10	7.4	10
Word Misuse	44	3.7	35
Typo	37	4.2	31
Awkward Phrasing	61	3.7	47
Run-on/Long Sent.	33	3.3	27

Table 2: Disfluency Error Statistics. *Percent of tokens is calculated out of all the sentences with the error of interest. The values are used to generate realistic errors from clean texts.

The disfluency error distribution is visualized in Figure 3, which plots the frequency of manually annotated errors across 100 randomly sampled sentences from the development split of the JFLEG dataset. L2 sentences have 76 grammar errors, 81 semantic errors, and 94 fluency errors as plotted in Figure 3a. The more advanced an L2 learner is in their language study, the less likely they will make low-level errors, yet beginner-level learners tend to make all types of errors. Therefore, it is not surprising that fluency errors have the highest number of occurrences. Additionally, the distribution of error subtypes in Figure 3b provides a detailed breakdown of the errors that make the sentence grammatically incorrect or non-native sounding. Word Misuse and Awkward Phrasing errors are particularly common. This is partially because of the lack of familiarity and exposure to the proper or natural way to use their L2. However, it can also be attributed to the error coding method, which labels an alternative usage of words in the correction rewrites as a Word Misuse error and labels longer range rearrangement/rewrites as Awkward Phrasing errors. Since the rewrites have minimal constraints, a higher degree of freedom would cause more diverse rewrites, and thus more errors.

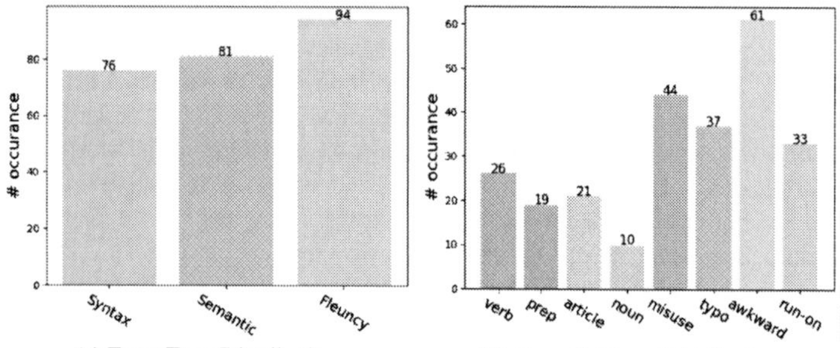

(a) Error Type Distribution (b) Error Subtype Distribution

Figure 3: Disfluency Error Distributions

3.3 Error Generation

3.3.1 Grammar Error Augmentation

After learning the distribution of disfluency errors in L2 sentences, we design algorithms to recreate the errors and inject them into clean, well-formed English sentences. For each type of sub-error, we first parse the clean sentences with the Berkeley Parser (Petrov et al., 2006) to determine the potential error injection sites. We create one grammar error per line using the script provided by Anastasopoulos et al. (2019). Lastly, the relative ratios of the grammatical errors as shown in the error subtype distribution plot in Figure 3b are used as weights to randomly sample the erroneous lines to form the synthetic Grammatical Error dataset.

3.3.2 Rule-based Typo Error Augmentation

We simulate typos with character-based swapping, substitution, insertion, and deletion edits. Swapping edits switch the order of two adjacent characters within a word. Substitution errors are generated using the statistics of most frequently switched letters on the English QWERTY keyboard Berry (2012). Lastly, insertion and deletion errors are generated at random. We only insert the typos in sentences with at least 4 words and words with at least 6 letters to avoid making the augmentation unnecessarily noisy. From Table 2, 4.2% of the tokens in a sentence contain typos, so we set the probability of randomly selecting a token to insert typos to match the real distribution.

3.3.3 Run-on Error Augmentation

Note that Run-on errors refer to both grammatically sound but confusing long sentences and ungrammatical run-on sentences with more than one main verb. We generate run-on or long sentences by first converting lines in the clean data with multiple sentences into one sentence joined by ',', ';', or ", and'". This is the most natural way to create run-on sentences, as the topic of each sentence in a line is similar. However, there is a limited number of lines with multiple sentences. So we perform a more aggressive data augmentation where each initial sentence S_i is appended by n randomly selected sentences from the same batch of size B. The number of sentences, n, to append to the initial sentence is determined as follows:

$$P(N = n \mid p, B) = \frac{p^n}{\sum_{i=1}^{B} p^i}, \tag{1}$$

where p is computed to match the realistic error distribution in Section 3.2.1. Specifically, if a sentence contains Run-on/Long Sentence errors, it has 1.22 of them on average, meaning that 1.22 extra sentences should be appended to the initial sentence.

3.3.4 Embedding-based Fluency Error Augmentation

Lastly, we group Word Misuse errors and Awkward Phrasing errors together, because it is often a fine line to determine when a phrase is "misused" or just not natural sounding enough. We use the Parrot[2] utterance augmentation framework to create paraphrases of the clean text in the same overall semantic space to simulate Word Misuse and Awkward Phrasing errors (Damodaran, 2021). Parrot is based on T5 and fine-tuned on paraphrase datasets. In the Parrot framework, the levels of adequacy and fluency can be adjusted to fit the goal of paraphrase generation. Adequacy is the degree to which the meaning of the sentence is preserved; whereas fluency measures how well-formed is the paraphrased sentence. Through preliminary experimentation, we set the adequacy and fluency thresholds to (0.3, 0.6) to generate Word Misuse errors and (0.7, 0.3) to generate Awkward Phrasing errors. For both generation tasks, we set Diversity to true in order to lessen the constraints on the generation. Parrot outputs the generated paraphrases in descending order of "diversity scores." We generate five paraphrases for each clean source sentence and randomly select one as the final output in order to introduce more nondeterministic variations in the generation process and encourage data diversity.

3.4 Error Combination

We propose two methods to combine different errors into one synthetic dataset. The first method simply generates one type of error per line and combines the lines into one dataset so that we have a multi-error dataset with single-error lines. The ratio of lines of each error type is determined by *% of lines* in Table 2. We call this method *Single-Error Mixture*. The second method models how L2 learners create errors more realistically. It compounds different errors in one line. We refer to this method as the *In-line Compounding*. Both combination schemes are explored in our experiments in different scenarios.

[2]`https://github.com/PrithivirajDamodaran/Parrot_Paraphraser`

4 Experimental Setup

4.1 Datasets

When choosing the source and target languages, the practical utility of our system is considered. English is the most common second language (Alemi, 2016), and Spanish is one of the most commonly translated languages[3]. Therefore, our work focuses on the English→Spanish translation direction. We use the English-Spanish Europarl dataset (Koehn, 2005) as the raw data to which we inject artificial errors. It contains 2,012,343 parallel sentence pairs.

To evaluate the robustness of the NMT model, we take 1,501 parallel sentences from the JFLEG corpus (28,106 words) (Napoles et al., 2017) and the JFLEG-es corpus (25,685 words) (Anastasopoulos et al., 2019). The JFLEG corpus is a selection of the GUG corpus, which is composed by L2 learners with a broad range of English proficiency levels and first languages, where the first languages of the writers are not disclosed (Heilman et al., 2014). In the JFLEG dataset, each disfluent sentence is annotated with four holistic fluency rewrites, making the JFLEG dataset unique as it corrects the disfluent sentences not only to void the grammar mistakes but also to make them natural-sounding. Anastasopoulos et al. (2019) extends the JFLEG into JFLEG-es dataset by manually translating the L2 sentences into Spanish, providing limited but valuable gold-standard translations.

4.2 Training Setup

Preprocessing To preprocess the data, we remove extra white spaces, preserve the casing, and tokenize with the SentencePiece[4] tokenizer into Byte-Pair-Encoding (BPE) with a vocab size of 50k (Sennrich et al., 2016). In each experiment, the L2 (disfluent) and correction (fluent) sentences are tokenized with the BPE model trained on the same training dataset used to train the NMT model. Then, the standard Fairseq preprocessing routine is used to further preprocess and binarize the data (Ott et al., 2019).

Training We use a simple transformer architecture with 4 encoder layers, 4 decoder layers, an embedding dimension of 512, a feed-forward dimension of 2048, 4 encoder attention heads, and 4 decoder attention heads. We apply a dropout of 0.3 and use the Adam optimizer with an epsilon value of 1e-6, betas of 0.9 and 0.98 (Kingma and Ba, 2015). We use the inverse square root learning rate scheduler following Vaswani et al. (2017) with an initial learning rate of 1e-7, 8000 warm-up steps to reach the target learning rate 4e-4. We train for 200000 steps and 8192 tokens per batch with an early stopping if the dev metric (BLEU score) does not improve in 4 epochs. During decoding, we use a beam size of 5.

Evaluation The evaluation results are measured with multiple metrics in order to present a more comprehensive set of comparisons. We use the detokenized BLEU score (Papineni et al., 2002) provided by SacreBLEU (Post, 2018), translation edit rate (TER), which measures the amount of editing required to match the reference (Snover et al., 2006), and BERTScore, which measures the contextualized embedding-based similarity (Zhang et al., 2019b). We evaluate the models on the disfluent L2 data and the fluency rewrite data from the JFLEG dataset (Napoles et al., 2017). The reference Spanish sentences are from the JFLEG-es dataset, which is a manual translation of the L2 sentences with the goal to recover L2 errors (Anastasopoulos et al., 2019).

4.3 Experiments

The baseline of our experiment is an NMT model trained on the clean Europarl English-Spanish data without error augmentation (exp #0 in Table 3).

To evaluate the effect of the grammatical error augmentation, we combine the 4 subtypes of grammar errors (exp #1 in Table 3) according to the distribution learned in Section 3.2.1 with the

[3] `www.focusfwd.com/10-most-translated-languages`

[4] `https://github.com/google/sentencepiece`

Single-Error Mixture method, as it allows us to explore different error ratios without repeating runs of the error generation script. The final error ratio reported in the results section is 5:4:4:2 for Verb Inflection, Preposition Misuse, Article Misuse, and Noun Form errors, respectively, which closely resembles the percentage of lines containing each error type as shown in Table 2.

In Experiments #2 and #3, we study the effect of Typo and Run-on errors generated following Section 3.3.2 and 3.3.3, respectively. The paraphrase dataset is used in Experiment #4, which combines the Word Misuse Error and the Awkward Phrasing Error types in a Single-Error Mixture fashion, as they are both line-level errors and cannot be easily compounded.

In Experiments #5 through #8, the '&' operator denotes errors combined with In-line Compounding, and '+' denotes errors combined with Single-Error Mixture. Using both methods during the error augmentation process imitates the realistic L2 learning process of compounding mistakes in one sentence but also allows for the efficient reuse of generated errors and avoids overloading too many errors in one sentence. For all error augmentation configurations, we add the clean data to the synthetic disfluent data to control for the noise contained in the training set inspired by Ye et al. (2022). Lastly, in Experiment #9, we sample 2M sentence pairs from the error combination of Experiment #8 to match the data size used in the baseline Clean model and run a controlled study to evaluate the effect of training dataset size.

5 Results & Analysis

Table 3 shows the detokenized BLEU (Papineni et al., 2002), TER (Snover et al., 2006), and BERTScore (Zhang et al., 2019b) of the model trained with different error augmentation methods. Overall, all models have better performance on the "easier" Fluent test set, while the Disfluent test set posts a harder challenge on the models.

#	Error Desc.	Size	Fluent			Disfluent			Δ
			BLEU	TER	BERTScore	BLEU	TER	BERTScore	BLEU
0	Clean	2.0M	**27.4**	60.8	**0.868**	25.4	62.5	0.858	2.0
1	Grammar (G)	5.0M	26.5	60.9*	0.866	25.7	61.8*	0.859	0.8
2	Typo (T)	3.9M	26.9*	62.3	0.867*	25.9*	62.4	0.861*	1.0
3	Run-on (R)	3.5M	26.8	63.2	0.865	25.7	64.1	0.858	1.1
4	Paraphrase (P)	3.0M	26.4	61.0	0.865	25.6	62.1	0.857	0.9
5	T & R	4.0M	26.7	62.8	0.866	26.2	62.2	0.862	0.5
6	P + G	6.0M	27.0	60.7	0.867	26.5	61.3	0.862	0.5
7	T & R + G	7.0M	27.2	60.6	**0.868**	27.0	**60.8**	**0.864**	**0.2**
8	T & R + G + P	9.0M	**27.4**	**60.4**	**0.868**	**27.2**	**60.8**	0.863	**0.2**
9	TRGP Control	2.0M	27.3	61.1	0.867	26.4	61.9	0.859	0.9

Table 3: NMT Performance on Fluent (manually corrected) and Disfluent (L2) sentences. Bold values mark best overall performance; '*' marks best results from single-error augmentation.

Baseline Clean Model The model trained on clean data (exp #1) achieves the best performance on the Fluent test set. This is because the sentences in the clean data are the most similar to the fluent manual corrections. When evaluated on the Disfluent L2 test set, however, the performance of the Clean model drops by 2 BLEU scores. This suggests that the L2 errors in disfluent data cause performance degradation when the model has not seen any noisy or out-of-domain data.

Single-Error Augmentation All models trained with one type of synthetic error outperform the Clean model on the Disfluent dataset, while generally performing not as well on the Fluent test set. Out of the four models trained with single error augmentation, the Typo model recovers the most from L2 noises, outperforming the Clean model by 0.5 BLEU. This behavior can be explained by the introduced typo words, generated from a realistic distribution described in Section 3.3.2, creating more tokens in the vocabulary and alleviating the performance degradation caused by OOV tokens. The poor performance on the Fluent set might be due to the single-source errors changing the data distribution drastically, causing the model to overfit to a one error type.

Error Diversity The models trained with a combination of several errors (exps #5–7) perform better than the other models trained on only one type of error. This suggests that diversifying the error type improves the robustness of the model. Note that although the Grammar model (exp #1) is trained with a combination of four types of grammar errors, the error subtypes are relatively simple. Thus, the combination of the four subtypes is not as diverse as, for example, Typo & Run-on Errors in exp #5, and definitely not as diverse as its superset: Typo & Run-on + Grammar Errors in exp #7. Lastly, we can see that although increasing the training data size will improve performance (2M in exp #9 vs. 9M in exp #8), it does not dictate the quality of the trained MT system, as exp #9 outperforms #0 by a large margin with the same amount of data.

Robustness to Disfluency The relative performance of each model on the Fluent and Disfluent test sets is also an informative measure of robustness. Ideally, a model robust to disfluent sentences should achieve the same performance on noisy, disfluent data as it does on clean, fluent data. As shown in Table 3, the lower the value of ΔBLEU, the smaller the performance drop with noisy data and thus the more robust the model. Single error models in experiments #1 through #4 show stronger robustness (ΔBLEU=0.95) than the Clean model (ΔBLEU=2.0). The combined error augmentation models are the most robust models with ΔBLEU=0.35.

Overall The combination of 'Typo & Run-on + Grammar + Paraphrase' errors (exp #8) not only outperforms all other models on the Disfluent dataset but also has comparable results to the Clean model evaluated on the Fluent dataset. It is able to recover most of the noise and degradation of the NMT system caused by L2 disfluency without sacrificing performance on regular fluent data. The model in exp #9 has the highest diversity and replicates the gold-standard L2 error distribution obtained in Section 3.2. Although other error combinations improve robustness, they do not contain full coverage of error types and deviate from the error distributions, thus resulting in less optimal performance. Therefore, accurately representing L2 errors contributes to the development of high-quality synthetic datasets, suggesting the potential for cognitively-motivated studies of human-generated corpora to better understand the process of L2 error formation.

6 Conclusion

In conclusion, our study shows that by specifically targeting the challenges faced by second-language learners of English, we can improve the robustness of neural machine translation models to disfluent data. We first created a realistic L2 error distribution and then produced synthetic data using the learned distributions to resemble real L2 errors. Our method of creating artificial errors similar to those made by L2 learners proved to be effective in improving the quality of the machine translation system, even without gold-labeled training data. This approach can be extended to other language pairs and used to improve the performance of machine translation systems for other language learners as well. Overall, this work opens up exciting avenues for future research in combining cognitive science theories to improve the robustness of NLP systems to disfluent L2 data.

7 Limitations

While our study shows promising results in improving the robustness of neural machine translation models to disfluent data, there are several limitations that should be acknowledged. Firstly, our method of creating artificial errors is based on a limited set of patterns observed in L2 data. It is possible that there are other patterns of disfluencies in L2 data that our method does not capture. This motivates an extensive study on written second language acquisition, which is out of scope for the current project but would be of great value to both the research community and potential users. Secondly, our study only focuses on the English→Spanish language pair. Although we are currently creating an L2 dataset in other typologically diverse languages, it is unclear how well our approach would generalize to other L2 and target languages.

References

Abdul Rauf, S., Rosales Núñez, J. C., Pham, M. Q., and Yvon, F. (2020). LIMSI @ WMT 2020. In *Proceedings of the Fifth Conference on Machine Translation*, pages 803–812, Online. Association for Computational Linguistics.

Alemi, M. (2016). General impacts of integrating advanced and modern technologies on teaching english as a foreign language. *International Journal on Integrating Technology in Education*, 5(1):13–26.

Anastasopoulos, A., Lui, A., Nguyen, T. Q., and Chiang, D. (2019). Neural machine translation of text from non-native speakers. In *Proceedings of the 2019 Conference of the North American Chapter of the Association for Computational Linguistics: Human Language Technologies, Volume 1 (Long and Short Papers)*, pages 3070–3080, Minneapolis, Minnesota. Association for Computational Linguistics.

Artetxe, M., Labaka, G., Agirre, E., and Cho, K. (2018). Unsupervised neural machine translation. In *International Conference on Learning Representations*.

Bahdanau, D., Cho, K., and Bengio, Y. (2014). Neural machine translation by jointly learning to align and translate. *arXiv preprint arXiv:1409.0473*.

Belinkov, Y. and Bisk, Y. (2018). Synthetic and natural noise both break neural machine translation. In *International Conference on Learning Representations*.

Benson, B. (1986). The markedness differential hypothesis: Implications for vietnamese speakers of english. *Markedness*, pages 271–289.

Berard, A., Calapodescu, I., and Roux, C. (2019). Naver labs europe's systems for the wmt19 machine translation robustness task. *arXiv preprint arXiv:1907.06488*.

Berry, N. (2012). Sloppy typing, fat fingers and atomic typos.

Chauhan, S., Saxena, S., and Daniel, P. (2022). Improved unsupervised neural machine translation with semantically weighted back translation for morphologically rich and low resource languages. *Neural Processing Letters*, 54(3):1707–1726.

Chen, H., Huang, S., Chiang, D., and Chen, J. (2017). Improved neural machine translation with a syntax-aware encoder and decoder. *arXiv preprint arXiv:1707.05436*.

Cheng, Y. and Cheng, Y. (2019). Semi-supervised learning for neural machine translation. *Joint training for neural machine translation*, pages 25–40.

Cheng, Y., Jiang, L., and Macherey, W. (2019). Robust neural machine translation with doubly adversarial inputs. *arXiv preprint arXiv:1906.02443*.

Cheng, Y., Tu, Z., Meng, F., Zhai, J., and Liu, Y. (2018). Towards robust neural machine translation. In *Proceedings of the 56th Annual Meeting of the Association for Computational Linguistics (Volume 1: Long Papers)*, pages 1756–1766, Melbourne, Australia. Association for Computational Linguistics.

Dahlmeier, D., Ng, H. T., and Wu, S. M. (2013). Building a large annotated corpus of learner english: The nus corpus of learner english. In *Proceedings of the eighth workshop on innovative use of NLP for building educational applications*, pages 22–31.

Damodaran, P. (2021). Parrot: Paraphrase generation for nlu.

Eckman, F. R. (1977). Markedness and the contrastive analysis hypothesis. *Language learning*, 27(2):315–330.

Hashemi, H. B. and Hwa, R. (2016). An evaluation of parser robustness for ungrammatical sentences. In *Proceedings of the 2016 Conference on Empirical Methods in Natural Language Processing*, pages 1765–1774.

Heilman, M., Cahill, A., Madnani, N., Lopez, M., Mulholland, M., and Tetreault, J. (2014). Predicting grammaticality on an ordinal scale. In *Proceedings of the 52nd Annual Meeting of the Association for Computational Linguistics (Volume 2: Short Papers)*, pages 174–180.

Hoang, V. C. D., Koehn, P., Haffari, G., and Cohn, T. (2018). Iterative back-translation for neural machine translation. In *Proceedings of the 2nd Workshop on Neural Machine Translation and Generation*, pages 18–24, Melbourne, Australia. Association for Computational Linguistics.

Hsu, C.-Y., Chen, P.-Y., Lu, S., Liu, S., and Yu, C.-M. (2022). Adversarial examples can be effective data augmentation for unsupervised machine learning. In *Proceedings of the AAAI Conference on Artificial Intelligence*, volume 36, pages 6926–6934.

Kingma, D. P. and Ba, J. (2015). Adam: A method for stochastic optimization. iclr. 2015. *arXiv preprint arXiv:1412.6980*, 9.

Koehn, P. (2005). Europarl: A parallel corpus for statistical machine translation. In *Proceedings of machine translation summit x: papers*, pages 79–86.

Koehn, P. (2020). *Neural machine translation*. Cambridge University Press.

Krashen, S. (1981). Second language acquisition. *Second Language Learning*, 3(7):19–39.

Lample, G., Conneau, A., Denoyer, L., and Ranzato, M. (2018). Unsupervised machine translation using monolingual corpora only. In *International Conference on Learning Representations*.

Li, X., Michel, P., Anastasopoulos, A., Belinkov, Y., Durrani, N., Firat, O., Koehn, P., Neubig, G., Pino, J., and Sajjad, H. (2019). Findings of the first shared task on machine translation robustness. In *Proceedings of the Fourth Conference on Machine Translation (Volume 2: Shared Task Papers, Day 1)*, pages 91–102, Florence, Italy. Association for Computational Linguistics.

Liu, Y., Wan, Y., Zhang, J.-G., Zhao, W., and Yu, P. S. (2021). Enriching non-autoregressive transformer with syntactic and semanticstructures for neural machine translation. *arXiv preprint arXiv:2101.08942*.

Napoles, C., Sakaguchi, K., and Tetreault, J. (2017). JFLEG: A fluency corpus and benchmark for grammatical error correction. In *Proceedings of the 15th Conference of the European Chapter of the Association for Computational Linguistics: Volume 2, Short Papers*, pages 229–234, Valencia, Spain. Association for Computational Linguistics.

Ng, H. T., Wu, S. M., Briscoe, T., Hadiwinoto, C., Susanto, R. H., and Bryant, C. (2014). The conll-2014 shared task on grammatical error correction. In *Proceedings of the Eighteenth Conference on Computational Natural Language Learning: Shared Task*, pages 1–14.

Ott, M., Edunov, S., Baevski, A., Fan, A., Gross, S., Ng, N., Grangier, D., and Auli, M. (2019). fairseq: A fast, extensible toolkit for sequence modeling. In *Proceedings of the 2019 Conference of the North American Chapter of the Association for Computational Linguistics (Demonstrations)*, pages 48–53, Minneapolis, Minnesota. Association for Computational Linguistics.

Papineni, K., Roukos, S., Ward, T., and Zhu, W.-J. (2002). Bleu: a method for automatic evaluation of machine translation. In *Proceedings of the 40th Annual Meeting of the Association for Computational Linguistics*, pages 311–318, Philadelphia, Pennsylvania, USA. Association for Computational Linguistics.

Petrov, S., Barrett, L., Thibaux, R., and Klein, D. (2006). Learning accurate, compact, and interpretable tree annotation. In *Proceedings of the 21st International Conference on Computational Linguistics and 44th Annual Meeting of the Association for Computational Linguistics*, pages 433–440.

Post, M. (2018). A call for clarity in reporting bleu scores. *arXiv preprint arXiv:1804.08771*.

Sennrich, R., Haddow, B., and Birch, A. (2015). Improving neural machine translation models with monolingual data. *arXiv preprint arXiv:1511.06709*.

Sennrich, R., Haddow, B., and Birch, A. (2016). Neural machine translation of rare words with subword units. In *Proceedings of the 54th Annual Meeting of the Association for Computational Linguistics (Volume 1: Long Papers)*, pages 1715–1725, Berlin, Germany. Association for Computational Linguistics.

Settles, B., Brust, C., Gustafson, E., Hagiwara, M., and Madnani, N. (2018). Second language acquisition modeling. In *Proceedings of the Thirteenth Workshop on Innovative Use of NLP for Building Educational Applications*, pages 56–65, New Orleans, Louisiana. Association for Computational Linguistics.

Snover, M., Dorr, B., Schwartz, R., Micciulla, L., and Makhoul, J. (2006). A study of translation edit rate with targeted human annotation. In *Proceedings of the 7th Conference of the Association for Machine Translation in the Americas: Technical Papers*, pages 223–231, Cambridge, Massachusetts, USA. Association for Machine Translation in the Americas.

Specia, L., Li, Z., Pino, J., Chaudhary, V., Guzmán, F., Neubig, G., Durrani, N., Belinkov, Y., Koehn, P., Sajjad, H., Michel, P., and Li, X. (2020). Findings of the WMT 2020 shared task on machine translation robustness. In *Proceedings of the Fifth Conference on Machine Translation*, pages 76–91, Online. Association for Computational Linguistics.

Stahlberg, F. (2020). Neural machine translation: A review. *Journal of Artificial Intelligence Research*, 69:343–418.

Vaswani, A., Shazeer, N., Parmar, N., Uszkoreit, J., Jones, L., Gomez, A. N., Kaiser, Ł., and Polosukhin, I. (2017). Attention is all you need. *Advances in neural information processing systems*, 30.

Ye, R., Wang, M., and Li, L. (2022). Cross-modal contrastive learning for speech translation. *arXiv preprint arXiv:2205.02444*.

Yuan, X., Pham, D., Davidson, S., and Yu, Z. (2022). ErAConD: Error annotated conversational dialog dataset for grammatical error correction. In *Proceedings of the 2022 Conference of the North American Chapter of the Association for Computational Linguistics: Human Language Technologies*, pages 76–84, Seattle, United States. Association for Computational Linguistics.

Zhang, M., Li, Z., Fu, G., and Zhang, M. (2019a). Syntax-enhanced neural machine translation with syntax-aware word representations. *arXiv preprint arXiv:1905.02878*.

Zhang, T., Kishore, V., Wu, F., Weinberger, K. Q., and Artzi, Y. (2019b). Bertscore: Evaluating text generation with bert. *arXiv preprint arXiv:1904.09675*.

The Role of Compounds in Human vs. Machine Translation Quality

Kristýna Neumannová kristyna.neumannova@gmail.com
Ondřej Bojar bojar@ufal.mff.cuni.cz
Charles University, Faculty of Mathematics and Physics, Institute of Formal and Applied Linguistics, Prague, Czech Republic

Abstract

We focus on the production of German compounds in English-to-German manual and automatic translation. On the example of WMT21 news translation test set, we observe that even the best MT systems produce much fewer compounds compared to three independent manual translations. Despite this striking difference, we observe that this insufficiency is not apparent in manual evaluation methods that target the overall translation quality (DA and MQM). Simple automatic methods like BLEU somewhat surprisingly provide a better indication of this quality aspect. Our manual analysis of system outputs, including our freshly trained Transformer models, confirms that current deep neural systems operating at the level of subword units are capable of constructing novel words, including novel compounds. This effect however cannot be measured using static dictionaries of compounds such as GermaNet. German compounds thus pose an interesting challenge for future development of MT systems.

1 Introduction

Assessing the quality of machine translation is a challenging task regularly tackled, e.g., in the manual evaluation of WMT translation task (Akhbardeh et al., 2021; Kocmi et al., 2022) or in WMT metrics task (Freitag et al., 2021, 2022). Various evaluation methods have been developed for this purpose. Manual evaluation in WMT has evolved from fluency and adequacy (Koehn and Monz, 2006) to direct assessment (DA, Graham et al., 2015) or MQM (Burchardt, 2013). Automatic evaluation is on the move from string matching techniques like BLEU (Papineni et al., 2002) or chrF (Popović, 2015) to embedding-based methods like COMET (Rei et al., 2020) or Prism (Thompson and Post, 2020). None of these approaches is particularly sensitive to specific subtle phenomena such as the presence or absence of compound words, a particular grammatical construction that is frequent in German. This paper focuses on German compounds, and how they occur in human and machine translations from English.

German has a highly productive word formation system mainly through compounding and derivation, especially for nouns (Barz, 2016, p. 2388). In this paper, we study German nominal compounds, which mostly consist of two constituents that are either complex or simple stems. The compounds in German are right-headed which means that the second element determines the morphosyntactic properties of the formed word. Additionally, semantically empty elements, called linking elements, can be added to the first stem of the compound (Barz, 2016, p. 2390).

Using compounds instead of multi-word expressions is a soft phenomenon related to text style, which can affect the perceived quality of the text. Native speakers regularly form new

Proceedings of Machine Translation Summit XIX, Vol. 1: Research Track, pages 248–260
September 4–8, 2023, Macau SAR, China.

compound words to fulfill the needs requested by a particular dialogue or discourse situation. We believe that machine translation systems, operating on subword units, are able to produce complex words like humans, even if they were not included in the training data.

We know that splitting and determining German compounds is a complex task. Therefore, we relied on a list of compounds extracted from the German adaptation of WordNet called GermaNet (Henrich and Hinrichs, 2011). Operating on a closed list of compounds may provide an advantage for the analysis. Considering that the use of compounds is a stylistic matter, the exact list provides us with the possibility to group the observations of the phenomenon.

In the paper, we study several aspects of the data and models concerning the production of German nominal compounds.

2 Related Work

Most of the previous work on MT dealing with German compounds was done in the "classical" statistical machine translation (SMT). We found only a few papers, see below, about German compounds in neural machine translation (NMT), almost all of which were published before the introduction of the Transformer model (Vaswani et al., 2017), the current state of the art. Our work focuses on the production of German compounds in Transformer models, a topic that has not been adequately studied yet.

2.1 Compounds in SMT

The most common approaches to SMT operated on whole words. Therefore, they did not handle morphologically rich or compounding languages very well and dedicated methods were needed for processing compounds (by splitting them) and producing compounds (by merging them from pieces).

One of the first empirical methods for handling compounds was introduced by Koehn and Knight (2003), splitting compounds into parts that had been separately observed in the training data. The frequency of the compound constituents in the training data was the main criterion for the split.

Henrich and Hinrichs (2011) used an adapted version of a German morphological analyzer SMOR (Schmid et al., 2004) to improve the German compound splitting algorithm for determining the constituents of compounds. They combined an updated SMOR with other splitters, such as a pattern-matching-based splitter that considers all potential modifiers and heads, along with linking elements. This approach extracted a list of nominal German compounds from the German word net called GermaNet. As mentioned, we use this list for our analysis.

Sugisaki and Tuggener (2018) introduced an unsupervised method for compound splitting based on the idea of morpheme productivity, distinguishing between free morphemes (can stand alone as words) and bound morphemes within a word (appear only as parts of words). They computed the ratio between the counts of bound and free morphemes and selected a splitting with the lowest one i.e., preferring words consisting primarily of otherwise free morphemes.

Daiber et al. (2015) utilize vector representations of compounds and their parts to identify which word is likely a compound (its embedding is not far from the vector calculated from its parts).

Popović et al. (2006) focused on both German-English and English-German translation. For English-German, they split all compounds, trained the SMT system to produce split compounds and merged them in a post-processing step based on corpus statistics of compounds and their parts.

Stymne (2009) built upon Popović et al. (2006), adding a method based on a special token indicating the need to merge, and a method based on POS. These methods were evaluated in two ways: the overall translation quality and the performance of merging algorithms (the number, type and quality of merges). It was shown that merging strategies could improve SMT quality; however, none of the investigated algorithms reached the number of compounds in the human-translated reference. The follow-up work (Stymne and Cancedda, 2011) additionally viewed the task as sequence labelling: words were labelled as to whether they should be joined or not.

Cap et al. (2014) synthesized new compounds by merging word parts based on their frequencies. Evaluation using BLEU did not show significant improvements which they sought for and validated compounds manually. Their method generated 100 more compounds (750 in total) than the baseline Moses decoder Koehn et al. (2007). Many of the generated compounds were correct translations of the source text even if they were not all confirmed by the reference translation.

2.1.1 Compounds in NMT

Neural MT reached the quality of SMT only after subword units such as Byte Pair Encoding (BPE, Sennrich et al., 2016) were invented. Splitting long words into smaller units in principle allows it to process as well as produce compounds in pieces without any dedicated focus. Weller-Di Marco and Fraser (2020) nevertheless tried explicit compound splitting as a pre-processing step, building upon Weller-Di Marco (2017) and Koehn and Knight (2003) but no significant improvement was observed.

Huck et al. (2017) investigated word segmentation strategies that incorporate more linguistic knowledge than the widely used BPE. One of the described strategies involved compound splitting and provided top-down segmentation that considers the frequency of the components, in contrast to BPE, which operates bottom-up. Compound splitting combined with suffix splitting improved BPE word segmentation in English-German translation, as evaluated by the BLEU score.

Macháček et al. (2018) examine linguistically-motivated or agnostic splits in German-to-Czech translation but observe no benefits from the motivated ones.

3 Experimental Setup

3.1 Data

In this section, we present the data that was used to analyse the presence or absence of German compounds in English-German translations, as well as the fixed dataset that was used to train our Transformer model. The compounds included in the systems' outputs and in the training data were identified based on a fixed list of compounds extracted from GermaNet.

3.1.1 GermaNet

GermaNet is a German word net that preserves the database format and structure of Princeton WordNet 1.5. Its central representation concept is the synset that groups synonyms of a given topic, such as *Streichholz* and *Zündholz* (matches for starting a fire). The word net captures semantic relations between the synsets and synonyms in them (Kunze and Lemnitzer, 2007). The authors distinguished two types of relations: lexical, such as synonymy and antonymy, and conceptual, like hyponymy, hypernymy, and others.

Henrich and Hinrichs (2011) presented a compound splitter to add semantic relations between compound constituents to GermaNet. For our analysis, we used only the list of nominal German compounds extracted from GermaNet (version v17.0, last updated in June 2022). The list contains 115,563 nominal German compounds with information on how they are split into two parts: the modifier and the head. The first part modifies the meaning of the second part, which carries the morphosyntactic features of the entire word (Barz, 2016, p. 2390). Compounds with more than two constituents can be recursively split by finding the split of its components in the GermaNet list.

3.1.2 WMT21

We used a dataset provided by the Sixth Conference on Machine Translation (WMT21, Akhbardeh et al., 2021) and tested our hypotheses on the outputs of systems submitted to the conference. Our own Transformer model was trained using the provided set of parallel training data and then tested on the Newstest2021 test set. The seven training parallel corpora were the same as those used for constrained systems submitted to WMT21. The constrained systems did not use any additional data except for the given corpora for training.

The news test set comprises around 1,000 sentences for all languages (1,002 for en-de). The authors of the test set guaranteed that the sentences were originally from the source language and then translated into the target language. Professional translation agencies performed the reference translations. Considering that English-German is a highly attractive language pair, it received special attention. A different translation agency provided a second reference, labelled "B"; however, it was found to be a post-edited version of one of the submitted systems, so it was discarded from the conference. The third reference translation was sponsored by Microsoft, labelled "C". The metric task organizers (Freitag et al., 2021) then provided a fourth reference, labelled "D".

3.2 Tools

Prior to identifying compounds in the outputs, we had to lemmatize the text. We used the UDPipe 2 (Straka, 2018) lemmatization method. In a small manual examination, we found that the pre-trained German GSD model[1] from the 2.10 version of Universal Dependencies models[2] is the best option for lemmatization of complex compounds.

Additionally, we used some minor tools during our analysis. For word segmentation, we used the subword-nmt (Sennrich et al., 2016) implementation to learn and apply BPE.[3] For estimating the overall translation quality of the outputs, we used the SacreBLEU (Post, 2018) implementation[4] of the BLEU metric.

3.3 Training of Vanilla Transformer

We selected FAIRSEQ (Ott et al., 2019) as the framework for training and evaluating Transformers. FAIRSEQ is an open-source tool used for sequence modelling. It allows researchers to train and evaluate their custom models for text-generating tasks such as translation, language modelling and summarization. It is written in PyTorch and designed to run on multiple GPUs.

We set aside 10% of the data for validation, as suggested by the translation example from FAIRSEQ.[5] Therefore, only 90% of the data was used for training. We trained several variations of the Transformer model. The modifications mainly concerned the creation of the subword dictionary, as summarized in Table 1.

We trained the models using the default FAIRSEQ Transformer configuration containing 6 decoder and 6 encoder layers, each with eight-headed attention. The setup differed from the default configuration in the following ways. The parameters were inspired by EdinSaar's submission to WMT21 (Tchistiakova et al., 2021). We operated on batches of a maximum size of 4,096 tokens. We used the Adam optimizer with setting $\beta_1 = 0.9$, $\beta_2 = 0.98$, and $\epsilon = 1e-9$. The dropout was set to 0.01. We utilized the GELU activation function. The learning rate was set to $3e - 4$ and scheduled with an *inverse_sqrt* scheduler. We set 16,000 warmup updates with an initial learning rate of $1e - 7$. The criterion for training was label-smoothed cross-

[1] https://universaldependencies.org/treebanks/de_gsd/index.html

[2] https://ufal.mff.cuni.cz/udpipe/2/models#universal_dependencies_210_models

[3] https://github.com/rsennrich/subword-nmt

[4] https://github.com/mjpost/sacreBLEU

[5] https://github.com/facebookresearch/fairseq/tree/main/examples/translation

system	seed	type of dictionary	size of dictionary
T40k	1	joint	40,000
T2x40k	1	separated	2 x 40,000
T10k	1	joint	10,000
T2x40k-2	1,000	separated	2 x 40,000

Table 1: Training setups of our Transformer model

entropy. The models were trained on a heterogeneous grid server that contains Quadro RTX 5000, GeForce GTX 1080 Ti, RTX A4000, and GeForce RTX 3090 cards. We utilized 8 GPU cards across several weeks to train the models.

4 Compounds in MT Outputs

In our analysis, we primarily rely on compounds that are contained in the GermaNet list and search for them in WMT21 translations. We compare the counts of compounds found in reference translations and state-of-the-art system outputs. We present counts of compounds and sentences containing at least one compound for each reference and output translation separately. We also report the number of compounds and sentences with compounds confirmed in one or more of the reference translations. The results are sorted by the decreasing number of found compounds and listed in Table 2.

Table 2 shows that human reference translations contain more compounds than any other MT system outputs. The best reference regarding the compound number is the reference "C", with 955 compounds found in 593 sentences. That is over 100 compounds more than in the best MT system. The source text for all the translations comprised 1,002 sentences, so more than half of them led to the generation of some compound in the best reference translation. Considering all sentences where at least one human translator used a compound, we get 756 sentences with 995 different compounds. For all translations, we have 898 out of 1,002 sentences where at least one compound occurred.

Considering only the number of produced compounds, the best MT system is the constrained system *Nemo*, with 842 compound occurrences in 559 sentences (see Table 2). 87% of the compounds are approved by references. Unconstrained systems that employ extra training data are expected to have better results than constrained systems. However, two constrained systems, *Nemo* and *UF*, each produced more compounds than any of the unconstrained systems. The worst system, *ICL*, contained 138 fewer compounds than the best MT system and 251 fewer compounds than the best human translation.

It is important to note that the same concept can be translated using various compounds, so even when the MT output contains a correct compound, it need not be confirmed by the reference. We mitigate this issue by considering four different human translations instead of only one, and also by reporting the number of sentences in which any compound appeared.

4.1 Novel Compounds

MT models operating on subword units have the potential to generate unseen words in their output. We first examined the number of compounds from GermaNet that were produced by systems but were not present in the training data. We found that there were no newly created compounds from GermaNet in the outputs of the constrained system. We expected this subset to be very small or empty, so it was not surprising.

We also looked at whether there were any compounds from GermaNet that were not present in the training data. We found that the training data did not include approximately 3.5% (4,200)

system	# compounds	in refs	# sents	in refs
ref-C	955		593	
ref-D	946		591	
ref-A	901		566	
ref-B	878		569	
C-Nemo	842	735	559	511
C-UF	802	710	532	487
UC-metricsystem2	801	670	533	476
UC-Online-B	798	705	532	484
UC-Facebook-AI	796	735	533	511
C-eTranslation	794	696	530	486
UC-VolcTrans-GLAT	792	756	533	521
UC-Online-W	791	741	533	515
UC-metricsystem1	790	698	530	486
UC-metricsystem3	787	641	518	475
UC-metricsystem5	783	674	531	480
C-WeChat-AI	783	707	527	493
UC-VolcTrans-AT	782	678	531	480
UC-Online-Y	776	658	522	464
UC-happypoet	770	668	526	473
UC-metricsystem4	769	685	515	475
C-Manifold	768	666	514	460
UC-Online-A	767	685	520	478
C-nuclear_trans	762	656	514	466
C-HuaweiTSC	761	673	516	473
C-UEdin	758	666	513	466
UC-Online-G	754	648	516	464
C-P3AI	740	655	505	467
C-BUPT_rush	731	627	495	443
C-ICL	704	595	485	426

Table 2: Compounds appearance in English-German translations in WMT 21 (counts of all appearances of compounds and counts of sentences with compounds plus its subsets approved by reference translations).

of the compounds from GermaNet. This set of compounds presents the upper bound to our observations: we are curious if the systems can produce compounds not seen in their training data, but our diagnosis method (the GermaNet list) offers only 4,200 compounds that could be noticed – and we have no idea if they are relevant to the test text.

Therefore, we decided to explore the subset of compounds produced by constrained systems but that were not present in the training data or the GermaNet list. However, there is no direct way to accomplish this. We collected all words that were not seen in the training data; note that we considered all words here, and manually verified which of them are compounds, see below.

Determining whether a word is a valid or conceivable German compound is not easy. We can consider all compounds produced by native speakers as proper German words. To identify valid novel words, we searched large monolingual corpora, such as Araneum Germanicum Maius (Benko, 2014) or the DWDS dictionary (Klein and Geyken, 2010). To include compounds used in German articles or web pages, we used Google search.

The constrained WMT21 systems produced a total of 304 unique new words that started with a capital letter, indicating that they were possible nouns. Approximately half of them were found by Google anywhere on the Internet. During the analysis, we discovered various groups of words. Some words were of foreign origins, such as the English verb *MACED* (capitalized because it was so in the source text), human names like *Shaquia* and *Bhadauria*, and geographic locations like *Mambourin*. Regarding compounds, we discovered an example of a joint English phrase, *Speakupfordemocracy*, and many German compounds. Out of 304 novel nouns, we manually determined 229 of them as compounds. The exact number of identified compounds and foreign words for each constrained system is displayed in Table 3 below.

We examined the German compounds and discovered many of them were made up of meaningful constituents but were neither included in the training corpus nor found by Google. Naturally, they were also not found in DWDS. Below, we list several instances of this phenomenon. Most of the examples make sense as two separate words, and combining them into a compound is possible (Example 1). We also provide examples of more complex words produced by the systems that do not have any known sense (see Example 2). Their two constituents can form proper German words (Examples 2d and 2e), but their concatenation is not known as a German compound. Finally, there are also examples that cannot be clearly divided into just two parts (for instance, 2b or 2c were formed from three meaning-bearing parts).

The systems also produced compounds that existed and were found by Google but were not contained in DWDS or Araneum Germanicum Maius. The examples of these rare words we found during the analysis are listed in Example 3. These words were also produced by humans in some texts or articles but did not belong to a common vocabulary. In total, 103 of 229 novel compounds were found by Google. This analysis provides several examples of the productivity of NMT models in terms of compounds. We examined these examples further and searched for them in a bigger German corpus, namely in *Deutsche Referenzkorpus* (DeReKo).[6] The DeReKo corpus revealed that beside all compounds from Example 3, Examples 1a and 1c can also be considered as existing compounds.

(1) Words not seen in DWDS or Araneum, made from known constituents
  a. *Kondolenzbotschaft* (a condolence message)
  b. *Gladiatorenmodus* (the mode of a gladiator)
  c. *Quarantäneentscheidung* (the decision on quarantine)

(2) Very complex words not seen in DWDS or Araneum, made from known constituents
  a. *Sanktionsüberwachungsteam* (a team for observing sanctions)
  b. *Gefangenenfreistellungsprogramm* (a program for releasing prisoners)
  c. *Passagierlokalisierungsformular* (a form for localizing travellers)
  d. *Notfallgesundheitsdirektorin* (a female director for emergency health issues)
  e. *Telekommunikationsnetzausrüstung* (equipment for telecommunication networks)

(3) Rare compounds found by Google but not seen in DWDS or Araneum
  a. *Flughafenvertrag* (airport contract)
  b. *Pandemiekrise* (pandemic crisis)
  c. *Kartoffelwurzeln* (potato root)
  d. *Republikanerkollege* (a Republican colleague)
  e. *Amateurfehler* (a layman's error)

[6]https://www.ids-mannheim.de/digspra/kl/projekte/korpora

system	# nouns	n. in ref	# comp.	c. in ref	# foreign
C-Manifold	106	52	69	22	34
C-HuaweiTSC	102	57	58	24	36
C-UF	101	58	60	24	36
C-WeChat-AI	95	54	51	19	35
C-UEdin	93	56	49	20	37
C-eTranslation	92	56	55	23	32
C-Nemo	87	51	44	17	38
C-nuclear_trans	87	47	44	13	35
C-P3AI	86	45	49	15	32
C-ICL	82	47	41	15	35
C-BUPT_rush	81	43	40	11	34

Table 3: Categories of novel words (nouns, out of which some were classified as compounds and some as foreign nouns) produced by constrained systems according to our manual analysis. We also report how many of them were confirmed by the reference ("in ref").

After discovering many newly produced compounds in systems' outputs, we also explored words produced by human translators in the references that were not contained in the training data in order to compare them. We are aware of the fact that comparing the vocabulary of human translations to training corpora might not be ideal for demonstrating productivity regarding composition. However, we can consider the huge training corpora as a sample of common vocabulary knowledge.

We detected several novel compounds from our examples also in the reference translations: The compounds *Kondolenzbotshaft* and *Gladiatorenmodus* (Examples 1a and 1b above) were found in references B and D, while references A and C contained a modification of the second compound, *Gladiatormodus*. Two of the complex compounds that seemed to have no established sense were also created by humans, namely the word *Sanktionsüberwachungsteam* (Example 2a) in references B and C and *Passagierlokalisierungsformular* (Example 2c) in references A, B, and C. We found three of the listed rare compounds (Examples 3) in the references – *Flughafenvertrag* (in references A, C, and D), *Pandemiekrise* (in references B and C) and *Kartoffelwurzeln* (in all references). We can assume that these words were created correctly and reflect the discourse situation of the source test text. Particular phrases in the source text encouraged the translators to create these compounds. However, we can not easily decide the correctness of the other novel words.

After providing a manual analysis and listing some examples, we grouped the observations together. Table 3 displays the number of novel nouns created by constrained MT systems, their cooccurrence with reference translations and their distribution into categories. We distinguished three categories: compounds, foreign words or names, and others, such as web domain names or meaningless words. Only the first two categories are listed in the table. We also counted how many of the novel compounds were also present in the reference translations. In most of the constrained systems, more than a half of novel nouns appeared to be compounds, as shown in Table 3.

To conclude, the MT systems are, same as humans, capable of generating novel words, although it did not seem so when relying on a fixed list of compounds. At the same time, the number of compounds in the translations is still higher for human translators than for the MT systems when we count both novel words and compounds found by GermaNet.

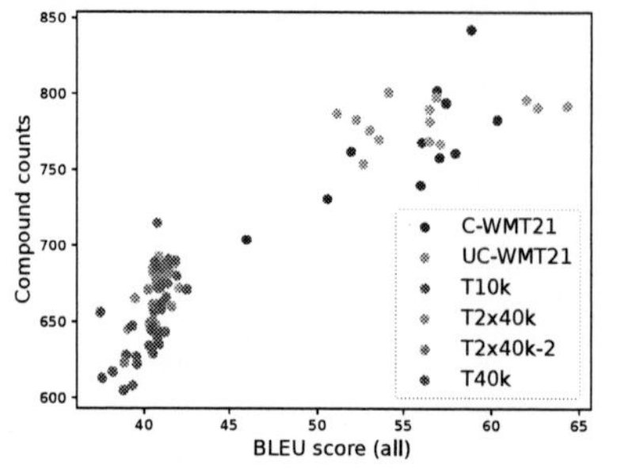

Figure 1: Comparison of BLEU scores (against 3 references) to the number of produced compounds for WMT21 systems and our systems.

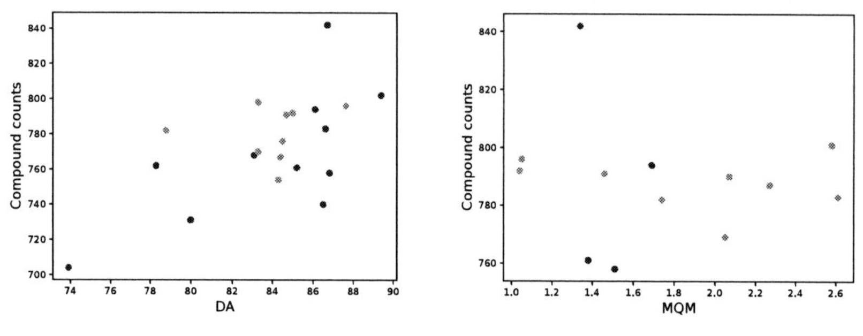

Figure 2: Comparison of human evaluation to the number of produced compounds for WMT21 systems. Legend same as in Figure 1.

4.2 Compounds vs. Overall Quality

We calculated BLEU scores for WMT21 systems to compare their overall translation quality with the number of produced compounds from GermaNet.

We visualised the relationship between both scores for all the constrained MT systems, including four versions of our Transformer, as shown in Figure 1. The graph showed the correlation between the overall quality of translations measured by BLEU and the number of generated compounds. The dependency shows an almost linear pattern. The Pearson correlation coefficient was 0.75 for constrained WMT21 systems, 0.41 for unconstrained, and 0.59 for all WMT21 systems combined. Thus, overall quality serves as a good indicator of *relative* performance in terms of compounds, although it does not reflect the human level.

To compare the number of produced compounds with human evaluation (DA and MQM), we presented the correlation in Figure 2. The Pearson correlation coefficient for DA and the compound number was 0.69 for constrained WMT21 systems, 0.17 for unconstrained, and 0.60 for all WMT21 systems combined. Regarding MQM and the compound number, the Pearson correlation coefficients were -0.24 for constrained WMT21 systems, -0.19 for unconstrained and -0.10 for all WMT21 systems combined.

In summary, these results indicate that the relationship between the number of produced compounds and human evaluation varies depending on the evaluation metric and the type of system used (constrained vs. unconstrained). BLEU score seems to reflect the presence or absence of compounds slightly better than DA and substantially better than MQM. Nonetheless, our study highlights the potential of using the number of produced compounds as an additional metric to evaluate the quality of machine translation systems.

5 Conclusion

We examined the production of German compounds in Transformer models in English-to-German MT. Our analysis revealed that reference translations consistently contain more compounds than MT systems. We confirmed that Transformers have the ability to generate new words including compounds but evaluating compound production using closed lists or existing general manual evaluation methods (DA, MQM) is not effective. This opens space for further exploration of compound production as well as their evaluation.

Acknowledgements

This research was partially supported by the grant 19-26934X (NEUREM3) of the Czech Science Foundation.

References

Akhbardeh, F., Arkhangorodsky, A., Biesialska, M., Bojar, O., Chatterjee, R., Chaudhary, V., Costa-jussa, M. R., España-Bonet, C., Fan, A., Federmann, C., Freitag, M., Graham, Y., Grundkiewicz, R., Haddow, B., Harter, L., Heafield, K., Homan, C., Huck, M., Amponsah-Kaakyire, K., Kasai, J., Khashabi, D., Knight, K., Kocmi, T., Koehn, P., Lourie, N., Monz, C., Morishita, M., Nagata, M., Nagesh, A., Nakazawa, T., Negri, M., Pal, S., Tapo, A. A., Turchi, M., Vydrin, V., and Zampieri, M. (2021). Findings of the 2021 conference on machine translation (WMT21). In *Proceedings of the Sixth Conference on Machine Translation*, pages 1–88, Online. Association for Computational Linguistics.

Barz, I. (2016). German. In Müller, P. O., Ohnheiser, I., Olsen, S., and Rainer, F., editors, *Word-Formation. An International Handbook of the Languages of Europe*, volume 4, pages 2387–2410. Mouton de Gruyter, Berlin.

Benko, V. (2014). Aranea: Yet another family of (comparable) web corpora. In Sojka, P., Horák, A., Kopeček, I., and Pala, K., editors, *Text, Speech and Dialogue*, pages 247–256, Cham. Springer International Publishing.

Burchardt, A. (2013). Multidimensional quality metrics: a flexible system for assessing translation quality. In *Proceedings of Translating and the Computer 35*, London, UK. Aslib.

Cap, F., Fraser, A., Weller, M., and Cahill, A. (2014). How to produce unseen teddy bears: Improved morphological processing of compounds in SMT. In *Proceedings of the 14th Conference of the European Chapter of the Association for Computational Linguistics*, pages 579–587, Gothenburg, Sweden. Association for Computational Linguistics.

Daiber, J., Quiroz, L., Wechsler, R., and Frank, S. (2015). Splitting compounds by semantic analogy. In *Proceedings of the 1st Deep Machine Translation Workshop*, pages 20–28, Praha, Czechia. ÚFAL MFF UK.

Freitag, M., Rei, R., Mathur, N., Lo, C.-k., Stewart, C., Avramidis, E., Kocmi, T., Foster, G., Lavie, A., and Martins, A. F. T. (2022). Results of wmt22 metrics shared task: Stop using bleu – neural metrics are better and more robust. In *Proceedings of the Seventh Conference on Machine Translation*, pages 46–68, Abu Dhabi. Association for Computational Linguistics.

Freitag, M., Rei, R., Mathur, N., Lo, C.-k., Stewart, C., Foster, G., Lavie, A., and Bojar, O. (2021). Results of the WMT21 metrics shared task: Evaluating metrics with expert-based human evaluations on TED and news domain. In *Proceedings of the Sixth Conference on Machine Translation*, pages 733–774, Online. Association for Computational Linguistics.

Graham, Y., Baldwin, T., and Mathur, N. (2015). Accurate evaluation of segment-level machine translation metrics. In *Proceedings of the 2015 Conference of the North American Chapter of the Association for Computational Linguistics: Human Language Technologies*, pages 1183–1191, Denver, Colorado. Association for Computational Linguistics.

Henrich, V. and Hinrichs, E. (2011). Determining immediate constituents of compounds in GermaNet. In *Proceedings of the International Conference Recent Advances in Natural Language Processing 2011*, pages 420–426, Hissar, Bulgaria. Association for Computational Linguistics.

Huck, M., Riess, S., and Fraser, A. (2017). Target-side word segmentation strategies for neural machine translation. In *Proceedings of the Second Conference on Machine Translation*, pages 56–67, Copenhagen, Denmark. Association for Computational Linguistics.

Klein, W. and Geyken, A. (2010). Das digitale wörterbuch der deutschen sprache (dwds). In *Lexicographica: International annual for lexicography*, pages 79–96. De Gruyter.

Kocmi, T., Bawden, R., Bojar, O., Dvorkovich, A., Federmann, C., Fishel, M., Gowda, T., Graham, Y., Grundkiewicz, R., Haddow, B., Knowles, R., Koehn, P., Monz, C., Morishita, M., Nagata, M., Nakazawa, T., Novák, M., Popel, M., Popović, M., and Shmatova, M. (2022). Findings of the 2022 conference on machine translation (wmt22). In *Proceedings of the Seventh Conference on Machine Translation*, pages 1–45, Abu Dhabi. Association for Computational Linguistics.

Koehn, P., Hoang, H., Birch, A., Callison-Burch, C., Federico, M., Bertoldi, N., Cowan, B., Shen, W., Moran, C., Zens, R., Dyer, C., Bojar, O., Constantin, A., and Herbst, E. (2007). Moses: Open source toolkit for statistical machine translation. In *Proceedings of the 45th Annual Meeting of the Association for Computational Linguistics Companion Volume Proceedings of the Demo and Poster Sessions*, pages 177–180, Prague, Czech Republic. Association for Computational Linguistics.

Koehn, P. and Knight, K. (2003). Empirical methods for compound splitting. In *10th Conference of the European Chapter of the Association for Computational Linguistics*, Budapest, Hungary. Association for Computational Linguistics.

Koehn, P. and Monz, C. (2006). Manual and automatic evaluation of machine translation between european languages. In *Proceedings on the Workshop on Statistical Machine Translation*, pages 102–121, New York City. Association for Computational Linguistics.

Kunze, C. and Lemnitzer, L. (2007). *Computerlexikographie: Eine Einführung*. Narr Francke Attempto Verlag.

Macháček, D., Vidra, J., and Bojar, O. (2018). Morphological and language-agnostic word segmentation for nmt. In *Proceedings of the 21st International Conference on Text, Speech and Dialogue—TSD 2018*, pages 277–284, Cham, Switzerland. Springer-Verlag.

Ott, M., Edunov, S., Baevski, A., Fan, A., Gross, S., Ng, N., Grangier, D., and Auli, M. (2019). fairseq: A fast, extensible toolkit for sequence modeling. In *Proceedings of NAACL-HLT 2019: Demonstrations*.

Papineni, K., Roukos, S., Ward, T., and Zhu, W.-J. (2002). Bleu: a method for automatic evaluation of machine translation. In *Proceedings of the 40th annual meeting of the Association for Computational Linguistics*, pages 311–318.

Popović, M. (2015). chrF: character n-gram F-score for automatic MT evaluation. In *Proceedings of the Tenth Workshop on Statistical Machine Translation*, pages 392–395, Lisbon, Portugal. Association for Computational Linguistics.

Popović, M., Stein, D., and Ney, H. (2006). Statistical machine translation of german compound words. In Salakoski, T., Ginter, F., Pyysalo, S., and Pahikkala, T., editors, *Advances in Natural Language Processing*, pages 616–624, Berlin, Heidelberg. Springer Berlin Heidelberg.

Post, M. (2018). A call for clarity in reporting BLEU scores. In *Proceedings of the Third Conference on Machine Translation: Research Papers*, pages 186–191, Belgium, Brussels. Association for Computational Linguistics.

Rei, R., Stewart, C., Farinha, A. C., and Lavie, A. (2020). COMET: A neural framework for MT evaluation. In *Proceedings of the 2020 Conference on Empirical Methods in Natural Language Processing (EMNLP)*, pages 2685–2702, Online. Association for Computational Linguistics.

Schmid, H., Fitschen, A., and Heid, U. (2004). SMOR: A German computational morphology covering derivation, composition and inflection. In *Proceedings of the Fourth International Conference on Language Resources and Evaluation (LREC'04)*, Lisbon, Portugal. European Language Resources Association (ELRA).

Sennrich, R., Haddow, B., and Birch, A. (2016). Neural machine translation of rare words with subword units. In *Proceedings of the 54th Annual Meeting of the Association for Computational Linguistics (Volume 1: Long Papers)*, pages 1715–1725, Berlin, Germany. Association for Computational Linguistics.

Straka, M. (2018). UDPipe 2.0 prototype at CoNLL 2018 UD shared task. In *Proceedings of the CoNLL 2018 Shared Task: Multilingual Parsing from Raw Text to Universal Dependencies*, pages 197–207, Brussels, Belgium. Association for Computational Linguistics.

Stymne, S. (2009). A comparison of merging strategies for translation of German compounds. In *Proceedings of the Student Research Workshop at EACL 2009*, pages 61–69, Athens, Greece. Association for Computational Linguistics.

Stymne, S. and Cancedda, N. (2011). Productive generation of compound words in statistical machine translation. In *Proceedings of the Sixth Workshop on Statistical Machine Translation*, pages 250–260, Edinburgh, Scotland. Association for Computational Linguistics.

Sugisaki, K. and Tuggener, D. (2018). German compound splitting using the compound productivity of morphemes. In Barbaresi, A., Biber, H., Neubarth, F., and Osswald, R., editors, *14th Conference on Natural Language Processing - KONVENS 2018*, pages 141–147. Austrian Academy of Sciences Press. 14th Conference on Natural Language Processing (KONVENS 2018), Vienna, Austria, 19-21 September 2018.

Tchistiakova, S., Alabi, J., Dutta Chowdhury, K., Dutta, S., and Ruiter, D. (2021). EdinSaar@WMT21: North-Germanic low-resource multilingual NMT. In *Proceedings of the Sixth Conference on Machine Translation*, pages 368–375, Online. Association for Computational Linguistics.

Thompson, B. and Post, M. (2020). Automatic machine translation evaluation in many languages via zero-shot paraphrasing. In *Proceedings of the 2020 Conference on Empirical Methods in Natural Language Processing (EMNLP)*, pages 90–121, Online. Association for Computational Linguistics.

Vaswani, A., Shazeer, N., Parmar, N., Uszkoreit, J., Jones, L., Gomez, A. N., Kaiser, L., and Polosukhin, I. (2017). Attention is all you need. *CoRR*, abs/1706.03762.

Weller-Di Marco, M. (2017). Simple compound splitting for German. In *Proceedings of the 13th Workshop on Multiword Expressions (MWE 2017)*, pages 161–166, Valencia, Spain. Association for Computational Linguistics.

Weller-Di Marco, M. and Fraser, A. (2020). Modeling word formation in English–German neural machine translation. In *Proceedings of the 58th Annual Meeting of the Association for Computational Linguistics*, pages 4227–4232, Online. Association for Computational Linguistics.

Benchmarking Dialectal Arabic-Turkish Machine Translation

Hasan Alkheder hasan.alkhder2@ogr.sakarya.edu.tr
Computer Engineering, Sakarya University, Serdivan, Türkiye

Houda Bouamor hbouamor@cmu.edu
Information Systems, Carnegie Mellon University Qatar, Doha, Qatar

Nizar Habash nizar.habash@nyu.edu
Computer Science, New York University Abu Dhabi, Abu Dhabi, UAE

Ahmet Zengin azengin@sakarya.edu.tr
Computer Engineering, Sakarya University, Serdivan, Türkiye

Abstract

Due to the significant influx of Syrian refugees in Turkey in recent years, the Syrian Arabic dialect has become increasingly prevalent in certain regions of Turkey. Developing a machine translation system between Turkish and Syrian Arabic would be crucial in facilitating communication between the Turkish and Syrian communities in these regions, which can have a positive impact on various domains such as politics, trade, and humanitarian aid. Such a system would also contribute positively to the growing Arab-focused tourism industry in Turkey. In this paper, we present the first research effort exploring translation between Syrian Arabic and Turkish. We use a set of 2,000 parallel sentences from the MADAR corpus containing 25 different city dialects from different cities across the Arab world, in addition to Modern Standard Arabic (MSA), English, and French. Additionally, we explore the translation performance into Turkish from other Arabic dialects and compare the results to the performance achieved when translating from Syrian Arabic. We build our MADAR-Turk data set by manually translating the set of 2,000 sentences from the Damascus dialect of Syria to Turkish with the help of two native Arabic speakers from Syria who are also highly fluent in Turkish. We evaluate the quality of the translations and report the results achieved. We make this first-of-a-kind data set publicly available to support research in machine translation between these important but less studied language pairs.[1]

1 Introduction

The rapid advancements in machine translation technology have significantly helped to break down language barriers and facilitate cross-cultural communication using distant languages, including Turkish and Arabic. Given that Syria and Iraq border Turkey to the south, there is cultural overlap and close ties between those nations and Turkey, making Arabic and Turkish two of the most widely spoken languages in the Middle East. Despite this, there has been no significant research or machine translation effort that specifically addresses the translation of

[1]The MADAR-Turk data set is available from `http://resources.camel-lab.com/`.

Proceedings of Machine Translation Summit XIX, Vol. 1: Research Track, pages 261–271
September 4–8, 2023, Macau SAR, China.

dialectal Arabic and Turkish. The presence of more than 4 million Syrian and Iraqi refugees in Turkey, as well as the massive spread of Turkish drama (dubbed TV series) in the Arab world (Kraidy and Al-Ghazzi, 2013), not to mention the growing tourism industry in Turkey catering to Arab tourists, reinforce the urgent need for developing machine translation capabilities between Turkish and Arabic and its dialects to promote communication and cultural exchange between the Arab countries and Turkey.

Efforts to develop neural machine translation between several language pairs including Turkish (Qumar et al., 2023) and Arabic (Gamal et al., 2022) have yielded promising results, improving translation quality and reducing the need for extensive linguistic knowledge. Building such systems requires a large amount of data, which currently does not exist for the Turkish and Arabic language pair – for Modern Standard Arabic (MSA), and more so for the dialects. Focusing on benchmarking, we present the first research effort exploring translation between Syrian Arabic and Turkish using a set of 2,000 parallel sentences from the MADAR corpus containing 25 different city dialects from various cities across the Arab world, in addition to MSA, English, and French. Additionally, we explore the translation performance into Turkish from other Arabic dialects and compare the results to the performance achieved when translating from Syrian Arabic. We make the data set publicly available.[1]

The paper is structured as follows. Section 2 presents some related work in Turkish and Arabic machine translation, and section 3 discusses the linguistic challenges of Arabic-Turkish translation. Section 4 details the MADAR-Turk data set creation process. Sections 5 and 6 present our benchmarking results and error analysis, respectively. We conclude and describe our future work in Section 7.

2 Related Work

2.1 Arabic-Turkish Resources

Due to the lack of parallel corpora between Arabic and Turkish, MT between this language pair did not receive much attention. A few researchers attempted to develop resources, models, and techniques to translate between these two languages. For instance, Durgar El-Kahlout et al. (2019) introduced an Arabic-to-Turkish statistical machine translation system in the news domains. This work included building parallel Turkish and Arabic corpora collected in different ways: manual translation by professional translators, web-based open-source Arabic-Turkish parallel texts, and using back-translation techniques to translate monolingual Arabic data by using existing machine translation systems. The corpus they created is small and does not include any dialectal Arabic examples.

The OpenSubtitles corpus (Lison and Tiedemann, 2016), a large dataset of TV and movie subtitles covering more than 60 languages, contains Standard Arabic-Turkish parallel texts comprising almost 28 million sentences. Baali et al. (2022) introduced an unsupervised approach to creating a Turkish-Arabic speech corpus from dubbed TV series videos. This corpus was not transcribed and therefore is not available in a text format.

Some research efforts explored Arabic and Turkish for different NLP tasks (Sliwa et al., 2018; Zampieri et al., 2020); however, these efforts employed non-parallel corpora.

A comprehensive survey of the corpora and lexical resources, publicly available for Turkish, is presented in Çöltekin et al. (2023). None of the resources described include dialectal Arabic.

2.2 Dialectal Arabic Parallel Resources

Previous research has focused on creating parallel dialectal data with other languages, but not with Turkish. For instance, MADAR (Bouamor et al., 2018) is the first city-level dialectal dataset including dialects from 25 cities, in addition to MSA, English, and French. MADAR was built on the Basic Traveling Expression Corpus (BTEC) (Takezawa et al., 2007). We draw inspiration from this effort and build on the MADAR corpus to leverage its parallelism benefits in our corpus development. We note that a Turkish version of the BTEC corpus was used for Turkish-English MT (Köprü, 2009; Mermer et al., 2010; Demir et al., 2012); however, to the best of our knowledge, it is not publicly available.

There have been many efforts in Arabic dialect machine translation (Salloum and Habash, 2011; Zbib et al., 2012; Meftouh et al., 2015; Harrat et al., 2017; Baniata et al., 2018; Kchaou et al., 2020; Sghaier and Zrigui, 2020). The work we present in this paper is intended to bridge a crucial gap in the Arabic dialect-Turkish language pairs; we hope this will lay the foundation for further exploration and research in this area.

3 Challenges of Arabic-Turkish Translation

While Ottoman Turkish used to be written in Arabic Script, Modern Turkish uses the Roman script, which adds to the many linguistic differences between Turkish and Arabic and its dialects in terms of morphology, syntax, and lexicon.

3.1 Orthography Differences

Arabic orthography, i.e., the way Arabic language information is encoded using its script, is different from Turkish orthography in the crucial detail of not specifying short vowels and doubling consonants, which are typically written with optional diacritical marks in Arabic. This leads to important ambiguities that pose a significant challenge for Arabic to Turkish MT. For example, the two Arabic words عِقْد *ςiqd*[2] 'necklace' and عَقْد *ςaqd* 'contract' are often written simply as عقد *ςaqd*, but they would be properly translated to Turkish as *kolye* and *sözleşme*, respectively.

3.2 Morphological Differences

Despite centuries of linguistic exchange and geographical proximity, Turkish and Arabic belong to distinct and separate language families. Turkish belongs to the Turkic language family, while Arabic belongs to the Semitic language family. Consequently, there are several morphological differences between the two languages. Most evident is that Arabic is morphologically rich and employs a combination of templatic and affixational morphology (including a number of clitics); while Turkish is heavily agglutinative in nature.

One example of the difference is the absence of the gender feature in Turkish, unlike Arabic's two-gender system. Also Turkish does not have a definite/indefinite distinction. For example, Turkish *büyük sultan* '[a/the] great [male/female] sultan' maps to four Arabic phrases that vary in gender and definiteness: سلطان عظيم *slTAn ςĎym*, السلطان العظيم *AlslTAn AlςĎym*, سلطانة عظيمة *slTAnħ ςĎymħ*, السلطانة العظيمة *AlslTAnħ AlςĎymħ*. We expect this to make mapping from Arabic to Turkish easier than the reverse. The gender neutrality of Turkish even extends to pronouns. For instance, Turkish *o* 'he/she' map to Arabic هو *hw* 'he' and هي *hy* 'she'.

Another important difference is that Arabic utilizes prepositions, but Turkish uses agglutinating postpositions, e.g., the postposition *+a* 'to' *büyük sultana* 'to [the] great sultan'. This compares with the Arabic preposition +ل *l+* in للسلطان العظيم *llslTAn AlςĎym* 'for the great sultan'.

For more information on Arabic and Turkish morphology, see (Habash, 2010) and (Oflazer, 1993).

[2]The Arabic transliteration is in the Habash-Soudi-Buckwalter (HSB) scheme (Habash et al., 2007).

3.3 Syntactic Differences

Syntactically, Turkish is a head-final language that uses a subject-object-verb (SOV) word order; while Arabic is a head-initial language that uses both VSO and SVO orders. For example, the Turkish sentence *çocuk süt içti* '[lit. child milk drank] the child drank milk', is translated as Arabic شرب الطفل الحليب *šrb AlTfl AlHlyb* '[lit. drank the-child the-milk]' or الطفل شرب الحليب *AlTfl šrb AlHlyb* '[lit. the-child drank the-milk]'.

Similarly, Turkish adjectives precede the nouns they modify, while Arabic adjectives follow, as in the Turkish example *büyük sultan* '[the] great sultan' mapping to Arabic السلطان العظيم *AlslTAn AlςĎym* '[lit. the-sultan the-great]', presented above.

Given the complex morphology of both Arabic and Turkish, one can expect many interactions between syntax and morphology in the context of translating between these languages. The examples of Arabic prepositional clitics and Turkish postpositional clitics (shown above) map to separate words when translated: Arabic prepositional clitic +ل *l+* 'for' maps to Turkish standalone postposition *için*, and Turkish postpositional suffix *+a* 'to' maps to the Arabic standalone preposition إلى Ǎlý.

3.4 Lexical Differences and Similarities

Due to the historical and geographical affinity between Arabic and Turkish, there are many words that are shared between the two languages. However, the majority of their lexicons are distinct from each other. Examples of Turkish words of Arabic origin include *kalem* 'pen' from قلم *qalam*, *kahve* 'coffee' from قهوة *qahwaħ*, *merhaba* 'hello' from مرحبا *mrHbA*, and *inşallah* 'God willing' from the phrase إن شاء الله *Ǎn šA' Allh*.

In addition, there are Turkish words that have made their way into standard Arabic such as Turkish *Gümrük* 'customs' and Arabic جمرك *jmrk* and also into dialectal Arabic, particularly Levantine, such as Turkish *Aferin* 'well done' becoming Arabic عفارم *ςfArm*. While the shared lexical items may be useful in translation, in principle, the differences in script, orthography, and morphology can limit their practical value.

3.5 Arabic Dialect Differences

Since we benchmark MT from a number of Arabic dialects, we should note that these varieties differ in many ways at all linguistic levels, including phonology, morphology, syntax, and lexicon (Bouamor et al., 2018; Salameh et al., 2018; Althobaiti, 2020). The differences can even be high within the same country and region. For instance, Salameh et al. (2018) show, as part of their work on dialect identification, that Damascus and Aleppo dialects are different from each other only by 32% and from Beirut dialect by 38%; and that the dissimilarity between the cluster enclosing the Tunisian cities of Tunis and Sfax and the cluster containing the rest of the dialects is more than 50%.

4 MADAR-Turk Data Set Creation

4.1 Data Selection

We used the MADAR Corpus (Bouamor et al., 2018), which was the first set of parallel sentences that include the dialects of 25 Arab cities in addition to English, French, and MSA. Table 1 lists the various cities in the corpus with their countries and regions. MADAR was built on the Basic Traveling Expression Corpus (BTEC) (Takezawa et al., 2007) which comprised about 20,000 English tourism-related sentences. BTEC is conversational in nature, has short sentences, and has translations in several languages, making it an attractive resource for build-

Region	Maghreb				Nile Basin	Levant		Gulf		Yemen
Sub-region	**Morocco**	**Algeria**	**Tunisia**	**Libya**	**Egypt/Sudan**	**South Levant**	**North Levant**	**Iraq**	**Gulf**	**Yemen**
Cities	Rabat Fes	Algiers	Tunis Sfax	Tripoli Benghazi	Cairo Alexandria Aswan Khartoum	Jerusalem Amman Salt	Beirut Damascus Aleppo	Mosul Baghdad Basra	Doha Muscat Riyadh Jeddah	Sana'a

Table 1: The MADAR resources include a variety of region, sub-region, and city dialects.

Turkish	Arabic
Orda, tam turizm ofisinin önünde.	موجود هنيك، قدام مكتب معلومات السياح بالزبط.
Daha önce burda öyle bir adres olduğunu hiç duymadım	ما سمعت بهيك عنوان هون من قبل.
Eczaneyi görene kadar düz git.	إمشي مباشرة لحد ما تشوف صيدلية.
Kahvaltı ne kadar?	بأديش الفطور؟
Sana nasıl yardımcı olabilirim?	كيف فيني ساعدك؟
Soldaki üçüncü aradan geç.	لف عالشمال بالدخلة التالتة.

Table 2: Examples of translation from the Damascus Arabic dialect to the Turkish language.

ing machine translation models. Bouamor et al. (2018) translated large portions of BTEC to five major city dialects representing distinct regions: Beirut (Levant), Doha (Gulf), Cairo (Egypt), Tunis, and Rabat (Maghreb); and they translated a smaller portion (2,000 sentences) to all 25 cities, which plus MSA constitute Corpus-26. In all their translations they started with English or French to avoid the priming effect of Standard Arabic on dialect speakers. In this paper, we work with the same smaller portion and add a Turkish translation to it. This allows us to benchmark translation to Turkish from all Arabic dialects.

4.2 Data Set Construction

Two native Arabic speakers from Syria who are highly fluent in Turkish translated all 2,000 sentences. We provided the translators with a set of guidelines, such as translating each sentence independently without considering the previous context, paying attention to the correctness of the punctuation, and avoiding sentence combinations. After confirming their adherence to these guidelines using an initial pilot set of 50 sentences, the translators proceeded to translate the remainder of the 2,000 sentences from the Damascus dialect into Turkish, from scratch. We specifically chose Damascus because our initial objective was to work on Syrian Arabic to Turkish MT. We expect, and acknowledge, a bias towards Damascus in the effort. Examples of translations from the Damascus dialect into Turkish are shown in Table 2.

4.3 Data Set Statistics

Table 3 presents examples of parallel sentences from the MADAR and MADAR-Turk corpora with their average lengths. We note a stark difference in the number of words per sentence in Turkish (6.9) compared to English (9.9), French (11.5), and most Arabic variants (around 7). This difference is expected due to the agglutinative nature of the Turkish language which results in longer words and fewer overall words per sentence.

Language | Dialect	Example	# words/sentence
Turkish	Eczaneyi görene kadar düz git.	6.9
English	Go straight until you see a drugstore.	9.9
French	Continuez tout droit jusqu'à ce que vous	11.5
MSA	استمر في السير في هذا الطريق حتى تجد صيدلية .	8.0
Aleppo	روح ساوي لبين ما تشوف صيدلية.	6.8
Alexandria	امشي على طول لحد ما تشوف صيدلية.	7.3
Algiers	امشي قبالة حتى تشوف صيدلية.	7.3
Amman	امشي دغري لعند ما تشوف صيدلية.	7.3
Aswan	امشي على طول لغاية متشوف صيدلية.	7.3
Baghdad	اطلع كبل لحد ما تشوف الصيدلية.	6.8
Basra	اطلع كبل لحد ما تشوف صيدلية.	6.6
Beirut	روح دغري لحتى تشوف صيدلية.	6.7
Benghazi	أمشي طول لعند ما تشوف الصيدلية.	7.2
Cairo	أمشي علطول لحد ما تلقي صيدلية.	7.2
Damsacus	إمشي مباشرة لحد ما تشوف صيدلية.	6.8
Doha	امش سيده لين تشوف صيدلية.	6.7
Fes	سير نيشان حتا تلقى الصيدلية.	7.3
Jeddah	امشي سيدا لين ما تلاقي الصيدلية.	6.7
Jerusalem	خليك ماشي دغري لتلاقي صيدلية.	7.0
Khartoum	أمشي دغري لغاية تشوف صيدلية.	7.4
Mosul	امشي كبل الى ان اتشوف صيدليه.	7.1
Muscat	روح سيده حتى تشوف الصيدلية.	7.3
Rabat	سير نيشان حتا تشوف صيدلية.	7.4
Riyadh	امش على طول لين تلقى صيدلية.	7.0
Salt	روح دغري حتى تشوف الصيدلية.	7.1
Sanaa	امشي طوالي لوما تبسر صيدليه.	7.1
Sfax	كمل القدام لين تارى الفارمسي.	6.8
Tripoli	برا طول لين تشوف صيدلية.	7.2
Tunis	امشي طول طول حتى لين تشوف صيدلية.	6.9

Table 3: Examples of parallel sentences from the MADAR and MADAR-Turk corpora with their average lengths.

5 Benchmarking Dialect Arabic to Turkish MT

We translated the various sentences from the MADAR data set into Turkish using *Google Translate*.[3] To evaluate the quality of the automatic translations, we compared them against the reference translations produced by the translators. We measure the translation quality using BLEU (Papineni et al., 2002). We use the SacreBleu implementation (Post, 2018) for evaluating automatic translations against the reference translations (lowercase=True, tokenize='intl'). The results are shown in Table 4. The Table has two parts: (a) organized by the city and (b) organized by region. The results show the following: of all the input languages, MSA has the highest BLEU score, followed by English, then the Riyadh dialect, then French. In contrast, the dialects of Sfax and Tunis (both Tunisian cities) have the lowest scores. Interestingly, English was not the highest, despite its widespread use and the availability of high-quality translation resources. One possible explanation for this result is that we used one reference translation that

[3]`https://translate.google.com/`

(a)

Region	Country	Variant	BLEU
Gulf	Oman	Muscat	23.60
Gulf	Qatar	Doha	20.49
Gulf	Saudi Arabia	Jeddah	20.58
Gulf	Saudi Arabia	Riyadh	**26.92**
Iraq	Iraq	Baghdad	21.46
Iraq	Iraq	Basra	20.25
Iraq	Iraq	Mosul	17.74
Levant	Jordan	Amman	21.84
Levant	Jordan	Salt	22.43
Levant	Lebanon	Beirut	15.81
Levant	Palestine	Jerusalem	22.47
Levant	Syria	Aleppo	21.27
Levant	Syria	Damsacus	26.18
Maghreb	Algeria	Algiers	14.79
Maghreb	Libya	Benghazi	18.54
Maghreb	Libya	Tripoli	16.07
Maghreb	Morocco	Fes	13.64
Maghreb	Morocco	Rabat	9.76
Maghreb	Tunisia	Sfax	8.30
Maghreb	Tunisia	Tunis	8.94
Nile Basin	Egypt	Alexandria	24.13
Nile Basin	Egypt	Aswan	21.95
Nile Basin	Egypt	Cairo	21.99
Nile Basin	Sudan	Khartoum	22.17
Yemen	Yemen	Sanaa	21.09
		MSA	**33.88**
		French	**26.22**
		English	**30.01**

(b)

Region	BLEU
Nile Basin	22.56
Levant	21.67
Yemen	21.09
Gulf	**22.90**
Iraq	19.82
Maghreb	12.86

Table 4: (a) BLEU scores for Google Translate output starting with texts from the various Arab cities in MADAR Corpus, plus Modern Standard Arabic (MSA), English, and French. (b) Average BLEU scores by Arabic dialectal region.

was originally translated from Arabic. The dialect of Damascus was not the best, even though that was the dialect we used when we generated the reference, because the model was developed independently by Google.

We also summarize in Table 4 (b) the differences across the different regions in the Arab world following the regional division that we explained in Table 1. The best performance is in the Gulf, followed by the Nile Basin, followed by the Levant, and the Maghreb appears in the last ranking.

Clearly, a lot more effort has to be done to aid Turkish translation from all these different languages, especially from Arabic.

Language / Dialect	Quality (1- 5)	Transliteration Error	Semantic Error	Morphology Error
English	4.45	4	33	7
French	4.38	2	38	9
MSA	4.26	4	44	8
Damascus	3.80	19	51	22
Tunis	2.74	42	77	30

Table 5: Results of manual evaluation and transliteration, semantic, and morphology errors.

Turkish Reference	Language/ Dialect	Input	Google Translate	Quality (1 - 5)	Transliteration Error	Semantic Error	Morphology Error
Orda, tam turizm ofisinin önünde.	English	It's over there, just in front of the tourist information.	Orada, turist bilgilerinin hemen önünde.	4		X	
	French	C'est là-bas, juste en face du bureau d'information touristique.	Orada, turizm danışma bürosunun hemen önünde.	5			
	MSA	هناك ، أمام بيانات السائح تماما.	Orada, turizm verilerinin hemen önünde.	4		X	
	Damascus	موجود هنيك، قدام مكتب معلومات السياح بالزبط.	Orada, turizm danışma bürosunun hemen önünde.	4		X	
	Tunis	اهوكا غادي، بالضبط قدام البيرو متاع الارشادات السياحية.	Ahuka Gadi, Peru'nun hemen önünde, turist rehberlerinin keyfini çıkarın.	1	X	X	
Bu biraz soğuk. Isıtabilir misin?	English	This is rather cold. Will you heat it up?	Bu oldukça soğuk. ısıtacak mısın?	5			
	French	C'est plutôt froid. Pouvez-vous le réchauffer?	Oldukça soğuk. Bunu ısıtabilir misin?	5			
	MSA	هذا بارد إلى حد ما . هل يمكن أن تقوم بتسخينه ؟	Bu biraz havalı. Isıtabilir misin?	3		X	
	Damascus	هاد بارد شوي. ممكن تسخنه؟	Bu soğuk. Isıtabilir misin?	5			
	Tunis	هذا بارد شوية. بش تسخنو؟	Bu biraz soğuk. Isınıyor musun?	3			X
Teşekkür ederim. Bu yeterli.	English	Thank you, that's enough.	Teşekkürler, bu kadar yeter.	5			
	French	Merci. Ce sera tout.	TEŞEKKÜRLER. Bu kadar.	5			
	MSA	شكراً ، هذا يكفي.	Teşekkürler, bu kadar yeter.	5			
	Damascus	شكراً. هيك بكفي.	teşekkür ederim. Bu yeterli.	5			
	Tunis	شكرا، يزي.	Teşekkürler, Yeezy.	3	X		

Table 6: Examples from the manual error analysis.

6 Error Analysis

In addition to the quantitative evaluation using BLEU, we conducted an error analysis on translations from the several languages we studied, specifically English, French, and MSA because these are standard languages, as well as the dialect of Damascus and Tunis (which was among the worst-performing in the evaluation).

We chose the same 100 sentences for these languages and evaluated their Turkish automatic translation outputs in two different ways. Firstly, we asked human evaluators to rate the translation quality on a scale of 1 to 5, where 5 represents a perfectly acceptable translation in Turkish that accurately covers the meaning and fluency of Turkish, and 1 represents a translation that is lacking in either accuracy or fluency in a way that makes it hard to read and has errors.

Additionally, we identify three types of errors: transliteration errors, semantic errors, and morphology errors. **Transliteration** errors refer to cases where the system failed to translate a word and produced a transliteration instead, e.g., Tunisian Arabic يزي *yzy* 'enough' is transliterated as *Yeezy* instead of Turkish *yeterli*. **Semantic** errors refer to cases where a word is translated with a different meaning than intended. For instance, the Damascus Arabic word نص (with ambiguous diacritization as *nuS∼* 'half' or *naS∼* 'text') is incorrectly translated in the context of the phrase نص قنينة *nS qnynħ* 'half bottle' as *şişe metni* 'bottle text' as opposed to the correct translation *yarım şişe* 'half bottle'. And **morphology** errors refer to cases where a word is translated with errors in morphological features. For example, the Tunisian Arabic verb نحب *nHb* 'I want' (Turkish reference *istiyorum*) is mistranslated as *seviyoruz* 'we love' (i.e. plural instead of singular morphology). This is most likely a result of confusion with the MSA reading of the Arabic word which also means 'we love'.

The summary of our results is given in Table 5. We provide examples in Table 6. English has the highest quality; which is expected given that it is a language with a wealth of resources and training data. Furthermore, we observe that, despite being the best-automated automated assessment using BLEU, MSA came in third place in terms of translation quality behind English and French. Lastly, the Tunisian dialect had the lowest quality and had the greatest errors compared to the other languages evaluated.

7 Conclusion and Future Work

We introduced MADAR-Turk, a set of 2,000 sentences from the MADAR corpus, translated from the Damascus dialect into Turkish. To the best of our knowledge, this is a first-of-a-kind human reference set for Dialectal Arabic-Turkish. Our study provides the first-ever benchmarking results on translation performance from Arabic dialects to Turkish. By producing this data set and making it publicly available, we hope to support ongoing efforts to improve translation and language access for individuals who speak Arabic dialects in the Turkish context.

In the future, we plan to continue expanding the human reference set to improve machine translation in the context of this resource-scarce language pair. We also plan to use this data set as part of developing improved methods for machine translation for low-resource language pairs.

Acknowledgments

We would like to express our sincere gratitude to Sara Almarmour and Ahad Hızıroğlu for their exceptional effort in translating the dataset used in this study. We are truly grateful for their assistance. We also thank the reviewers for their valuable feedback and comments.

References

Althobaiti, M. J. (2020). Automatic Arabic dialect identification systems for written texts:A survey. *CoRR*, abs/2009.12622.

Baali, M., El-Hajj, W., and Ali, A. (2022). Creating speech-to-speech corpus from dubbed series. ArXiv preprint arXiv:2203.03601.

Baniata, L. H., Park, S., Park, S.-B., et al. (2018). A neural machine translation model for arabic dialects that utilizes multitask learning (mtl). *Computational intelligence and neuroscience*, 2018.

Bouamor, H., Habash, N., Salameh, M., Zaghouani, W., Rambow, O., Abdulrahim, D., Obeid, O., Khalifa, S., Eryani, F., Erdmann, A., and Oflazer, K. (2018). The MADAR Arabic dialect corpus and lexicon. In *Proceedings of the Eleventh International Conference on Language Resources and Evaluation (LREC 2018)*, Miyazaki, Japan. European Language Resources Association (ELRA).

Çöltekin, Ç., Doğruöz, A. S., and Çetinoğlu, Ö. (2023). Resources for turkish natural language processing: A critical survey. *Language Resources and Evaluation*, 57(1):449–488.

Demir, S., El-Kahlout, İ. D., Unal, E., and Kaya, H. (2012). Turkish paraphrase corpus. In *Proceedings of the Eighth International Conference on Language Resources and Evaluation (LREC'12)*, pages 4087–4091, Istanbul, Turkey. European Language Resources Association (ELRA).

Durgar El-Kahlout, İ., Bektaş, E., Erdem, N. Ş., and Kaya, H. (2019). Translating between morphologically rich languages: An Arabic-to-Turkish machine translation system. In *Proceedings of the Fourth Arabic Natural Language Processing Workshop*, pages 158–166, Florence, Italy. Association for Computational Linguistics.

Gamal, D., Alfonse, M., Jiménez-Zafra, S. M., and Aref, M. (2022). Survey of arabic machine translation, methodologies, progress, and challenges. In *2022 2nd International Mobile, Intelligent, and Ubiquitous Computing Conference (MIUCC)*, pages 378–383. IEEE.

Habash, N., Soudi, A., and Buckwalter, T. (2007). On Arabic Transliteration. In van den Bosch, A. and Soudi, A., editors, *Arabic Computational Morphology: Knowledge-based and Empirical Methods*, pages 15–22. Springer, Netherlands.

Habash, N. Y. (2010). *Introduction to Arabic natural language processing*, volume 3. Morgan & Claypool Publishers.

Harrat, S., Meftouh, K., and Smaïli, K. (2017). Machine translation for arabic dialects (survey). *Information Processing & Management.*

Kchaou, S., Boujelbane, R., and Hadrich-Belguith, L. (2020). Parallel resources for Tunisian Arabic dialect translation. In *Proceedings of the Fifth Arabic Natural Language Processing Workshop*, pages 200–206, Barcelona, Spain (Online). Association for Computational Linguistics.

Köprü, S. (2009). AppTek Turkish-English machine translation system description for IWSLT 2009. In *Proceedings of the 6th International Workshop on Spoken Language Translation: Evaluation Campaign*, pages 19–23, Tokyo, Japan.

Kraidy, M. M. and Al-Ghazzi, O. (2013). Neo-ottoman cool: Turkish popular culture in the arab public sphere. *Popular Communication*, 11(1):17–29.

Lison, P. and Tiedemann, J. (2016). Opensubtitles2016: Extracting large parallel corpora from movie and tv subtitles. In *Proceedings of the Tenth International Conference on Language Resources and Evaluation (LREC 2016)*, pages 923–929. European Language Resources Association.

Meftouh, K., Harrat, S., Jamoussi, S., Abbas, M., and Smaili, K. (2015). Machine translation experiments on padic: A parallel arabic dialect corpus. In *Proceedings of the 29th Pacific Asia conference on language, information and computation*, pages 26–34.

Mermer, C., Kaya, H., and Doğan, M. U. (2010). The TÜBİTAK-UEKAE statistical machine translation system for IWSLT 2010. In *Proceedings of the 7th International Workshop on Spoken Language Translation: Evaluation Campaign*, pages 183–188, Paris, France.

Oflazer, K. (1993). Two-level description of Turkish morphology. In *Sixth Conference of the European Chapter of the Association for Computational Linguistics*, Utrecht, The Netherlands. Association for Computational Linguistics.

Papineni, K., Roukos, S., Ward, T., and Zhu, W.-J. (2002). BLEU: a Method for Automatic Evaluation of Machine Translation. In *Proceedings of the Conference of the Association for Computational Linguistics (ACL)*, pages 311–318, Philadelphia, Pennsylvania, USA.

Post, M. (2018). A call for clarity in reporting BLEU scores. In *Proceedings of the Third Conference on Machine Translation: Research Papers*, pages 186–191, Brussels, Belgium. Association for Computational Linguistics.

Qumar, S. M. U., Azim, M., and Quadri, S. (2023). Neural machine translation: A survey of methods used for low resource languages. In *2023 10th International Conference on Computing for Sustainable Global Development (INDIACom)*, pages 1640–1647. IEEE.

Salameh, M., Bouamor, H., and Habash, N. (2018). Fine-grained Arabic dialect identification.

Salloum, W. and Habash, N. (2011). Dialectal to Standard Arabic Paraphrasing to Improve Arabic-English Statistical Machine Translation. In *Proceedings of the First Workshop on Algorithms and Resources for Modelling of Dialects and Language Varieties*, pages 10–21, Edinburgh, Scotland.

Sghaier, M. A. and Zrigui, M. (2020). Rule-based machine translation from tunisian dialect to modern standard arabic. *Procedia Computer Science*, 176:310–319. Knowledge-Based and Intelligent Information and Engineering Systems: Proceedings of the 24th International Conference KES2020.

Sliwa, A., Ma, Y., Liu, R., Borad, N., Ziyaei, S., Ghobadi, M., Sabbah, F., and Aker, A. (2018). Multi-lingual argumentative corpora in english, turkish, greek, albanian, croatian, serbian, macedonian, bulgarian, romanian and arabic. In *Proceedings of the Eleventh International Conference on Language Resources and Evaluation (LREC 2018)*.

Takezawa, T., Kikui, G., Mizushima, M., and Sumita, E. (2007). Multilingual Spoken Language Corpus Development for Communication Research. *Computational Linguistics and Chinese Language Processing*, 12(3):303–324.

Zampieri, M., Nakov, P., Rosenthal, S., Atanasova, P., Karadzhov, G., Mubarak, H., Derczynski, L., Pitenis, Z., and Çağrı Çöltekin (2020). Semeval-2020 task 12: Multilingual offensive language identification in social media (offenseval 2020).

Zbib, R., Malchiodi, E., Devlin, J., Stallard, D., Matsoukas, S., Schwartz, R., Makhoul, J., Zaidan, O. F., and Callison-Burch, C. (2012). Machine translation of Arabic dialects. In *Proceedings of the 2012 Conference of the North American Chapter of the Association for Computational Linguistics: Human Language Technologies*, pages 49–59, Montréal, Canada. Association for Computational Linguistics.

Context-aware Neural Machine Translation for English-Japanese Business Scene Dialogues

Sumire Honda pu.sumirehonda@gmail.com
Computational Linguistics, University of Potsdam, Potsdam, Germany
Patrick Fernandes pfernand@cs.cmu.edu
Language Technologies Institute, Carnegie Mellon University, Pittsburgh, USA
Instituto de Telecomunicações, Instituto Superior Técnico, Lisbon, Portugal
Chrysoula Zerva chrysoula.zerva@tecnico.ulisboa.pt
Instituto de Telecomunicações, Instituto Superior Técnico, Lisbon, Portugal

Abstract

Despite the remarkable advancements in machine translation, the current sentence-level paradigm faces challenges when dealing with highly-contextual languages like Japanese. In this paper, we explore how *context-awareness* can improve the performance of the current Neural Machine Translation (NMT) models for *English-Japanese business dialogues* translation, and what kind of context provides meaningful information to improve translation. As business dialogue involves complex discourse phenomena but offers scarce training resources, we adapted a pretrained mBART model, finetuning on multi-sentence dialogue data, which allows us to experiment with different contexts. We investigate the impact of larger context sizes and propose novel context tokens encoding extra-sentential information, such as speaker turn and scene type. We make use of *Conditional Cross-Mutual Information* (CXMI) to explore how much of the context the model uses and generalise CXMI to study the impact of the *extra-sentential context*. Overall, we find that models leverage both preceding sentences and extra-sentential context (with CXMI increasing with context size) and we provide a more focused analysis on honorifics translation. Regarding translation quality, increased source-side context paired with scene and speaker information improves the model performance compared to previous work and our context-agnostic baselines, measured in BLEU and COMET metrics. [1]

1 Introduction

Traditionally NMT models such as Transformers (Maruf et al., 2021) approach the task of machine translation (MT) focusing on individual sentences without considering the surrounding information, such as previous utterances or underlying topics. As a result, the output often lacks discourse coherence and cohesion, which is problematic for MT applications such as chat translation systems (Farajian et al., 2020; Bawden et al., 2018). Thus, it is still an open research question to what degree these models can take advantage of contextual information to produce more accurate translations.

To answer this question, several context-aware NMT (Tiedemann and Scherrer, 2017; Voita et al., 2019; Maruf et al., 2019; Xu et al., 2021) studies have been conducted by adding

[1]Code available at: `https://github.com/su0315/discourse_context_mt`

Proceedings of Machine Translation Summit XIX, Vol. 1: Research Track, pages 272–285
September 4–8, 2023, Macau SAR, China.

surrounding sentences to the models and testing if it helps to capture better specific linguistic phenomena requiring context (e.g. coreference resolution). However, there is limited work on discourse or dialogue datasets, and most of it is focused on high-resource or Indo-European (IE) languages (Liu et al., 2021). Therefore, there is a need to investigate how well do the proposed approaches capture discourse phenomena in non-IE or low-resource languages.

This work aims to address the aforementioned gap by focusing on English-Japanese (En-Ja) translation for business dialogue scenarios in order to examine if current context-aware NMT models (Tiedemann and Scherrer, 2017) actually use the additional context, and what kind of context is useful regarding the translation of linguistic phenomena pertaining to Japanese discourse, such as honorifics. We specifically propose the use of novel extra-sentential information as additional context and show that it improves translation quality. Overall, the main contributions of this study are threefold: (1) We demonstrate that it is possible to adapt a (non-context-aware) large pretrained model (mBART; Liu et al. (2020); Tang et al. (2021)) to attend to context for business dialogue translation and propose an **improved attention mechanism** (CoAttMask) with significant performance gains for source-side context, even on small datasets; (2) we propose **novel extra-sentential information** elements such as speaker turn and scene type, to be used as additional source-side **context**; and (3) we compare the use of context between our context-aware models using CXMI (Fernandes et al., 2021), a mutual-information-based metric and perform a more focused analysis on the translation of **honorifics**.

2 Related Work

2.1 Context-aware MT

Context-aware MT lies between sentence-level MT and document-level MT, as the former assumes the translation of a single sentence from source to target language with no other accessible content, and the latter implies the translation of a sequence of sentences from a document, assuming access to the whole document. Context-aware MT lies close to the definition of document-level MT, as it requires access to context either in the form of preceding sentences or other type of information regarding the topic and setup of the text to be translated, that can aid in its translation.

Several methods using a transformer-based architecture (Vaswani et al., 2017) have been proposed for context-aware NMT, frequently categorised into single-encoder and multi-encoder models (Sugiyama and Yoshinaga, 2019). Single-encoder models concatenate the source sentence with (a) preceding sentence(s) as the contexts, with a special symbol to distinguish the context and the source or target in an encoder (Tiedemann and Scherrer, 2017). Multi-encoder models pass the preceding sentence(s) used as context through a separate encoder modifying the Transformer architecture (Voita et al., 2018; Tu et al., 2018). According to Sugiyama and Yoshinaga (2019), the observed performance gap between the two models is marginal, but the single-encoder models are relatively simpler architectures without modifying sequence-to-sequence transformers.

Apart from concatenating preceding sentences on the source-side, some works focus on the target-side context, i.e., show some benefits from attempting to decode multiple sequential sentences together (Su et al., 2019; Mino et al., 2020). Depending on the use-case, source-side, target-side, or a combination of contexts has proven beneficial (Agrawal et al., 2018; Chen et al., 2021; Fernandes et al., 2021). Additionally, some works focused more on context related to discourse phenomena, with Liang et al. (2021a) proposing the use of variational autoencoders to model dialogue phenomena such as speaker role as latent variables (Liang et al., 2021b). We examine here a simpler approach, that directly encodes such speaker and scene information and allows the model to use it as additional context. In more recent work, the impact of pretraining on larger out-of-domain (OOD) data has also been studied to aid in downstream MT tasks with limited resources (Voita et al., 2019; Liang et al., 2022).

For English-Japanese translation, there have been some context-aware NMT studies that used variations of single-encoder models in the news and dialogue domain (Sugiyama and Yoshinaga, 2019; Ri et al., 2021; Rikters et al., 2020). Specifically for dialogue, Rikters et al. (2020) experimented with context-aware MT that employs source-side factors on Ja-En (Japanese-English) and En-Ja (English-Japanese) discourse datasets. They propose to concatenate the preceding sentence(s) from the same document followed by a tag-token to separate the context from the original sentence and use binary token-level factors on top of this to signify whether a token belongs to the context or source sentence.

2.2 Japanese Honorifics in NMT

For into-Japanese MT, specific discourse phenomena such as honorifics constitute a core challenge when translating from languages that do not include such phenomena, like English (Hwang et al., 2021; Sennrich et al., 2016). Japanese honorifics differ to English because different levels of honorific speech are used to convey respect, deference, humility, formality, and social distance, using different types of verbal inflexions. Besides, the desired formality is decided depending on social status and context and may involve more extensive changes in utterances compared to other languages (Fukada and Asato, 2004). Feely et al. (2019) proposed formality-aware NMT, conditioning the model on a manually selected formality level to evaluate honorifics. They evaluate the formality level of the translated sentences using their formality classifier, showing improvements. Instead of explicitly selecting the formality level, we evaluate the impact of our context representations on the correct translation of honorifics, inspired by Fernandes et al. (2023).

3 Datasets

We use Business Scene Dialogue corpus (BSD) (Rikters et al., 2019) as the main dataset. Additionally, only to compare the performance in a certain setup with the main dataset, we also use AMI Meeting Parallel Corpus (AMI) (Rikters et al., 2020) as a supplemental dataset. They are both document-level parallel corpora consisting of different scenes (dialogue sequence scenarios) or meetings and include both out-of-English and into-English translations, of which we use the English-Japanese translation direction. We focus our analysis on the BSD dataset, as it contains more scenarios and extra-sentential information which we use as additional context.

In the main dataset BSD, each document consists of a business scene with a scene tag (face-to-face, phone call, general chatting, meeting, training, and presentation), and each sentence has speaker information that indicates who is speaking. Contents of BSD are originally written either in English or Japanese by bilingual scenario writers who are familiar with business scene conversations and then translated into the other language to create a parallel corpus.

As for AMI, the contents are translations to Japanese from 100 hours of meeting recordings in English. Since it originates from naturally occurring dialogue it contains shorter utterances than BSD, including multiple single-word sentences with filler and interjection words. The data split statistics for BSD and AMI are shown in Table 1. The domain of BSD and AMI is similar, however, AMI does not include scene information and the number of documents (scenarios) is smaller.

	BSD	Train	Dev	Test	**AMI**	Train	Dev	Test
Sentences		20,000	2051	2120		20,000	2000	2000
Scenarios		670	69	69		30	5	5

Table 1: Data split statistics for BSD and AMI dataset

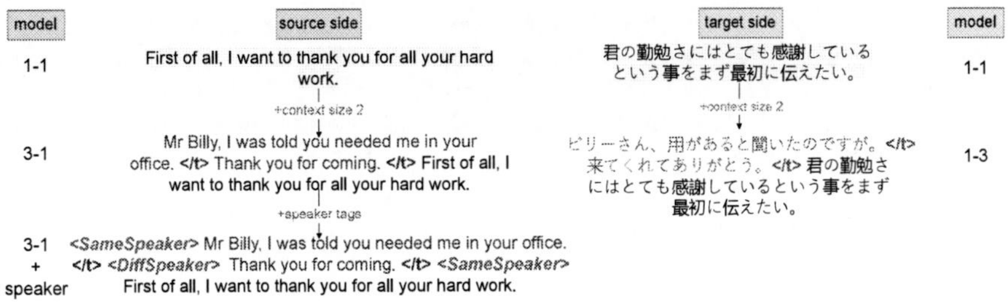

Figure 1: Context-extended inputs on source and target side. Coloured text corresponds to added context, **bold** signifies context separators and ***bold-italics*** speaker-related context tags.

4 Methodology

In this section, we analyse our context-aware NMT approach in a dialogue setup in two steps: firstly, we consider what type of information might be useful as context and how it should be encoded to generate useful input representations, and secondly, we discuss modifications in the original encoder-decoder architecture that facilitate learning to attend to context even when tuning on small datasets.

4.1 Encoding Context

We adapt the method of Tiedemann and Scherrer (2017) and experiment with encoding contexts both on source-side and target-side. Unlike Tiedemann and Scherrer (2017) who considers a single preceding sentence, we experiment with up to five preceding sentences, motivated by the findings of Fernandes et al. (2021); Castilho et al. (2020). We intercept a separator token `</t>` following every context sentence as shown in Figure 1.

We compare the context-aware models to the context-agnostic model, finetuned on our dataset. Henceforth, in this work, we will refer to the context-agnostic model as a 1-1 model, meaning that the model's source-side input is only 1 source sentence, and the target-side input is also only 1 target sentence during the training. For the context-aware models, this paper uses the naming convention of 2-1, 3-1, 4-1, and 5-1 for source context-aware models and 1-2, 1-3, 1-4, and 1-5 for target context-aware models. Note that in this work we use the gold data (human-generated translations of previous sentences) to represent the target context. Although the accessibility of target-side context data is limited in real-world translation tasks, there are some relevant use cases. For example, in a chatbot system where a human can edit the predicted translation in preceding sentences before the current sentence translation, the gold label of preceding target-side sentences is accessible.

Speaker Information: Delving deeper into the dialogue scenario, we also explore whether speaker-related information can provide useful context. In a dialogue dataset with multiple speakers, each speaker may utter a varying number of sentences per turn, and as such using a fixed context window implies potentially including multiple speakers in the context. Since aspects such as discourse style, politeness, honorifics in Japanese (Feely et al., 2019) or even topic distribution can be tied to specific speakers, knowing when a speaker changes in the context can be particularly informative. Speaker information has been used to improve user experience in simultaneous interpretation (Wang et al., 2022), but to the best of our knowledge, it has not been explored as a contextual feature for MT.

Hence, we consider two speaker types: (1) the one who utters the sentence to be translated – and who may have communicated more sentences in the context window – (same speaker) and (2) any other speaker(s) with utterances within the context window (different speaker), between which we do not differentiate. In other words, we only encode information about whether there has been **a change of speakers** within the context. We achieve this by concatenating either a special token <DiffSpeak> (Different speaker) or a <SameSpeak> (Same speaker) to each sentence (utterance) of the context as shown in the last row of Figure 1. This example also highlights the potential difference in speaker formality: the boss uses more casual expressions compared to the employee.

Scene Information: Similar to speaker information, we consider the information associated with the dialogue scene and its potential impact on the translation if used as context. We hence experiment with an additional special token representing the scene tag in BSD dataset. Following BSD dataset scene tags explained in §3, we prepared six additional tokens; <face-to-face conversation>, <phone call>, <general chatting>, <meeting>, <training>, and <presentation>. One of the tags is concatenated at the very beginning of each source input to signify the scene of the dialogue. For example, the scene tag of conversation in Figure 1 is <face-to-face conversation>, so the 2-1 model's input will be "<face-to-face conversation> *Thank you for coming.* </t> *First of all, I want to thank you for all your hard work.*". Such information could provide a useful signal regarding the speaker style, such as honorifics and formality, or even scene-specific terminology.

4.2 Context-aware Model Architecture

To encode context we rely on the Tiedemann and Scherrer (2017) approach, which we adapt to optimise performance for the BSD dataset. Due to the small size of available datasets for the business dialogue scenarios it is difficult to train a context-aware transformer architecture from scratch. Instead, we opt for fine-tuning a multi-lingual large pretrained model.

Baseline: All the models for En-Ja translation in this experiment are finetuned with mBART50 (Liu et al., 2020; Tang et al., 2021) with our proposed architectural modification for context-aware models described in the following paragraphs. We train all models until convergence on the validation set and use a `max_token_length` of size 128 for the baseline model, and 256 for the context-aware ones [2]. mBART is one of the state-of-the-art multilingual NMT models, with a Transformer-based architecture (Vaswani et al., 2017). It follows BART (Lewis et al., 2020) Seq2Seq pretraining scheme and is pretrained in 50 languages, including Japanese and English, using multilingual denoising auto-encoder strategy.

Target context-aware model: To consider context on the target side we essentially decode the target-context as shown in Figure 1 instead of a single sentence. To apply the Tiedemann and Scherrer (2017)'s context-aware approach to the target-side, the baseline model architecture was modified to prevent the loss function from accounting for mispredicted context and optimising instead only for the original target sentence.

Source context-aware model: Contrary to (Tiedemann and Scherrer, 2017; Bawden et al., 2018) we found that directly using the extended source inputs resulted in significantly lower performance for all context sizes, when compared to the original context-agnostic model (see Table 2). We attribute this inconsistency in our findings to the small size of the BSD dataset which might be insufficient for tuning a large pretrained model towards a context-aware setup.

To address this issue, a new architecture Source **Co**ntext **Att**ention **Mask** Model (CoAttMask) is proposed. In this approach, we pass the context-extended input to the encoder part of the model but mask the encoder outputs that correspond to the context when passed to the decoder. As shown in the yellow block in Figure 2, after the context-extended input is passed to the encoder, we mask the context-related part when passing the encoded input to the decoder to compute cross attention. As such, the context is leveraged to compute better input representations through self-attention in the transformer but does not further complicate the

[2]All hyperparameters are at: `https://github.com/su0315/discourse_context_mt`

decoding process. Table 2 shows that the CoAttMask model successfully outperformed the baseline model architecture (without CoAttMask).

5 Evaluation

5.1 Metrics for Overall Performance

To report the performance of the MT models, we report BLEU (Papineni et al., 2002) and COMET (Rei et al., 2020) scores. We use COMET as the primary metric since it has shown to be more efficient in assessing MT quality, better capturing valid synonyms and paraphrases (Smith et al., 2016) as well as discourse phenomena in longer text (Maruf et al., 2021).

5.2 Metric for Context Usage – CXMI –

Although COMET can capture more semantic features than BLEU, it is still difficult to assess how much context-aware NMT models actually use the additional contexts to improve predictions. To that end, we use Conditional Cross Mutual Information (CXMI) (Bugliarello et al., 2020; Fernandes et al., 2021). CXMI measures the entropy (information gain) of a context-agnostic machine translation model and a context-aware machine translation model. The CXMI formula can be seen in Eq. (1), where C signifies additional context, Y the target, X the source, H_{qMT_A} the entropy of a context-agnostic machine translation model, and H_{qMT_C} the entropy of context-aware machine translation model. Thus, a positive CXMI score indicates a useful contribution of context to predicting the correct target (increasing the predicted score of the correct target words). This can be estimated with Eq. (2), over a test dataset with N sentences, when $y^{(i)}$ is i^{th} target sentence and $x^{(i)}$ the ith source sentence in each document (Fernandes et al., 2021).

$$CXMI(C \to Y|X) = H_{qMT_A}(Y|X) - H_{qMT_C}(Y|X,C) \tag{1}$$

$$\approx -\frac{1}{N}\sum_{i=1}^{N} \log \frac{q_{MT_A}(y^{(i)}|x^{(i)})}{q_{MT_C}(y^{(i)}|x^{(i)},C^{(i)})} \tag{2}$$

In this experiment, CXMI is calculated between context-aware models with preceding sentence(s), speaker information, and scene information and each corresponding baseline model that lacks the respective context. To compute CXMI, a single model that can be tested with both context-agnostic inputs and context-extended inputs is required. We hence train the models with dynamic context size, such that during training the model can see anywhere from 0 to k context sentences (Fernandes et al., 2021).

5.3 *Honorifics P-CXMI*

To evaluate how much additional context is actually used to improve translation with respect to honorifics, we also compute P-CXMI, an extension of CXMI that allows us to measure the impact

Context Size	Baseline	CoAttMask
0	0.724	-
1	0.661	0.724
2	0.665	0.724
3	0.662	**0.727**
4	0.658	**0.727**

Table 2: Performance of CoAttMask model in COMET. **Bold** scores signify the performance improved 1-1 model

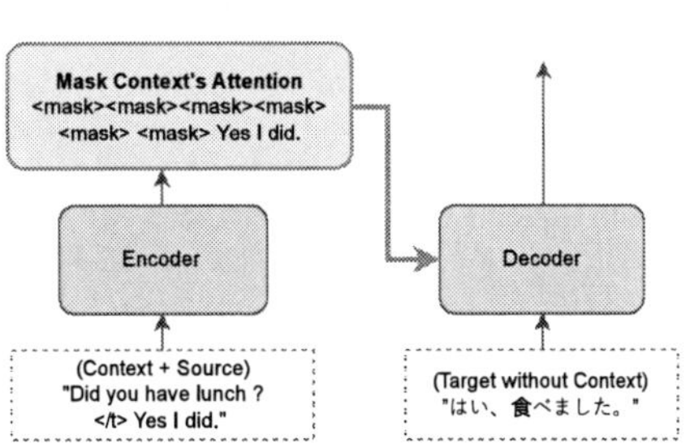

Figure 2: CoAttMask Architecture

of context on specific translations or words in a translation instead of over the whole corpus (Fernandes et al., 2023). We define *Honorifics P-CXMI* for token-level honorific expressions, which we calculate only for cases where the gold label is an honorific expression. While CXMI is calculated on the corpus level, averaged over the number of sentences, *Honorifics P-CXMI* is calculated for each honorific token and averaged over the number of the honorific tokens in the testset. As such, it is not directly comparable to the CXMI values (Fernandes et al., 2023).

Inspired by Japanese honorific word lists proposed in Fernandes et al. (2023) and Farajian et al. (2020), the following tokens are selected as the main honorific expressions (based on frequency of use and non-ambiguous functionality in the sentence) [3] "です (desu)", "でした (deshita)", "ます (masu)", "ました (mashita)", "ません (masen)", "ましょう (mashou)","でしょう (deshou)","ください (kudasai)","ございます (gozaimasu)","おります(orimasu)", "致します (itashimasu)", "ご覧 (goran)", "なります (narimasu)", "伺 (ukaga)", "頂く (itadaku)", "頂き (itadaki)", "頂いて (itadaite)", "下さい (kudasai)", "申し上げます (moushiagemasu)". Those tokens are mainly categorized as three types of honorifics: respectful (sonkeigo, 尊敬語), humble (kenjogo, 謙譲語), polite (teineigo, 丁寧語).

6 Experimental Results

We compare our work to previous approaches evaluated on BSD, namely this of Rikters et al. (2019) who combined multiple En-Ja datasets to train a model for En-Ja dialogue translation and Rikters et al. (2021) who also used a context-aware variant of Tiedemann and Scherrer (2017) combined with factors to encode dialogue context. Additionally, we compare with our context agnostic baseline. Table 3 shows that tuning mBART on the BSD data already outperformed the previous studies by more than 9 points in terms of BLEU, highlighting the impact of pretraining on large multilingual data. For the context-aware models, four types of models are compared for different context sizes; (1) Preceding Sentences Model (§6.1); (2) Speaker Information Model; 3) Scene Information Model; and (4) Speaker & Scene Information Model (§6.2).

6.1 Context-aware Models: Preceding Sentences

As seen in Table 3, as we increase the size of the context used, the CXMI score consistently increases indicating better leveraging of the context provided for the prediction of the target words. However, this increased attention to context is only reflected in small gains in the overall performance for specific context sizes. Specifically, for the source-side context only the models with larger context of 3 and 4 sentences improved for BLEU and COMET, as opposed to previous work that observes gains on single sentence context and often decreasing performance for larger context sizes (Tiedemann and Scherrer, 2017; Voita et al., 2018; Rikters et al., 2020; Ri et al., 2021; Nagata and Morishita, 2020). We hypothesize that this relates to our stronger baseline, and the specifics of the dialogue translation task: shorter utterances on average and multiple speakers which could lead to useful context lying further away in the dialogue history.

For the target-side context most variants either under-performed or performed similarly to the context-agnostic model. Indeed, while we notice an increased usage of context as we increase the target context size (see Figure 3), this does not seem to lead to improved performance. Further supported by the findings in §6.3 on the AMI dataset, it seems that using context on the source side is more beneficial for such small dialogue datasets and we focus our analysis and experiments more on the source side. However, it would be interesting to consider further adapting target-side context or explore pre-training on larger corpora as a way to mitigate this in future work (Liang et al., 2022; Su et al., 2019).

Focusing on CXMI as shown in Table 3 and Figure 3, our experiments corroborate the main findings of Fernandes et al. (2021). We can see that for both target and source the biggest jump

[3]Modified for the mBART50 tokenizer.

	Model (context size)	BLEU ↑	COMET ↑	CXMI ↑
Baselines	Rikters et al. (2019) (0)	13.53	-	-
	Rikters et al. (2021) (0)	12.93	-	-
	Rikters et al. (2021) (1)	14.52	-	-
	Ri et al. (2021) (1)	17.11	-	-
	1-1 (0)	26.04	0.725	0
Source context	2-1 (1)	25.87	0.724	0.32
	3-1 (2)	25.41	0.724	0.36
	4-1 (3)	**26.09**	**0.727**	0.38
	5-1 (4)	**26.09**	**0.727**	0.39
Target context	1-2 (1)	25.85	0.72	0.65
	1-3 (2)	**26.08**	0.702	0.76
	1-4 (3)	25.77	0.704	0.83
	1-5 (4)	24.96	0.71	0.88

Table 3: Score comparison between preceding sentences models and 1-1 model. **Bold** scores signify the performance improved baseline (BLEU, COMET)

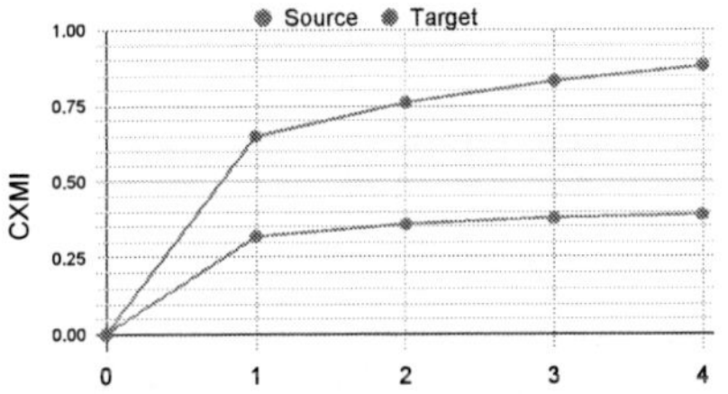

Figure 3: CXMI for source and target context-aware models in each context size

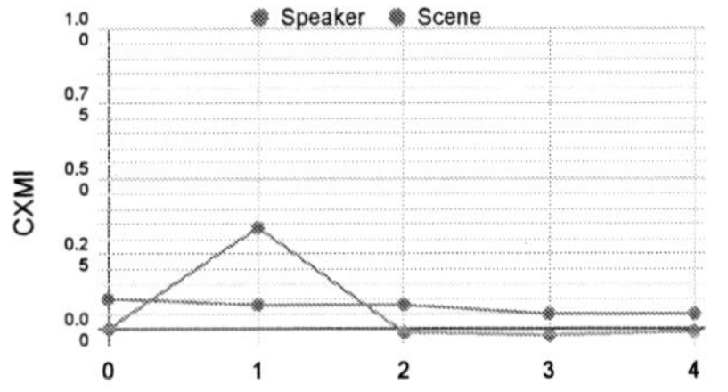

Figure 4: CXMI for speaker and scene model in each context size

in context usage is when we increase the context size from 0 to 1, but unlike Fernandes et al. (2021) we subsequently observe small but consistent increases for each context size (ascending).

Table 4 shows the result of *Honorifics CXMI* between source-side preceding sentences models and 1-1 model. With respect to the translation of honorifics, *Honorifics CXMI* scores for all context sizes show positive score, indicating that the provision of additional context helps the model to attribute higher density to the correct honorific translation. In other words, the model can leverage additional context to improve the prediction of honorific expressions.

Looking at the improved scores for each context size and honorific expression separately, we found that in all cases, it was the translation of the honorific token "伺 (ukaga)" that benefited the most. "伺 (ukaga)" is an honorific token that is a component of "伺う(ukagau)", a verb meaning "go" or "ask" in Japanese honorific expression. In particular, "伺う(ukagau)" is one of the humble (kenjogo, 謙譲語) expressions, and the humble is used in a business email or very formal speech (Liu and Kobayashi, 2022). These honorific expressions are used strictly by speakers to refer to themselves when they address a superior in business settings (Rahayu, 2013). As such, previous utterances that would reveal the relation of the speaker to the addressee are necessary to obtain the correct translation. Table 5 demonstrates the correction in the use of "伺 (ukaga)" when using a context window of size 2. The baseline model predicts "申します" instead of "伺 (ukaga)", leading to a semantically inappropriate translation meaning *"I'm (Takada)"* while with additional context it correctly predicts the "伺 (ukaga)" token.

	2-1	3-1	4-1	5-1
Honorifics CXMI ↑	0.05	0.07	0.06	0.06

Table 4: *Honorifics CXMI* between source-side preceding sentences models and 1-1 model

Source Sentence	Reference Sentence	1-1 Model Prediction	3-1 Model Prediction
I, Takada from Company I will <u>go</u> to your place at 5 o'clock in the afternoon tomorrow.	明日の午後５時に、わたくし、I社の高田が<u>伺います</u>。	明日の午後5時に、I社の高田と申します。	私、I社の高田が明日の午後5時に御社へお<u>伺いします</u>。

Table 5: Comparison between a context-agnostic model (1-1) and a context-aware model (3-1) in predicting honorific token "伺". (<u>Underlined</u> words signify that the 3-1 model improved the 1-1 model in predicting the correct token.)

6.2 Extra-sentential context:

For the following experiments, we focus on further enhancing the source-side context by adding scene and speaker information as discussed in §4.1. We first explore their usefulness separately, concatenating to the context either speaker tags or scene tags, as shown in Table 6 and Figure 4.

Speaker Information Models: When adding speaker information ("With Speaker", Table 6) the model seems to be obtaining slightly better performance on BLEU scores but not COMET. Additionally, with respect to the CXMI (see Figure 4), the speaker information seems to be useful for the model predictions only when using a single sentence of context. In other words, the model benefits only from knowing whether the previous utterance originated from the same speaker or not. While this finding is quite intuitive (a change of speaker could indicate a switch in style and formality) it is still unclear why this does not hold for larger context windows.

Note that while the benefits of using the speaker turn information seem limited, there are further aspects to be explored that were out of scope in this work. Specifically, given sufficient training data one could use a separate tag for each speaker in case of ≤ 2 speakers, either using abstract speaker tags, or even the speaker names, potentially helping toward pronoun translation.

	Preceding Sentences		With Speaker		With Scene		With Speaker & Scene	
Model (Context Size)	BLEU↑	COMET↑	BLEU↑	COMET↑	BLEU↑	COMET↑	BLEU↑	COMET↑
1-1 (0)	26.04	0.725	-	-	**26.19**	**0.726**	-	-
2-1 (1)	25.87	0.724	25.94	0.718	**26.18**	0.727	**26.18**	**0.730**
3-1 (2)	25.41	0.724	26.09	0.722	26.26	0.727	<u>**26.41**</u>	<u>**0.740**</u>
4-1 (3)	26.09	0.727	26.03	0.722	**26.27**	**0.731**	26.07	0.730
5-1 (4)	26.09	0.727	**26.39**	0.726	26.1	**0.728**	26.15	0.720

Table 6: Score comparison among preceding sentence models (w/o speaker and scene information), and models with addition of speaker and scene tags. **Bold** scores signify the best performance for each context size and <u>underlined</u> ones the best performance overall.

Scene Information Model: Unlike the speaker information, scene information can be added when the context size is zero too, since it does not need preceding sentences.

In contrast to speaker information models, "With Scene" models outperformed "Preceding Sentences" models for both BLEU and COMET on all context sizes, including when used with no additional context. Additionally, CXMI remains positive for all context sizes with a small decrease when the context size is larger. Hence, we can conclude that scene information helps towards the correct translation especially when limited context is available.

Speaker and Scene Model: We finally investigate if combining scene and speaker information can further improve performance. Indeed, for smaller context windows (speaker & scene models 2-1 and 3-1) outperformed their respective scene-only and speaker-only versions. Also, the 3-1 speaker & scene model obtained the best performance overall. Hence, while speaker information on its own did not improve performance, the combination of speaker information and scene information outperformed the models without them. This finding indicates that for specific scenarios (scenes), speaker turn might provide more useful signal. Indeed, depending on the scene the speakers may change more or less frequently signifying a necessary change of style (e.g. compare a presentation scene versus the phone call one). It would be interesting to further explore the relationship between the speaker switch frequency and scene type in the future.

6.3 Performance on the AMI dataset

To examine the context-aware model's performance on a similar dataset, we also tested the trained preceding sentences models using AMI dataset introduced in §3. Table 7 shows the performance of the context-aware models on increasing context size. Both context-aware and context-agnostic models obtain higher scores on the AMI dataset, compared to BSD. We notice however that we obtain small performance boosts for some context-aware combinations. More importantly, CXMI findings corroborate those on BSD: as the context size gets larger, CXMI increases both on source and target side. The similar CXMI trends reinforce our findings, hinting that they are not artifacts of a specific dataset, but rather a property of the language pair.

	Baseline	Source Side				Target Side			
	1-1	2-1	3-1	4-1	5-1	1-2	1-3	1-4	1-5
BLEU	32.46	**32.8**	32.12	**32.61**	32.05	32.13	31.22	31.29	**32.56**
COMET	0.852	**0.858**	0.846	**0.854**	0.846	0.848	0.833	0.833	0.85
CXMI	-	0.24	0.27	0.31	0.34	0.07	0.17	0.25	0.48

Table 7: Score comparison between preceding sentences models and 1-1 models with AMI dataset. **Bold** scores signify the performance improved over the baseline (BLEU, COMET).

7 Conclusion and Future Work

This paper explored to what degree encoded context can improve NMT performance for English-Japanese dialogue translation, and what kind of context provides useful information. With our proposed method, we were able to tune mBART on small dialogue datasets and obtain improved MT performance using context. We found that source-side context was more beneficial towards performance and that complementing our source-side context with scene and speaker-turn tags provided further performance improvements. We further analyse the impact of our proposed context-aware methods on the translations obtained, with a focus on translation of Japanese honorifics. In future work, we aim to further investigate context for dialogue translation, expanding to a multilingual setup, larger datasets, and additional extra-sentential context.

Acknowledgements

This work was supported by EU's Horizon Europe Research and Innovation Actions (UTTER, contract 101070631), by the Portuguese Recovery and Resilience Plan through project C645008882-00000055 (NextGenAI, Center for Responsible AI), and by Computational Linguistics, University of Potsdam, Germany.

References

Agrawal, R. R., Turchi, M., and Negri, M. (2018). Contextual handling in neural machine translation: Look behind, ahead and on both sides. In *Proceedings of the 21st Annual Conference of the European Association for Machine Translation*, pages 11–20.

Bawden, R., Sennrich, R., Birch, A., and Haddow, B. (2018). Evaluating discourse phenomena in neural machine translation. In *Proceedings of the 2018 Conference of the North American Chapter of the Association for Computational Linguistics: Human Language Technologies, Volume 1 (Long Papers)*, pages 1304–1313, New Orleans, Louisiana. Association for Computational Linguistics.

Bugliarello, E., Mielke, S. J., Anastasopoulos, A., Cotterell, R., and Okazaki, N. (2020). It's easier to translate out of English than into it: Measuring neural translation difficulty by cross-mutual information. In *Proceedings of the 58th Annual Meeting of the Association for Computational Linguistics*, pages 1640–1649, Online. Association for Computational Linguistics.

Castilho, S., Popović, M., and Way, A. (2020). On context span needed for machine translation evaluation. In *Proceedings of the Twelfth Language Resources and Evaluation Conference*, pages 3735–3742, Marseille, France. European Language Resources Association.

Chen, L., Li, J., Gong, Z., Duan, X., Chen, B., Luo, W., Zhang, M., and Zhou, G. (2021). Improving context-aware neural machine translation with source-side monolingual documents. In *IJCAI*, pages 3794–3800.

Farajian, M. A., Lopes, A. V., Martins, A. F. T., Maruf, S., and Haffari, G. (2020). Findings of the WMT 2020 shared task on chat translation. In *Proceedings of the Fifth Conference on Machine Translation*, pages 65–75, Online. Association for Computational Linguistics.

Feely, W., Hasler, E., and de Gispert, A. (2019). Controlling Japanese honorifics in English-to-Japanese neural machine translation. In *Proceedings of the 6th Workshop on Asian Translation*, pages 45–53, Hong Kong, China. Association for Computational Linguistics.

Fernandes, P., Yin, K., Martins, A. F., and Neubig, G. (2023). When does translation require context? a data-driven, multilingual exploration. *Proceedings of the 61st Annual Meeting of the Association for Computational Linguistics*.

Fernandes, P., Yin, K., Neubig, G., and Martins, A. F. T. (2021). Measuring and increasing context usage in context-aware machine translation. In *Proceedings of the 59th Annual Meeting of the Association for Computational Linguistics and the 11th International Joint Conference on Natural Language Processing (Volume 1: Long Papers)*, pages 6467–6478, Online. Association for Computational Linguistics.

Fukada, A. and Asato, N. (2004). Universal politeness theory: application to the use of japanese honorifics. *Journal of pragmatics*, 36(11):1991–2002.

Hwang, Y., Kim, Y., and Jung, K. (2021). Context-aware neural machine translation for korean honorific expressions. *Electronics*, 10(13):1589.

Lewis, M., Liu, Y., Goyal, N., Ghazvininejad, M., Mohamed, A., Levy, O., Stoyanov, V., and Zettlemoyer, L. (2020). BART: Denoising sequence-to-sequence pre-training for natural language generation, translation, and comprehension. In *Proceedings of the 58th Annual Meeting of the Association for Computational Linguistics*, pages 7871–7880, Online. Association for Computational Linguistics.

Liang, Y., Meng, F., Chen, Y., Xu, J., and Zhou, J. (2021a). Modeling bilingual conversational characteristics for neural chat translation. In *Proceedings of the 59th Annual Meeting of the Association for Computational Linguistics and the 11th International Joint Conference on Natural Language Processing (Volume 1: Long Papers)*, pages 5711–5724.

Liang, Y., Meng, F., Xu, J., Chen, Y., and Zhou, J. (2022). Scheduled multi-task learning for neural chat translation. In *Proceedings of the 60th Annual Meeting of the Association for Computational Linguistics (Volume 1: Long Papers)*, pages 4375–4388.

Liang, Y., Zhou, C., Meng, F., Xu, J., Chen, Y., Su, J., and Zhou, J. (2021b). Towards making the most of dialogue characteristics for neural chat translation. In *Proceedings of the 2021 Conference on Empirical Methods in Natural Language Processing*, pages 67–79.

Liu, M. and Kobayashi, I. (2022). Construction and validation of a Japanese honorific corpus based on systemic functional linguistics. In *Proceedings of the Workshop on Dataset Creation for Lower-Resourced Languages within the 13th Language Resources and Evaluation Conference*, pages 19–26, Marseille, France. European Language Resources Association.

Liu, S., Sun, Y., and Wang, L. (2021). Recent advances in dialogue machine translation. *Information*, 12(11):484.

Liu, Y., Gu, J., Goyal, N., Li, X., Edunov, S., Ghazvininejad, M., Lewis, M., and Zettlemoyer, L. (2020). Multilingual denoising pre-training for neural machine translation. *Transactions of the Association for Computational Linguistics*, 8:726–742.

Maruf, S., Martins, A. F., and Haffari, G. (2019). Selective attention for context-aware neural machine translation. In *Proceedings of the 2019 Conference of the North American Chapter of the Association for Computational Linguistics: Human Language Technologies, Volume 1 (Long and Short Papers)*, pages 3092–3102.

Maruf, S., Saleh, F., and Haffari, G. (2021). A survey on document-level neural machine translation: Methods and evaluation. *ACM Comput. Surv.*, 54(2).

Mino, H., Ito, H., Goto, I., Yamada, I., and Tokunaga, T. (2020). Effective use of target-side context for neural machine translation. In *Proceedings of the 28th International Conference on Computational Linguistics*, pages 4483–4494, Barcelona, Spain (Online). International Committee on Computational Linguistics.

Nagata, M. and Morishita, M. (2020). A test set for discourse translation from Japanese to English. In *Proceedings of the Twelfth Language Resources and Evaluation Conference*, pages 3704–3709, Marseille, France. European Language Resources Association.

Papineni, K., Roukos, S., Ward, T., and Zhu, W.-J. (2002). Bleu: a method for automatic evaluation of machine translation. In *Proceedings of the 40th Annual Meeting of the Association for Computational Linguistics*, pages 311–318, Philadelphia, Pennsylvania, USA. Association for Computational Linguistics.

Rahayu, E. T. (2013). The japanese keigo verbal marker. *Advances in Language and Literary Studies*, 4(2):104–111.

Rei, R., Stewart, C., Farinha, A. C., and Lavie, A. (2020). COMET: A neural framework for MT evaluation. In *Proceedings of the 2020 Conference on Empirical Methods in Natural Language Processing (EMNLP)*, pages 2685–2702, Online. Association for Computational Linguistics.

Ri, R., Nakazawa, T., and Tsuruoka, Y. (2021). Zero-pronoun data augmentation for Japanese-to-English translation. In *Proceedings of the 8th Workshop on Asian Translation (WAT2021)*, pages 117–123, Online. Association for Computational Linguistics.

Rikters, M., Ri, R., Li, T., and Nakazawa, T. (2019). Designing the business conversation corpus. In *Proceedings of the 6th Workshop on Asian Translation*, pages 54–61, Hong Kong, China. Association for Computational Linguistics.

Rikters, M., Ri, R., Li, T., and Nakazawa, T. (2020). Document-aligned japanese-english conversation parallel corpus. In *Proceedings of the Fifth Conference on Machine Translation*, pages 637–643, Online. Association for Computational Linguistics.

Rikters, M., Ri, R., Li, T., and Nakazawa, T. (2021). Japanese–english conversation parallel corpus for promoting context-aware machine translation research. *Journal of Natural Language Processing*, 28(2):380–403.

Sennrich, R., Haddow, B., and Birch, A. (2016). Controlling politeness in neural machine translation via side constraints. In *Proceedings of the 2016 Conference of the North American Chapter of the Association for Computational Linguistics: Human Language Technologies*, pages 35–40.

Smith, A., Hardmeier, C., and Tiedemann, J. (2016). Climbing mont BLEU: The strange world of reachable high-BLEU translations. In *Proceedings of the 19th Annual Conference of the European Association for Machine Translation*, pages 269–281.

Su, J., Zhang, X., Lin, Q., Qin, Y., Yao, J., and Liu, Y. (2019). Exploiting reverse target-side contexts for neural machine translation via asynchronous bidirectional decoding. *Artificial Intelligence*, 277:103168.

Sugiyama, A. and Yoshinaga, N. (2019). Data augmentation using back-translation for context-aware neural machine translation. In *Proceedings of the Fourth Workshop on Discourse in Machine Translation (DiscoMT 2019)*, pages 35–44, Hong Kong, China. Association for Computational Linguistics.

Tang, Y., Tran, C., Li, X., Chen, P.-J., Goyal, N., Chaudhary, V., Gu, J., and Fan, A. (2021). Multilingual translation from denoising pre-training. In *Findings of the Association for Computational Linguistics: ACL-IJCNLP 2021*, pages 3450–3466.

Tiedemann, J. and Scherrer, Y. (2017). Neural machine translation with extended context. In *Proceedings of the Third Workshop on Discourse in Machine Translation*, pages 82–92, Copenhagen, Denmark. Association for Computational Linguistics.

Tu, Z., Liu, Y., Shi, S., and Zhang, T. (2018). Learning to remember translation history with a continuous cache. *Transactions of the Association for Computational Linguistics*, 6:407–420.

Vaswani, A., Shazeer, N., Parmar, N., Uszkoreit, J., Jones, L., Gomez, A. N., Kaiser, L. u., and Polosukhin, I. (2017). Attention is all you need. In Guyon, I., Luxburg, U. V., Bengio, S., Wallach, H., Fergus, R., Vishwanathan, S., and Garnett, R., editors, *Advances in Neural Information Processing Systems*, volume 30. Curran Associates, Inc.

Voita, E., Sennrich, R., and Titov, I. (2019). When a good translation is wrong in context: Context-aware machine translation improves on deixis, ellipsis, and lexical cohesion. In *Proceedings of the 57th Annual Meeting of the Association for Computational Linguistics*, pages 1198–1212.

Voita, E., Serdyukov, P., Sennrich, R., and Titov, I. (2018). Context-aware neural machine translation learns anaphora resolution. In *Proceedings of the 56th Annual Meeting of the Association for Computational Linguistics (Volume 1: Long Papers)*, pages 1264–1274, Melbourne, Australia. Association for Computational Linguistics.

Wang, X., Utiyama, M., and Sumita, E. (2022). A multimodal simultaneous interpretation prototype: Who said what. In *Proceedings of the 15th Biennial Conference of the Association for Machine Translation in the Americas (Volume 2: Users and Providers Track and Government Track)*, pages 132–143, Orlando, USA. Association for Machine Translation in the Americas.

Xu, H., Xiong, D., Van Genabith, J., and Liu, Q. (2021). Efficient context-aware neural machine translation with layer-wise weighting and input-aware gating. In *Proceedings of the Twenty-Ninth International Conference on International Joint Conferences on Artificial Intelligence*, pages 3933–3940.

A Context-Aware Annotation Framework for Customer Support Live Chat Machine Translation

Miguel Menezes lmenezes@campus.ul.pt
INESC-ID, Unbabel, University of Lisbon, Lisbon, Portugal
Amin Farajian amin@unbabel.com
Unbabel, Lisbon, Portugal
Helena Moniz helena@unbabel.com
INESC-ID, Unbabel, University of Lisbon, Lisbon, Portugal
João Graça joao@unbabel.com
Unbabel, Lisbon, Portugal

Abstract

To measure context-aware machine translation (MT) systems quality, existing solutions have recommended human annotators to consider the full context of a document. In our work, we revised a well known Machine Translation quality assessment framework, Multidimensional Quality Metrics (MQM), (Lommel et al., 2014) by introducing a set of nine annotation categories that allows to map MT errors to source document contextual phenomenon, for simplicity sake we named such phenomena as **contextual triggers**.

Our analysis shows that the adapted categories set enhanced MQM's potential for MT error identification, being able to cover up to 61% more errors, when compared to traditional non-context core MQM's application. Subsequently, we analysed the severity of these MT "contextual errors", showing that the majority fall under the critical and major levels, further indicating the impact of such errors. Finally, we measured the ability of existing evaluation metrics in detecting the proposed MT "contextual errors". The results have shown that current state-of-the-art metrics fall short in detecting MT errors that are caused by **contextual triggers** on the source document side. With the work developed, we hope to understand how impactful context is for enhancing quality within a MT workflow and draw attention to future integration of the proposed contextual annotation framework into current MQM's core typology.

Keywords

Context-aware error typologies; Machine Translation; Customer Support; Test-Suites; Translation Quality Workflows and Automation; Automatic metrics.

1 Introduction

In past decades, the staggering growth in demand for shared knowledge has led to an increase in translation requests, exceeding human translators' work capacity. In order to accommodate to such request, many enterprises are now integrating MT systems to their workflow that allegedly provide human-like translations in record time. However, despite often claims of

Proceedings of Machine Translation Summit XIX, Vol. 1: Research Track, pages 286–297
September 4–8, 2023, Macau SAR, China.

human-parity (Xiong et al., 2017), there are plenty of work in the field (Wan et al., 2022; Singh and Singh, 2022) that dispel such allegations, even showing that, under certain circumstances, state-of-the art conventional approaches under-perform and are unable to deal with language nuances, translating words instead of "meanings". Aware of Neural Machine Translation (NMT) limitations, in the last few years, new approaches have been devised to leverage document context for finer-grained MT outputs. Despite sharing similar believes, we suspect that researchers have only now begun to scratch the surface on such complex subject matter, especially when it is not yet clear that context-aware MT systems are indeed able to account for context within a document (Yin et al., 2021). Yet, there is scarce research into document-level MT quality assessment (QA) metrics for more reliable evaluations (Castilho et al., 2020, 2021). Taking into account the present scenario, we propose a framework that deals strictly with context issues instead of relying on more traditional QA metrics regarded as less suitable for document-level NMT assessment. To properly understand the weight of context within a document, we used the previously MQM annotated WMT-Chat-task EN-PT/BR dataset [1], from live chat customer support interactions, creating the perfect test environment for our research, that strives for more equitable and accurate QA MT metrics.

2 State-of-the-Art

It is widely acknowledged that document context is critical for resolving a wide range of translation problems, nevertheless, the sentence-based translation approach remains the most salient characteristic of the prevailing MT paradigm (Post and Junczys-Dowmunt, 2023). This method, in which documents are dismembered in self contained elements (independent sentences) for better translation management, fails in several accounts. First off, the MT system may translate words or phrases based solely on their individual usage, rather than considering their placement in the document as a whole, and second, it largely fails to maintain intersentential relationships within a document (Bawden, 2018). Such behavioral pattern ends up compromising essential textual parameters: cohesion and coherence, giving rise to a warped source text representation. Realizing the limitations of sentence-level MT, in recent years, new proposals have surfaced, encouraging a paradigm shift. Context aware MT models have started to be implemented and designed to leverage contextual information in a document (Zhang et al., 2018; Lopes et al., 2020; Yin et al., 2021), exposing the importance of context in improving MT quality (Nayak et al., 2022), leading to new challenges: how to evaluate the quality of contextual MT models and how to identify if contextual MT models are actually using context?

2.1 Source Contextual Phenomena and Contextual MT Errors Identification.

It can be challenging to identify context-dependent sentences in a document, as well as to detect MT errors caused by a lack of intersentential context in the source document. The difficulty lies in the fact that the definition of context can be problematic as well as circumscribing what is context in a document. Moreover, MT errors that are linked to contextual phenomenon in a source document are often neglected, since, at first sight, they can only be recognized when juxtaposing source and target documents. This comes to show that, to properly assess quality in an MT output, it is essential to acknowledge the importance of the source document, and realize that a source sentence has the potential to bring about a certain set of MT errors that can be mapped to contextual phenomena. We have defined this phenomena as **contextual triggers**, a phenomenon previously observed by Navrátil et al. (2012), when dealing with methods for syntactic source reordering developed for EN-DE, and whose concept support the core aspect for the devised context MT error annotation.

[1] https://github.com/WMT-Chat-task/data-and-baselines

2.2 Context-Aware Typologies

Contextual mechanisms used for developing state-of-the-art context-aware MT models or used for MT QA have been repeatedly explored and studied, with most researchers focusing on the same well-defined contextual categories subset i) anaphoric pronouns, ii) gender and number agreement, iii) lexical ambiguity, iv) ellipsis, v) terminology, vi) discourse connectives, and vii) deixis (Yin et al., 2021; Post and Junczys-Dowmunt, 2023; Castilho et al., 2021). The aforementioned set of contextual categories make up the general framework of analysed issues widely investigated in the literature (Voita et al., 2019; Yin et al., 2021; Lopes et al., 2020). For our research, we aim at analysing and applying these canonical contextual mechanisms that have been continuously addressed for document-level NMT, furthermore, and since previous categories frameworks were developed with generic domains in mind, thus not completely covering the contextual nuances for user generated content in spontaneous dialogues, we have introduce a set of less explored categories that are particularly relevant for the analysed dataset domain, **live chat customer support solutions**. The categories are: Discourse Markers, Greetings, Multiword-Expressions, Named Entities and Register. In tables 2 and 3, we present the complete description of our annotation framework, coupled with examples. Table 2 reflects the mainstream categories accounted for on document-level QA. Table 3, on the other-hand, shows our set of complementary context-categories that can further enhance the identification of **contextual triggers**.

2.3 Metrics for Context Evaluation

Typologies on context are scarce, not suitable for spontaneous dialogues and user generated content. The same applies to context evaluation metrics, that are affected by lack of context examples. One can then assume that insufficient studies on the context evaluation metrics as well as insufficient training data for contextual MT evaluation have detrimental consequences in MT QA results. This section will cover QA in general and how it has been applied to context.

Currently, MT outputs quality evaluation is performed relying on both automatic evaluation metrics, e.g., COMET (Rei et al., 2020), chrF (Popović, 2015), SacreBLEU (Post, 2018) as well as on human judgments, using, for example, the MQM Framework Typology (Lommel et al., 2014). MQM with its hierarchic error typology framework, easily adapted by users according to particular needs with a total of 100 issue types with various levels of granularity, has not been created to have in mind contextual MT errors, which does not prevent it from being applied to QA of context-aware MT models (Freitag et al., 2021, 2022), leading to unreliable results. We regard current MQM framework as unfit to fully deal with contextual nuances, creating potential biases in document-level NMT QA results.

Moreover, concerning automatic document-level NMT QA, the current practice is to resort to existing pretrained models e.g., BERTScore (Zhang et al., 2020) and COMET (Rei et al., 2020) by simply providing several sentences of context to the pretrained model, allowing the pretrained model to use surrounding context. We hypothesize that this technique of leveraging existing sentence-level metrics might not be conducive to robust enough models capable of covering the complete spectrum of contextual errors.

3 Multilingual Virtual Agents for Customer Service (MAIA) Corpus

For our research, we used the MAIA corpus (Farinha et al., 2022), made available for the WMT 2022 Shared Task on Chat Translation, containing genuine bilingual customer support interaction (chat conversation between customer support agents and customers). Such content is planned on-the-fly and written on-line, usually coupled with abbreviations, emoticons, idiomatic expressions and grammatical and typographical errors. We took advantage of this ideal test environment to i) understand how context is conveyed in a document, ii) pinpoint lexical structures linked to contextual information, iii) create an annotation framework that allows to measure context in a document, with the needed plasticity to be added to more traditional quality measure metrics iv) give the first steps on creating a multilingual test suite with contextual annotations for real customer support data.

Maia Corpus	EN-PT/BR
Number of conversations	28
Number of agent segments	509
Number of customer segments	609
Number of total (customer and agent) segments	1168

Table 1: Statistics of the dataset used for context annotation.

4 Contextual Annotation Framework.

Recent context-aware MT models progress calls for developing new evaluation solutions that cover contextual errors. Our framework allows to identify and classify contextual discourse structures linked to MT errors. This section will initially describe the most frequently addressed contextual categories in the literature, followed by our new set of contextual categories found to be relevant for the customer support live chat domain data. Note that the framework was created with the possibility to be accustomed to other domains.

4.1 Building a Context-Aware Typology

To devise a contextual framework, we built on previous works, such as the Document-Level Machine Translation Evaluation (DELA) by Castilho et al. (2021) that introduces several meaningful contextual related issues, *e.g.*, Agreement; Ellipsis; Gender Agreement; Lexical Ambiguity; Terminology; and Number. Using a corpora-based analyses approach of an ecological dataset, we aimed to explore the standard categories proposed in the literature. Consequently, we extended our analysis to consider less explored contextual categories, such as, **Discourse Markers, Greetings, Multiword Expressions, Named Entities and Register**, which have a significant impact in the chat domain. The identification of the contextual issues entailed an annotation step where the **contextual triggers** were identified and categorized. To the best of our knowledge, our research is the first to focus on contextual issues for MT for the customer support chat domain. Next, we will introduce all the contextual categories that compose our framework, starting with the more explored-canonical categories, followed by the new proposed categories, see Tables 2 and 3.

4.2 The Annotation Process

The annotation process was performed by a Portuguese annotator with a background in translation and with previous experience in contextual issues annotation. Concerning the test sets, we used the official submissions of the WMT-Chat-2022 shared task for the EN-PT/BR language pairs, translated by two MT systems: Baseline and Unbabel-IST. Note that, the dataset used came already with a prior MQM non-contextual annotation performed for the WMT 2022 Chat Shared Task. Both MT systems are based on the large multilingual pre-trained models. The Baseline model, uses a vanilla M2M-100 model, Fan et al. (2021), while the Unbabel-IST model uses a fine-tuned version of mBART50, Liu et al. (2020). For the fine-tuning data, it uses the in-domain parallel validation set provided by the shared task organizers and a generic parallel corpus. For our analysis, only the sentences requiring context with a MT issue/error have been considered. For those, the annotator performed as follows: i) identified the **contextual trigger** that caused the MT error, ii) categorized it, providing a translation, iii) identified

Category	Example and Explanation
Agreement: Targets gender and number agreements.	*Source:* Por quanto tempo vou poder ficar afastada? *Target:* How long will I be able to stay away? *Source:* While your account is on pause, you will not be billed for a new month subscription. *Target:* Enquanto sua conta estiver em pausa, você não será cobrado/a para um novo mês de assinatura.
	Explanation: Gender agreement: masculine cobrado/ feminine cobrada beyond the sentence level. In the example, only by accessing previous information (context afastada) we are able to understand that we need the feminine translation cobrado/a.
Lexical ambiguity: Refers to the polysemy of words in distinct contexts.	*Source:* Thanks so much for your interest in partnering with us *Target:* Obrigado por seu interesse em colaborar connosco! *Source:* Someone on our Corporate team will reach out *Target:* Alguém em nossa equipe corporativa chegará. (Glosa: will arrive).
	Explanation: The translation of "reach out" requires information that lies beyond the sentence, assuming a complete different meaning from arriving. Correct Translation: Alguém em nossa equipe corporativa "**entrará em contacto**". Glosa: will contact you
Ellipsis: Refers to omission of word(s) within a sentence. Syntactically, the linguistic information is recovered.	*Source:* It looks like this inquiry requires further investigation, and we'll need to log into a few different systems. *Target:* Parece que esta pesquisa requer mais investigação e precisaremos de entrar em alguns sistemas diferentes. *Source:* Quando [-] forem consultar a principal questão é sobre os créditos não expirarem mais *Target:* When they go to consult, the main question is about the credits do not expire more
	Explanation: the elliptical pronoun **[-]**, wrongly translated as **they**, is only recovered accessing previous sentences: "**we**'ll need to log into a few different systems". Correct translation: When **you** go to consult (...).
Terminology: Targets terms that constitute a set of vocabulary within a specialized field of knowledge.	*Source:* On your phone or tablet, open the #PRS_ORG# app. *Target:* No seu telefone ou tablet, abra a aplicação #PRS_ORG# . *Source:* At the top right, tap More. *Target:* Na parte superior direita, clique em Mais. *Source:* Tap history. *Target:* Tap história.
	Explanation: Contextually, the word "history" is a term and should be translated as **histórico**. In this case, the MT does not recognizes "history" as a term.

Table 2: Conventionally context categories used for annotation.

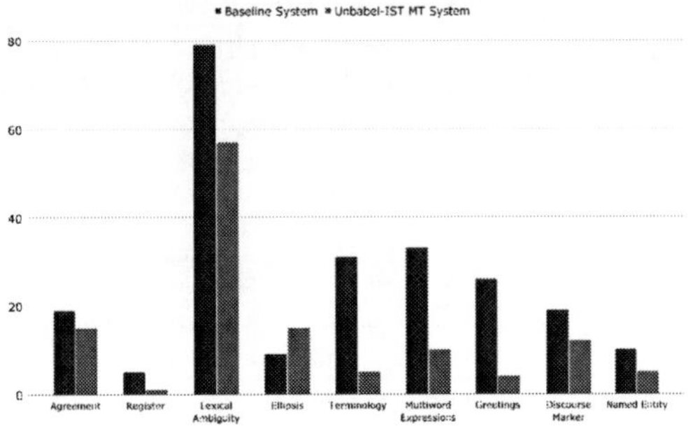

Figure 1: Contextual categories error distribution for each MT model

the turn that serves as anchor to disambiguate the issue, and iv) attributed a level of severity for each issue.

5 Results

In this section we analysed the errors and characterized them according to the Context Aware Typologies Framework that we developed, providing an error and severity analysis, whilst, simultaneously, contrasting our annotation with the MQM's non-contextual annotation performed previously for the WMT 2002 Chat Shared Task.

5.1 Context Dependent Segments

From the dataset with 1168 sentences, we identified 197 sentences (17% of the dataset) with MT errors that can be mapped to **contextual triggers** for the Baseline model, and 123 sentences for the Unbabel-IST model (10% of the dataset).

5.2 Contextual Categories Distribution

Figure 1 displays the contextual categories distribution linked to the MT errors in our dataset. As seen in Figure 1, the most prevalent MT errors are induced by *Lexical Ambiguities* in the source document, 76 MT errors for the baseline MT system and 56 MT errors for the Unbabel-IST model. Taking into account the overall MT errors linked to our contextual categories per MT model, we observe that the presence of lexical ambiguities in the source document accounts for 34% of the overall contextual MT errors for the baseline MT system, and 45.50% for the Unbabel-IST model. Note that, since the percentages were calculated taking into account the MT overall contextual errors outputs **for each MT model** (the baseline MT system outputted 231 contextual errors, the Unbabel-IST model 124), the percentage values reflect the weight that each category has within those subsets (the overall contextual errors for each system). Concerning the category *Terminology*, the Baseline showed 31 MT errors, accounting 13% of the overall MT contextual error, and 5 MT errors for the Unbabel-IST system, accounting 4% of the overall MT contextual error. This difference can be explained by the fact that the second model was fine-tuned with the in-domain data and was specialized to this domain, and not necessarily by its ability in handling the contextual terminology errors.

For the category *Multiword Expressions*, the Baseline model reports 33 MT errors, 14% of the total contextual errors for this model, whilst the Unbabel-IST system reports, 10 MT errors, accounting 9%. *Agreement* is a very present error category within the analysed dataset. This category is particularly relevant, since it deals with gender agreement, and it is considered a

Category	Example and Explanation
Discourse Markers: Fillers or other words that are used to indicate dialogue interactions. Different discourse markers convey different meanings for the fluidity of a dialogue.	*Source:* Thank you please try the following steps: *Target:* Obrigado, por favor, tente os seguintes passos: *Source:* Delete cache, restart your device *Target:* Delete cache, reiniciar o seu dispositivo *Source:* Tá bom *Target:* It is good *Explanation:* The expression "Tá bom" should have been translated as an acknowledgment discourse marker, such as "**ok**", instead it is literally translated as "it is good".
Greetings: Conventionalized expressions used as part of our daily lives when greeting, well-wishing and leaving a conversation. These structures are dependent on the degree of politeness and cultural awareness.	*Source:* Bom dia. *Target:* Good day. *Source:* Gostaria de saber melhor como funciona os créditos. *Target:* I would like to know better how the credits work. *Explanation:* The expression "Bom dia", can be translated in EN as "Good day" meaning "it is a good day", but it should have been translated as a greeting "Good morning", "Hello". Since greetings are culturally and language dependent, they are are negatively influenced when contextual information is scarce.
Multiword-expressions: Compounded units, e.g., phrasal-verbs, they act as a single unit. These structures can either be solved within a sentence or require contextual information to be disambiguate.	*Source:* Cancelei meu plano mas mesmo assim me cobraram. *Target:* I cancelled my plan but still they charged me. *Source:* Thank you for reaching #PRS_ORG#! *Target:* Obrigado por entrar em contacto com #PRS_ORG#! *Source:* Let me check on that for you. *Target:* Deixe-me verificar isso para você. *Source:* Please hold while I pull up your account. *Target:* Por favor, mantenha enquanto eu retirei sua conta. *Explanation:* The Multiword-expression "pull up" was translated as "retirar" (to withdraw), but in the specific context the correct translation would be: enquanto **acesso** à tua conta (glosa: whilst I access you account).
Named Entity (NE): Linguistic structures which refers to, e.g., a book title , a person's name, an address, a credit card number.	*Source:* Boa tarde, não consigo comprar livros com nenhum cartão de crédito apenas com cartão de oferta. *Target:* Good afternoon, I can't buy books with no credit card only with offer card. *Source:* O último foi hoje, à pouco e chama-se A única mulher. *Target:* The last was today, shortly, and it is called the only woman. *Explanation:* The NE, a book title ("A única mulher"), is not identified within the sentence and should not have been translated, since the user is looking for the book in Portuguese, but the original book´s name was translated.
Register: Degrees of politeness where speakers adapt their discourse according to the audience.	*Source:* How can I help you today? *Target:* Como posso te ajudar hoje? *Explanation:* In the example, "help you / **ajudar-te**" is not appropriate, since it is using a very informal second person singular. The correct translation would be: Como posso **ajudá-lo/la**?, a third person singular.

Table 3: New set of contextual categories triggers.

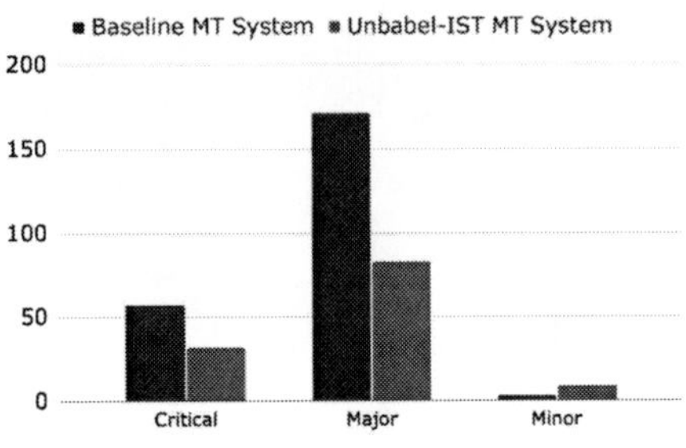

Figure 2: Contextual error severities for each MT model

critical error. For this case, the Baseline shows 19 gender agreement MT errors, about 8% of the MT contextual errors for this model, whilst the Unbabel-IST model shows 15 MT gender agreement errors, about 12% of the complete set of MT contextual errors, All things considered, although we see that the Unbabel-IST model produces significantly fewer contextual errors, this can be simply due to the domain-adaptation effect and not necessarily in its capability to deal with the contextual phenomena.

5.3 Categories (Not) Covered by the Core MQM Framework

In our research, we have noticed that core MQM typology used for the WMT-2022 chat shared task moderately identifies some contextual issues, in part because annotators were instructed to, if possible, account for some dependencies within the dataset. Nevertheless, 36.1%, for the Baseline and 42% for Unbabel-IST of the contextual issues annotated by the Context-Aware Typology were not considered during the WMT-2022 chat shared task MQM annotation. Concerning the contextual issues identified by the MQM, they were tagged as **Mistranslations** in most cases, without specifying the underlying cause, e.g., an absence of context at a sentence level. As such, **Multiword Expressions, Discourse Markers, Lexical Ambiguities and Greeting** errors, according to MQM analysis results, were annotated as **Mistranslations**. Moreover, these errors fall for the most part within the critical and major error severity, compromising customer/agent communication fluidity.

5.4 Contextual Categories Distribution Severities

As Figure 2 displays, most contextual issues fall under the severity Critical, 24.6% for the Baseline, 25.8% for the Unbabel-IST MT model; and Major, 74% for the Baseline, 66% for the Unbabel-IST MT model. These errors severely compromise understanding and communication, impacting customer support reliability. Concerning the Minor severity, those values present strictly residual numbers, reinforcing the importance of contextual issues.

5.5 Contextual Error Severities by Categories and MT Model

As seen from the charts in Figure 3, there is a considerable difference between models concerning the total of contextual issues. Nevertheless, there are similar patterns regarding some categories. According to the tables, lexical ambiguity issues, considered a Major error, are common and make a considerable amount of the issues for both models. The category *Agreement* shows a sizable value for both models, being considered for most cases a Critical issue. *Terminology*, *Multiword Expressions* and *Discourse Markers* are categories particularly interesting to observe, due to their disparity between the baseline and Unbabel-IST model. This difference validates the hypothesis that models trained with in-domain datasets are more robust,

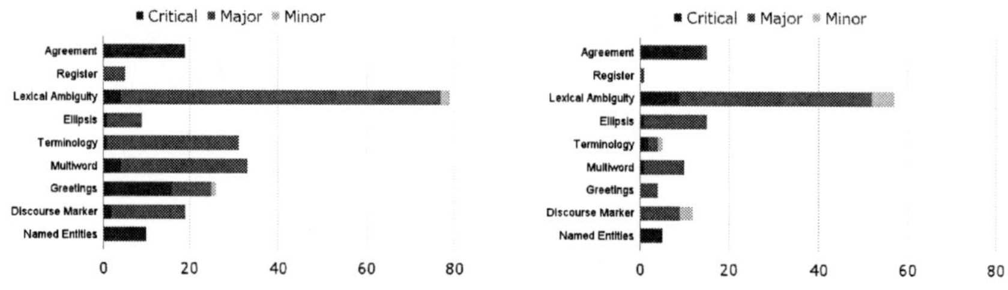

(a) baseline

(b) Unbabel-IST

Figure 3: Distribution of error categories and their severities of a) the baseline MT system, and b) the Unbabel-IST system.

outweighing some contextual issues. Nevertheless, despite showing significant quality output improvements, robust models still fall short in detecting contextual nuances, substantiating, and validating future research in document-level MT models.

6 Automatic Metrics of MT Evaluation and Contextual Errors

Measuring the ability of the current state-of-the-art MT evaluation metrics in detecting the contextual errors is the first crucial step for developing new automated quality evaluation solutions for the MT systems using our proposed typology. Hence, we measured the correlation of these metrics with the MQM annotations of the MAIA test-set. To have a reliable term of comparison, in addition to the contextual annotations, we also measured the correlation of the metrics on the original MQM annotations based on the existing framework.

For the metrics, we used COMET (Rei et al., 2020) that is trained to predict the human translation quality judgments of the MT outputs. It evaluates the translations in isolation without considering their contexts at all. Very recently, Vernikos et al. (2022) introduced an extension of this metric (i.e., Doc-COMET) that incorporates context when evaluating the MT outputs. Vernikos et al. (2022) show that Doc-COMET obtains a higher system-level Pearson correlation with human judgments compared to its original sentence-level counterpart on TED talks and News domains for En-DE, En-RU, and ZH-EN language pairs.

Since the system-level analysis does not provide detailed insights on the ability of the metrics in capturing the contextual errors, we focused our analysis on the sentence-level correlation of the metrics with human judgments on the MAIA dataset. Given that our framework is tailored for the contextual errors only, for our analysis we concentrated on the samples that contain at least one contextual error in the output of the MT system. We also made sure that errors that do not have a contextual background have no reflection on the automatic metrics results. To this aim, and to not lose the context, we first obtained the scores of all the sentences of the test-set with each metric, and then used only the segments with contextual errors, 197 sentences, for the baseline model, and 123 sentences for the Unbabel-IST model.

Table 4 shows the sentence-level Pearson correlations of the two metrics for both MT systems. As the results suggest, both COMET and Doc-COMET have a lower correlation with the MQM scores of our annotation framework. This, however, is expected mainly because the COMET models were trained on the data annotated with the existing MQM annotation framework. Moreover, we clearly see that there is no reliable correlation between DocCOMET and the human judgments of both frameworks on the sentence level. This can be justified by the fact that the COMET models were not trained on any document-level annotations, hence they

Metric	Baseline	Unbabel-IST
Correlation with the existing error annotation framework		
COMET	0.35	0.35
Doc-COMET	0.13	0.07
Correlation with our contextual error annotation framework		
COMET	0.25	0.06
Doc-COMET	-0.07	-0.19

Table 4: Sentence-level Pearson correlation of COMET and Doc- COMET metrics with MQM annotations on a subset of the test-set that contains at least one contextual error. The annotations are done with the existing framework and our new contextual errors framework.

cannot detect contextual errors accurately.
These findings show that in order to measure the quality of the MT systems on the contextual errors, new datasets, metrics and tools need to be developed that not only cover the existing sentence-level errors, but also can cover the contextual errors that none of the current resources cover, and usually are categorized as severe errors (i.e., either critical or major).

7 Conclusion

With our research, we have shown the significance of context for the MT. Similarly, we exposed the inadequacy in conventional QA metrics for reliable qualitative assessments, since current QA models and frameworks show to be weak and deceptive as they have not been created to have in mind contextual MT errors. We have displayed first attempts in overcoming QA models and frameworks shortcomings in the form of contextual errors test-suites, but also those are scarce in terms of contextual typologies coverage and focus on common analysed domains. We instead propose an alternative contextual framework for document level MT QA, covering a relatively untapped domain in terms of contextual errors analysis. Our framework shows significant gains of an average of 61% more contextual errors coverage than more conventional QA metrics, highlighting the fact that most of such contextual errors are deemed as critical and major, thus strengthening our beliefs that the field of QA for context aware MT is far from being effectively dealt with, on the one hand, and that contextual error severely compromise MT outputs, on the other hand.

8 Future Work

We are well aware of several research limitations in our work, as such, we intend to address these in future work. We aim to apply our framework to different domains and different language pairs, for that, we plan to resort to a team of expert annotators, allowing us to extensively put to test and validate our framework.

Acknowledgments

This work was partially supported by national funds through Fundação para a Ciência e a Tecnologia (FCT), under project UIDB/50021/2020; by the Portuguese Recovery and Resilience Plan through project C645008882-00000055, Center for Responsible AI; by the project Multilingual AI Agents Assistants (MAIA), contract number 045909. This work was also supported by the FCT PhD grant with the reference 2022.12091.BD.

References

Bawden, R. (2018). *Going beyond the sentence: Contextual machine translation of dialogue*. PhD thesis, Université Paris-Saclay (ComUE).

Castilho, S., Cavalheiro Camargo, J. L., Menezes, M., and Way, A. (2021). DELA corpus - a document-level corpus annotated with context-related issues. In *Proc. of the Sixth Conference of WMT*, pages 566–577.

Castilho, S., Popović, M., and Way, A. (2020). On context span needed for machine translation evaluation. In *Proc. of the Twelfth LREC*, pages 3735–3742, Marseille, France. European Language Resources Association.

Fan, A., Bhosale, S., Schwenk, H., Ma, Z., El-Kishky, A., Goyal, S., Baines, M., Celebi, O., Wenzek, G., Chaudhary, V., Goyal, N., Birch, T., Liptchinsky, V., Edunov, S., Grave, E., Auli, M., and Joulin, A. (2021). Beyond english-centric multilingual machine translation. 22(1).

Farinha, A. C., Farajian, M. A., Buchicchio, M., Fernandes, P., C. de Souza, J. G., Moniz, H., and Martins, A. F. T. (2022). Findings of the WMT 2022 shared task on chat translation. In *Proc. of the Seventh Conference on Machine Translation*, pages 724–743, Abu Dhabi, UAE.

Freitag, M., Rei, R., Mathur, N., Lo, C.-k., Stewart, C., Avramidis, E., Kocmi, T., Foster, G., Lavie, A., and Martins, A. F. T. (2022). Results of WMT22 metrics shared task: Stop using BLEU – neural metrics are better and more robust. In *Proc. of the Seventh Conference on Machine Translation (WMT)*, pages 46–68, Abu Dhabi, UAE.

Freitag, M., Rei, R., Mathur, N., Lo, C.-k., Stewart, C., Foster, G., Lavie, A., and Bojar, O. (2021). Results of the WMT21 metrics shared task: Evaluating metrics with expert-based human evaluations on TED and news domain. In *Proc. of the Sixth Conference of WMT*, pages 733–774.

Liu, Y., Gu, J., Goyal, N., Li, X., Edunov, S., Ghazvininejad, M., Lewis, M., and Zettlemoyer, L. (2020). Multilingual denoising pre-training for neural machine translation. *Transactions of the ACL*, 8:726–742.

Lommel, A., Uszkoreit, H., and Burchardt, A. (2014). Multidimensional quality metrics (mqm): A framework for declaring and describing translation quality metrics. *Tradumàtica*, (12):0455–463.

Lopes, A., Farajian, M. A., Bawden, R., Zhang, M., and Martins, A. F. T. (2020). Document-level neural MT: A systematic comparison. In *Proc. of the 22nd Annual Conference of the European Association for Machine Translation*, pages 225–234, Lisboa, Portugal. European Association for Machine Translation.

Navrátil, J., Visweswariah, K., and Ramanathan, A. (2012). A comparison of syntactic reordering methods for english-german machine translation. In *Proc. of COLING 2012*, pages 2043–2058.

Nayak, P., Haque, R., Kelleher, J. D., and Way, A. (2022). Investigating contextual influence in document-level translation. *Information*, 13(5):249.

Popović, M. (2015). chrF: character n-gram F-score for automatic MT evaluation. In *Proc. of the Tenth Workshop on Statistical Machine Translation*, pages 392–395, Lisbon, Portugal.

Post, M. (2018). A call for clarity in reporting BLEU scores. In *Proc. of the Third Conference on Machine Translation: Research Papers*, pages 186–191, Brussels, Belgium.

Post, M. and Junczys-Dowmunt, M. (2023). Escaping the sentence-level paradigm in machine translation. *arXiv preprint arXiv:2304.12959.*

Rei, R., Stewart, C., Farinha, A. C., and Lavie, A. (2020). COMET: A neural framework for MT evaluation. In *Proc. of the 2020 Conference on Empirical Methods in Natural Language Processing*, pages 2685–2702.

Singh, S. M. and Singh, T. D. (2022). Low resource machine translation of english–manipuri: A semi-supervised approach. *Expert Systems with Applications*, 209:118187.

Vernikos, G., Thompson, B., Mathur, P., and Federico, M. (2022). Embarrassingly easy document-level MT metrics: How to convert any pretrained metric into a document-level metric. In *Proc. of the Seventh Conference on Machine Translation (WMT)*, pages 118–128, Abu Dhabi, UAE.

Voita, E., Sennrich, R., and Titov, I. (2019). When a good translation is wrong in context: Context-aware machine translation improves on deixis, ellipsis, and lexical cohesion. In *Proc. of the 57th Annual Meeting of the ACL*, pages 1198–1212, Florence, Italy.

Wan, Y., Yang, B., Wong, D. F., Chao, L. S., Yao, L., Zhang, H., and Chen, B. (2022). Challenges of neural machine translation for short texts. *Computational Linguistics*, 48(2).

Xiong, W., Droppo, J., Huang, X., Seide, F., Seltzer, M., Stolcke, A., Yu, D., and Zweig, G. (2017). Achieving human parity in conversational speech recognition.

Yin, K., Fernandes, P., Pruthi, D., Chaudhary, A., Martins, A. F., and Neubig, G. (2021). Do context-aware translation models pay the right attention? *arXiv preprint arXiv:2105.06977.*

Zhang, J., Luan, H., Sun, M., Zhai, F., Xu, J., Zhang, M., and Liu, Y. (2018). Improving the transformer translation model with document-level context. *arXiv preprint arXiv:1810.03581.*

Zhang, T., Kishore, V., Wu, F., Weinberger, K. Q., and Artzi, Y. (2020). Bertscore: Evaluating text generation with bert. In *8th International Conference on Learning Representations, ICLR 2020, Addis Ababa, Ethiopia, April 26-30, 2020*. OpenReview.net.

Targeted Data Augmentation Improves Context-aware Neural Machine Translation

Harritxu Gete[1,2] hgete@vicomtech.org
Thierry Etchegoyhen[1] tetchegoyhen@vicomtech.org
Gorka Labaka[2,3] gorka.labaka@ehu.eus

[1]Vicomtech Foundation, Basque Research and Technology Alliance (BRTA)
[2]University of the Basque Country UPV/EHU
[3]HiTZ Basque Center for Language Technologies - Ixa

Abstract

Progress in document-level Machine Translation is hindered by the lack of parallel training data that include context information. In this work, we evaluate the potential of data augmentation techniques to circumvent these limitations, showing that significant gains can be achieved via upsampling, similar context sampling and back-translations, targeted on context-relevant data. We apply these methods on standard document-level datasets in English-German and English-French and demonstrate their relevance to improve the translation of contextual phenomena. In particular, we show that relatively small volumes of targeted data augmentation lead to significant improvements over a strong context-concatenation baseline and standard back-translation of document-level data. We also compare the accuracy of the selected methods depending on data volumes or distance to relevant context information, and explore their use in combination.

1 Introduction

Neural Machine Translation (NMT) models (Sutskever et al., 2014; Bahdanau et al., 2015; Vaswani et al., 2017) are typically trained and used to translate sentences in isolation, ignoring their context of occurrence. This limitation impends the accurate translation of linguistic phenomena that depend on context information, such as discursive coreference or coherence, among others (Bawden et al., 2018; Lopes et al., 2020). A number of approaches have been devised in NMT to extend the modeling window beyond isolated sentences. These approaches range from extending the input by including context sentences (Tiedemann and Scherrer, 2017) to architectural variants (Jean et al., 2017; Zhang et al., 2018; Voita et al., 2019b; Li et al., 2020). Despite the improvements achieved by these methods, the lack of training data that includes contextual information is hindering progress in the field, with only relatively recent efforts to provide large parallel datasets that preserve document boundaries (Barrault et al., 2019).

Data augmentation is one of the main methods to increase machine translation coverage at the sentence level, typically via back-translation of monolingual data (Sennrich et al., 2016a) or comparable data mining (Sharoff et al., 2014). For document-level NMT, fewer studies have addressed the use of data augmentation to tackle the aforementioned scarcity. Back-translation at the document level has been shown to help context-aware NMT (Junczys-Dowmunt, 2019; Sugiyama and Yoshinaga, 2019; Huo et al., 2020), but its use has been limited to bulk back-translation rather than targeting contextual phenomena. Other data augmentation methods such

Proceedings of Machine Translation Summit XIX, Vol. 1: Research Track, pages 298–312
September 4–8, 2023, Macau SAR, China.

as data alteration based on coreference resolvers (Stojanovski et al., 2020; Hwang et al., 2021) have also been shown to be useful for the task. Overall, it is currently unclear whether data augmentation that do not rely on bulk back-translation or external tools can provide any benefits for context-aware NMT.

In this work, we explore different approaches to data augmentation for context-aware NMT, which, to the best of our knowledge, have not yet been studied in depth. We thus evaluate the use of upsampling, context sampling and back-translations, targeted on context-relevant data. Our experiments focus on pronoun translation with a single context sentence, to provide initial results in a constrained experimental protocol, and are evaluated on standard datasets, namely ContraPro (Müller et al., 2018) for English-German and the large-scale pronoun test set for English-French (Lopes et al., 2020). We show that significant gains can be achieved by each method over a strong baseline, with relatively small quantities of augmented data, and provide a detailed analysis of these methods in isolation and in combination.

2 Related work

A variety of studies have tackled context-aware approaches within the framework of NMT, analysing the improvements that these models can provide over non-contextual baselines (Li et al., 2020; Ma et al., 2020; Lopes et al., 2020; Lupo et al., 2022; Majumde et al., 2022; Sun et al., 2022). One of the first methods proposed for the task is the concatenation of context sentences to the sentence to be translated (Tiedemann and Scherrer, 2017). This simple approach is still one of the most efficient methods to perform context-aware neural machine translation, matching or outperforming more sophisticated ones (Lopes et al., 2020). Alternative methods have involved refining the context-agnostic translations (Xiong et al., 2019; Voita et al., 2019a; Mansimov et al., 2021), or modelling context information with specific NMT architectures (Jean et al., 2017; Zhang et al., 2018; Li et al., 2020; Wang et al., 2017; Tan et al., 2019).

The growing interest in context-aware NMT models has increased the need for parallel data where context information is preserved. Dedicated efforts have been made to increase the availability of this type of data, for instance in recent shared tasks in the WMT series (Barrault et al., 2019). However, context boundaries might not always be recoverable, ensuring continuous contextual information in sentence-aligned datasets can be a costly task, and most of the available relevant data might be limited to specific domains. Data augmentation might thus complement the existing datasets for the variety of possible language pairs and domains.

Over the years, specific efforts have been made to create synthetic data to improve NMT at the sentence-level (Fadaee et al., 2017; Li et al., 2019; Li and Specia, 2019; Xia et al., 2019; Liu et al., 2021). The most widespread method is the use of back-translations, a technique introduced to NMT by Sennrich et al. (2016a) that exploits monolingual corpora by machine-translating target language data into the source language. For document-level NMT, back-translation has been shown to be effective in capturing contextual information, both by translating the original data sentence by sentence (Junczys-Dowmunt, 2019) or by using context-aware models (Sugiyama and Yoshinaga, 2019). In the same vein, Huo et al. (2020) find that document-level models benefit even more from back-translations than their sentence-level counterparts. To our knowledge, back-translations targeted on specific phenomena, as proposed by Fadaee and Monz (2018) for sentence-level models, have not been investigated for context-aware NMT and we include this approach among our data augmentation methods.

Monolingual data have also been exploited for document-level NMT via context-level decoders (Voita et al., 2019b) or systems that learn to improve the translations generated by sentence-level models (Voita et al., 2019a). Other methods augment document-level parallel data by creating synthetic sentence sequences via the concatenation of varying numbers of sentences extracted from aligned document pairs (Popel et al., 2019; Popel, 2020; Nowakowski et al., 2022). Other forms of data augmentation are antecedent-free augmentation (Stojanovski et al., 2020), which creates new training examples by modifying cases where the antecedent is not present in the available context, or the more recent method of Hwang et al. (2021), which generates faulty data and trains NMT models via contrastive learning. In both cases, a coreference analysis needs to be performed on document pairs. Finally, data augmentation has also been performed for sentence-level models by mining large volumes of comparable data (Sharoff et al., 2014). This type of data has been shown to increase the quality of NMT models for low-resource languages, independently or in combination with back-translations (Gete and Etchegoyhen, 2022). To our knowledge, using similar data for contextual data augmentation has not yet been explored, and we include a variant of this method in our analysis.

Context-aware models are particularly suited to improve the translation of phenomena that directly depend on context information, such as intersentential anaphora resolution, discourse coherence or terminological consistency (Müller et al., 2018). We evaluate our approach on the specific task of adequately translating pronouns in context, for which several specific test sets have been created (Guillou and Hardmeier, 2016; Bawden et al., 2018; Guillou et al., 2018; Müller et al., 2018; Lopes et al., 2020; Gete et al., 2022).

3 Methodology

We aim to generate synthetic parallel data that include relevant information for the translation of specific contextual phenomena. This involves (i) identifying context blocks in document-level data, i.e. parallel sequences consisting of a sentence and its previous context sentence in the source and target languages, and (ii) sampling blocks that contain elements whose translation typically requires context information. Although our approach could be applied to other contextual phenomena as well, we selected pronouns as our linguistic category of interest, specifically the translation of pronouns from English into German and French, given their relevance for document-level translation and the availability of contrastive test sets for precise evaluations (Müller et al., 2018; Lopes et al., 2020). In particular, for English-German, we focused on the pronoun *it* which can be translated as *es* (neutral gender), *er* (masculine) or *sie* (feminine). For English-French, in addition to *it*, which can be translated as *elle* (feminine) or *il* (masculine), we also included *they*, which can be translated as *elles* (feminine) or *ils* (masculine).

We first identify context blocks where the targeted elements occur in the source (src_i) and target (tgt_i) sentences and the preceding source sentence (src_{i-1}) is available. More specifically, we extracted context blocks that met one of the following conditions: (i) *it* in src_i and *es/er/sie* in tgt_i (EN-DE) (ii) *it* in src_i and *elle/il* in tgt_i (EN-FR) (iii) *they* in src_i and *elles/ils* in tgt_i (EN-FR). Under this approach, we might sample data where the antecedent of the pronoun is found in the block, but might also extract blocks where the antecedent is not included. These instances can also be useful as they might help balance the data in case of bias. This extraction method avoids having to use coreference annotation tools, which simplifies the data extraction process. To avoid introducing ambiguity in the sampled data, we discarded cases where more than one pronominal translation with different genders appeared in the target sentence.

After sampling the blocks of interest, we create new ones by either duplicating the sampled blocks (*upsampling*), replacing the context sentences randomly or via sentence embedding similarity (*context sampling*), or back-translating the target language blocks (*targeted back-translation*). We describe each method in more details below.

Upsampling. This method (hereafter, UP-SAMP) is the simplest, and consists in repeating the selected blocks multiple times and adding them to the training data. This type of data augmentation could lead to overfitting, i.e. overtraining the model on the upsampled data and learning specific patterns which might be irrelevant in other cases. It may thus happen that the model achieves higher accuracy on the selected data but does not generalise well to other data.

Context Sampling. To avoid the overfitting that may arise from upsampling, context sampling uses context blocks as a basis to create synthetic data. To do this, the sentences src_i and tgt_i remain unchanged, but the English source context (src_{i-1}) is replaced by another sentence from the corpus. To select the substitute sentence, we first retrieve blocks which contain the same target pronoun and may thus contain varying but useful context. We then select the replacement context sentence among the retrieved blocks via one of two methods: random sampling (RDM-SAMP) and similarity sampling (SIM-SAMP). Random sampling is meant to evaluate unconstrained substitution by randomly selecting any context sentence within the candidate blocks. Note that the antecedent is likely to be replaced by a semantically unrelated one, which could impact the final quality of the model. Similarity sampling is performed by selecting the most similar context in terms of cosine similarity using pretrained sentence embeddings.[1]

Targeted Back-translation. Our final method is targeted back-translation (T-BT), where we back-translate specific portions of document-level monolingual data, selecting (tgt_{i-1}, tgt_i) blocks where tgt_i contains one of the targeted pronouns. As in bilingual data extraction, if the sentence contains a pronoun, the pronoun corresponding to the other gender cannot appear in the sentence. The selected blocks are translated into the source language using a context-agnostic NMT model and blocks where the back-translation does not contain a translation of the targeted pronoun are discarded.

4 Experimental setup

4.1 Data

All selected datasets were normalised, tokenised and truecased using Moses (Koehn et al., 2007) scripts and segmented with BPE (Sennrich et al., 2016b), using 32,000 operations. Table 1 describes corpora statistics, indicating the amount of data with context information (DOC-LEVEL) and without (SENT-LEVEL), for parallel and monolingual datasets.

	EN-DE	EN-FR		DE	FR
	DOC-LEVEL	SENT-LEVEL	DOC-LEVEL	DOC-LEVEL	DOC-LEVEL
TRAIN	5,852,458	11,221,790	234,738	58,979,140	106,830,385
DEV	2,999	4,992	5,818	-	-
TEST	6,002	-	1,210	-	-

Table 1: Corpora statistics (number of sentences)

Parallel corpora. For English-German, we follow the setup of Müller et al. (2018) and selected the data from the WMT 2017 news translation task, using newstest2017 and newstest2018 as test sets and the union of newstest2014, newstest2015 and newstest2016 for validation. For English-French, we follow Lopes et al. (2020) and use publicly available sentence-level parallel data to train baseline models. We used Europarl v7, NewsCommentary v10, CommonCrawl, UN, Giga from WMT 2017 and the IWSLT17 TED Talks (Cettolo et al., 2012) processed at the sentence-level. We then fine-tune context-aware models on the document-level IWSLT17 dataset, using the test sets from 2011 to 2014 as dev sets, and 2015 as test sets.

Monolingual corpora. We use NewsCrawl2021 (Barrault et al., 2021) as German monolingual data and OpenSubtitles2018 (Lison et al., 2018) for French.

[1]Embeddings were computed with all-MiniLM-L6-v2 (https://www.sbert.net/docs/pretrained_models.html).

EN-DE		EN-FR	
it→*es*	221,327	*it*→*elle*	3,539
it→*er*	40,238	*it*→*il*	13,252
it→*sie*	105,906	*they*→*elles*	2,886
		they→*ils*	14,967
TOTAL	367,471		34,644

Table 2: Extracted context data per target category (number of sentences)

Contrastive tests. We evaluate our models using two sets of contrastive tests, both created from OpenSubtitles2018[2] excerpts and aiming to assess a model's ability to rank correct translations over incorrect ones. ContraPro (Müller et al., 2018) enables testing the ability of a model to identify the correct German translation of the English anaphoric pronoun *it* as *es*, *sie* or *er*. It contains 4,000 examples per pronoun and, for 80% of them, the sentence-based antecedent distance is superior to 0. The EN-FR large-scale pronoun test set (hereafter, LSCP) (Lopes et al., 2020) is similar, but in addition to assessing the translation of *it* as *elle* or *il*, it includes the translation of *they* as *elles* or *ils*. It consists of 3,500 examples for each type of pronoun and almost 60% of the examples need contextual information to make the correct choice.

4.2 Models

All models follow the Transformer-base architecture (Vaswani et al., 2017) and were trained with the MarianNMT toolkit (Junczys-Dowmunt et al., 2018). The embeddings for source, target and output layers were tied and optimisation was performed with Adam (Kingma and Ba, 2015), with $\alpha = 0.0003$, $\beta_1 = 0.9$, $\beta_2 = 0.98$ and $\epsilon = 10^{-9}$. As baselines, we trained sentence-level models and 2to1 models. The latter is a context-aware approach that extends the input by concatenating the previous sentence without any changes to the model architecture (Tiedemann and Scherrer, 2017), including an additional sentence break token between the context and the current sentence.

For English-German, both the sentence-level model and the 2to1 baseline were trained with the available document-level corpora, and the parameters of the 2to1 model were initialised with those of the sentence-level model. For English-French, due to the lower data volumes, a sentence-level model was first trained with sentence-level data. Following Müller et al. (2018), this model was then fine-tuned with document-level data to obtain a 2to1 model. In addition, 2to1 models are trained also on the augmented data, with varying quantities and different data distributions to balance or maintain the distribution of pronouns in the original datasets.

5 Optimal Variants

We first aimed to establish the optimal selection of data along two lines: (i) balancing the distribution of pronominal categories vs. maintaining an unbalanced distribution, and (ii) varying the amounts of sampled data with each method.

5.1 Distribution Balance

As shown in Table 2, the distribution per pronominal category in the extracted context blocks is unbalanced. To balance the data, we increased the representation of the least represented categories to reach the volumes of the most represented one. For English-French, given the relatively lower data volumes, we raised the amounts of data to a minimum of 45K for all categories, rather than just matching the volumes of the most represented one. For each method, we compared balancing with data augmentation maintaining the original distribution of the

[2]Note that training data were filtered so as not to include examples of the contrastive tests.

training data. To maintain the distribution, n blocks were created for each extracted block, choosing the smallest n so that the amount of data reached the amount in the balanced data. These quantities were reached with $n = 1$ for English-German and $n = 5$ for English-French.

For comparison purposes, we also include results from untargeted back-translation, i.e. standard back-translation of document-level monolingual data. We trained a BT-SMALL model with the same amount of data added to balance the distribution (296K in total for English-German and 145K for English-French) and a larger version, BT-LARGE, with 1.1M and 765K back-translations for English-German and English-French, respectively. Note that, in this case, no selection of the data is performed, so the final distribution does not necessarily maintain the original distribution and is not necessarily balanced.

	TOTAL	ES	ER	SIE	Δ
2TO1	0.58	**0.92**	0.38	0.43	0.54
UP-SAMP (B)	**0.69**	0.81	**0.70**	0.55	0.26
UP-SAMP (O)	0.62	0.91	0.43	0.52	0.48
RDM-SAMP (B)	0.64	0.83	0.55	0.53	0.30
RDM-SAMP (O)	0.58	0.90	0.37	0.48	0.53
SIM-SAMP (B)	0.65	0.82	0.62	0.51	0.31
SIM-SAMP (O)	0.61	0.91	0.42	0.49	0.49
T-BT (B)	0.66	0.71	0.66	**0.60**	0.11
T-BT (O)	0.62	0.88	0.41	0.57	0.47
BT-SMALL	0.59	0.91	0.39	0.48	0.52
BT-LARGE	0.59	**0.92**	0.39	0.47	0.53

Table 3: English-German accuracy results. (B) and (O) indicate balancing and maintaining the original data distribution, respectively. Δ is the difference in accuracy between best and worst categories. Best results for each category are shown in bold.

	TOTAL	ELLE	IL	ELLES	ILS	Δ
2TO1	0.84	0.80	0.92	0.67	0.98	0.31
UP-SAMP (B)	**0.87**	0.90	0.85	0.77	0.96	0.19
UP-SAMP (O)	0.86	0.82	0.92	0.71	0.98	0.27
RDM-SAMP (B)	0.86	0.90	0.83	0.78	0.95	0.17
RDM-SAMP (O)	0.84	0.79	0.91	0.68	0.98	0.30
SIM-SAMP (B)	**0.87**	0.89	0.84	0.78	0.96	0.18
SIM-SAMP (O)	0.85	0.80	0.91	0.69	0.98	0.29
T-BT (B)	0.85	**0.91**	0.79	**0.83**	0.86	0.12
T-BT (O)	0.85	0.76	**0.94**	0.72	0.98	0.26
BT-SMALL	0.84	0.79	0.92	0.65	**0.99**	0.33
BT-LARGE	0.84	0.79	0.92	0.65	**0.99**	0.34

Table 4: English-French accuracy results. (B) and (O) indicate balancing and maintaining original data distribution, respectively. Δ is the difference in accuracy between best and worst categories. Best results for each category are shown in bold.

The results for this first set of experiments are provided in Tables 3 and 4. Balancing reduces the difference in accuracy between the different genders, to a marked extent, and although it has a negative impact on the most represented categories (*es* in German, *il* and *ils* in French), it markedly increases the accuracy for the less represented ones. Overall, balancing clearly improves over keeping the original data distribution, and we thus opted to balance all datasets in the remaining experiments. Of note are the significant total improvements obtained in English-German, and the smaller ones for English-French, where the baseline 2to1 method already achieves relatively high accuracy. The use of untargeted back-translations, whether in smaller or larger quantities, performed on a par with the baseline, maintaining a distribution of scores very similar to the original one. In both cases, this method was outperformed by targeted data augmentation methods, in all but the top-scoring cases for each language pair (*es* in English-German and *ils* in English-French), where it achieved marginally better scores.

5.2 Data Size

We then turned to measuring the impact of different volumes of augmented data. For English-German, we started from the minimal balanced data size and augmented the data by increments of 100,000, up to 500,000 per category; for English-French, given the smaller amounts, the increments were made on a 10,000 basis, starting from 15,000 and up to 45,000, with an additional increase reaching 200,000 instances per category, to test the impact of larger datasets. Note that not all data increases were feasible with T-BT, as there were not enough data meeting the targeted sampling criteria. Therefore, for this method, the maximum available data were 226,651 instances per pronoun category in English-German and 126,905 in English-French.

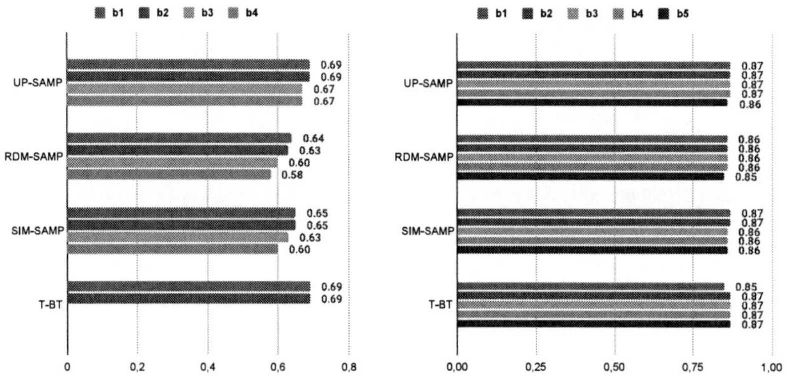

Figure 1: Accuracy results for English-German (left) and English-French (right) as a factor of augmented data size. For English-German, b1=221,327, b2=300K, b3=400K and b4=500K except for T-BT, where b2=226,651. For English-French, b1=15K, b2=25K, b3=35K, b4=4K and b5=200K except for T-BT, where b5=126,905.

Accuracy results obtained with varying amounts of augmented data are shown in Figure 1. Increasing the data size brought no improvement or was detrimental for all models except for the English-French T-BT. Adding data beyond what was needed for data balancing did not improve the upsampling and contextual sampling models, even in a more data-sparse scenario such as English-French. This might be caused by the overfitting arising from upsampling and the noise introduced by sampling methods with incorrect contexts, although a more detailed analysis, beyond the scope of this work, would be needed to establish the determining factors for this behaviour. In the case of T-BT, for English-German the results remained identical, which is not unexpected considering that very little data could be added. In the case of English-French, where there was less initial data, increasing up to 25K instances per category improved accuracy. In what follows, therefore, we opted for the smallest data sizes for each model, except for English-French T-BT where we selected 25K cases per pronominal category.

6 Method Comparison

In this section, we compare the methods selected in the previous section, i.e. balanced 221,327 for English-German and balanced 15K for English-French, except for English-French T-BT, with 25K selected. Additionally, for each language pair we trained a combined model (COMB) where we merged the augmentation blocks from each method and selected a random sample maintaining distribution balance. We discarded the option of using the combination of all data, as this would have resulted in unbalanced data distributions.

6.1 Comparative Accuracy

Accuracy results, including total and pronoun-specific results, are shown in Figure 2. All data augmentation methods improve over both the sentence-level and the 2to1 baselines, although the improvements are more marked in English-German, where the baselines are less accurate than in English-French. The high scores obtained by the English-French baselines may be due to several factors. On the one hand, as previously mentioned, this test set contains over 40% of examples where the context is not necessary to make a correct translation. On the other hand, this is a less varied test than the corresponding test for English-German, since it only includes subject pronouns whose antecedent is a noun. Although a more detailed analysis would be needed to confirm this conjecture, the uniformity and relative simplicity of antecedent-pronoun configuration might be a relevant factor for the rather high scores obtained by the baseline. Improving over these baseline results might thus be a challenge for any method on this test set.

The sampling methods are better at preserving the distribution of the most frequent pronouns, with upsampling outperforming both random and similarity sampling for English-German. For this language pair, T-BT is outperformed by upsampling in most cases but performs better than all other methods on translation of *sie*, the less accurately translated category overall. The combination provides balanced results across categories and achieves the best results on the initially least represented *er* category, but also loses accuracy for the most frequent *es* pronoun. Similar results are obtained for English-French, where it obtains the best results for *elle* and *elles*, and the worst for *il* and *ils*. T-BT and COMB obtain the most balanced results, to the detriment of *ils*, the category with the best results with the other methods.

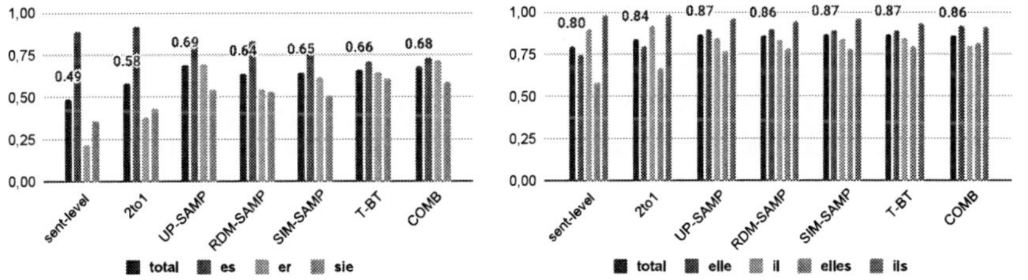

Figure 2: Accuracy results in English-German (left) and English-French (right) for all selected models. Numerical results are indicated for total accuracy.

6.2 Impact of Distance

The results so far indicate that accuracy increases when using the selected data augmentation methods, overall and per category. However, since the contrastive test sets include data where the relevant pronoun antecedent can occur within the same sentence, the extent to which the observed improvements come from an actual improved use of the preceding context is unclear.

In Figure 3, we compare results for cases where the antecedent is in the same sentence

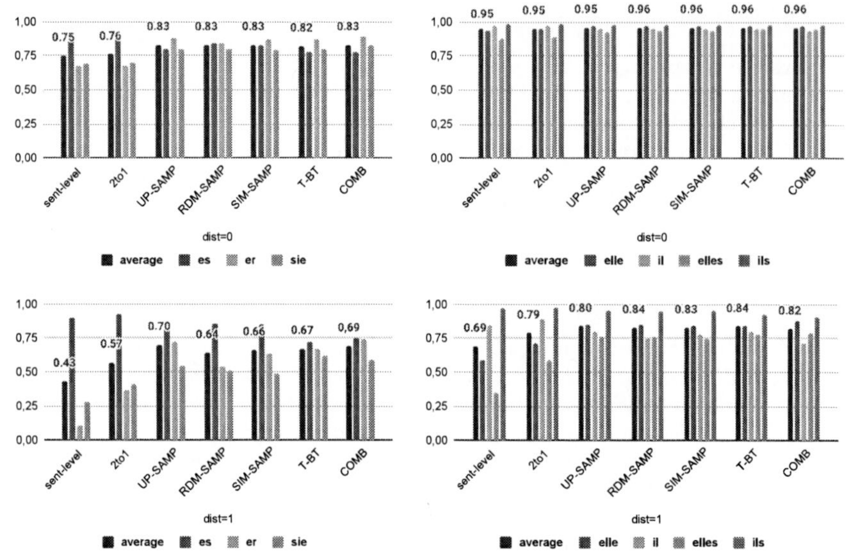

Figure 3: Accuracy results as a factor of antecedent distance in English-German (left) and English-French (right). Numerical results are indicated for average accuracy.

(dist=0) or in the preceding context sentence (dist=1). Here, we indicate the average across categories instead of total accuracy, since categories are distributed differently in the test set depending on antecedent distance. For both language pairs, the improvements are markedly larger across categories when the relevant context is in the preceding sentence, although all methods also match or improve over the baselines when the antecedent occurs within the same sentence. These results thus indicate that the selected data augmentation methods do improve context appraisal beyond the current sentence, with additional improvements at the sentence level. Untangling the precise impact of the augmented data in both cases would require additional experiments which we leave for future work.

6.3 Impact on translation metrics

Finally, since data augmentation may impact the resulting models in terms of general translation quality, we computed BLEU (Papineni et al., 2002) scores on both sentence-level and document-level test sets. The scores were computed with the SacreBLEU[3] toolkit (Post, 2018) and statistical significance was computed via paired bootstrap resampling (Koehn, 2004). The results are shown in Table 5.

Overall, T-BT was the optimal method preserving general translation quality, improving over both baselines in most cases. These differences are more marked in the case of English-French, where T-BT was the only method that improved over the two baselines in all cases. Upsampling induced BLEU loss across the board in English-German when compared to the sentence-level baseline, a result which may be due to the overfitting resulting from this method. Both random and similarity sampling performed worse than T-BT in general, although they slightly improved over the 2to1 baselines on several test sets. Finally, COMB obtained relatively balanced results across test sets, outperforming both baselines in most cases.

[3]signature: nrefs:1—case:mixed—eff:no—tok:13a—smooth:exp—version:2.0.0

The different methods we examined in this work do not seem to negatively impact the models' general translation capability, and may even improve over both sentence-level and 2to1 models in this respect. Combining these results with those achieved on the contrastive test sets, it appears that the data augmentation techniques evaluated in this work can thus contribute to improving translation quality of context-aware NMT models overall.

	EN-DE			EN-FR	
	wmt2017	wmt2018	ContraPro	iwslt17	ContraPro
SENTENCE-LEVEL	27.7	41.1	22.7	41.2	27.7
2TO1	26.8	40.7	23.4	42.6	28.7
UP-SAMP	26.8†	40.1†‡	24.8†‡	42.6†	29.2†‡
RDM-SAMP	27.4‡	40.7	24.5†‡	42.2†‡	29.1†‡
SIM-SAMP	27.5‡	40.4†	24.7†‡	42.4†	29.1†‡
T-BT	28.0‡	41.7†‡	**24.9**†‡	**42.9**†‡	**29.7**†‡
COMB	27.8‡	41.1	**25.0**†‡	42.4†	29.3†‡
BT-SMALL	28.3†‡	41.7†‡	24.1†‡	42.4†	28.9†‡
BT-LARGE	**28.8**†‡	**42.4**†‡	24.4†‡	42.2†	28.8†‡

Table 5: BLEU results. † and ‡ indicate statistically significant results ($p < 0.05$) against the sentence-level and 2to1 baselines, respectively; best performing systems, without statistically significant differences between them, are shown in bold.

7 Conclusions

In this work, we described three different data augmentation techniques for context-aware NMT and evaluated them in isolation and in combination over standard sentence-level and document-level test sets. Specifically, we created synthetic data centred on improving pronoun translation in English-German and English-French, as a test case for an approach which could be applied to other contextual phenomena as well, provided they feature overt elements that may be targeted.

The methods we examined included upsampling, context sampling with both random and similar context substitution, and back-translations, all targeted on specific data featuring different pronominal types. All methods improved over a strong concatenation baseline, in terms of accuracy on contrastive test sets, while also achieving parity or improving in terms of BLEU scores in most cases. Accuracy improvements were markedly larger on the English-German contrastive sets, as high scores could already be obtained by the baseline on the English-French test sets. We leave for future work an exploration of alternative contrastive datasets and models with a wider contextual window. We demonstrated that balancing the data and using minimal volumes was optimal overall, and showed that the improvements were mainly obtained by leveraging contextual information in preceding sentences. All methods were shown to perform markedly better than simply back-translating document-level data, indicating that targeted data augmentation might be a research path worth exploring further for context-aware NMT.

Finally, among the selected methods, targeted back-translation proved a simple and effective approach which performed well across the board, although it can be outperformed in terms of accuracy on specific categories. This method does not require external tools such as coreference resolvers and can significantly improve the results of a 2to1 model with relatively small amounts of data, as measured in contrastive evaluations as well as evaluations in terms of BLEU. The combination of data from the different examined methods may also be considered a viable alternative, as it resulted in balanced improvements over categories overall.

References

Bahdanau, D., Cho, K., and Bengio, Y. (2015). Neural machine translation by jointly learning to align and translate. In *3rd International Conference on Learning Representations, ICLR 2015, San Diego, CA, USA, May 7-9, 2015, Conference Track Proceedings*.

Barrault, L., Bojar, O., Bougares, F., Chatterjee, R., Costa-jussa, M. R., Federmann, C., Fishel, M., Fraser, A., Freitag, M., Graham, Y., Grundkiewicz, R., Guzman, P., Haddow, B., Huck, M., Yepes, A. J., Koehn, P., Kocmi, T., Martins, A., Morishita, M., and Monz, C., editors (2021). *Proceedings of the Sixth Conference on Machine Translation*, Online. Association for Computational Linguistics.

Barrault, L., Bojar, O., Costa-jussà, M. R., Federmann, C., Fishel, M., Graham, Y., Haddow, B., Huck, M., Koehn, P., Malmasi, S., Monz, C., Müller, M., Pal, S., Post, M., and Zampieri, M. (2019). Findings of the 2019 conference on machine translation (WMT19). In *Proceedings of the Fourth Conference on Machine Translation (Volume 2: Shared Task Papers, Day 1)*, pages 1–61, Florence, Italy. Association for Computational Linguistics.

Bawden, R., Sennrich, R., Birch, A., and Haddow, B. (2018). Evaluating discourse phenomena in neural machine translation. In *Proceedings of the 2018 Conference of the North American Chapter of the Association for Computational Linguistics: Human Language Technologies, Volume 1 (Long Papers)*, pages 1304–1313, New Orleans, Louisiana. Association for Computational Linguistics.

Cettolo, M., Girardi, C., and Federico, M. (2012). WIT3: Web inventory of transcribed and translated talks. In *Proceedings of the 16th Annual conference of the European Association for Machine Translation*, pages 261–268, Trento, Italy. European Association for Machine Translation.

Fadaee, M., Bisazza, A., and Monz, C. (2017). Data augmentation for low-resource neural machine translation. In *Proceedings of the 55th Annual Meeting of the Association for Computational Linguistics (Volume 2: Short Papers)*, pages 567–573, Vancouver, Canada. Association for Computational Linguistics.

Fadaee, M. and Monz, C. (2018). Back-translation sampling by targeting difficult words in neural machine translation. In *Proceedings of the 2018 Conference on Empirical Methods in Natural Language Processing*, pages 436–446, Brussels, Belgium. Association for Computational Linguistics.

Gete, H. and Etchegoyhen, T. (2022). Making the most of comparable corpora in neural machine translation: a case study. *Lang. Resour. Evaluation*, 56(3):943–971.

Gete, H., Etchegoyhen, T., Ponce, D., Labaka, G., Aranberri, N., Corral, A., Saralegi, X., Ellakuria, I., and Martin, M. (2022). TANDO: A corpus for document-level machine translation. In *Proceedings of the Thirteenth Language Resources and Evaluation Conference*, pages 3026–3037, Marseille, France. European Language Resources Association.

Guillou, L. and Hardmeier, C. (2016). PROTEST: A test suite for evaluating pronouns in machine translation. In *Proceedings of the Tenth International Conference on Language Resources and Evaluation (LREC'16)*, pages 636–643, Portorož, Slovenia. European Language Resources Association (ELRA).

Guillou, L., Hardmeier, C., Lapshinova-Koltunski, E., and Loáiciga, S. (2018). A pronoun test suite evaluation of the English–German MT systems at WMT 2018. In *Proceedings of the Third Conference on Machine Translation: Shared Task Papers*, pages 570–577, Belgium, Brussels. Association for Computational Linguistics.

Huo, J., Herold, C., Gao, Y., Dahlmann, L., Khadivi, S., and Ney, H. (2020). Diving deep into context-aware neural machine translation. In *Proceedings of the Fifth Conference on Machine Translation*, pages 604–616, Online. Association for Computational Linguistics.

Hwang, Y., Yun, H., and Jung, K. (2021). Contrastive learning for context-aware neural machine translation using coreference information. In *Proceedings of the Sixth Conference on Machine Translation*, pages 1135–1144, Online. Association for Computational Linguistics.

Jean, S., Lauly, S., Firat, O., and Cho, K. (2017). Neural machine translation for cross-lingual pronoun prediction. In *Proceedings of the Third Workshop on Discourse in Machine Translation*, pages 54–57, Copenhagen, Denmark. Association for Computational Linguistics.

Junczys-Dowmunt, M. (2019). Microsoft translator at WMT 2019: Towards large-scale document-level neural machine translation. In *Proceedings of the Fourth Conference on Machine Translation (Volume 2: Shared Task Papers, Day 1)*, pages 225–233, Florence, Italy. Association for Computational Linguistics.

Junczys-Dowmunt, M., Grundkiewicz, R., Dwojak, T., Hoang, H., Heafield, K., Neckermann, T., Seide, F., Germann, U., Fikri Aji, A., Bogoychev, N., Martins, A. F. T., and Birch, A. (2018). Marian: Fast neural machine translation in C++. In *Proceedings of ACL 2018, System Demonstrations*, pages 116–121, Melbourne, Australia.

Kingma, D. P. and Ba, J. (2015). Adam: A method for stochastic optimization. In *International Conference on Learning Representations (ICLR)*.

Koehn, P. (2004). Statistical significance tests for machine translation evaluation. In *Proceedings of the 2004 Conference on Empirical Methods in Natural Language Processing*, pages 388–395, Barcelona, Spain. Association for Computational Linguistics.

Koehn, P., Hoang, H., Birch, A., Callison-Burch, C., Federico, M., Bertoldi, N., Cowan, B., Shen, W., Moran, C., Zens, R., et al. (2007). Moses: Open source toolkit for statistical machine translation. In *Proceedings of the 45th Annual Meeting of the Association for Computational Linguistics*, pages 177–180, Prague, Czech Republic.

Li, B., Liu, H., Wang, Z., Jiang, Y., Xiao, T., Zhu, J., Liu, T., and Li, C. (2020). Does multi-encoder help? a case study on context-aware neural machine translation. In *Proceedings of the 58th Annual Meeting of the Association for Computational Linguistics*, pages 3512–3518, Online. Association for Computational Linguistics.

Li, G., Liu, L., Huang, G., Zhu, C., and Zhao, T. (2019). Understanding data augmentation in neural machine translation: Two perspectives towards generalization. In *Proceedings of the 2019 Conference on Empirical Methods in Natural Language Processing and the 9th International Joint Conference on Natural Language Processing (EMNLP-IJCNLP)*, pages 5689–5695, Hong Kong, China. Association for Computational Linguistics.

Li, Z. and Specia, L. (2019). Improving neural machine translation robustness via data augmentation: Beyond back-translation. In *Proceedings of the 5th Workshop on Noisy User-generated Text (W-NUT 2019)*, pages 328–336, Hong Kong, China. Association for Computational Linguistics.

Lison, P., Tiedemann, J., and Kouylekov, M. (2018). OpenSubtitles2018: Statistical rescoring of sentence alignments in large, noisy parallel corpora. In *Proceedings of the Eleventh International Conference on Language Resources and Evaluation (LREC 2018)*, Miyazaki, Japan. European Language Resources Association (ELRA).

Liu, Q., Kusner, M., and Blunsom, P. (2021). Counterfactual data augmentation for neural machine translation. In *Proceedings of the 2021 Conference of the North American Chapter of the Association for Computational Linguistics: Human Language Technologies*, pages 187–197, Online. Association for Computational Linguistics.

Lopes, A., Farajian, M. A., Bawden, R., Zhang, M., and Martins, A. F. T. (2020). Document-level neural MT: A systematic comparison. In *Proceedings of the 22nd Annual Conference of the European Association for Machine Translation*, pages 225–234, Lisboa, Portugal. European Association for Machine Translation.

Lupo, L., Dinarelli, M., and Besacier, L. (2022). Focused concatenation for context-aware neural machine translation. In *Proceedings of the Seventh Conference on Machine Translation (WMT)*, pages 830—842, Abu Dhabi. Association for Computational Linguistics.

Ma, S., Zhang, D., and Zhou, M. (2020). A simple and effective unified encoder for document-level machine translation. In *Proceedings of the 58th Annual Meeting of the Association for Computational Linguistics*, pages 3505–3511, Online. Association for Computational Linguistics.

Majumde, S., Lauly, S., Nadejde, M., Federico, M., and Dinu, G. (2022). A baseline revisited: Pushing the limits of multi-segment models for context-aware translation. *arXiv preprint arXiv:2210.10906v2*.

Mansimov, E., Melis, G., and Yu, L. (2021). Capturing document context inside sentence-level neural machine translation models with self-training. In *Proceedings of the 2nd Workshop on Computational Approaches to Discourse*, pages 143–153, Punta Cana, Dominican Republic and Online. Association for Computational Linguistics.

Müller, M., Rios, A., Voita, E., and Sennrich, R. (2018). A large-scale test set for the evaluation of context-aware pronoun translation in neural machine translation. In *Proceedings of the Third Conference on Machine Translation: Research Papers*, pages 61–72, Brussels, Belgium. Association for Computational Linguistics.

Nowakowski, A., Pałka, G., Guttmann, K., and Pokrywka, M. (2022). Adam mickiewicz university at wmt 2022: Ner-assisted and quality-aware neural machine translation. In *Proceedings of the Seventh Conference on Machine Translation (WMT)*, pages 326—334, Abu Dhabi. Association for Computational Linguistics.

Papineni, K., Roukos, S., Ward, T., and Zhu, W.-J. (2002). Bleu: a method for automatic evaluation of machine translation. In *Proceedings of the 40th Annual Meeting of the Association for Computational Linguistics*, pages 311–318, Philadelphia, Pennsylvania, USA. Association for Computational Linguistics.

Popel, M. (2020). CUNI English-Czech and English-Polish systems in WMT20: Robust document-level training. In *Proceedings of the Fifth Conference on Machine Translation*, pages 269–273, Online. Association for Computational Linguistics.

Popel, M., Macháček, D., Auersperger, M., Bojar, O., and Pecina, P. (2019). English-Czech systems in WMT19: Document-level transformer. In *Proceedings of the Fourth Conference on Machine Translation (Volume 2: Shared Task Papers, Day 1)*, pages 342–348, Florence, Italy. Association for Computational Linguistics.

Post, M. (2018). A call for clarity in reporting BLEU scores. In *Proceedings of the Third Conference on Machine Translation: Research Papers*, pages 186–191, Brussels, Belgium. Association for Computational Linguistics.

Sennrich, R., Haddow, B., and Birch, A. (2016a). Improving neural machine translation models with monolingual data. In *Proceedings of the 54th Annual Meeting of the Association for Computational Linguistics (Volume 1: Long Papers)*, pages 86–96, Berlin, Germany. Association for Computational Linguistics.

Sennrich, R., Haddow, B., and Birch, A. (2016b). Neural machine translation of rare words with subword units. In *Proceedings of the 54th Annual Meeting of the Association for Computational Linguistics (Volume 1: Long Papers)*, pages 1715–1725, Berlin, Germany. Association for Computational Linguistics.

Sharoff, S., Rapp, R., Zweigenbaum, P., and Fung, P. (2014). Building and using comparable corpora. In *Springer Berlin Heidelberg*.

Stojanovski, D., Krojer, B., Peskov, D., and Fraser, A. (2020). ContraCAT: Contrastive coreference analytical templates for machine translation. In *Proceedings of the 28th International Conference on Computational Linguistics*, pages 4732–4749, Barcelona, Spain (Online). International Committee on Computational Linguistics.

Sugiyama, A. and Yoshinaga, N. (2019). Data augmentation using back-translation for context-aware neural machine translation. In *Proceedings of the Fourth Workshop on Discourse in Machine Translation (DiscoMT 2019)*, pages 35–44, Hong Kong, China. Association for Computational Linguistics.

Sun, Z., Wang, M., Zhou, H., Zhao, C., Huang, S., Chen, J., and Li, L. (2022). Rethinking document-level neural machine translation. In *Findings of the Association for Computational Linguistics: ACL 2022*, pages 3537–3548, Dublin, Ireland. Association for Computational Linguistics.

Sutskever, I., Vinyals, O., and Le, Q. V. (2014). Sequence to sequence learning with neural networks. In *Advances in neural information processing systems*, pages 3104–3112.

Tan, X., Zhang, L., Xiong, D., and Zhou, G. (2019). Hierarchical modeling of global context for document-level neural machine translation. In *Proceedings of the 2019 Conference on Empirical Methods in Natural Language Processing and the 9th International Joint Conference on Natural Language Processing (EMNLP-IJCNLP)*, pages 1576–1585, Hong Kong, China. Association for Computational Linguistics.

Tiedemann, J. and Scherrer, Y. (2017). Neural machine translation with extended context. In *Proceedings of the Third Workshop on Discourse in Machine Translation*, pages 82–92, Copenhagen, Denmark. Association for Computational Linguistics.

Vaswani, A., Shazeer, N., Parmar, N., Uszkoreit, J., Jones, L., Gomez, A. N., Kaiser, L., and Polosukhin, I. (2017). Attention is all you need. In *Advances in Neural Information Processing Systems 30: Annual Conference on Neural Information Processing Systems 2017, December 4-9, 2017, Long Beach, CA, USA*, pages 5998–6008.

Voita, E., Sennrich, R., and Titov, I. (2019a). Context-aware monolingual repair for neural machine translation. In *Proceedings of the 2019 Conference on Empirical Methods in Natural Language Processing and the 9th International Joint Conference on Natural Language Processing (EMNLP-IJCNLP)*, pages 877–886, Hong Kong, China. Association for Computational Linguistics.

Voita, E., Sennrich, R., and Titov, I. (2019b). When a good translation is wrong in context: Context-aware machine translation improves on deixis, ellipsis, and lexical cohesion. In *Proceedings of the 57th Annual Meeting of the Association for Computational Linguistics*, pages 1198–1212, Florence, Italy. Association for Computational Linguistics.

Wang, L., Tu, Z., Way, A., and Liu, Q. (2017). Exploiting cross-sentence context for neural machine translation. In *Proceedings of the 2017 Conference on Empirical Methods in Natural Language Processing*, pages 2826–2831, Copenhagen, Denmark. Association for Computational Linguistics.

Xia, M., Kong, X., Anastasopoulos, A., and Neubig, G. (2019). Generalized data augmentation for low-resource translation. In *Proceedings of the 57th Annual Meeting of the Association for Computational Linguistics*, pages 5786–5796, Florence, Italy. Association for Computational Linguistics.

Xiong, H., He, Z., Wu, H., and Wang, H. (2019). Modeling coherence for discourse neural machine translation. In *The Thirty-Third AAAI Conference on Artificial Intelligence, AAAI 2019, The Thirty-First Innovative Applications of Artificial Intelligence Conference, IAAI 2019, The Ninth AAAI Symposium on Educational Advances in Artificial Intelligence, EAAI 2019, Honolulu, Hawaii, USA, January 27 - February 1, 2019*, pages 7338–7345. AAAI Press.

Zhang, J., Luan, H., Sun, M., Zhai, F., Xu, J., Zhang, M., and Liu, Y. (2018). Improving the transformer translation model with document-level context. In *Proceedings of the 2018 Conference on Empirical Methods in Natural Language Processing*, pages 533–542, Brussels, Belgium. Association for Computational Linguistics.

Target Language Monolingual Translation Memory based NMT by Cross-lingual Retrieval of Similar Translations and Reranking

Takuya Tamura s2120744_@_u.tsukuba.ac.jp
Xiaotian Wang s2320811_@_u.tsukuba.ac.jp
Takehito Utsuro utsuro_@_iit.tsukuba.ac.jp
Deg. Prog. Sys.&Inf. Eng., Grad. Sch. Sci.&Tech., University of Tsukuba, Japan

Masaaki Nagata masaaki.nagata_@_ntt.com
NTT Communication Science Laboratories, NTT Corporation, Japan

Abstract

Retrieve-edit-rerank (Hossain et al., 2020) is a text generation framework composed of three steps: retrieving for sentences using the input sentence as a query, generating multiple output sentence candidates, and selecting the final output sentence from these candidates. This simple approach has outperformed other existing and more complex methods. This paper focuses on the retrieving and the reranking steps. In the retrieving step, we propose retrieving similar target language sentences from a target language monolingual translation memory using language-independent sentence embeddings generated by mSBERT or LaBSE. We demonstrate that this approach significantly outperforms existing methods that use monolingual inter-sentence similarity measures such as edit distance, which is only applicable to a parallel translation memory. In the reranking step, we propose a new reranking score for selecting the best sentences, which considers both the sentence length normalized log-likelihood of each candidate and the sentence embeddings based similarity between the input and the candidate. We evaluated the proposed method with English-to-Japanese translation of the ASPEC and English-to-French translation of the EU bookshop corpus. The proposed method significantly exceeded the baseline in BLEU score, especially observing a 1.4-point improvement in the EU bookshop dataset over the original retrieve-edit-rerank method.

1 Introduction

Many studies have incorporated translation memories (TM), a set of high-quality bilingual sentences, into the NMT model in recent years. Bulte and Tezcan (2019) and Tezcan et al. (2021) proposed a NFR (Neural Fuzzy Repair) model that improves translation accuracy by incorporating TM into NMT. The model retrieves a similar source sentence from the set of source language sentences in the TM based on edit distance and sent2vec (Pagliardini et al., 2018), and concatenates the translation of a similar source sentence with the input source sentence to the NMT model. Since this model only requires preprocessing of the input to the NMT model, TM can be incorporated without modifying the model's architecture. Therefore, it is highly compatible with existing NMT models and portable in terms of implementation. On the other hand, due to the limitation of input sentence length, the number of similar sentences available

Proceedings of Machine Translation Summit XIX, Vol. 1: Research Track, pages 313–323
September 4–8, 2023, Macau SAR, China.

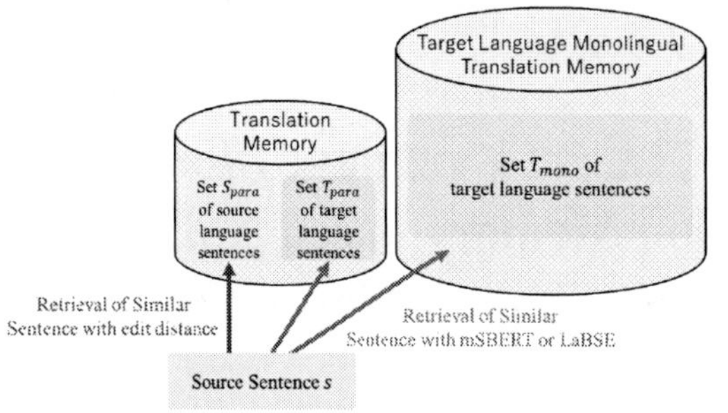

Figure 1: Retrieval of Similar Sentences from Translation Memory

for these methods is limited to one or two at most, and the retrieved similar sentences are not fully utilized. Also, if many informative similar sentences are obtained during inference, it is difficult to use all of them.

Hossain et al. (2020) proposed the retrieve-edit-rerank framework to overcome this limitation. They proposed a method that (1) retrieves multiple sentences from the training data using the input sentence as a query, (2) inputs the concatenation of the source and retrieved sentences into the model to generate multiple candidate sentences, and (3) extract the best sentence from the multiple candidates by choosing the sentence that maximizes the log-likelihood. In this paper, we focus on the (1) retrieval step and the (3) reranking step. As for the retrieval step, we compared monolingual inter-sentence similarity measures such as edit distance to cosine similarity based on language-independent sentence embedding with Multilingual Sentence-BERT (mSBERT) (Reimers and Gurevych, 2020) and LaBSE (Feng et al., 2022). Here, as shown in Figure 1, the edit distance requires the parallel corpus as the retrieval target, while the methods based on multilingual sentence embedding only requires a monolingual corpus of target language sentences. In the reranking step, we proposed a new reranking score for selecting the best sentences. This reranking score takes into account both the log-likelihood of each candidate with normalization by sentence length and the sentence embedding based similarity between the input and the candidate. We used the English-Japanese corpus of Asian Scientific Paper Excerpt Corpus (ASPEC) (Nakazawa et al., 2016) and the English-French corpus of EU bookshop corpus (EUbookshop) (Skadiņš et al., 2014; Tiedemann, 2012) to evaluate our method and found that the proposed method achieved significantly higher translation accuracy in all settings.

In summary, our contributions are as follows

1. In the framework of NFR (Figure 2), the use of similar sentences retrieved by language-independent sentence embedding generation models such as mSBERT and LaBSE significantly improved translation accuracy compared to conventional edit distance based retrieval methods (Table 2).
2. In the reranking phase of retrieve-edit-rerank (Figure 3), which selects the best sentence from multiple candidate output sentences, translation accuracy significantly improved by using a reranking score that takes into account both the log-likelihood of output with normalization by sentence length and the sentence embedding based similarity between the input and output candidate sentences (Table 3).

2 Related Work

As an NMT using the retrieve-edit framework, Bulte and Tezcan (2019) and Tezcan et al. (2021) proposed NFR (Neural Fuzzy Repair), a method to incorporate translation memory (TM) into

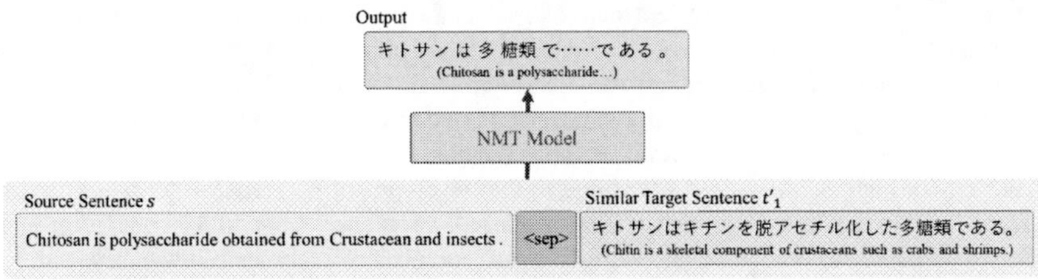

Figure 2: Framework of Translation with a Similar Target Sentence by NFR

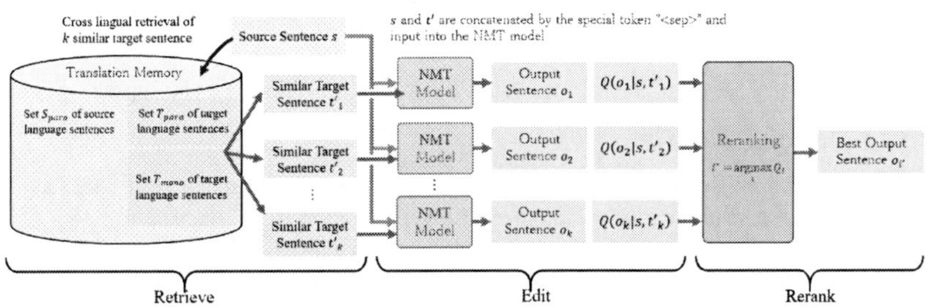

Figure 3: The Inference Framework of Retrieve-Edit-Rerank Model

NMT. They proposed a method that first retrieves similar source sentences based on edit distance using the input source sentence as the query, then concatenates the translation of the similar source sentence and the input source sentence and enters them into an LSTM-based NMT model. In this method, they achieved state-of-the-art in English-German and English-Hungarian translations. In addition, Xu et al. (2020) introduced word-by-word Fuzzy Matching to improve the accuracy of English-to-French translation using the Transformer model. They used cosine similarity of sentence embeddings as a similarity measure between an input sentence and the source language sentence. Among Bulte and Tezcan (2019), Tezcan et al. (2021), and Xu et al. (2020), both Tezcan et al. (2021) and Xu et al. (2020) introduced sentence embedding based similarity measure such as sent2vec for matching of the input sentence and similar source language sentences. However, they limit the search to the source language side of the training data. This information source is the same as the data used for training the baseline models, and the available quantity of data has not significantly increased. Our approach, on the other hand, is based on multilingual sentence embedding methods such as mSBERT and LaBSE and its information source for retrieving similar target sentences is the monolingual translation memory of target language sentences that is much larger than the training parallel data. Cai et al. (2021) also proposed a method that uses a monolingual corpus of the target language, rather than a bilingual corpus, as a target for retrieving similar sentences. They proposed a learnable retrieval model which is jointly optimized with the NMT model and performed similar sentence retrieval by MIPS (Maximum Inner Product Search). Although this approach achieves high performance, the model has to be built upon an architecture consisting of a Retrieval Model and a Translation Model. As a result, it eliminates the advantage of NFR where one can leverage the existing Transformer architecture and simply expand the input. Our approach, on the other hand, can be formalized as introducing the reranking phase of retrieve-edit-rerank into the architecture of the NFR framework, where it can be seen as leveraging the existing Transformer architecture in the edit phase of retrieve-edit-rerank framework.

For translation and summarization tasks, Hossain et al. (2020) proposed a method to generate multiple candidate output sentences and select the best output sentence by reranking them according to log-likelihood. They achieved a significant improvement in accuracy by combining NFR and retrieve-edit-rank frameworks. Despite the simplicity and versatility of this method, however, the improvement in translation accuracy due to the reranking is small.

In recent years, dense retrieval methods enabled us to retrieve semantically similar sentences with high accuracy and speed due to the development of Transformer-based language models. Reimers and Gurevych (2019) proposed a sentence embedding generation model, Sentence-BERT, to embed semantically similar sentences close to each other in vector space based on the pre-trained BERT (Devlin et al., 2019). More recently, Feng et al. (2022) proposed a multilingual sentence embedding generation model, LaBSE. These multilingual sentence embeddings can be retrieved quickly using approximate nearest neighbor search methods such as FAISS (Johnson et al., 2019).

3 Retrieval of Similar Sentences from Translation Memory (Retrieve)

3.1 Translation Memory

A translation memory (TM) is a set of high-quality bilingual sentence pairs that have been manually translated in the past. Computer-Aided Translation (CAT) is used as a tool to assist manual translation. If the source language sentence is already stored in the TM, it can be translated without error simply by replacing it with the target language sentence. Even when there is no exact match, a sentence with a certain degree of similarity (similar sentence) may be helpful during translation. In recent years, incorporating TM into NMT has been studied. In this paper, we define "similar target sentence" as a target language translation of a source language sentence similar to the input source language sentence ("similar source sentence").

Hereafter in this paper, a translation memory is defined as a set of pairs of a source language sentence s and a target language sentence t. Also, let S_{para} be a set of input source language sentences, T_{para} be a set of target language sentences, and T_{mono} be a monolingual translation memory of target language sentences. As shown in Figure 1, the original NFR requires the parallel corpus as the retrieval target and similar source sentences in the source language side S_{para} of the parallel translation memory are retrieved based on the edit distance. The proposed method, on the other hand, is based on multilingual sentence embedding methods such as mSBERT and LaBSE and only requires a monolingual corpus of target language sentences, where similar target sentences are retrieved not only from the target language side T_{para} of the parallel translation memory but also from the monolingual translation memory T_{mono} of target language sentences.

3.2 Similarity Measure based on Edit Distance

The edit distance is defined as the minimum number of operations required to convert one string into another string by inserting, deleting, or replacing. This paper followed Bulte and Tezcan (2019) and adopted the following similarity score of Vanallemeersch and Vandeghinste (2015),

$$sim_{ed}(x, y) = 1 - \frac{\Delta_{ed}(x, y)}{\max(|x|, |y|)}$$

where $\Delta_{ed}(x, y)$ is the edit distance between two sentences x, y, and $|x|$ is the number of tokens in x. When x and y perfectly match, the similarity score takes the maximum value $sim_{ed}(x, y) = 1$. Since the edit distance can only be calculated between two sentences of the same language, the retrieval is limited to the source sentences S_{para} in the TM. Therefore, the translation of "similar source sentences" is considered to be "similar target sentences". In addition, the computational cost during retrieval for large translation memories is significantly high because similarity must be calculated and compared on a brute-force basis when retrieving similar sentences by edit distance. Therefore, following Bulte and Tezcan (2019), we also adopted a method to calculate edit distance only for candidate set[1] of similar sentences retrieved using the similarity measure $containment_{max}$ provided by a Python library $SetSimilaritySearch$ (sss). The $containment_{max}$ is defined for the set of unique tokens v_x and v_y contained in each source sentence x and y respectively as follows:

$$containment_{max}(v_x, v_y) = \frac{||v_x \cap v_y||}{\max(||v_x||, ||v_y||)}$$

3.3 Similarity Measure based on Multilingual Sentence Embeddings

In this section, we describe a similarity measure based on multilingual sentence embedding. Sentence embedding is a mapping of a sentence to a vector of real numbers, which is used for document classification, sentiment analysis and bilingual sentence retrieval. In this paper, we used Multilingual Sentence-BERT[23] (Reimers and Gurevych, 2020) and LaBSE (Feng et al., 2022) as the sentence embedding generation model. Sentence-BERT (SBERT) was trained on NLI datasets and achieved high accuracy in STS tasks. It is extended to Multilingual SBERT by knowledge distillation using monolingual English SBERT and parallel sentences. LaBSE is also a sentence embedding generation model trained on large-scale monolingual and bilingual texts and achieved state-of-the-art accuracy in the BUCC task of bilingual sentence retrieval. We defined the similarity measure sim_{se} based on multilingual sentence embeddings between two sentences x and y as follows, where $E(x)$ is the sentence embedding for the sentence x[4]:

$$sim_{se}(x, y) = \frac{E(x) \cdot E(y)}{|E(x)||E(y)|}$$

4 Generation with NMT Model (Edit)

4.1 Training

As shown in Figure 2[5], we trained the translation model using the same procedure as Bulte and Tezcan (2019) and Tezcan et al. (2021). Specifically, we first retrieve k-best similar target sentences $t'_1, t'_2, \ldots, t'_k$ from the TM by edit distance or sentence embeddings, using the source language sentence s as a query. As in NFR model, for each of t'_i $(i = 1, \ldots, k)$, we concatenated s and t'_i with a special token "⟨sep⟩" and entered them to the translation model as below together with the reference target language translation t.

$$\text{Input} \quad : \quad s \ \langle \text{sep} \rangle \ t'_i, \qquad \text{Reference} \quad : \quad t$$

Thus, for each source language sentence s, we entered k parallel sentences to the translation model for training.

4.2 Inference

Figure 3 shows the inference procedure for the retrieve-edit-rerank model. First, we search for k-best similar target sentences $t'_1, t'_2, \ldots, t'_k$ in the TM using edit distance or sentence embeddings. We then decode k times using the translation model to obtain the k output candidates o_i

[1]Candidates are limited to those satisfying the similarity lower bound of 0.5.

[2]`https://github.com/UKPLab/ sentence-transformers`

[3]In the implementation of this paper, we used `paraphrase-multilingual-mpnet-base-v2`.

[4]For the retrieve-edit-rerank machine translation, we have to extract k similar sentences from $T_{para} \cup T_{mono}$ using the input source sentence s as a query. We used FAISS (Johnson et al., 2019), a library for approximate nearest neighbor search on GPUs, to extract k-best similar sentences.

[5]Figure 2 illustrates the inference procedure by Bulte and Tezcan (2019), where only the translation of the source sentence with the highest similarity is used as the "similar target sentence".

	ASPEC (En→Ja)	EUbookshop (En→Fr)	
Train	100,000	100,000	1,000,000
Dev	1,790	2,000	
Test	1,812	2,000	
Target Language Monolingual TM (including the target language side of Train)	2,000,000 (Ja)	8,421,120 (Fr)	

Table 1: Statistics of the Datasets

$(i = 1, \ldots, k)$ and calculate the reranking score Q_i of o_i $(i = 1, \ldots, k)$ based on the decoder's output probability p_{MT}.

5 Reranking Outputs by Reranking Scores (Rerank)

In the reranking step, out of the k output candidates o_i $(i = 1, \ldots, k)$, we select the i^*-th output candidate o_{i^*} whose score Q_{i^*} is the largest among the k output candidates:

$$i^* = \underset{i=1,2,\ldots,k}{\arg\max}\, Q_i$$

We compared three reranking scores in this paper. The first is a reranking score based on the log-likelihood of the output candidate (Hossain et al., 2020).

$$Q_i^{(\mathrm{Hossain})} = Q(s, t'_i, o_i) = \log_2 p_{MT}(o_i|s, t'_i)$$

Here, the p_{MT} represents the output probability of o_i when s, t'_i is input to the trained NMT model. It is calculated as follows:

$$p_{MT}(o_i|s, t'_i) = \prod_l p_{MT}(o_i^{(l)}|s, t'_i, o_i^{(<l)})$$

where, supposing that $o_i^{(<l)}$ represents the token sequence already output at the l-th step and $o_i^{(l)}$ represents the token output by the decoder at the l-th step, $p_{MT}(o_i^{(l)}|s, t'_i, o_i^{(<l)})$ represents the output probability at the l-th step of decoding.

The second is the proposed method, which is based on the average log-likelihood with normalization by sentence length. Here, let $|deSW(o_i)|$ be the number of words after detokenizing the subwords of the output candidate o_i.

$$Q_i^{(\mathrm{proposed1})} = Q(s, t'_i, o_i) = \frac{\log_2 p_{MT}(o_i|s, t'_i)}{|deSW(o_i)|}$$

The third is another proposed method, which takes into account the average log-likelihood normalized by sentence length and the similarity between input and output candidates using multilingual sentence embeddings. In the subsequent experiments, we chose $\alpha = 0.4$ as the optimal value based on the development data. Furthermore, the similarity measure sim_{se} employed in this context is derived from LaBSE.

$$Q_i^{(\mathrm{proposed2})} = Q(s, t'_i, o_i) = \alpha \frac{\log_2 p_{MT}(o_i|s, t'_i)}{|deSW(o_i)|} + (1 - \alpha)\, sim_{se}(s, o_i)$$

6 Experiments

6.1 Datasets

In this paper, to evaluate the proposed method, we used the English-Japanese corpus of Asian Scientific Paper Excerpt Corpus (ASPEC)[6] (Nakazawa et al., 2016) and the English-French corpus of the EU bookshop corpus (EUbookshop)[7] (Skadiņš et al., 2014; Tiedemann, 2012), which

[6] https://jipsti.jst.go.jp/aspec/

[7] https://opus.nlpl.eu/EUbookshop.php

is based on publications from various European institutions. The translation direction was from English to Japanese and from English to French, respectively. Only 100,000 or 1,000,000 randomly sampled sentences from each corpus were used as training data for the translation models, while the rest and the target language side of the training data were used as the monolingual translation memories. Table 1 shows the detailed numbers of sentences in these datasets. We tokenize the corpus using Moses tokenizer[8] for both English and French sentences and using MeCab[9] for Japanese. We then split it into sub-words using byte pair encoding BPE[10] (Sennrich et al., 2016) with applying 32,000 merge operations.

6.2 Setting

For the retrieval of similar sentences, we compared three different methods: $SetSimilaritySearch$ + edit distance (sss+ed), mSBERT, and LaBSE. With sss+ed, only the similar source sentences in the source language side of the training data (i.e., only 100,000 or 1,000,000 sentences shown in Table 1) are retrieved, while with the proposed methods with mSBERT and LaBSE, the similar target sentences not only in the target language side of the training data but also in the monolingual translation memory of target language sentences (i.e., 2,000,000 or 8,421,120 sentences shown in Table 1) are retrieved. During training, we compared the normal method without similar sentence retrieval (w/o retrieval) with a method that uses up to four similar sentences (top 1 to top 4). During inference, we compared three methods: a method that does not use similar sentences (w/o retrieval), a method that uses only the similar translation of the topmost 1 sentence as in the original NFR (top 1), a method that reranks based on $Q^{(\text{Hossain})}$, and two proposed methods that rerank based on $Q^{(\text{proposed1})}$ and $Q^{(\text{proposed2})}$. In those reranking methods, we use the number k of output candidates as $k = 32$. In addition, we define the oracle as selecting the one with the highest Sentence-BLEU out of the output candidates for each input sentence to investigate the upper bound of translation accuracy improvement due to reranking. In the comparison of retrieval methods in Table 2, we consider sss+ed as the baseline. In the comparison of reranking methods in Table 3, on the other hand, for each retrieval method, we consider the method that uses only the similar translation of the topmost 1 sentence (top 1) as the first baseline (baseline 1) and that based on $Q^{(\text{Hossain})}$ as the second baseline (baseline 2)[11].

6.3 Results

The results of training the translation model by retrieving similar translations using each retrieval method are shown in Table 2. The number of similar sentences used for training is set to $k = 1, 2, 3, 4$, and the number of similar sentences used for inference is set to $k = 1$. Without the retrieval of similar translations, the ASPEC, EUbookshop (100K), and EUbookshop (1M) BLEUs were 26.2, 20.2, and 26.9 points, respectively, whereas the sss+ed BLEUs were up to 26.4, 20.2, and 28.6 points, respectively, and significantly improved only for EUbookshop (1M). On the other hand, LaBSE showed significantly higher BLEU than sss+ed in all cases, with maximums of 27.1, 21.0, and 30.6 points. The highest BLEUs were obtained for both mSBERT and LaBSE when the topmost two or three sentences were used, and it can be confirmed that the accuracy conversely decreases when the topmost four sentences are used.

[8] https://www.statmt.org/moses/

[9] https://github.com/neologd/mecab-ipadic-neologd

[10] https://github.com/rsennrich/subword-nmt

[11] The encoder and decoder were 6 layers each, with 512 hidden dimensions, 2,048 dimensions in the FF layer and 8 multi-heads. We also adopted a warm-up of 6,000 steps and trained 30 epochs with a batch size of 32 sentences. Then, the BLEU score was measured against the test data at the number of epochs with the highest BLEU score against the development data.

	# of Similar Sentences		ASPEC (En→Ja)	EUbookshop (En→Fr)	
			# Training Data		
	Training	Inference	100,000	100,000	1,000,000
w/o retrieval	-	-	26.2	20.2	26.9
sss+ed (baseline)	top 1	top 1	26.4	20.2	28.6
	top 2		26.2	19.5	28.2
	top 3		26.1	18.3	27.6
	top 4		25.7	16.4	27.0
mSBERT	top 1	top 1	25.8	20.5	29.9†
	top 2		26.5	20.8	29.9†
	top 3		26.4	19.9	29.6†
	top 4		26.2	19.0	29.4†
LaBSE	top 1	top 1	25.8	20.9	30.2†
	top 2		**27.1**†	**21.0**†	30.3†
	top 3		26.5	20.4	**30.6**†
	top 4		26.3	19.3	30.0†

Table 2: Results of Comparing Retrieval Methods by the Translation Accuracies in BLEU (Topmost 1 similar sentence to be used during inference. "w/o retrieval" for vanilla Transformer without using similar sentences, sss+ed for a method using edit distance as NFR. † for significant (p<0.05) difference with the BLEU of sss+ed (baseline) when # of similar sentences in training is the same.)

Dataset	Retrieval Method	w/o reranking: w/o retrieval	w/o reranking: top 1 (baseline 1)	w/ reranking (k = 32): $Q^{(\text{Hossain})}$ (baseline 2)	$Q^{(\text{proposed1})}$	$Q^{(\text{proposed2})}$	oracle
ASPEC (En→Ja)	w/o retrieval	26.2	-	-	-	-	-
	sss+ed	-	26.2	26.6	26.8	27.0	28.5†‡
	mSBERT	-	26.5	26.4	26.9	27.2	29.7†‡
	LaBSE	-	27.1	27.4	28.1†	**28.3**†‡	31.8†‡
EUbookshop (En→Fr, 100k)	w/o retrieval	20.2	-	-	-	-	-
	sss+ed	-	20.2	20.3	20.3	20.3	20.3
	mSBERT	-	20.8	19.9	22.1†‡	22.4†‡	25.2†‡
	LaBSE	-	21.0	19.6	21.7‡	**22.5**†‡	25.6†‡
EUbookshop (En→Fr, 1M)	w/o retrieval	26.9	-	-	-	-	-
	sss+ed	-	28.2	28.2	28.2	28.2	28.3
	mSBERT	-	29.9	30.4	31.0†	31.4†‡	34.0†‡
	LaBSE	-	30.3	30.3	31.0	**31.7**†‡	34.2†‡

Table 3: Results of Comparing Retrieval/Reranking Methods by the Translation Accuracies in BLEU (Topmost 2 similar sentences to be used during training. "w/o retrieval" for vanilla Transformer without using similar sentences, "top 1" for a method using the most similar target sentence as NFR. $Q^{(\text{Hossain})}$ for the reranking score based on log-likelihood of the output candidate, $Q^{(\text{proposed1})}$ for the reranking score with length normalization of $Q^{(\text{Hossain})}$, $Q^{(\text{proposed2})}$ for the reranking score with $Q^{(\text{proposed1})}$ and the similarity between input and output candidates. Oracle for selecting the sentence with the highest Sentence-BLEU from output candidates. † for significant (p<0.05) difference with the BLEU of "top 1" (baseline 1) when the retrieval method is the same, ‡ for significant (p<0.05) difference with the BLEU of $Q^{(\text{Hossain})}$ (baseline 2) when the retrieval method is the same.)

Then, the results of reranking following the framework of retrieve-edit-rerank are shown in Table 3. First, when we focus on the reranking method using $Q^{(\text{Hossain})}$, no significant improvement in BLEU was obtained for any of the reranking methods. On the other hand, the reranking method using $Q^{(\text{proposed1,2})}$ did not improve BLEU significantly for sss+ed, but significantly improved BLEU in many cases when using mSBERT and LaBSE. The oracle that retrieves the sentence with the highest Sentence-BLEU shows an upper bound for reranking, but it is lower for sss+ed than for mSBERT and LaBSE, suggesting that there is little room for further improvement[12].

[12]For $Q^{(\text{proposed2})}$ with mSBERT/LaBSE, the percentages of similar target sentences retrieved from target language monolingual TM (excluding the target language side of the training data) that give the largest score through reranking are 97.6/95.5, 99.0/98.9, and 87.9/87.6 (ASPEC, EUbookshop 100k and 1M),

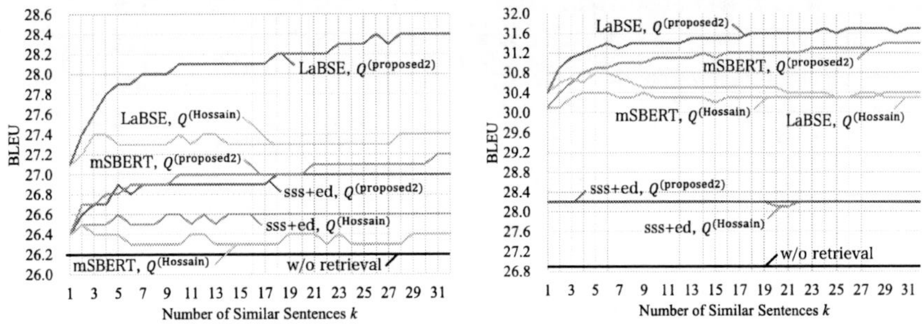

(a) for ASPEC (En→Ja)   (b) for EUbookshop (En→Fr, 1M)

Figure 4: The Changes in BLEU Scores for the Number of Similar Sentences k for Each Retrieval Method

6.4 Impact of the Number of Similar Target Sentences used for Reranking

Figure 4 shows the changes in BLEU scores when the number of similar translations k used for reranking is changed. As an overall trend, the reranking method based on $Q^{(\text{proposed2})}$ yields significantly higher BLEU than the method based on $Q^{(\text{Hossain})}$. In particular, for EUbookshop (1M) in Figure 4b, using LaBSE and $Q^{(\text{proposed2})}$, BLEU improves almost monotonically as k increases, reaching 31.7 points at $k = 32$. On the other hand, using $Q^{(\text{Hossain})}$ improves to 30.8 points at $k = 5$ and 6, but drops to 30.3 points at $k = 32$. In terms of corpus differences, only the method using LaBSE achieves significantly higher BLEUs than the baseline of sss+ed in ASPEC in Figure 4a, while both mSBERT and LaBSE achieve significantly higher BLEU scores than sss+ed in EUbookshop (1M) in Figure 4b. This difference may be derived from the difference of the training of the models of mSBERT and LaBSE. While mSBERT is multilingualized by distilling the model to measure the similarity of English sentences, LaBSE is more suitable for bilingual sentence retrieval because LaBSE was originally trained using bilingual data. In addition, in terms of the number of sentences per language included in the LaBSE's training data, the Japanese language ranks at third following English and Russian, suggesting that it is more suitable for tasks involving the Japanese language than mSBERT. Finally, focusing on the differences in retrieval methods, sss+ed has the smallest range of change in BLEU due to reranking compared to the other retrieval methods, with little or no effect from reranking. This is mainly because sss+ed's retrieval target was limited to 100K/1M sentences of the source language side of the parallel translation memory and did not find high-quality similar target sentences. This suggests that the cross-language retrieval method based on mSBERT and LaBSE sentence embedding can find a much larger number of high-quality similar sentences than sss+ed.

6.5 Example

Table 4 shows a concrete example of the results of an evaluation experiment using ASPEC. This example describes "the absorption of glucose in the small intestine of a mouse". In the table, "Similar Target Sentences selected through Reranking" shows the similar sentences with which the largest score Q_{i^*} is obtained through reranking among the $k = 32$ output candidates, and "Output" shows the output results from the NMT model. The Sentence-BLEU for each sentence

while they are 98.0/94.2, 99.3/98.9, and 86.7/87.8 for oracle. These percentages are mostly close to the percentages of the numbers of the sentences within the target language monolingual TMs (excluding the target language side of the training data) against the total numbers of the target language sentences to be retrieved (i.e., 95.0, 98.8, and 88.1 for ASPEC, EUbookshop 100k and 1M, respectively).

Input	Study of the effect on the glucose absorption power , the TCDD exposed C57BL / 6J mouse increased the glucose absorption power in the intestinum tenue .		
Reference	グルコース吸収能に対する影響を検討した結果，ＴＣＤＤ暴露Ｃ５７ＢＬ／６Ｊマウスは小腸におけるグルコース吸収能が増加した．		
	Similar Target Sentence selected through Reranking	**Output**	**Sentence-BLEU**
w/o Similar Sentence	N/A	グルコース吸収能に対する効果の研究では，ＴＣＤＤがＰＢＬ／６Ｊマウスに暴露されたものは小腸のグルコース吸収能を増加させた．	21.0
sss+ed + top 1	また，ポンプ光と信号光との間の偏光角を変化させて，スイッチングに与える影響を実験により確認した．	耐糖能吸収能への影響の研究では，ＴＣＤＣＤが５７ＢＬ／６Ｊを搭載したが，小腸では耐糖吸収能は増加していた．	18.8
sss+ed $+Q^{(\text{Hossain})}$	また，ハタケシメジ投与は糞中胆汁酸排せつ量と，コレステロールを胆汁酸に変換するコレステロール７α－ヒドロキシラーゼの活性を上昇させた．	耐糖能吸収能への影響の研究では，ＴＣＤＣＤが５７ＢＬ／６Ｊを搭載したＴＣＤＤは小腸中での耐糖吸収能を増加した．	24.5
sss+ed $+Q^{(\text{proposed2})}$	また，ハタケシメジ投与は糞中胆汁酸排せつ量と，コレステロールを胆汁酸に変換するコレステロール７α－ヒドロキシラーゼの活性を上昇させた．	耐糖能吸収能への影響の研究では，ＴＣＤＣＤが５７ＢＬ／６Ｊを搭載したＴＣＤＤは小腸中での耐糖吸収能を増加した．	24.5
LaBSE + top 1	グルコースとしょ糖間の相互転化を触媒する細菌性（大腸菌）キシロースイソメラーゼの発現によって，発育中のジャガイモ塊茎の代謝におけるヘキソースの役割について調べた．	グルコース吸収電力に対する影響の研究，ＴＣＤＤがＣＭＳ／６Ｊマウスに暴露されたＣＣＤは小腸のグルコース吸収電力を増加させた．	14.0
LaBSE $+Q^{(\text{Hossain})}$	ヤギにおけるコレシストキニン（ＣＣＫ）の食欲減退効果を評価する目的で，２２時間粗食させた５頭の去勢ヤギに，塊状注入もしくは連続注入で第三脳室内にＣＣＫ（硫酸エステルＣＣＫ－８）を投与した．	グルコース吸収電力に対する効果の研究，ＴＣＤＤがＣｕｐ５７ＢＬ／６Ｊマウスに暴露された．	24.0
LaBSE $+Q^{(\text{proposed2})}$	正常マウスやＫＫ－Ａｙマウスを用いて，小腸におけるα－グルコシル二糖類の消化／吸収能力を比較した．	グルコース吸収電力，ＴＣＤＤ露光ＣＭＳ／６Ｊマウスのグルコース吸収電力に対する影響を研究した結果，小腸におけるグルコース吸収電力を増加させた．	**27.3**

Table 4: Examples of Results of Experiments with ASPEC

is calculated. Focusing on the similar sentences retrieved by sss+ed, the target language translation of the most similar source language sentence (i.e., top 1) is not a sentence in the biological field, and the similar target sentences selected through reranking by $Q^{(\text{Hossain})}$ and $Q^{(\text{proposed2})}$, although they are sentences in the biological field, do not have much information relevant to the reference sentence in terms of the content. On the other hand, when we focus on the similar sentences retrieved by LaBSE, we find that even the "top 1" sentence describes "glucose(グルコース)" and the similar target sentence selected through reranking by $Q^{(\text{proposed2})}$ describes "the absorption of sugars in mice (マウスにおける糖類の吸収)", which is the most relevant to the content of the reference translation. The highest value of Sentence-BLEU of the output candidate is also obtained by LaBSE+$Q^{(\text{proposed2})}$.

7 Conclusion

In this study, within the retrieve-edit-rerank framework, we introduced a method for cross-lingual retrieval of similar translations through multilingual sentence embedding, along with an enhanced reranking method. We demonstrated that utilizing vector neighborhood search, based on language-agnostic sentence embedding generation models like mSBERT and LaBSE, contributed to a significant improvement in translation accuracy within this framework. This proved more effective than the retrieval technique based on edit distance employed in the previous research. Moreover, we applied multiple similar sentences to generate various candidate translations, subsequently selecting the optimal translation through an automatic reranking process. The reranking score considered both the output log-likelihood normalized for the length of the reconstituted subword sentences, and the cosine similarity between the input and output candidate sentences through sentence embeddings. This methodology has led to a significant enhancement in translation accuracy.

References

Bulte, B. and Tezcan, A. (2019). Neural fuzzy repair: Integrating fuzzy matches into neural machine translation. In *Proc. 57th ACL*, pages 1800–1809.

Cai, D., Wang, Y., Li, H., Lam, W., and Liu, L. (2021). Neural machine translation with monolingual translation memory. In *Proc. 59th ACL and 11th IJCNLP*, pages 7307–7318.

Devlin, J., Chang, M.-W., Lee, K., and Toutanova, K. (2019). BERT: Pre-training of deep bidirectional transformers for language understanding. In *Proc. NAACL-HLT*, pages 4171–4186.

Feng, F., Yang, Y., Cer, D., Arivazhagan, N., and Wang, W. (2022). Language-agnostic BERT sentence embedding. In *Proc. 60th ACL*, pages 878–891.

Hossain, N., Ghazvininejad, M., and Zettlemoyer, L. (2020). Simple and effective retrieve-edit-rerank text generation. In *Proc. 58th ACL*, pages 2532–2538.

Johnson, J., Douze, M., and Jégou, H. (2019). Billion-scale similarity search with GPUs. *IEEE Transactions on Big Data*, 7(3):535–547.

Nakazawa, T., Yaguchi, M., Uchimoto, K., Utiyama, M., Sumita, E., Kurohashi, S., and Isahara, H. (2016). ASPEC: Asian scientific paper excerpt corpus. In *Proc. 10th LREC*, pages 2204–2208.

Pagliardini, M., Gupta, P., and Jaggi, M. (2018). Unsupervised learning of sentence embeddings using compositional n-gram features. In *Proc. NAACL-HLT*, pages 528–540.

Reimers, N. and Gurevych, I. (2019). Sentence-BERT: Sentence embeddings using Siamese BERT-networks. In *Proc. EMNLP and 9th IJCNLP*, pages 3982–3992.

Reimers, N. and Gurevych, I. (2020). Making monolingual sentence embeddings multilingual using knowledge distillation. In *Proc. EMNLP*, pages 4512–4525.

Sennrich, R., Haddow, B., and Birch, A. (2016). Neural machine translation of rare words with subword units. In *Proc. 54th ACL*, pages 1715–1725.

Skadiņš, R., Tiedemann, J., Rozis, R., and Deksne, D. (2014). Billions of parallel words for free: Building and using the EU bookshop corpus. In *Proc. 9th LREC*, pages 1850–1855.

Tezcan, A., Bulté, B., and Vanroy, B. (2021). Towards a better integration of fuzzy matches in neural machine translation through data augmentation. *Informatics*, 8(1):1–27.

Tiedemann, J. (2012). Parallel data, tools and interfaces in OPUS. In *Proc. 8th LREC*, pages 2214–2218.

Vanallemeersch, T. and Vandeghinste, V. (2015). Assessing linguistically aware fuzzy matching in translation memories. In *Proc. 18th EAMT*, pages 153–160.

Xu, J., Crego, J., and Senellart, J. (2020). Boosting neural machine translation with similar translations. In *Proc. 58th ACL*, pages 1580–1590.

Towards Zero-Shot Multilingual Poetry Translation

Wai Lei Song nlp2ct.jacky@gmail.com
Haoyun Xu nlp2ct.haoyun@gmail.com
Derek F. Wong derekfw@um.edu.mo
Runzhe Zhan nlp2ct.runzhe@gmail.com
Lidia S. Chao lidiasc@um.edu.mo
Shanshan Wang* nlp2ct.shanshan@um.edu.mo
NLP^{2}CT Lab, Department of Computer and Information Science, University of Macau

Abstract

The application of machine translation in the field of poetry has always presented significant challenges. Conventional machine translation techniques are inadequate for capturing and translating the unique style of poetry. The absence of a parallel poetry corpus and the distinctive structure of poetry further restrict the effectiveness of traditional methods. This paper introduces a zero-shot method that is capable of translating poetry style without the need for a large-scale training corpus. Specifically, we treat poetry translation as a standard machine translation problem and subsequently inject the poetry style upon completion of the translation process. Our injection model only requires back-translation and easily obtainable monolingual data, making it a low-cost solution. We conducted experiments on three translation directions and presented automatic and human evaluations, demonstrating that our proposed method outperforms existing online systems and other competitive baselines. These results validate the feasibility and potential of our proposed approach and provide new prospects for poetry translation.

1 Introduction

The process of translating poetry presents an intricate challenge within the field of machine translation. The prevalence of the neural machine translation (NMT) paradigm (Vaswani et al., 2017), which necessitates copious amounts of data to effectively train a model capable of producing accurate translations (Koehn and Knowles, 2017). Unfortunately, the availability of parallel corpora that can be leveraged towards the training of a robust poetry translation system is currently inadequate. On the other hand, poetry is a manifestation of the unique imagination and creativity of the poet, as well as their distinctive writing style. As Chakrabarty et al. (2021) has pointed out, although NMT systems may succeed in translating the essence meaning of the poetry, the translation process inevitably disregards the writing style.

As a result, two distinct research paths have emerged within the field of poetry translation. In an effort to preserve the poet's distinctive writing style, Genzel et al. (2010) initially employed statistical machine translation, with a focus on maintaining the rhythm of the original

*Corresponding Author.

Proceedings of Machine Translation Summit XIX, Vol. 1: Research Track, pages 324–335
September 4–8, 2023, Macau SAR, China.

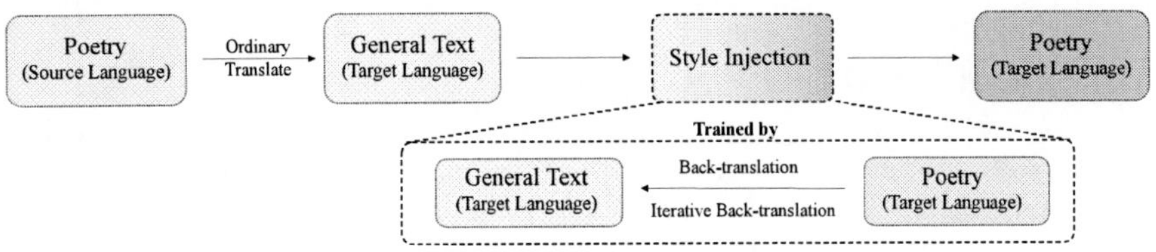

Figure 1: An illustration of the proposed zero-shot poetry translation method.

work. This approach was subsequently refined by Ghazvininejad et al. (2018), who introduced the additional constraints of rhythm and rhyme into neural poetry translation. This yielded an acceptability rate of 78.2% in terms of translation quality. Additionally, Yang et al. (2019) explored the use of unique tokens to govern the structure of the translated poetry. Meanwhile, From the perspective of overcoming the low-resource challenge, researchers have been proved to be an effective method by utilizing out-of-domain data, such as song lyrics (Shen et al., 2020; Liu et al., 2019). However, the existence of gaps in genre and writing style between poetry and other forms of text, improvements made to current poetry do not necessarily result in significant advancements. This is because these methods remain limited to enhancing the representation of general domain text, rather than enabling the model to comprehend the intricate patterns present in poetry. Encouragingly, as Chakrabarty et al. (2021) has provided poetic parallel corpora and demonstrated that fine-tuning with such data can greatly enhance the model's ability to adapt in poetry translation. Regrettably, the collection of parallel text and the construction of corpora are prohibitively expensive for research purposes. To address the aforementioned concerns in a cost-effective manner, we proposed a novel zero-shot method for poetry translation that consists of two stages. During the first stage, the model concentrates on learning to translate general domain text, thereby guaranteeing the preservation of the meaning of the source sentence and the fluency of the generated translation. In the second stage, the model acquires the ability to inject poetic style into the sentences generated in the first stage, resembling the process of style transfer (Huang et al., 2020; Li et al., 2020; Malmi et al., 2020). To achieve this goal, we collected over 2 million poetry texts in the target languages, including English, Portuguese, and Chinese. We utilized a back-translation approach to separate the poetic style, resulting in a pseudo-parallel corpus that goes from general text to poetry text. Our proposed method outperforms several competitive baselines, as evidenced by both automatic evaluation metrics and human evaluation results.

The contributions of our work are as follows:

- We are the first to propose a new approach for poetry translation without requiring a parallel poetry corpus. And the proposed method can be extended to other language pairs with monolingual data.
- We proposed a new human evaluation framework for poetry translation (Section 3.3) and invited several professional poets to evaluate the translation results.
- We will release the collected monolingual data and the created pseudo-parallel corpus for the purpose of research.

2 Methodology

To overcome the current absence of parallel poetry corpus, a zero-shot poetry translation method was proposed. As displayed in Figure 1, the proposed approach comprises of two distinct stages:

ordinary translation and style injection.

2.1 Related work

Poetry translations continue to predominantly rely on parallel corpora. To address this, one potential approach is to explore alternative datasets that share similar attributes to train the model effectively (Shen et al., 2020; Liu et al., 2019). Utilizing a multilingual parallel poetry corpus for fine-tuning pre-trained models has demonstrated promising results, indicating that poetry within a language family can be more effectively modeled through this approach (Chakrabarty et al., 2021). Furthermore, by leveraging the available dataset, modifying the model's mechanism or incorporating specific notations can enhance its ability to grasp the underlying structure of the poem more effectively (Ghazvininejad et al., 2018; Yang et al., 2019).

Text style transfer is the process of modifying the style of a sentence by rephrasing the original sentence in a different style while retaining its original meaning (Toshevska and Gievska, 2021). Until now, recent research has focused on a certain area of style transfer, such as Personal style (Pennebaker et al., 2003; Argamon et al., 2003; Peersman et al., 2016), Formality (Sheikha and Inkpen, 2010; Heylighen and Dewaele, 1999), Politeness (Brown et al., 1987; Andersson and Pearson, 1999; Chhaya et al., 2018), Offensiveness Pavlopoulos et al. (2019); Zampieri et al. (2019), Genre (Dewdney et al., 2001) and Sentiment (Russell, 1980; Susanto et al., 2020). Indeed, there are various methods utilized in different areas for achieving text style transfer. These methods may vary depending on the specific domain or application. Establishing a pseudo-parallel corpus by using an augmentation method such as back-translation is one direction of style transfer (Zhang et al., 2020b). Representation learning involves feeding sentences with a particular input style into the encoder while embedding the target style into the decoder. This enables the generation of desired outputs with different styles (Zhang et al., 2018; Liu et al., 2020). One approach to text style transfer involves removing certain words or adjusting the latent representation of a sentence, followed by regenerating the sentence to alter its style (Li et al., 2018; Sudhakar et al., 2019). The advantage of this method lies in its effectiveness in effectively changing the style compared to representation learning methods. However, one common challenge is that the model may struggle to maintain the same meaning of the sentences and may introduce grammar errors during the style transfer process.

2.2 Formulation

Given a poetry text $\mathbf{x}$ in the source language, the neural poetry translation model parameterized with θ generates the translation $\hat{\mathbf{y}}$ in the target language based on the conditional probability:

$$\hat{\mathbf{y}} = \arg\max \prod_{i=1}^{I} \log P(y_i | y_{<i}, \mathbf{x}; \theta) \tag{1}$$

Through the comparison of the golden truth $\mathbf{x}$ and the model hypothesis $\mathbf{y}$, the optimization of the model parameters θ occurs during the training process. We argue that the acquisition of robust parameters θ, necessary for the production of high-quality poetry translation $\mathbf{y}$, is a formidable task due to the aforementioned challenges. The primary obstacle in poetry translation lies in the model's requirement to not only translate the intended meaning accurately but also to adhere to the structural and stylistic conventions of the target language's poetry. This poses a significant translated challenge in terms of wording and sentence structure. Furthermore, directly translating the source language poetry text may result in the loss of the poem's intended meaning, due to the agency of the poetry text. This risk of meaning loss is further compounded by the inherent difficulty in producing high-quality translations when working with a single line of a poem at a time, as this approach lacks the necessary contextual and structural information to accurately convey the intended meaning, regardless of whether the source

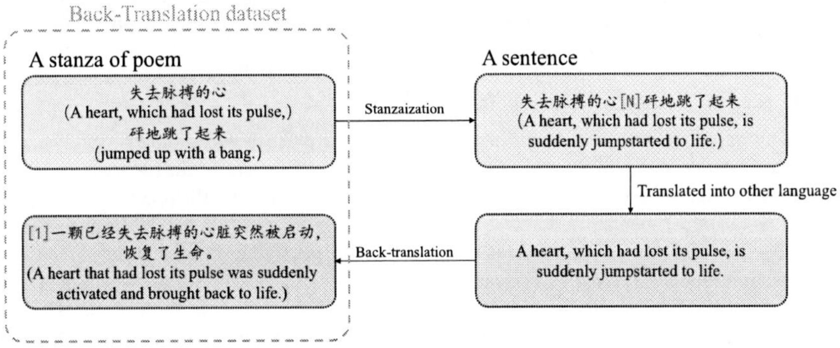

Figure 2: An illustration of poetry stanzaization process and back-translation process. The token known as "[number] serves the purpose of indicating the number of line breaks present in the original poems.

language or target language text is read.

Consequently, to address these challenges, as displayed in Figure 1, a two-stage translation approach is proposed, utilizing two distinct models, namely θ_{trans} and θ_{style}. In the first stage, model θ_{trans} is employed to translate the source sentence $\mathbf{x}$ into ordinary text $\hat{y}_{\text{general}}$. In the subsequent stage, model θ_{style} is utilized to inject the ordinary text with poetic style, producing the poetic text $\hat{y}$.

2.3 Poetry Stanzaization

A stanza is a fundamental poetry unit comprised of poetic lines that follow a specific principle or set of principles, such as syntax, meter, alliteration, lineation, or arc of thought. In some poetry styles, a stanza is created through end rhymes. The identification of stanzas is based on their intervals and other units of lines before and after them, often mirroring the first stanza. Stanzas possess a periodic nature, directing readers through a poem's text with their organized lines and transitions between stanzaic intervals. The line serves as both a rhythmical and structural unit, perceptible to both readers and listeners of poetry. Traditional mechanisms of closure are employed to delimitate stanzas from each other. As a unit of measure, a stanza is connected to adjacent units to form higher-level structures, while functioning as a structure built of lower-level poetic lines.

In order to guarantee the preservation of the meaning of poetry during the two-stage translation process, it is suggested that the stanza be encoded with the assistance of an additional signal. More specifically, as shown in Figure 2, the verse (or stanza) contains two lines. Therefore, a stanzaization process was utilized to properly handle the poem. the two sentences are concatenated into "A heart, which had lost its pulse, is suddenly jumpstarted to life." The token "[N]" is primarily utilized to represent the place after the stanzaization process, where the line break occurs. Furthermore, it is utilized to guarantee the model's consistent translation of an equivalent number of lines of poetry, thereby ensuring the consistency of evaluation conditions. In addition, when applying the stanzaization process to poetic works that are often written in a prose-like style, the resulting outcomes will typically consist of long sentences. To prevent the issue of excessively long spliced sentences, any sentence exceeding 100 words will be divided into shorter sentences based on punctuation or the natural ending point of the original sentence. The objective is to maximize the preservation of the sentence's meaning while minimizing the frequency of sentence cuts.

2.4 Stage I: Ordinary Translation

To acquire an ordinary translation model θ_{trans}, there exist three candidate systems, namely online system[1], in-house trained system, and pre-trained system[23]. In order to ascertain the preferred choice of an ordinary translation model, we employed English-to-Chinese translation tasks as our experimental framework. Our team opted to utilize the WMT'17 English⇒Chinese shared task data[4] to train our in-house systems, with the intention of securing a competitive translation model. In order to evaluate the performance of these systems, we compared them using the WMT'17 English⇒Chinese test set and determined their F-score via BERTScore Zhang et al. (2020a). Our results indicate that the online system achieved the highest performance on the test set[5], and as such, we have selected it to serve as the translation model for the first stage of our method for all languages.

2.5 Stage II: Style Injection

The utilization of Back-Translation (BT) is a prevalent technique in establishing a pseudo-parallel corpus that serves as an input for training the style injection model. One advantage of the BT method is that it only requires easily obtainable monolingual data, thereby reducing the need for costly parallel corpus construction. It is widely recognized that the era, experience, and emotional state of poets play a profound role in the style of their poemsYu and Liu (2021). Nonetheless, Rabinovich et al. (2017) research has revealed that sentences generated by machine translation tend to adopt the stylistic features of the machine translation process itself, rather than the specific style of the original author. Therefore, another benefit is that sentences generated through BT tend to adopt the stylistic features of machine translation, which can facilitate the injection of poetic style into the translated sentences. To illustrate, Figure 2 displayed the use of an online system to apply the BT method and establish a pseudo-parallel poetry corpus.

The monolingual poetry text $\mathbf{y}_{\text{poe}}$ in the target language is subjected to the BT method through an online system, resulting in the generation of an ordinary text $\mathbf{y}^*_{\text{general}}$, which can be formulated as: $\mathbf{y}_{\text{poe}} \rightarrow \mathbf{x}_{\text{general}} \rightarrow \mathbf{y}^*_{\text{general}}$. The sentence pair $\{\mathbf{y}^*_{\text{general}}, \mathbf{y}_{\text{poe}}\}$, comprising the original poetry text $\mathbf{y}_{\text{poe}}$ and its back-translated counterpart $\mathbf{y}^*_{\text{general}}$, is employed as the source and target data for training the style injection model θ_{style}. Furthermore, we incorporate an additional measure to our methodology by placing a distinct token labeled "[number]" at the beginning of each sentence. This token is used to indicate the number of lines present in each stanza, thereby providing an added layer of control over the overall structure of the poetic style. For example, as shown in Figure 2,"[1]" denotes that there are two lines in the current stanza. If only one line in the stanza the token will display "[0]".

One potential weakness of poetry stanzaization is that it will decrease the amount of training data because it merges multiple lines into one training instance. For example, the 1.6M modern Chinese poetry lines become 30K long sentences after applying the stanzaization process.

[1]https://fanyi.baidu.com

[2]https://huggingface.co/Helsinki-NLP/opus-mt-en-zh

[3]https://huggingface.co/facebook/m2m100_418M

[4]http://www.statmt.org/wmt17/translation-task.html

[5]Pre-trained: 0.742; In-house:0.809; Baidu Online System: 0.832

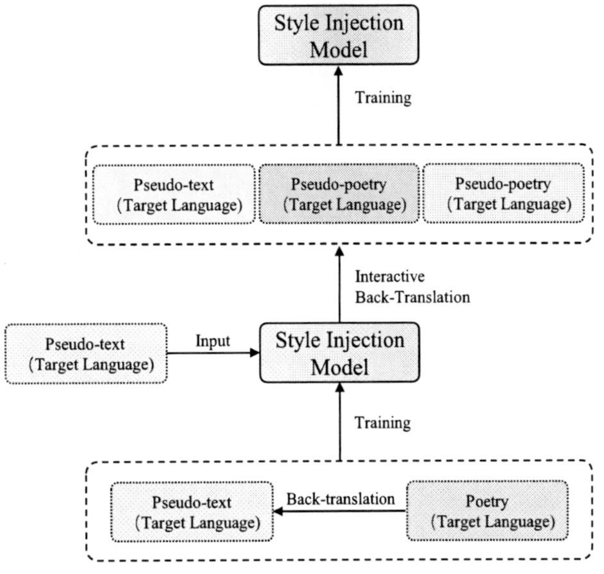

Figure 3: An illustration of Iterative Back-translation (IBT) process.

We have noted that certain words found within poems possess additional nuances of meaning that cannot be accurately conveyed through the back-translation process. Additionally, the act of performing back-translations may also result in alterations to the original intended meaning. Consequently, it is not uncommon for some of the generated sentences to contain erroneous meanings. Hence, we further use Iterative Back-translation Hoang et al. (2018) to augment the data for training θ_{style}. Hoang et al. (2018) introduced the Iterative Back-translation (IBT) methodology, and according to his approach, duplicating the bilingual corpus and appending it to the corpus dataset can be advantageous to the training model without any detrimental impact. Intuitively, the back-translation method is utilized to generate the pseudo-parallel dataset. The act of implementing the iterative back-translation method to enrich the dataset holds the potential to improve the model's capabilities and enhance its overall performance. As shown in Figure 3, IBT repeats the BT process to establish an extensive pseudo-parallel corpus for building a better translation system, and augmenting the pseudo-data by IBT is also a direct and inexpensive method. It is also helpful to improve the robustness of the style injection system by providing diverse pseudo-data.

3 Experimental Settings

We conduct experiments on English, Portuguese, and Chinese poetry translation task to verify the effectiveness of the proposed method.

3.1 Dataset

In this study, we have compiled a comprehensive collection of poetry in different languages. Specifically, a significant corpus of 1.6M sentences of modern Chinese poetry was collected, which was subsequently subjected to the process of stanzaization, resulting in a final compilation of 300k lines. Regarding the English and Portuguese poetry, we have refrained from

Lanugage	Split	Train	Dev	Test
Chinese	BT	300K	3K	876
	ConPP	300K		
	UnPP	300K		
	PSen	275K		
English	BT	290K	1K	100
	ConPP	270K		
	UnPP	270K		
	PSen	270K		
Portuguese	BT	380K	1K	100
	ConPP	350K		
	UnPP	350K		
	PSen	350K		

Table 1: Statistics of the pseudo-parallel corpora used to train style injection model. The BT corpus $\{\mathbf{y}^*_{\text{general}}, \mathbf{y}_{\text{poe}}\}$ is built by back-translation. The ConPP $\{\mathbf{y}^*_{\text{general}}, \mathbf{y}'_{\text{poe}}\}$, UnPP $\{\mathbf{y}^*_{\text{general}}, \hat{\mathbf{y}}_{\text{poe}}\}$, and PSen $\{\mathbf{y}^-_{\text{general}}, \mathbf{y}_{\text{poe}}\}$ refer to Controllable Pseudo-Poems corpus, Uncontrollable Pseudo-Poems corpus, and Pseudo-Sentences corpus respectively. These corpora are built by iterative back-translation.

categorizing them based on style and instead collected a total of 290K and 380K stanzas, respectively. The primary sources of data for this compilation were online platforms, including forums[6][7], website[8][9], and other online resources[10][11].

Table 1 shows the statics of pseudo-parallel data used to train style injection model θ_{style}, including BT data and several IBT data variants.

- **Controllable Pseudo-Poems (ConPP)**: The synthetic parallel corpus $\{\mathbf{y}^*_{\text{general}}, \mathbf{y}'_{\text{poe}}\}$ is built by applying iterative translation to translate the $\mathbf{y}^*_{\text{general}}$ by prepending a "[number]" token before the $\mathbf{y}_{\text{poe}}$, which eventually produces a new synthetic parallel corpus as: $\mathbf{y}^*_{\text{general}} \rightarrow \mathbf{y}'_{\text{poe}}$.
- **Uncontrollable Pseudo-Poems (UnPP)**: The synthetic parallel corpus $\{\mathbf{y}^*_{\text{general}}, \hat{\mathbf{y}}_{\text{poe}}\}$ is built by applying iterative translation to translate the $\mathbf{y}^*_{\text{general}}$ without prepending the "[number] token before the $\hat{\mathbf{y}}_{\text{poe}}$.
- **Pseudo-Sentences (PSen)**: The synthetic parallel corpus $\{\mathbf{y}^-_{\text{general}}, \mathbf{y}_{\text{poe}}\}$ is built by applying iterative translation to translate the $\mathbf{y}_{\text{poe}}$ into the $\mathbf{y}^-_{\text{general}}$ in the IBT process, which can be formulated as: $\mathbf{y}_{\text{poe}} \rightarrow \mathbf{y}^-_{\text{general}}$.

To create the test sets for both the one-stage and two-stage models, a random selection of 200 English poems (comprising 876 stanzas in total) was made from the English-Chinese Poetry Translation Website[12]. The test set of Portuguese poems and English poems translated

[6]http://www.chinawriter.com.cn/
[7]https://poets.org/poems
[8]http://www.zgshige.com/
[9]https://allpoetry.com/
[10]http://vvchem.com/
[11]https://www.luso-poemas.net/
[12]www.poetrysky.com

from English and Chinese respectively, are randomly selected 100 stanzas in total. As for the training of the various style injection models, the aforementioned test set was employed, with a random selection of 3,000 stanzas of modern Chinese poetry, 1,000 stanzas of English and Portuguese poetry serving as the validation set.

3.2 Model Training

Transformer architecture Vaswani et al. (2017) implemented by *fairseq* toolkit[13] is used to train the in-house NMT system, style injection and iterative back-translation models with shared vocabulary of 30K BPE Sennrich et al. (2015) tokens. Both the encoder and decoder block consist of 6 layers with 8 attention heads. The embedding size and hidden size are set to 512. We train all the models with a learning rate of 3e-5 and use 16K tokens per batch.

3.3 Evaluation

As for the automatic evaluation, we use BLEU and BERTScore to evaluate the performance of different MT systems. Furthermore, the evaluation method BERTScore calculates a sentence's score depending on the contextualized embedding similarity of references and system results, which could better understand each token's meaning during the sentence than the BLEU method, and more similar to the human evaluation score Zhang et al. (2020a). We report the recall score (BS.R), precision score (BS.P), and F1 (BS.F) score of the BERTScore respectively. For human evaluation, given the absence of any preceding research on evaluation metrics for poetry translation, our study relied upon human evaluation as a way to acquire more objective and authentic evaluations. We invited experts in the field of modern Chinese poetry to modify the evaluation framework proposed by Yi et al. (2018), and proposed a new evaluation framework that comprises five distinct perspectives:

- **Poeticity**: The translated poem exhibits a structure and poetic quality that is consistent with the poetry style of the target language.
- **Fluency**: The translated poem employs the diction and grammar that are characteristic of the poetry in the target language.
- **Coherence**: The meaning translated in the content of the translated poem is equivalent to that of the original poem in the source language.
- **Meaningfulness**: Translating poetry entails conveying a significant meaning and message.
- **Overall Impression**: For the overall impression score of the translated poem.

We randomly selected 30 Chinese poems and then asked four experts in the field of poetry to evaluate four types of translation generated by humans, the online system, "BT" model, and "IBT:ALL" model, respectively. The evaluation was conducted in a blind way, i.e., the experts did not know the type of translation during the evaluation process.

4 Main Results

Table 2 illustrates that the injection of poetic style using the model trained with all the IBT variants, following the utilization of the online translation system, outperforms the one-stage and other two-stage baselines. This superiority is further confirmed by the results of the human evaluation presented in Table 3, despite all the automatic translation methods being unable to surpass human translation. The automatic evaluation and human evaluation results serve as evidence for the efficacy of the two-stage translation approach, with particular emphasis on the effectiveness of the style injection model compare to the online system.

[13]https://github.com/pytorch/fairseq/

	English ⇒ Modern Chinese				Chinese ⇒ English				English ⇒ Portuguese			
	BLEU	**BS.P**	**BS.R**	**BS.F**	**BLEU**	**BS.P**	**BS.R**	**BS.F**	**BLEU**	**BS.P**	**BS.R**	**BS.F**
One-stage Neural Poetry Translation												
Pre-trained Transformer	7.62	71.4	70.1	70.6	11.46	81.6	81.2	81.3	12.82	74.8	75.3	75.0
Baidu Online system	14.23	74.6	74.7	74.5	18.87	83.5	83.5	83.4	18.62	77.0	77.8	77.4
Two-stage Neural Poetry Translation												
BT	11.69	76.4	76.1	76.2	19.05	85.5	85.0	85.2	18.64	78.0	78.6	78.2
IBT:All	14.04	**78.3**	**77.7**	**77.9**	19.34	**86.5**	**85.8**	**86.1**	19.04	78.7	78.7	78.5
IBT:PSen	12.08	76.7	76.4	76.5	**19.54**	86.2	85.7	86.0	17.70	**79.0**	**79.1**	**78.9**
IBT:ConPP	12.29	76.8	76.6	76.6	18.28	85.4	85.1	85.2	**19.72**	78.9	79.0	78.8
IBT:UnPP	**14.35**	78.2	77.6	**77.9**	17.93	86.2	85.7	86.0	18.81	78.3	78.6	78.3

Table 2: Statistics of the pseudo-parallel corpora used to train style injection model. The BT corpus $\{\mathbf{y}^*_{\text{general}}, \mathbf{y}_{\text{poe}}\}$ is built by back-translation. The ConPP $\{\mathbf{y}^*_{\text{general}}, \mathbf{y}^{'}_{\text{poe}}\}$, UnPP $\{\mathbf{y}^*_{\text{general}}, \hat{\mathbf{y}}_{\text{poe}}\}$, and PSen $\{\mathbf{y}^{-}_{\text{general}}, \mathbf{y}_{\text{poe}}\}$ refer to Controllable Pseudo-Poems corpus, Uncontrollable Pseudo-Poems corpus, and Pseudo-Sentences corpus respectively. These corpora are built by iterative back-translation. The IBT:ALL refers train style injection model by using all corpus.

5 Analysis

As shown in Table 2, regarding the second stage of neural poetry translation, it was observed that the scores achieved for the English and Chinese poems were higher than those attained for the Portuguese poems. This may be attributed to the fact that the stylistic obviously differences between the Chinese and English poems were more pronounced. Consequently, the stylistic injected in these poems became more evident. Nonetheless, it is important to take into consideration that the golden poems were translated by a translator who may not possess a thorough understanding of the poetic style in the target language. As such, we speculate that better results can be achieved in terms of transferring poetic style by leveraging the additional Chinese poetry that has been translated from other languages during the training process.

	Poeticity	Fluency	Coherence	Meaningfulness	Impression
Human Translation	**3.54**	**3.76**	**3.79**	**3.65**	**3.69**
Baidu Online System	2.95	3.06	3.05	2.91	3.00
BT	3.15	3.17	3.23	<u>3.21</u>	3.21
IBT:ALL	<u>3.17</u>	<u>3.18</u>	<u>3.25</u>	3.16	<u>3.24</u>

Table 3: Human evaluation of the selected 30 poems (English⇒Modern Chinese). **Bold** values denote the highest scores of each evaluation perspective, and <u>underlined</u> values denote the highest scores of each evaluation perspective among the neural poetry translation systems.

Based on the results of the human evaluation, Table 3 demonstrates that the models' capacity to translate modern Chinese poetry exceeds that of the most advanced online translation systems. The "BT" model stands out for its superior capacity to conserve the meaning of poetry, while the "IBT:ALL" model particularly excels in preserving the poetic nature of the text. This may be attributed to the continuous superimposition of poetic imagery during the process of data enhancement, which enables the "IBT:ALL" model to effectively capture the poeticity of the text. Conversely, the process of data enhancement may introduce incomplete or even incorrect meanings, which can impact the ability of the "IBT:ALL" model to preserve the meaning of poetry during translation, thus rendering it inferior to the "BT" model in this regard.

6 Conclusions and Future Work

This paper introduces a zero-shot poetry translation method, which reduces the difficulty of the whole poetry translation by splitting the process of translating the meaning of the poem and translating the poetic meaning in poetry translation. The proposed method also avoids the disadvantage of lack of parallel poetry corpus and reduces the cost of training. The experimental results, derived from both automatic and human evaluation, provide evidence of the efficacy of our proposed method. In the poetry translation, the model achieved superior outcomes in comparison to contemporary online systems. Moreover, the proposed technique was evaluated by humans and found to inject poetic meaning into the translated poems, thereby bringing them closer to the standards of human translation and aligning more closely with human expectations for poetry. Moving forward, our future work will focus on exploring the potential of our proposed method on more languages.

Acknowledgement

This work was supported in part by the Science and Technology Development Fund, Macau SAR (Grant Nos. FDCT/0070/2022/AMJ, FDCT/060/2022/AFJ), the Multi-year Research Grant from the University of Macau (Grant No. MYRG2020-00054-FST), and the Research Program of Guangdong Province (Grant No. 2220004002576). This work was performed in part at SICC which is supported by SKL-IOTSC, and HPCC supported by ICTO of the University of Macau.

References

Andersson, L. M. and Pearson, C. M. (1999). Tit for tat? the spiraling effect of incivility in the workplace. *Academy of management review*, 24(3):452–471.

Argamon, S., Koppel, M., Fine, J., and Shimoni, A. R. (2003). Gender, genre, and writing style in formal written texts. *Text & Talk*, 23(3):321–346.

Brown, P., Levinson, S. C., and Levinson, S. C. (1987). *Politeness: Some universals in language usage*, volume 4. Cambridge university press.

Chakrabarty, T., Saakyan, A., and Muresan, S. (2021). Don't go far off: An empirical study on neural poetry translation. In *Proceedings of the 2021 Conference on Empirical Methods in Natural Language Processing*, pages 7253–7265, Online and Punta Cana, Dominican Republic. Association for Computational Linguistics.

Chhaya, N., Chawla, K., Goyal, T., Chanda, P., and Singh, J. (2018). Frustrated, polite, or formal: Quantifying feelings and tone in email. In *Proceedings of the Second Workshop on Computational Modeling of People's Opinions, Personality, and Emotions in Social Media*, pages 76–86.

Dewdney, N., Van Ess-Dykema, C., and MacMillan, R. (2001). The form is the substance: Classification of genres in text. In *Proceedings of the ACL 2001 Workshop on Human Language Technology and Knowledge Management*.

Genzel, D., Uszkoreit, J., and Och, F. (2010). "poetic" statistical machine translation: Rhyme and meter. In *Proceedings of the 2010 Conference on Empirical Methods in Natural Language Processing*, pages 158–166, Cambridge, MA. Association for Computational Linguistics.

Ghazvininejad, M., Choi, Y., and Knight, K. (2018). Neural poetry translation. In *Proceedings of the 2018 Conference of the North American Chapter of the Association for Computational Linguistics: Human Language Technologies, Volume 2 (Short Papers)*, pages 67–71, New Orleans, Louisiana. Association for Computational Linguistics.

Heylighen, F. and Dewaele, J.-M. (1999). Formality of language: definition, measurement and behavioral determinants. *Interner Bericht, Center "Leo Apostel", Vrije Universiteit Brüssel*, 4.

Hoang, V. C. D., Koehn, P., Haffari, G., and Cohn, T. (2018). Iterative back-translation for neural machine translation. In *Proceedings of the 2nd Workshop on Neural Machine Translation and Generation*, pages 18–24, Melbourne, Australia. Association for Computational Linguistics.

Huang, Y., Zhu, W., Xiong, D., Zhang, Y., Hu, C., and Xu, F. (2020). Cycle-consistent adversarial autoencoders for unsupervised text style transfer. *arXiv preprint arXiv:2010.00735*.

Koehn, P. and Knowles, R. (2017). Six challenges for neural machine translation. In *Proceedings of the First Workshop on Neural Machine Translation*, pages 28–39, Vancouver. Association for Computational Linguistics.

Li, J., Jia, R., He, H., and Liang, P. (2018). Delete, retrieve, generate: A simple approach to sentiment and style transfer. *arXiv preprint arXiv:1804.06437*.

Li, J., Li, Z., Mou, L., Jiang, X., Lyu, M. R., and King, I. (2020). Unsupervised text generation by learning from search. *arXiv preprint arXiv:2007.08557*.

Liu, D., Fu, J., Zhang, Y., Pal, C., and Lv, J. (2020). Revision in continuous space: Unsupervised text style transfer without adversarial learning. In *Proceedings of the AAAI Conference on Artificial Intelligence*, volume 34, pages 8376–8383.

Liu, Z., Fu, Z., Cao, J., de Melo, G., Tam, Y.-C., Niu, C., and Zhou, J. (2019). Rhetorically controlled encoder-decoder for modern chinese poetry generation. In *Proceedings of the 57th Annual Meeting of the Association for Computational Linguistics*, pages 1992–2001.

Malmi, E., Severyn, A., and Rothe, S. (2020). Unsupervised text style transfer with padded masked language models. *arXiv preprint arXiv:2010.01054*.

Pavlopoulos, J., Thain, N., Dixon, L., and Androutsopoulos, I. (2019). Convai at semeval-2019 task 6: Offensive language identification and categorization with perspective and bert. In *Proceedings of the 13th international Workshop on Semantic Evaluation*, pages 571–576.

Peersman, C., Daelemans, W., Vandekerckhove, R., Vandekerckhove, B., and Van Vaerenbergh, L. (2016). The effects of age, gender and region on non-standard linguistic variation in online social networks. *arXiv preprint arXiv:1601.02431*.

Pennebaker, J. W., Mehl, M. R., and Niederhoffer, K. G. (2003). Psychological aspects of natural language use: Our words, our selves. *Annual review of psychology*, 54(1):547–577.

Rabinovich, E., Patel, R. N., Mirkin, S., Specia, L., and Wintner, S. (2017). Personalized machine translation: Preserving original author traits. In *Proceedings of the 15th Conference of the European Chapter of the Association for Computational Linguistics: Volume 1, Long Papers*, pages 1074–1084, Valencia, Spain. Association for Computational Linguistics.

Russell, J. A. (1980). A circumplex model of affect. *Journal of personality and social psychology*, 39(6):1161.

Sennrich, R., Haddow, B., and Birch, A. (2015). Neural machine translation of rare words with subword units. *arXiv preprint arXiv:1508.07909*.

Sheikha, F. A. and Inkpen, D. (2010). Automatic classification of documents by formality. In *Proceedings of the 6th international conference on natural language processing and knowledge engineering (nlpke-2010)*, pages 1–5. IEEE.

Shen, L., Guo, X., and Chen, M. (2020). Compose like humans: Jointly improving the coherence and novelty for modern chinese poetry generation. In *2020 International Joint Conference on Neural Networks, IJCNN 2020, Glasgow, United Kingdom, July 19-24, 2020*, pages 1–8. IEEE.

Sudhakar, A., Upadhyay, B., and Maheswaran, A. (2019). Transforming delete, retrieve, generate approach for controlled text style transfer. *arXiv preprint arXiv:1908.09368*.

Susanto, Y., Livingstone, A. G., Ng, B. C., and Cambria, E. (2020). The hourglass model revisited. *IEEE Intelligent Systems*, 35(5):96–102.

Toshevska, M. and Gievska, S. (2021). A review of text style transfer using deep learning. *IEEE Transactions on Artificial Intelligence*, page 1–1.

Vaswani, A., Shazeer, N., Parmar, N., Uszkoreit, J., Jones, L., Gomez, A. N., Kaiser, L., and Polosukhin, I. (2017). Attention is all you need. In Guyon, I., von Luxburg, U., Bengio, S., Wallach, H. M., Fergus, R., Vishwanathan, S. V. N., and Garnett, R., editors, *Advances in Neural Information Processing Systems 30: Annual Conference on Neural Information Processing Systems 2017, December 4-9, 2017, Long Beach, CA, USA*, pages 5998–6008.

Yang, Z., Cai, P., Feng, Y., Li, F., Feng, W., Chiu, E. S.-Y., and Yu, H. (2019). Generating classical Chinese poems from vernacular Chinese. In *Proceedings of the 2019 Conference on Empirical Methods in Natural Language Processing and the 9th International Joint Conference on Natural Language Processing (EMNLP-IJCNLP)*, pages 6155–6164, Hong Kong, China. Association for Computational Linguistics.

Yi, X., Sun, M., Li, R., and Yang, Z. (2018). Chinese poetry generation with a working memory model. *arXiv preprint arXiv:1809.04306*.

Yu, M. and Liu, C. (2021). "creation" and "production": Reflections on microsoft xiaobing's poetry writing software. *Modern Literary Magazine (05) p.158-165*.

Zampieri, M., Malmasi, S., Nakov, P., Rosenthal, S., Farra, N., and Kumar, R. (2019). Predicting the type and target of offensive posts in social media. *arXiv preprint arXiv:1902.09666*.

Zhang, T., Kishore, V., Wu, F., Weinberger, K. Q., and Artzi, Y. (2020a). Bertscore: Evaluating text generation with BERT. In *8th International Conference on Learning Representations, ICLR 2020, Addis Ababa, Ethiopia, April 26-30, 2020*. OpenReview.net.

Zhang, Y., Ge, T., and Sun, X. (2020b). Parallel data augmentation for formality style transfer. *arXiv preprint arXiv:2005.07522*.

Zhang, Y., Xu, J., Yang, P., and Sun, X. (2018). Learning sentiment memories for sentiment modification without parallel data. *arXiv preprint arXiv:1808.07311*.

Leveraging Highly Accurate Word Alignment for Low Resource Translation by Pretrained Multilingual Model

Jingyi Zhu s2120801_@_u.tsukuba.ac.jp
Minato Kondo s2320743_@_u.tsukuba.ac.jp
Takuya Tamura s2120744_@_u.tsukuba.ac.jp
Takehito Utsuro utsuro_@_iit.tsukuba.ac.jp
Deg. Prog. Sys.&Inf. Eng., Grad. Sch. Sci.&Tech., University of Tsukuba, Japan

Masaaki Nagata masaaki.nagata_@_ntt.com
NTT Communication Science Laboratories, NTT Corporation, Japan

Abstract

Recently, there has been a growing interest in pretraining models in the field of natural language processing. As opposed to training models from scratch, pretrained models have been shown to produce superior results in low-resource translation tasks. In this paper, we introduced the use of pretrained seq2seq models for preordering and translation tasks. We utilized manual word alignment data and mBERT-based generated word alignment data for training preordering and compared the effectiveness of various types of mT5 and mBART models for preordering. For the translation task, we chose mBART as our baseline model and evaluated several input manners. Our approach was evaluated on the Asian Language Treebank dataset, consisting of 20,000 parallel data in Japanese, English and Hindi, where Japanese is either on the source or target side. We also used in-house 3,000 parallel data in Chinese and Japanese. The results indicated that mT5-large trained with manual word alignment achieved a preordering performance exceeding 0.9 RIBES score on Ja-En and Ja-Zh pairs. Moreover, our proposed approach significantly outperformed the baseline model in most translation directions of Ja-En, Ja-Zh, and Ja-Hi pairs in at least one of BLEU/COMET scores.

1 Introduction

In recent years, there has been a growing body of research on sequence-to-sequence (seq2seq) models that are based on pretraining (Xue et al., 2021; Liu et al., 2020; Lin et al., 2020). Since the introduction of the Transformer architecture (Vaswani et al., 2017), the quality of machine translation has greatly improved. However, when it comes to low-resource translation tasks, the performance of this type of parameter randomization model often suffers due to the limited size of available datasets (Sennrich and Zhang, 2019; Lee et al., 2022; Zhu et al., 2022).

To address this challenge, many researchers have proposed using unsupervised methods, such as mapping monolingual vector embeddings to a common cross-lingual embedding space (Lin et al., 2020; Sen et al., 2019), or leveraging large-scale pretraining models that have been successfully applied to various NLP tasks (Devlin et al., 2019; Brown et al., 2020).

Proceedings of Machine Translation Summit XIX, Vol. 1: Research Track, pages 336–347
September 4–8, 2023, Macau SAR, China.

In this paper, we propose applying a pretrained seq2seq model for preordering and translation tasks. Specifically, we investigate different sizes of mT5s (Xue et al., 2021) and mBART (Liu et al., 2020), in order to evaluate their performance on preordering when using manual word alignment data. For the translation process, we choose mBART as our baseline model, and we evaluate the translation results using both the original sequence and the generated preordering sequence as input. Our approach was evaluated on the Asian Language Treebank dataset (Riza et al., 2016), consisting of 20,000 parallel data in Japanese, English and Hindi, where Japanese is either on the source or target side. To compare the effects on different datasets, we also used the in-house data which comprised 3,000 parallel data in Chinese and Japanese. The results indicated that mT5-large trained with manual word alignment achieved a preordering performance exceeding 0.9 when evaluated using the RIBES score on Ja-En and Ja-Zh pairs. Moreover, our proposed approach significantly outperformed the baseline model in most of the translation directions of language pairs of Ja-En, Ja-Zh, and Ja-Hi in terms of at least one of the BLEU(Papineni et al., 2002) and COMET (wmt20-comet-da) (Rei et al., 2020) scores.

2 Related Work

In recent years, researchers have conducted more and more studies on seq2seq models based on pretraining. While learning the rules of sequence generation remains the most crucial feature of these models, some studies have explored the application of preordering to training, resulting in improved results. Kawara et al. (2018) discussed the importance of maintaining consistency between input source word order and output target word order for improved translation accuracy in neural machine translation (NMT) models. Murthy et al. (2019) proposed a transfer learning approach for NMT that trains the model on an assisting source-target language pair and improves translation quality in extremely low-resource scenarios. However, both methods rely on separately pretraining a translation model using a large-scale parallel corpus and handle preordering based on the syntax tree. In contrast, Zhu et al. (2022) proposed a framework for low-resource translation that focuses on preordering and highly accurate word alignment using an SMT model. Their solution outperformed the Transformer model, but they did not explore the use of large-scale pretrained seq2seq models.

Our work focused on low-resource translation tasks and utilizes large-scale pretrained multilingual models for fine-tuning the preordering and translation procedures.

3 Seq2seq Models

In general, seq2seq models take a sequence of tokens as input from the source sequence $S = s_1, s_2, \dots, s_k$ and produce a sequence of tokens as output for the target sequence $T = t_1, t_2, \dots, t_m$, where $s_i(i = 1, \dots, k)$ and $t_j(j = 1, \dots, m)$ represent the tokens in the source and target sequences, respectively.

In terms of structure, seq2seq models consist of an encoder and a decoder (Hochreiter and Schmidhuber, 1997). The encoder converts the input sequence into a high-dimensional vector representation, while the decoder maps the high-dimensional vectors to the output dictionary based on the encoder's output. This framework has been applied to various tasks, including machine summarization (Shi et al., 2021), question-answering systems (Yin et al., 2016), and machine translation (Sutskever et al., 2014). Since seq2seq models can learn the rules governing the input and output sequences, we aim to use them for preordering and translation.

4 Seq2seq Models for Preordering

4.1 Preordering Process

While preordering is commonly utilized in statistical-based translation systems, it is also possible to implement preordering in seq2seq systems. The preordering procedure entails arranging the tokens in a source sequence to those of the tokens in its target sequence before translation is performed. An example of transferring a Japanese sentence is shown in Figure 1.

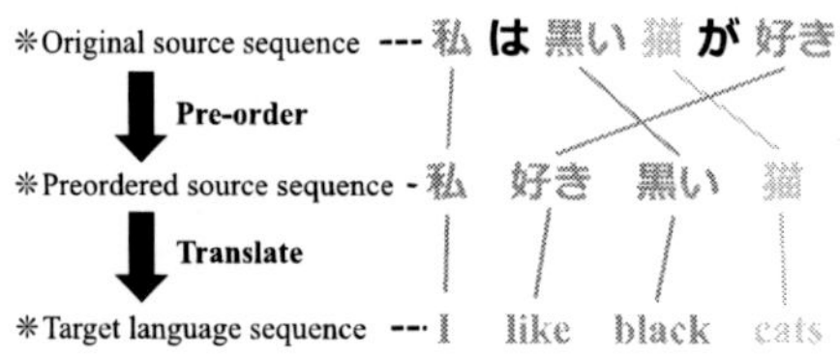

Figure 1: Transform the word order of the source Japanese language to the target English language before translation.

Regarding the preordering procedure, we use mT5 (Xue et al., 2021) and mBART (Liu et al., 2020), which are kinds of state-of-the-art seq2seq models. Both models have encoder-decoder structures based on self-attention, with a minor variation in their pretraining tasks.

4.2 Reordered Training Data

As our preordering method is entirely based on the seq2seq model, it is necessary to construct the required training data, which is produced by manual word alignment data.

Formally, word alignment can be defined as: given a sentence $X = \{x_1, x_2, ..., x_m\}$ in the source language and its corresponding parallel sentence $Y = \{y_1, y_2, ..., y_n\}$ in the target language, the word alignment are set of pairs of source and target words using the following equation:

$$Alignment = (< x_i, y_j >: x_i \in X, y_j \in Y) \tag{1}$$

The aligned pair of words x_i and y_j are semantically similar within the context of the sentence.

Having those word alignments, for the model input, we use the original source sequence. On the output side, we simply ignore the NULL-aligned tokens, which were not aligned with any tokens on the target side. For instance, the Japanese sentence " 私 (I) は 黒い (black) 猫 (cat) が 好き (like) " can be easily preordered into the English order of " 私 (I) 好き (like) 黒い (black) 猫 (cat)" with the alignments of (私-*I*), (黒い-*black*), (猫-*cat*), and (好き-*like*) based on the word alignment. Therefore, we ignore " は" and " が" in the preordered sequence because they were not aligned to any tokens. After removing " は" and " が" from the output side of the preordered sequence, the training pair becomes " 私 (I) は 黒い (black) 猫 (cat) が 好き (like)" and " 私 (I) 好き (like) 黒い (black) 猫 (cat)". We use such training pairs to train order transformation seq2seq neural networks.

We utilized two types of word alignment data to generate our training data. The first type is based on manual word alignment data, while the second type is derived from the word alignment data generated by mBERT (Devlin et al., 2019). To automatically extract word alignment from parallel corpus data, we employed the AWESoME-align (Dou and Neubig, 2021), which is capable of unsupervised fine-tuning by adjusting the embedding distribution of the output from a multilingual BERT in order to achieve accurate word alignments. One significant advantage of this approach is that it eliminates the need for manual word alignment data.

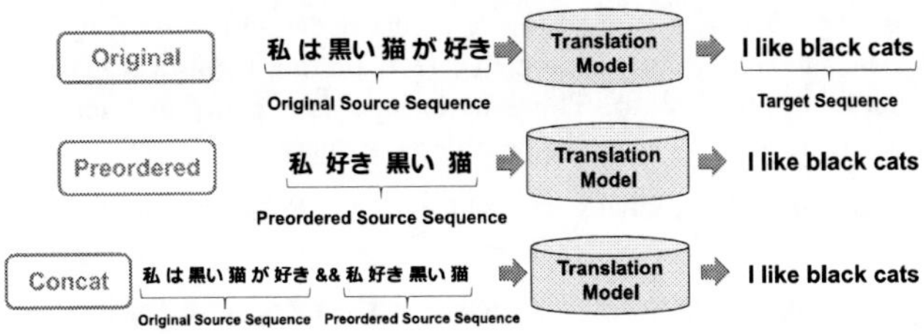

(a) The normal input type, which inputs the sequence to the model directly, including the original input, preordered input, and concatenated input. A distinct translation model will be trained for each of the original input, preordered input, and concatenated input, resulting in a total of three translation models for the normal input type. 'Concat' represents for 'Concatenated'

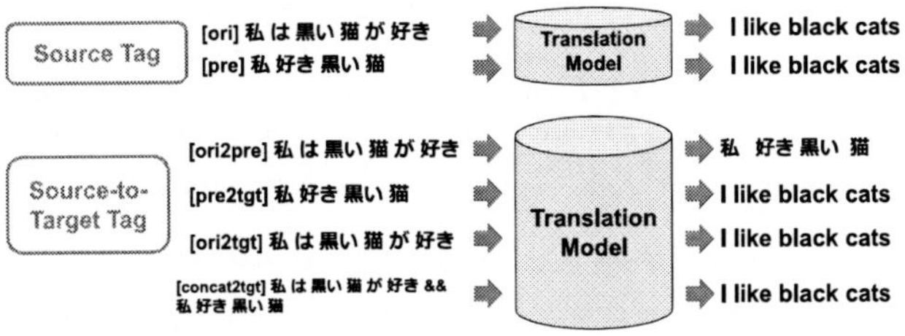

(b) The tagged input type, which places the unique tag before each input sequence, including source tag input and source-to-target tag input. A total of two translation models will be trained for the tagged input type, where one model is trained for each source tag input and source-to-target tag input.

Figure 2: Two input types of **(a) Normal Input** and **(b) Tagged Input**.

5 Seq2seq Model for Translation

5.1 Training Pattern

We utilize mBART as the primary translation model for the translation process. In order to compare the results of several input variations, we experimented with various "training patterns", consisting of the normal input type and the tagged input type. Normal input type refers to sequences directly fed into the model, including the original input, preordered input, and concatenated input, as shown in Figure 2 (a). On the other hand, tagged input type includes a sequence type tag at the beginning of each sequence, which includes the source tag input and the source-to-target tag input as shown in Figure 2 (b).

For normal input type, we trained translation models using the original input, preordered input, and concatenated input separately. In other words, we trained three models and tested the translation accuracy of each pattern of input. Original input uses the original source language sequence as input and outputs the target language sequence as shown in "original" of Figure 2 (a). We see this pattern of the input as the seq2seq translation baseline.

- **Original input**: Original source sequence ⇒ Target language sequence

In order to verify whether the utilization of preordering in isolation can result in an enhancement of translation accuracy, we use the preordered source language sequence as input and output the corresponding target language sequence as shown in "preorder" of Figure 2 (a).

- **Preordered input**: Preordered source sequence ⇒ Target language sequence

In addition to this, we also attempted to use a concatenation approach by combining the sequences of the original and preorder together and splitting them using learnable symbols as shown in "concat" of Figure 2 (a). This kind of input is intended to leverage the information from both the original sequence and the preordered sequence.

- **Concatenated input**: Original source sequence && Preordered source sequence ⇒ Target language sequence

For tagged input, we aim to verify whether the translation accuracy improves by increasing the amount of training data. To achieve this, we differentiated the input types by mixing original, preordered, and concatenated sequences, while each sequence is prefixed with a corresponding tag to facilitate this process. For each of the source tag input and the source-to-target tag input, a separate translation model is trained respectively. In other words, for the tagged input type, a total of two models are trained. Source tag input uses both original and preordered source language sequences as input but carries the sequence type tag at the head of the sequence (for example, using [ori] and [pre] to represent the original sequence and preordered sequence) as shown in "source tag" of Figure 2 (b). It stands to reason that the actual amount of training data is twice the baseline due to the mixture of inputs from the original and preordered sequences.

- **Source tag input**: [ori] Original source sequence ⇒ Target language sequence

  [pre] Preordered source sequence ⇒ Target language sequence

In addition to the previously mentioned training mode, we also experimented with a source-to-target tag input to maximize the amount of training data using our method as shown in "source-to-target tag" of Figure 2 (b). This training pattern combines four inputs: from original source sequence to preordered source sequence, from original source sequence to target language sequence, from preordered source sequence to target language sequence, and from concatenated sequence to target language sequence. To enable the model to distinguish between the types of input and output corresponding sequences, we added tags [ori2pre], [pre2tgt], [ori2tgt], and [concat2tgt] to each kind of sequences, respectively. The reason we tried this input method is that, unlike the source tag input, which only outputs from the source language sequence to the target language sequence, the process of learning preordering is added during the translation model training, allowing the model to more appropriately learn the rules for generation from the source language sequence to the target language sequence. Note that the training data of source-to-target tag input is fourth the baseline because we mixed four kinds of inputs and outputs.

- **Source-to-target tag input**: [ori2pre] Original source sequence ⇒ Preordered source sequence

  [ori2tgt] Original source sequence ⇒ Target language sequence

  [pre2tgt] Preordered source sequence ⇒ Target language sequence

  [concat2tgt] Original source sequence && Preordered source sequence ⇒ Target language sequence

5.2 Test Pattern

In the generation stage, to each of the trained translation models described in the previous section, we input test data comprised of corresponding input pattern, which is referred to as "test pattern"[1].

[1]The correspondence between the training and test patterns are shown in the columns of "Training Pattern" and "Test Pattern" in Table 5.

Since each training pattern of the normal input type has its own translation model trained on its corresponding input data, we directly input the corresponding pattern of test data into the model to obtain the translation results. For example, we input the test data of the test pattern of the original input into the model, which is trained with the training pattern of the original input, to obtain the translation results.

During the training of the translation models of the tagged input type, it can be considered that we trained multiple models with different test patterns, inputs, which allows us to translate inputs of multiple test patterns simultaneously during testing.

For the source tag input, we input both the original and preordered sequences with tags during training, which enables us to evaluate the translation accuracy of the original or preordered sequences separately when conducting translation evaluation on the test set. For example, we add the [ori] tag before the original test data sequence, or the [pre] tag before the preordered test data sequence, and input either of them into the model trained with the training pattern of the source tag input to obtain the respective translation results.

For the source-to-target tag input, we simultaneously input the original, preordered, and concatenated sequences with tags during training. Therefore, when evaluating the translation accuracy of the test data, we can evaluate the translation accuracy of the original, preordered, or concatenated sequences separately. For example, we add the [ori2tgt] tag before the original test data sequence, the [pre2tgt] tag before the preordered test data sequence, or the [concat2tgt] tag before concatenated test data sequence and input either of them into the model trained with the training pattern of the source-to-target tag input to obtain the respective translation results. Although we added the process of generating the preordered sequence from the original sequence in the training process of source-to-target tag input, we did not add the accuracy of this process in our paper as we focused solely on the translation results[2]. The preordered sequence (which is evaluated through preordered input or concatenated input) used in testing source-to-target tag input is generated by mT5 rather than mBART.

6 Experiments

6.1 Dataset

In our seq2seq experiments, we utilized ALT[3] Japanese-XX (English and Hindi) and in-house Chinese-Japanese parallel datasets as our primary datasets. It is worth noting that in ALT, manual word alignment data is not available for language pairs other than Ja-En, so we only conduct manual word alignment on this pairs. The dataset was partitioned into training, validation, and test sets. Each subset of the ALT dataset contains 18K, 1K, and 1K parallel sequence pairs respectively, while the in-house dataset includes 2K, 0.5K, and 0.5K parallel sequence pairs. The amount of training data for each training pattern is presented in Table 1.

6.2 Preordering Setting

We created training data for seq2seq preordering by manual word alignment as described in Section 4.2. We compare preordering results using RIBES (Isozaki et al., 2010) between mT5-small, mT5-base, mT5-large and mBART-large (*mbart-large-50*)[4][5]. The preordered sequence

[2]We also evaluated the performance of preordering obtained through source-to-target tag input. However, the precision obtained was not as high as that obtained through mT5-large.

[3]`https://www2.nict.go.jp/astrec-att/member/mutiyama/ALT/`

[4]All pretrained seq2seq models are downloaded from the public Huggingface library.

[5]Each model was trained for 40,000 steps with a training batch size of 16 and a learning rate of 3e-5. Additionally, we trained another mT5-large with a batch size of 32 because it achieved the best preordering result with a batch size of 16. We also attempted to train mT5-large with a batch size of 64, but the preordering result was lower than when training with a batch size of 32.

Input Type	Training Pattern	Training Data	
		Ja-XX	Ja-Zh
Normal	Original	18K	2K
	Preorder	18K	2K
	Concatenated	18K	2K
Tagged	Source	36K	4K
	Source-to-target	72K	8K

Table 1: The number of training data for each training pattern. 'XX' represents for English and Hindi.

Language Pairs	Precision	Recall	F1
Ja-En	0.79	0.60	0.68
Ja-Zh	0.84	0.68	0.75

Table 2: Precision, Recall, and F1 scores of AWESoME-align compared with manual word alignment in the language pairs of Ja-En and Ja-Zh.

was generated using the model with the maximum BLEU score against the validation set. The preordering process was executed on the NVIDIA RTX A6000 with CUDA 11.3.

For AWESoME-align, which automatically extracts word alignments, we only use the original parallel corpus to fine-tune due to its unsupervised nature. Furthermore, the parameters are not shared between different language pairs, meaning we fine-tune each language pair with a different instance of AWESoME-align. Regarding hyperparameters, we fine-tune each language pair for 10 epochs with a batch size of 16 and a learning rate of 3e-5. The accuracy of word alignments extracted by AWESoME-align has been presented in Table 2. In this table, manual word alignment is considered as the reference. However, since manual word alignment data is only available for Ja-En and Ja-Zh, we have reported the results only for those language pairs.

6.3 Translation Setting

We trained the mBART translation models using Fairseq[6]. Each model was trained for 40,000 steps with a maximum input length of 1,024 and a learning rate of 3e-5, which were the same as those used for the preordering process. We selected the model with the minimum label-smoothed cross-entropy loss during the generation stage on the validation set to generate the target translation. We used the preordered sequences generated by mT5-large, which was trained with a batch size of 32, as inputs for the mBART models. The translation process was executed on the NVIDIA RTX TITAN with CUDA 10.3.

7 Results

7.1 Preordering Performance

The RIBES columns in Table 3 display the comparison of RIBES scores for different seq2seq models to generate the preordered sequence. The results demonstrate that the RIBES score for mT5-large models trained with manual word alignment exceeds 0.9, regardless of the batch size used during training (i.e., 16 or 32). Table 4 reports the comparison of RIBES scores for transferring the original source sequence to the preordered source sequence using mT5-large when trained with manual word alignment or generated word alignment. Under our experimental conditions, the unigram precision is not equal to a hundred as the generated preordered sequence tends to include more tokens than the reference preordered sequence. It is obvious

[6]https://github.com/facebookresearch/fairseq

Preordering Model	# Parameters	Training Batch Size	BLEU Ja⇒En	BLEU En⇒Ja	RIBES Ja⇒En	RIBES En⇒Ja
Oracle	-	-	34.82	34.27	-	-
mT5-small	300M	16	21.44	26.06	0.876	0.872
mT5-base	580M	16	24.38	27.68	0.895	0.889
mT5-large	1200M	16	24.83	28.48	0.901	0.905
		32	25.22	28.34	0.904	0.909
mBART-large	610M	16	23.28	27.28	0.883	0.894

Table 3: BLEU scores of using mBART as the translation model for translating Ja-En pairs when applying the preordered training/test pattern in normal input type among different preordering models, and RIBES results of seq2seq model trained by manual word alignments of transferring Japanese order into English order and opposite.

	Ja⇒En		En⇒Ja		Ja⇒Zh		Zh⇒Ja		Ja⇒Hi	Hi⇒Ja
Alignment used	M	A	M	A	M	A	M	A	A	A
RIBES	0.904	0.896	0.909	0.904	0.927	0.883	0.919	0.894	0.883	0.877
Unigram Precision	0.91	0.88	0.92	0.91	0.89	0.75	0.83	0.77	0.86	0.85
Normalized Kendall's Tau	0.93	0.93	0.94	0.93	0.96	0.96	0.97	0.96	0.92	0.92
Brevity Penalty	0.96	0.94	0.95	0.97	0.93	0.96	0.95	0.98	0.96	0.98

Table 4: RIBES scores when transferring the original source sequence to preordered source sequence using mT5-large. 'Alignment used' means manual word alignment or mBERT-based generated word alignment is used for training preordering. 'M' is short for 'Manual', while 'A' represents 'AWESoME'.

from the table that mT5-large models trained with manual word alignment outperformed those trained with generated word alignment.

7.2 Translation Performance

Table 4(a) illustrates the BLEU (Papineni et al., 2002) and COMET (wmt20-comet-da) (Rei et al., 2020) for each translation direction with different word alignments. Our proposed approach when trained with manual word alignment significantly outperformed the baseline model in most of the translation directions of language pairs of Ja-En, Ja-Zh, and Ja-Hi in terms of at least one of the BLEU and COMET (wmt20-comet-da) scores. Moreover, even with mBERT-based generated word alignment, our proposed approach significantly outperformed the baseline model in the translation directions of Ja to En, Zh to Ja, Ja to Hi, and Hi to Ja in terms of the COMET score. Our findings suggest that when utilizing manual word alignment as preordering training data, concatenated inputs exhibit the highest BLEU or COMET scores compared to other input patterns. However, when using the AWESoME word alignment, the original input mostly yields the best BLEU results, while concatenated inputs mostly generate the best COMET results. For the better results illustrated in concatenated inputs when using manual word alignment, we speculate that this could be due to the models learning the relative positions between the source and target languages by combining the original and more highly accurate preordered sequences as the concatenated input. When utilizing AWESoME word alignment, it is predictable that the preordered sequence contains more noisy positional information than manual word alignments. During the generation process, those erroneous positional information inevitably impact the output quality. However, due to the implementation of multiple input manners, the model could still achieve a higher precise output based on the original input. To conduct comparison experiments, we employed the **oracle** approach as shown in Table 4(b), which involves preordering the source test set according to the target test set using manual

(a) Preordering by mT5

Alignment	Input Type	Training Pattern	Test Pattern	Preorder Model	BLEU Ja-En ⇒	BLEU Ja-En ⇐	BLEU Ja-Zh ⇒	BLEU Ja-Zh ⇐	BLEU Ja-Hi ⇒	BLEU Ja-Hi ⇐	COMET Ja-En ⇒	COMET Ja-En ⇐	COMET Ja-Zh ⇒	COMET Ja-Zh ⇐	COMET Ja-Hi ⇒	COMET Ja-Hi ⇐
-	Normal	Original (Baseline)	Original (Baseline)	-	25.7	29.3	14.1	17.9	30.0	19.3	47.9	54.4	67.9	54.4	16.2	29.1
Manual	Normal	Preorder	Preorder	mT5	25.2	28.3	14.2	18.5†	-	-	47.9	51.0	63.2	53.2	-	-
		Concat	Concat	mT5	25.6	29.6	**14.7**†	19.2†	-	-	49.2	53.4	65.1	58.5	-	-
	Tagged	Source	Original	-	25.8	29.2	14.2	18.0	-	-	48.7	52.2	**66.2**	55.6	-	-
			Preorder	mT5	25.5	28.5	14.0	17.8	-	-	48.5	50.1	63.0	55.3	-	-
		S-T	Original	-	25.8	28.9	14.0	18.8†	-	-	46.8	52.7	64.3	58.4	-	-
			Preorder	mT5	25.1	28.2	13.7	18.3	-	-	46.4	51.0	61.5	57.3†	-	-
			Concat	mT5	**25.9**	**29.7**	14.4	**19.4**†	-	-	**49.8**†	**54.2**	63.5	**60.2**†	-	-
AWESoME	Normal	Preorder	Preorder	mT5	23.9	28.3	13.7	18.2	29.4	18.6	46.7	50.6	61.6	53.6	18.4	29.0
		Concat	Concat	mT5	25.7	**29.8**	14.0	**19.4**†	30.0	19.4	49.9†	53.2	**64.7**	53.6	18.1	**31.6**†
	Tagged	Source	Original	-	**26.1**	29.4	**14.3**	19.0†	**30.1**	19.6	**50.0**†	53.0	64.4	56.7	17.7	30.3
			Preorder	mT5	24.6	28.8	13.5	19.0†	**30.1**	19.0	46.3	50.1	61.7	56.7	**19.1**†	30.0
		S-T	Original	-	26.0	29.2	12.8	18.5†	28.8	**19.7**	46.9	52.7	63.4	57.0	13.4	30.2
			Preorder	mT5	24.1	28.2	12.0	18.6†	29.3	19.2	42.1	50.1	59.7	55.4	15.9	29.2
			Concat	mT5	25.8	29.6	12.9	18.9†	29.5	19.6	47.0	**54.3**	63.6	**57.8**†	15.6	31.3†

(b) Preordering by Oracle

Alignment	Input Type	Training Pattern	Test Pattern	Preorder Model	BLEU Ja-En ⇒	BLEU Ja-En ⇐	BLEU Ja-Zh ⇒	BLEU Ja-Zh ⇐	BLEU Ja-Hi ⇒	BLEU Ja-Hi ⇐	COMET Ja-En ⇒	COMET Ja-En ⇐	COMET Ja-Zh ⇒	COMET Ja-Zh ⇐	COMET Ja-Hi ⇒	COMET Ja-Hi ⇐
Manual	Normal	Preorder	Preorder	Oracle	34.8	34.3	17.2	22.7	-	-	54.5	56.1	67.3	62.0	-	-
		Concat	Concat	Oracle	35.5	35.7	17.8	22.9	-	-	56.3	59.1	69.8	65.1	-	-
	Tagged	Source	Preorder	Oracle	33.6	33.6	16.1	20.9	-	-	53.6	56.2	64.8	58.4	-	-
		S-T	Preorder	Oracle	33.7	33.5	15.9	20.8	-	-	52.6	55.8	63.8	61.3	-	-
			Concat	Oracle	35.0	35.0	16.1	22.0	-	-	55.8	58.9	67.4	63.4	-	-
AWESoME	Normal	Preorder	Preorder	Oracle	36.8	34.3	18.4	22.6	36.0	24.4	54.6	54.2	65.6	55.9	24.7	30.3
		Concat	Concat	Oracle	40.3	36.2	19.0	23.5	36.8	26.0	58.3	58.8	69.7	63.5	26.8	37.5
	Tagged	Source	Preorder	Oracle	36.6	33.9	17.2	21.9	35.4	23.7	52.2	54.8	64.3	60.3	23.9	30.0
		S-T	Preorder	Oracle	36.2	33.2	16.1	21.3	34.7	24.2	48.6	52.8	62.1	58.1	20.9	30.4
			Concat	Oracle	39.1	35.4	16.7	21.9	35.4	24.9	55.4	58.9	67.5	63.1	24.0	36.5

Table 5: BLEU and COMET scores between the different training/test patterns. The results are translated by mBART. 'mT5' represents 'mT5-large'. 'Oracle' represents preordering the source test set according to the target test set using manual or AWESoME word alignment data, instead of generating the preordered sequences using the seq2seq model. Results in bold indicate the best BLEU or COMET results in a specific translation direction using different word alignments. 'Concat' represents 'concatenated' and 'S-T' represents 'Source-to-target'. † for a significant difference ($p < 0.05$) from the baseline.

or AWESoME word alignment data, instead of generating the preordered sequences using the seq2seq model. Although this result is not practical, it still demonstrates the potential of applying our preordering method to the seq2seq model.

Table 3 displays the BLEU scores of different models when using the preordered training/test pattern in normal input type for translating Ja-En pairs[7]. The translation quality coin-

[7]The number of model parameters are from https://github.com/google-research/

Japanese original sequence	彼 は 金曜日 の 夜 に サウス メルボルン の 停車場 から トラム を 盗ん だ こと でも 訴え られ て いる 。
English target reference sequence	He is also accused of stealing a tram on Friday night , from South Melbourne depot .
Oracle (manual) preordered sequence	彼 て いる でも 訴え られ でも 盗ん だ こと トラム に 金曜日 夜 から サウス メルボルン 停車場 。
Oracle (AWESoME) preordered sequence	彼 いる でも 訴え でも 盗ん を トラム に 金曜日 夜 から サウス メルボルン 停車場。
Generated preordered sequence (manual)	彼 られ て いる でも 訴え こと 盗ん だ トラム から 停車場 の サウス メルボルン に 金曜日 夜 。
Generated preordered sequence (AWESoME)	彼 いる でも 訴え こと 盗んを トラム から の 停車場 サウス メルボルン に 金曜日 夜。
Baseline translation	He is also accused of stealing a tram from a South Melbourne station on Friday night .
Tagged source-to-target concatenate input by oracle (manual)	He is also accused of stealing a tram on Friday night from a South Melbourne escalator .
Tagged source-to-target concatenate input by oracle (AWESoME)	He is also accused of stealing the tram on Friday night from South Melbourne exit .
Tagged source-to-target concatenate input by mT5 (manual)	He is also accused of stealing a tram from a depot in South Melbourne on Friday night .
Tagged source-to-target concatenate input by mT5 (AWESoME)	He is also accused of stealing the tram from a lane at South Melbourne on Friday night .
Chinese original sequence	此外 , 国外 对 出口 企业 实施 严格 的 责任 标准 。
Japanese target reference sequence	この ほか 、 国際 市場 で は 輸出 企業 に 、 厳格 な 責任 を 課す よう に なっ た 。 (Additionally, the international market has come to require strict responsibility to exporting companies.)
Oracle (manual) preordered sequence	此外 , 国外 出口 企业 对 严格 的 责任 实施 。
Oracle (AWESoME) preordered sequence	此外 , 国外 出口 企业 对 严 格 的 责任 实施 。
Generated preordered sequence (manual)	此外 , 国外 出口 企业 对 严格 责任 标 准 实施 。
Generated preordered sequence (AWESoME)	此外 , 国外 出口 企业 对 严 格 的 责任 标准 实施 。
Baseline translation	さらに 、 海外 から の 輸出 企業 に 対し て は 厳格 な 責任 基準 が 定め られ て いる 。
Tagged source-to-target concatenate input by oracle (manual)	さらに 、海外 へ の 輸出 企業 に 対し て は 厳格 な 責任管理 を 行っ て いる 。
Tagged source-to-target concatenate input by oracle (AWESoME)	さらに、 海外 へ の 輸出 企業 に 対し て 厳格 な 責任基準 が 課さ れ て いる 。
Tagged source-to-target concatenate input by mT5 (manual)	さらに 、海外 へ の 輸出 企業 に 対し て は 厳格 な 責任基準 を 実施 し て いる 。
Tagged source-to-target concatenate input by mT5 (AWESoME)	さらに、 海外 から の 輸出 企業 に 対し 厳格 な 責任基準 を 課さ れ て いる 。

Table 6: Results of preordering generated by mT5-large.

cides with the preordering performance. The better the preordering quality is, the higher the final translation quality is.

7.3 Specific Results

We have included our experimental results in Table 6 to compare the differences between translations by oracle and seq2seq models. In the first example, the meaningful words ' 金曜日 夜 (Friday night)' and 'サウス メルボルン 停車場 (South Melbourne depot)' were generated in the opposite position. This led to errors in the final translation results when evaluated by the BLEU score, although the transposition of the meaningful words in this example did not affect the semantics of the output text. In the second example, the generated preordered Chinese sequence retained more tokens than the oracle sequence. For example, the Chinese token '标准 (standard)' has the same meaning as '基準' in Japanese. The reference abandoned this word because it was unaligned with any token in the Japanese sequence, while the generated preordered sequence retained it. This resulted in a surplus of translation content compared to the reference Japanese. We also observed that when generating a preordered sequence through a preordering model trained with manual word alignment data, the Chinese conjunction token ' 的' is omitted. However, during the translation process, the decoder is able to appropriately incorporate this token (with 'な' in Japanese) based on the surrounding context. Overall, these examples highlight the importance of paying attention to the position or number of tokens in the preordered sequence, as they can have a significant impact on the final translation quality.

8 Conclusion

In this paper, we propose the utilization of seq2seq multilingual pretrained models for preordering and translation. Specifically, we use manual and mBERT-based word alignment to train mT5-large in generating preordering sequences, and mBART for performing translation. We compare the translation accuracy under various training/test patterns during translation. Our approach is evaluated on ALT Ja-En, Ja-Hi pairs, and in-house Zh-Ja pairs. The results indicate that our proposed approach significantly outperformed the baseline model in most translation directions of Ja-En, Ja-Zh, and Ja-Hi pairs in at least one of BLEU/COMET scores. In future work, we will further explore which kind of input aspect is the most impactful for improving translation tasks.

`multilingual-t5` and (Xue et al., 2021).

References

Brown, T., Mann, B., Ryder, N., Subbiah, M., Kaplan, J. D., Dhariwal, P., Neelakantan, A., Shyam, P., Sastry, G., Askell, A., Agarwal, S., Herbert-Voss, A., Krueger, G., Henighan, T., Child, R., Ramesh, A., Ziegler, D., Wu, J., Winter, C., Hesse, C., Chen, M., Sigler, E., Litwin, M., Gray, S., Chess, B., Clark, J., Berner, C., McCandlish, S., Radford, A., Sutskever, I., and Amodei, D. (2020). Language models are few-shot learners. In *Advances in Neural Information Processing Systems*, volume 33, pages 1877–1901.

Devlin, J., Chang, M.-W., Lee, K., and Toutanova, K. (2019). BERT: Pre-training of deep bidirectional transformers for language understanding. In *Proceedings of the 2019 Conference of the North American Chapter of the Association for Computational Linguistics: Human Language Technologies, Volume 1 (Long and Short Papers)*, pages 4171–4186.

Dou, Z.-Y. and Neubig, G. (2021). Word alignment by fine-tuning embeddings on parallel corpora. In *Proceedings of the 16th Conference of the European Chapter of the Association for Computational Linguistics: Main Volume*, pages 2112–2128.

Hochreiter, S. and Schmidhuber, J. (1997). Long short-term memory. *Neural Comput.*, 9(8):1735–1780.

Isozaki, H., Hirao, T., Duh, K., Sudoh, K., and Tsukada, H. (2010). Automatic evaluation of translation quality for distant language pairs. In *Proceedings of the 2010 Conference on Empirical Methods in Natural Language Processing*, pages 944–952.

Kawara, Y., Chu, C., and Arase, Y. (2018). Recursive neural network based preordering for English-to-Japanese machine translation. In *Proceedings of ACL 2018, Student Research Workshop*, pages 21–27.

Lee, E.-S., Thillainathan, S., Nayak, S., Ranathunga, S., Adelani, D., Su, R., and McCarthy, A. (2022). Pre-trained multilingual sequence-to-sequence models: A hope for low-resource language translation? In *Findings of the Association for Computational Linguistics: ACL 2022*, pages 58–67.

Lin, Z., Pan, X., Wang, M., Qiu, X., Feng, J., Zhou, H., and Li, L. (2020). Pre-training multilingual neural machine translation by leveraging alignment information. In *Proceedings of the 2020 Conference on Empirical Methods in Natural Language Processing (EMNLP)*, pages 2649–2663.

Liu, Y., Gu, J., Goyal, N., Li, X., Edunov, S., Ghazvininejad, M., Lewis, M., and Zettlemoyer, L. (2020). Multilingual denoising pre-training for neural machine translation. *Transactions of the Association for Computational Linguistics*, 8:726–742.

Murthy, R., Kunchukuttan, A., and Bhattacharyya, P. (2019). Addressing word-order divergence in multilingual neural machine translation for extremely low resource languages. In *Proceedings of the 2019 Conference of the North American Chapter of the Association for Computational Linguistics: Human Language Technologies, Volume 1 (Long and Short Papers)*, pages 3868–3873.

Papineni, K., Roukos, S., Ward, T., and Zhu, W.-J. (2002). Bleu: a method for automatic evaluation of machine translation. In *Proceedings of the 40th Annual Meeting of the Association for Computational Linguistics*, pages 311–318.

Rei, R., Stewart, C., Farinha, A. C., and Lavie, A. (2020). COMET: A neural framework for MT evaluation. In *Proceedings of the 2020 Conference on Empirical Methods in Natural Language Processing (EMNLP)*, pages 2685–2702.

Riza, H., Purwoadi, M., Gunarso, Uliniansyah, T., Ti, A. A., Aljunied, S. M., Mai, L. C., Thang, V. T., Thai, N. P., Chea, V., Sun, R., Sam, S., Seng, S., Soe, K. M., Nwet, K. T., Utiyama, M., and Ding, C.

(2016). Introduction of the asian language treebank. In *2016 Conference of The Oriental Chapter of International Committee for Coordination and Standardization of Speech Databases and Assessment Techniques (O-COCOSDA)*, pages 1–6.

Sen, S., Gupta, K. K., Ekbal, A., and Bhattacharyya, P. (2019). Multilingual unsupervised NMT using shared encoder and language-specific decoders. In *Proceedings of the 57th Annual Meeting of the Association for Computational Linguistics*, pages 3083–3089.

Sennrich, R. and Zhang, B. (2019). Revisiting low-resource neural machine translation: A case study. In *Proceedings of the 57th Annual Meeting of the Association for Computational Linguistics*, pages 211–221.

Shi, T., Keneshloo, Y., Ramakrishnan, N., and Reddy, C. K. (2021). Neural abstractive text summarization with sequence-to-sequence models. *ACM/IMS Trans. Data Sci.*, 2(1).

Sutskever, I., Vinyals, O., and Le, Q. V. (2014). Sequence to sequence learning with neural networks. In *Proceedings of the 27th International Conference on Neural Information Processing Systems - Volume 2*, NIPS'14, page 3104–3112.

Vaswani, A., Shazeer, N., Parmar, N., Uszkoreit, J., Jones, L., Gomez, A. N., Kaiser, L. u., and Polosukhin, I. (2017). Attention is all you need. In *Advances in Neural Information Processing Systems*, volume 30.

Xue, L., Constant, N., Roberts, A., Kale, M., Al-Rfou, R., Siddhant, A., Barua, A., and Raffel, C. (2021). mT5: A massively multilingual pre-trained text-to-text transformer. In *Proceedings of the 2021 Conference of the North American Chapter of the Association for Computational Linguistics: Human Language Technologies*, pages 483–498.

Yin, J., Jiang, X., Lu, Z., Shang, L., Li, H., and Li, X. (2016). Neural generative question answering. In *Proceedings of the Workshop on Human-Computer Question Answering*, pages 36–42.

Zhu, J., Wei, Y., Tamura, T., Utsuro, T., and Nagata, M. (2022). A framework for low resource language translation based on SMT and highly accurate word alignment. In *Proceedings of the 28th Annual Conference of the Association for Natural Language Processing*, pages 1312–1316.

Pivot Translation for Zero-resource Language Pairs Based on a Multilingual Pretrained Model

Kenji Imamura kenji.imamura@nict.go.jp
Masao Utiyama mutiyama@nict.go.jp
Eiichiro Sumita eiichiro.sumita@nict.go.jp
National Institute of Information and Communications Technology, Hikari-dai, Seika-cho, Soraku-gun, Kyoto, 619-0289, Japan

Abstract

A multilingual translation model enables a single model to handle multiple languages. However, the translation qualities of unlearned language pairs (i.e., zero-shot translation qualities) are still poor. By contrast, pivot translation translates source texts into target ones via a pivot language such as English, thus enabling machine translation without parallel texts between the source and target languages.

In this paper, we perform pivot translation using a multilingual model and compare it with direct translation. We improve the translation quality without using parallel texts of direct translation by fine-tuning the model with machine-translated pseudo-translations. We also discuss what type of parallel texts are suitable for effectively improving the translation quality in multilingual pivot translation.

1 Introduction

Multilingual neural network models are models in which multiple languages are learned in a single model, and are useful for machine translation and cross-lingual language processing. Multilingual models utilize resources of similar languages (e.g., those in the same language family) and thus provide a relatively high degree of accuracy for even low-resource languages.[1] Machine translation is performed according to a combination of a source language and a target language, and therefore, language-specific models require a model for each possible combination of languages. By contrast, a multilingual model can handle all combinations of source and target languages and is therefore easier to manage. The potential usefulness of the multilingual model has led to the development of several encoder–decoder models pretrained using parallel corpora.

For example, a multilingual translation model pretrained with the OPUS-100 corpus (Zhang et al., 2020)[2] has been developed. This is a multilingual model that translates between English and any of 100 languages (i.e., an English-centric model). The M2M-100 model (Fan

[1]Under high-resource conditions, language-specific models are generally more accurate than multilingual models. This is called the curse of multilinguality.

[2]`https://github.com/bzhangGo/zero/tree/master/docs/multilingual_laln_lalt#pretrained-multilingual-models-many-to-many`

Proceedings of Machine Translation Summit XIX, Vol. 1: Research Track, pages 348–359
September 4–8, 2023, Macau SAR, China.

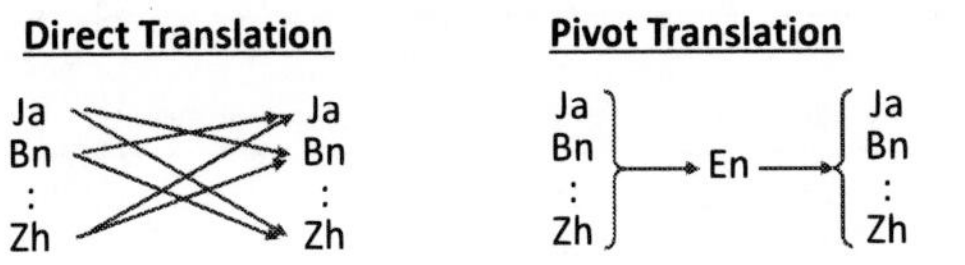

Figure 1: Direct translation and pivot translation.

et al., 2020)[3] also handles 100 languages. It is pretrained in 2,200 directions by adding parallel corpora that do not include English. The NLLB-200 models (Team et al., 2022)[4], which are extended from the M2M-100 model, handle around 200 languages and pretrained from parallel corpora of over 2,600 language pairs. Although the mBART models (Liu et al., 2020; Lewis et al., 2020) are also encoder–decoder pretrained models, they are trained using monolingual corpora only.

If we handle 100 languages for translation, this results in a total of 9,900 translation directions. Even if a multilingual translation model is used, translation quality for language pairs not trained by parallel corpora (called the zero-shot translation (Johnson et al., 2017)) is likely to be insufficient for practical use.

Pivot translation (Utiyama and Isahara, 2007; Cohn and Lapata, 2007) is a known method of achieving moderate quality translation in language pairs for which it is difficult to obtain parallel corpora. The method uses a pivot language between the source and target languages. Source texts are first translated into the pivot language, and then the pivot texts are translated into the target language (Figure 1). English is often used as the pivot language given the benefit of its rich set of parallel corpora. Although pivot translation is often used in statistical machine translation, it is also applicable to neural machine translation. By applying a multilingual pretrained model to the pivot translation, a single model can achieve a practical level of translation, even between languages without parallel corpora (zero-resource language pairs; between non-English languages in most cases).

In this paper, we apply pivot translation based on a multilingual pretrained model to zero-resource language pairs. This study aims to clarify the following points.

Q1 Comparison of the translation quality of pivot and direct translation. If parallel corpora exist, which has better translation quality? In creating new parallel corpora for zero-resource language pairs, should we prefer pivot or direct translation?

Q2 Pivot translation is performed in two stages: translation from the source language to the pivot (first stage), and then translation from the pivot to the target language (second stage). We can use different models in each stage. In regard to improvement, which model should be addressed first, the former or the latter?

Q3 Using pivot translation, we can create pseudo-parallel corpora (i.e., synthetic parallel corpora) between all language pairs of the supported languages if we have monolingual corpora. When we use pseudo-parallel corpora to fine-tune a multilingual model, what level of translation quality can be achieved with respect to manually created parallel corpora?

Q4 When generating pseudo-parallel corpora, which monolingual corpus should be used as the original language, the source, pivot, or target language?

[3] `https://github.com/facebookresearch/fairseq/tree/main/examples/m2m_100`

[4] For example, `https://huggingface.co/facebook/nllb-200-3.3B`

XX Language	Family[5]	Script[5]	CC-100 (monolingual)	OPUS-100 (En-XX)	CCAligned (En-XX)
English (En)	Indo-European	Latin	1,858 M	-	-
Japanese (Ja)	Japonic	Chinese and Kana	393 M	1.0 M	15.0 M
Bengali (Bn)	Indo-European	Bengali-Assamese	54 M	1.0 M	3.5 M
Indonesian (Id)	Austronesian	Latin	969 M	1.0 M	15.7 M
Khmer (Km)	Austroasiatic	Khmer	6.6 M	0.1 M	0.4 M
Lao (Lo)	Kra-Dai	Lao	2.6 M	-	0.2 M
Malay (Ms)	Austronesian	Latin	66 M	1.0 M	5.4 M
Myanmar (My)	Sino-Tibetan	Burmese	2.0 M	0.02 M	0.3 M
Thai (Th)	Kra-Dai	Thai	295 M	1.0 M	10.7 M
Tagalog (Tl)	Austronesian	Latin	27 M	-	6.6 M
Vietnamese (Vi)	Austroasiatic	Latin	939 M	1.0 M	12.4 M
Chinese (Zh)	Sino-Tibetan	Simplified Chinese	169 M	1.0 M	15.2 M

Table 1: Training corpus sizes of the languages used in this paper for the basic model. The values indicate the number of sentences.

Hereafter, Section 2 describes the English-centric multilingual pretrained model used in this study. Section 3 investigates the above questions through experiments.

2 Multilingual Pretrained Model Used in This Study

For this study, we newly trained an English-centric model to focus on translating zero-resource language pairs. We call this the "basic model." Specifically, this model corresponds to the 103 languages covered by the CC-100 corpus (Conneau et al., 2020; Wenzek et al., 2020), and the OPUS-100 corpus (Aharoni et al., 2019; Tiedemann, 2012) or the CCAligned v1 corpus (El-Kishky et al., 2020). CC-100 is a monolingual corpus, and OPUS-100 and CCAligned are parallel corpora. All corpora are based on Web crawl data. Table 1 shows the corpus sizes used for training the basic model (only the languages used in this paper). The number of sentences in CC-100 is for monolingual sentences. OPUS-100 and CCAligned are the number of parallel sentences between English (En) and one of the languages other than English (XX languages).

2.1 Procedure for Building the Basic Model

We built the basic model using the following procedure.

1. Following the method of Wang et al. (2020), the word embeddings of the mBART-50 model were extended to the 109 languages covered by the CC-100 corpus. The extended embeddings were randomly initialized.

2. All corpora were tokenized by SentencePiece (Kudo and Richardson, 2018) using the model attached to mBART-50 (250K subwords). Then, denoising training was additionally performed on the above extended model using the CC-100 corpus. This is the same as the training of the mBART-50.

3. The model was trained using parallel sentences from/to English in the OPUS-100 and CCAligned corpora. Because the corpus sizes for each language pair are substantially different, we applied temperature sampling (Arivazhagan et al., 2019) in the training (inverse

[5] `https://en.wikipedia.org/`

XX Language	En → XX BLEU	En → XX ChrF2	XX → En BLEU	XX → En ChrF2
Japanese (Ja)	26.0	36.0	26.2	57.2
Bengali (Bn)	9.5	44.5	28.2	56.8
Indonesian (Id)	41.8	67.5	43.0	67.6
Khmer (Km)	52.7 †	47.6	27.0	55.2
Lao (Lo)	27.7 †	24.9	6.3	27.7
Malay (Ms)	44.1	69.1	44.5	68.3
Myanmar (My)	40.9 †	36.2	19.3	49.1
Thai (Th)	53.0 †	48.2	26.9	56.4
Tagalog (Tl)	30.7	59.1	39.2	63.3
Vietnamese (Vi)	39.7	57.8	36.0	61.9
Chinese (Zh)	35.0	31.0	24.8	56.2
Average Score (11 Languages)	36.5	47.4	29.2	56.3
(FYI) Average Score of M2M-100	28.5	40.9	26.0	52.0

Table 2: Translation quality between English (En) and foreign languages (XX) in the basic model. † mark indicates the BLEU scores tokenized into characters because sacreBLEU cannot tokenize the languages. The language-dependent default tokenizers of sacreBLEU were used for other languages.

temperature coefficient $1/T = 0.7$). Namely, we down-sampled training sentences in the language pairs of the large corpora, and up-sampled them in the language pairs of the small corpora.

The basic model has the same structure as the mBART-50 model except for the word embedding table. Thus, the encoder and decoder consist of 12 layers each, 1,024 hidden dimensions, 4,096 FFN dimensions, 16 heads, and 250K word embeddings. Note that the source and target language IDs must be given during translation because the mBART-50 requires the source and target language tags.

2.2 Translation Quality between English and Foreign Languages in the Basic Model

Table 2 lists the quality of translation between English and the selected languages targeted in this study using the basic model.

The Asian Language Treebank (ALT) Parallel Corpus (Riza et al., 2016), which is used in the experiments described in the next section, was translated by the basic model using the direct translation, and the translation qualities were evaluated by sacreBLEU (Post, 2018). Note that several languages are not supported by the tokenizers in sacreBLEU. We used sacreBLEU to evaluate translations in such languages using the character tokenization († marks in Table 2). In addition, we also report the ChrF scores (Popović, 2015) ($\beta = 2$; notated as ChrF2), which are independent of the tokenizers.

For reference, the results of the M2M-100 model (Fan et al., 2020) evaluated on the same test set are also listed at the bottom of the table. The results indicate that translation quality of the basic model is, in the limited languages, better than that of the M2M-100 model on average.

3 Translation Experiments

In this study, we conducted translation experiments between Japanese (Ja) and languages other than English (XX).

Corpus	#Sentences Training	Dev.	Test	Remarks
ALT	18,088	1,000	1,018	
ASPEC-JC	669,923	2,090	2,107	
ASPEC-JE	670,000	-	-	English only, selected from 3M sentences.

Table 3: Corpus size for fine-tuning

3.1 Experimental Settings

3.1.1 Corpora

In our experiments, the following parallel corpora were used to compare a zero-resource condition with a condition when direct parallel corpora exist. The corpus sizes are shown in Table 3. The sizes of the training sets indicate those after removing translations with significantly different lengths.

In the low-resource experiments, we used the ALT Parallel Corpus (Riza et al., 2016)[6]. This is a multilingual corpus that covers English (En), Japanese (Ja), Bengali (Bn), Indonesian (Id), Khmer (Km), Lao (Lo), Malay (Ms), Myanmar (My), Thai (Th), Tagalog (Tl), Vietnamese (Vi), and Simplified Chinese (Zh). This corpus contains translations from the same English WikiNews texts. Therefore, translations are also provided between languages other than English. Hence, translation experiments were conducted between Japanese and languages other than English.

In the mid-resource experiments, we used the Asian Scientific Paper Excerpt Corpus (ASPEC) (Nakazawa et al., 2016)[7], which is based on scientific paper abstracts. The ASPEC-JC corpus is a parallel corpus of Japanese and Chinese, and it does not have English counterparts. We mainly use it to evaluate the effectiveness of pseudo-translations. To generate pseudo-translations from English texts in the same domain, we also used the English part of the ASPEC-JE corpus, which is a Japanese–English parallel corpus. To match the size with ASPEC-JC, we selected 670K sentences from the entire corpus.

These corpora were tokenized by the SentencePiece model attached with the mBART-50 model, in the same way as the basic model.

3.1.2 Comparison of Methods/Systems

In this study, we compare the direct and pivot translations (Figure 1). The multilingual pre-trained model described in Section 2 is called the basic model. We compare the translation results of the basic model with those of models fine-tuned on the parallel corpora (Figure 2). Fine-tuning was performed using the parallel corpora described in Section 3.1.1.

- **+Direct Parallel Model:**
  The model fine-tuned using the direct parallel corpora of Japanese and the XX languages. In this case, we used the direct translation method because the corpora do not go through the pivot.[8]

- **+XX $\rightarrow$ En Model:**
  The model fine-tuned using the parallel corpora from the XX languages to English. The

[6] `https://www2.nict.go.jp/astrec-att/member/mutiyama/ALT/`

[7] `https://jipsti.jst.go.jp/aspec/`

[8] Translation qualities among languages that have not been fine-tuned are significantly degraded due to catastrophic forgetting. Therefore, pivot translation cannot be applied.

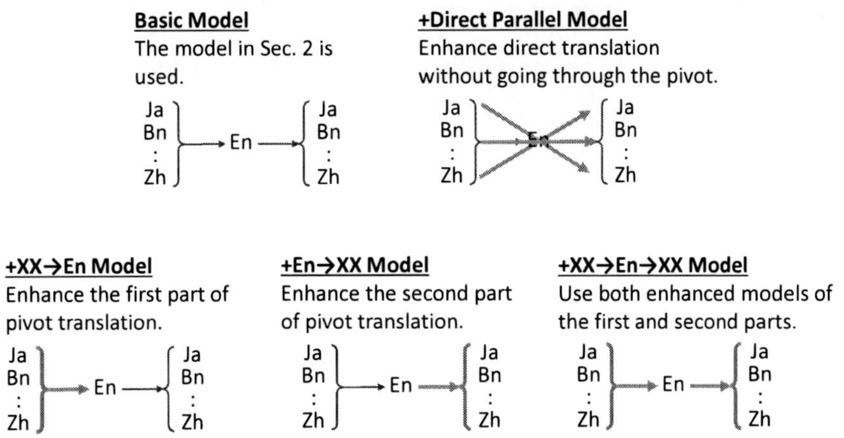

Figure 2: Types of fine-tuned models.

first stage of pivot translation was enhanced. The basic model was used in the second stage of pivot translation.

- **+En → XX Model:**
  The model fine-tuned using the parallel corpora from English to the XX languages. The second stage of pivot translation was enhanced. The basic model was used in the first stage of pivot translation.

- **+XX → En → XX Model:**
  The +XX → En and +En→XX models were used for the first and second stages of pivot translation, respectively.

3.1.3 Pseudo-translations

Using pivot translation, we can perform machine translation even for zero-resource language pairs. Therefore, we can construct direct parallel corpora by machine translation from monolingual corpora. In this study, we also compare the cases fine-tuned by manual translation and pseudo-translations.

All pseudo-translations were generated by the basic model. Although word sampling (Imamura et al., 2018; Edunov et al., 2018) improves translation quality during back-translation (Sennrich et al., 2016) because of increasing the translation diversity, we must switch the translation methods depending on the direction. For the sake of simplicity, we used one-best translations for pseudo-translations in our experiments.[9]

3.1.4 Other Settings

The hyperparameters used during fine-tuning and testing are listed in Table 4. We used one-best translations in both stages of pivot translation.

We used BLEU (Papineni et al., 2002) and ChrF (Popović, 2015) for the evaluation using sacreBLEU (Post, 2018).

[9]In back-translation (target-to-source), final translation quality improves when we increase translation diversity using word sampling. By contrast, one-best translation is preferred in sequence-level knowledge distillation (source-to-target) (Kim and Rush, 2016; Kim et al., 2019)). To apply this distinction, it is necessary to switch the generating method depending on the translation direction.

Type	Value
Fine-tuning	Temperature sampling (Arivazhagan et al., 2019): $1/T = 0.7$, Loss: label_smoothed_cross_entropy=0.1, Dropout: 0.3, Warmup: around one epoch, LR: 0.00008, inverse_sqrt, Early stopping: ten epochs, Batch size: 8K tokens, Adam optimizer ($\beta_1 = 0.9$, $\beta_2 = 0.99$, $\epsilon = 10^{-6}$)
Test (Inference)	Beam width: 10 One-best translation

Table 4: List of hyperparameters.

3.2 Experimental Results

Tables 5 and 6 present the results for the ALT and ASPEC-JC corpora, respectively. The results of the ALT corpus show the average scores on all XX languages. No. 2 is the baseline result using pivot translation.

3.2.1 Pivot Translation vs. Direct Translation

Regardless of language direction, the BLEU scores of the direct translation using the basic model (No. 1) in the ALT and ASPEC-JC corpora are extremely low. This is caused by zero-shot translation. However, when we use pivot translation with the same model (No. 2), the BLEU scores improve by over 12 points. Namely, moderate transition can be obtained even for the zero-resource language pairs.

By contrast, when we fine-tune the model using the direct parallel corpus (No. 6a), the BLEU scores improved by more than 3 points and 18 points in the ALT and ASPEC-JC corpora, respectively, when compared with the results of No. 2. These scores were not the highest in the results of the ALT corpus. We assume that this is because the number of parallel sentences was small (18K sentences), and the improvement obtained using pivot translation with the English-centric model surpassed these results. By contrast, the BLEU scores for the ASPEC-JC corpus were the highest. If we can acquire a corpus of medium size, we should prepare a direct parallel corpus to improve the translation quality.

3.2.2 First and Second Stages of Pivot Translation

No. 3a and 4a in Table 2 are the results of the fine-tuned basic models using the parallel corpora between English and XX languages. No. 3a and 4a enhanced the first and second stages of pivot translation, respectively.

Compared with the baseline results, the results of No. 2 and 3a are not significantly different. By contrast, the BLEU score of No. 4a improved the score of No. 2 by over 4 points. In other words, the translation quality was efficiently improved when we enhanced the second stage of pivot translation. This is because the basic model was trained using corpora of Web crawl data, and their domain was different from that of the test set. Therefore, the quality of the output sentences was improved by the domain adaptation of the second stage of pivot translation.

No.	Model	Translation Method	Ja → XX BLEU (Avr.)	Ja → XX ChrF2 (Avr.)	XX → Ja BLEU (Avr.)	XX → Ja ChrF2 (Avr.)
1	Basic Model	Direct	0.5	6.3	0.1	0.8
2	Basic Model	Pivot	27.0	40.4	17.3	26.9
3a	+XX → En (Manual)	Pivot	26.8	40.0	18.8	28.3
4a	+En → XX (Manual)	Pivot	**33.1**	**45.6**	21.4	30.2
5a	+XX → En → XX (Manual)	Pivot	32.9	45.4	**23.1**	**32.0**
6a	+Direct Parallel (Manual)	Direct	32.2	44.8	21.2	30.3

Table 5: Translation results for the ALT corpus. The bold values indicate the highest score among the models and methods.

No.	Model	Translation Method	Ja → Zh BLEU	Ja → Zh ChrF2	Zh → Ja BLEU	Zh → Ja ChrF2
1	Basic Model	Direct	0.0	0.0	0.1	0.2
2	Basic Model	Pivot	19.4	17.6	12.0	21.8
3b	+XX → En (Pseudo)	Pivot	19.6	17.7	12.4	22.2
4b	+En → XX (Pseudo)	Pivot	26.8	23.2	19.2	27.8
5b	+XX → En → XX (Pseudo)	Pivot	27.2	23.6	19.8	28.4
6b	+Direct Parallel (Pseudo)	Direct	31.0	26.4	24.5	32.9
6a	+Direct Parallel (Manual)	Direct	**37.6**	**32.0**	**33.4**	**41.6**

Table 6: Translation results for the ASPEC-JC corpus. The bold values indicate the highest score among the models and methods.

3.2.3 Data Augmentation Generated by Machine Translation

The results for No. 3a, 4a, 5a, and 6a in Tables 5 and 6 are the results of the fine-tuned models with the manually created parallel corpora. The results for No. 3b, 4b, 5b, and 6b in the tables are the results of the fine-tuned models with the pseudo-parallel corpora generated by machine translation.

When we enhance the first stage of the pivot translation using the pseudo-translations (No. 3b), the translation quality rarely changed from that of the baseline (No. 2).

By contrast, the translation qualities were significantly improved when we enhanced the second stage of pivot translation (No. 4b) or fine-tuned using the direct parallel corpus (No. 6b) despite using pseudo-data, even though the quality scores did not reach those of manual translation (No. 6a). However, the pseudo-translations can be generated from monolingual corpora. If we actively use pseudo-translations, the translation quality can be improved even for zero-resource language pairs.

3.2.4 Original Language of Pseudo-Translations

When we generate pseudo-translations from monolingual corpora, either the source, target, or pivot language can be used as the original language. In the experiments described in this section, we created pseudo-translations from various original languages and fine-tuned the basic model. When the source or target language was used as the original one, the ASPEC-JC training set was used. When the pivot language was used as the original one, the English part of ASPEC-JE

No.	Model	Translation Method	Original Language	Ja → Zh BLEU	Ja → Zh ChrF2	Zh → Ja BLEU	Zh → Ja ChrF2
3b	+ XX → En	Pivot	Source	19.6	17.7	12.4	22.2
3c			Pivot	20.1	17.9	12.8	23.1
4b	+ En → XX	Pivot	Target	26.8	23.2	19.2	27.8
4c			Pivot	19.2	17.4	11.6	21.5
5b	+ XX → En → XX	Pivot	Source & Target	27.2	23.6	19.8	28.4
5c			Pivot	19.8	17.5	12.3	22.9
6b	+ Direct Parallel	Direct	Target	31.0	26.4	24.5	32.9
6c			Pivot	21.7	19.2	15.0	24.9
6d			Source	20.4	18.4	13.1	23.0

Table 7: Translation qualities when pseudo-translations with different original languages are used. The underlined values indicate the highest score of the same model/translation method.

was used.

Table 7 presents the translation quality results obtained on ASPEC-JC and is summarized as follows.

- In the +XX → En model, the pseudo-translations generated from the pivot language (i.e., the translations from the pivot to the source language) had a higher translation quality.
- In the +En → XX model, the quality of the pseudo-translations generated from the target language (i.e., translations from the target to the pivot language) was significantly higher.
- In the +XX → En → XX model, the quality of the pseudo-translations generated from the source and target languages (i.e., translations from the target to the pivot and from the source to the pivot language) was significantly higher.
- In the +Direct Parallel model, the translation quality was highest in the order of the target, pivot, and source languages.

For all these results, the translation qualities were high when we fine-tuned the model with the pseudo-translations translated in the direction opposite that to be tested. Even in pivot translation, the monolingual corpora of the target languages should be collected, if possible.

4 Conclusions

Using the pivot translation, we can translate texts even for zero-resource language pairs. Moreover, we can improve the translation quality without changing the zero-resource condition because we can generate pseudo-parallel corpora from monolingual corpora.

In this study, we applied pivot translation to zero-resource language pairs using a multilingual pretrained model. The answers to the questions studied in this work are summarized as follows.

A1 Comparing pivot translation with direct translation, the quality of pivot translation is higher than that of direct translation when the parallel corpus size is very small. When the corpus size is large, the quality of direct translation increases. If we can acquire a corpus of medium size, we should prepare a direct parallel corpus to improve the translation quality.

A2 Comparing the first and second stages of pivot translation, it is better to enhance the second stage to improve quality.

A3 It is possible to improve translation quality using pseudo-translations generated by pivot translation.

A4 When generating pseudo-translations, it is better to generate them from monolingual corpora of the target language.

The fact that zero-resource language pairs can be translated is helpful when we extend our machine translation to new languages. For example, we can check the quality of a newly created parallel corpus by back-translation, or we can post-edit pseudo-translations to create direct parallel corpora.

We plan to extend multilinguality while appropriately using direct and pivot translation.

Acknowledgment

Part of this work was conducted under the commissioned research program 'Research and Development of Advanced Multilingual Translation Technology' in the 'R&D Project for Information and Communications Technology (JPMI00316)' of the Ministry of Internal Affairs and Communications (MIC), Japan.

References

Aharoni, R., Johnson, M., and Firat, O. (2019). Massively multilingual neural machine translation. In *Proceedings of the 2019 Conference of the North American Chapter of the Association for Computational Linguistics: Human Language Technologies, Volume 1 (Long and Short Papers)*, pages 3874–3884, Minneapolis, Minnesota. Association for Computational Linguistics.

Arivazhagan, N., Bapna, A., Firat, O., Lepikhin, D., Johnson, M., Krikun, M., Chen, M. X., Cao, Y., Foster, G., Cherry, C., Macherey, W., Chen, Z., and Wu, Y. (2019). Massively multilingual neural machine translation in the wild: Findings and challenges. *arXiv e-print*, 1907.05019.

Cohn, T. and Lapata, M. (2007). Machine translation by triangulation: Making effective use of multi-parallel corpora. In *Proceedings of the 45th Annual Meeting of the Association of Computational Linguistics*, pages 728–735, Prague, Czech Republic. Association for Computational Linguistics.

Conneau, A., Khandelwal, K., Goyal, N., Chaudhary, V., Wenzek, G., Guzmán, F., Grave, E., Ott, M., Zettlemoyer, L., and Stoyanov, V. (2020). Unsupervised cross-lingual representation learning at scale. In *Proceedings of the 58th Annual Meeting of the Association for Computational Linguistics*, pages 8440–8451, Online. Association for Computational Linguistics.

Edunov, S., Ott, M., Auli, M., and Grangier, D. (2018). Understanding back-translation at scale. In *Proceedings of the 2018 Conference on Empirical Methods in Natural Language Processing*, pages 489–500, Brussels, Belgium. Association for Computational Linguistics.

El-Kishky, A., Chaudhary, V., Guzmán, F., and Koehn, P. (2020). CCAligned: A massive collection of cross-lingual web-document pairs. In *Proceedings of the 2020 Conference on Empirical Methods in Natural Language Processing (EMNLP)*, pages 5960–5969, Online. Association for Computational Linguistics.

Fan, A., Bhosale, S., Schwenk, H., Ma, Z., El-Kishky, A., Goyal, S., Baines, M., Celebi, O., Wenzek, G., Chaudhary, V., Goyal, N., Birch, T., Liptchinsky, V., Edunov, S., Grave, E., Auli, M., and Joulin, A. (2020). Beyond english-centric multilingual machine translation. *arXiv e-print*, 2010.11125.

Imamura, K., Fujita, A., and Sumita, E. (2018). Enhancement of encoder and attention using target monolingual corpora in neural machine translation. In *Proceedings of the 2nd Workshop on Neural Machine Translation and Generation*, pages 55–63, Melbourne, Australia. Association for Computational Linguistics.

Johnson, M., Schuster, M., Le, Q., Krikun, M., Wu, Y., Chen, Z., Thorat, N., Viégas, F., Wattenberg, M., Corrado, G., Hughes, M., and Dean, J. (2017). Google's multilingual neural machine translation system: Enabling zero-shot translation. *Transactions of the Association for Computational Linguistics*, 5(0):339–351.

Kim, Y. and Rush, A. M. (2016). Sequence-level knowledge distillation. In *Proceedings of the 2016 Conference on Empirical Methods in Natural Language Processing*, pages 1317–1327, Austin, Texas. Association for Computational Linguistics.

Kim, Y. J., Junczys-Dowmunt, M., Hassan, H., Fikri Aji, A., Heafield, K., Grundkiewicz, R., and Bogoychev, N. (2019). From research to production and back: Ludicrously fast neural machine translation. In *Proceedings of the 3rd Workshop on Neural Generation and Translation*, pages 280–288, Hong Kong. Association for Computational Linguistics.

Kudo, T. and Richardson, J. (2018). SentencePiece: A simple and language independent subword tokenizer and detokenizer for neural text processing. In *Proceedings of the 2018 Conference on Empirical Methods in Natural Language Processing: System Demonstrations*, pages 66–71, Brussels, Belgium. Association for Computational Linguistics.

Lewis, M., Liu, Y., Goyal, N., Ghazvininejad, M., Mohamed, A., Levy, O., Stoyanov, V., and Zettlemoyer, L. (2020). BART: Denoising sequence-to-sequence pre-training for natural language generation, translation, and comprehension. In *Proceedings of the 58th Annual Meeting of the Association for Computational Linguistics*, pages 7871–7880, Online. Association for Computational Linguistics.

Liu, Y., Gu, J., Goyal, N., Li, X., Edunov, S., Ghazvininejad, M., Lewis, M., and Zettlemoyer, L. (2020). Multilingual denoising pre-training for neural machine translation. *Transactions of the Association for Computational Linguistics*, 8:726–742.

Nakazawa, T., Yaguchi, M., Uchimoto, K., Utiyama, M., Sumita, E., Kurohashi, S., and Isahara, H. (2016). ASPEC: Asian scientific paper excerpt corpus. In *Proceedings of the Tenth International Conference on Language Resources and Evaluation (LREC'16)*, pages 2204–2208, Portorož, Slovenia. European Language Resources Association (ELRA).

Papineni, K., Roukos, S., Ward, T., and Zhu, W.-J. (2002). Bleu: a method for automatic evaluation of machine translation. In *Proceedings of the 40th Annual Meeting of the Association for Computational Linguistics*, pages 311–318, Philadelphia, Pennsylvania, USA. Association for Computational Linguistics.

Popović, M. (2015). chrF: character n-gram F-score for automatic MT evaluation. In *Proceedings of the Tenth Workshop on Statistical Machine Translation*, pages 392–395, Lisbon, Portugal. Association for Computational Linguistics.

Post, M. (2018). A call for clarity in reporting BLEU scores. In *Proceedings of the Third Conference on Machine Translation: Research Papers*, pages 186–191, Brussels, Belgium. Association for Computational Linguistics.

Riza, H., Michael Purwoadi, G., Uliniansyah, T., Ti, A. A., Aljunied, S. M., Mai, L. C., Thang, V. T., Thai, N. P., Chea, V., Sun, R., Sam, S., Seng, S., Soe, K. M., Nwet, K. T., Utiyama, M., and Ding, C. (2016). Introduction of the asian language treebank. In *Oriental COCOSDA*.

Sennrich, R., Haddow, B., and Birch, A. (2016). Improving neural machine translation models with monolingual data. In *Proceedings of the 54th Annual Meeting of the Association for Computational Linguistics (Volume 1: Long Papers)*, pages 86–96, Berlin, Germany. Association for Computational Linguistics.

Team, N., Costa-jussà, M. R., Cross, J., Çelebi, O., Elbayad, M., Heafield, K., Heffernan, K., Kalbassi, E., Lam, J., Licht, D., Maillard, J., Sun, A., Wang, S., Wenzek, G., Youngblood, A., Akula, B., Barrault, L., Gonzalez, G. M., Hansanti, P., Hoffman, J., Jarrett, S., Sadagopan, K. R., Rowe, D., Spruit, S., Tran, C., Andrews, P., Ayan, N. F., Bhosale, S., Edunov, S., Fan, A., Gao, C., Goswami, V., Guzmán, F., Koehn, P., Mourachko, A., Ropers, C., Saleem, S., Schwenk, H., and Wang, J. (2022). No language left behind: Scaling human-centered machine translation. *arXiv e-print*, 2207.04672.

Tiedemann, J. (2012). Parallel data, tools and interfaces in opus. In Chair), N. C. C., Choukri, K., Declerck, T., Doğan, M. U., Maegaard, B., Mariani, J., Moreno, A., Odijk, J., and Piperidis, S., editors, *Proceedings of the Eight International Conference on Language Resources and Evaluation (LREC'12)*, Istanbul, Turkey. European Language Resources Association (ELRA).

Utiyama, M. and Isahara, H. (2007). A comparison of pivot methods for phrase-based statistical machine translation. In *Human Language Technologies 2007: The Conference of the North American Chapter of the Association for Computational Linguistics; Proceedings of the Main Conference*, pages 484–491, Rochester, New York.

Wang, Z., K, K., Mayhew, S., and Roth, D. (2020). Extending multilingual BERT to low-resource languages. In *Findings of the Association for Computational Linguistics: EMNLP 2020*, pages 2649–2656, Online. Association for Computational Linguistics.

Wenzek, G., Lachaux, M.-A., Conneau, A., Chaudhary, V., Guzmán, F., Joulin, A., and Grave, E. (2020). CCNet: Extracting high quality monolingual datasets from web crawl data. In *Proceedings of the Twelfth Language Resources and Evaluation Conference*, pages 4003–4012, Marseille, France. European Language Resources Association.

Zhang, B., Williams, P., Titov, I., and Sennrich, R. (2020). Improving massively multilingual neural machine translation and zero-shot translation. *arXiv e-print*, 2004.11867.

Character-level NMT and language similarity

Josef Jon jon@ufal.mff.cuni.cz
Ondřej Bojar bojar@ufal.mff.cuni.cz
Charles University, Faculty of Mathematics and Physics, Institute of Formal and Applied Linguistics, Prague, Czech Republic

Abstract

We explore the effectiveness of character-level neural machine translation using Transformer architecture for various levels of language similarity and size of the training dataset on translation between Czech and Croatian, German, Hungarian, Slovak, and Spanish. We evaluate the models using automatic MT metrics and show that translation between similar languages benefits from character-level input segmentation, while for less related languages, character-level vanilla Transformer-base often lags behind subword-level segmentation. We confirm previous findings that it is possible to close the gap by finetuning the already trained subword-level models to character-level.

1 Introduction

Character-level NMT has been studied for a long time, with mixed results compared to subword segmentation. In the MT practitioner's discourse, it has sometimes been assumed that character-level systems are more robust to domain shift and better in the translation of morphologically rich languages. Recent studies (Libovický et al., 2022) show that there are no conclusive proofs for these claims.

At the same time, character-level systems have been reliably shown to be robust against source-side noise. In terms of general translation quality, they often either underperform or are on par with their subword-level counterparts (Libovický et al., 2022). Also, both training and inference speeds are lower and memory requirements are higher due to longer sequence lengths (mostly because of the quadratic complexity of the Transformer attention mechanism with respect to the input length (Vaswani et al., 2017)) unless specialized architectures are used.

In this work, we present experiments on a specific use-case of translation of related languages. We train bilingual Transformer translation models to translate between Czech and Croatian, German, Hungarian, Slovak, or Spanish. We vary the training dataset size, vocabulary size and model depth and study the effects. We show that in the baseline configuration with vanilla `Transformer-base`, character-level models outperform subword-level models in terms of automated evaluation scores only in closely related Czech-Slovak translation pair. Finally, we confirm that it is possible to obtain a better quality of the char-level translation for less related languages by first training a subword-level model and in the later stage of the training switching to character-level processing.

2 Related work

Libovický et al. (2022) analyze the body of the work on character-level NMT and show that in most cases, it still falls behind in many aspects compared to the subword-level counterpart.

Proceedings of Machine Translation Summit XIX, Vol. 1: Research Track, pages 360–371
September 4–8, 2023, Macau SAR, China.

Since they provide a comprehensive overview of the field up to today, we will only very briefly list the most influential works in this section, and refer the reader to the detailed analysis in Libovický et al. (2022).

In one of the earliest works, Chung et al. (2016) use RNN with character segmentation on the decoder side. Lee et al. (2017) use CNN for fully character-level NMT. Costa-jussà et al. (2017) apply a similar approach to byte-level translation. Gupta et al. (2019) and Ngo et al. (2019) explore character-level MT using the Transformer model. Recent work on character-level NMT includes Li et al. (2021); Banar et al. (2021) and Gao et al. (2020).

Libovický and Fraser (2020) show that problems with slow training and worse final translation quality for character-level NMT models can be largely mitigated by first training with subword segmentation and subsequently finetuning on character-segmented text. However, a problem of lower speed (due to longer sequence length) persists, which can make both the training and inference prohibitively costly and slow, especially for models that make use of a larger context than only one sentence.

Our work specifically targets character-level translation of closely related languages. In WMT 2019 Similar Language translation task (Barrault et al., 2019), Scherrer et al. (2019) show that character-level NMT is effective for translation between closely related Portuguese and Spanish and in Multilingual Low-Resource Translation for Indo-European Languages task at WMT21 (Akhbardeh et al., 2021), Jon et al. (2021) successfully apply character-level NMT to translation between Catalan and Occitan.

3 System description

3.1 Data

We evaluate our models on translation from Czech to German, Spanish, Croatian, Hungarian and Slovak and vice-versa. We train on MultiParaCrawl (Bañón et al., 2020)[1] corpus. It is based on Paracrawl, which is English-centric (each language in the original dataset is aligned only to English). MultiParaCrawl aligns the sentences in the other languages that have the same English translation. This introduces mis-alignments into the dataset (it is possible that two sentences with different meanings in other languages have the same English translation), but we nevertheless use it to have a comparable training corpus for all the languages. We sample subsets for each language pair in sizes of 50k, 500k, and 5M sentences (Croatian corpus only has about 800k sentences in total, so we use only the 50k and 500k sizes). We use FLORES-200 (Team et al., 2022) as validation and test sets (we keep the original splits). We note that this test set is created by translating the same English test into all the languages and not translating the two tested languages between each other – this might mean that the effect of language similarity is somewhat subdued in this setting.

We segment the text using SentencePiece with the given vocabulary size (32k, 4k, or character-level model), with 99.95% character coverage and UTF-8 byte fallback for unknown characters. The segmentation models are trained on the whole 5M datasets, jointly for each pair.

Language similarity We use chrF score (Popović, 2015), traditionally used to compute translation quality, as a language similarity metric. It is a character-level metric and we hypothesize that character-level similarity is an important aspect for our experiments. We compute chrF score of the Czech FLORES-200 test set relative to all the other languages (Table 1). We also show the lexical similarity score provided by the UKC database[2], which is based on a number of cognates between languages in their contemporary vocabularies (Bella et al., 2021).

[1]https://opus.nlpl.eu/MultiParaCrawl.php

[2]http://ukc.disi.unitn.it/index.php/lexsim/

Language	chrF	LexSim
sk	36.7	16.5
hr	22.7	8.2
es	16.5	2.6
hu	16.3	2.9
de	15.4	3.7

Table 1: UKC LexSim and chrF score-based similarities of the testsets, i.e. chrF score of untranslated Czech testset compared to the other languages.

Pair	Lang	% skip	Avg len
cs-de	cs	0.43	88.2
	de	0.64	100.3
cs-es	cs	0.30	84.5
	es	0.50	95.5
cs-hr	cs	1.21	127.1
	hr	1.30	131.7
cs-hu	cs	0.26	76.4
	hu	0.45	83.0
cs-sk	cs	0.25	74.9
	sk	0.29	77.4

Table 2: Percentage of examples exceeding the training source length limit (400 characters) and average sentence character lengths for all the training datasets for character-level training.

3.2 Model

We trained Transformer (Vaswani et al., 2017) models to translate to Czech from other languages (Hungarian, Slovak, Croatian, German and Spanish) and vice-versa using MarianNMT (Junczys-Dowmunt et al., 2018).

Our baseline model is `Transformer-base` (512-dim embeddings, 2048-dim ffn) with 6 encoder and 6 decoder layers. We also train two other versions of `Transformer-base`: with 16 encoder + 6 decoder layers and with 16 encoder + 16 decoder layers. For other hyperparameters, we use the default configuration of MarianNMT. We evaluate the models on the validation set each 5000 updates and we stop the training after 20 consecutive validations without improvement in either chrF or cross-entropy. We use Adam optimizer (Kingma and Ba, 2017) and one shared vocabulary and embeddings for both source and target.

Similarly to Libovický and Fraser (2020), we compared training char-level models from scratch to starting the training from subword-level models (both with 4k and 32k vocabularies) and switching to character-level processing after subword-level training converged. They obtained better results with a more complex curriculum learning scheme, while we only finetune the pre-trained model.

We performed a length analysis on the character level for all the datasets. Based on this, we set the maximum source sequence length for training and inference to 400 for all the systems. We skip longer training examples. In the worst case (Croatian to Czech), 1.3 % of the examples are skipped. Table 2 shows average character lengths and percentage of the skipped training examples in all directions. For inference, we normalize the output score by the length of the hypothesis as implemented in Marian. We search for the optimal value of the length normalization constant on the validation set in the range of 0.5 to 4.0.

3.3 Evaluation

We use SacreBLEU (Post, 2018) to compute BLEU and chrF scores. We set $\beta = 2$ for chrF in all the experiments (i.e. chrF2, the default in SacreBLEU). For COMET (Rei et al., 2020)[3] scores we use the original implementation and the `wmt20-comet-da` model.

[3] `https://github.com/Unbabel/COMET`

3.4 Hardware

We ran the experiments on a grid comprising of Quadro RTX 5000, GeForce GTX 1080 Ti, RTX A4000, or GeForce RTX 3090 GPUs. We trained a total of about 170 models with training times ranging from 10 hours to 14 days, depending on the dataset, model, and GPUs used.

4 Results

4.1 Subwords vs. characters

We compare BLEU, chrF and COMET scores for Transformer-base trained on different training dataset sizes and with different segmentations in all the language directions in Table 3 and the same results are plotted in Figure 1. First and foremost, the character-level models provide the best results for the most similar language pair, Czech-Slovak (sk), across training data sizes and translation directions. For example, with a 50k dataset, the character-level model achieves a COMET score of 0.8834 and 0.8429 in Czech-to-Slovak and Slovak-to-Czech translations, respectively. The scores are better compared to those of 4k and 32k vocab models with the same training dataset. This trend continues with larger datasets; the character-level model outperforms in both the 500k and 5M datasets, although for the largest datasets, the results are very similar across vocabulary sizes.

However, for the other language pairs, the results are mixed, and subword-level models often outperform character-level models, particularly with larger training dataset sizes. For instance, in Czech-to-Hungarian (hu) translations with a 5M dataset, the 32k vocab model achieves a COMET score of 0.6531 which is better than the 0.6263 score of the character-level model. The same pattern is observed in Czech-to-German (de) translations with the 32k vocab model outperforming the character-level model in the 5M dataset with a COMET score of 0.6275 against 0.5955.

For all the other languages (aside from Slovak), training on the 50k dataset fails to produce usable translation model at any vocabulary size, even for the second most similar language, Croatian. However, as we show in the next section, we can see the benefits of char-level translation of Czech-Croatian when finetuning charl-level model from subword-level model.

The results are more favorable for subword-level models with increasing training set sizes, probably due to the sparsity of the longer subwords in smaller datasets which results in worse quality of the embeddings. We also see that generally, character-level models perform better in terms of chrF (char-level metric) than BLEU and COMET. For example, see Czech-to-Spanish, 5M dataset: character model has the best chrF score (although by a small margin), but the worst BLEU and COMET scores.

4.2 Finetuning

We took an alternative approach to training character-level models from scratch by fine-tuning the subword-level models. We only finetuned the models in the direction from Czech to the target language. Starting from the last checkpoint of the subword-level training, we switched the dataset to a character-split one. Since SentencePiece models include all the characters in their vocabularies, there was no need to adjust them. We proceeded with the same hyperparameters, including the optimizer parameters, after resetting the early-stopping counters.

We present the results in Tables 4 and 5 for models finetuned from 4k and 32k subword models, respectively. We see that in cases where training a char-level model from scratch didn't perform well compared to a subword-level one, finetuning from subword-level helps to attain the quality of the subword-level and even surpass it in some cases. For example, Czech-to-Croatian char level model without finetuning obtains COMET score of -1.4055, but after finetuning from 4k model, the score increases to -0.2671, which is also better than the -1.0112 of the 4k model alone.

Lang	Dataset	Vocab	Czech → Lang BLEU	Czech → Lang CHRF	Czech → Lang COMET	Lang → Czech BLEU	Lang → Czech CHRF	Lang → Czech COMET
sk	50k	char	**23.1**	**53.1**	**0.8834**	**23.4**	**53.1**	**0.8429**
		4k	21.1	51.7	0.6989	21.6	51.8	0.7054
		32k	20.1	50.5	0.5155	20.1	50.2	0.5226
	500k	char	**27.8**	**56.4**	**1.0737**	**27.2**	**56.1**	**1.0165**
		4k	27.0	55.8	1.0574	26.7	55.8	1.0018
		32k	26.8	55.6	1.0342	26.3	55.4	0.9893
	5M	char	**28.7**	**57.0**	**1.1035**	**28.4**	**56.8**	**1.0419**
		4k	28.6	56.9	1.1012	28.1	56.5	1.0333
		32k	**28.7**	56.9	1.0973	28.2	56.6	1.0376
hu	50k	char	0.6	21.0	-1.4054	0.3	18.1	-1.4137
		4k	1.9	25.4	-1.3256	1.5	24.2	-1.2826
		32k	**3.0**	**28.3**	**-1.2141**	**2.1**	**25.5**	**-1.2116**
	500k	char	**13.3**	**45.8**	**0.1812**	**12.3**	**42.2**	0.1892
		4k	12.7	44.7	0.1371	**12.3**	41.2	**0.2414**
		32k	12.4	43.4	0.0852	11.8	40.6	0.1658
	5M	char	17.4	**50.8**	0.6263	17.7	46.9	0.6999
		4k	17.7	50.3	0.6447	18.4	**47.4**	0.7283
		32k	**18.3**	50.6	**0.6531**	**18.6**	47.2	**0.7325**
de	50k	char	0.4	22.5	-1.5904	0.4	18.5	-1.4006
		4k	2.2	29.2	-1.3982	2.0	25.7	-1.2548
		32k	**4.7**	**33.7**	**-1.2014**	**4.7**	**29.9**	**-1.0102**
	500k	char	18.0	50.6	0.3185	**18.0**	**47.3**	0.4657
		4k	**19.2**	**50.9**	**0.3568**	**18.0**	**47.3**	**0.5533**
		32k	**19.2**	50.3	0.3155	17.6	46.1	0.4517
	5M	char	24.1	55.2	0.5955	23.1	**52.0**	0.8322
		4k	24.3	55.2	0.6043	23.0	51.9	0.8648
		32k	**25.2**	**55.7**	**0.6275**	**23.4**	51.8	**0.8838**
es	50k	char	0.2	23.0	-1.4847	0.2	18.3	-1.3952
		4k	2.3	28.4	-1.329	1.4	24.0	-1.2688
		32k	**4.6**	**32.6**	**-1.1684**	**2.8**	**27.3**	**-1.0927**
	500k	char	16.0	**46.6**	**0.1857**	0.4	18.1	-1.3986
		4k	15.6	45.7	0.1765	**11.7**	**41.2**	**0.3451**
		32k	**15.8**	45.4	0.0976	11.5	40.2	0.2395
	5M	char	19.3	**49.5**	0.4602	14.6	44.2	0.6394
		4k	20.0	49.3	0.4911	**15.7**	44.9	0.7160
		32k	**20.4**	49.4	**0.5074**	**15.7**	**45.1**	**0.7186**
hr	50k	char	0.2	21.2	-1.4055	0.2	16.9	-1.4397
		4k	4.8	34.0	-1.0112	4.6	30.3	-1.0283
		32k	**7.7**	**38.1**	**-0.7048**	**5.3**	**31.3**	**-0.9501**
	500k	char	19.6	**51.6**	0.6403	18.0	47.3	0.5469
		4k	**19.7**	51.2	**0.6922**	**19.3**	**48.2**	**0.6772**
		32k	19.2	50.5	0.6160	19.3	47.6	0.6170

Table 3: Test set scores for Transformer-base models (6 encoder and 6 decoder layers) trained from scratch. Bold are the best results within the same training dataset.

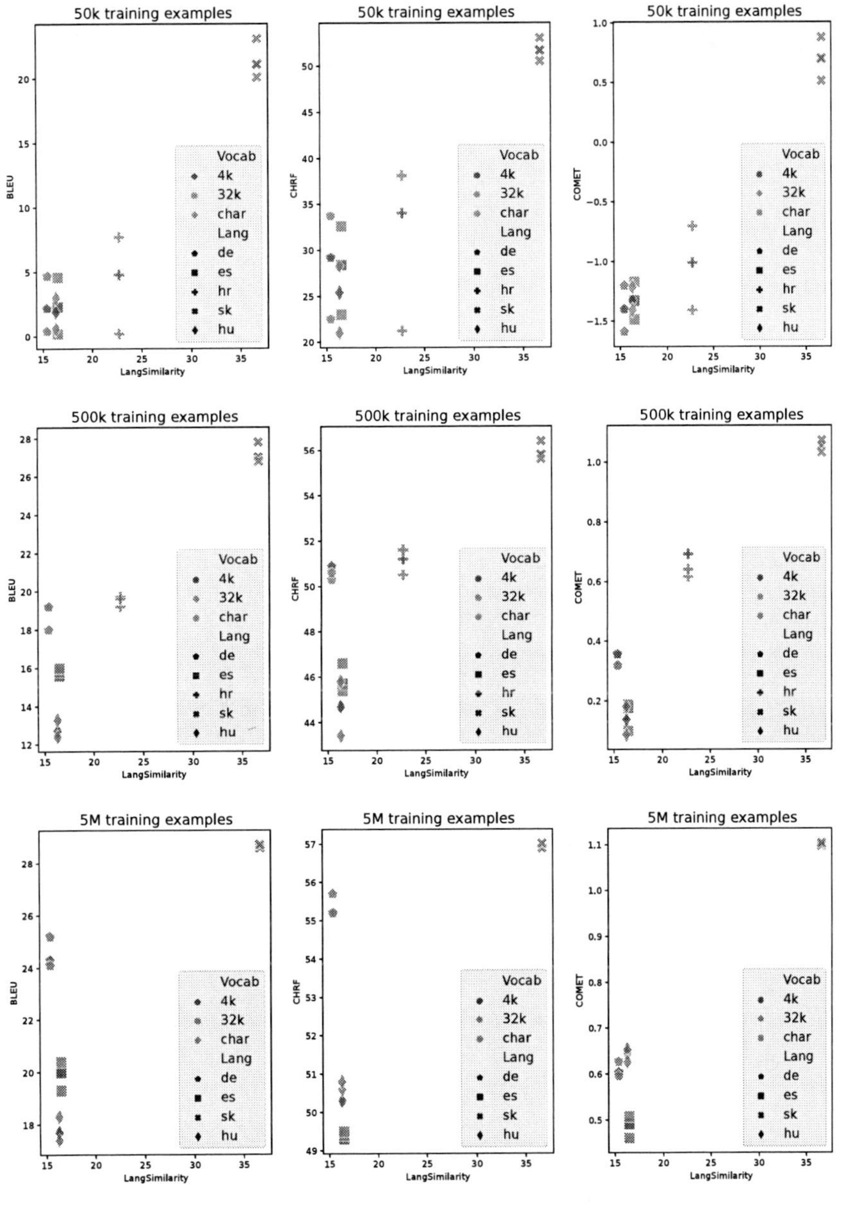

Figure 1: Relationship between language similarity scores (chrF of the untranslated test set source) and BLEU, chrF and COMET scores, depending on vocabulary size. First row are the results for 50k sentence train set, second row for 500k train set and third row for 5M train set.

		Score			$\Delta(char)$			$\Delta(4k)$		
Lang	Dataset	BLEU	CHRF	COMET	BLEU	CHRF	COMET	BLEU	CHRF	COMET
sk	50k	21.8	52.4	0.8750	−1.3	−0.7	−0.0084	0.7	0.7	0.1761
	500k	27.6	56.3	1.0720	−0.2	−0.1	−0.0017	0.6	0.5	0.0146
	5M	28.8	57.0	1.1017	0.1	0.0	−0.0018	0.2	0.1	0.0005
hu	50k	1.7	22.8	-1.3850	1.1	1.8	0.0204	−0.2	−2.6	−0.0594
	500k	13.4	46.0	0.2555	0.1	0.2	0.0743	0.7	1.3	0.1184
	5M	18.2	51.2	0.6726	0.8	0.4	0.0463	0.5	0.9	0.0279
de	50k	2.9	30.7	-1.4227	2.5	8.2	0.1677	0.7	1.5	−0.0245
	500k	19.3	51.3	0.3966	1.3	0.7	0.0781	0.1	0.4	0.0398
	5M	24.7	55.6	0.6214	0.6	0.4	0.0259	0.4	0.4	0.0171
es	50k	1.8	27.5	-1.4024	1.6	4.5	0.0823	−0.5	−0.9	−0.0734
	500k	16.3	46.4	0.2276	0.3	−0.2	0.0419	0.7	0.7	0.0511
	5M	19.8	49.5	0.5038	0.5	0.0	0.0436	−0.2	0.2	0.0127
hr	50k	10.3	42.9	-0.2671	10.1	21.7	1.1384	5.5	8.9	0.7441
	500k	20.6	52.4	0.7382	1.0	0.8	0.0979	0.9	1.2	0.0460

Table 4: Results of char-level models for translation from Czech finetuned from 4k subword-level models. Numbers under $\Delta(char)$ show the difference between fine-tuned model scores compared to the char-level model trained from scratch, under $\Delta(4k)$ difference from the model that served as the initial checkpoint for the finetuning.

		Score			$\Delta(char)$			$\Delta(32k)$		
Lang	Dataset	BLEU	CHRF	COMET	BLEU	CHRF	COMET	BLEU	CHRF	COMET
	50k	21.2	52.2	0.8697	−1.9	−0.9	−0.0137	1.1	1.7	0.3542
sk	500k	27.5	56.2	1.0723	−0.3	−0.2	−0.0014	0.7	0.6	0.0381
	5M	29	57.2	1.1011	0.3	0.2	−0.0024	0.3	0.3	0.0038
	50k	2.2	24.8	-1.358	1.6	3.8	0.0474	−0.8	−3.5	−0.1439
hu	500k	12.7	45.7	0.1832	−0.6	−0.1	0.0020	0.3	2.3	0.0980
	5M	18	51.0	0.6589	0.6	0.2	0.0326	−0.3	0.4	0.0058
	50k	4.5	33.3	-1.3335	4.1	10.8	0.2569	−0.2	−0.4	−0.1321
de	500k	19.4	51.4	0.3775	1.4	0.8	0.0590	1.4	0.8	0.0590
	5M	24.8	55.6	0.6274	0.7	0.4	0.0319	−0.4	−0.1	−0.0001
	50k	3.3	30.9	-1.3182	3.1	7.9	0.1665	−1.3	−1.7	−0.1498
es	500k	15.8	46.2	0.1854	−0.2	−0.4	−0.0003	0.0	0.8	0.0878
	5M	19.6	49.4	0.4875	0.3	−0.1	0.0273	−0.8	0.0	−0.0199
hr	50k	8.9	41.3	-0.4144	8.7	20.1	0.9911	1.2	3.2	0.2904
	500k	20.5	52.0	0.7181	0.9	0.4	0.0778	1.3	1.5	0.1021

Table 5: Results of char-level models for translation from Czech finetuned from 32k subword-level models. Numbers under $\Delta(char)$ show the difference between fine-tuned model scores compared to the char-level model trained from scratch, under $\Delta(32k)$ difference from the model that served as the initial checkpoint for the finetuning.

Lang	Dataset	Vocab	16-enc/6-dec BLEU	16-enc/6-dec CHRF	16-enc/6-dec COMET	16-enc/16-dec BLEU	16-enc/16-dec CHRF	16-enc/16-dec COMET
sk	50k	char	**21.9**	**52.4**	**0.8475**	**21.9**	**52.0**	**0.8001**
		4k	20.2	51.0	0.6444	19.3	50.1	0.5262
		32k	19.6	50.1	0.5308	20.1	50.4	0.5764
	500k	char	**27.4**	**56.0**	**1.0621**	**27.4**	**56.1**	**1.0618**
		4k	26.5	55.6	1.0432	26.6	55.6	1.0469
		32k	26.2	55.4	1.0319	26.2	55.4	1.0194
	5M	char	**28.6**	**57.0**	**1.1016**	**28.5**	**56.9**	**1.1013**
		4k	**28.6**	56.9	1.1015	28.3	56.7	1.0920
		32k	28.2	56.7	1.0916	28.4	56.8	1.0986
hu	50k	char	2.8	26.2	-1.3086	2.9	25.2	-1.3019
		4k	2.8	26.4	-1.2933	2.5	26.6	-1.2995
		32k	**3.0**	**28.3**	**-1.2445**	**3.1**	**27.5**	**-1.2623**
	500k	char	**12.9**	**45.7**	**0.0855**	11.8	**43.4**	**-0.0212**
		4k	11.1	42.0	-0.1612	11.1	41.8	-0.1580
		32k	11.4	42.3	-0.0943	**12.0**	42.5	-0.0934
	5M	char	17.3	**50.7**	**0.6280**	**17.6**	**50.1**	0.6102
		4k	17.3	49.8	0.6140	17.4	49.8	0.6045
		32k	**17.7**	49.9	**0.6280**	17.5	50.0	**0.6409**
de	50k	char	**5.7**	**35.4**	**-1.2272**	**5.0**	**33.0**	-1.2836
		4k	3.5	31.5	-1.3532	3.2	31.0	-1.3571
		32k	4.8	34.2	-1.2328	3.8	32.9	**-1.2819**
	500k	char	**18.9**	**51.1**	**0.3203**	**18.6**	**51.0**	**0.3155**
		4k	17.1	49.1	0.1909	16.6	48.4	0.1292
		32k	17.7	48.8	0.1595	17.5	49.0	0.1624
	5M	char	24.1	**55.4**	0.6146	24.1	**54.9**	0.6007
		4k	24.6	55.3	0.6138	24.1	54.8	0.6006
		32k	**24.8**	55.2	**0.6178**	**24.3**	54.7	**0.6055**
es	50k	char	4.6	32.8	**-1.2302**	**4.5**	31.3	**-1.2476**
		4k	4.1	30.7	-1.2826	3.3	30.0	-1.2983
		32k	**5.1**	**33.6**	-1.1571	**4.5**	**32.6**	-1.1992
	500k	char	**15.5**	**45.7**	**0.1277**	**14.8**	**45.6**	**0.0684**
		4k	15.0	44.6	0.0258	14.3	43.8	-0.0695
		32k	14.6	44.1	-0.0454	**14.8**	44.1	-0.0491
	5M	char	**20.1**	**49.7**	**0.4917**	**19.8**	**49.1**	0.4679
		4k	19.3	48.8	0.4712	19.6	49.0	0.4582
		32k	20.0	48.9	0.4670	19.9	49.0	**0.4708**
hr	50k	char	**10.3**	**42.3**	**-0.4010**	**9.5**	**40.4**	**-0.4877**
		4k	5.7	35.5	-0.9234	4.5	33.3	-1.0641
		32k	7.8	37.9	-0.7439	6.7	35.8	-0.8185
	500k	char	**19.3**	**51.6**	**0.6619**	**20.1**	**51.6**	**0.6795**
		4k	18.0	50.0	0.5527	18.6	50.2	0.5224
		32k	18.0	49.6	0.5050	18.3	49.6	0.5208

Table 6: Test set scores for deeper models (16 encoder layers, 6 decoder layers and 16 encoder layers, 16 decoder layers). Bold are the best results within the same training dataset and same model architecture.

Similar, although small increases compared to training from scratch can be seen across all the language pairs, with the exception of Czech-Slovak. For this pair, the translation quality of the character-level model trained from scratch is already much higher on the 50k and 500k datasets. Finetuning from either 32k or 4k models hurts the quality in this case, which could be expected.

After the finetuning, the char-level Croatian model clearly outperforms both 4k and 32k subword models on the 50k dataset in all the metrics. As this did not occur with other, less similar languages, we hypothesize that language similarity is again an important factor in favor of character-level translation.

4.3 Model size

Previous work suggests that character-level processing in Transformers requires the use of deeper models to reach the same performance as subword-level processing. We present experiments with increasing depth of the model in Table 6. All the models are trained in the direction Czech to target. The model sizes are described in Section 3.2. We observe improvements in character-level translation compared to subword-level models of the same depth, but not compared to the `Transformer-base` models (the results are actually often worse than for the base model). For instance, in German (de) target language with the 500k dataset, the character-level model using 16 encoder layers and 6 decoder layers yielded a COMET score of 0.3203. In contrast, the 4k and 32k vocab subword-level models achieved lower scores of 0.1909 and 0.1595, respectively. Similar patterns can be observed for other languages and datasets as well. However, the vanilla Transformer-base with 4k (Table 3) obtained COMET of 0.3568, still outperforming even the deeper character-level model. The baseline models outperform the deeper models with 4k and 32k vocabularies, often by a large margin, while performance at char-level remains similar or only slightly worse (compare corresponding rows in Table 3 and Table 6).

We hypothesize that the absence of improvements is caused by small dataset sizes and non-optimal hyperparameter choices. The results however suggest that deeper models are better suited for character-level translation, even though they mostly fail to outperform the shallower models in our setting.

5 Conclusions

We trained standard Transformer models to translate between languages with different levels of similarity both on subword-segmented and character-segmented data. We also varied the model depth and the training set size. We show that character-level models outperform subword-segmented models on the most closely related language pair (Czech-Slovak) as measured by automated MT quality metrics. Finetuning models trained with subword-level segmentation to character-level increases the performance in some cases. After finetuning, character-level models surpass the quality of subword-level models also for Czech-Croatian. Other, less similar language pairs reach similar preformances for both subword- and character-level models.

Acknowledgements

This research was partially supported by grant 19-26934X (NEUREM3) of the Czech Science Foundation and by the Charles University project GAUK No. 244523.

References

Akhbardeh, F., Arkhangorodsky, A., Biesialska, M., Bojar, O., Chatterjee, R., Chaudhary, V., Costa-jussa, M. R., España-Bonet, C., Fan, A., Federmann, C., Freitag, M., Graham, Y., Grundkiewicz, R., Haddow, B., Harter, L., Heafield, K., Homan, C., Huck, M., Amponsah-

Kaakyire, K., Kasai, J., Khashabi, D., Knight, K., Kocmi, T., Koehn, P., Lourie, N., Monz, C., Morishita, M., Nagata, M., Nagesh, A., Nakazawa, T., Negri, M., Pal, S., Tapo, A. A., Turchi, M., Vydrin, V., and Zampieri, M. (2021). Findings of the 2021 conference on machine translation (WMT21). In *Proceedings of the Sixth Conference on Machine Translation*, pages 1–88, Online. Association for Computational Linguistics.

Banar, N., Daelemans, W., and Kestemont, M. (2021). Character-level transformer-based neural machine translation. In *Proceedings of the 4th International Conference on Natural Language Processing and Information Retrieval*, NLPIR 2020, page 149–156, New York, NY, USA. Association for Computing Machinery.

Bañón, M., Chen, P., Haddow, B., Heafield, K., Hoang, H., Esplà-Gomis, M., Forcada, M. L., Kamran, A., Kirefu, F., Koehn, P., Ortiz Rojas, S., Pla Sempere, L., Ramírez-Sánchez, G., Sarrías, E., Strelec, M., Thompson, B., Waites, W., Wiggins, D., and Zaragoza, J. (2020). ParaCrawl: Web-scale acquisition of parallel corpora. In *Proceedings of the 58th Annual Meeting of the Association for Computational Linguistics*, pages 4555–4567, Online. Association for Computational Linguistics.

Barrault, L., Bojar, O., Costa-jussà, M. R., Federmann, C., Fishel, M., Graham, Y., Haddow, B., Huck, M., Koehn, P., Malmasi, S., Monz, C., Müller, M., Pal, S., Post, M., and Zampieri, M. (2019). Findings of the 2019 conference on machine translation (WMT19). In *Proceedings of the Fourth Conference on Machine Translation (Volume 2: Shared Task Papers, Day 1)*, pages 1–61, Florence, Italy. Association for Computational Linguistics.

Bella, G., Batsuren, K., and Giunchiglia, F. (2021). A database and visualization of the similarity of contemporary lexicons. In *Text, Speech, and Dialogue: 24th International Conference, TSD 2021, Olomouc, Czech Republic, September 6–9, 2021, Proceedings*, page 95–104, Berlin, Heidelberg. Springer-Verlag.

Chung, J., Cho, K., and Bengio, Y. (2016). A character-level decoder without explicit segmentation for neural machine translation. In *Proceedings of the 54th Annual Meeting of the Association for Computational Linguistics (Volume 1: Long Papers)*, pages 1693–1703, Berlin, Germany. Association for Computational Linguistics.

Costa-jussà, M. R., Escolano, C., and Fonollosa, J. A. R. (2017). Byte-based neural machine translation. In *Proceedings of the First Workshop on Subword and Character Level Models in NLP*, pages 154–158, Copenhagen, Denmark. Association for Computational Linguistics.

Gao, Y., Nikolov, N. I., Hu, Y., and Hahnloser, R. H. (2020). Character-level translation with self-attention. In *Proceedings of the 58th Annual Meeting of the Association for Computational Linguistics*, pages 1591–1604, Online. Association for Computational Linguistics.

Gupta, R., Besacier, L., Dymetman, M., and Gallé, M. (2019). Character-based nmt with transformer.

Jon, J., Novák, M., Aires, J. P., Varis, D., and Bojar, O. (2021). CUNI systems for WMT21: Multilingual low-resource translation for Indo-European languages shared task. In *Proceedings of the Sixth Conference on Machine Translation*, pages 354–361, Online. Association for Computational Linguistics.

Junczys-Dowmunt, M., Grundkiewicz, R., Dwojak, T., Hoang, H., Heafield, K., Neckermann, T., Seide, F., Germann, U., Aji, A. F., Bogoychev, N., Martins, A. F. T., and Birch, A.

(2018). Marian: Fast neural machine translation in C++. In *Proceedings of ACL 2018, System Demonstrations*, pages 116–121, Melbourne, Australia. Association for Computational Linguistics.

Kingma, D. P. and Ba, J. (2017). Adam: A method for stochastic optimization.

Lee, J., Cho, K., and Hofmann, T. (2017). Fully character-level neural machine translation without explicit segmentation. *Transactions of the Association for Computational Linguistics*, 5:365–378.

Li, J., Shen, Y., Huang, S., Dai, X., and Chen, J. (2021). When is char better than subword: A systematic study of segmentation algorithms for neural machine translation. In *Proceedings of the 59th Annual Meeting of the Association for Computational Linguistics and the 11th International Joint Conference on Natural Language Processing (Volume 2: Short Papers)*, pages 543–549, Online. Association for Computational Linguistics.

Libovický, J. and Fraser, A. (2020). Towards reasonably-sized character-level transformer NMT by finetuning subword systems. In *Proceedings of the 2020 Conference on Empirical Methods in Natural Language Processing (EMNLP)*, pages 2572–2579, Online. Association for Computational Linguistics.

Libovický, J., Schmid, H., and Fraser, A. (2022). Why don't people use character-level machine translation? In *Findings of the Association for Computational Linguistics: ACL 2022*, pages 2470–2485, Dublin, Ireland. Association for Computational Linguistics.

Ngo, T.-V., Ha, T.-L., Nguyen, P.-T., and Nguyen, L.-M. (2019). How transformer revitalizes character-based neural machine translation: An investigation on Japanese-Vietnamese translation systems. In *Proceedings of the 16th International Conference on Spoken Language Translation*, Hong Kong. Association for Computational Linguistics.

Popović, M. (2015). chrF: character n-gram F-score for automatic MT evaluation. In *Proceedings of the Tenth Workshop on Statistical Machine Translation*, pages 392–395, Lisbon, Portugal. Association for Computational Linguistics.

Post, M. (2018). A call for clarity in reporting BLEU scores. In *Proceedings of the Third Conference on Machine Translation: Research Papers*, pages 186–191, Brussels, Belgium. Association for Computational Linguistics.

Rei, R., Stewart, C., Farinha, A. C., and Lavie, A. (2020). COMET: A neural framework for MT evaluation. In *Proceedings of the 2020 Conference on Empirical Methods in Natural Language Processing (EMNLP)*, pages 2685–2702, Online. Association for Computational Linguistics.

Scherrer, Y., Vázquez, R., and Virpioja, S. (2019). The University of Helsinki submissions to the WMT19 similar language translation task. In *Proceedings of the Fourth Conference on Machine Translation (Volume 3: Shared Task Papers, Day 2)*, pages 236–244, Florence, Italy. Association for Computational Linguistics.

Team, N., Costa-jussà, M. R., Cross, J., Çelebi, O., Elbayad, M., Heafield, K., Heffernan, K., Kalbassi, E., Lam, J., Licht, D., Maillard, J., Sun, A., Wang, S., Wenzek, G., Youngblood, A., Akula, B., Barrault, L., Gonzalez, G. M., Hansanti, P., Hoffman, J., Jarrett, S., Sadagopan, K. R., Rowe, D., Spruit, S., Tran, C., Andrews, P., Ayan, N. F., Bhosale, S., Edunov, S., Fan, A., Gao, C., Goswami, V., Guzmán, F., Koehn, P., Mourachko, A., Ropers, C., Saleem,

S., Schwenk, H., and Wang, J. (2022). No language left behind: Scaling human-centered machine translation.

Vaswani, A., Shazeer, N., Parmar, N., Uszkoreit, J., Jones, L., Gomez, A. N., Kaiser, L., and Polosukhin, I. (2017). Attention is all you need.

Negative Lexical Constraints in Neural Machine Translation

Josef Jon jon@ufal.mff.cuni.cz
Dušan Variš varis@ufal.mff.cuni.cz
Michal Novák mnovak@ufal.mff.cuni.cz
João Paulo Aires aires@ufal.mff.cuni.cz
Ondřej Bojar bojar@ufal.mff.cuni.cz
Institute of Formal and Applied Linguistics, Faculty of Mathematics and Physics, Prague, Czech Republic

Abstract

This paper explores negative lexical constraining in English to Czech neural machine translation. Negative lexical constraining is used to prohibit certain words or expressions in the translation produced by the neural translation model. We compared various methods based on modifying either the decoding process or the training data. The comparison was performed on two tasks: paraphrasing and feedback-based translation refinement. We also studied to which extent these methods "evade" the constraints presented to the model (usually in the dictionary form) by generating a different surface form of a given constraint.We propose a way to mitigate the issue through training with stemmed negative constraints to counter the model's ability to induce a variety of the surface forms of a word that can result in bypassing the constraint. We demonstrate that our method improves the constraining, although the problem still persists in many cases.

1 Introduction

In general, lexically constrained neural machine translation (NMT) is a method that allows enforcing presence or absence of certain words or phrases in the translation output . Positively constrained translation is more common and is used, for example, in named entities translation (Li et al., 2019; Yan et al., 2019), terminology integration (Dinu et al., 2019; Jon et al., 2021), or interactive machine translation (Knowles and Koehn, 2016).

Negative constraining serves different purposes. In this paper, we focus on two use-cases: (1) paraphrase generation and (2) refining translation based on feedback. Paraphrasing aims to produce a new translation hypothesis that differs from the original translation without significant changes in meaning. On the other hand, translation refinement involves replacing specific tokens in the original translation. These tokens can be selected either manually by the user or automatically using techniques like word-level quality estimation (Kepler et al., 2019). Negative constraining is particularly well-suited for translation refinement, while it can be one of the solutions for paraphrase generation.

After providing a summary of related work (Section 2), we proceed to describe the two tasks in detail (Section 3). Next, we delve into the methods we employ to achieve negative constraining (Section 4). The results are presented in Section 5, followed by a manual analysis of the outputs in Section 6.

Proceedings of Machine Translation Summit XIX, Vol. 1: Research Track, pages 372–384
September 4–8, 2023, Macau SAR, China.

2 Related work

There are three dominant approaches to constrained NMT. The earliest ones were based on replacing the constrained expressions in the source sentence with placeholders, ensuring that the placeholders are copied into the translation produced by the model and, finally, replacing the placeholders in the target with the desired expression (Crego et al., 2016; Hanneman and Dinu, 2020).

The second class of methods is based on modifying the decoding mechanism in such way that only translations including (or not including) the specified words or phrases can be produced in the final output (Anderson et al., 2017; Hasler et al., 2018; Chatterjee et al., 2017; Hokamp and Liu, 2017; Post and Vilar, 2018; Hu et al., 2019a).

The third class of methods revolves around altering the source input in the training data, allowing the NMT model to learn how to incorporate the constraints. This is typically done by either appending the constraints to the end of the source sentence as a suffix or intertwining them with the source sentence and distinguishing them from its tokens using factors (Dinu et al., 2019; Song et al., 2019; Chen et al., 2020; Jon et al., 2021; Bergmanis and Pinnis, 2021b,a).

Currently, most of the research in the field focuses on positive lexical constraints, often used for terminology integration. In contrast, there is a relatively less emphasis on negative constraining, despite its applications in areas like paraphrase generation (Hu et al., 2019b; Kajiwara, 2019). These works apply a method developed by Post and Vilar (2018) and later improved by Hu et al. (2019a). This method modifies the beam search decoding algorithm so that the beam in each time step includes the best hypotheses that satisfy from zero to the full number of pre-defined constraints. When using only negative constraints, the algorithm effectively boils down to filtering out hypotheses that would introduce any word (or phrase) from the list of constraints.

3 Task description

We carry out experiments with negative constraints in the two following tasks:

Paraphrase generation is often achieved through translation, where negative constraints come in handy for indicating the desired differences in the paraphrased output. To create a paraphrase of a source sentence, we go through multiple rounds of translation, each time disallowing some of the words generated in the previous pass. These restricted words or expressions should be replaced by synonymous expressions by the MT model, thereby creating a paraphrase of the original translation. As an example, consider the sentence *"He dodged the ball."* as the initial translation from a foreign language into English. When the word *"dodge"* is employed as the negative constraint, the system is expected to generate a paraphrase of the original translation (e.g. *"He avoided the ball."*) in the second pass.

Feedback-based translation refinement involves using external feedback to assess the model's output, for example, through user feedback in an interactive setting. After the initial translation is presented, the user can identify certain words as mistranslated. These words are then excluded from the subsequent output, prompting the model to generate a potentially improved translation. As obtaining human constraints can be costly, we translate the source without any constraints and analyze the tokens present in the MT output but not in the reference. In the next translation pass, we constrain the model to avoid using these "unconfirmed" tokens and evaluate the resulting translation.

In practice, word-level quality estimation (QE) systems can partially replace user feedback by highlighting potentially problematic tokens. In our work, we use references as a proxy for an oracle QE.

4 Proposed methods

We define a constraint as a sequence of consecutive subwords, which may represent either a single word or a multi-word expression. Each input example can have a list of multiple constraints that need to be satisfied. To incorporate these constraints into the translation process, we implement the following methods.

Beam filtering This method is based on an existing implementation where a hypothesis containing any forbidden subword is dropped from the beam search.[1] For each input sentence, a list of constraints (where each constraint represents a single subword) is provided. During beam search, any time a hypothesis that contain a constraint from the list is generated, it is removed. Optionally, it is removed only if the log probability of the subword is falls below a specified threshold. This method is referred to as the "subword method", and we extend it to support multi-subword expressions ("multi-subword method"). Instead of filtering after a single subword is generated, we store subwords corresponding to each constraint in a list of lists. For example:

- **Constraint 1:** decoding **Segmentation:** _deco ding
- **Constraint 2:** beam search **Segmentation:** _be am _search
- **Subword method:** [_deco, ding, _be, am, _search]
- **Multi-subword method:** [[_deco, ding], [_be, am, _search]]

Each hypothesis tracks its progress through the constraints, and it is removed only when a complete constraint is met. In other words, the hypothesis is removed only when all the subwords forming a single constraint are generated subsequently.[2]

Score penalty Another technique we experimented with is modifying the output probability of the subwords that form the constrained expression during the decoding. For this technique, we provided a list of constraints along with each input sentence. We created a mask with a penalty value for each subword present in the vocabulary. In our implementation, the penalty value was global, meaning each subword had either no or the same specified penalty. This mask was then summed with the output logits at each decoding step. To handle multi-subword constraints, we used a trie structure to track the progress through each constraint in each beam, similar to the approach used in (Hu et al., 2019a).

In the trie structure, each node represents a subword that is part of a constraint. The node contains a list of vocabulary IDs that, if generated in the next decoding step, would complete the constraint. When the subword represented by a node is produced, the penalty is added to the scores of these IDs in the next step.

Learned constraints A different approach to constraining involves modifying the training data to bias the model. The objective is to prevent the model from producing the constraint expressions that are directly provided with the input sentence. In our experiments, we separate the list of constraints from the source sentence by a special <sep> token, whereas the individual constraints within the list are separated by a special <c> token. For example:

- This is a sentence where we want to use synonyms for dog and cat. <sep> dog <c> cat

We train a model on the original dataset and the use this model to translate the source side of the dataset. Tokens present in the translation but not in the reference are extracted and used as "synthetic" constraints for training data, similar to the approach in the *Translation refinement* task. The resulting training dataset with "synthetic" constraints is then utilized to train a model capable of handling negative constraints in its input.

[1]Implemented here: `https://github.com/XapaJIaMnu/marian-dev/tree/paraphrases_v2`

[2]Link to the github repository of our code, removed for review.

constraints	WMT20		Multi-ref	
	BLEU	COMET	BLEU	COMET
Yes	30.8	0.6067	46.5	0.5971
No	30.7	0.6071	46.7	0.5944

Table 1: Comparison of the baseline models trained with and without constraints present in the training data. No constraints were present in the test set, showing that even the model exposed to the input constraints can be used in a "default" mode (no input constraints).

5 Experiments

In this section, we compare the performance of the methods on the tasks presented earlier.

5.1 Datasets and tools

We use CzEng 2.0 (Kocmi et al., 2020) dataset, all the authentic parallel sentences (61M), as the training dataset. We use WMT `newstest-2019` (Barrault et al., 2019) and `newstest-2020` (Barrault et al., 2020) for development and final evaluation respectively. We also used a subset of 50 examples from English-Czech `newstest-2011` which contains a large number of references (about 15M reference sentences in total, averaging 300k references per source sentence) introduced by Bojar et al. (2013) for part of the experiments. For evaluation on this multi-reference dataset (denoted "Multi-ref" in the following), we randomly picked up to 1,000 references for each source sentence to compute BLEU score and 20 references to compute COMET (the COMET scores are computed separately for each reference and averaged).

We use SentencePiece (Kudo and Richardson, 2018) for subword segmentation and UDPipe (Straka and Straková, 2017) for lemmatization. The models are trained with Marian (Junczys-Dowmunt et al., 2018) using default hyperparameters for Transformer-base architecture. BLEU (Papineni et al., 2002) scores are obtained by SacreBLEU (Post, 2018).[3] For COMET (Rei et al., 2020) scores, we evaluate with the *wmt20-comet-da* model. As the references in the Multi-ref test set are tokenized, we detokenized them using Sacremoses.[4]

5.2 Baseline

Our baseline model is a Transformer-base trained on CzEng 2.0 with negative constraints. This model is specifically trained to use negative constraints provided as part of the input, as described earlier in the *Learned constraints* section of Section 4. This approach enables more accurate comparison with other methods of incorporating constraints. Table 1 illustrates that when no constraints are provided at test time, the translation quality in terms of automated metrics is similar to a vanilla model without constraints.

5.3 Paraphrasing

In this task, our goal is to produce paraphrases that are diverse enough from the original translation. We thus opt for a multi-reference evaluation.

We create negative constraints by translating the source sentences of Multi-ref with the baseline model. The translations are then tokenized, removing punctuation and common Czech stopwords[5]. The remaining set of tokens serve as negative constraints.

[3]SacreBLEU signature: BLEU+case.mixed+lang.en-cs+numrefs.1+smooth.exp+test.wmt20+tok.13a+version.1.4.14

[4]`https://github.com/alvations/sacremoses`

[5]Prohibiting them by a constraint would hinder generation of grammaically fluent sentences.

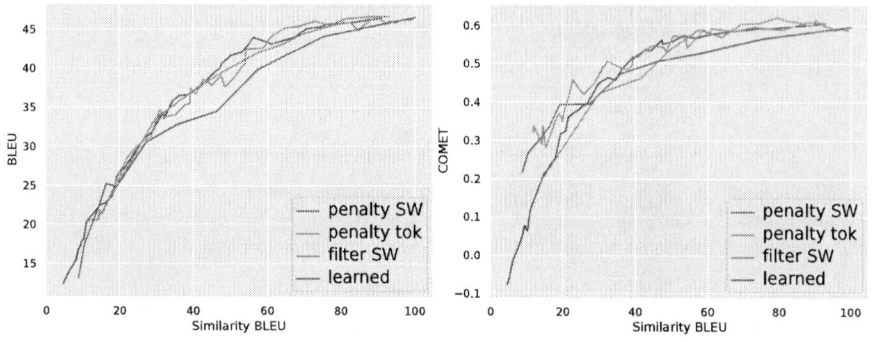

Figure 1: Correlation between either BLEU (left) or COMET (right) scores and similarity of translation to the baseline translation for paraphrasing.

	Single subword				Whole token			
Penalty	**↑BLEU**	**↓Sim**	**↑COMET**	**↓Cvg**	**↑BLEU**	**↓Sim**	**↑COMET**	**↓Cvg**
0	46.5	100	0.5991	1.00	46.5	100	0.5991	1.00
0.1	**46.5**	**83.6**	**0.5999**	0.84	**46.7**	**92.9**	**0.6078**	0.94
0.2	**45.9**	**76.4**	**0.5946**	0.76	**46.6**	**88.0**	**0.6123**	0.89
0.5	45.1	70.6	0.5917	0.70	**46.0**	**72.9**	**0.5991**	0.73
1	41.6	50.2	0.5616	0.52	42.6	58.9	0.5939	0.62
2	32.5	29.7	0.4469	0.32	35.5	39.1	0.4988	0.46
3	20.2	10.9	0.1203	0.18	26.8	20.5	0.3869	0.30

Table 2: Results of the *score penalty* method on the paraphrasing task. We boldface variants where we deem the degradation small enough (BLEU or COMET close enough to their baseline value or even better).

In this task, our focus is on examining the relationship between the reference-based translation quality metrics (BLEU and COMET) and the similarity of the translation with the baseline translation. The objective is to generate sentences that are as distinct as possible while minimizing the negative impact on translation quality. The correlation for all the methods is depicted in Figure 1. Sampling across a range of thresholds (see below) generates various output variants. We arrange them on the x-axis based on their similarity with the unconstrained translation ("Similarity BLEU"). The y-axis then represents the automatically assessed translation quality. The curves' concave shape confirms that there is no sudden drop in quality as we paraphrase. However, even with the very permissive scoring against the Multi-ref references, both BLEU and COMET inevitably decline as we deviate further from the initial translations.

Tables 2–4 present the translation scores as well as the similarity of the paraphrase to the first translation (Similarity BLEU, denoted "Sim" here) for several thresholds. Each threshold controls the number of tokens to be paraphrased, affecting the similarity. However, its exact meaning differs for each method, as explained below. Coverage ("Cvg") indicates the ratio of constraint tokens that were produced in the translation (ignoring the casing).

The results for the *score penalty* method are presented in Table 2. *Penalty* represents the log probability that is subtracted from the logits for constrained tokens in each decoding step. Two variants of the method are compared. *Single subword* is the simpler variant, penalizing

	Single subword				Whole token			
Thrshld	↑BLEU	↓Sim	↑COMET	↓Cvg	↑BLEU	↓Sim	↑COMET	↓Cvg
0	7.2	2	-0.3388	0.07	8.7	2.8	0.0621	0.09
-0.1	20.4	13.7	0.1919	0.17	18.1	10.5	0.2448	0.14
-0.2	33.5	29.9	0.4285	0.37	33.9	26.8	0.4595	0.31
-0.5	42.0	57.6	0.5938	0.60	41.7	53.3	0.5544	0.52
-1	**45.9**	**82.6**	**0.6146**	0.83	45.1	**77.8**	**0.6059**	0.76
-1.5	**45.7**	**92.3**	**0.6011**	0.91	**46.1**	**89.8**	**0.6076**	0.87
-2	**46.2**	**95.5**	**0.5901**	0.96	**46.2**	**93.3**	**0.5774**	0.93
-3	**46.3**	**99.2**	**0.5931**	0.99	**46.3**	**99.1**	**0.5906**	0.99

Table 3: Results of the *beam filtering* method on the paraphrasing task. Boldfacing as in Table 2.

Ratio	BLEU	Sim	COMET	Cvg
0	46.5	100	0.5991	1.00
single	45.4	81.4	0.5582	0.83
0.1	44.1	75.1	0.5685	0.76
0.2	39.9	57.6	0.5287	0.63
0.4	32.8	35.9	0.4796	0.43
0.6	24.8	19.1	0.4034	0.25
0.8	22.3	14.3	0.3193	0.18
1	13.1	8.7	0.2194	0.12

Table 4: Results of the *learned* method on the paraphrasing task. We do not boldface any row because the BLEU and COMET scores immediately degrade.

each subword found among the constraints. On the other hand, in the *Whole token* variant, the multi-subword implementation is used. The penalty is applied only when a whole constraint is completed in the hypothesis (in our configuration, the whole constraint will always be a single word, due to the constraint generation algorithm). The *penalty* parameter allows us to control the resulting paraphrase similarity: the higher its value, the more disadvantaged are the constrained tokens during decoding. We observe no significant degradation of translation up until about 88 BLEU similarity (0.89 coverage). Even at 72.9 BLEU similarity (0.73 coverage), the degradation is minimal. Multi-subword implementation yields better results than the single-subword implementation, allowing us to reach slightly lower coverage with comparable degradation, and it even appears to improve the baseline metric levels (BLEU of 46.7 and COMET of 0.6123 instead of the baseline 46.5 and 0.5991, respectively).

For the *beam filtering* method, the results are presented in Table 3. The controlling parameter is a threshold log probability, removing the hypotheses that use the constraint with a probability below the threshold. Opposed to the previous method, the lower its value, the more permissive the algorithm is, keeping the hypotheses with less probable constraints in the beam search. Again, two variants (single- and multi-subword) are implemented. For similar paraphrases, there are no notable score differences. However, as translations become more dissimilar, the multi-subword implementation performs better. Overall, *beam filtering* and *score penalty* methods show similar performance. An improvement in overall quality in terms of COMET is again observed when deviating somewhat from the baseline output (COMET slightly above 0.60 compared to 0.59).

Results for the *learned* constraints method are displayed in Table 4. We consider content

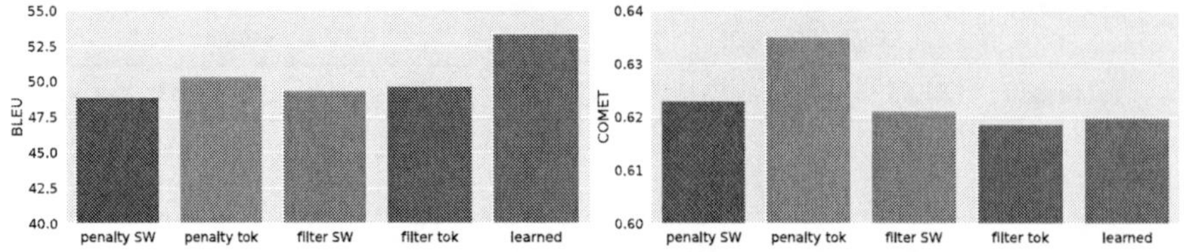

Figure 2: The best results obtained by each method on the *translation refinement* task, either in terms of BLEU (left) or COMET (right) scores. These results were computed using the best found setting of the control parameter for each method.

	Single subword				Whole token			
Penalty	**BLEU**	**Sim**	**COMET**	**Cvg**	**BLEU**	**Sim**	**COMET**	**Cvg**
0	46.5	100	0.5991	1	46.5	100	0.5991	1
0.1	46.9	95.4	**0.6144**	0.93	47.0	96.5	0.6104	0.95
0.5	48.5	80.6	0.6024	0.70	48.7	85.1	0.6237	0.76
1	**48.6**	68.9	0.5754	0.50	48.5	74.3	**0.6302**	0.59
2	47.1	57	0.5773	0.30	48.6	63.9	0.6011	0.43
3	48.2	53.3	0.5617	0.19	49.4	61.4	0.5790	0.33
3.5	48.1	50.8	0.5226	0.15	**49.4**	57.1	0.5695	0.22

Table 5: Results of the *score penalty* method on the refinement task.

words from the baseline translation as potential negative constraints, resulting in a full set of conceivable constraints for a sentence. The method's control parameter is the ratio of total constraints to those actually used. For example, with 6 available constraints for a sentence and a ratio of 0.5, we select only 3 constraints. "Singl" in the ratio column indicates that only one constraint was used for each sentence. The selection is based on token-level model scores from the baseline translation, where scores of subwords comprising a token are summed. The lowest log probability tokens are constrained first, effectively preventing the usage of words that the baseline model hesitates to produce. We chose this sampling approach after observing large result variances when using randomly sampled constraints. However, we acknowledge that this selection method is not optimal, as several random runs led to significantly better BLEU and COMET scores. The learned constraints underperform compared to other approaches, likely because the decoding-based methods offer more precise control over which constraints to use (penalty or threshold).

5.4 Translation refinement

Unlike the paraphrasing task, where the relationship between similarity and translation quality is relevant, the translation refinement task solely aims to improve the absolute quality of translation. The best scores achieved with optimal control parameters are presented in Figure 2.

Results for *score penalty* and *beam filtering* methods are presented in Tables 5 and 6, showing the similar performance to each other, as already observed in the previous task.

In the *learned constraints* method (Table 7), the BLEU scores improve with an increasing ratio of constraints, while the COMET scores do not follow the same trend.

The *learned constraints* method outperformed others significantly in terms of BLEU score. The *score penalty* method achieved a slightly better COMET score with the best penalty value.

	Single subword				Whole token			
Thrshld	BLEU	Sim	COMET	Cvg	BLEU	Sim	COMET	Cvg
0	47.4	48.7	0.4755	0.03	49.4	50.1	0.5771	0.05
-0.1	47.9	52.4	0.6012	0.19	**49.6**	53.4	0.5814	0.16
-0.2	48.7	59.5	0.6163	0.37	48.7	56.7	**0.6192**	0.31
-0.3	**49.4**	65.7	0.5976	0.46	48.5	63.7	0.6179	0.42
-1	47.1	88	**0.6100**	0.83	47.7	85.4	0.6109	0.76
-2	46.3	96.9	0.5932	0.97	46.5	95	0.5813	0.93
-3.5	46.3	99.2	0.5931	0.99	46.3	99.2	0.5931	0.99

Table 6: Results of the *beam filtering* method on the refinement task.

ratio	BLEU	Sim	COMET	Cvg
0	46.5	100	0.5991	1.00
single	47.6	82.3	0.6123	0.75
0.1	46.8	94.4	0.6058	0.92
0.2	47.0	83	**0.6212**	0.75
0.4	47.4	72.5	0.6026	0.56
0.6	48.7	65.7	0.5922	0.38
0.8	51.2	58.8	0.6103	0.21
1	**53.4**	55.4	0.5746	0.08

Table 7: Results of the *learned* method on the refinement task.

We believe this is again due to the decoding methods providing more precise control over the enforcement of constraints compared to the learned method.

In Table 8 we present results for the two best scoring methods on a better-known test set for comparison, *newstest20* (Barrault et al., 2020). The *learned* method provides better results than the *score penalty* method on this dataset.

6 Manual analysis

Our results show that the methods tend to overlook some negative constraints and still produce prohibited words. Both the *score penalty* and *beam filtering* methods require pushing the thresholds quite far to satisfy all constraints. Conversely, the *learned* method is more attentive to constraining but results in quick degradation of translation quality. To gain insights into the system behavior, we examined the outputs and present typical examples for each class in Figure 3. These examples are from the *translation refinement* task using the *learned* method, with constraints being tokens present in the baseline translation but not in the reference. The first example showcases a clear failure of the method, as the constraint is ignored without any apparent reason. The second example is challenging, as it requires knowledge of the Czech transcription of the name *Assam* based on its English transcription.

The *Reference* error example illustrates a situation, where the the meaning of the reference translation that we use to generate the negative constraints slightly deviates from the source sentence, resulting in a constraint difficult to satisfy. The reference translation replaces the term *two-thirds* (*dvoutřetinovou*) with a different term, *needed* (*potřebnou*), which leads to *dvoutřetinovou* being selected as a constraint. Since it is difficult to translate *two-thirds majority* differently from the baseline translation, the model fails to do so. This issue could be addressed

	Learned		Score penalty		
ratio	BLEU	COMET	penalty	BLEU	COMET
single	31.5	**0.6183**	0.2	30.6	**0.6033**
1	**38.5**	0.5973	0.1	**30.8**	0.6028
baseline	30.9	0.6067			

Table 8: Results of best performing methods on newstest20. Results obtained using best-performing parameters for both metrics separately are shown.

Model	Constraints	BLEU	Surface Form Cvg	Lemma Cvg
SF	no	30.9	1.00	0.96
SF	SF	38.5	0.09	0.34
Stem	no	30.9	1.00	0.96
Stem	Stem	36.9	0.22	0.39

Table 9: Comparison of surface form and lemma coverage (Cvg) for models trained with either surface form or stemmed constraints. Evaluated on `newstest-2020`.

by using a validation dataset with more accurate reference translations.

In the *Segmentation* error example, the constraint is circumvented by employing a different subword segmentation of the output. Sinve we use SentencePiece without prior tokenization, adding a quotation mark („) at the beginning of a token results in a different segmentation that is not accounted for by the constraints (as the constraints are provided to the model with pre-existing segmentation).

The *Inflection* example demostrates a scenario where the model managed to avoid generating a constraint in a specific form but did not avoid producing the constrained term itself. Out of 8 constraints, 4 are fulfilled with a different inflected form in the constrained translation (in addition, one constraint is produced with a different spelling: *diskusi/diskuzi*). This behavior is undesirable because such circumvention can still lead to a potentially problematic translation. However, in certain cases, like paraphrasing, it may be deemed acceptable.

The extent of this behavior is presented in Table 9. We conduct a comparison between coverage at the surface form level and coverage at the lemma level. The evaluation is based on the *translation refinement* task on `newstest-2020`, using the *learned* method with a constraint usage ratio of 1.0. For the lemma-level coverage assessment, both the constraints and constrained translation were lemmatized. This ensures that even when the constraint is generated in a different surface form, it is considered covered. It is important to note that our lemmatization method is context-dependent, and in some cases, different lemmas may be produced for the same word in a sentence and in the constraint list, leading to some imprecision in these results.

At the surface level, the coverage is 0.09, indicating that 91% of the constraints are correctly satisfied. However, at the lemma level, the coverage increases to 0.34, which means that another 25% of the constraints appear in the translation in a different surface form, not detected by the previous method of computing coverage. We attempted to mitigate this behavior by training the model to use stemmed constraints (*Stem* model in Table 9). Our goal was to leverage the language modeling capability of the NMT model to account for all the possible word forms. While this approach partially works, reducing the gap between surface form and lemma coverage to 17 instead of 25, the overall performance is inferior (BLEU of 36.9 instead of 38.5).

Source	Base translation	Constraints	Constrained translation	Error
Michael Jackson's former bodyguard has claimed the late singer cultivated some of his eccentricities with the deliberate intention of **riling up** the media.	Bývalý bodyguard Michaela Jacksona tvrdil, že zesnulý zpěvák pěstoval některé z jeho výstředností s úmyslem rozzuřit média.	bodyguard, tvrdil, pěstoval, své, výstřednosti, s, úmyslem, **rozzuřit**, média	Bývalý osobní strážce Michaela Jacksona tvrdí, že zesnulý zpěvák pěstuje některé z jeho výstředností se záměrem **rozzuřit** sdělovací prostředky.	Not satisfied
And Modi's government has created an uproar by instituting a national registry of citizens and setting up detention camps in the border state of Assam.	A Modiho vláda vyvolala pozdvižení zavedením národního registru občanů a zřízením zadržovacích táborů v pohraničním státě **Assam**	Modiho, vyvolala, pozdvižení, zavedením, zadržovacích, **Assam**	A Módího vláda způsobila rozruch vytvořením národního registru občanů a zřízením zajateckých táborů v pohraničním státě **Assam**.	Challenging
Neither chamber of Congress appears to have the two-thirds majority needed to override the president's opposition.	Zdá se, že ani jedna kongresová komora nemá **dvoutřetinovou** většinu potřebnou k překonání prezidentovy opozice.	kongresová, komora, **dvoutřetinovou**, překonání	Zdá se, že ani jedna z kongresových komor nemá **dvoutřetinovou** většinu potřebnou k potlačení prezidentovy opozice.	Reference
_Last _year , _construction _of _Q id di y a _" ent er tain ment _city " _was _launched _near _Ri y ad h.	_Po bl í ž _Ri já du _byla _v _loňském _roce _zahájen a _výstavba **_útvar ového** _města _Q id di y a	**_útvar ového**	Po bl í ž _Ri já du _byla _v _loňském _roce _zahájen a _výstavba _„ **ú t var ového** _města " _Q id di y a	Segmentation
A Pittsburgh native whose real name was Malcolm James Myers McCormick, Miller's lyrics included frank discussion of his depression and drug use.	Domorodec z Pittsburghu, jehož pravé jméno bylo Malcolm James Myers McCormick, Millerovy texty zahrnovaly upřímnou diskusi o jeho depresi a užívání drog.	**domorodec**, pravé, **Millerovy**, **texty**, zahrnovaly, upřímnou, **diskusi**, **depresi**	**Domorodce** z Pittsburghu, jehož skutečné jméno bylo Malcolm James Myers McCormick, **Millerův text** obsahoval otevřenou **diskuzi** ohledně **deprese** a užívání drog.	Inflection

Figure 3: Examples of baseline and constrained translations with interesting behavior. The columns show the English source sentence, baseline translation into Czech, list of constraints, and the final constrained translation. The last column contains a type of error observed. The Segmentation example is shown in subword units for explanation purposes.

7 Conclusion

We conducted a thorough investigation into NMT decoding with negative lexical constraints, addressing two tasks: paraphrasing and interactive translation refinement. Our comparison of various approaches revealed that it is indeed possible to restrict the NMT model from generating specific words in its output. However, none of the methods provided flawless results. By examining the errors made by the most effective approach, we identified instances where the model evades the constraints in morphologically rich languages by producing slightly different surface forms of the prohibited words. While we proposed a simple solution by training the model to use stemmed constraints, it adversely impacts the overall translation quality. Despite these challenges, our research sheds light on the potential of using negative constraints in NMT decoding and highlights areas for further improvement.

Acknowledgements

This work was partially supported by the Charles University project GAUK No. 244523, the grant 825303 (Bergamot) of the European Union's Horizon 2020 research and innovation programme, the grant 19-26934X (NEUREM3) of the Czech Science Foundation and the grant FW03010656 of the Technology Agency of the Czech Republic.

References

Anderson, P., Fernando, B., Johnson, M., and Gould, S. (2017). Guided open vocabulary image captioning with constrained beam search. In *Proceedings of the 2017 Conference on Empirical Methods in Natural Language Processing*, pages 936–945, Copenhagen, Denmark. Association for Computational Linguistics.

Barrault, L., Biesialska, M., Bojar, O., Costa-jussà, M. R., Federmann, C., Graham, Y., Grundkiewicz, R., Haddow, B., Huck, M., Joanis, E., Kocmi, T., Koehn, P., Lo, C.-k., Ljubešić, N., Monz, C., Morishita, M., Nagata, M., Nakazawa, T., Pal, S., Post, M., and Zampieri, M. (2020). Findings of the 2020 conference on machine translation (WMT20). In *Proceedings of the Fifth Conference on Machine Translation*, pages 1–55, Online. Association for Computational Linguistics.

Barrault, L., Bojar, O., Costa-jussà, M. R., Federmann, C., Fishel, M., Graham, Y., Haddow, B., Huck, M., Koehn, P., Malmasi, S., Monz, C., Müller, M., Pal, S., Post, M., and Zampieri, M. (2019). Findings of the 2019 conference on machine translation (WMT19). In *Proceedings of the Fourth Conference on Machine Translation (Volume 2: Shared Task Papers, Day 1)*, pages 1–61, Florence, Italy. Association for Computational Linguistics.

Bergmanis, T. and Pinnis, M. (2021a). Dynamic terminology integration for COVID-19 and other emerging domains. In *Proceedings of the Sixth Conference on Machine Translation*, pages 821–827, Online. Association for Computational Linguistics.

Bergmanis, T. and Pinnis, M. (2021b). Facilitating terminology translation with target lemma annotations. In *Proceedings of the 16th Conference of the European Chapter of the Association for Computational Linguistics: Main Volume*, pages 3105–3111, Online. Association for Computational Linguistics.

Bojar, O., Macháček, M., Tamchyna, A., and Zeman, D. (2013). Scratching the surface of possible translations. In Habernal, I. and Matoušek, V., editors, *Text, Speech, and Dialogue*, pages 465–474, Berlin, Heidelberg. Springer Berlin Heidelberg.

Chatterjee, R., Negri, M., Turchi, M., Federico, M., Specia, L., and Blain, F. (2017). Guiding neural machine translation decoding with external knowledge. In *Proceedings of the Second Conference on Machine Translation*, pages 157–168, Copenhagen, Denmark. Association for Computational Linguistics.

Chen, G., Chen, Y., Wang, Y., and Li, V. O. (2020). Lexical-constraint-aware neural machine translation via data augmentation. In Bessiere, C., editor, *Proceedings of the Twenty-Ninth International Joint Conference on Artificial Intelligence, IJCAI-20*, pages 3587–3593. International Joint Conferences on Artificial Intelligence Organization. Main track.

Crego, J., Kim, J., Klein, G., Rebollo, A., Yang, K., Senellart, J., Akhanov, E., Brunelle, P., Coquard, A., Deng, Y., Enoue, S., Geiss, C., Johanson, J., Khalsa, A., Khiari, R., Ko, B., Kobus, C., Lorieux, J., Martins, L., Nguyen, D.-C., Priori, A., Riccardi, T., Segal, N., Servan, C., Tiquet, C., Wang, B., Yang, J., Zhang, D., Zhou, J., and Zoldan, P. (2016). Systran's pure neural machine translation systems.

Dinu, G., Mathur, P., Federico, M., and Al-Onaizan, Y. (2019). Training neural machine translation to apply terminology constraints. In *Proceedings of the 57th Annual Meeting of the Association for Computational Linguistics*, pages 3063–3068, Florence, Italy. Association for Computational Linguistics.

Hanneman, G. and Dinu, G. (2020). How should markup tags be translated? In *Proceedings of the Fifth Conference on Machine Translation*, pages 1160–1173, Online. Association for Computational Linguistics.

Hasler, E., de Gispert, A., Iglesias, G., and Byrne, B. (2018). Neural machine translation decoding with terminology constraints. In *Proceedings of the 2018 Conference of the North American Chapter of the Association for Computational Linguistics: Human Language Technologies, Volume 2 (Short Papers)*, pages 506–512, New Orleans, Louisiana. Association for Computational Linguistics.

Hokamp, C. and Liu, Q. (2017). Lexically constrained decoding for sequence generation using grid beam search. In *Proceedings of the 55th Annual Meeting of the Association for Computational Linguistics (Volume 1: Long Papers)*, pages 1535–1546, Vancouver, Canada. Association for Computational Linguistics.

Hu, J. E., Khayrallah, H., Culkin, R., Xia, P., Chen, T., Post, M., and Van Durme, B. (2019a). Improved lexically constrained decoding for translation and monolingual rewriting. In *Proceedings of the 2019 Conference of the North American Chapter of the Association for Computational Linguistics: Human Language Technologies, Volume 1 (Long and Short Papers)*, pages 839–850, Minneapolis, Minnesota. Association for Computational Linguistics.

Hu, J. E., Rudinger, R., Post, M., and Durme, B. V. (2019b). Parabank: Monolingual bitext generation and sentential paraphrasing via lexically-constrained neural machine translation.

Jon, J., Aires, J. P., Varis, D., and Bojar, O. (2021). End-to-end lexically constrained machine translation for morphologically rich languages. In *Proceedings of the 59th Annual Meeting of the Association for Computational Linguistics and the 11th International Joint Conference on Natural Language Processing (Volume 1: Long Papers)*, pages 4019–4033, Online. Association for Computational Linguistics.

Junczys-Dowmunt, M., Grundkiewicz, R., Dwojak, T., Hoang, H., Heafield, K., Neckermann, T., Seide, F., Germann, U., Aji, A. F., Bogoychev, N., Martins, A. F. T., and Birch, A. (2018). Marian: Fast neural machine translation in C++. In *Proceedings of ACL 2018, System Demonstrations*, pages 116–121, Melbourne, Australia. Association for Computational Linguistics.

Kajiwara, T. (2019). Negative lexically constrained decoding for paraphrase generation. In *Proceedings of the 57th Annual Meeting of the Association for Computational Linguistics*, pages 6047–6052, Florence, Italy. Association for Computational Linguistics.

Kepler, F., Trénous, J., Treviso, M., Vera, M., and Martins, A. F. T. (2019). OpenKiwi: An open source framework for quality estimation. In *Proceedings of the 57th Annual Meeting of the Association for Computational Linguistics: System Demonstrations*, pages 117–122, Florence, Italy. Association for Computational Linguistics.

Knowles, R. and Koehn, P. (2016). Neural interactive translation prediction. In *Conferences of the Association for Machine Translation in the Americas: MT Researchers' Track*, pages 107–120, Austin, TX, USA. The Association for Machine Translation in the Americas.

Kocmi, T., Popel, M., and Bojar, O. (2020). Announcing czeng 2.0 parallel corpus with over 2 gigawords. *CoRR*, abs/2007.03006.

Kudo, T. and Richardson, J. (2018). SentencePiece: A simple and language independent subword tokenizer and detokenizer for neural text processing. In *Proceedings of the 2018 Conference on Empirical Methods in Natural Language Processing: System Demonstrations*, pages 66–71, Brussels, Belgium. Association for Computational Linguistics.

Li, X., Yan, J., Zhang, J., and Zong, C. (2019). Neural name translation improves neural machine translation. In Chen, J. and Zhang, J., editors, *Machine Translation*, pages 93–100. Springer Singapore.

Papineni, K., Roukos, S., Ward, T., and Zhu, W.-J. (2002). Bleu: a method for automatic evaluation of machine translation. In *Proceedings of the 40th Annual Meeting of the Association for Computational Linguistics*, pages 311–318, Philadelphia, Pennsylvania, USA. Association for Computational Linguistics.

Post, M. (2018). A call for clarity in reporting BLEU scores. In *Proceedings of the Third Conference on Machine Translation: Research Papers*, pages 186–191, Brussels, Belgium. Association for Computational Linguistics.

Post, M. and Vilar, D. (2018). Fast lexically constrained decoding with dynamic beam allocation for neural machine translation. In *Proceedings of the 2018 Conference of the North American Chapter of the Association for Computational Linguistics: Human Language Technologies, Volume 1 (Long Papers)*, pages 1314–1324, New Orleans, Louisiana. Association for Computational Linguistics.

Rei, R., Stewart, C., Farinha, A. C., and Lavie, A. (2020). COMET: A neural framework for MT evaluation. In *Proceedings of the 2020 Conference on Empirical Methods in Natural Language Processing (EMNLP)*, pages 2685–2702, Online. Association for Computational Linguistics.

Song, K., Zhang, Y., Yu, H., Luo, W., Wang, K., and Zhang, M. (2019). Code-switching for enhancing NMT with pre-specified translation. In *Proceedings of the 2019 Conference of the North American Chapter of the Association for Computational Linguistics: Human Language Technologies, Volume 1 (Long and Short Papers)*, pages 449–459, Minneapolis, Minnesota. Association for Computational Linguistics.

Straka, M. and Straková, J. (2017). Tokenizing, POS tagging, lemmatizing and parsing UD 2.0 with UDPipe. In *Proceedings of the CoNLL 2017 Shared Task: Multilingual Parsing from Raw Text to Universal Dependencies*, pages 88–99, Vancouver, Canada. Association for Computational Linguistics.

Yan, J., Zhang, J., Xu, J., and Zong, C. (2019). The impact of named entity translation for neural machine translation. In Chen, J. and Zhang, J., editors, *Machine Translation*, pages 63–73. Springer Singapore.

Post-editing of Technical Terms based on Bilingual Example Sentences

Elsie K. Y. Chan elsie.chan@mail.com
John S. Y. Lee jsylee@cityu.edu.hk
Department of Linguistics and Translation, City University of Hong Kong

Chester Cheng chester.cheng@gmail.com
Department of Translation, The Chinese University of Hong Kong

Benjamin K. Tsou rlbtsou@cityu.edu.hk
Department of Linguistics and Translation, City University of Hong Kong
Chilin (HK), Ltd.

Abstract

As technical fields become ever more specialized, and with continuous emergence of novel technical terms, it may not be always possible to avail of bilingual experts in the field to perform translation. This paper investigates the performance of bilingual non-experts in Computer-Assisted Translation. The translators were asked to identify and correct errors in MT output of technical terms in patent materials, aided only by example bilingual sentences. Targeting English-to-Chinese translation, we automatically extract the example sentences from a bilingual corpus of English and Chinese patents. We identify the most frequent translation candidates of a term, and then select the most relevant example sentences for each candidate according to semantic similarity. Even when given only two example sentences for each translation candidate, the non-expert translators were able to post-edit effectively, correcting 67.2% of the MT errors while mistakenly revising correct MT output in only 17% of the cases.

1 Introduction

Post-editing of machine translation (MT) system output is now commonly incorporated as part of the workflow in the translation industry, since it can produce higher quality texts than manual translation (Garcia, 2011; Green et al., 2013). For texts in scientific or technical domains, it would be ideal to have bilingual domain experts to perform the post-editing. Given the large number of specialized domains and language pairs, however, translators with the required skills are unfortunately not always available. It is therefore important to understand whether those without the full linguistic or technical background could still perform post-editing adequately. While previous research has explored the feasibility of monolingual post-editing (Mitchell et al., 2013), few studies have investigated how well bilingual non-experts can post-edit MT output of technical texts.

This paper evaluates the performance of bilingual novice translators in identifying and correcting MT errors in technical term translation. To simulate a realistic scenario with time constraints, the translators are aided with only a small number of bilingual example sentences from a database of patents. These example sentences are automatically retrieved from PatentLex, a

Proceedings of Machine Translation Summit XIX, Vol. 1: Research Track, pages 385–392
September 4–8, 2023, Macau SAR, China.

large corpus of English and Chinese patents (Lu et al., 2009; Tsou et al., 2019), to illustrate the most likely translation candidates. Results show that, despite their unfamiliarity with the domain, the translators managed to correct a majority (67.2%) of the MT errors, and mistakenly revised correct MT output in less than 17% of the cases.

The rest of the paper is organized as follows. After sketching the research background (Section 2), we describe the translation texts and bilingual example sentences (Section 3). We then define the translation task (Section 4) and report the results (Section 5).

2 Research Background

Although MT systems can often provide high-quality output, high-stakes translation assignments still require manual verification and editing. This can be a challenging task, especially in technical translation when the human translator is not an expert in the field. In this case, the translator may need to consult existing bilingual examples in context, in order to evaluate different translation options of a term (Bowker and Barlow, 2008). Previous research has studied how well bilingual concordancing can assist novice translators in post-editing MT output of patents (Lee et al., 2020). An in-domain bilingual corpus was shown to yield better translation quality than a general-domain one, but MT outputs from Google and Baidu outperformed the post-edited versions in terms of both BLEU score and term accuracy. However, these results may not be conclusive because of possible variations in the concordancing process. The post-editing outcome could be significantly affected by the skills of the individual subjects in discerning relevant bilingual examples, and the amount of time and effort invested.

Our study mitigates these confounding factors by controlling the post-editing time and the set of bilingual examples provided (Section 4). We use PatentLex, a very large corpus of over 300K comparable Chinese and English patents registered in separate jurisdictions, curated within a 10 year period (Lu et al., 2009; Tsou et al., 2019). This corpus has served as the dataset in two Chinese-English patent MT competitions, organized by NTCIR in Tokyo in 2009 and 2010, and won second place in the 2019 Game Changer Innovation Contest organized by TAUS in Singapore. Reflecting its high quality, MT models trained on this corpus have been shown to outperform generic MT tools such as Google, Baidu and Microsoft in patent translation.

3 Data

3.1 Translation materials

We selected 12 patents in English from PatentLex as the materials for this experiment. The professionally translated Chinese versions of these 12 patents served as the gold translation. We used *Google Translate* and *Baidu Fanyi* to automatically translate one passage from each patent (see example in Table 1). In each English passage, two technical terms were highlighted for our subjects to attempt translation. One term required post-editing, and the other term did not:

Post-editing (PE) required The MT system gave a Chinese translation that differed from the gold translation and was incorrect, and therefore required post-editing. For example, the word 进入 *jinru* 'access' in the MT outputs in Table 1 should be revised to 接入 *jieru* 'access'.

Post-editing (PE) unnecessary The Chinese translation given by the MT system was the gold translation or an acceptable alternative, and therefore did not require post-editing. For example, no change was required for the word 组织 *zuzhi* 'tissue' in the MT outputs in Table 1, since it was the gold translation.

Description	Text	Post-editing required	Post-editing unnecessary
Source	Furthermore, by placement of the cuff below the ***access*** site, the fluid collected above the cuff balloon can expose the ***tissue*** on the ***access*** site.	n/a	n/a
MT output (Google)	此外，通过将套囊放置在进入部位下方，收集在套囊气球上方的流体可使暴露部位上的组织暴露。	进入 *jinru* 'access'	组织 *zuzhi* 'tissue'
MT output (Baidu)	此外，通过将袖带放置在进入部位下方，袖带气囊上方收集的液体可以暴露进入部位的组织。	进入 *jinru* 'access'	组织 *zuzhi* 'tissue'
Gold translation (PatentLex)	此外，通过将囊套放置在接入部位下方，囊套气球上所收集的流体可使接入部位上的组织暴露。	接入 *jieru* 'access'	组织 *zuzhi* 'tissue'

Table 1: Excerpt from a passage in the original English patent, its human (gold) translation in Chinese from PatentLex, and the MT output from Google and Baidu. For each highlighted term in the English passage ('access' and 'tissue'), the subjects were asked to decide whether and how to post-edit the MT translation (*jinru* and *zuzhi*), based on bilingual examples (Table 2). The gold translation was not provided to the subjects.

3.2 Bilingual examples

Since the subjects were non-experts, they needed to examine bilingual example sentences to determine whether post-editing was needed. To support the subjects in making well-informed decisions, these examples should include the most likely translation candidates and illustrate the typical context in which the candidate could be used. For each PE-required word and each PE-unnecessary word, we used LexiScan (Tsou et al., 2019) to find the most frequent Chinese renditions in the database. For each rendition, we retrieved all bilingual example pairs and ranked them according to cosine similarity with the source sentence.

In principle, if there were no time constraint, the more examples are viewed by translators, the higher the post-editing accuracy could be expected. In practice, however, translators are under time pressure to deliver their assignments quickly. To simulate a realistic scenario, we provided only 12 bilingual example pairs for each term, comprising 2 examples for each of the 6 most frequent Chinese renditions. Table 2 shows the 6 renditions of the highlighted term 'access' in the example passage in Table 1, as well as one of the two bilingual example pairs provided to the subjects for each rendition.

4 Experimental set-up

4.1 Subjects

Our study involved 61 students enrolled in a Master of Arts programme in translation studies in Hong Kong. Most of them newly or recently completed their undergraduate studies with a non-science major, and were therefore unlikely to be familiar with the subject domain of the translation materials (Section 3.1).

The students were divided into two groups of 20 students each and one group of 21 students. Each student was asked to complete a translation task: answer a distinctive set of 4 translation questions designed in the same format, without the use of any dictionary or reference sources other than the MT outputs (Section 3.1) and bilingual examples (Section 3.2)

Translation candidate	Bilingual example pairs
访问 *fangwen* 'access'	The bioreactor further includes a second substrate, wherein the second substrate is positioned adjacent to the first surface of the first substrate and defines a plurality of connection channels, each of the connection channels being formed so as to be in fluid communication with a corresponding one of the inlet port, the outlet port, the auxiliary port, and the ***access*** port.
	所述生物反应器进一步包括一第二基片，其中所述第二基片位于邻近所述第一基片的所述第一表面处，并界定多个连接通道，每个所述连接通道的形成以使所述输入口、所述输出口、所述辅助口和所述访问口中相应的一个进行液体传送为宜。
接入 *jieru* 'access' (Gold)	It would be desirable to provide a laparoscopic ***access*** apparatus that would maintain a seal against the escape of gas from within a body cavity, that would enable large tissue samples to be withdrawn through the catheter without damage to the pressure seal, and that would also adapt to a variety of instrument sizes and configurations that are to be passed into and out of the catheter.
	因此需要提供一种剖腹接入装置，该装置能够维持密封防止气体从体腔内逸出，能够使大的组织取样通过导管取出而不损坏压力密封，还能够适合进出导管的多种器械尺寸和结构。
存取 *cunqu* 'access'	With a chosen area of the bottle designed to be flexible, a membrane switch, or any other type of pressure sensor, can be fitted to respond to the change of internal pressure within the bottle, when the ***access*** seal is broken, thus providing a method of interfacing the action of opening the bottle with a circuit.
	由于所选择的瓶区域设计为柔性的，所以膜片开关或任何其它类型的压力传感器可被固定，以在打破存取密封时相应于瓶的内部压力变化，从而提供使开启瓶的动作与电路连接的方法。
进入 *jinru* 'access'	The percutaneous ***access*** sheath may be used in conjunction with a deployment catheter, which is provided with a balloon at its distal end.
	可以与在其远端设置有气囊的扩展导管相结合地使用经皮进入套管。
入口 *rukou* 'access'	As disclosed herein, the ribbon holder includes a cover to allow ***access*** to the through passage whereby the ribbons can be placed into the passage transversely thereof.
	如这里所揭示的，所述光缆支架包括一个压盖，可形成进入通道内的入口来置入所述光缆的横截面。
接近 *jiejin* 'access'	The clamp is structured to contact the diaphragm along a perimeter portion and allow ***access*** to a center portion of the diaphragm.
	该夹具沿周边部分接触振动膜，并且允许接近振动膜的中心部分。

Table 2: Bilingual example pairs for the word 'access' in the passage in Table 1, intended to illustrate the usage context of the top six translation candidates *fangwen*, *jieru*, *cunqu*, *jinru*, *rukou* and *jiejin*

provided on the question paper.

4.2 Translation task

The study was conducted on paper, in the form of 3 typed question papers (namely, Post-editing Exercises A, B and C) each containing 4 translation questions. The 12 distinctive translation questions (namely, Sentences A1-A4; B1-B4; C1-C4) correspond to different text segments taken from 12 selected patents covering varied technical domains.

Regarding the 4 questions in each of the 3 question papers, each question contains: (1) a distinctive patent excerpt in English taken from the corpus of PatentLex, which contains two specific words being highlighted; (2) the corresponding automatic MT translations in Chinese by *Google Translate* and *Baidu Fanyi*, to be used as the reference for the translation task; and (3) for each highlighted word, 12 bilingual English-Chinese sentences taken from other patents from PatentLex that contain the same English word, to be used as the reference for their translation task. For the two highlighted words in each patent excerpt, one is PE-required and the other PE-unnecessary, a fact which was not made known to the subjects. The 12 questions altogether feature 24 highlighted English words to be translated into Chinese with the MT translations and PatentLex bilingual sentences as the only reference sources.

The subjects were asked to work independently on their own translation task, which features texts from filed patents on technical domains that are likely to be unfamiliar to them. After a brief introduction by the instructor, the subjects were given 30 minutes to determine 'the most appropriate translation' of the highlighted English words in Chinese, and another 5 minutes to input their answers on a designated Google Form.

4.3 Manual assessment

The subjects' translations gathered via the designated Google Form were reviewed by two human judges, both native speakers of Chinese. One judge was an experienced translation teacher and professional translator with a PhD in translation studies, who administered the experiment. The other judge was a PhD candidate in Translation with considerable experience working with translation of English-Chinese technical texts.

The judges considered all the translations provided by the subjects and on average accepted 1.5 alternative translations (ranging from 0 to 3) for each highlighted English word, in addition to the gold translation presumably provided by professionals. The judges reconciled the final decision through discussion.

5 Results

Our post-editing study involved 488 instances of term translation from English to Chinese. These included 244 instances that required post-editing (PE) (left side of Table 3) and 244 instances for which post-editing was unnecessary (right side of Table 3). Overall, the subjects achieved 75.4% accuracy by correctly revising 164 of the 244 PE-required instances, and correctly keeping the MT output in 204 of the 244 PE-unnecessary instances. The quality of the post-edited translation was thus higher than the MT output (without post-editing), which had 50% accuracy among the 488 instances. This result shows that, even without the provision of necessary contextual information of the patent excerpts, the subjects were fairly able to deduce the meaning of the highlighted words from the MT translations and bilingual sentences provided and consequently infer either the gold translations or acceptable translations.

5.1 PE-required cases

As shown in Table 3, out of the 244 PE-required cases, the subjects correctly post-edited 164 translations, representing an average accuracy rate of 67.2%. The result is fairly satisfactory,

Text	Post-editing required				Post-editing unnecessary			
	Term	Cor.	Inc.	Cor. %	Term	Cor.	Inc.	Cor. %
A1	access	20	0	100.0%	tissue	12	8	60.0%
A2	reservoir	18	2	90.0%	simulation	19	1	95.0%
A3	access	17	3	85.0%	data	19	1	95.0%
A4	reservoir	4	16	20.0%	body	16	4	80.0%
B1	configuration	10	11	47.6%	slot	13	8	61.9%
B2	operation	2	19	9.5%	system	14	7	66.7%
B3	function	17	4	81.0%	module	19	2	90.5%
B4	act	15	6	71.4%	surface	20	1	95.2%
C1	control	12	8	60.0%	barrier	20	0	100.0%
C2	position	17	3	85.0%	transaction	18	2	90.0%
C3	amount	18	2	90.0%	functional group	16	4	80.0%
C4	switch	14	6	70.0%	solution	18	2	90.0%
Total		164	80	67.2%		204	40	83.6%

Table 3: Post-editing results: number of correct (cor.) and incorrect (inc.) instances among post-editing required terms and post-editing unnecessary terms

given the fact that most subjects did not possess a technical or science background.

Falling slightly below the said average are the translations for 'control' (C1), with a passing 60% (the gold translation being 对照 *duizhao* as in 对照器件 *duizhao qijian* 'control devices'; both MT translations being 控制 *kongzhi* as in 控制装置 *kongzhi zhuangzhi*, which is considered marginally acceptable); while the remaining 40% are inaccurate (调节 *diaojie*) and imprecise (对照变量 *duizhao bianliang*) renderings. Faring less well is 'configuration' (B1, with an accuracy rate of 47.6%), which refers to paper notes in folded shape, form, state or arrangement (形状 *xingzhuang* being the gold translation; 配置 *peizhi* - the MT translation - and *zhuangtai* - proposed rendering by 2 subjects - are considered marginally acceptable); the wrong translations attempted (构形, 结构, 模型, 装置) indicate unacceptable collocation with the word 'note' and inadequate comprehension of context.

A more challenging word is 'reservoir' (A4), with mere 20% accuracy. The obvious reason is that in that particular context, 'reservoir' refers to a sample of aqueous body (水体 *shuiti* being the gold translation) which can be as large as 'Umberumberka Reservoir' (水库 *shuiku* being the gold translation) or as small as that on 'laboratory film balances.' Both judges found it difficult to find one Chinese word that collocates with both sample types: both the MT translation (储层 *chuceng*) and the other attempted translations by the subjects (储器, 储罐, 储液器, 储水器, 蓄水池) appear out of place. The judges suggested that different translations be adopted for the specific 'Reservoir' (水库 *shuiku*) and the generic 'reservoir' (贮库 *zhuku* being an acceptable alternative by 3 subjects; or 储体 *chuti* or 采样来源 *caiyang laiyuan* proposed by the judges) for better textual cohesion and consistency.

The worst performance is for 'operation' (B2), with a meagre 9.5% accuracy rate. Although the respective terms 'interventionist operation' and 'endovascular operations' may appear distinguishing, only 2 out of 21 subjects could infer the gold translation (手术 *shoushu*). 10 subjects adopted the MT version (操作 *caozuo*), which is imprecise for a technical patent, while the rest proposed incoherent translations (操作系统, 操刀, 生产, 运行, 作业, 装置, 反应), reflecting inadequate comprehension caused probably by a lack of technical knowledge and vocabulary.

It is worth noting that a good number of the MT translations were considered to be marginally to reasonably acceptable by the two judges, even though they deviate from their respective gold translations. Examples include those in A2 (储层 *chuceng* vs. 油藏 *youcang* 'reservoir'), A3 (访问 *fangwen* vs. 存取 *cunqu* 'access'), B1 (配置 *peizhi* vs. 形状 *xingzhuang* 'configuration'), B3 (功能 *gongneng* vs. 函数 *hanshu* 'function'), C1 (控制 *kongzhi* vs. 对照 *duizhao* 'control'), C2 (头寸 *toucun* vs. 立场 *lichang* 'position') and C4 (交换 *jiaohuan* vs. 切换 *qiehuan* 'switch'). All in all, the MT translations and PatentLex bilingual sentences provided, albeit decontextualized and containing one supposedly wrong translation that deviates from the gold standard, are found to be fairly helpful to the subjects for completing their post-editing task with a satisfactory accuracy rate under stringent conditions – translating 8 words used in a technical sense taken from 4 decontextualized patent excerpts within 30 minutes without access to dictionaries or translators' normal reference tools, not to mention the fact that most of the subjects did not possess a technical or science background.

5.2 PE-unnecessary cases

Out of the 244 PE-unnecessary cases, the subjects correctly kept the MT versions, which are the same as the gold translation, in 204 cases, representing a high average accuracy rate of 83.6%. This illustrates the overall efficiency of the selected MT and PatentLex texts and the subjects' post-editing capability. However the accuracy scores for 'tissue' (A1, 60%), 'slot' (B1, 61.9%) and 'system' (B2, 66.7%), albeit middling in absolute terms, are relatively lower. Below is an analysis of the translation errors, which points to the significance of contextual understanding and subject knowledge for the translator.

For 'tissue,' the wrongly attempted translations (组织部位, 体组织, 织物, 薄纸) reflect the subjects' failure to comprehend the context or subject matter – tracheal tissue (组织 *zuzhi* in the MT version) being exposed in relation to a medical device. For 'slot' as in 'note entry slot' (the MT version being 槽 *cao* as in 钞票进槽 *chaopiao jincao*), the unacceptable renderings proposed (狭槽, 槽缝, 狭缝, 缝隙, 缝) reflect imprecision or mis-collocation on the part of the subjects.

The term 'system' refers to a 模拟系统 *moni xitong* 'simulation system' for simulating an 'interventional operation' (模拟介入操作 *moni jieru caozuo* in the MT version) and 'endovascular operations' (血管内操作 *xueguan nei caozuo* in the MT version) using a device (装置 *zhuangzhi* and 设备 *shebei* in the MT versions) equipped with the patented invention. The subjects who correctly kept the MT translations of this term understood that it concerns medical operations. However, the wrong translations 装置 *zhuangzhi* and 装备 *zhuangbei* for 'system' show that the subjects concerned failed to notice that the said Chinese versions should be reserved for 'device' in the same sentence, while the other wrong translations 环境 *huanjing* and 方法 *fangfa* indicate the other subjects' inadequate understanding of the context and technical subject.

6 Conclusion

As technical fields become ever more specialized, and with continuous emergence of novel technical terms, it may not be always possible to avail of bilingual experts in the field to perform translation. In the age of artificial intelligence, translators are increasingly expected to function as post-editors. This paper has investigated the performance of bilingual but non-expert translators in post-editing. Targeting English-to-Chinese translation of technical terms in patents, we asked translators to post-edit these terms in MT output, aided only by bilingual example sentences that were automatically extracted from the PatentLex database.

The results show that, even in the absence of dictionaries and field knowledge, the subjects were in general fairly able to deduce word meaning and produce acceptable translations (75.4%) in decontextualized technical texts with the help of MT translations and the bilingual corpus of PatentLex. In particular, they corrected a majority (67.2%) of the MT errors, and mistakenly revised correct MT output in less than 17% of the cases. The understanding of context and field knowledge remains crucial for highly accurate and professional translation. In the future, we plan to conduct larger-scale experiments to further shed light on the increasing efficiency and reliability of MT translation and bilingual corpora as indispensable tools for translators.

Acknowledgments

We gratefully acknowledge support from the Strategic Research Grant (projects #7005709 and #7005803) at City University of Hong Kong; and from Hong Kong's Innovation and Technology Commission (ITC) grant to Chilin (HK) Ltd for the PaTTA project (ITC/ESS Project: B/E019/20).

References

Bowker, L. and Barlow, M. (2008). A comparative evaluation of bilingual concordancers and translation memory systems. In Rodrigo, E. Y., editor, *Topics in Language Resources for Translation and Localisation*, pages 1–22. John Benjamins, Philadelphia, PA.

Garcia, I. (2011). Translating by post-editing: is it the way forward? *Machine Translation*, 25:217–237.

Green, S., Heer, J., and Manning, C. D. (2013). The Efficacy of Human Post-Editing for Language Translation. In *Proc. CHI.*

Lee, J., Tsou, B., and Cai, T. (2020). Using Bilingual Patents for Translation Training. In *Proc. 28th International Conference on Computational Linguistics (COLING).*

Lu, B., Tsou, B. K., Zhu, J., Jiang, T., and Kwong, O. Y. (2009). The Construction of a Chinese-English Patent Parallel Corpus. In *Proc. MT Summit XII: Third Workshop on Patent Translation*, pages 17–24.

Mitchell, L., Roturier, J., and O'Brien, S. (2013). Community-based post-editing of machine-translated content: monolingual vs. bilingual. In *Proc. MT Summit XIV Workshop on Post-editing Technology and Practice.*

Tsou, B. K., Chow, K., Nie, J., and Yuan, Y. (2019). From the cultivation of comparable corpora to harvesting from them: A quantitative and qualitative exploration. In *Proc. 12th Workshop on Building and Using Comparable Corpora.*

A Filtering Approach to Object Region Detection in Multimodal Machine Translation

Ali Hatami ali.hatami@insight-centre.org
Paul Buitelaar paul.buitelaar@insight-centre.org
Mihael Arcan mihael.arcan@insight-centre.org
Insight SFI Research Centre for Data Analytics,
Data Science Institute, University of Galway, Ireland

Abstract

Recent studies in Multimodal Machine Translation (MMT) have explored the use of visual information in a multimodal setting to analyze its redundancy with textual information. The aim of this work is to develop a more effective approach to incorporating relevant visual information into the translation process and improve the overall performance of MMT models. This paper proposes an object-level filtering approach in Multimodal Machine Translation, where the approach is applied to object regions extracted from an image to filter out irrelevant objects based on the image captions to be translated. Using the filtered image helps the model to consider only relevant objects and their relative locations to each other. Different matching methods, including string matching and word embeddings, are employed to identify relevant objects. Gaussian blurring is used to soften irrelevant objects from the image and to evaluate the effect of object filtering on translation quality. The performance of the filtering approaches was evaluated on the Multi30K dataset in English to German, French, and Czech translations, based on BLEU, ChrF2, and TER metrics.

1 Introduction

In recent years, neural network-based models have been widely used in translation tasks. Neural Machine Translation (NMT) represents remarkable performance in terms of fluency and precision compared with the previous generations of machine translation (Cho et al., 2014a). Recurrent Neural Network (RNN) with an attention mechanism has found broad application in NMT due to its capability to capture long-term dependencies between the most relevant parts of the source sentence (Cho et al., 2014b). The transformer model has demonstrated remarkable improvements in machine translation tasks. The cross-attention mechanism as a crucial component of the transformer-based model enhances the model's ability to capture semantic dependencies by combining self-attention, which allows source words to interact with themselves, with attention mechanisms involving target words (Vaswani et al., 2017).

Most current NMT models have shown incredible improvements in the quality of translations, but they rely solely on parallel text corpora for training. However, recent studies (Yao and Wan, 2020; Zhao et al., 2022; Wang and Xiong, 2021) in NMT have increasingly focused on using visual as well as textual content to enhance the quality of translations. Multimodal Machine Translation (MMT), a subarea of NMT, has been introduced to utilise visual information extracted from other modalities, such as images or videos, to translate an aligned sentence

Proceedings of Machine Translation Summit XIX, Vol. 1: Research Track, pages 393–405
September 4–8, 2023, Macau SAR, China.

Figure 1: The use of an image helps the translation model disambiguate the word *seal* in the sentence "*Two boys watch a seal.*" and select the correct translation from English to German.

in a source language into the target language. Similar to other multimodal tasks, MMT aims to enhance the model's ability by using visual content as an additional source of information to better understand and translate the source text. The idea behind MMT is to incorporate visual information to assist with word sense disambiguation in the input text.

Despite the fact that text-only NMT models, particularly the hidden states in the attention mechanism, consider contextual information, word sense disambiguation remains an open challenge for NMT (Tang et al., 2018). For example, as shown in Figure 1, the word "*seal*" in the English sentence "*Two boys watch a seal.*" is an ambiguous word and could have at least two different translations in German: (1) "*Zwei Jungs gucken sich einen Seehund an.*", and (2) "*Zwei Jungs gucken sich ein Siegel an.*". The Word *Seehund* in (1) refers to a fish-eating aquatic mammal, and *Siegel* in (2) is a piece of wax with an individual design stamped into it. Given the word "*seal*", the context of the source text does not provide enough information to disambiguate the words in English, and both translated texts in German are correct. However, the aligned image with the source text can provide additional information for disambiguation of the source text. Due to this, visual information can enrich text-only NMT models by leveraging additional information to disambiguate input words and provide correct translations on the target side.

Despite the importance of using visual context, visual resources such as images and videos contain a large amount of information that might not be helpful in the translation step. This additional information does often not help on improving the performance of a translation model and in some cases, it even drops the translation quality. So the recent studies on MMT focus more on finding a suitable approach to reduce the negative effects of rich visual information and enrich the translation model with the related information. To overcome the challenge mentioned above, this work focuses on identifying related visual information in the image encoder before using it in the translation model. Our approach is based on matching identified objects within the images with the captions in the text to detect which identified objects are relevant and useful in the translation process. Therefore, we apply a filtering approach that blurs irrelevant object regions on the image to reduce their negative effects on the translation model.

2 Related Work

There are various approaches proposed to integrate visual information with text-only translation models. These approaches typically utilise a visual attention mechanism in either the decoder or encoder to capture the relationships between words in a sentence and image features. The common method involves extracting visual information by employing Convolutional Neural Networks (CNN) and then integrating this information with textual features (Yao and Wan, 2020).

Regarding visual features, existing studies on MMT employ two types of visual features: global and local visual features. Global features represent the entire image as a single vector without attention to the spatial layout of the image (Calixto and Liu, 2017). On the other hand, local features describe an image as a sequence of equally sized patches (Calixto et al., 2017). Global and local features represent different information about the image based on texture. Local features are extracted from multiple points in the image and are more robust to clutter than global features (Lisin et al., 2005). CNNs can be used to extract both global and local features from the image (Zheng et al., 2019).

In some studies, global image features are used in the encoder in addition to word sequences, to use both types of features in the decoding stage (Huang et al., 2016). Alternatively, they can be used to initialise the hidden parameters of the encoder and decoder in RNN (Calixto and Liu, 2017). In Caglayan et al. (2017), element-wise multiplication is used to initialise the hidden states of the encoder/decoder in the attention-based model. In Zhou et al. (2018), a visual attention mechanism is used to link visual and corresponding text semantically.

Despite the successful use of multimodal information in MMT, visual features do not always improve the translation quality of the integrated model, especially when textual features are highly informative (Caglayan et al., 2019). Therefore, recent studies on MMT focus more on the quality of the visual modality used as auxiliary information in the translation model (Zhao et al., 2022; Wang and Xiong, 2021), specifically in selecting relevant information and integrating this visual information with textual modality (Caglayan et al., 2016).

Several approaches have been proposed to improve the quality of visual modality in MMT. For instance, Yao and Wan (2020) proposed a multimodal transformer-based self-attention mechanism to encode relevant information in images. To capture various relationships, Yin et al. (2020) proposed a graph-based multimodal fusion encoder. Ive et al. (2019) introduced a translate-and-refine mechanism by using images in a second-stage decoder to refine the text-only NMT model in ambiguous words. Calixto et al. (2019) employed a latent variable model to extract the multimodal relationships between image and text modalities. Recent methods try to reduce the noise of visual information and select visual features related to the text. For example, Wang and Xiong (2021) used object-level visual modelling to mask irrelevant objects and specific words in the source text to analyse visual feature learning. Zhao et al. (2022) employed object detection in the image encoder to extract visual features of object regions from an image and then applied it to a doubly-attentive decoder model.

In our study, we utilised blur filtering on the initial image to conceal irrelevant objects while preserving the relevant ones. Our approach differs from previous works such as Zhao et al. (2022); Wang and Xiong (2021); Yin et al. (2020) in that our blur filter prioritises relevant objects over irrelevant ones. However, it's important to note that the irrelevant objects are only partially blurred, so the MMT model does not completely disregard them. Additionally, by applying the filter to the entire image, the model gains knowledge about the relative positions of all objects in relation to each other.

3 Methodology

In this section, we explain the main steps of our approach: i) detect object regions from images, ii) align object regions with captions and iii) blur irrelevant object regions.

3.1 Object Region Detection

For the image encoder, we use an object detection model to extract object-level features from the input image. As shown in Figure 2, the encoder first uses a bottom-up attention-based object detection model (Anderson et al., 2018) to detect n objects from the image. The bottom-up attention mechanism detects a set of image regions, with each region represented by a pooled convolutional features vector. This mechanism is based on Faster R-CNN (Ren et al., 2015) with ResNet-101 (He et al., 2016) pre-trained on Visual Genome (Krishna et al., 2017) to detect

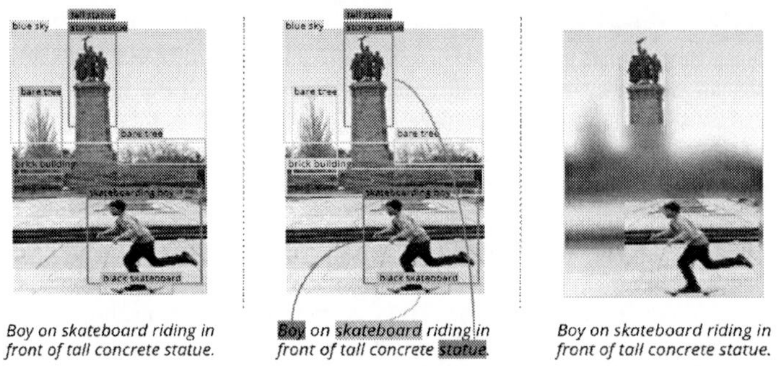

Figure 2: Our proposed image filtering approach involves three steps (left to right): (1) detecting all possible objects from the image, (2) aligning words in the text with identified object classes for irrelevant object detection, (3) applying blur filtering on irrelevant objects.

1,400 objects and 600 object attributes. The bottom-up attention mechanism first generates a fixed-length feature vector for each region proposal in the image. Then, these region proposals are classified using the Faster R-CNN model, and for each identified object, the model returns its object class, object attribute, and bounding box. For example, Figure 2 shows the objects identified from the image including *statue*, *skateboard*, and *boy* as object classes and *tall*, *stone*, and *skateboarding* as object attributes.

3.2 Object Region and Caption Alignment

After obtaining the identified objects, we explore different strategies to align the identified object classes with words in the text captions to be translated. As we discussed, the redundancy of information in the image side is one of the important challenges for MMT. As shown in Figure 2, some of these objects such as *statue*, *skateboard*, and *boy* are important for translating *"Boy on skateboard riding in front of tall concrete statue."*, while other detected objects are not mentioned in the caption to be translated. Thus, finding the relevant visual in regard to the caption plays an important role in MMT tasks. In this work, we used string matching, lemma matching and word embedding similarity approaches to find matching objects that are mentioned in the text caption.

String matching is a technique used to compare two strings and determine whether they match for a specific word or sequence of words within a larger body of text. In this work, we used string matching to align each word in the text caption with the detected object classes in the image. This is an important step in selecting relevant visual information for the translation process. To perform string matching, the words in the text caption are compared with each detected object class to determine whether they match or not.

String matching is a simple approach that compares the overlap of a word or a sequence of words in the caption with the exact string of the object class. However, this can be a limitation, as the words in the captions can be inflected, opposite to the lexicalised object classes that are always in their nominative form. Therefore, we used lemma matching, which is more flexible than string matching. Lemma matching is used for matching the nominative form of words (known as lemmas) in the text caption with the base form of identified object classes. This is particularly useful in cases where there may be variations in the form of words such as plural. For example, using string matching, the word *statues* in the caption was not matched with the nominative form *statue* provided by the object detection tool. Applying lemma matching, we could align *statue* with the object class.

	Training	Validation	Test 2016	Test 2017	Test 2018
Number of Sentences	29,000	1,014	1,000	1,000	1,071
English (words/sent)	13.0	13.1	13.0	11.4	12.9
German (words/sent)	12.4	12.7	12.1	10.8	11.5
French (words/sent)	14.1	14.2	14.0	12.6	13.8
Czech (words/sent)	10.2	10.2	10.5	-	10.2

Table 1: The summary of the Multi30k dataset includes the number of sentences and the average words per sentence for each language.

Furthermore, we leverage word embeddings to align words in the caption with the object detection classes, where each word is represented as a dense vector of real numbers, where each dimension of the vector corresponds to a feature of the word. Using word embeddings, we can find matching words between the text caption and the object classes by computing the similarity between their corresponding vectors. This approach allows us to capture semantic similarities between words, even if they are not exact matches. For instance, the words "*girl*" and "*woman*" can be semantically related using word embeddings, whereas string and lemma matching fail to identify their connection.

In this work, we use two different word embedding methods, GloVe and BERT. GloVe (Pennington et al., 2014) is a word embedding model that aims to capture the semantic and syntactic relationships between words. Unlike GloVe, BERT (Devlin et al., 2019) is a context-based model. BERT is a language model that learns the representation of the contextual relationship between the words in a sentence, known as contextual word embeddings. For example, in GloVe, the word "*bank*" would have the same vector representation in phrases like "*bank account*" and "*bank of the river*" However, in BERT, each word is represented based on the context of the other words in the sentence. To compute the similarity between each word in the caption with all object classes, we use the cosine similarity. This metric measures the cosine of the angle between two vectors and ranges between 0 and 1. A cosine similarity of 1 indicates that two vectors are identical, while a cosine similarity of 0 indicates that they are completely dissimilar.

For each word embedding model, we perform experiments using various cosine similarity thresholds. We select the optimal threshold for each method based on the translation BLEU score. Through empirical observation, we found that thresholds of 0.8 for GloVe and 0.98 for BERT yielded the best translation results. Once the matching between each word in the text caption and the identified object classes is finished, the relevant object classes can be chosen for applying blur filtering on irrelevant objects.

3.3 Irrelevant Object Region Filtering

After selecting the relevant objects for each matching technique, we apply a blur filter to the region boxes of the irrelevant objects in the original image. There are two benefits by using a blur filter for the irrelevant objects in the original image. Firstly, the blur filter helps the model to focus on the relevant objects more than the irrelevant objects. Nevertheless, as we only partially blur the irrelevant objects, the MMT model does not completely ignore them. Secondly, applying the filter to the whole image allows the model to learn the positional information of all relevant objects in the image.

For blur filtering, we use Gaussian blur (also called Gaussian smoothing), a convolution technique widely used in computer vision as a pre-processing step for noise reduction and eliminating details from the image (Ibrahim. et al., 2021). Gaussian blur is a linear low-pass filter that uses a Gaussian function to calculate the pixel value. Equation 1 shows the Gaussian blur filter with a two-dimensional Gaussian function.

$$G(x,y) = \frac{1}{2\pi\sigma^2} e^{\frac{-x^2+y^2}{2\sigma^2}} \quad (1)$$

Where *(x,y)* are the coordinates of the pixel, and σ is the standard deviation of the Gaussian distribution. The standard deviation (σ) is a parameter that changes the radius of the Gaussian function and controls the blur intensity. The intensity of blurring refers to the degree or level of blur applied to an image or specific areas within an image. It determines how much the details in the image are smoothed or obscured. By increasing the radius, the Gaussian function considers more neighbouring pixels, leading to an increased degree of intensity. A higher intensity of blurring results in a stronger and more noticeable blur effect, while a lower intensity produces a milder or less pronounced blur. After filtering out irrelevant objects and keeping relevant ones in the original image, we use the ResNet-101 model pre-trained on ImageNet (Deng et al., 2009), to extract visual features from the filtered image. We used the Python Imaging Library (PIL)[1] to apply blur filtering to the image. We perform the experiment with different blur intensities (10, 25, and 75) for the English to German translation task. Based on the BLUE scores for all matching strategies, we determine that a blur intensity of 75 produces the best results.

4 Experimental Setup

This section provides insights into the dataset used in this work, translation evaluation metrics and neural architecture of our model including text/image encoder and decoder.

4.1 Dataset

We used the Multi30K (Elliott et al., 2016) dataset in this work to train and evaluate our models. Multi30K is an extension of the Flickr30K Entities dataset that consists of 29,000 images with paired descriptions expressed in one English sentence and translated sentences in German, French, and Czech (Elliott et al., 2017). The training set of the dataset contains captions aligned with the images. Multi30K also provides three test sets: the 2016 and 2017 test sets, each with 1,000 images, and the 2018 test set with 1,071 images. Table 1 summarises the dataset, including the number of sentences and the average number of words per sentence for each language.

4.2 Object Detection Framework

We use the bottom-up attention (Anderson et al., 2018) mechanism to detect objects in the image encoder to extract all possible objects from an input image. This object detection model is based on the Faster R-CNN model (Ren et al., 2015) and can be used to extract class, attribute and region box for each object. This object detection model is a pre-trained model on Visual Genome (Krishna et al., 2017) to detect 1,400 objects and 600 attributes. For this work, we use the default settings[2] for Faster R-CNN model to extract 36 objects for each image (Anderson et al., 2018). Figure 2 shows an example of the output of the object detection model that extracts object region boxes for an image with the associated object classes and attributes. In this example, object detection model identifies multiple objects from the image and returns a pair of words for each object (attribute class) including: *blue sky, tall statue, stone statue, bare tree, brick building, skateboarding boy, black skateboard.*

4.3 Word Embeddings

We used word embedding methods to align words in the text caption with the detected object classes. Specifically, we utilised GloVe and BERT word embedding models to find relevant object classes for words in the English caption. For this work, we used pre-trained GloVe 50d

[1]`https://github.com/python-pillow/Pillow`

[2]`https://github.com/airsplay/py-bottom-up-attention`

English → German	BLEU ↑	ChrF2 ↑	TER ↓
Text-only NMT	32.5	57.7	53.7
Basline MMT	35.3 ± 1.5	60.9 ± 1.1	50.2 ± 1.5
String matching	**36.9 ± 1.6***	**61.4 ± 1.1***	**49.1 ± 1.7***
Lemma matching	36.3 ± 1.6*	61.2 ± 1.2	**49.1 ± 1.7***
GloVe matching	36.3 ± 1.7*	61.0 ± 1.2	49.5 ± 1.7*
BERT matching	36.2 ± 1.6*	60.9 ± 1.2	49.4 ± 1.6*
English → French	**BLEU ↑**	**ChrF2 ↑**	**TER ↓**
Text-only NMT	53.8	69.7	33.6
Baseline MMT	**56.8 ± 1.7**	**72.6 ± 1.2**	30.8 ± 1.5
String matching	56.6 ± 1.7	**72.6 ± 1.2**	**30.6 ± 1.4**
Lemma matching	56.0 ± 1.8	72.1 ± 1.2	31.6 ± 1.6
GloVe matching	56.7 ± 1.6	72.5 ± 1.2	30.7 ± 1.4
BERT matching	56.5 ± 1.7	72.5 ± 1.2	31.1 ± 1.4
English → Czech	**BLEU ↑**	**ChrF2 ↑**	**TER ↓**
Text-only NMT	26.0	48.7	58.0
Baseline MMT	29.4 ± 1.5	52.1 ± 1.2	53.7 ± 1.6
String matching	29.0 ± 1.5	51.7 ± 1.2	54.5 ± 1.6
Lemma matching	**29.6 ± 1.7**	**52.4 ± 1.2**	**53.0 ± 1.7**
GloVe matching	29.2 ± 1.7	51.8 ± 1.2	53.8 ± 1.7
BERT matching	28.7 ± 1.6	51.6 ± 1.2	54.3 ± 1.6

Table 2: BLEU, ChrF2 and TER scores for baseline and proposed models for English to German, French and Czech on the 2016 test set ($*$ represents a statistically significant result compared to baseline MMT at a significance level of $p < 0.05$).

word embedding to extract word vectors for the words in the text caption and identified object classes. Additionally, we used the pre-trained BERT-base-uncased to extract vectors for each word. This model is trained on lower-cased text, which allows it to generalise better to unseen text with different capitalisation patterns.

4.4 Neural Machine Translation

In this section, we introduce the text-only and multimodal NMT models used in this work.

4.4.1 Text-only NMT

We train a text-only transformer model as a baseline model for our experiment. This model uses only the text captions of the images. OpenNMT (Klein et al., 2018) toolkit is used to train the text-only model on English to German, French and Czech of Multi30k dataset. The architecture of the model includes a 6-layer transformer with an attention mechanism for both the encoder and decoder. We trained the model for 50K steps on the training dataset and set the parameters of the model to the default configuration of OpenNMT. We used Sentencepiece Kudo and Richardson (2018) to split words into sub-word units.

4.4.2 Multimodal NMT

We used the Doubly-Attentive Decoder RNN (Calixto et al., 2017) as the baseline model for our multimodal architecture. The Doubly-Attentive Decoder employs a single decoder RNN that integrates two separate attention mechanisms, one for the source-language words and another for the visual features. The decoder RNN with a Doubly-Attentive mechanism considers the previous hidden state of the decoder and previously generated word, along with two distinct attention mechanisms that handle the source sentence and image separately. For this study, we used the default configuration[3] of the Doubly-Attentive Decoder RNN. The visual features,

[3]https://github.com/iacercalixto/MultimodalNMT

English → German	BLEU ↑	ChrF2 ↑	TER ↓
Text-only NMT	25.0	53.2	63.7
Baseline MMT	28.2 ± 1.6	55.4 ± 1.1	59.6 ± 1.7
String matching	28.8 ± 1.6	55.6 ± 1.2	60.0 ± 1.9
Lemma matching	**29.1 ± 1.7***	55.7 ± 1.1	**59.0 ± 1.8**
GloVe matching	28.6 ± 1.6	**55.8 ± 1.2**	59.9 ± 1.8
BERT matching	28.4 ± 1.6	**55.8 ± 1.2**	60.0 ± 1.9
English → French	**BLEU ↑**	**ChrF2 ↑**	**TER ↓**
Text-only NMT	47.0	65.2	40.2
Baseline MMT	**48.4 ± 1.8**	**66.9 ± 1.2**	38.2 ± 1.7
String matching	47.8 ± 1.9	66.6 ± 1.3	**38.0 ± 1.6**
Lemma matching	47.4 ± 1.7	66.1 ± 1.3	39.2 ± 1.6
GloVe matching	47.6 ± 1.8	66.8 ± 1.3	38.6 ± 1.6
BERT matching	47.7 ± 1.9	66.8 ± 1.2	38.5 ± 1.6

Table 3: BLEU, ChrF2 and TER scores for baseline and proposed models for English to German and French on the 2017 test set ($*$ represents a statistically significant result compared to baseline MMT at a significance level of $p < 0.05$).

with a dimension of 2,048, were obtained by inputting images to a pre-trained ResNet-101 and extracting the activations of the res4f layer. The hidden state dimension of the visual model was set to 500 for both the 2-layer GRU encoder and the 2-layer GRU decoder. The model also set the dimension of the source word embedding to 500, batch size to 400, beam size to 5, text dropout to 0.3, and image region dropout to 0.5. After training the model for 25 epochs using stochastic gradient descent with ADADELTA (Zeiler, 2012) and a learning rate of 0.002, we selected the model of epoch 16 based on comparing the BLEU scores of the final models on the test datasets.

4.5 Evaluation Metrics

We report the translation scores using three metrics: BLEU (Papineni et al., 2002), ChrF2 (Popović, 2015), and TER (Snover et al., 2006). BLEU score is based on the precision of n-grams (contiguous sequences of words) in the candidate translation compared to the reference translations. ChrF2 measures the similarity between the character n-grams in the reference translation and the candidate translation produced by the machine translation system. It is particularly useful for evaluating the quality of machine translations for languages with complex writing systems, where word-based metrics like BLEU may not be as effective. TER measures the number of edits (insertions, deletions, and substitutions) required to transform a machine translation output into a reference translation produced by a human translator.

5 Results

In this section, we present the results of our experiments, where we trained our models on the Multi30k dataset and evaluated the translation quality using the BLEU, ChrF2, and TER metrics. We compare the translation quality of our proposed models, which utilise different matching approaches, i.e., string, lemma, GloVe, and BERT, with MMT baseline models across three different test sets. The text-only NMT model was trained solely on text captions without images. The MMT baseline model was trained on both text captions and original images without applying any filtering of irrelevant objects. We report the results for English-German, English-French, and English-Czech translation pairs. Comparing the text-only NMT and the MMT models, the latter statistically significant ($p < 0.05$) outperform the text-only models.

Table 2 presents the translation results of the 2016 test set from English into German,

English → German	BLEU ↑	ChrF2 ↑	TER ↓
Text-only NMT	24.0	50.8	66.0
Baseline MMT	26.4 ± 1.4	52.9 ± 1.0	63.8 ± 1.6
String matching	26.6 ± 1.4	53.3 ± 1.0	63.8 ± 1.6
Lemma matching	26.9 ± 1.3	53.3 ± 1.0	63.1 ± 1.6
GloVe matching	**27.2 ± 1.3***	**53.8 ± 1.0***	**63.0 ± 1.7**
BERT matching	27.0 ± 1.4	53.4 ± 1.0*	63.3 ± 1.6
English → French	**BLEU ↑**	**ChrF2 ↑**	**TER ↓**
Text-only NMT	31.5	55.3	43.0
Baseline MMT	**34.1 ± 1.4**	**57.6 ± 1.0**	51.0 ± 1.7
String matching	33.7 ± 1.4	57.3 ± 1.0	**50.7 ± 1.4**
Lemma matching	32.8 ± 1.3	56.9 ± 1.0	51.3 ± 1.3
GloVe matching	33.8 ± 1.4	**57.6 ± 1.0**	51.1 ± 1.3
BERT matching	33.7 ± 1.4	57.5 ± 1.0	51.2 ± 1.7
English → Czech	**BLEU ↑**	**ChrF2 ↑**	**TER ↓**
Text-only NMT	20.0	44.4	67.1
Baseline MMT	23.4 ± 1.4	46.7 ± 1.0	64.2 ± 1.6
String matching	23.5 ± 1.3	46.7 ± 1.0	63.8 ± 1.6
Lemma matching	**23.7 ± 1.3**	46.8 ± 1.1	**63.7 ± 1.6**
GloVe matching	23.6 ± 1.3	46.3 ± 1.1	64.1 ± 1.5
BERT matching	23.4 ± 1.3	**46.9 ± 1.0**	64.4 ± 2.0

Table 4: BLEU, ChrF2 and TER scores for baseline and proposed models for English to German, French and Czech on the 2018 test set ($*$ represents a statistically significant result compared to baseline MMT at a significance level of $p < 0.05$).

French, and Czech. String matching resulted in a one-point improvement in the BLEU score compared to the baseline MMT, as verified by the ChrF2 and TER metrics which was statistically significant at a significance level of $p < 0.05$. However, no significant improvements were observed in the proposed approaches for English to French translation. Lemma matching showed a slight improvement in English to Czech translation for three metrics. In Table 3, we can see the translation results for the 2017 test set from English to German and French. The use of lemma matching led to an improvement of 0.9 points in terms of the BLEU score compared to the baseline MMT. However, it was unexpected to find that for the English to French translation direction, the baseline MMT model outperformed the proposed models with blurred irrelevant objects. Table 4 presents the results of translating the 2018 test set from English to German, French and Czech. GloVe matching showed a 0.8-point improvement in terms of the BLEU score compared to the MMT baseline. This improvement is supported by ChrF2 and TER metrics. Other matching approaches demonstrated slight improvements. However, for English to French and Czech translation direction, we only observe minor improvements using the proposed matching approaches.

Figure 3 shows a few examples for the English to German translation direction, where our filtered approach improved over the baseline MMT approach. In the first example, our approach can guide the translation system to translate *riding* into *reitet*, with the meaning of *riding a horse*. The baseline MMT model translated *riding* into *fährt*, with the meaning of *driving a car*. In the second example, the baseline MMT system ignores translating the word *barefoot*, while the filtered MMT model provides the right translation, i.e. *barfüßiges*. Within the last example, the baseline MMT model translates the word *plastic* into *Gewändern*, in the meaning as *garment* or *rob*. The filtered MMT model, on the other hand, provides the right translation as a compound word, i.e., *Plastickstühlen* (en. *plastic chairs*).

Source (En)	A cowboy **riding** on the back of a bronco in a competition.
Reference (De)	Ein Cowboy **reitet** ein Wildpferd in einem Wettbewerb.
Baseline_MMT (De)	Ein Cowboy fährt bei einem Wettkampf auf einem Pferd.
Filtered_MMT (De)	Ein Cowboy reitet auf dem Rücken eines Wettkampfs in einem Rennen.
Source (En)	A young **barefoot** girl in a pink dress is jumping outside.
Reference (De)	Ein **barfüßiges** junges Mädchen in einem rosa Kleid springt im Freien.
Baseline_MMT (De)	Ein kleines Mädchen in einem rosa Kleid springt draußen.
Filtered_MMT (De)	Ein junges barfüßiges Mädchen in einem rosa Kleid springt im Freien.
Source (En)	Two men in white **plastic chairs** sitting in a doorway.
Reference (De)	Zwei Männer auf weißen **Plastikstühlen** sitzen in einem Eingang.
Baseline_MMT (De)	Zwei Männer in weißen Gewändern sitzen in einer Türöffnung.
Filtered_MMT (De)	Zwei Männer in weißen Plastikstühlen sitzen auf einem Eingang.

Figure 3: Examples for baseline and Filtered-based (string matching) MMT models to translate from English to German. Red and blue words indicate incorrect and correct translations, respectively.

6 Conclusion

Recent studies in Neural Machine Translation have focused on utilising visual information to enhance the quality of translation tasks. However, the success of Multimodal Machine Translation systems is highly dependent on the quality of the visual content used alongside textual datasets. Visual resources like images and videos contain a large amount of visual information, and some of it is irrelevant to the caption translation task. Hence, one of the major challenges in Multimodal Machine Translation is to separate the relevant information from the irrelevant one.

In this study, to improve the translation of the image captions, we propose to use object detection in the image encoder to prioritise relevant objects within the image. For each detected object, we extract its class, attribute, and regional box. Then, we utilise string, lemma matching, and pre-trained word embeddings, such as GloVe and BERT, to align the detected object classes in images with the words in text captions. Our experiments show that blurring irrelevant objects of images statistically significantly improves the performance of the baseline model in English to German translation. However, we observe minor improvements in translations from English to Czech, where the translations from English to French do not show any improvements. For our future work, we plan to leverage visual scene graphs in Multimodal Machine Translation. A visual scene graph is a data structure that represents visual scenes as a graph, where nodes correspond to objects and edges correspond to their relationships. It encodes the objects in the scene and the relationships among them, such as the attributes and locations of the objects and the spatial relationships between them. This representation allows for a rich and structured visual understanding of images.

Acknowledgements

This publication has emanated from research conducted with the financial support of Science Foundation Ireland (SFI) under Grant Number SFI/12/RC/2289_P2, co-funded by the European Regional Development Fund. For the purpose of Open Access, the author has applied a CC BY public copyright licence to any Author Accepted Manuscript version arising from this submission. We would like to thank the anonymous reviewers for their insights on this work.

References

Anderson, P., He, X., Buehler, C., Teney, D., Johnson, M., Gould, S., and Zhang, L. (2018). Bottom-up and top-down attention for image captioning and visual question answering. In *2018 IEEE/CVF Conference on Computer Vision and Pattern Recognition (CVPR)*, pages 6077–6086, Los Alamitos, CA, USA. IEEE Computer Society.

Caglayan, O., Aransa, W., Bardet, A., García-Martínez, M., Bougares, F., Barrault, L., Masana, M., Herranz, L., and van de Weijer, J. (2017). LIUM-CVC submissions for WMT17 multimodal translation task. In *Proceedings of the Second Conference on Machine Translation*, pages 432–439, Copenhagen, Denmark. Association for Computational Linguistics.

Caglayan, O., Aransa, W., Wang, Y., Masana, M., García-Martínez, M., Bougares, F., Barrault, L., and van de Weijer, J. (2016). Does multimodality help human and machine for translation and image captioning? In *Proceedings of the First Conference on Machine Translation: Volume 2, Shared Task Papers*, pages 627–633, Berlin, Germany. Association for Computational Linguistics.

Caglayan, O., Madhyastha, P., Specia, L., and Barrault, L. (2019). Probing the need for visual context in multimodal machine translation. In *Proceedings of the 2019 Conference of the North American Chapter of the Association for Computational Linguistics: Human Language Technologies, Volume 1 (Long and Short Papers)*, pages 4159–4170, Minneapolis, Minnesota. Association for Computational Linguistics.

Calixto, I. and Liu, Q. (2017). Incorporating global visual features into attention-based neural machine translation. In *Proceedings of the 2017 Conference on Empirical Methods in Natural Language Processing*, pages 992–1003, Copenhagen, Denmark. Association for Computational Linguistics.

Calixto, I., Liu, Q., and Campbell, N. (2017). Doubly-attentive decoder for multi-modal neural machine translation. In *Proceedings of the 55th Annual Meeting of the Association for Computational Linguistics (Volume 1: Long Papers)*, pages 1913–1924, Vancouver, Canada. Association for Computational Linguistics.

Calixto, I., Rios, M., and Aziz, W. (2019). Latent variable model for multi-modal translation. In *Proceedings of the 57th Annual Meeting of the Association for Computational Linguistics*, pages 6392–6405, Florence, Italy. Association for Computational Linguistics.

Cho, K., van Merriënboer, B., Bahdanau, D., and Bengio, Y. (2014a). On the properties of neural machine translation: Encoder–decoder approaches. In *Proceedings of SSST-8, Eighth Workshop on Syntax, Semantics and Structure in Statistical Translation*, pages 103–111, Doha, Qatar. Association for Computational Linguistics.

Cho, K., van Merriënboer, B., Gulcehre, C., Bahdanau, D., Bougares, F., Schwenk, H., and Bengio, Y. (2014b). Learning phrase representations using RNN encoder–decoder for statistical machine translation. In *Proceedings of the 2014 Conference on Empirical Methods in Natural Language Processing (EMNLP)*, pages 1724–1734, Doha, Qatar. Association for Computational Linguistics.

Deng, J., Dong, W., Socher, R., Li, L.-J., Li, K., and Li, F.-F. (2009). Imagenet: a large-scale hierarchical image database. *IEEE Conference on Computer Vision and Pattern Recognition*, pages 248–255.

Devlin, J., Chang, M., Lee, K., and Toutanova, K. (2019). BERT: pre-training of deep bidirectional transformers for language understanding. In Burstein, J., Doran, C., and Solorio, T., editors, *Proceedings of the 2019 Conference of the North American Chapter of the Association for Computational Linguistics: Human Language Technologies, NAACL-HLT 2019, Minneapolis, MN, USA, June 2-7, 2019, Volume 1 (Long and Short Papers)*, pages 4171–4186. Association for Computational Linguistics.

Elliott, D., Frank, S., Barrault, L., Bougares, F., and Specia, L. (2017). Findings of the Second Shared Task on Multimodal Machine Translation and Multilingual Image Description. In *Proceedings of the Second Conference on Machine Translation*, Copenhagen, Denmark.

Elliott, D., Frank, S., Sima'an, K., and Specia, L. (2016). Multi30K: Multilingual English-German image descriptions. In *Proceedings of the 5th Workshop on Vision and Language*, pages 70–74, Berlin, Germany. Association for Computational Linguistics.

He, K., Zhang, X., Ren, S., and Sun, J. (2016). Deep residual learning for image recognition. In *2016 IEEE Conference on Computer Vision and Pattern Recognition (CVPR)*, pages 770–778, Los Alamitos, CA, USA. IEEE Computer Society.

Huang, P.-Y., Liu, F., Shiang, S.-R., Oh, J., and Dyer, C. (2016). Attention-based multimodal neural machine translation. In *Proceedings of the First Conference on Machine Translation: Volume 2, Shared Task Papers*, pages 639–645, Berlin, Germany. Association for Computational Linguistics.

Ibrahim., N. M., ElFarag., A. A., and Kadry., R. (2021). Gaussian blur through parallel computing. In *Proceedings of the International Conference on Image Processing and Vision Engineering - IMPROVE*, pages 175–179. INSTICC, SciTePress.

Ive, J., Madhyastha, P., and Specia, L. (2019). Distilling translations with visual awareness. In *Proceedings of the 57th Annual Meeting of the Association for Computational Linguistics*, pages 6525–6538, Florence, Italy. Association for Computational Linguistics.

Klein, G., Kim, Y., Deng, Y., Nguyen, V., Senellart, J., and Rush, A. (2018). OpenNMT: Neural machine translation toolkit. In *Proceedings of the 13th Conference of the Association for Machine Translation in the Americas (Volume 1: Research Track)*, pages 177–184, Boston, MA. Association for Machine Translation in the Americas.

Krishna, R., Zhu, Y., Groth, O., Johnson, J., Hata, K., Kravitz, J., Chen, S., Kalantidis, Y., Li, L., Shamma, D. A., Bernstein, M. S., and Fei-Fei, L. (2017). Visual genome: Connecting language and vision using crowdsourced dense image annotations. *Int. J. Comput. Vis.*, 123(1):32–73.

Kudo, T. and Richardson, J. (2018). SentencePiece: A simple and language independent subword tokenizer and detokenizer for neural text processing. In *Proceedings of the 2018 Conference on Empirical Methods in Natural Language Processing: System Demonstrations*, pages 66–71, Brussels, Belgium. Association for Computational Linguistics.

Lisin, D., Mattar, M., Blaschko, M., Benfield, M., and Learned-Miller, E. (2005). Combining local and global image features for object class recognition. In *CVPR*, pages 47–47. Max-Planck-Gesellschaft.

Papineni, K., Roukos, S., Ward, T., and Zhu, W.-J. (2002). Bleu: a method for automatic evaluation of machine translation. In *Proceedings of the 40th Annual Meeting of the Association for Computational Linguistics*, pages 311–318, Philadelphia, Pennsylvania, USA. Association for Computational Linguistics.

Pennington, J., Socher, R., and Manning, C. (2014). GloVe: Global vectors for word representation. In *Proceedings of the 2014 Conference on Empirical Methods in Natural Language Processing (EMNLP)*, pages 1532–1543, Doha, Qatar. Association for Computational Linguistics.

Popović, M. (2015). chrF: character n-gram F-score for automatic MT evaluation. In *Proceedings of the Tenth Workshop on Statistical Machine Translation*, pages 392–395, Lisbon, Portugal. Association for Computational Linguistics.

Ren, S., He, K., Girshick, R., and Sun, J. (2015). Faster r-cnn: Towards real-time object detection with region proposal networks. In Cortes, C., Lawrence, N., Lee, D., Sugiyama, M., and Garnett, R., editors, *Advances in Neural Information Processing Systems*, volume 28. Curran Associates, Inc.

Snover, M., Dorr, B., Schwartz, R., Micciulla, L., and Makhoul, J. (2006). A study of translation edit rate with targeted human annotation. In *Proceedings of the 7th Conference of the Association for Machine Translation in the Americas: Technical Papers*, pages 223–231, Cambridge, Massachusetts, USA. Association for Machine Translation in the Americas.

Tang, G., Sennrich, R., and Nivre, J. (2018). An analysis of attention mechanisms: The case of word sense disambiguation in neural machine translation. In *Proceedings of the Third Conference on Machine Translation: Research Papers*, pages 26–35, Brussels, Belgium. Association for Computational Linguistics.

Vaswani, A., Shazeer, N., Parmar, N., Uszkoreit, J., Jones, L., Gomez, A. N., Kaiser, L. u., and Polosukhin, I. (2017). Attention is all you need. In Guyon, I., Luxburg, U. V., Bengio, S., Wallach, H., Fergus, R., Vishwanathan, S., and Garnett, R., editors, *Advances in Neural Information Processing Systems*, volume 30. Curran Associates, Inc.

Wang, D. and Xiong, D. (2021). Efficient object-level visual context modeling for multimodal machine translation: Masking irrelevant objects helps grounding. In *Thirty-Fifth AAAI Conference on Artificial Intelligence, AAAI 2021, Thirty-Third Conference on Innovative Applications of Artificial Intelligence, IAAI 2021, The Eleventh Symposium on Educational Advances in Artificial Intelligence, EAAI 2021, Virtual Event, February 2-9, 2021*, pages 2720–2728. AAAI Press.

Yao, S. and Wan, X. (2020). Multimodal transformer for multimodal machine translation. In *Proceedings of the 58th Annual Meeting of the Association for Computational Linguistics*, pages 4346–4350, Online. Association for Computational Linguistics.

Yin, Y., Meng, F., Su, J., Zhou, C., Yang, Z., Zhou, J., and Luo, J. (2020). A novel graph-based multimodal fusion encoder for neural machine translation. In *Annual Meeting of the Association for Computational Linguistics*.

Zeiler, M. D. (2012). ADADELTA: an adaptive learning rate method. *Computing Research Repository (CoRR)*, abs/1212.5701.

Zhao, Y., Komachi, M., Kajiwara, T., and Chu, C. (2022). Region-attentive multimodal neural machine translation. *Neurocomputing*, 476:1–13.

Zheng, Y., Huang, J., Chen, T., Ou, Y., and Zhou, W. (2019). CNN classification based on global and local features. In Kehtarnavaz, N. and Carlsohn, M. F., editors, *Real-Time Image Processing and Deep Learning 2019*, volume 10996, page 109960G. International Society for Optics and Photonics, SPIE.

Zhou, M., Cheng, R., Lee, Y. J., and Yu, Z. (2018). A visual attention grounding neural model for multimodal machine translation. In *Proceedings of the 2018 Conference on Empirical Methods in Natural Language Processing*, pages 3643–3653, Brussels, Belgium. Association for Computational Linguistics.

Author Index

Association for Computational Linguistics
209 N. Eighth Street
Stroudsburg, Pennsylvania 18360

ISBN 978-1-7138-9040-9

CURRAN ASSOCIATES INC.
proceedings.com